A HISTORY OF THE SOUTH

VOLUMES IN THE SERIES

Volume XI

THE NEW SOUTH
1945–1980

Winner of the Jules and Frances Landry Award
for 1995

A HISTORY

OF

THE SOUTH

Volume XI

EDITORS

WENDELL HOLMES STEPHENSON

E. MERTON COULTER

The
New South
1945–1980

BY NUMAN V. BARTLEY

LOUISIANA STATE UNIVERSITY PRESS

THE LITTLEFIELD FUND FOR SOUTHERN
HISTORY OF THE UNIVERSITY OF TEXAS

1995

Typeface: New Baskervillle
Typesetter: Impressions, a division of Edwards Bros., Inc.
Printer and binder: Thomson-Shore, Inc.

LIBRARY OF CONGRESS CATALOGING-IN-PUBLICATION DATA

Bartley, Numan V.
    The new South, 1945–1980 / by Numan V. Bartley.
        p.   cm. — (A history of the South : v. 11)
    Includes bibliographical references (p.   ) and index.
    ISBN 0-8071-2038-3 (cl : alk. paper)
    1. Southern States—History—1951–   I. Title.   II. Series.
F216.2.B36   1995
975'.043—dc20   95-19542
                                                                        CIP

The paper in this book meets the guidelines for permanence and durability of
the Committee on Production Guidelines for Book Longevity of the Council on
Library Resources. ⊗

PUBLISHER'S PREFACE

A HISTORY OF THE SOUTH is sponsored by Louisiana State University and the Trustees of the Littlefield Fund for Southern History at the University of Texas. More remotely, it is the outgrowth of the vision of Major George W. Littlefield, C.S.A., who established a fund at the University of Texas in 1914 for the collection of materials on Southern history and the publication of a "full and impartial study of the South and its part in American history." Trustees of the Littlefield Fund began preparations in 1937 for the writing of the history that Major Littlefield contemplated. Meanwhile, a plan had been conceived at Louisiana State University for a history of the South as a part of that institution's comprehensive program to promote interest, research, and writing in the field of Southern history.

As the two undertakings harmonized in essentials, the planning groups united to become joint sponsors of *A History of the South*. Wendell Holmes Stephenson, professor of American history at Louisiana State University, and Charles W. Ramsdell, professor of American history at the University of Texas, were chosen to edit the series. They had been deeply involved in planning the work, and it was appropriate that they should be selected to edit it. Upon the death of Professor Ramsdell in 1943, E. Merton Coulter, professor of history at the University of Georgia, was named his successor.

To date, nine of the ten volumes originally planned have been published. The most recent, *The Emergence of the New South*, by George B. Tindall, appeared in 1967 and covered the period from 1913 to 1945. By the 1980s it had become apparent that the very substantial and significant changes that had taken place in the South since the end of World War II demanded an additional volume. By joint agreement of the Trustees of the Littlefield Fund and Louisiana State University, Numan V. Bartley, E. Merton Coulter Professor of History at the University of Georgia, was asked to undertake the assignment. The result is this Volume XI of *A History of the South,* published nearly sixty years after the enterprise was initiated.

AUTHOR'S PREFACE

THE Great Depression of the 1930s, the New Deal, and the Second World War profoundly altered the course of southern development. A predominantly rural region became increasingly urban and metropolitan. A colonial economy geared to the production of agricultural staples and other raw materials grew more diversified. A low-wage section so stricken with poverty that President Franklin D. Roosevelt labeled it "the Nation's No. 1 economic problem" achieved a rising level of material prosperity. "Looking at the South as a whole," a perceptive journalist wrote in 1943, "one fact stands out like a landmark: the war has wrought a long-overdue economic revolution in the region, and the changes that have come will outlast the war." [1]

During the postwar years, southerners struggled to steer, to block, or simply to accommodate the massive forces that the upheavals of the late 1930s and the early 1940s had set in motion. The depopulation of the southern countryside, the disintegration of the region's folk cultures, and the dissolution of conventional relationships and standards of behavior exacted a heavy toll in human suffering. At the same time, an expanding economy and a more flexible social system offered vastly greater opportunities for individual achievement. The difficult but often rewarding transition from an indisputable position as "the Nation's No. 1 economic problem" in the late 1930s to membership in the prospering Sunbelt South in the late 1970s was a complex and sometimes paradoxical process.

At the beginning of World War II, southern society had its own insular cultures that rested on the sense of roots, place, and tra-

[1] Franklin D. Roosevelt to members of the conference, July 5, 1938, in National Emergency Council, *Report on Economic Conditions of the South* (1938), 1; Selden Menefee, *Assignment, U.S.A.* (New York, 1943), 65.

dition anchored by family, church, and community. The southern
social environment, in David M. Potter's words, "retained a personalism in the relations of man to man" and a "relation of people
to one another [that] imparted a distinctive texture as well as a
distinctive tempo to their lives." The regional sense of roots and
place rested on relatively structured and insulated communities
that encouraged social stability and family loyalty. Such communities offered little in the way of equality, and they dampened
social mobility and unmitigated individualism. Community obligations and duties defined the scope of the socially based, predominantly masculine, "hell of a fellow" individualism that was a
part of the southern tradition.[2]

By 1980 the South had become far more dynamic. The decimation of plantation agriculture, of mill villages and mining
camps, and of black and white communities and the consequent
migration of people into the cities eroded the foundations of
southern folk cultures. Such developments broadened opportunities for individuals, undermined racial and gender proscrip-
tions, and stimulated individual ambitions. An autonomous individualism that elevated achievement, self-fulfillment, and material
gain sustained a regional commitment to economic growth and
development. Fundamental changes in the way southerners lived
their lives, earned their livelihoods, and interpreted the events
around them brought conflicts and disruptions that were often
resolved—or at least addressed—in the public arena of politics.

The pages that follow aim to examine the sweeping transformation that occurred. Their preparation has left me in the debt
of many people. Michael Cassity of the University of Wyoming,
James C. Cobb of the University of Tennessee, Glenn T. Eskew of
Georgia State University, David R. Goldfield of the University of
North Carolina at Charlotte, and Dewey W. Grantham of Vanderbilt University kindly read and commented on the manuscript.

[2] David M. Potter, "The Enigma of the South," in *Myth and Southern History,* ed. Patrick
Gerster and Nicholas Cords (Chicago, 1974), 186; W. J. Cash, *The Mind of the South* (New
York, 1941), 52; Richard M. Weaver, "Two Types of American Individualism," in *The
Southern Essays of Richard M. Weaver,* ed. George M. Curtis III and James J. Thompson, Jr.
(Indianapolis, 1987), 77–103. In the following pages, the South is defined as the states of
the former Confederacy plus Kentucky and Oklahoma.

Lester D. Stephens, formerly chair of the Department of History at the University of Georgia, was supportive in a variety of ways. A fellowship from the National Endowment for the Humanities provided me with an uninterrupted year of research. Most of all, I am indebted to Morraine Matthews Bartley, who not only put up with a rather too lengthy project but chipped in with criticisms, proofreading, and good humor.

CONTENTS

CHAPTER I

WORLD WAR II AND
THE POSTWAR SOUTH

A T THE beginning of World War II the South was a land beset by crisis. The Great Depression had deepened the region's rural poverty and exposed the bankruptcy of staple-crop plantation agriculture. Southern cities, which historian David R. Goldfield has described as the urban "basket cases" of the 1930s, were only relatively better off than the southern countryside. In 1938 President Franklin D. Roosevelt proclaimed the South "the Nation's No. 1 economic problem," and the administration-sponsored *Report on Economic Conditions of the South* presented evidence to support the president's observation. The report portrayed a population ravaged by an inadequate diet, poor health, unacceptable housing, and inferior public services. Earlier in the 1930s H. L. Mencken had ventured to identify the "worst American state" according to such criteria as wealth, education, health, and public safety. Southern states dominated the competition. Mencken's presumptuous judgment of the region differed in tone from the sympathetic assessment in the *Report on Economic Conditions of the South,* but the two evaluations were the same in substance. The southern region ranked at the bottom of virtually any national socioeconomic index.[1]

Since the 1870s the South had been in the anomalous position of being, in economist Gavin Wright's words, a "low-wage region in a high-wage country," and the lowest incomes normally went

---

[1] David R. Goldfield, "The Urban South: A Regional Framework," *American Historical Review,* LXXXVI (1981), 1030; National Emergency Council, *Report on Economic Conditions of the South* (1938), 1; Charles Angoff and H. L. Mencken, "The Worst American State," *American Mercury,* XXIV (1931), 1–16, 175–88, 355–71.

to farmers and African Americans. "To-day as for years past," a liberal southern critic of the status quo stated in 1940, "the South remains a single-crop, plantation economy," and indeed the great cotton belt that stretched through ten states from North Carolina to Texas was one of the world's most specialized agricultural zones. Two-thirds of the southern population lived on the land or in hamlets of fewer than 2,500 people, and well over one-third of the work force and an even higher proportion of the population drew their livelihoods from agriculture. As Leonard Reissman has observed, "Prior to 1940 the South could fairly be described, with one or two states excepted, as a predominately rural region here and there dotted with cities." [2]

Black southerners constituted 25 percent of the region's population and almost 30 percent of its work force. They held the hardest, dirtiest, lowest-paying jobs, and critics in the South and elsewhere frequently commented on the linkage between the meager wages paid to black workers and the low wages that typified the regional economy. A reproachful commentary in 1941 lamented, "The inescapable fact is that the poorer whites compete with the Negroes for jobs and consequently the wage paid the Negro sets the regional standard." Even if significant numbers of businessmen, managers, professionals, and skilled workers reached a standard of living that did not differ markedly from that of persons in the same occupations elsewhere in the nation, the South ranked among the poorest regions in the Western world. [3]

[2] Gavin Wright, *Old South, New South: Revolutions in the Southern Economy Since the Civil War* (New York, 1986), 50; Katharine Du Pre Lumpkin, *The South in Progress* (New York, 1940), 17; David Wayne Ganger, "The Impact of Mechanization and the New Deal's Acreage Reduction Programs on Cotton Farmers During the 1930s" (Ph.D. dissertation, University of California at Los Angeles, 1973); William C. Holey, Ellen Winston, and T. J. Woofter, Jr., *The Plantation South, 1934–1937* (Freeport, N.Y., 1940); Howard W. Odum, *Southern Regions of the United States* (Chapel Hill, N.C., 1936); Merle Prunty, Jr., "Recent Quantitative Changes in the Cotton Regions of the Southeastern States," *Economic Geography*, XXVII (1951), 189–208; Leonard Reissman, "Urbanization in the South," in *The South in Continuity and Change*, ed. John C. McKinney and Edgar T. Thompson (Durham, N.C., 1965), 79.

[3] Arthur F. Raper and Ira De A. Reid, *Sharecroppers All* (Chapel Hill, N.C., 1941), 232; Douglas F. Dowd, "A Comparative Analysis of Economic Development in the American South and West," *Journal of Economic History*, XVI (1956), 558–74; Anna Rochester, *Why*

The Roosevelt administration's *Report on Economic Conditions of the South* identified the central problem as the region's position as an economic colony of the Northeast. The South produced low-cost raw materials for northern industry while providing a market, albeit a limited one, for high-value manufactured goods. Absentee ownership of southern transportation and industry drained profits away from the region and produced the discriminatory freight rates and basing-point pricing policies that limited southern development. Outside control of capital and credit contributed to high interest rates and further retarded progress. The report also traced the South's difficulties to its staple-crop economy and its concentrated land ownership—both closely associated with plantation agriculture—but saw those factors as secondary to the dependence that economic colonialism inflicted.[4]

The report joined an expanding body of research that ascribed the region's economic woes to outside forces. "The effect is to keep the South poor," one such study reported in 1940, "and to put the people at the mercy of an impersonal outside economic power." Economically as well as socially and politically, the southern scene was dismal, any number of critics reported, and absentee domination sharply circumscribed the potential for improvement.[5]

Such dire prospects lay behind the despair articulate southerners frequently expressed on the eve of America's entry into World War II. Five of the thirteen southern states quartered less manufacturing employment in 1939 than they had in 1909, and as economist Clarence H. Danhof has observed, there was "widespread pessimism" regarding new economic development in the region. Arthur F. Raper and Ira De A. Reid, two social scientists associated with the Institute for Research in Social Science at the University of North Carolina, entitled their devastating critique of southern society *Sharecroppers All*. Most southerners were effec-

---

Farmers Are Poor: The Agricultural Crisis in the United States (New York, 1940), 55–70; Paul E. Mertz, *New Deal Policy and Southern Rural Poverty* (Baton Rouge, 1978); Arthur Goldschmidt, "The Development of the U.S. South," *Scientific American*, CCIX (1963), 224–34.

[4] National Emergency Council, *Report on Economic Conditions of the South,* esp. 45–60.

[5] Lumpkin, *The South in Progress,* 29.

tively sharecroppers, they wrote, "because most Southern communities are essentially feudalistic." Although written from a New Deal reform perspective, their portrait of the region was so gloomy as to suggest hopelessness. As the cotton plantations and other regional institutions "crumble from forces within and without," southerners were "making the adjustment—downward," they concluded.[6]

Their pessimism was characteristic of the literature of the period. In her 1940 novel, *The Heart Is a Lonely Hunter,* Carson McCullers presented a sympathetic picture of the white and black underclass but offered little hope that they would join hands in support of reform. The oppressive culture of the wasteland, mill-town South that she portrayed offered little but frustration for labor-union organizers and black proponents of racial justice. Such would-be reformers were too estranged from community values to be effective. Also writing in 1940, James McBride Dabbs, a churchman, planter, teacher, and author, and later the president of the Southern Regional Council, despaired, "I do not see that we shall make any radical change in this community—and this is the south—in generations, perhaps in centuries."[7]

Three years later, Lillian E. Smith made much the same point in her "Two Men and a Bargain." "Once upon a time, down South," Smith wrote, "a rich white made a bargain with a poor white," namely, "You boss the nigger, and I'll boss the money." As a consequence of the bargain, whites "segregated southern money from the poor white and they segregated southern manners from the rich white and they segregated southern churches from Christianity and they segregated southern minds from honest thinking and they segregated the Negro from everything." Buttressed by the "strange fruit" that was southern culture, the bargain proved

[6] Clarence H. Danhof, "Four Decades of Thought on the South's Economic Problems," in *Essays in Southern Economic Development,* ed. Melvin L. Greenhut and W. Tate Whitman (Chapel Hill, N.C., 1964), 13; Raper and Reid, *Sharecroppers All,* v, vii, 28. See also Arthur F. Raper, *Preface to Peasantry: A Tale of Two Black Belt Counties* (Chapel Hill, N.C., 1936).

[7] Carson McCullers, *The Heart Is a Lonely Hunter* (New York, 1940); James McBride Dabbs, "Is a Christian Community Possible in the South?" *Christian Century,* LVII (1940), 876.

to be both enduring and successful: "The South had no Negro problem, it was all settled." [8]

At the same time, the gradual expansion of cities, industry, and commerce undermined traditional practices. In 1941 William Alexander Percy, whose Trail Lake plantation spread across three thousand acres of the Mississippi Delta, bemoaned the disintegration of southern culture and moral cohesion. In his gracefully written *Lanterns on the Levee,* Percy grieved that "the world I know is crashing to bits." Time-tested patterns of living fell into desuetude: "Manners used to be a branch of morals, now they were merely bad; poverty used to be worn with style and dignity, now it was a stigma of failure." The "old Southern way of life" disintegrated, and the future offered little beyond "catastrophe." [9]

Percy's distress over the decline of old values and the emergence of a starkly materialistic ethic received classic expression in William Faulkner's *The Hamlet,* published in 1940. Flem Snopes, the spiritual and intellectual leader of the pestiferous Snopes clan, brought to Yoknapatawpha County the neighborliness of the marketplace and the ethics of material acquisitiveness. The Snopes tribe was by and large a ruthless, materialistic, and avaricious lot who disdained family loyalty and community values. *The Hamlet* presented some of Faulkner's most evocative descriptions of nature, and those passages underscored the seemingly alien character of the Snopesian invasion. In Faulkner's novel, the subversive effect of middle-class materialism implied ruinous consequences for traditional southern folk culture. [10]

Other writers arrived at similar conclusions on the basis of quite different assumptions. North Carolina journalist Wilbur J. Cash, whose *The Mind of the South* appeared in 1941, was profoundly pessimistic, but his overriding concern was that the South had changed too little. Like a great tree, southern culture developed new limbs and branches, but its "tap root" was firmly planted in antebellum soil. The region's "characteristic vices in the past"—

[8] Lillian E. Smith, "Two Men and a Bargain: A Parable of the Solid South," *South Today,* Spring, 1943, pp. 5–14.

[9] William Alexander Percy, *Lanterns on the Levee: Recollections of a Planter's Son* (New York, 1941), Foreword, 312.

[10] William Faulkner, *The Hamlet* (New York, 1940).

racism, intolerance, and violence among them—remained "its characteristic vices today." C. Vann Woodward's biography *Tom Watson* had found in history an explanation "for the tragedy of a section," and although Cash wrote his historical analysis of southern culture from a contrary interpretative perspective, he arrived at a similar conclusion: the southern historical legacy was largely tragic. Rather than "being modernized," Cash observed, the South "in many ways . . . has actually always marched away, as to this day it continues to do, from the present toward the past." [11]

Embattled black southerners—indeed African Americans nationally—had limited options. "We black and they white. They got things and we ain't. They do things and we can't. It's just like living in jail. Half the time I feel like I'm on the outside of the world peeping in through a knot-hole in the fence." Thus Bigger Thomas, the central character in Richard Wright's *Native Son*, summarized black life. Although Wright set his novel of 1940 in Chicago, its inspiration came from the author's experiences growing up in the South. There, according to Wright, the black masses turned for solace to religion or alcohol or indigenous black music and folk culture, or they occupied themselves with day-to-day survival and sometimes with the search for ameliorative reform, while more affluent Negroes adopted the "style of their bourgeois oppressors" and cooperated with the white elite "to keep their groaning brothers in line, for that was the safest course of action."

Wright continued, "I lived the first seventeen years of my life in the South without so much as hearing of or seeing one act of rebellion from any Negro, save the Bigger Thomases." Only an occasional Bigger Thomas "became estranged from the religion and the folk culture of his race," thereby becoming a "bad nigger." In the South such people "were shot, hanged, maimed, lynched, and generally hounded until they were either dead or their spirits broken." In Chicago, Bigger Thomas, imprisoned on death row at the end of the novel, could only equate racial justice with the destruction of America's exploitative system and the establishment of communist brotherhood. Earlier in the novel, Big-

[11] W. J. Cash, *The Mind of the South* (New York, 1941), 439, x; C. Vann Woodward, *Tom Watson, Agrarian Rebel* (New York, 1938), Preface.

ger's friend Gus had advised, "Aw, nigger, quit thinking about it. You'll go nuts." [12]

In Yoknapatawpha County and elsewhere in southern literature, historian Daniel J. Singal has written, "What stood revealed was a South tormented and paralyzed, trapped in an intricate web, largely of its own making, which tied together sexuality, avarice, and aggression with the 'higher' facets of southern life until they were all hopelessly tangled. Instead of a repository of glory and innocence, the past was now seen as a fatalistic curse upon the present that no southerner could wholly escape." Much of the literature of the southern renaissance tended to be the mirror image of the literature of the American West. In the Western, men confronted challenges directly and overcame them; in the Southern, men were often impotent and less effective than women in coping with the complexities besetting them. "Where the Western hero acted," historian Robert Wiebe has written, "the characters in the Southern talked." Where the Western was free from the constraining past, the Southern was overwhelmed by it. Where the protagonist in the Western usually solved his problems, the cast in the Southern almost never solved theirs. [13]

Southerners during the 1930s and 1940s did wrestle with the massive problems afflicting the region. The myth of the Lost Cause, with its cavaliers and belles, retreated before the rediscovery of the poor whites, the emerging redefinition of African Americans and their place in national and especially southern life, and the general swell of proletarian literature that grew from the depression. Ralph W. McGill has described the "mighty surge of discussion, debate, self-examination, confession and release" generated by New Deal idealism and southern critical realism. "Few towns," McGill noted, "were too small to have their study groups." Black southerners debated alternative strategies and during the war years sometimes supported the Double V campaign that called for victory over fascism abroad and over racism at home. Yet problems were more obvious than solutions. As Raper and Reid de-

[12] Richard Wright, *Native Son* (New York, 1940), 23, ix–xiii.

[13] Daniel Joseph Singal, *The War Within: From Victorian to Modernist Thought in the South, 1919–1945* (Chapel Hill, N.C., 1982), 154; Robert H. Wiebe, "Modernizing the Republic," in *The Great Republic,* by Bernard Bailyn *et al.* (Lexington, Mass., 1977), 1155.

scribed the situation in *Sharecroppers All,* "Southerners are in the midst of a wilderness of transition—yesterday is not yet dead, tomorrow is not fully born." [14]

To northern soldiers who trained in the South during World War II, the region's "backwardness" was obvious. "I looked out on shabby unpainted shacks and people in rags, all of them barefoot," a Massachusetts native traveling south to a marine training camp reported. "No Taras, no Scarletts, no Rhetts; just Tobacco Road. And this was Virginia, the state of Robert E. Lee." Viewing the omnipresent pine trees, mules, wagons, and cotton gins, a trainee from Minneapolis likened his train trip through the Deep South to "punishment in some myth: we were condemned to ride forever through the same southern landscape." Even the language was different; northern and southern soldiers were "continually amazed at the other's inability to speak English." Black recruits from the North were particularly appalled, often equating the region with hell itself. "The white civilians hate us," a black soldier explained, "and we in turn despise them." That German prisoners of war often received better treatment than African-American soldiers did was particularly galling. A black marine commented, "You ain't in the United States now. This is North Carolina." [15]

Still, the nonsouthern soldiers flocking to the South for military training were an integral part of the impact of World War II on the region. The accelerating breakdown of plantation agriculture drove tenants and laborers off the land, and they joined the exodus to the cities by the small farmers and by the squatters who

[14] Ralph W. McGill, *The South and the Southerner* (Boston, 1964), 159; J. Wayne Flynt, *Dixie's Forgotten People: The South's Poor Whites* (Bloomington, Ind., 1979), 74–92; Shields McIlwaine, *The Southern Poor-White: From Lubberland to Tobacco Road* (Norman, Okla., 1939); Sylvia Jenkins Cook, *From Tobacco Road to Route 66: The Southern Poor White in Fiction* (Chapel Hill, N.C., 1976); Richard M. Dalfiume, *Desegregation of the U.S. Armed Forces: Fighting on Two Fronts, 1939–1953* (Columbia, S.C., 1969); Bryon R. Skinner, "The Double 'V': The Impact of World War II on Black America" (Ph.D. dissertation, University of California at Berkeley, 1978); Raper and Reid, *Sharecroppers All,* 141.

[15] William Manchester, *Goodbye Darkness: A Memoir of the Pacific War* (Boston, 1979), 120; Samuel L. Hynes, *Flights of Passage: Reflections of a World War II Aviator* (New York, 1988), 29; Walter Bernstein, *Keep Your Head Down* (New York, 1945), 6; Phillip McGuire, *Taps for a Jim Crow Army: Letters from Black Soldiers in World War II* (Santa Barbara, Calif., 1983), 69; Bill Downey, *Uncle Sam Must Be Losing the War* (San Francisco, 1982), 66.

had earlier tried to weather the depression by settling on unoccupied land. War industries provided jobs on a sufficient scale to create what some employers perceived as labor shortages. "For the first time since the 'War between the States,' " *Fortune* magazine reported in 1943, "almost any native of the Deep South who wants a job can get one." Whites had far greater access to decent employment than black southerners, but the wartime expansion of the southern labor market was impressive. "What the army was taking," an Alabamian informed novelist John Dos Passos, "wasn't a drop in the bucket to the drain into war industry." [16]

Journalist Selden Menefee predicted that "many thousands of ex-farmers and sharecroppers who have learned new skills in the war centers will want to use them after the war, instead of returning to farm work at subsistence standards of living." The prophecy held equally for the soldiers who had opportunities for travel and training and who as veterans qualified for benefits under the GI Bill. It held, too, for the women whose work in war industries was, as another touring journalist reported, the "first break they have had in the old routine of cooking, dishwashing, and childbearing." The factories, military bases, and construction projects that appeared throughout the region caused severe housing shortages in the cities and strained social services. They also created "sin towns" like Phenix City, Alabama, where the "principal industry . . . is sex, and its customer is the Army." [17]

The feverish activity reoriented the southern economy. Throughout the war, the South, as historian George B. Tindall has pointed out, "remained more campground than arsenal." The region in 1940 contained 27 percent of the nation's people and 28 percent of its land area, but it received only 17.5 percent of the nation's investment in wartime industrial development. That percentage nevertheless represented some $4.5 billion, most of it provided by the federal government. The national government

---

[16] "The Deep South Looks Up," *Fortune,* July, 1943, p. 95; Neil A. Wynn, *The Afro-American and the Second World War* (New York, 1975), 39–59; John Dos Passos, *State of the Nation* (Boston, 1944), 76.

[17] Selden Menefee, *Assignment, U.S.A.* (New York, 1943), 65; Agnes E. Meyer, *Journey Through Chaos* (New York, 1943), 171; Bernstein, *Keep Your Head Down,* 32; Frank F. Mathias, *G.I. Jive: An Army Bandsman in World War II* (Lexington, Ky., 1982), 17.

9

thus delivered the means to mobilize an agricultural economy for war production both by supplying the capital for plant construction and by constituting an insatiable military market for the output of the federally sponsored factories. In the underdeveloped and capital-starved southern economy, the federal largess had formidable consequences.[18]

During the years of World War II, the construction and expansion of factories doubled the region's industrial plant over what it had been in 1939 and substantially if less impressively expanded manufacturing capacity. Industrial employment increased from 1.6 million workers to a high, in late 1943, of 2.8 million. Although pay scales in the South were well below national norms, the requirements of the Fair Labor Standards Act of 1938 and the policies of the War Labor Board during the war years forced southern wages upward. Federal agencies also attempted to eliminate wage differentials based on race and gender.[19]

The building of ships and planes yielded the most obvious industrial bonanza. The shipbuilding facilities in Pascagoula, Mississippi, vaulted that community's population from 4,000 people in 1940 to 30,000 in 1944. The Mobile metropolitan district, also primarily as a result of naval production, virtually doubled in population, from 115,000 in 1940 to 200,000 in 1944. The great aircraft factories in Dallas–Fort Worth and Atlanta-Marietta, along with airplane assembly plants in other southern cities, further fueled urban growth. Ordnance plants appeared throughout the region; the making of ammunition and explosives was the most geographically scattered of southern wartime industries. Coal production expanded in the Upper South, and the petroleum and chemical industries grew enormously in the Southwest—especially in Texas, the southern state that experienced the largest economic gain from wartime spending.[20]

[18] George Brown Tindall, *The Emergence of the New South, 1913–1945* (Baton Rouge, 1967), 695; Calvin B. Hoover and B. U. Ratchford, *Economic Resources and Policies of the South* (New York, 1951), 120–25; Frederick L. Deming and Weldon A. Stein, *Disposal of Southern War Plants* (Washington, D.C., 1949), 12–23.

[19] Hoover and Ratchford, *Economic Resources and Policies of the South*, 120–21; Gavin Wright, *Old South, New South*, 198–238; Richard Polenberg, *One Nation Divisible: Class, Race, and Ethnicity in the United States Since 1938* (New York, 1980), 74–77.

[20] Frederic C. Lane, *Ships for Victory: A History of Shipbuilding Under the U.S. Maritime Com-

A somewhat greater infusion of funds—about $4.75 billion—
went into military installations and related housing. The South
was the great training ground for the nation's military forces. As
a result of the proliferation of military bases and other public
projects, government payrolls in 1944 accounted for some 25 percent of salaries and wages in the region. The purchasing power
flowing from federal payrolls created markets for local enterprises, although it may not have warranted a northern soldier's
remark, that "this whole draft business is just a southern trick . . .
put over by southern merchants to hold the big trade they get
from the training camps." Such circumstances induced the governor of Alabama to declaim in 1944 that his state enjoyed a
"prosperity such as its people have never known before" and perhaps justified historian Morton Sosna's observation that "World
War II probably had a greater impact on the South than the Civil
War." [21]

From 1940 to 1945, approximately one-quarter of the region's
farm population—some four million people—left the land. As historian Pete Daniel has observed, "The armed forces and defense
work became the resettlement administration for rural southerners." It was little wonder that longtime residents of Pascagoula and
such other sleepy little towns as Panama City, Florida, Orange,
Texas, and Wilmington, North Carolina, felt inundated by the
flood of newly arriving families or that many established citizens
were "inclined to blame the breakdown of community controls in
places like Mobile on the shiftlessness of their country cousins."
It was told how southerners from the "back counties" stacked
their meager belongings on old trucks and wagons, piling on as
well their "crate of fowls and . . . brood of flaxen-haired children
with smeared mouths and puffy eyes" as they set off "to take a job

mission in World War II (Baltimore, 1951), 437–38; Hoover and Ratchford, Economic Resources and Policies of the South, 121–22; Deming and Stein, Disposal of Southern War Plants,
15–16.

[21] Hoover and Ratchford, Economic Resources and Policies of the South, 45–62; John Temple
Graves, The Fighting South (New York, 1943), 104; Chauncey Sparks, "The Impact of the
War on Alabama," in War Comes to Alabama (Tuscaloosa, Ala., 1943), 5; Morton Sosna,
"More Important Than the Civil War? The Impact of World War II on the South," in
Perspectives on the American South: An Annual Review of Society, Politics, and Culture, Vol. IV,
ed. James C. Cobb and Charles R. Wilson (New York, 1987), 145.

in a war plant." A Washington *Post* writer, in a report on wartime conditions in the South entitled *Journey Through Chaos,* described a "large proportion" of the new immigrants in the shipbuilding centers along the Gulf Coast as "primitive, illiterate backwoods people" who brought with them "their native habits of living" and had to be taught "what it means to use gas stoves and sinks and toilets." Their "cultural patterns," she reported, "remind one of America's most primitive existence one hundred years or more ago." [22]

Given how distasteful middle-class observers found the practices of the newly arrived, the population influx spawned social conflict, much of it finding outlet in racial discord. Academic studies have examined the outbreak of race riots in Mobile, Beaumont, Texas, and elsewhere, the "alarming rise in mutinies by black soldiers in southern camps and bases," and the upsurge in lynching during and just after the war. White defenders of the old order fretted about outside interference in southern racial matters and the nascent disruption of the region's traditional "harmonious" race relations. The members of the South Carolina house of representatives passed a resolution declaring "our belief in and our allegiance to established white supremacy as now prevailing in the South" and pledging "our lives and our sacred honor to maintain it, whatever the cost, in war and in peace." In 1943 Howard W. Odum reported "that the South and the Negro . . . faced their greatest crisis since the days of the reconstruction and that many of the same symbols of conflict and tragedy that were manifest in the 1840's were evident again a hundred years later." [23]

[22] Hoover and Ratchford, *Economic Resources and Policies of the South,* 90–91; Pete Daniel, *Breaking the Land: The Transformation of Cotton, Tobacco, and Rice Cultures Since 1880* (Urbana, Ill., 1985), 243; Menefee, *Assignment, U.S.A.,* 53; Dos Passos, *State of the Nation,* 68; Meyer, *Journey Through Chaos,* 170, 197, 210; Marvin W. Schlegel, *Conscripted City: Norfolk in World War II* (Norfolk, Va., 1951); Bernadette Kuehn Loftin, "A Social History of the Mid-Gulf South, 1930–1950" (Ph.D. dissertation, University of Southern Mississippi, 1971).

[23] James A. Burran III, "Racial Violence in the South During World War II" (Ph.D. dissertation, University of Tennessee, 1977), v; James A. Burran III, "Urban Racial Violence in the South During World War II: A Comparative Overview," in *From the Old South to the New: Essays on the Transitional South,* ed. Walter J. Fraser, Jr., and Winfred B. Moore, Jr. (Westport, Conn., 1981), 167–77; Skinner, "The Double 'V'"; Harvard Sitkoff, "Racial Militancy and Interracial Violence in the Second World War," *Journal of American History,*

Racial issues became more salient in both the South and the nation. The war effort promoted national unity and blurred traditional ethnic differences at the same time that it exacerbated racial tensions. The logic of a war against Nazi Germany encouraged reevaluation of racial beliefs at home and hastened the triumph of "liberal environmentalism" as at least the titular racial creed of the nation. "The gradual destruction of the popular theory behind race prejudice," Gunnar Myrdal wrote in his epic work on interracial relations, "is the most important of all social trends in the field." Justifications for white supremacy—and for de jure segregation—rapidly lost intellectual respectability.[24]

Myrdal, a Swedish sociologist whose profoundly influential *An American Dilemma* appeared in 1944, was optimistic about the direction and future course of American race relations. In this he was not alone. "More progress has been made, in this five-year period, toward a realistic understanding of the issues involved in what we still call 'the race problem' than in the entire period from the Civil War to 1940," a journalist wrote in 1946. In the following year, an English visitor called attention to the growing number of both popular and scholarly books that treated black people fairly. During the war black thespians began to appear in film roles that differed fundamentally from Hollywood's usual stereotyped casting. "There is bound to be," Myrdal predicted, "a redefinition of the Negro's status in America as a result of this War."[25]

LVIII (1971), 661–81; Charles S. Johnson *et al.*, *To Stem This Tide: A Survey of Racial Tension Areas in the United States* (Boston, 1943); Wynn, *The Afro-American and the Second World War*, 60–78; Resolution quoted in *Take Your Choice: Separation or Mongrelization*, by Theodore G. Bilbo (Poplarville, Miss., 1947), 220; Howard W. Odum, *Race and Rumors of Race* (Chapel Hill, N.C., 1943), 4.

[24] Polenberg, *One Nation Divisible*, 77–85; George M. Fredrickson, *The Black Image in the White Mind: The Debate on Afro-American Character and Destiny, 1817–1914* (New York, 1971), 330; Gunnar Myrdal, *An American Dilemma: The Negro Problem and Modern Democracy* (New York, 1944), 1003; David W. Southern, *Gunnar Myrdal and Black-White Relations: The Use and Abuse of "An American Dilemma," 1944–1969* (Baton Rouge, 1987).

[25] Carey McWilliams, "What We Did About Racial Minorities," in *While You Were Gone: A Report on Wartime Life in the United States*, ed. Jack Goodman (New York, 1946), 98; D. W. Brogan, *American Themes* (New York, 1947); Thomas Cripps, *Slow Fade to Black: The Negro in American Film, 1900–1942* (New York, 1977), 375–80; Skinner, "The Double 'V,'" 205–35; Wynn, *The Afro-American and the Second World War*, 79–98; Richard M. Dalfiume, "The 'Forgotten Years' of the Negro Revolution," *Journal of American History*, LV (1969), 90–

The expectations of black southerners expanded as wartime developments eroded regional folk culture and race etiquette. A survey that Charles S. Johnson, a black sociologist at Fisk University, conducted in 1944 found that "the great majority of southern Negroes are becoming increasingly dissatisfied with the present pattern for race relations and want a change." The impressions of journalists and other observers conformed with Johnson's findings. When William T. Couch of the University of North Carolina Press asked a black historian to compile and edit a series of essays in which prominent African Americans addressed the question of "what the Negro wants," he learned to his astonishment that all the contributors wanted integration. To obtain a wide range of opinion, Rayford W. Logan, the editor of the collection, solicited essays from four people generally regarded as conservative, five known as liberal, and five judged radical. The contributors differed on numerous points, but they were unanimous in their rejection of racial segregation. Couch, a progressive editor usually counted among white southern liberals, published *What the Negro Wants* in 1944, but he included a publisher's introduction spelling out his disagreement with much that was in the volume. Virginius Dabney, the liberal editor of the Richmond *Times-Dispatch*, sympathized with Couch's predicament and confided that recent events "have made me realize all too vividly that the war and its slogans have roused in the breasts of our colored friends hopes, aspirations and desires which they formerly did not entertain, except in the rarest instances." [26]

Before the war's end, the federal government—or at least the executive and judicial branches of it—moved haltingly toward the rediscovery of the Fourteenth and Fifteenth Amendments. As the nation prepared for war, President Roosevelt issued an executive order requiring nondiscriminatory employment in defense industries and training programs. The President's Committee on

---

106; Myrdal, *An American Dilemma,* 997. See also Buell G. Gallagher, *Color and Conscience: The Irrepressible Conflict* (New York, 1946), and Margaret Halsy, *Color Blind: A White Woman Looks at the Negro* (New York, 1946).

[26] Charles S. Johnson, "The Present Status of Race Relations in the South," *Social Forces,* XXIII (1944), 27–32; Rayford W. Logan, ed., *What the Negro Wants* (Chapel Hill, N.C., 1944); Dabney quoted in *The War Within,* by Singal, 299.

Fair Employment Practice lacked the enforcement powers and often the will to establish any noticeable equality in the workplace, but Roosevelt's action was an important symbolic commitment to expanding opportunities for black wage earners. The vigorously pro–civil rights position championed by first lady Eleanor Roosevelt further identified the executive office with black advancement.[27]

During the 1930s the United States Supreme Court had begun to require that "separate but equal" facilities be equal as well as separate. In 1938 the Court held in *Gaines* v. *Canada* that Missouri was in violation of the Constitution because it maintained a law school for whites but none for blacks. Missouri instead provided a fund for the payment of out-of-state tuition for African Americans who wished to study law. In the suit, which was brought with the support of the National Association for the Advancement of Colored People, the Court required that Missouri either provide a "separate but equal" law school or admit Gaines to the white school. The NAACP also sponsored a series of cases during the 1930s and 1940s seeking salary equality for black public-school teachers. The NAACP lawyers were successful, and the pay of black teachers did increase throughout the southern region, although full equality in salaries was not achieved until much later.[28]

The most important NAACP initiative, at least as measured by the outcry of white southern politicians, was *Smith* v. *Allwright,* in which the Supreme Court declared white primary elections unconstitutional. Limiting the electorate in Democratic party primary elections to white voters appealed to supporters of white supremacy because, as V. O. Key, Jr., explained, the practice "drew the color line sharply and cleanly." Throughout the South, defenders of the old order deplored the Court's decision, and the legislatures in four states—Alabama, Arkansas, Mississippi, and South Carolina—adopted measures to circumvent the ruling.[29]

[27] Louis Ruchames, *Race, Jobs, and Politics: The Story of FEPC* (New York, 1953); Merl E. Reed, *Seedtime for the Modern Civil Rights Movement: The President's Committee on Fair Employment Practice* (Baton Rouge, 1991).

[28] Mark V. Tushnet, *The NAACP's Legal Strategy Against Segregated Education, 1925–1950* (Chapel Hill, N.C., 1987), 70–76.

[29] V. O. Key, Jr., *Southern Politics in State and Nation* (New York, 1949), 625; Steven F. Lawson, *Black Ballots: Voting Rights in the South, 1944–1969* (New York, 1976), 23–54.

The economic disasters of the 1930s and the demographic and economic upheavals of the war years helped generate pressures for political change. The fortunes of an older generation of Negro-baiting southern demagogues declined. Governor Eugene Talmadge, Georgia's "wild man from Sugar Creek," and Mississippi's Senator Theodore Bilbo, perhaps the most vituperative of all the demagogues, died after winning elections in 1946. Senator Ellison D. "Cotton Ed" Smith of South Carolina lost his bid for reelection in 1944, and Senator W. Lee "Pass the Biscuits, Pappy" O'Daniel of Texas chose not to seek reelection when his term expired after the war.

Southern politics continued periodically to offer entertainment to the nation at large. In Georgia, Eugene Talmadge died after winning election to his fourth term as governor but before being reinstated in the office, and his death touched off a wild scramble for the statehouse. The Georgia legislature, on the basis of fraudulent write-in ballots, chose his son Herman as governor, and the Talmadge forces seized the state executive offices. Outgoing Governor Ellis G. Arnall denounced the "putsch" of January, 1947, and attempted to run the government from the lobby of the capitol building. Melvin E. Thompson, the incoming lieutenant governor, claimed to be the legitimate heir to the office and established a government-in-exile in downtown Atlanta. After the competing forces had wrangled for weeks, the state supreme court ruled that Thompson was the acting governor.[30]

In Texas a Democratic senatorial runoff primary in 1948 between former Governor Coke Stevenson and Lyndon B. Johnson was classic even by southern standards. The voters divided their ballots virtually equally between the two candidates, both of whom called in additional returns from kept counties. For a week the lead seesawed between the two contestants as "late returns" continued to arrive. Robert Dallek, a biographer of Johnson, has concluded that "no one could be sure who won," but Johnson was ultimately declared the victor by a margin of eighty-seven votes.[31]

[30] Harold Paulk Henderson, *The Politics of Change in Georgia: A Political Biography of Ellis Arnall* (Athens, Ga., 1991), 171–89; Ellis Gibbs Arnall, *What the People Want* (Philadelphia, 1947), 12.

[31] Robert Dallek, *Lone Star Rising: Lyndon Johnson and His Times, 1908–1960* (New York, 1991), 327.

When Oklahomans voted in 1949 to continue prohibition, Mississippi and Oklahoma remained the only two bone-dry southern states. Gunnar Myrdal reported that he saw in Mississippi "more hard drinking" than he had ever before witnessed, confirming Will Rogers' observation that Mississippians hold "faithful and steadfast to prohibition as long as the voters can stagger to the polls." Practical about such matters, the Mississippi state government taxed illegal booze, just as Louisiana in 1948 began to tax illegal slot machines. It was hardly surprising when Fred Allen introduced to his national radio audience Senator Beauregard Claghorn, a Deep South statesman who never went to Yankee Stadium and attended baseball games at the Polo Grounds only when "a southpaw's pitchin'." [32]

Yet the wartime administrations of reform governors like Ellis Arnall of Georgia and Robert S. Kerr of Oklahoma suggested new directions in regional politics. The reelection in 1944 of the South's most prominent political liberals—Senator Claude Pepper of Florida and Senator Lister Hill of Alabama—deepened the impression some had of an incipient leftward trend in regional politics. Large numbers of conservatives continued to hold office, and they rallied to the defense of southern tradition. At the same time, urban and industrial expansion propelled the demand for still more economic growth. [33]

The discriminatory freight-rate system that had long burdened industrial development came under mounting attack. In the 1930s the Southern Governors' Conference launched a campaign against railroad pricing policies that offered low rates for the shipment of raw materials and unfinished products to the North but set high freight charges for the transportation of finished products manufactured in the South. Southern elites had accepted the system because it provided relatively inexpensive transportation for the products of southern plantations, forests, and mines. By

[32] James R. Scales and Danney Goble, *Oklahoma Politics: A History* (Norman, Okla., 1982), 261; Rogers quoted in *An American Dilemma*, by Myrdal, 458; Claghorn character quoted in New York *Times*, May 4, 1946.

[33] All the articles in two issues of *Journal of Politics*, X (1948) were devoted to the "southern political scene, 1938–1948" and assessed the state of southern politics and government.

the 1940s business and political leaders increasingly perceived that freight-rate discrimination impeded the expansion and diversification of southern industry. Governor Arnall, who claimed the practice particularly curtailed opportunities for small businessmen, argued successfully before the Supreme Court that the nation's antitrust laws extended to the system. The Interstate Commerce Commission backed down in 1945 and during the early postwar years established a uniform schedule of freight rates. The rapid growth of the motortruck network made victory in the contest over rail rates less important for southern industry than it might have been, but at the very least it was of considerable symbolic significance.[34]

State governments were especially energetic in trying to sell the South as a congenial location for business and industry. Mississippi Governor Hugh L. White had successfully sponsored a Balance Agriculture with Industry program in the 1930s. Although BAWI lapsed during the early years of World War II, the legislature revived it in 1944. Under the program, Mississippi communities provided factory buildings, exemptions from property taxes, and other inducements for industrialists. Eventually, all the southern states adopted comparable plans and created industry-chasing agencies. As such programs matured in the 1950s, they sometimes came under criticism for being too generous with concessions. The Alabama Planning and Industrial Development Board assured corporations that new industries "never pay any property taxes" and that a factory could "make a profit on its taxes." Such blandishments, an Alabama chamber of commerce executive charged, invited northern criticism and federal regulation and were "likely to be resented by our existing industries."[35]

[34] Robert S. Lively, *The South in Action: A Sectional Crusade Against Freight Rate Discrimination* (Chapel Hill, N.C., 1949); J. V. Norman, "Brief History of the Efforts of the Southern Governors Conference to Obtain a Parity of Rates," July 5, 1946, in Executive Papers of Governor Chauncey Sparks, File 219, Alabama Department of Archives and History, Montgomery. Arnall and a number of Atlanta business leaders are quoted in Atlanta *Journal,* May 21, 1945.

[35] James C. Cobb, *The Selling of the South: The Southern Crusade for Industrial Development, 1936–1980* (Baton Rouge, 1982), 3–63; Glenn E. McLaughlin and Stefan Robock, *Why Industry Moves South: A Study of Factors Influencing the Recent Location of Manufacturing Plants in the South* (Washington, D.C., 1949); Albert Lepawsky, "Governmental Planning in the

In most cases the new developmental agencies grew from the state planning commissions that had been established under the New Deal. Although during the early postwar years few of the agencies were as generous to manufacturers as the one in Mississippi, all advertised the virtues of their states, provided assistance for companies establishing new plants or expanding old ones, and in varying degrees helped train workers, provided low-cost or free land, constructed plants, and offered tax abatements. Local urban-development groups created industrial parks and supplemented the subsidies. The attempt to lure outside investment to the capital-starved South was hardly new, but it was only in the 1940s that the southern states established the programs that were to mature during the postwar years into well-staffed, handsomely financed commissions.

The policy of public subsidies to private industry had its limitations. Historian James C. Cobb has concluded that aid the southern states bestowed in encouraging development was "most appealing to industries such as textiles, apparel, footwear, hosiery, and furniture where intense competition made all costs, and therefore all savings, significant." As a result, the development programs, especially during their early decades, contributed to the expansion of the region's traditional low-wage, labor-intensive industrial base. Nevertheless, state subsidy provisions, like the abolition of discriminatory freight rates, charted new directions for the evolution of the southern economy.[36]

Growth advocates divided over strategy in the midforties. Governor Arnall and former Texas congressman Maury Maverick, chairman of the national Small War Plants Corporation, allied themselves with those championing a homemade modern South, with internally generated capital and local ownership. At the

---

South," *Journal of Politics*, X (1958), 536–67; Leland H. Jones to John M. Ward, March 15, 1960, in Frank Murray Dixon Papers, Alabama Department of Archives and History.

[36] James C. Cobb, *Industrialization and Southern Society, 1877–1984* (Lexington, Ky., 1984), 43; Gavin Wright, *Old South, New South*, 257–64; W. Paul Brann, "Industrial Financing in the South," in *Raising the Income and Productivity of the South* (Frankfort, Ky., 1961), 29–33; George I. Whitlatch, "The Role of State Economic Development Agencies," in *Raising the Income and Productivity of the South*, 75–78; James R. Rinehart, "Rates of Return on Municipal Subsidies to Industry," in *Essays in Southern Economic Development*, ed. Greenhut and Whitman, 473–87.

Southern Governors' Conference in New Orleans in December, 1945, George C. Biggers, the general manager of the Atlanta *Journal* and an ally of Arnall, took to task southern businessmen who sat "with . . . hands folded, complacently waiting for the damn Yankee to come down here and build factories and open new businesses." He called such inaction defeatist, because it ensured that the region would remain a "colonial economy indefinitely." Instead, Biggers asserted, Dixie "should pay more attention to the development of its own industries; to the investment of its own capital." Southerners themselves should promote "improved education and technical training" and should launch enterprises capable of turning to advantage the expanded home markets and the enlarged skilled and semiskilled work force that wartime economic growth had created. Biggers acknowledged the need to bring in investment from outside the region, and he noted the importance of a favorable business environment in encouraging either "local capital or foreign capital," but he saw the greatest potential in homegrown economic progress.[37]

Arnall's most innovative effort in behalf of an indigenous industrial revolution was his plan to create in Georgia a Reconstruction Finance Corporation modeled on the federal agency of the same name. The "little RFC" would have had authority to issue $100 million in debentures to raise capital for public and private projects that would contribute to economic development. The legislature, however, never approved its establishment.[38]

The campaign for locally originated industrial capitalism rapidly dissipated. Not only did old-guard conservatives oppose the program but it garnered little concrete support from the expanding business and professional, urban and suburban middle class that was the driving force behind industrial development and government efficiency. Economic boosterism was essentially a market-oriented creed championed by real-estate dealers, construction

[37] Ellis Gibbs Arnall, *The Shore Dimly Seen* (New York, 1946); Arnall, *What the People Want*; Ellis Gibbs Arnall, "Revolution Down South," *Collier's*, July 17, 1945, pp. 17ff.; Biggers quoted in Atlanta *Journal*, December 9, 1945; Newspaper Clippings File, File 80b-1945, Tuskegee Institute Archives, esp. Richmond *Times-Dispatch*, December 18, 1945.

[38] Numan V. Bartley, *The Creation of Modern Georgia* (2nd ed.; Athens, Ga., 1990), 194–97.

companies, retailers, public utilities, bankers, and media executives, as well as lawyers, doctors, and other professionals. Writing
in 1952 journalist Samuel Lubell explained, "The fever for new
industry probably runs strongest among the rising middle class in
the Southern cities. The young lawyer searching for clients, the
college graduate seeking a supervisory post in the mills, merchants and salesmen with something to sell, bankers hunting new
investment outlets for growing deposits, doctors building their
practice, all the numerous property holders who hope the cities
they live in will grow out to the land they own and strike them
rich—all are building their dream castles upon the growth of industry." Local ownership of the process was not a particularly grip-
ping concern.[39]

The southern states channeled their efforts into cajoling northern corporations to expand into the region. "Hell, what we've
been selling is peace and order," an industrial promoter informed
an Arkansas journalist, "telling 'em that what we've got down here
is stability—friendly politicians who are not going to gut a business
with taxes, and workers who are grateful for a job and are not
going to be stirring up trouble." A Mississippi editor commented,
"A Northerner with new ideas might get a quick brushoff or
worse, but a Northerner with a new factory deserved the best of
southern hospitality." As a nonsouthern executive employed in
the South by a nonsouthern corporation observed, "We've been
welcomed by local businessmen and praised as public benefac-
tors."[40]

The return of veterans to civilian life reinforced the campaign
for economic growth and government efficiency. In addition to
whatever broadening influence they may have absorbed from wartime travel and to whatever skill they may have acquired during
their service, veterans had access to the bounty of the GI Bill. The
veterans improved the southern work force, and they often
showed an impatience with traditional practices. In communities

[39] Samuel Lubell, *The Future of American Politics* (Garden City, N.Y., 1952), 119; Carl Abbott, *The New Urban America: Growth and Politics in Sunbelt Cities* (Chapel Hill, N.C., 1981),
140–52.

[40] Harry S. Ashmore, *An Epitaph for Dixie* (New York, 1958), 119; Hodding Carter, *Southern
Legacy* (Baton Rouge, 1950), 158; McLaughlin and Robock, *Why Industry Moves South*, 106.

throughout the region, "GI revolts" rose against courthouse cliques and urban political machines. The participants wanted honest elections, good government, and greater economic opportunity. Among the best known of the GI revolts were the successful campaigns led by a former lieutenant colonel, Sidney S. McMath, to oust the corrupt machine based in the gambling resort of Hot Springs, Arkansas, and by a former colonel, deLesseps S. Morrison, to overturn the patronage-and-favor Old Regular city administration in New Orleans. The GI revolts, in Cobb's words, "heralded a gradual but ongoing process of political and institutional modernization."[41]

The emplacement of merit systems for state employees was a crucial step toward the professionalization of state bureaucracies. In 1939 the United States Congress amended the Social Security Act to require a merit system for state employees connected with federal grant-in-aid programs. Thus began the gradual "modernization and professionalization of the administrative branch of government in the South" that, as political scientist Edward M. Wheat has pointed out, played a central role in the transformation of the region. In Alabama Governor Frank M. Dixon had before civil service reform quipped that "the chief duty of the governor of Alabama is running an employment agency." The highly personalized spoils system common throughout the South in earlier years was not without its virtues, but professional staffing was far more effective in nurturing growth policies and rationalized procedures.[42]

The economic growth ethos was a rising force in southern politics. Governor McMath of Arkansas and Governor Gordon Browning of Tennessee were among those who in the early post-

[41] Key, *Southern Politics*, 189–204; Jim Lester, *A Man for Arkansas: Sid McMath and the Southern Reform Tradition* (Little Rock, Ark., 1976); Edward F. Haas, *DeLesseps S. Morrison and the Image of Reform: New Orleans Politics, 1946–1961* (Baton Rouge, 1974), 6–40; Richard M. Bernard, "Metropolitan Politics in the American Sunbelt," in *Searching for the Sunbelt: Historical Perspectives on a Region*, ed. Raymond A. Mohl (Knoxville, Tenn., 1990), 69–84; Cobb, *Industrialization and Southern Society*, 51.

[42] Edward M. Wheat, "The Bureaucratization of the South: From Traditional Fragmentation to Administrative Incoherence," in *Contemporary Southern Politics*, ed. James F. Lea (Baton Rouge, 1988), 263–81; Tindall, *The Emergence of the New South*, 490–93; Dixon quoted in "The Merit System in Alabama State Government," in *Public Administration Survey* (University, Ala., 1960), 2.

war years identified industrial development with businesslike government efficiency and state-sponsored internal improvements. Luther H. Hodges, governor of North Carolina during the 1950s, explained in his *A Businessman in the Statehouse,* "Industrialization, then, with all its advantages to the people and to the state, became the number one goal of my administration." Advocates of economic growth were racial segregationists, but they were inclined to defend white supremacy only so far as it did not conflict with pocketbook preoccupations. Many were conscious of the South's national image and saw the danger of zealous inflexibility in race relations.[43]

On some issues they were relatively progressive, but their program, it has been remarked, "was not to subsidize or support have-nots or have-littles, but to subsidize the institutional and individual creators of wealth." Compared with the old-guard conservatives, business-oriented political moderates were more willing to support public education and to deal with metropolitan problems. As the chief advocates for southern cities, they frequently battled for reapportionment, constitutional reform, proportional distribution of state funds, and other such normally hopeless causes. Most of all, they sought to apply sound business standards to government and to achieve a good atmosphere for industrial development.[44]

Just as the moderate proponents of economic growth emerged from World War II with a vision of a New South led by businessmen, the region's liberals envisioned a more democratic and pluralistic South wherein organized labor, small farmers, and African Americans participated in shaping postwar development. Benefiting from the popularity of the New Deal and President Roosevelt, southern liberalism held the promise of becoming a significant force in regional affairs. During the war, opinion polls consistently reported southerners to be the most New Dealish and the most

[43] Luther H. Hodges, *Businessman in the Statehouse: Six Years as Governor of North Carolina* (Chapel Hill, N.C., 1962), 32; William C. Havard and Loren P. Beth, *The Politics of Mis-Representation: Rural-Urban Conflict in the Florida Legislature* (Baton Rouge, 1962), 113; Numan V. Bartley, *The Rise of Massive Resistance: Race and Politics in the South During the 1950s* (Baton Rouge, 1969), 22–25.

[44] Earl Black and Merle Black, *Politics and Society in the South* (Cambridge, Mass., 1987), 29.

"liberal" of sectional groups in the United States. When in late 1944 Mark F. Ethridge, publisher of the Louisville *Courier-Journal,* surveyed the prospects for southern liberalism in a letter to Ralph McGill, he confidently predicted a revival of New Deal reform. "The swing of the post-war world *will* be to the left," Ethridge wrote, confident that the South was "on the march" toward democracy and social justice.[45]

At approximately the same time Clark H. Foreman, president of the Southern Conference for Human Welfare, presented his analysis of the state of southern liberalism. Tory conservatives dominated regional politics, Foreman conceded, but they did not represent the southern people. "There is another South composed of the great mass of small farmers, the sharecroppers, the industrial workers white and colored, for the most part disfranchised by the poll tax and without spokesmen either in Congress, in their state legislatures or in the press. This latter South comprises about 80% of the population." Were these people to be mobilized, Foreman concluded, there would be "good ground for maintaining that the South can become in a very short time, the most liberal region in the Nation." Not every liberal prophecy was so sanguine, but at the end of World War II liberal expectations were high.[46]

Traditionally the numerical strength of southern liberalism had its roots in Populism. "The alignment that most often forces its way into southern factional politics," V. O. Key stated in the late 1940s, "is the old Populist battle of the poor white farmer against the plantation regions." Key concluded that "fundamentally within southern politics there is a powerful strain of agrarian liberalism, now re-enforced by the growing unions of the cities," that should "not be underestimated." The expanding southern work-

[45] Everett Carll Ladd, Jr., *Transformations of the American Party System: Political Coalitions from the New Deal to the 1970s* (New York, 1975), 129–77; Alfred O. Hero, Jr., *The Southerner and World Affairs* (Baton Rouge, 1965), 369–73; Mark Ethridge to Ralph W. McGill, September 7, 1944, in McGill Papers, Box 3, Emory University Libraries. A more pessimistic appraisal is presented by Charles W. Eagles in *Jonathan Daniels and Race Relations: The Evolution of a Southern Liberal* (Knoxville, Tenn., 1982).

[46] Clark H. Foreman and James Dombrowski, "Memo for the CIO Executive Board," November 13, 1944, in Records of the Southern Conference for Human Welfare, Box 43, Tuskegee Institute Archives.

ing class, itself fed by the decimation of rural society, had social and consanguineous ties—and often shared political predilections—with its country cousins. Although local African-American leaders often endorsed an accommodationist strategy, the growing discontent of black southerners made them particularly susceptible to liberal alternatives. Much of the radicalism of the 1930s—apparent in the Southern Tenant Farmers' Union and the Alabama Sharecroppers Union—dissolved during the war years, yet those years were also pregnant with harbingers of liberal change.[47]

The Depression and the New Deal invigorated southern liberalism by heightening awareness of economic issues and class-related political alignments, and the patronage and spending policies of the Roosevelt administration augmented liberal leadership. The federal government filled influential positions with left-leaning political activists who had rarely found preferment in southern state governments. Federal largess also disposed pragmatic politicians to align themselves with the Roosevelt administration in support of federally financed programs and projects. Lyndon Johnson often sought in private conversations to persuade doubters with the argument "What are you worried about? It's not coming out of your pocket. Any money that's spent down here on New Deal projects, the East is paying for." [48]

New Deal and wartime idealism as well as internal changes in the South created what Clark Foreman described in 1944 as a "fairly large group of the most progressive ministers, editors, educators and writers that can be found anywhere in the United States." Liberal journalists and politically active women were particularly prominent. At the end of World War II, such newspapers as the Louisville *Courier-Journal,* the Nashville *Tennessean,* the Raleigh *News and Observer,* and the Atlanta *Constitution* were friendly toward New Deal reformers. Within the Southern Conference for

[47] Key, *Southern Politics,* 302, 670; Myrdal, *An American Dilemma,* 503–12, 727–33, 781–88; Anthony P. Dunbar, *Against the Grain: Southern Radicals and Prophets, 1929–1959* (Charlottesville, Va., 1981); Patricia Ann Sullivan, "Gideon's Southern Soldiers: New Deal Politics and Civil Rights Reform, 1933–1948" (Ph.D. dissertation, Emory University, 1983); Lee Finkle, "The Conservative Aims of Militant Rhetoric: Black Protest During World War II," *Journal of American History,* LX (1973), 692–713.

[48] Sullivan, "Gideon's Southern Soldiers," 39–65; Johnson quoted in *The Years of Lyndon Johnson,* by Robert A. Caro (New York, 1983), 471–72.

Human Welfare, women occupied a substantial number of the policy-making positions.[49]

During the 1940s disfranchisement came under more sustained attack. The National Committee to Abolish the Poll Tax, an organization comprising mainly southern white and black reformers and supported largely by northern labor unions, lobbied Congress. The banning of the poll tax promised immediate enlargement of the white working-class vote and, more broadly, the setting of a precedent for federal protection of voting rights. Legislation against the poll tax passed in the House of Representatives on a number of occasions between 1940 and 1949 but consistently failed to overcome southern opposition in the Senate.[50]

The campaign was successful in drawing attention to the stunted condition of democratic institutions in the South. Governor Arnall pushed through constitutional revisions eliminating the poll tax in Georgia in 1945. Georgia's action left only seven southern states with the tax, and two of those—South Carolina and Tennessee—abandoned it in the early fifties. Of more immediate significance was the Supreme Court's decision in *Smith* v. *Allwright*. That ruling in 1944 against all-white primaries promised not only the reentry of blacks into southern politics but also a considerable enlargement of the political influence of less affluent citizens generally. State NAACP chapters and local black political associations responded by initiating campaigns to register black voters.[51]

In the spring of 1946 the Congress of Industrial Organizations began its long-envisaged campaign to organize the southern working class. Philip F. Murray, president of the six-million-member union, pronounced the project the "most important drive of its kind ever undertaken by any labor organization in the history of this country." The CIO established headquarters in Atlanta for its Southern Organizing Committee and poured organizers and re-

[49] Foreman and Dombrowski, "Memo for the CIO Executive Board"; Myrdal, *An American Dilemma*, 469.

[50] Lawson, *Black Ballots*, 55–85; *Outside the Magic Circle: The Autobiography of Virginia Foster Durr*, ed. Hollinger F. Barnard (University, Ala., 1985), 152–70; Frederic D. Ogden, *The Poll Tax in the South* (University, Ala., 1958).

[51] O. Douglas Weeks, "The White Primary, 1944–1948," *American Political Science Review*, XLII (1948), 500–510; Lawson, *Black Ballots*, 23–54.

sources into the campaign that journalists labeled Operation Dixie. The National Farmers' Union, with veteran New Dealer Aubrey Williams as director of organization, had already begun its drive to organize the small farmers of the region. Stetson Kennedy, the most articulate propagandist for the Southern Conference for Human Welfare, explained that progress for ordinary southerners rested on "unionization of the region's farmers, the further unionization of its labor, and a coalition of the two."[52]

The executive board of the CIO had in 1944 recognized the Southern Conference for Human Welfare as the "natural and appropriate spearhead of liberal forces in the South." Created in 1938 in response to the Roosevelt administration's *Report on Economic Conditions of the South,* the Conference had languished before being revitalized in the midforties. By the end of 1946 the Conference had more than ten thousand members and a budget over $200,000. State conferences with paid executive secretaries were active in six southern states, a large committee in Washington lobbied for liberal causes and promoted projects of national scope, and an office in New York raised funds or, as the executive secretary of the Conference phrased it, acted "to reclaim for the southern people a tiny percentage of the wealth drained from them to the financial center of the nation."[53]

The Southern Conference occupied a strategic position in the liberal front. Its membership included many of the more advanced liberals in the South, and its program of "political and industrial democracy" offered direction for the regional liberal movement. Conference spokespeople projected a vision of unionized workers with access to the ballot who would not only gain higher wages, better working conditions, and a voice in their own economic affairs but also replace the South's predominantly Bour-

[52] Murray quoted in New York *Times,* April 11, 1946; Paul David Richards, "The History of the Textile Workers Union of America, CIO, in the South, 1937 to 1945" (Ph.D. dissertation, University of Wisconsin at Madison, 1978), 216–17; Philip S. Foner, *Organized Labor and the Black Worker, 1619–1981* (New York, 1982), 277–81; John Salmond, *A Southern Rebel: The Life and Times of Aubrey Willis Williams, 1890–1965* (Chapel Hill, N.C., 1983), 177–212; Stetson Kennedy, *Southern Exposure* (Garden City, N.Y., 1946), 47.

[53] Thomas A. Krueger, *And Promises to Keep: The Southern Conference for Human Welfare, 1938–1948* (Nashville, 1967), 125; James A. Dombrowski, "Southern Conference for Human Welfare," *Common Ground,* Summer, 1946, pp. 15–25.

bon congressional delegation with New Deal liberals. "We are not going to do anything fundamentally in the South," a correspondent wrote Clark Foreman, "without organization of the little people, and that is not going to be accomplished except through a widespread, democratic and UNIVERSAL labor movement that will be strong [enough] to prevail against the red herrings of race, communism, CIO, etc. etc. There flatly isn't any other way than through power." [54]

In early 1946 the Southern Conference officially rejected racial discrimination as "fundamentally undemocratic, unAmerican and unChristian," but its leaders regarded race relations as an economic rather than a social issue. Because "segregation was created and has been maintained to serve the economic and political purpose of keeping southern labor divided and cheap," Stetson Kennedy argued, the "Southern Negro must be emancipated economically and politically before he can be emancipated socially." In any event, a direct attack on segregation was not politically feasible. In the South of the midforties, Kennedy stated, the "case for economic and even political equality" could "be argued on the street corner—yes, even in a Klan meeting—without necessarily making oneself a candidate for lynching." The case for social equality was not heard as serenely.[55]

Substantial numbers of black southerners were in agreement with the Conference's strategy. Ralph J. Bunche maintained that racial justice "will never be accomplished at the Southern polls, not at least until labor, farm and industrial, black and white, has become so strongly organized and so bold as to present a forceful challenge to the authority of entrenched interests." Wartime and

[54] Tarleton Collier to Clark H. Foreman, June 12, 1942, in Southern Conference for Human Welfare Collection, Box 35, Atlanta University Center; Charles H. Martin, "The Rise and Fall of Popular Front Liberalism in the South: The Southern Conference for Human Welfare, 1938–1948," in *Perspectives on the American South: An Annual Review of Society, Politics, and Culture*, Vol. III, ed. James C. Cobb and Charles R. Wilson (New York, 1985), 119–44; Numan V. Bartley, "The Southern Conference and the Shaping of Post–World War II Southern Politics," in *Developing Dixie: Modernization in a Traditional Society*, ed. Winfred B. Moore, Jr., Joseph F. Tripp, and Lyon G. Tyler, Jr. (Westport, Conn., 1988), 179–97.

[55] Press Release, January 24, 1946, in Southern Conference for Human Welfare Collection, Box 35; Stetson Kennedy, "Total Equality and How to Get It," *Common Ground*, Winter, 1946, p. 63; Kennedy, *Southern Exposure*, 349.

postwar prosperity strengthened the position of black civil rights advocates, but labor-oriented and working-class blacks continued to espouse the "doctrine of labor solidarity." As Myrdal noted, the proposition "that the whole caste problem is 'basically' economic" remained a widely accepted strategic tenet. Charles Johnson, in another survey of southern race relations conducted in 1945, observed that the "trend toward substitution of worker solidarity for racial solidarity" might prove "in the long run to be the most significant of the forces" affecting black life.[56]

The premier black reform organization was the National Association for the Advancement of Colored People. The NAACP, basking in the prestige attending its judicial victories in cases like *Smith* v. *Allwright,* increased both its southern and national membership in the 1940s. Between 1939 and 1948, its membership in South Carolina went from eight hundred to more than fourteen thousand, and in other states the association experienced similar if less spectacular growth. Although biracial, the NAACP membership in the South was overwhelmingly black, and the group, both in the South and nationally, appealed most strongly to bourgeois blacks and especially black professionals. The NAACP was an avowed friend of the labor movement and in the midforties frequently cooperated with the Southern Conference for Human Welfare. Nevertheless, the civil rights individualism that was the association's goal differed in kind from the grass-roots aims of the Conference.[57]

Moderate liberals constituted the basic membership of the Southern Regional Council and such women's groups as the League of Women Voters. The Southern Regional Council, created in 1944 largely by white and black educators, journalists, and

[56] Myrdal, *An American Dilemma,* 789–90, p. 790 Bunche quoted; Ralph J. Bunche, *The Political Status of the Negro in the Age of FDR,* ed. Dewey W. Grantham (Chicago, 1973), 24–46; W. E. Burghardt Du Bois, "My Evolving Program for Negro Freedom," in *What the Negro Wants,* ed. Logan, 31–70; A. Philip Randolph, "March on Washington Movement Presents Program for the Negro," in *What the Negro Wants,* 133–62; Willard S. Townsend, "One American Problem and a Possible Solution," in *What the Negro Wants,* 163–92; Charles S. Johnson, "Social Changes and their Effect on Race Relations in the South," *Social Forces,* XXIII (1945), 347.

[57] Myrdal, *An American Dilemma,* 794–800; Tushnet, *The NAACP's Legal Strategy,* 105–60; Robert L. Zangrando, *The NAACP Crusade Against Lynching, 1909–1950* (Philadelphia, 1980), 166–209; *A Man Called White: The Autobiography of Walter White* (New York, 1948).

religious leaders, had a heavily white membership. A nonpolitical agency that did not seek mass membership, the council in the late 1940s still enrolled approximately 3,500 people. The sponsor of human rights councils in a number of southern states, the council was the most traditional of mainstream liberal organizations. It sought to improve race relations within a segregated society through research and education, as well as through behind-the-scenes efforts to foster racial moderation among southern political and economic leaders. Ultimately the approach proved vain, and in 1951 the board of directors endorsed racial desegregation as the organization's goal.[58]

The liberal coalition—both real and potential—manifested more than its share of internal contradictions. A wide range of committed activists, political pragmatists, and well-meaning moderates sometimes shared little beyond opposition to the policies and practices of the old regime. Neopopulists, labor liberals, racial reformers, and middle-class progressives searched for new directions in southern politics without possessing much in the way of strategic unity.

Traditional rural-oriented neopopulist liberalism lacked clear ideological content. It reflected a common-folk distrust of the rich and powerful and a preference for common-folk policies and campaign styles. Rural liberals favored economic expansion, but their agenda, Earl Black and Merle Black have observed, concerned "less a politics of economic growth than of redistributing fixed resources." Defending the interests of the have-nots in southern society, they pursued ends more attuned to the small farmers of the countryside than to the proliferating working class in the cities. Distrustful of the middle-class complexion of state bureaucracies and lacking the resources of their better-placed adversaries, they tended to oppose merit systems, centralized purchasing agencies, and competitive bidding procedures. At the same time, they demonstrated a realistic understanding that economic growth without the restructuring of economic and political power was apt

[58] "The Southern Regional Council, 1944–1964," *New South,* January, 1964, pp. 1–32; Odum, *Race and Rumors of Race,* 185–292; Anthony L. Newberry, "Without Urgency or Ardor: The South's Middle-of-the-Road Liberals and Civil Rights, 1945–1960" (Ph.D. dissertation, Ohio University, 1982), 67–69, 137–47.

to result in greater wealth and control at the top of the social order.[59]

Labor liberals similarly feared that economic growth without political and industrial democracy would offer limited benefits to the southern masses. Unlike the neopopulists, who occupied a traditional if circumscribed niche in regional politics, the labor liberals were unmistakably dependent on outside support. The Southern Conference's fond dream of political and industrial democracy hung on the readiness of national labor unions to allocate nonregional funds and resources for the organization of southern workers. Federal patronage and spending, more than anything else, provided whatever unity the unstable liberal coalition possessed. Even such moderately liberal organizations as the Southern Regional Council relied upon outside foundations for financial assistance.

The tortured southern political universe of truncated electorates, one-party politics, rotten borough legislatures, white-supremacy policies, and insulated conservative policy makers was too thoroughly entrenched to be overturned—or at least to be overturned nonviolently—without outside assistance. As Foreman was aware, disfranchisement provisions largely prevented black southerners from casting ballots and sharply curtailed the political influence of landless farmers, working-class families, and the less affluent generally. Because of the limited membership in labor unions and reformist farmer organizations, the southern masses remained generally disorganized and isolated. The malapportioned legislatures strengthened southern conservatism, and the one-party system, as Key pointed out, benefited the haves at the expense of the have-nots.[60]

County elites were the leading beneficiaries of the southern political system, and they were its foremost defenders. Political scientist Jasper Berry Shannon penned in the late forties the classic portrait of the county-seat elite—the planter, banker, merchant, and usually old-family governing class that dictated the gen-

[59] Black and Black, *Politics and Society in the South*, 28.

[60] Key, *Southern Politics*, esp. 489–532; Alexander Heard and Donald S. Strong, comps., *Southern Primaries and Elections, 1920–1949* (University, Ala., 1950); Tindall, *The Emergence of the New South*, 632–49.

eral direction of southern public affairs. "The economy of the South, together with its traditional developments," Shannon wrote, "has created a governing class which has disfranchised its political opposition and thereby effectively placed itself in the saddle of the Democratic party" in a one-party region.[61]

The heartland of the old regime was the great plantation belt spreading from southside Virginia into eastern Texas. There the descendants of slaves were a substantial percentage of the population and a larger percentage of the labor force. The ghosts of the antebellum aristocracy haunted the land, and planters usually stood near the top of the social order. The planter class and its county-seat allies had led the South into secession, turned back the Reconstruction experiment, defeated the Populists in the 1890s, disfranchised the masses of southern voters, and established the conventions that ruled southern public life.[62]

Traditional plantations relied heavily on cheap labor, and so too in the underdeveloped southern economy did a wide range of labor-intensive industries. Gavin Wright has concluded that when defenders of the "southern way of life" resisted intrusions from outside into regional affairs, "the economic underpinning was the separate low-wage labor market, and the implicit coalition included not just planters but lumber and sawmill operators, textile millowners, and other employers." Because smaller, labor-intensive enterprises tended to locate in towns and rural nonfarm areas, industrialization often strengthened the forces of Bourbon democracy. The merchants, bankers, and businessmen of the county-seat regime were usually themselves employers, and their wives maintained staffs of maids, cooks, and yardmen. Southern liberals tirelessly repeated that segregation was at bottom a device to keep southern labor "cheap and divided," and there was more than a little truth in their analysis.[63]

The elite of the county seats and larger countryside towns were the primary champions of lost-cause mythology, white supremacy,

[61] Jasper Berry Shannon, *Toward a New Politics in the South* (Knoxville, Tenn., 1949), 65.

[62] Key, *Southern Politics*, 3–12.

[63] Gavin Wright, *Old South, New South*, 259; James C. Cobb, "Beyond Planters and Industrialists: A New Perspective on the New South," *Journal of Southern History*, LIV (1988), 45–68.

plantation labor relations, and a status-based social order, all of which were part of a broader paternalism. County elites, Shannon noted, held to a "feudal" ideology that "conceives of each man belonging to an hierarchical order of inequality in which his peculiar faculties equip him to perform a unique role in some part of the hierarchy." Gunnar Myrdal similarly commented on the conservative preference for a "social order which established an ideal division of labor and of responsibility in society between the sexes, the age groups, the social classes and the two races." A closely knit family with obligations and duties, authority and submission, and rights and responsibilities according to each member's position within it came close to being the ideal model for a society.[64]

The ideology was reactionary. As the redefinition of the place of black people in American life was making the idea of white supremacy intellectually indefensible and as the diversification and mechanization of agriculture and the increasing technological sophistication of business were lessening the need for cheap labor, changes sweeping over the South were also rapidly eroding paternal social relations. Many southern conservatives chose to defend the old order in the teeth of such transformations. Mississippi journalist Hodding Carter observed that the South's more conservative leadership "seemed to believe that American political and economic history had ended with Grover Cleveland." But more fundamentally, Shannon insisted, they had accepted neither the principle of free labor nor the Thirteenth Amendment. Regional conservatism, as Myrdal put it, had "preserved an ideological allegiance not only to *status quo,* but to *status quo ante.*" [65]

Old-guard conservatives defended disfranchisement, malapportionment, and one-party politics as proper and desirable methods for preserving the southern way of life. As an influential legislator in Alabama explained, the state Democratic party had to "protect Alabama from the mass registration of negroes . . .

[64] Shannon, *Toward a New Politics in the South,* 2–3; Myrdal, *An American Dilemma,* 442; Keith F. McKean, *Cross Currents in the South* (Denver, 1960); John Dollard, *Caste and Class in a Southern Town* (3rd ed.; Garden City, N.Y., 1957).

[65] Carter, *Southern Legacy,* 149; Shannon, *Toward a New Politics in the South,* 64–65; Myrdal, *An American Dilemma,* 441; James McBride Dabbs, *The Southern Heritage* (New York, 1959).

which, if allowed to happen, will destroy democracy in Alabama government." County elites tended to be suspicious of mass public education, cities, bureaucracies, and most social services. In state legislatures, where they and their lawyer agents were typically over-represented, they favored horse trading, interpersonal give-and-take, and decentralized nodes of power over rationalized administrative procedures.[66]

Marketplace ethics and the economic changes taking place in the region influenced many county-seat conservatives. More than a few were themselves investors in industry and commerce. Thus, they often supported economic growth despite their skepticism about, as one study has worded it, "rapid economic development that might topple or challenge local and state power structures." They preferred importing industry from outside to being discommoded by locally originated urban industrial development. Above all, county-seat conservatives treasured social stability and the racial and gender conventions that anchored it.[67]

Discontented blacks, resurgent liberals, and modernizing urban businessmen and bureaucrats laid plans for recasting the southern political agenda while apprehensive guardians of the old order pondered strategies for defending traditional practices. Liberals and moderates debated the future of the South in journals like *Common Cause*. African-American intellectuals and activists charted new directions for race relations in *What the Negro Wants*. Industrial promoters issued countless pamphlets and flyers ballyhooing the "good business atmosphere" in the region. George Biggers described the South as "the nation's no. 1 economic opportunity," in a phrase coined in response to Roosevelt's characterization of it as "the Nation's No. 1 economic problem." Richard M. Weaver, a North Carolina native writing in the Agrarian tradition, expressed the Bourbon view of southern civilization, and he warned of the chaotic consequences of "unregulated competition, unplanned industrial expansion" and an "unlimited number of

[66] Gessner T. McCorvey to Frank M. Dixon, January 28, 1949, in Dixon Papers; Havard and Beth, *The Politics of Mis-Representation*, 33–34, 111–12.

[67] Black and Black, *Politics and Society in the South*, 27; Daniel J. Elazar, *American Federalism* (2nd ed.; New York, 1972), 93–154; Bartley, *The Rise of Massive Resistance*, 18–20; William H. Nicholls, *Southern Tradition and Regional Progress* (Chapel Hill, N.C., 1960).

groups and individuals engaged in self-promotion." Events in the South continued to fascinate academicians, and southern novelists solidified their position as the dominant force in American fiction. Interestingly, the literature of the midforties tended to be optimistic and upbeat, at least in comparison with the despairing tone so frequently in evidence a half decade before.[68]

Richard Wright's autobiographical *Black Boy,* which appeared in 1945, dealt frankly with the daunting impediments a white-supremacy social order placed in the path of black people struggling for survival and dignity, and it concluded with Wright's departing the South. "Yet, deep down," Wright wrote, "I knew that I could never really leave the South, for there had been slowly instilled into my personality and consciousness, black though I was, the culture of the South." Even though he went "without a single backward glance," he concluded on a far more hopeful note than he had in *Native Son.*[69]

Gunnar Myrdal's *An American Dilemma* devoted most of two substantial volumes to sketching the enormous problems faced by blacks, especially in the South, but predicted the coming triumph of the "American Creed of liberty, equality, justice, and fair opportunity for everybody." [70]

Faulkner's first postwar novel, *Intruder in the Dust,* was a mostly optimistic work that varied considerably from the Southern that Faulkner had helped create. As one critic remarked, "Chick is the first white character in Faulkner's Southern saga to make a positive act, not only of atonement for his region's past, but also toward racial justice for the nation's future." In the book, a white boy, Chick, joins forces with a white woman and a black man to clear another black man of a murder charge. Faulkner, or at least the character Gavin Stevens, expressed a moderately conservative

[68] Southern Regional Council, *The South: America's Opportunity Number One* (Atlanta, 1945); Southern Regional Council, "Business Magazine Calls South 'New Industrial Frontier,' " *New South,* January, 1946; Richard M. Weaver, "The South and the Revolution of Nihilism," in *The Southern Essays of Richard M. Weaver,* ed. George M. Curtis III and James J. Thompson, Jr. (Indianapolis, 1987), 184; Richard M. Weaver, *The Southern Tradition at Bay: A History of Postbellum Thought,* ed. George Core and M. E. Bradford (New Rochelle, N.Y., 1968).

[69] Richard Wright, *Black Boy: A Record of Childhood and Youth* (New York, 1945), 284, 281.

[70] Myrdal, *An American Dilemma,* lxx, 997–1024.

but hopeful view of the future of race relations: "I'm defending Sambo from the North and East and West—the outlanders [who would set back black progress] by forcing on us laws based on the idea that man's injustice to man can be abolished overnight by police . . . I only say that the injustice is ours, the South's. We must expiate and abolish it ourselves, alone and without help nor even (with thanks) advice." By the time Faulkner returned to his Snopes trilogy, in 1957, with *The Town*, the Snopes clan had mellowed to where in some respects it had become more comical than sinister.[71]

The liberal program received its classic expression in Stetson Kennedy's *Southern Exposure*, which appeared in 1946. Although much of the book spelled out the respects in which "all's hell on the southern front," Kennedy was enthusiastic about liberal prospects. The reactionary opposition of the "new slavocracy" was formidable, but in contrast to the 1860s, "this time the bulk of the South's people stand ready to fight *for* freedom." History demonstrated, Kennedy argued, that "the plain people of the South—whites and Negroes, farmers and laborers—can work together in the same economic and political organizations and co-operate with similar coalitions nationally for the betterment of all." Kennedy presented the Southern Conference's economic analysis of the origins and purposes of segregation and disfranchisement and hailed its strategy of achieving political and industrial democracy through grass-roots organization with the backing of national liberals.[72]

V. O. Key's *Southern Politics in State and Nation,* published toward the end of the 1940s, assumed a moderate liberal perspective. After unraveling the "unfathomable maze formed by tradition, caste, race, poverty," Key concluded that "an underlying liberal drive permeates southern politics."[73]

The southern old guard found its spokesman in Charles Wallace Collins, an Alabama planter who spent his professional life

[71] F. Garvin Davenport, Jr., *The Myth of Southern History: Historical Consciousness in Twentieth-Century Southern Literature* (Nashville, 1967), 130; William Faulkner, *Intruder in the Dust* (New York, 1949), 131–32; William Faulkner, *The Town* (New York, 1957).

[72] Kennedy, *Southern Exposure,* 127, 19, 357, 47.

[73] Key, *Southern Politics,* 644, 670.

as a lawyer in Washington, D.C. His *Whither Solid South?* which appeared in 1947, was widely read by southern conservatives and became the bible of the Dixiecrats. It depicted the enormous power wielded by forces bent on destroying southern civilization but also optimistically explained how to repulse the assault. According to Collins, two "virulent" forces threatened the region. One was the black movement that was "on the offensive." Although the book rested on white supremacy assumptions, Collins acknowledged that the black leadership was intelligent, well organized, and competent. The other threat emanated from groups supporting "State capitalism," which the Soviet Union's "system of Five-Year Plans" had carried to its "logical and ultimate conclusion." In Collins' judgment, influential admirers of the Soviet system, self-seeking federal bureaucrats, cynical politicians, African Americans, the CIO, and northern church groups misled by "over-simplified slogans" had turned their crusade for black equality and state capitalism to the South, which was the most important bastion of conservative opposition to their plans. Collins outlined strategies of resistance and expressed confidence that the southern people would never permit racial amalgamation or police-state capitalism.[74]

Moderate proponents of economic development, liberal advocates of reform, and conservative defenders of the social and political status quo correctly gauged the enormous impact of World War II. Political and intellectual elites of various ideological persuasions analyzed the opposition and predicted victory for their side. Many appeared blithely sanguine about the prospects of their causes despite the formidable obstacles that they perceived it necessary to overcome. The political struggles of the late 1940s determined the validity of their prophecies and defined the parameters of postwar southern political and social change.

[74] Charles Wallace Collins, *Whither Solid South? A Study in Politics and Race Relations* (New Orleans, 1947), 252, 64, 180, 189.

CHAPTER II

THE RISE AND FALL OF POSTWAR
LIBERALISM

I N LATER years observers sometimes looked back with nostalgia on the decade following World War II. "It was a kind of lovely moment, the period between 1945 and 1954," a commentator wrote in the mid-1970s, "when everything seemed to be working but when the hard issues, not only in the South but elsewhere, had not been faced." A journalist in Mississippi recalled the decade as a "halcyon period for the exponents of gradualism," an era when political demagoguery declined and a "new climate" of racial tolerance gained acceptance. In comparison with the turmoil attending the great civil rights struggles of the 1950s and 1960s, the early postwar years do appear less stressful and disruptive. But to politically active southerners at the time, the mid- and late 1940s were an era of sharp social and ideological conflict when liberals and others struggled for political power in the modernizing South.[1]

National forces generated much of the liberal resurgence. In 1943 the Congress of Industrial Organizations created its Political Action Committee to promote voter registration and turnout among working people and to support the campaigns of progressive candidates. The following year CIO-PAC leaders and independent liberals formed the National Citizens Political Action Committee to mobilize support from nonunionists. Among the leading organizers of NC-PAC were Calvin B. Baldwin and Palmer

---

[1] Peter Schrag, "The New South—Again; or, The View from Inside the Carpetbag," in *The Rising South: Changes and Issues,* ed. Donald R. Noble and Joab L. Thomas (University, Ala., 1976), 111; Hodding Carter III, *The South Strikes Back* (Garden City, N.Y., 1959), 12–13.

Weber, both of Virginia, and Clark H. Foreman, of Georgia. Foreman, who was also president of the Southern Conference for Human Welfare, led an energetic campaign to resurrect the Conference from its wartime doldrums, and during 1945 and 1946 it expanded both its membership and its financing.[2]

A central goal of the Southern Conference was to unite the disparate liberal forces in the region. Although oriented toward the CIO, the Conference endeavored to rally southern progressives generally. In an effort to ease the continuing feud between the CIO and the American Federation of Labor, the Conference included on its board of directors three members from the CIO and three from the AFL, as well as representatives from the Railroad Brotherhoods, United Mine Workers, National Farmers' Union, Southern Regional Council, Highlander Folk School, Southern Negro Youth Congress, and National Council of Negro Women. Former Vice-President Henry A. Wallace, University of North Carolina president Frank P. Graham, several editors of prominent black- and white-circulation newspapers, and a number of clergymen also served on the Conference board. The CIO executive board, the National Association for the Advancement of Colored People, and other change-oriented groups passed resolutions endorsing the Conference program.[3]

Most of all, the Conference sought to organize support for a program of labor organization, particularly the CIO's Operation Dixie. At the national CIO convention in 1940, president John L. Lewis had identified the South as "one of the unfinished jobs ahead of labor in America." Southern wages were the lowest in the nation, the region contained the smallest number of organized workers, and the expansion of northern branch plants into the South made the region a threat to unionism elsewhere. The

[2] Patricia Ann Sullivan, "Gideon's Southern Soldiers: New Deal Politics and Civil Rights Reform, 1933–1948" (Ph.D. dissertation, Emory University, 1983), 98–113; James Caldwell Foster, *The Union Politic: The CIO Political Action Committee* (Columbia, Mo., 1975), 16–75.

[3] "Southern Conference for Human Welfare Officers and Board of Representatives," November 30, 1946, in Southern Conference for Human Welfare Collection, Box 35, Atlanta University Center; Thomas A. Krueger, *And Promises to Keep: The Southern Conference for Human Welfare, 1938–1948* (Nashville, 1967), 122–26; Stetson Kennedy, *Southern Exposure* (Garden City, N.Y., 1946), 36–61.

South was also the home base of legions of anti-union, anti–New Deal congressional Democrats, who in alliance with conservative Republicans made Congress a citadel of social and political reaction. Hence, political and industrial democracy in the South was a crucial variable in the national political equation.[4]

Operation Dixie began in the spring of 1946, and the AFL inaugurated a competing southern drive. The CIO's effort focused on labor in traditional southern industries like textiles, lumber and wood products, and tobacco. The core of the CIO's southern membership, clearly exaggerated at 400,000, was in such consolidated national manufacturing as automobiles, steel, and rubber, in which stronger northern unions could protect their southern brethren. The traditional southern industries were usually smaller and, whether owned in the South or not, were less likely to be branch plants of already unionized northern corporations. They often relied on cheap labor to maintain their competitive position, and they normally adopted a paternal role in their relations with their employees. In the attempt to unionize such firms, the CIO faced a not inconsiderable challenge.

The CIO created a Southern Organizing Committee headed by Van A. Bittner of the steelworkers, although deputy director and later director George Baldanzi of the textile workers managed the committee's day-to-day affairs. Headquartered in Atlanta, the organizing committee operated with a staff of approximately 250 organizers and a budget of a million dollars. Most of the organizers were native southerners and veterans of World War II. The Textile Workers Union of America sent its entire organizing force southward and invested some four million dollars in the effort, and other member unions contributed resources, including a hundred or so organizers. The organizing committee formed a community-relations staff headed by Virginia reformer Lucy Randolph Mason to generate local support for—or at least to soften local hostility to—the campaign.[5]

---

[4] "Mr. Lewis Said," in Textile Workers Union of America Papers, Series A, File 10A, State Historical Society of Wisconsin, Madison.

[5] Barbara S. Griffith, *The Crisis of American Labor: Operation Dixie and the Defeat of the CIO* (Philadelphia, 1988), esp. 3–45; F. Ray Marshall, *Labor in the South* (Cambridge, Mass., 1967), 246–69; Philip S. Foner, *Organized Labor and the Black Worker, 1619–1981* (New

Operation Dixie faced a range of opponents. Hostile company owners and managers truculently combated organizing efforts, sometimes threatening to close plants or to fire workers associated with labor organizers, sometimes expanding welfare provisions for workers to undermine the union's appeal, and almost invariably linking unions with racial integration, Communism, un-Christian values, and outside control of local affairs. Indeed, nonsouthern managers became adept at tarring southern labor organizers as outside agitators. Groups on the order of the Southern States Industrial Council and the Christian-American Association, sometimes joined by local chambers of commerce, carried on ceaseless propaganda campaigns, and the Texas Manufacturers' Association raised more than three million dollars to protect the liberty and independence of working people. *Militant Truth* and other religiously affiliated antiunion publications normally appeared in communities where labor organizers were active. As the editors of *Militant Truth* explained, the CIO's principal aim was "to arouse class-hatred and race-hatred for the purpose of creating strikes, riots, bloodshed, anarchy and revolution."[6]

Most important, the CIO faced the unbending hostility of the county-seat establishment. By attempting to mobilize ordinary white and black workers, the CIO threatened not only the low-wage economy but the entire paternal social order. Labor organizers, like black civil rights advocates, were quite literally "agitators," Jasper Berry Shannon observed, "for they question or attack values which have been set for three or four generations in the hard concrete of custom."[7]

County-elite opposition ensured the hostility of law-enforcement officers. Gunnar Myrdal had written of how southern "peace officers" behaved "as the agents of the planters and other white employers," and union organizers were the object of constant police harassment. After all, a Georgia county sheriff explained to a

---

York, 1982), 277–81; Paul David Richards, "The History of the Textile Workers Union of America, CIO, in the South, 1937–1945" (Ph.D. dissertation, University of Wisconsin at Madison, 1978), 216–17; Research Department, "Economic Notes," October 9, 1954, in Textile Workers Union Papers, Series A, File 1A.

[6] Quoted in *The Crisis of American Labor*, by Griffith, 109.

[7] Jasper Berry Shannon, *Toward a New Politics in the South* (Knoxville, Tenn., 1949), 51.

CIO staffer, "You been associating with niggers and white trash—you ain't seen no decent people since you got here." The police chief of Jackson, Mississippi, may or may not have been facetious in telling Lucy Mason that an organizer should "go to the chamber of commerce and get its approval" and "should also see the managers of the companies and ask them if they objected to his organizing their employees." The close cooperation, Stetson Kennedy wrote, "between so-called public officials and law officers with anti-union employers was everywhere apparent."[8]

As if such resistance were not impediment enough, Operation Dixie divided southern liberals and bred destructive internal conflict. The organizing drive that some hoped would rally southern reformers resulted instead in the disaggregation and ultimate decimation of liberalism in the region. In rapid succession the Southern Organizing Committee denounced the Southern Conference for Human Welfare, participated in a disruptive feud with the AFL, and launched a bitter civil war within the CIO.

All these conflicts originated in the North. The South increasingly became a battleground where northern ideologues skirmished. Southern liberals were sometimes dismayed by the rancor of northern ideological schisms. Virginia Foster Durr scoffed, "For a bunch of unions in New York to be fighting each other over socialism and Trotskyism and Lovestoneism and communism—well, it meant exactly as much to me as whether you got saved by total immersion or dipping." The nominal issue of such conflicts was Communism.[9]

The pressure of developments outside the labor movement pushed union leaders toward a vigilant anticommunism. The CIO had since its inception been under attack from conservatives, and during the war years it had become ever more closely allied with the Democratic party. The death of Roosevelt in the spring of 1945 brought Harry S. Truman to office and inaugurated a period of strained relations between national party managers and the

[8] Gunnar Myrdal, *An American Dilemma: The Negro Problem and Modern Democracy* (New York, 1944), 536; Lucy Randolph Mason, *To Win These Rights: A Personal Story of the CIO in the South* (New York, 1952), 74, 116; Kennedy, *Southern Exposure*, 295.

[9] *Outside the Magic Circle: The Autobiography of Virginia Foster Durr*, ed. Hollinger F. Barnard (University, Ala., 1985), 166.

CIO leadership. Some union executives, already fearful of a postwar conservative reaction like that following World War I, took steps to preserve the organization's national political influence and to accommodate the rabid anticommunism that mushroomed in Democratic ruling circles as Cold War policies took shape.

Concurrently, a growing number of northern liberals who during the 1930s and into the 1940s had supported unionization and broad social reform increasingly identified the public welfare with economic growth, corporate prosperity, and national development, and they viewed international Communism as the most potent threat to their goals. Cold War liberals for a time kept the new president at arm's length, but they heartily endorsed his global anticommunism. The CIO was part of the liberal coalition, and union leaders could hardly fail to be influenced by the evolving outlook of their political allies.[10]

The internal dynamics of the labor movement further encouraged anticommunist obsessions. A long-simmering feud divided the leadership of the CIO's constituent internationals into a moderate and bureaucratic right wing, a radical and idealistic left wing, and a centrist faction that had normally supported the left. During World War II the CIO evolved from a new and militant movement into an accepted, established, and successful institution. Its officialdom served on and worked closely with federal wartime agencies and particularly the National War Labor Board. The experience in national planning kindled what Nelson Lichtenstein has referred to as a "bureaucratic imperative" that led "these officials to rely upon increasingly bureaucratic and undemocratic methods of institutional control." Their overriding concern was with managing a formidable and complex organization, with projecting a favorable national image, and with mounting defenses against the

[10] Mary Sperling McAuliffe, *Crisis on the Left: Cold War Politics and American Liberals, 1947–1954* (Amherst, Mass., 1978), 10–61; Foster, *The Union Politic*, 49–94; Alonzo L. Hamby, *Beyond the New Deal: Harry S. Truman and American Liberalism* (New York, 1973), 3–194; Richard Klimmer, "Liberal Attitudes Toward the South, 1930–1965" (Ph.D. dissertation, Northwestern University, 1976); Harvey A. Levenstein, *Communism, Anticommunism, and the CIO* (Westport, Conn., 1981), 208–52; Bruce J. Schulman, *From Cotton Belt to Sunbelt: Federal Policy, Economic Development, and the Transformation of the South, 1938–1980* (New York, 1991), 3–134.

allegation that the CIO was outside the American mainstream. They moved toward a job-conscious business unionism of the sort the AFL represented as they recruited members into a growing and respectable institution. The union's negotiators more and more regularly fought for contracts with welfare, health, and retirement provisions, thus strengthening its position as the source of social benefits for its own membership while subordinating its earlier commitment to the welfare of workers as a class. The upshot was the ascendancy of the right-wing unionists.[11]

The conservative impulse within the CIO found outlet in an anticommunist crusade. The leadership of the left-wing unions included Communists, and they had antagonized other union officials with their often mindless efforts to support international Communist policies. Of greater significance was the definition of Communism adopted by anticommunist union leaders as well as anticommunist ideologues outside the labor movement. Max M. Kampelman, a political scientist and a "close friend and associate" of Senator Hubert H. Humphrey, provided a standard accounting of the constituency of "Communist domination" in his *The Communist Party vs. the CIO*. Kampelman deemed "Communist strength" to depend on five types of people: the "Party member," the "fellow-traveler," the "sympathizer," the "opportunist," and the "liberal . . . who is willing to associate politically with Communists." Such an enumeration placed beyond the pale almost any proponent of mass social change.[12]

The Association of Catholic Trade Unionists injected the Church into an anticommunist lobbying effort within the CIO. Protestant evangelists organized workers' prayer groups to encourage Christians rather than Communists to become labor leaders. Most important of all, the left-wing radicals and their militant reformism simply became an embarrassment to labor bureaucrats in an age of postwar unity and prosperity. The centrist unions

[11] Nelson Lichtenstein, *Labor's War at Home: The CIO in World War II* (Cambridge, Mass., 1982), 140–245, p. 178 quoted; Frank Emspak, "The Break-Up of the Congress of Industrial Organizations (CIO), 1945–1950" (Ph.D. dissertation, University of Wisconsin, 1972).

[12] Max M. Kampelman, *The Communist Party vs. the CIO: A Study in Power Politics* (New York, 1957), vii (Foreword by Hubert H. Humphrey), 5–6.

44

moved toward an alliance with the right wing that became ever more hostile toward the left wing. The civil war within the CIO affected Operation Dixie directly, but perhaps more damaging still was its absorption of the energy and resources of the northern unions sponsoring the southern drive.[13]

Left-wing unions, the National Citizens Political Action Committee, and the Southern Conference for Human Welfare refused to abandon the commitment to popular-front cooperation that sought to ally radicals, liberals, and moderates in support of a broad reform program. The main impact of harping on Communism, Clark Foreman warned, was "to divide us, to make us attack each other instead of getting on with the job of democracy." Red-baiting was a "negative and undemocratic policy," he stated, and the leadership of both the Southern Conference and the left-wing unions rejected the "exclusion of any Americans because of their political beliefs," since that betrayed a lack of confidence "in the membership's ability to continue charting its course by the expressed majority will." Popular-front reformers argued that, rather than worrying about the influence of the limited number of Communists in the labor movement, liberals might more profitably direct their attention to organizing southern labor and opening the voting booths to southern workers.[14]

Operation Dixie began just as the right wing was asserting its authority over CIO policy. Van Bittner and George Baldanzi were right-wing stalwarts, and the Southern Organizing Committee reflected their outlook. So distrustful were left-wing unionists that

[13] Examining the question of Communism in labor unions from various perspectives are Douglas P. Seaton's *Catholics and Radicals: The Association of Catholic Trade Unionists and the American Labor Movement, from Depression to Cold War* (Lewisburg, Pa., 1981); William G. McLoughlin's *Billy Graham: Revivalist in a Secular Age* (New York, 1960), 101; Lichtenstein's *Labor's War at Home;* Levenstein's *Communism, Americanism, and the CIO;* Emspak's "The Break-Up of the Congress of Industrial Organizations"; Griffith's *The Crisis of American Labor;* Horace Huntley's "Iron Ore Miners and Mine Mill in Alabama, 1933–1952" (Ph.D. dissertation, University of Pittsburgh, 1977); and Randall Lee Patton's "Southern Liberals and the Emergence of a 'New South,' 1938–1950" (Ph.D. dissertation, University of Georgia, 1990).

[14] Manuscript of Speech by Clark H. Foreman Delivered Before the Georgia CIO Industrial Union Council, September 26, 1947, in Southern Conference Collection, Box 36; Clark H. Foreman to Roger Baldwin, May 19, 1942, in Southern Conference Collection, Box 35; Sam Carruthers to William B. Monroe, May 6, 1947, in Southern Conference Collection, Box 37. See Patton, "Southern Liberals and the Emergence of a 'New South.' "

they considered declining to take part in the drive. On its eve, food and tobacco union officials sponsored a meeting of popular-front unionists to debate participation. Their decision to join the campaign came with the determination to outorganize their right-wing rivals. The spirit of competition may have had its positive side, but it was a sharply split CIO that undertook an assault on the citadel of Dixie.[15]

Ideological conflict was a prominent factor influencing the CIO's southern organizing campaign. Bittner promptly made plain that the Southern Organizing Committee had no intention of cooperating with popular-front liberals. Shortly before Operation Dixie began, he declared in Atlanta, "No crowd, whether Communist, Socialist, or anybody else is going to mix up in this organizing drive. That goes for the Southern Conference for Human Welfare. . . . This drive is a CIO affair." The specific incident that provoked Bittner was a fund-raising rally in New York City. The executive secretary of the Southern Conference's New York arm was Branson Price, a North Carolinian residing in New York. Hard driving and competent, Price had developed a highly effective operation in New York and had recruited prominent public personalities to participate in fund-raising activities under the slogan Lend a Hand for Dixieland. In April, 1946, her group joined with left-wing union officials and black militants to sponsor a Help Organize the South rally in Harlem to raise funds for Operation Dixie. Bittner responded by denouncing the Southern Conference and other popular front groups.[16]

If Bittner was hoping to reduce the southern organizing drive's vulnerability to red-baiting from outside the CIO, he was to be disappointed. In May, the AFL initiated a competing drive at a conference in Asheville, North Carolina. The local AFL newspaper welcomed the delegates to a "gathering of freemen unfettered by Russian apron-strings" and called upon them to counter the southern schemes of the CIO, "which gets its inspiration from

[15] Griffith, *The Crisis of American Labor*, 27, 148–49.

[16] Bittner quoted in New York *Times*, April 19, 1946; Washington *Post*, April 19, 1946; *New York Post Daily Magazine*, August 29, 1946; Clark H. Foreman Interview, in Southern Oral History Program, File B-3, Southern Historical Collection, University of North Carolina at Chapel Hill.

Moscow." George Googe, southern director of the AFL and head of the federation's regional organizing campaign, impugned the CIO's "political manipulators, who wish to undermine our present American form of government as well as life." George Meany, secretary-treasurer of the federation, censured the "CIO-Communist drive in the South." William Green, the organization's president, invited southern manufacturers to "grow and cooperate with us or fight for your life against Communist forces." A disgruntled delegate complained that the conference seemed to be doing too little planning and too much "talking about the CIO all the time." [17]

Compared with the CIO's campaign, the AFL's southern effort enjoyed distinct advantages. Federation craft unions had long existed in the South, and although the claimed membership of 1.8 million was inflated, the federation had a well-established network of locals upon which to base a drive. Not only did the AFL have a traditional presence in the South, it represented less of a menace to southern tradition. Its easy acceptance of racially segregated locals, its concern for the interests of skilled—and overwhelmingly white male—workers, its willingness to cooperate with management, and its moderate political inclinations posed little basic threat to the regional status quo. AFL delegates at their 1946 national convention voted against both the continuation of the fair employment practices committee and the enactment of an Equal Rights Amendment, as well as for the work of the House Committee on Un-American Activities. Southern-based employers, if unionization became inevitable, normally preferred the AFL, sometimes, as labor historian F. Ray Marshall has written, taking "measures to insure that AFL unions represented their employees." [18]

Conscious of such advantages, the AFL made a substantial southern commitment. Affiliated unions deployed some 280 organizers, and Googe commanded a staff of 50. The federation

[17] *The Labor Advocate* (published by the Asheville Central Labor Council), May, 1946; Googe and delegate quoted in Charlotte *News,* May 14, 1946; Meany and Green quoted in New York *Times,* May 12, 1946.
[18] "Executive Council Report," *Labor Journal,* October 10, 1946; Marshall, *Labor in the South,* 266; "Labor Drives South," *Fortune,* November, 1946, pp. 134ff.

contended that by June, 1947, the drive had netted a half million new members, but that figure was wishful. Federation officials conceived their southern campaign as a war on the CIO and never evinced the CIO's level of enthusiasm for the venture. Despite the AFL's accommodationist policies, federation organizers too faced antilabor law enforcement, propaganda, and sometimes violence. Within a year of the campaign's inception, Googe reported that it was at a virtual standstill.[19]

The CIO battled the AFL, rejected cooperation with southern liberals, attacked its own left wing, and faced the determined hostility of southern conservatives and employers. Under such conditions, Operation Dixie made fitful progress. In June, 1947, the Southern Organizing Committee announced that 280,000 workers had joined during the first year, but it was no less prone to exaggeration than the AFL. In the key state of North Carolina, the CIO had by June, 1947, won sixty-six National Labor Relations Board elections covering 15,000 workers. During the same period it won fifty-seven of seventy-seven elections in Tennessee, but sixty-four of the contests involved firms with fewer than 200 employees. A vigorous effort in Texas resulted in only 14,500 new members. The Textile Workers Union had by June, 1947, won seventy-six elections covering 23,000 workers; it had lost sixty-seven involving almost 42,000. The campaign recorded gains in branch plants of northern firms and in the tobacco industry, but elsewhere progress was limited.[20]

For CIO officials who had dreamed of signing a million new members in the South, Operation Dixie was failing to justify its substantial cost. At the CIO's national convention in November, 1946, the executive board imposed what Bittner referred to as "disastrous" cuts on the Southern Organizing Committee's budget. The committee had to dismiss about half its organizers. Individual unions within the CIO employed many of the discharged staffers, but the drain of manpower exacerbated the al-

[19] Marshall, *Labor in the South*, 246–54.

[20] *Ibid.*, 264; Randall L. Patton, "The CIO and the Search for a 'Silent South,' " *Maryland Historian*, XIX (1988), 7; Griffith, *The Crisis of American Labor;* Research Department, "Feudal Tactics Thwart Effort to Organize and Sap Vitality of Unions," in Textile Workers Union Papers, Series A, File 1A.

ready substantial problems facing Operation Dixie. The committee responded during the first half of 1947 by recruiting some thousand part-time volunteers to work with the remaining regulars. A shortage of funds continued to plague the drive until late 1948, when the national convention of the CIO allotted the campaign a monthly levy of two cents per member. By then, Operation Dixie's moment had passed.[21]

Congressional enactment of the Taft-Hartley Labor Management Relations Act in June, 1947, was a blow to the southern campaigns of the CIO and the AFL alike. The law's passage was part of a general conservative resurgence, and one of its immediate purposes was to impede unionization in the South. The anticommunist features of Taft-Hartley further isolated left-wing unions. The law neutralized labor unity by banning supportive actions like secondary boycotts and, as a leading labor historian has noted, "made it much more difficult for strong unions to use their organization muscle to aid the unionization effort of weaker groups." Its provisions complicated and slowed the union certification process. "Appeals to the National Labor Relations Board are hopeless because of the time consumed," Emil Rieve, president of the Textile Workers Union, concluded. "The N.L.R.B. doesn't give decisions in these cases; it performs autopsies."[22]

The Taft-Hartley Act also permitted states to set right-to-work requirements. By the end of 1947 a majority of the southern states—seven of the thirteen—had passed open-shop laws or ratified constitutional amendments. By prohibiting union shops, the right-to-work states of Arkansas, Florida, Georgia, North Carolina, Tennessee, Texas, and Virginia assured workers the freedom to choose whether or not to belong to unions that were their authorized bargaining agencies. The right-to-work enactments divided workers, destabilized union membership, gave companies an opportunity to discriminate against union members, and cre-

---

[21] Bittner quoted in *Labor in the South*, by Marshall, 257–59; Griffith, *The Crisis of American Labor*, 41–44; Joseph Y. Garrison, "Paul Revere Christopher, Southern Labor Leader, 1910–1974" (Ph.D. dissertation, Georgia State University, 1977), 161–67; Lawrence E. Davies in New York *Times*, November 26, 1948.

[22] Seaton, *Catholics and Radicals*, 215–17; Lichtenstein, *Labor's War at Home*, 238–41, p. 239 quoted; Rieve quoted by John F. Day in Louisville *Courier-Journal*, October 22, 1950.

ated a host of other problems. Under these arrangements, an organizer recalled, "any mill that wanted to could beat the union." In the wake of Taft-Hartley, the AFL abandoned its flagging southern drive. The CIO struggled doggedly on until the spring of 1953.[23]

The Southern Conference for Human Welfare, after having been jilted by Bittner and the Operation Dixie organizing committee, adopted "as its primary concern the establishment of actual majority rule in the South." The Conference continued to cooperate with and receive funds from left-wing unions, and union officials remained on its board, but it had few ties with the regional effort to increase union membership. Instead the Conference lobbied against the poll tax and state antilabor legislation, promoted the interests of the National Farmers' Union in the South, identified and encouraged liberals to become candidates in elections, participated in local voter registration drives, and opposed and publicized antiblack brutalities. These activities presumably contributed to the organization's improving fortunes as both membership and finances expanded.[24]

Yet the promiscuous range of activity dissipated the Conference's limited resources without promising the kind of decisive liberal breakthrough that Operation Dixie had seemed to herald. The heightening hostility of the Truman administration toward southern liberalism and the widening rift between popular-front liberals and Cold War liberals portended ominous consequences.

[23] J. R. Dempsey, *The Operation of the Right-to-Work Laws* (Milwaukee, 1961), 24–93; "Taft-Hartley Law and NLRB," in Textile Workers Union Papers, Series A, File 1A; Lawrence Rogin Interview, in Southern Oral History Program, Labor History Series, File E-13, p. 48 quoted, Southern Historical Collection.

[24] "Resolutions Adopted by the Board of Representatives," May 28, 1946, in Carl Braden and Anne Braden Papers, Box 18, State Historical Society of Wisconsin. The discussion of the Southern Conference for Human Welfare is based primarily on manuscript sources, but see also Charles H. Martin, "The Rise and Fall of Popular Front Liberalism in the South: The Southern Conference for Human Welfare, 1938–1948," in *Perspectives on the American South: An Annual Review of Society, Politics, and Culture*, Vol. III, ed. James C. Cobb and Charles R. Wilson (New York, 1985), 119–44; Numan V. Bartley, "The Southern Conference and the Shaping of Post–World War II Southern Politics," in *Developing Dixie: Modernization in a Traditional Society*, ed. Winfred B. Moore, Jr., Joseph F. Tripp, and Lyon G. Tyler, Jr. (Westport, Conn., 1988), 179–97; Sullivan, "Gideon's Southern Soldiers"; Krueger, *And Promises to Keep*; and Patton, "Southern Liberals and the Emergence of a 'New South.' "

All the same, the situation afforded the Southern Conference an opportunity to mobilize and lead a southern popular-front movement that looked toward a return to New Deal priorities. Committed to the proposition that only the empowerment of the masses of citizens could provide the foundation for a soundly structured liberalism, some Conference members came to perceive politics as the path to political and industrial democracy. "I am convinced," Clark Foreman wrote, "that the best hope for the future lies in the building of a sound progressive party which, perhaps, will not command relatively more attention this year than did the Republican Party in 1856, but which will, nevertheless, create a solid opposition." Foreman, Virginia Durr, Branson Price, and other nationally oriented officials set about to align the Conference with the broader struggle over the direction of liberal policy.[25]

The recognized leader of the popular front was Henry A. Wallace. After Truman dismissed Wallace as secretary of commerce in September, 1946, Wallace became more outspoken in his criticisms of Truman's policies. By the end of the year, popular-front liberals had created the Progressive Citizens of America, and early in 1947 the Cold War liberals formed the Americans for Democratic Action. During 1947 the ADA established chapters in several southern states to compete with Southern Conference state committees. In Foreman's judgment, the "present administration" had abandoned the New Deal, had adopted a policy of cooperation with old-guard southern conservatives, and had become consumed with promoting democracy in Poland while ignoring the obstacles to democracy in Texas, Virginia, and Alabama. "The human needs and the political aspirations of the Southern people," the Conference board vowed, "will not be frustrated by reactionary programs of either traditional party."[26]

To Truman, Wallace and his collaborators were "Reds, phonies and . . . 'parlor pinks' [who] seem to be banded together and are

[25] Clark H. Foreman to Frank P. Graham, February 13, 1948, in Frank Porter Graham Papers, Southern Historical Collection; Sullivan, "Gideon's Southern Soldiers," 239–48.

[26] Clark H. Foreman, "The Election and the South" (Draft of speech before the National Council of Negro Women, November 15, 1946), in Southern Conference Collection, Box 35; "Resolution Adopted by the Board of Representatives," April 19, 1947, in Southern Conference Collection, Box 37.

becoming a national danger." The danger was not least to Truman's own plans for reelection in 1948. His political advisers estimated from polling data collected during 1947 that Wallace would, as a third-party candidate, receive approximately 10 percent of the presidential vote, most of it from Democratic partisans. The neutralization of the threat Wallace presented became a central political preoccupation. With the implementation of Cold War measures, administration policy makers became ever more antagonistic toward Wallace and his anti–Cold War popular-front allies. By the time Clark Clifford in November, 1947, penned his well-known memorandum on strategy for the election, the solution to the Wallace problem was "to identify him and isolate him in the public mind with the Communists." The Americans for Democratic Action "assumed the prime responsibility for challenging" Wallace and his "Communist-dominated unions and individuals well-known as CP apologists."[27]

In November, 1946, the Conference held its annual convention in New Orleans. "The Conference was undoubtedly at the strongest position in its history when the convention ended," a delegate remarked. Among the speakers at the racially desegregated meeting were Claude Pepper, senator from Florida; Walter White, executive secretary of the NAACP; Mary McLeod Bethune, president of the National Council of Negro Women; and Ellis Arnall, governor of Georgia. The growth of the Conference had led to the creation of a tax-exempt Southern Conference Education Fund, with Foreman serving as president of both the Conference and the fund, and James A. Dombrowski as administrator of both. During the World War II doldrums, Dombrowski had labored tirelessly to keep the Conference afloat, and he and some longtime members thought the body owed him a considerable debt. Dombrowski was also meticulous, slow, and provincial—hardly the per-

[27] Truman Diary, September 19, 1946, in *Mr. President,* by William Hillman (New York, 1952), 28; Gael Sullivan, "Re Wallace Situation" (Memorandum for the president), June 2, 1947, "The Major Findings" (Analysis of public-opinion polls), December, 1947, Clark Clifford, Memorandum for the President, November 19, 1947, p. 6, Americans for Democratic Action Publicity Department, "Henry A. Wallace: The First Three Months," all in Clark Clifford Papers, Political File, Harry S. Truman Library, Independence, Mo.; James I. Loeb Oral History Interview, June 26, 1970, Clark Clifford Oral History Interview, April 19, 1971, both in Truman Library.

son to direct a campaign to rally the southern popular front. In New Orleans, a board meeting heavy with Foreman loyalists kept Dombrowski on as administrator of the fund but replaced him with the aggressive Branson Price as administrator of the Southern Conference.[28]

Dombrowski objected, and the subsequent controversy brought to a head the underlying divisions within the Conference. Right-wing unionists led by Lucy Mason of the Southern Organizing Committee seized upon the issue as a way to oppose the Conference's drift into the Wallace camp. In addition to insisting on a review of the personnel changes, Mason argued that the Conference should abandon its political aspirations, sharply scale back its activities, and become a "small, militant, standard-bearing organization" reiterating to southerners the evils of segregation and other social injustices. William Mitch, a district director of the United Mine Workers, headed a small but energetic socialist group that opposed the appointment of Price. Aubrey Williams, publisher of the *Southern Farmer* and a leader of the Farmers' Union, numbered among those who supported the reappointment of Dombrowski because of personal friendship and a sense of obligation.[29]

Ultimately Dombrowski accepted selection as administrator of only the education fund, which drifted away to become a small and harmless antisegregation agency of the sort Mason had thought the Conference should be. The departure of labor unionists from the Conference accelerated, as did that of Democratic party loyalists and of liberals who because of belief or expediency chose to abandon the popular front. As the Conference became more closely identified with Wallace, funding problems grew. Union contributions declined sharply, and the Conference was more than ever dependent on money raised in the North and particularly in New York City, where the schism within the liberal camp

[28] Margaret Fisher to Clark H. Foreman, December 29, 1946, in Southern Conference Collection, Box 35; "Fourth Biennial Convention: Southern Conference for Human Welfare," November 28–30, 1946, in Braden Papers, Box 18.

[29] Lucy R. Mason, "Memorandum to Board of Representatives," April 19, 1947, in Braden Papers, Box 18; William Mitch to Clark H. Foreman, December 10, 1946, in Southern Conference Collection, Box 35.

made fund raising treacherous. Internal dissension, membership defections, and declining finances crippled Conference activities. Edmonia W. Grant, a black woman, was the compromise choice as Conference administrator, and she presided over the organization's decline. Foreman's faction joined forces with Progressive Citizens of America and worked to incorporate the Conference into Wallace's third-party campaign.[30]

The controversy occurred against a background of criticism by champions of anticommunism. Two weeks before the Conference's convention, the Young Men's Business Club of New Orleans endorsed a report by its Americanism committee condemning the Conference for its "definite communistic tendencies." The club offered accurate and impressive evidence to support its assertions: "The SCHW advocates the repeal of the poll tax, the passing of the FEPC bill, better living conditions for the working man, civil liberties, racial equality and more." The "real aim" of the Conference had to be "mass Revolution." It was no surprise when the New Orleans *States,* the Nashville *Banner,* and other conservative newspapers capitalized on the report and the publicity over the convention to attack the Conference. But when Ralph W. McGill and the Atlanta *Constitution* led in accusing the organization of being "badly tainted at the top with Communism and fellow travelling," Conference members had a measure of the swelling anticommunist tide.[31]

The Cold War escalated with congressional approval of the Truman Doctrine in March, 1947. The containment policy and Truman's accompanying pronouncements set in sharp contrast an aggressive international Communist conspiracy and the American defense of the free world. In the same month, Truman established by executive order the Federal Employee Loyalty Program to purge from government popular-front liberals and other opponents of Cold War policies. The Justice Department and the Fed-

[30] Krueger, *And Promises to Keep,* 142–76; Sullivan, "Gideon's Southern Soldiers," 214–48.

[31] Report in *Action: Official Publication of the Young Men's Business Club of New Orleans,* November 13, 1946, in Southern Conference Collection, Box 35; Ralph W. McGill in Atlanta *Constitution,* December 3, 1946. See also press clippings in Records of the Southern Conference for Human Welfare, Box 1, Tuskegee Institute Archives.

eral Bureau of Investigation became more vigorous in their search for subversives. The FBI's inclusion of interracial association among the criteria of subversion made left-wing unions and other popular-front groups prime suspects. Durr observed, "We were surrounded by the FBI." Congress joined the campaign through its investigating committees and particularly through its House Committee on Un-American Activities. Historian Richard M. Freeland was essentially accurate when he wrote that "in 1947, as much as in 1917 or 1941, the American people were being mobilized for world war." In the mobilization, the suppression of dissent was by no means directed only at Communists and subversives—or more correctly, Communism and subversion were defined in such ways as to encompass substantial numbers of Americans.[32]

The House Un-American Activities Committee intervened significantly for the first time in southern affairs in June, 1947. That spring Wallace had set out on an ambitious national speaking tour to rally opposition to Truman's policies. The Conference sponsored Wallace's appearances in the South. From there, he traveled to Washington, D.C., where the Conference staged a huge National Welcome Rally as the final event of the tour. Shortly before the rally, the Un-American Activities Committee released its "Report on Southern Conference for Human Welfare." The Committee searched for Communists in the Southern Conference and, finding none, concluded that the Conference was "perhaps the most deviously camouflaged Communist-front organization" in the nation. The report appeared during the the month of the enactment of Taft-Hartley and the unveiling of the Marshall Plan. Whereas the Truman Doctrine drew limited popular applause, the

[32] C. Girard Davidson Oral History Interview, July 17, 1972, pp. 45–50, in Truman Library; Clark H. Foreman to Tom C. Clark, November 4, 1947, in Southern Conference Collection, Box 36; Myles Horton to J. Howard McGrath, January 31, 1951, in Highlander Research and Education Center Papers, Box 33, State Historical Society of Wisconsin; *Outside the Magic Circle: The Autobiography of Virginia Foster Durr,* 188; Richard M. Freeland, *The Truman Doctrine and the Origins of McCarthyism: Foreign Policy, Domestic Politics, and Internal Security, 1946–1948* (New York, 1972), 226; Athan Theoharis, "The Escalation of the Loyalty Program," in *Politics and Policies of the Truman Administration,* ed. Barton J. Bernstein (Chicago, 1970), 243–68; Paul Boyer, *By the Bomb's Early Light: American Thought and Culture at the Dawn of the Atomic Age* (New York, 1985); David Caute, *The Great Fear: The Anti-Communist Purge Under Truman and Eisenhower* (New York, 1978).

Marshall Plan met with widespread support. The "Communist-front" Conference, left-wing unions, and similar groups faced ever mounting difficulties.[33]

Conference members organized two further tours in the South for Wallace, and the results of them attested to the region's changing political climate. In the fall of 1947, Wallace visited eight southern cities. Arranging the itinerary was difficult because Wallace refused to address racially segregated audiences. In the earlier tour, the meetings the Southern Conference had sponsored were integrated, but on at least one occasion Wallace made a side trip under the auspices of a different group and talked before a segregated gathering. This time the Conference stressed in its promotional literature, "*No racial segregation.*" As a result, a number of cities had to be dropped from the itinerary because public officials refused to permit racially integrated events. For the first time, Conference organizers encountered real difficulty finding prominent people willing to identify with it. Nevertheless, Wallace attracted impressive crowds in Atlanta, Norfolk, and elsewhere. "The Wallace meetings demonstrated," Edmonia Grant exulted, "that SCHW can be a mass political organization."[34]

One year later, in the fall of 1948, Wallace again toured the South. By then, he was an announced candidate for the presidency, and Foreman had resigned from the Conference to devote full time to the Progressive party campaign. The collapsing

[33] "Report on Southern Conference for Human Welfare," Committee on Un-American Activities, 80th Cong., 1st Sess., Report 592, June 16, 1947, p. 17. The conference publicized a rebuttal of the report's accusations: Walter Gellhorn, "Report on a Report of the House Committee on Un-American Activities," *Harvard Law Review*, LV (1947), 1193–1234. Press treatment of the report is surveyed in *Citizens in Action* (published by the Southern Conference Washington Committee), June 27, 1947. Wallace's southern tour is described in "Report of the Administrator," n.d., in Southern Conference Collection, Box 37. The best study of Wallace's campaign for president is Curtis D. MacDougall's *Gideon's Army* (3 vols.; New York, 1965); the best study of his southern campaign is Sullivan's "Gideon's Southern Soldiers." See also McAuliffe, *Crisis on the Left;* Norman D. Markowitz, *The Rise and Fall of the People's Century: Henry A. Wallace and American Liberalism, 1941–1948* (New York, 1973); and Richard J. Walton, *Henry Wallace, Harry Truman, and the Cold War* (New York, 1976).

[34] Edmonia W. Grant to chairmen of state committees, October 5, 1947, in Southern Conference Collection, Box 25; Edmonia W. Grant to Clark H. Foreman, September 14, 1947, in Southern Conference Collection, Box 36; Memorandum, Edmonia W. Grant to board members, January 23, 1948, in Braden Papers, Box 18.

Southern Conference had no role in Wallace's swing through the region, but Durr, Price, and other Conference loyalists handled arrangements for the tour. Wallace's appearances were on the whole disasters; hostile whites greeted the former vice-president with demonstrations and disruptions, with epithets of Communist and nigger lover, and with occasional barrages of eggs and tomatoes. Wallace received his unfriendliest reception in North Carolina, where Jonathan Daniels and the Raleigh *News and Observer* led the media assault. A journalist captured the trend of events in reporting that "for the first time in two days, he was able to make a completely audible speech." Even when Wallace's orations were audible, though, his audiences seemed to be evincing good manners, and perhaps curiosity, rather than enthusiasm.[35]

By late 1948 the popular front's message was no longer welcome in the South. The Truman administration and the ADA had successfully isolated Wallace, Truman had delivered his civil rights message to Congress, and the States' Rights Democrats had risen to the defense of the segregated southland, all of which placed pressure on those in the South who actually practiced racial equality. Foreign policy crises involving Czechoslovakia and Berlin further discredited opposition to the Cold War. The Wallace campaign fared even more poorly in the South than elsewhere. The effort to rally a popular-front movement through a third-party political campaign failed ignominiously. Shortly after the election, a small group of hard-core Conference members at the "final meeting of the Board of Representatives" in Richmond announced that "the Board of the SCHW had decided to suspend the operations of the Conference."[36]

Within a year of the demise of the Conference, Operation Dixie effectively collapsed. The *Southern Textile News* proclaimed in October, 1949, that "the widely touted, blatantly advertised, all-out frontal attack on the unorganized South, and principally the textile industry, has undoubtedly failed. Its failure was spectacular."

[35] John N. Popham in New York *Times*, September 1, 1948; MacDougall, *Gideon's Army*, 707–44; Sullivan, "Gideon's Southern Soldiers," 296–351.

[36] MacDougall, *Gideon's Army*, 707–44; "Minutes of the Final Meeting of the Board of Representatives," November 21, 1948, in Braden Papers, Box 18. See also Markowitz, *The Rise and Fall of the People's Century*, 276–77.

Union officers privately agreed that the assessment was accurate. A labor historian has reported that by 1949 "the CIO's position in the South had not improved much over what it had been in 1946 in spite of the expenditure of a great deal of money." Officials of the textile union were even more discouraged. At a meeting of southern state directors in 1949, executive vice-president William Pollock pointed out, "There are 650,000 textile workers in the southern states and 74,000 of them are members. We are gradually being liquidated in the South."[37]

The liquidation turned out not to be very gradual. Ironically, the organizing drive of the CIO that aimed to bridge sectional differences by bringing the South into the national labor movement foundered in part because of sectional differences in the textile union. In 1951 president Rieve and other officers who leaned toward the New England unions insisted that their southern counterparts demand a significant wage increase and a cost-of-living clause to match the increases negotiated in New England, so as to help "close the growing gap in wages and fringe benefits in the two areas of the country." Because the textile industry was in a slump, southern unionists, who tended to look to Baldanzi for leadership, argued that their locals were not strong enough to risk a confrontation with the textile companies. The national officers insisted, however, and the southern unions launched a major strike involving the largest unionized firms in the region and half the total southern membership. Textile executives, with demand for their products off, grasped the opportunity for battle. In Danville, Virginia, as elsewhere, union officials "found the entire community mobilized against the strike, and the company guided in its actions by a firm of public relations experts and community specialists." To make matters worse, national officials were miserly in dispensing relief funds, at least according to southern unionists. The strike was crushed. In the following year the strain between Baldanzi and Rieve became a break, and Baldanzi

[37] Frank A. Constangy, "CIO's Operation Dixie Is Dismal Failure," *Southern Textile News*, October 15, 1949; Emspak, "The Break-Up of the Congress of Industrial Organizations," 299; "Minutes of Meeting of TWUA Southern State Directors," May 5, 1949, in Textile Workers Union Papers, Series A, Box 19.

led most of what remained of the southern textile unionists into the AFL.[38]

The struggle between right-wing and left-wing unions flared into open warfare during the late 1940s. In the spring of 1948, right-wing and centrist unions began openly to raid left-wing locals. The most dramatic and revealing case involved the left-wing food and tobacco Local 22, the union's largest local and the bargaining agent at what was reputed to be the world's largest tobacco factory in Winston-Salem, North Carolina. Organized during World War II, Local 22 launched a strike in 1947 that attracted widespread attention. The five thousand or so black employees for the most part supported it and joined the picket lines, but most of the five thousand or so whites continued to report to work.

The Winston-Salem *Journal* launched an attack on the local. The banner headline Communist-Union Collusion Is Exposed in City captured the flavor of the stories the newspaper ran. The House Un-American Activities Committee scurried to investigate the extent of Communist infiltration into the cigarette industry. The Southern Organizing Committee distanced itself from the strike and withheld financial aid. The black community sided with the strikers and during the conflict elected Kenneth Williams a city alderman, the first southern black city official in the twentieth century to be seated after defeating a white opponent. The strikers eventually agreed to a negotiated settlement in which they won a significant number of their demands.[39]

Thereafter right-wing unions mounted a full-scale assault on food and tobacco. The Southern Organizing Committee and the North Carolina staff of the CIO backed the United Transport Services of America, which succeeded in replacing food and tobacco

[38] "Report on Southern Strike," June 26, 1951, in Textile Workers Union Papers, Series A, Box 1; Patton, "Southern Liberals and the Emergence of a 'New South,'" 142–55; Joseph D. Pedigo Interview, in Southern Oral History Program, Labor History Series, File E-11, Southern Historical Collection.

[39] Winston-Salem *Journal*, May 19, 1947; Bob Korstad, "Those Who Were Not Afraid: Winston-Salem, 1943," in *Working Lives: The "Southern Exposure" History of Labor in the South*, ed. Marc S. Miller (New York, 1980), 184–99; Southern Conference for Human Welfare, "Report on Strike at R. J. Reynolds Tobacco Company," July 23, 1947, in Southern Conference Collection, Box 39.

locals at some North Carolina firms. In 1949 United Transport set its sights on Local 22, labeling it a Communist organization and petitioning the National Labor Relations Board to conduct an election. The ballot offered workers a choice among United Transport, Local 22, and "no union." With the two unions in internecine combat, the local white business community damning both, and the workers divided along racial lines, a narrow plurality voted for "no union." [40]

Throughout the South right and center unions conducted similar campaigns. "We don't have raids in the CIO," Baldanzi explained. "We have revolts of workers against Communist domination." In Alabama, the workers' revolt included a concerted attack by the steelworkers on the left-wing mine, mill, and smelters union. The organizing committee clashed with the racially egalitarian packinghouse workers centered in Texas, conducting a formal investigation of its activities and attempting to freeze its treasury. At times Operation Dixie seemed more effective at busting unions than at organizing them. Nationally, the CIO was even more ruthless, making the decision at its 1949 convention to expel the left-wing internationals and thereby casting from the congress more than a million unionists.[41]

With the expulsion of the left wing, the CIO's commitment to racial equality languished. Left-wing officials, more so than their rivals, took seriously the vision of an interracial political and industrial democracy. "The left-led CIO unions," a union executive explained, sought to overcome differences between "men and women, black and white, skilled and unskilled," and to propel the workers toward understanding "their status as '*workers*' as the most

[40] Foner, *Organized Labor and the Black Worker*, 261–82; Philip S. Foner, *Women and the American Labor Movement: From World War I to the Present* (New York, 1980), 402–10; Griffith, *The Crisis of American Labor*, 150–55; Robert Korstad and Nelson Lichtenstein, "Opportunities Found and Lost: Labor, Radicals, and the Early Civil Rights Movement," *Journal of American History*, LXXV (1988), 786–811.

[41] Baldanzi quoted in "The Break-Up of the Congress of Industrial Organizations," by Emspak, 280; Huntley, "Iron Ore Miners and Mine Mill in Alabama," 123–225; Robert J. Norrell, "Caste in Steel: Jim Crow Careers in Birmingham, Alabama," *Journal of American History*, LXXIII (1986), 669–94; Rick Halpern, "Fort Worth's Packinghouse Workers, 1937–1954," in *Organized Labor in the Twentieth-Century South*, ed. Robert H. Zieger (Knoxville, Tenn., 1991), 158–82; David Burgess Interview, in Southern Oral History Program, Labor History Series, File E-1, Southern Historical Collection.

important" so as not to "allow other 'peripheral' differences to keep them from unity to win their common goal." The left-wing unions were consistently more likely than others to hire black and female organizers, choose black and female officers, and object to job discrimination. The tobacco workers not only relied on black members but much of the leadership was black and often female; Miranda Smith served on the international's executive board, occupying the highest position a black woman had ever held in the labor movement.[42]

Right-wing unions and the Southern Organizing Committee attempted to avert controversy by limiting the visibility of black unionists, and they disparaged the left wing for disregarding southern usages. In the Birmingham area the steelworkers rarely protested against policies of white supremacy; one study has reported that unionization created "greater restrictions on black opportunity than had existed before the 1930s." The left-wing mine, mill union had a creditable racial record, but after the steelworkers captured its locals, the leadership became entirely white. To be sure, inasmuch as unions were virtually the only local institutions blacks and whites shared, they were a positive force in southern race relations, and some CIO and occasionally AFL locals endeavored to promote enlightened racial policies. Nevertheless, the evidence supports the conclusion of Philip S. Foner that by the early 1950s "segregation was becoming so widespread at functions sponsored by CIO affiliates in the South that it was the practice to hold most meetings on a segregated basis."[43]

Black unionists attempted to arrest the CIO's drift from interracial solidarity by organizing the National Negro Labor Council. Paul Robeson, an actor and singer who had participated in membership and fund-raising drives for the Southern Conference for Human Welfare, spoke at the council's formational meeting in 1950 and was one of a number of black popular-front liberals identified with the body. The council cooperated on occasion with left-wing unions that the CIO had expelled. Active primarily in

[42] Karl Korstad, "An Account of the 'Left-Led' CIO Unions' Efforts to Build Unity Among the Workers in Southern Factories During the 1940s," in Textile Workers Union Papers, Series A, Box 12.

[43] Norell, "Caste in Steel," 679; Foner, *Organized Labor and the Black Worker*, 292.

the North, it sponsored black labor councils whose charge was to press for racial equality within CIO-affiliated unions. Both CIO officialdom and conservative black organizations repudiated the National Negro Labor Council, and predictably a congressional committee hastened to investigate and to pronounce it a conduit for "pro-Communist ideology." The council and its arms did not survive the antagonism directed toward them. By the midfifties, the CIO's outlook was largely indistinguishable from the AFL's, and the two unions merged into the AFL-CIO.[44]

Operation Dixie failed to establish political and industrial democracy or to build a strong union movement in the South. In 1953 an estimated 17 percent of the region's nonagricultural workers held union membership, about the same percentage who were unionists at the beginning of the organizing drives. The members often worked in southern plants of northern corporations, where national contracts signed in the North protected them, or they were skilled craftsmen in AFL brotherhoods. They were also more likely than other workers to be employed in capital-intensive "new industries," particularly those connected with national defense.[45]

Considerably more often than not, unionists were the relatively well paid workers who least needed union protection. With the partial exception of such workers as those in tobacco and petroleum—and the coal miners, who had created a strong union prior to World War II—employees in traditional southern industries largely remained outside the labor movement. The South contained islands of union strength, as had been the situation at the close of World War II, but as a force for social and political change, unions were in a position to contribute rather little to the shaping of the modern South.

The collapse of Wallace's campaign ended prospects for a vigorously assertive, grass-roots liberal political movement in the region. The truncated southern electorate was a formidable curb on the efforts of the Southern Conference for Human Welfare to

<hr>

[44] Manning Marable, *Race, Reform, and Rebellion: The Second Reconstruction in Black America, 1945–1982* (Jackson, Miss., 1984), 31–33; Foner, *Organized Labor and the Black Worker*, 293–311.

[45] Marshall, *Labor in the South*, 270–352.

unite "the working people and the farmers . . . to get justice from their government," but the experience of the Wallace campaign outside the South suggested that the attempt was foredoomed. The denouement of popular-front politics occurred in 1950, when the two remaining public figures closely associated with the Southern Conference were turned out of office. Senator Frank P. Graham, the honorary president of the Conference, and Senator Claude Pepper, a friend of the Conference who supported Wallace in 1948, succumbed to the virulent red-baiting and race-baiting of their challengers. In both North Carolina and Florida, the victorious candidates in the Democratic primary elections excoriated the red "birds of a feather" for being followers of Wallace and of Communism and urged that "white people wake up" to the threat of racial intermingling. Willis D. Smith, the victor in North Carolina, modeled his runoff strategy on the Florida Program that Representative George A. Smathers developed. Journalist Samuel Lubell described the outcome of the two elections as the "most crushing setbacks Southern liberalism has suffered since the coming of Franklin Roosevelt."[46]

In 1938 when Pepper was elected to his first full term in the Senate, President Roosevelt attempted to purge leading southern conservatives from the Democratic party. In 1950 President Truman helped persuade Smathers to become a candidate in order to purge a liberal from the Senate. In Gunnar Myrdal's words, southern liberalism got "its power from outside the South" and "mainly from Washington." When Foreman and his associates set about to expand the Southern Conference into a force in regional affairs, they could count on support from the White House. After Truman became president, however, southern New Dealers were no longer welcome. Maury Maverick—a Texas New Dealer who had kept clear of the popular front—complained that an "old FDR man just can't get near the White House." Truman wrote back, "It has always been said that you could never have an Irish

[46]Press Release, June 27, 1947, in Southern Conference Collection, Box 36; Robert Sherrill, *Gothic Politics in the Deep South: Stars of the New Confederacy* (New York, 1968), 136–73; Warren Ashby, *Frank Porter Graham, a Southern Liberal* (Winston-Salem, N.C., 1980), 260–65; Samuel Lubell, *The Future of American Politics* (2nd ed.; Garden City, N.Y., 1956), 106–16, p. 107 quoted.

Band because every member wants to be a leader and that is what the trouble is with the so-called F.D.R. people, who started at the top and who never polled a precinct or became elected in their lives—a great bunch—at least they're great on ballyhoo."[47]

Foreman later reflected rather bitterly, "Actually, the cold war was fought largely in the U.S., and it was a war in which the weapons were fear and defamation. Many organizations and people surrendered their principles and their interests because they were told that unless they did so they would be guilty of helping the Russians." Certainly, Foreman's grievance was not without basis: the anticommunist crusade was the crucial factor in the destruction of the popular front. But equally fundamentally the Truman administration and the Americans for Democratic Action helped reshape American liberalism in a manner that made grass-roots, popular-front New Deal reform not only treasonous but also passé. Wartime and postwar prosperity and the surge toward national consensus in the face of war and Cold War enemies combined with developing intellectual trends to undermine the assumptions upon which the programs of Operation Dixie and the Southern Conference were based. Civil rights, and most especially black civil rights, moved to the top of the liberal reform agenda.[48]

Lillian E. Smith embodied crucial features of the liberal transformation in her brief essay "Two Men and a Bargain." The bargain whereby the poor white would "boss the nigger" and the rich white would "boss the money" made the poor white "boss of everything but wages and hours and prices and jobs and credit and the vote—and his own living." The poor white was "free to lynch and flog, to burn and threaten," and to conform to the wisdom that "there's nothing so good for folks as to go to church on Sundays," but by 1943 both the poor white and the poor black were beginning to realize that they traveled "down the road that went nowhere." Southerners were talking of Christian brother-

[47] John Egerton, "Courtly Champion of America's Elderly," *New York Times Magazine,* November 29, 1981; Myrdal, *An American Dilemma,* 456, 466; Maury Maverick to Harry S. Truman, May 7, 1948, Harry S. Truman to Maury Maverick, May 12, 1948, both in Papers of Harry S. Truman, President's Secretary's Files, Political File, Truman Library.

[48] Clark H. Foreman to Thomas A. Krueger, December 19, 1967, in Southern Conference Collection, Box 1.

hood, poor whites were joining poor blacks in labor unions, and new questions were being asked "about money and wages and jobs and hours and things like that." The rich white "blamed it on the damyankee and the New Deal and the communist and Mrs. Roosevelt," but clearly the "bargain was breaking." Up to that point, Smith's parable rested on mainstream liberal assumptions. Not until the concluding paragraphs did an inner voice disclose that as "long as you have segregation none of these things can happen." The inner voice was the "seed of hate and fear and guilt," and it fed on the "strange fruit" of a southern culture shaped by white supremacy. What the voice made clear was that labor unions and voting and things like that were idle unless southerners overcame the more basic problem of racial segregation. A second voice—"sometimes it sounded as quiet and simple as Jesus; and sometimes as plain-written as the Bill of Rights"—urged them to do just that. In Smith's view, the resolution of the Manichaean conflict between the two inner voices of the individual white southern mind was the key to southern change. The South would not be redeemed by broad programs of social reform, she wrote in an article the following year; rather, "it can change as rapidly as each of us can change his own heart." [49]

Myrdal's *An American Dilemma* achieved its almost instant status as a classic in part because it gave explicit expression to the emerging trends in liberal thought. The "Negro problem" *was* the "dilemma" of American democracy, and Myrdal's analysis of it codified the outlook of liberal reformers. "The American Negro problem is a problem in the heart of the American," Myrdal wrote. "It is there that the decisive struggle goes on." Although the "Negro genius" was "imprisoned in the Negro problem," the problem itself was a "white man's problem." At issue was morality: "At bottom our problem is the moral dilemma of the American—the conflict between his moral valuations on various levels of consciousness and generality." Individual white Americans were torn between their belief in the "American Creed of liberty, equality, justice, and fair opportunity for everybody" and their practice of

[49] Lillian E. Smith, "Two Men and a Bargain: A Parable of the Solid South," *South Today*, Spring, 1943, pp. 5–14; Smith, "Addressed to White Liberals," *New Republic*, CXI (1944), 332.

racial oppression. Myrdal found that whites often discussed racial issues in terms of right and wrong. Therefore, "to view the Negro problem as primarily a moral issue" coincided "with popular thinking."[50]

Published in 1944, *An American Dilemma* broke with much of the scholarship of the 1930s by placing its stress on the competition and hostility between working-class whites and blacks rather than on their basic compatibility of interests. The white working class lacked the "psychological identification" with class position that might have made "interest solidarity" a feasible option. Instead, the "lower class whites have been the popular strength" behind antiblack public policies, and the "hatred of lower class whites toward Negroes" was the foundation upon which the appeal of white supremacy rested. The more natural ally for blacks was the "upper class of white people," the "people with economic and social security who are truly a 'noncompeting group.'" Better-educated whites of substance, according to Myrdal, were noticeably more tolerant than poorly educated and economically insecure lower-income whites. Myrdal also argued that "it is the upper class Negroes who have felt and expressed most clearly and persistently the Negro protest against segregation." Through organizations like the NAACP, they had formulated the most "clearly conceived tactical plan" for racial progress. The basic problem was the racism of ordinary southern whites, and the solution was to uplift them and educate them, thereby weaning them from their psychological commitment to white supremacy. "The problem for political liberalism," Myrdal wrote, "appears to be first to lift the masses to security and education and then to work to make them liberal."[51]

A product of the time, *An American Dilemma* endorsed black civil equality and was optimistically confident that Americans would find the way out of their dilemma democratically. The book was so inclusive, so perceptive, and so gracefully written that—except from a racist standpoint—it was difficult to criticize. To Myrdal, racism was a moral question—a matter of right and wrong—rather

[50] Myrdal, *An American Dilemma,* lxix–lxxi, 28.
[51] *Ibid.,* 68–69, 73, 597–98, 795.

than the product of socioeconomic and ideological forces. Racism was personal rather than institutional; it was a matter of individual psychology—a person was prejudiced or was not—rather than a consequence of group power and position within the social structure. Myrdal put the ameliorative influence of education ahead of the reorganization of society and the redistribution of wealth and power. He argued that the racism—the immorality—of working-class whites was the central impediment to racial progress and that, among blacks, the "theory of labor solidarity" was essentially "escapist in nature" rather than reformist. The evidence suggested to him that African-American civic progress was dependent on the leadership of black elites and the cooperation of affluent whites rather than on the organized militancy of the economically disadvantaged.[52]

Few of these propositions were new. Conservatives and racial gradualists had often invoked the individual nature of prejudice and the entrenched racism of lower-class whites as pretexts for maintaining the social status quo. Critics had often employed moral arguments to attack peculiar southern racial practices. Myrdal's ability to combine the two arguments was both a tribute to his intellectual acuity and a sign of the times. Deemphasized, denigrated, or discarded in Myrdal's analysis were most of the assumptions that undergirded the Roosevelt administration's *Report on Economic Conditions of the South* and that drove the programs of the Southern Conference and the early CIO.

Northern Cold War liberals led in reformulating national liberal priorities. Committed to a foreign policy that required massive public expenditures and ever proliferating programs, liberals promoted a military Keynesianism designed to produce weaponry and expand the gross national product. The peculiar career of the anticommunist crusade made liberals even more cautious about domestic reform. By proclaiming a former vice-president of the United States, two United States senators, and a host of once

[52] *Ibid.*, 793. See also David W. Southern, *Gunnar Myrdal and Black-White Relations: The Use and Abuse of "An American Dilemma," 1944–1969* (Baton Rouge, 1987); John Horton, "Order and Conflict Theories of Social Problems as Competing Ideologies," *American Journal of Sociology,* LXXI (1966), 701–13; and Judith Caditz, *White Liberals in Transition: Current Dilemmas in Ethnic Integration* (New York, 1976).

prominent New Deal officials Communists or fellow travelers, Truman and the Cold War liberals elevated the issue of Communist influence in the Democratic party and in government into a national concern, and Senator Joseph R. McCarthy and the Republicans responded by questioning the loyalty of northern liberals. The liberals were in the bizarre position of waging cold and hot wars on Communism abroad while trying to protect themselves from charges that they were procommunist. It is little wonder that liberalism lost much of its substance and direction. As one scholar has summarized the situation, "In this age, which commonly equated ideological radicalism with Communist subversion, little remained of radical political and social criticism." [53]

Black civil rights organizations enhanced their national prestige while narrowing their programs and incorporating the anticommunist impulse into their policies. The NAACP fired the militant W. E. B. Du Bois, a popular-front liberal who supported Wallace, from his position as research director and embraced the anticommunist crusade. In 1950 the association created a committee to "investigate and study the ideological composition and trends of the membership and leadership of local units . . . and expel any unit, which, in the judgment of the Board of Directors, . . . comes under Communist or other political control or domination." As Robert L. Zangrando has noted, "The NAACP and other civil rights activists long committed to working within a traditional, legal framework tried to protect their reputations and save their programs by espousing the 'American Way' and guarding against bad companions." Another scholar has remarked, "Accommodation, anti-communism, and tacit allegiance to white liberals and labour bureaucrats became the principal tenets of black middle-class politics for the next decade." [54]

[53] Charles C. Alexander, *Holding the Line: The Eisenhower Era, 1952–1961* (Bloomington, Ind., 1975), 156. See also Godfrey Hodgson, *America in Our Time* (New York, 1976); Allen J. Matusow, *The Unraveling of America: A History of Liberalism in the 1960s* (New York, 1984); Boyer, *By the Bomb's Early Light;* Caute, *The Great Fear;* and Richard H. Pells, *The Liberal Mind in a Conservative Age: American Intellectuals in the 1940s and 1950s* (New York, 1985).

[54] Langston Hughes, *Fight for Freedom: The Story of the NAACP* (New York, 1962), 149; Robert L. Zangrando, *The NAACP Crusade Against Lynching, 1909–1950* (Philadelphia, 1980), 191; Marable, *Race, Reform, and Rebellion,* 25. See also *The Autobiography of W. E. B. Du Bois* (New York, 1968), 361–79.

Doubtless it was true, as Zangrando has concluded, that "the late 1940s turned out to be far less conducive to civil rights than contemporaries hoped and assumed." Yet the NAACP continued to lead the black civil rights campaign. The organization pressed its legal attack on segregation and achieved increasingly significant victories. Whatever its limitations, it was at the forefront of national liberalism, and during the 1950s no other reform group had an equal impact on developments in the South.[55]

More broadly, the national liberal establishment tended to be cautious, indecisive, and often sectional in its approach. The concern for economic reform and for the redistribution of wealth abated as liberals identified national and international corporate expansion with the growth of democratic values. Whereas liberals had once believed the southern colonial economy to be at the center of the region's difficulties, they came to view corporate business development as an engine of southern progress. As racial issues, and most especially segregation in the South, moved to the top of the agenda for national reform, what had been the nation's number-one economic problem took on the aspect of the nation's number-one moral problem and an embarrassment in Cold War diplomacy.[56]

The result was a pursuit of what Robert F. Burk has termed "symbolic equality." According to Burk, "The preoccupation of civil rights supporters and politicians with the moral image of the nation as reflected in its official actions led to the twin conclusions that civil rights policy must focus upon the reformation of white racial attitudes and that such a reformation could be achieved most painlessly through the removal of discriminatory sanctions and the projection of an official image of racial equality." The problem came to seem not so much the disadvantaged state of the black American population, or even of black southerners; it was the blatant racial proscription that was most openly practiced in the South. Southern de jure segregation marred the nation's

[55] Zangrando, *The NAACP Crusade Against Lynching*, 209; Mark V. Tushnet, *The NAACP's Legal Strategy Against Segregated Education, 1925–1950* (Chapel Hill, N.C., 1987).

[56] Anthony P. Dunbar, *Against the Grain: Southern Radicals and Prophets, 1929–1959* (Charlottesville, Va., 1981), 199–260; Schulman, *From Cotton Belt to Sunbelt*, 63–173.

democratic image abroad and blemished white America's sense of moral rectitude at home.[57]

Yet while labeling segregation the nation's most significant domestic problem, liberals did relatively little about it. The contentment with "symbolic equality" led liberals to embrace what historian Richard Klimmer has described as an "essentially legalistic strategy which was defined in a way to most directly respond to a group . . . long scorned—the black middle class." When the political elite of the South reacted to this modest and gradualist policy with hostility, the issue became even more sectional, with white southerners cast as the moral culprits. The effect, according to the same historian, was to link the movement for black civil rights with a "comprehensive hostility toward the South, which portrayed the region as the root of ignorance and violence in American society."[58]

Southern liberals landed in a difficult position. During the early postwar years, New Dealish political liberals fared relatively well. The election in 1946 of James E. Folsom as governor of Alabama and in 1948 of Earl K. Long as governor of Louisiana and Fuller Warren as governor of Florida placed neopopulist liberals in the three statehouses. In 1948 the voters of North Carolina chose as their governor W. Kerr Scott, who was another rurally oriented, if less colorful, liberal. In 1946 John Sparkman won a seat as senator from Alabama in a special election, and in 1948 the voters reelected him to a full term. In the same year, two New Dealers—Estes Kefauver of Tennessee and Lyndon B. Johnson of Texas—won senatorial elections. Two business-oriented progressives—Sidney S. McMath, in Arkansas and Gordon Browning in Tennessee—won governorships, and a Senate seat went to another, Robert S. Kerr of Oklahoma. Such elections offered hope for a non-popular-front moderate liberal alternative. As liberalism became increasingly fixated on race relations and the South came

[57] Robert F. Burk, *The Eisenhower Administration and Black Civil Rights* (Knoxville, Tenn., 1984), 10; Peter J. Kellogg, "Civil Rights Consciousness in the 1940s," *The Historian*, XLII (1979), 18–41.

[58] Richard Klimmer, "Liberal Attitudes Toward the South, 1930–1965" (Ph.D. dissertation, Northwestern University, 1976), 116, 95.

under attack from outside the region, left-leaning politicians found themselves ever more isolated and ineffective. Senator Olin D. Johnston, a vigorous segregationist from South Carolina and a New Dealer, complained in 1948 that Truman "seems to have finally succeeded in getting himself tied hand and foot by the ultraconservatives—except for the race issue." That of course was the rub. Economic reform had gone out of style, and the new liberal fashion was to define objectives in racial terms.[59]

Most political liberals retreated to safer electoral terrain. Alabama's Senator Lister Hill resigned his position of Democratic whip and, as his biographer has commented, "began his retreat from the Democratic party's national leadership ranks." Hill and Sparkman were among those who moved to the right. A few officeholders from the peripheral South, like Lyndon Johnson and Kefauver, as well as A. S. "Mike" Monroney, who was elected as a senator from Oklahoma in 1950, managed to maintain their national standing while continuing to win at the polls, but their ranks thinned. Indeed, the very word *liberal* gradually disappeared from the southern political lexicon, except as a term of opprobrium.[60]

Similarly, white middle-class liberals attempted to redefine their position. A few who had championed the New Deal—such as journalist John Temple Graves of Alabama—were sufficiently unnerved by the menace of racial change that they shifted from liberalism to reaction. In the presidential election of 1948 Graves supported the Dixiecrat candidate. Some, such as Richmond editor Virginius Dabney, forswore reform and opted for conservatism. Most liberals searched for a middle way, perhaps, as in the case of Atlanta's Ralph McGill, a "little left of center." Those who did not adjust often suffered. Aubrey Williams' once flourishing farm journal folded because the publisher advocated racial justice and was active in the "Communist-front" Southern Conference Education Fund. As southern politics moved rightward, so too did the middle of the road. The titles of two studies of southern lib-

[59] Robert A. Garson, *The Democratic Party and the Politics of Sectionalism, 1941–1948* (Baton Rouge, 1974), 270.

[60] Virginia Van der Veer Hamilton, *Lister Hill, Statesman from the South* (Chapel Hill, N.C., 1987), 150; Patton, "Southern Liberals and the Emergence of a 'New South.' "

eralism tell the story: "Southern Apologists: A Liberal Image," and "Without Urgency or Ardor: The South's Middle-of-the-Road Liberals."[61]

Former liberals became moderates. They often extenuated their stance by citing the hostilities and violent proclivities of lower-income whites, their own expectation that economic development and education would eventually solve the race problem, and their unwillingness to sever their communications with southern conservatives. In rejecting northern intervention in southern social affairs but failing to win support for gradualism from regional conservatives, the moderates chose a course that often produced paralysis. Although they afforded the region a veneer of respectability during the 1950s, the position they arrived at fell into disrepute thereafter. As McGill candidly reflected, "The self-styled moderate turned out to be one who stood on the sidelines wringing his hands and urging both parties in conflict to be calm."[62]

The midcentury South, Morton Sosna has noted, was an "uncomfortable place" for the white liberals who remained. The Southern Regional Council performed a signal service as a rallying point for white advocates of racial reform. Individualists like Lillian Smith and churchmen like James McBride Dabbs and Will Campbell continued the struggle and sought to appeal to the conscience of the white South. The new southern liberalism failed to attract popular support, and as a critic has with some validity pointed out, "It was a progressivism shorn of any economic critique and absolutely unmarked by the radical protest of the past decade."[63]

[61] Steven R. Moore, "The Shadow and the Spotlight: Ralph McGill and Liberalism in the South, 1933–1950" (M.A. thesis, University of Georgia, 1988), 72; John Salmond, *A Southern Rebel: The Life and Times of Aubrey Willis Williams, 1890–1965* (Chapel Hill, N.C., 1983), 198–214; Dorothy C. Kinsella, "Southern Apologists: A Liberal Image" (Ph.D. dissertation, St. Louis University, 1971); Anthony L. Newberry, "Without Urgency or Ardor: The South's Middle-of-the-Road Liberals and Civil Rights, 1945–1960" (Ph.D. dissertation, Ohio University, 1982).

[62] Ralph W. McGill, *The South and the Southerner* (Boston, 1963), 283. See also John T. Kneebone, *Southern Liberal Journalists and the Issue of Race, 1920–1944* (Chapel Hill, N.C., 1985).

[63] Morton Sosna, *In Search of the Silent South: Southern Liberals and the Race Issue* (New York, 1977), 166; Dunbar, *Against the Grain*, 221.

Even more difficult was the position of the white working class. Whatever the failures of popular-front liberals, they presented a program that offered benefits to white workers. Unless blacks and whites alike participated in labor organizations, the unions would not have the strength to improve working conditions and the two races could be used as strikebreakers against each other. The Southern Conference for Human Welfare tried to enlist both blacks and whites in a political movement that would materially benefit both. After the demise of the popular front, postwar liberals offered white workers little aside from contempt and the right to compete for scarce jobs with black workers. By defining liberalism not in terms of the redistribution of wealth, power, and privilege but as an issue of individual morality, the new American left sharply narrowed the liberal agenda.

Henry A. Wallace led the popular-front liberals to destruction with his third-party campaign in 1948, but he was not alone in challenging the major-party system. Also on the hustings was J. Strom Thurmond, the States' Rights Democratic candidate. Thurmond offered a far different program, and he too faced formidable opposition.

73

CHAPTER III

THE DIXIECRATS AND SOUTHERN CONSERVATISM

IN *The Mind of the South,* Wilbur J. Cash described the South as "not quite a nation within a nation, but the next thing to it." Certainly, a great many southerners conceived of the region as a civilization with a distinct way of life. As racial segregation came under increasing national criticism, white southern conservatives responded with an impassioned defense of tradition. Sociologist Howard W. Odum, writing in the spring of 1948, lamented the "unbelievable revival of the old bitterness" that led to an "increase in narrow sectionalism as opposed to earlier trends toward interregional arrangements." According to Odum, the region's "defensive attitudes" grew from three contemporary developments. The South had "changed more rapidly than ... the rest of the United States"; there had been an "almost complete and revolutionary change in many aspects of Negro life and culture"; and there had been "relatively little change in Southern culture." The New Deal and World War II had altered the direction of southern history and had amplified the influence of national forces in southern affairs. Whether or not African Americans had changed their "life and culture," their aspirations had clearly expanded. Southern political and social institutions—perhaps even "Southern [white] culture"—had remained remarkably stable. The result was the "defensive attitudes" of whites concerning civil rights for black southerners.[1]

In February, 1948, President Harry S. Truman asked Congress to enact a civil rights program. That summer the national Dem-

[1] W. J. Cash, *The Mind of the South* (New York, 1941), viii; Howard W. Odum, "Social Change in the South," *Journal of Politics,* X (1948), 242, 250, 253.

ocratic convention approved a civil rights plank endorsing Truman's proposals. Truman called upon Congress to eliminate poll-tax requirements for voting, to create a statutory fair employment practices committee, to make lynching a federal offense, and to end segregation in interstate transportation. The president's recommendations were hardly revolutionary. None put the underlying structure of racial segregation in serious jeopardy. Indeed, as Ralph W. McGill observed, had southern politicians not reacted so vehemently, African Americans would "have protested the proposals as weak and mealy-mouthed." There was virtually no prospect that Congress would pass the measures anyway. After black groups pressed for more concrete federal progress in civil rights, Truman in the summer of 1948 issued executive orders banning discrimination in the armed forces and in the federal bureaucracy. These actions were modest, but Truman's message to Congress and the Democratic party's approbation gave impetus to the liberal commitment to civil rights and focused the ire of southern conservatives.[2]

The Democratic convention, held in Philadelphia in July, poignantly demonstrated the isolation of the political South. The region's delegates insisted on a reaffirmation of the rights of states, and Dan Moody, former governor of Texas, introduced the most significant of several state rights resolutions. Every delegate from the eleven states of the former Confederacy voted for the resolution; virtually no one else did. The Americans for Democratic Action responded with a resolution commending Truman's civil rights program. The vote on this plank was relatively close; the Truman administration supported a compromise proposal and the southern members received support from western and border-state delegates. Nevertheless, the ADA's resolution carried.

"The attitude of this convention towards Alabama and the South this afternoon," Grover C. Hall, editor of the Montgomery

[2] Ralph W. McGill, "Will the South Ditch Truman?" *Saturday Evening Post,* May 22, 1948, p. 88; Donald R. McCoy and Richard T. Ruetten, *Quest and Response: Minority Rights and the Truman Administration* (Lawrence, Kans., 1973), 31–147. Copies of Truman's message to Congress, of Executive Orders 9980 and 9981, and other relevant material can be found in the President's Committee on Civil Rights Records, Harry S. Truman Library, Independence, Mo.

Advertiser, wrote, "was cold, forbidding, and contemptuous." On the following day, the delegates from Mississippi and half of those from Alabama stomped out of the convention. Of the remaining participants from the former Confederate states, 263 cast votes for Senator Richard B. Russell of Georgia while the convention overwhelmingly selected Truman as the party's presidential candidate. As historian Robert A. Garson has observed, "The convention was so split that nobody even thought to move, as is customary, to make the nomination unanimous."[3]

Truman's civil rights program had a direct linkage with the postwar spasm of racial mayhem in the South. During World War II, racial violence was not uncommon nationally, but only in the South did it continue after the war. The wartime social and economic disruptions in the region, the return of some 400,000 African-American veterans, and the voting drives and other black protest activities contributed to the antiblack rampage in the region during late 1945 and through much of 1946. In Georgia, Texas, and South Carolina, white groups killed blacks who had voted or had participated in civil rights events. In northern Louisiana, eastern North Carolina, and the Mississippi Delta, lynch mobs murdered black veterans. Particularly gruesome was a multiple lynching in Walton County, Georgia. After an altercation between a white landowner and a black former employee, a gang of whites summarily executed the offending black, his wife, his sister, and her husband. In most cases, "law enforcement" officials had at least indirect complicity in the lynchings, but as Governor Millard Caldwell explained about what a county sheriff had done during a lynching in Florida, "Stupidity and ineptitude are not sufficient grounds for removal of an elected official by the governor." No one was convicted of any of the murders.[4]

The postwar antiblack violence in the South gained widespread publicity. Outraged African Americans and other civil rights ad-

[3] Grover C. Hall in Montgomery *Advertiser,* July 15, 1948; Robert A. Garson, *The Democratic Party and the Politics of Sectionalism, 1941–1948* (Baton Rouge, 1974), 232–80, p. 280 quoted.

[4] James Albert Burran III, "Racial Violence in the South During World War II" (Ph.D. dissertation, University of Tennessee, 1977), 257–90; Caldwell quoted in *New South,* January, 1946, p. 9.

vocates demanded that the federal government take action. The episode that crystallized civil rights sentiment occurred in Columbia, Tennessee, near Nashville. In February, 1946, a conflict between a black veteran and a white radio repairman escalated into a virtual war between the white and black communities. Blacks fired on and wounded the town's police chief and his three patrolmen; state police in their freestyle search for weapons manhandled black citizens and destroyed black property. Before the conflict ended, state and local officials had arrested some hundred blacks and four whites; twenty-six of the blacks were charged with capital offenses. Eventually, everyone arrested was acquitted or saw the charges dropped; the only fatalities were two blacks who were shot while attempting to escape.[5]

In the summer of 1946, civil rights, labor, religious, and veterans groups formed the National Emergency Committee Against Mob Violence to lobby for national action. The Truman administration showed little enthusiasm, but such a coalition was difficult to ignore, and even the president's more conservative advisers agreed that something had to be done. Truman fell back on the tried and tested expedient of appointing an investigative committee. Created by executive order in December, 1946, the President's Committee on Civil Rights was chaired by Charles E. Wilson, president of General Electric, and its membership included an array of well-connected citizens. It was also a committee of politically acceptable composition: insiders referred to it as Noah's Ark because it included two African Americans, two Jews, two women, two Catholics, two labor leaders, two businessmen, and two southerners. The southerners were Frank P. Graham and M. E. Tilley, the latter of the Women's Society of Christian Services.

The bold recommendations the committee delivered in its report in October, 1947, doubtless went beyond what the Truman administration had expected. Among its six general proposals was a call for the "elimination of segregation, based on race, color, creed, or national origin, from American life." Graham and Tilley

---

[5] Guy B. Johnson, "What Happened at Columbia," *New South*, May, 1946, pp. 1–8; Burran, "Racial Violence," 229–56.

submitted a minority report that disagreed with some of the committee's advice, but they did not dissent from the general tenor
of the committee's report.[6]

Governor J. Strom Thurmond of South Carolina insisted that
the report "gathered dust" until political considerations led Truman's advisers to revive it. Thurmond's perception held more
than a grain of truth. Truman had scant interest in black rights,
but the changing complexion of liberalism made it politically impossible for a Democratic president to ignore them. The Truman
camp's strategy of ostracizing Henry A. Wallace as keeping company with Communists required a complement; the Democrats
who might have voted for Wallace needed a reason to vote for
Truman, and civil rights was the issue of the hour. Congressman
Frank W. Boykin of Alabama quoted the president as saying,
"Frank, I don't believe in this civil rights program any more than
you do, but we've got to have it to win." The issue promised to
rally liberals to the Truman cause and to solidify Democratic support among black voters. Not only could the South in Clark Clifford's words "be considered safely Democratic" but as Clifford
later calculated, "The Negro votes in the crucial states will more
than cancel out any votes the President may lose in the South."[7]

Southern conservatives were fully aware of the region's
changed standing in partisan affairs. To Alabama's Frank M.
Dixon, the national Democratic party had become an "unholy
alliance of left-wingers, pseudo-liberals and radicals of as many
hues as Joseph's coat." Governor Ben T. Laney of Arkansas de-

[6] *To Secure These Rights: The Report of the President's Committee on Civil Rights* (New York,
1947), 166; Executive Order 9808, December 5, 1946, in Philleo Nash Papers, White
House File, Truman Library; William C. Berman, *The Politics of Civil Rights in the Truman
Administration* (Columbus, Ohio, 1970), 41–78; Robert L. Zangrando, *The NAACP Crusade
Against Lynching, 1909–1950* (Philadelphia, 1980), 166–87.

[7] J. Strom Thurmond, "President Truman's So-Called Civil Rights Program" (Manuscript
of speech delivered at Columbia, S.C., March 17, 1948), in Benjamin Travis Laney Papers,
in possession of Mrs. Ben T. Laney, Magnolia, Ark.; Boykin quoted in *Quest and Response*,
by McCoy and Ruetter, 149; Clark Clifford, Memorandum for the President, November
19, 1947, Clark Clifford, Memorandum for the President, August 17, 1948, both in Clark
Clifford Papers, Political File, Truman Library; Berman, *The Politics of Civil Rights*, 79–135;
Barton J. Bernstein, "The Ambiguous Legacy: The Truman Administration and Civil
Rights," in *The Politics of Civil Rights in the Truman Administration*, ed. Barton J. Bernstein
(Chicago, 1970), 278–90.

scribed the party's convention in 1948 as "beyond description. The South and Southern Democracy as we know it is in the hands of a foreign element." The South simply was without a place, another state rights advocate argued, in a national coalition dominated by northern urban machines, radical labor leaders, and African Americans. "The Democratic party has always stood for states' rights and white supremacy," Senator Russell contended, "and for this reason the southern people have given it their unswerving and devoted support." In 1948 the party broke with its past, and the conservative leadership in the South responded with anguish and hostility.[8]

The conservative political establishment had trouble devising a strategy of opposition. Having turned back the liberal threat posed by Operation Dixie, Bourbons again found the southern social system under attack. This time the danger emanated from within their own Democratic party, led by a border-state politician who had Confederate grandparents and who had been nominated as vice-president in 1944 in large part owing to his southern conservative support. "As the presidential election of 1948 approaches," Jasper Berry Shannon wrote, "the elite of county seatdom are ill at ease for they feel betrayed in their own household by one of their own kind, and most of all by their own political church, the Democratic party." For the first time since 1928, the Democratic party had seriously trod on southern conservative sensibilities, and it had not only touched the tender nerve of civil rights but had done so at a time when the party gave the appearance of being considerably less intimidating than it had been under Roosevelt.[9]

To some southern conservatives, the Truman administration's program was simply the most outrageous of a long list of federal intrusions. Well before Truman's civil rights message, southern congressional conservatives had formed an alliance with Repub-

[8] Dixon quoted in *The Dixiecrat Movement: Its Role in Third Party Politics*, by Emile B. Ader (Washington, D.C., 1955), 14; Ben Laney to Lawrence H. Derby, July 19, 1948, Shelby Myrick, "Will Southern Democracy Revolt," February 8, 1948, both in Laney Papers; Russell quoted in David Daniel Potenziani, "Look to the Past: Richard B. Russell and the Defense of Southern White Supremacy" (Ph.D. dissertation, University of Georgia, 1981), 75.

[9] Jasper Berry Shannon, *Toward a New Politics in the South* (Knoxville, Tenn., 1949), 52.

licans in an antireform coalition, and other southern Democrats had called for a revolt from national party policies. In large numbers, southern congressional Democrats supported the measures that eviscerated the Farm Security Administration, the Civilian Conservation Corps, the National Youth Administration, the Works Progress Administration, and the President's Committee on Fair Employment Practice. Their votes were crucial to the passage of the Smith-Connally Act, a wartime antilabor law, and the Taft-Hartley Act. It was southern Democratic legerdemain that made the House Committee on Un-American Activities a standing committee. In the Senate, southern Democrats had conducted filibusters that prevented enactment of laws against the poll tax and against lynching.[10]

At the state level, disgruntled Democrats talked of abandoning the national organization and creating an independent southern Democratic party. During the war years, Governor Sam H. Jones of Louisiana, Governor Dixon of Alabama, and Senator W. Lee O'Daniel of Texas were among those who declared that the South had nothing to lose but the chains by which it was bound to the national party. In 1944 anti–New Deal Democrats fleetingly won control of the party machinery in Texas and nominated electors pledged to vote against Roosevelt. Abortive uprisings also occurred in Mississippi and South Carolina. In every case, Democratic loyalists won control of the state organization. Dissident elements cast eighty-nine votes for Senator Harry Flood Byrd of Virginia rather than for Roosevelt at the party convention in 1944, and they led the fateful campaign to substitute Truman for Wallace as the vice-presidential candidate. The straying Texas electors, labeled the Texas Regulars and pledged to Byrd, carried 12 percent of the state's presidential vote.[11]

[10] Garson, *The Democratic Party and the Politics of Sectionalism*, 31–219; Robert Edward Hayes, "Senatorial Voting Behavior with Regard to the 'Southern Interest' " (Ph.D. dissertation, University of Colorado, 1964); Mary Hedge Hinchey, "The Frustration of the New Deal Revival, 1944–1946" (Ph.D. dissertation, University of Missouri, 1965); Will Maslow, "FEPC—A Case History in Parliamentary Maneuvers," *University of Chicago Law Review*, XIII (1946), 407–33; R. Alton Lee, *Truman and Taft-Hartley: A Question of Mandate* (Lexington, Ky., 1966); Susan M. Hartmann, *Truman and the Eightieth Congress* (Columbia, Mo., 1971).

[11] Alexander Heard, *A Two-Party South?* (Chapel Hill, N.C., 1952), 251–78; Jasper Berry Shannon, "Presidential Politics in the South," *Journal of Politics*, X (1948), 464–89.

During 1948 the festering estrangement between southern conservatives and the national Democratic establishment broke into open political conflict. A sizable segment of the South's Bourbon leadership attempted to restructure the Democratic party. The States' Rights Democrats created what Alexander Heard described as the "most vociferous minority political movement in the South since the Populists." States' Rights partisans—Dixiecrats as journalists nicknamed them—did not attempt to create a third party but sought to take over the southern state Democratic parties and to turn the Democratic state party apparatus against the national Democrats. "The significant competition engendered by the Dixiecrats," Heard pointed out, "occurred *within* the Democratic party rather than *with* it." The Dixiecrat strategy was to gain control of the party organizations in as many southern states as possible and to make Dixiecrat candidates the nominees of the Democratic party. Defining the national Democratic party as simply a federation of independent state parties, the Dixiecrats maintained that they represented the true Democratic party.[12]

The States' Rights movement was profoundly reactionary. Both national parties called for civil rights reform in the South; the Dixiecrats preferred to reconstitute the party system. The South, as Odum noted, was rapidly changing; the States' Rights solution was to block social and political reformation. African Americans within and outside the South called for a broader range of civil rights; Dixiecrats promised the maintenance of segregation. Rejecting the nationalizing tendencies of the New Deal and World War II, Dixiecrats preached the independence of southern state politics. The Dixiecrats sought to enlist southern white conservatives in their campaign and thereby to weld together a politically conservative Solid South.[13]

[12] Heard, *A Two-Party South?* 20, 23.

[13] The discussion of the Dixiecrats draws on material in the Frank Murray Dixon Papers, Alabama Department of Archives and History, Montgomery, and on the Benjamin Travis Laney Papers. The best general study of the Dixiecrat movement is Garson's *The Democratic Party and the Politics of Sectionalism*. The most thorough examination of the Dixiecrat campaign is Ann Mathison McLaurin's "The Role of the Dixiecrats in the 1948 Election" (Ph.D. dissertation, University of Oklahoma, 1972). Other valuable studies include Richard Calvin Ethridge's "Mississippi's Role in the Dixiecrat Movement" (Ph.D. dissertation, Mississippi State University, 1971); James G. Banks's "Strom Thurmond and the Revolt Against

The Dixiecrats appeared to be confident that only leadership and organization were needed to accomplish their purpose. Much as members of the Southern Conference for Human Welfare often viewed the South as a great liberal giant waiting to be awakened, the Dixiecrat leadership was ready to see the region's people—by which were meant its white people—as an organic entity. "We people of the south know the horrors of the carpetbag rule," Ben Laney wrote in characterizing southerners as a "people who believe in the rights of the states and who do not care for many of the so-called modern reform ideas." The South had become too dependent on the federal spending machine the New Deal created, and the region contained too large a "federal patronage group," but these were tractable problems. After all, the States' Rights Democrats placed their faith in, as Dixon put it, the "wisdom of the people to govern themselves," not the authority of a "powerful central government"; the issue was the ancient one "of a highly centralized police state, as opposed to local self-government." [14]

Race was of course at the center of the Dixiecrat campaign. Truman's civil rights program, according to Senator James O. Eastland of Mississippi, proved "that organized mongrel minorities control[led] the government" and were attempting "to Harlemize the country." Most of the States' Rights leaders regarded such explicit racial rhetoric as self-defeating. Thurmond insisted, "The South's fight is not being waged on the theory of white supremacy but on State sovereignty." Many agreed that the "Negro question" was "merely an incident to the States' Rights move-

Modernity" (Ph.D. dissertation, Kent State University, 1970); Glen Jeansonne's *Leander Perez, Boss of the Delta* (Baton Rouge, 1977); Sarah McCulloh Lemmon's "The Ideology of the 'Dixiecrat' Movement," *Social Forces,* XXX (1951), 162–71; William G. Carleton's "The Fate of Our Fourth Party," *Yale Review,* XXXVIII (1949), 449–59; Ader's *The Dixiecrat Movement;* and Emile B. Ader's "Why the Dixiecrats Failed," *Journal of Politics,* XV (1953), 356–69. The analyses by V. O. Key, Jr., in *Southern Politics in State and Nation* (New York, 1949), and by Heard, in *A Two-Party South?* have withstood the test of time remarkably well, except that both minimized the significance of the Dixiecrats.

[14] Ben Laney to Horace C. Wilkinson, April 12, 1948, in Laney Papers; Curtis Douglas to Frank M. Dixon, January 24, 1949, Frank M. Dixon to Edward S. Hemphill, July 28, 1948, Copy of Speech by Frank M. Dixon in Little Rock, October 17, 1948, all in Dixon Papers.

ment, although a most important incident." To Frank Dixon, Truman's program had relatively little to do with race: the antilynching proposal was "to establish federal police power and a federal police," the measure against the poll tax aimed "to establish federal control of elections," and the fair employment practices committee sought "to secure a strangle hold on American ways of life and the conduct of American business." But even the Dixiecrats who proclaimed "how much we want to keep the States' Rights movement off the Negro proposition" had difficulty avoiding it, in part because regular southern Democrats so frequently employed racism in their defense of party loyalty.[15]

Leadership for the States' Rights campaign came from state politicians—including seven governors and former governors—and from business people. Senator Eastland and several representatives supported the Dixiecrat movement, but most southern members of Congress remained at least nominally loyal to the national party. The Southern States Industrial Council, which claimed five thousand member businesses, along with the Arkansas Free Enterprise Association, the Associated Industries of Florida, and a few other state business associations, played an active role in the campaign. The business groups served smaller enterprises, many of them in traditional southern industries, for which cheap labor had a telling effect on the balance sheet. All the business associations active in the movement were proponents—usually leaders—of right-to-work campaigns. R. Kirby Longino, president of the Southern States Industrial Council, was not atypical in ranking the minimum wage on the same level as the fair employment practices committee in the threat posed to the "future of small business." Sarah McCulloh Lemmon was clearly correct in arguing that the Dixiecrats sought "to defend the [low-

---

[15] Eastland quoted in "The Ideology of the 'Dixiecrat' Movement," by Lemmon, 165; J. Strom Thurmond to Ben Laney, April 12, 1948, in Laney Papers; Gessner T. McCorvey to C. M. Stanley, August 26, 1948, Gessner T. McCorvey to Frank M. Dixon and Horace C. Wilkinson, August 21, 1948, Frank M. Dixon to Richmond *Times-Dispatch*, August 14, 1948, Frank M. Dixon to Birmingham *News*, September 4, 1948, all in Dixon Papers; Hodding Carter, "Civil Rights Issue as Seen in the South," *New York Times Magazine*, March 21, 1948.

wage] economic system" . . . as well as to protect the South from civil rights.[16]

States' Rights Democrats were not in complete agreement on how the movement's goals would be accomplished. Thurmond, who headed the Dixiecrat ticket, took the campaign seriously. Merritt Gibson, the national campaign director, once remarked, "That damned fool really thinks he's going to be elected." Thurmond and his fellow optimists reasoned that by denying both the national Democratic and Republican candidates a majority in the electoral college, the southern electors could force Congress to select one of the top three candidates. In that event, the Republicans might prefer a southern Democrat to a national Democrat and the national Democrats might prefer a southern Democrat to a Republican. Thus could J. Strom Thurmond become the leader of the free world.[17]

The realists within the movement harbored few such illusions. Their aims were comparable to those of the popular-front liberals; much as Henry Wallace and his followers wished to demonstrate the dependence of the Democratic party on liberal-radical support, the Dixiecrats hoped to dramatize the South's indispensability to the party. If the southern electors deadlocked the electoral college, the situation would provide an opportunity for reviving the compromise of 1877. If Truman lost—and the public-opinion polls indicated he would—then the party, in the words of a Louisiana Dixiecrat, faced "bankruptcy in 1948 and we of the South must be prepared to accept the receivership." Governor Fielding Wright of Mississippi suggested that "one certain way to get rid of rats is to let the ship sink, and those rats will desert." A decisive national party defeat would, Ben Laney reasoned, discredit the civil rights issue and its proponents and provide the opportunity for the southern states to take the "proper step for the re-construction of a true Democratic Party in America."[18]

---

[16] R. Kirby Longino, "The Revolt of the South," February 18, 1948, in Laney Papers; Lemmon, "The Ideology of the 'Dixiecrat' Movement," 171.

[17] Gibson quoted in "The Role of the Dixiecrats," by McLaurin, 95.

[18] John U. Barr to Horace C. Wilkinson, May 24, 1948, in Laney Papers; Wright quoted by John N. Popham in New York *Times*, February 13, 1948; Laney to Wilkinson, April 12, 1948, in Laney Papers; Frank M. Dixon to Donald Comer, August 13, 1948, Frank M. Dixon to Laurie C. Battle, July 6, 1948, both in Dixon Papers.

Most fundamentally of all, the true believers among the Dixie-crats wanted a separate southern party. Having achieved partisan independence, the political South would, if they had their way, either go it alone in national affairs or align with northern conservatives. "The plan would be," Charles Wallace Collins wrote, "to organize a southern party on a southern platform." The power of such an organization, Collins explained, "would dwarf into insignificance that of the Negroes and the New York City radicals." In his more grandiose moments, Collins envisaged a renewed southern nationalism with an indigenous arts and literature that replaced the "Tobacco Road philosophers in New York City." Frank Dixon stated, "It has always been my idea that eventually we would have to come to the formation of a separate southern party." [19]

President Truman delivered his civil rights message to Congress on February 2, 1948. Four days later the Southern Governors' Conference convened in Florida for a special meeting on educational problems, and the president's program was an inescapable topic of discussion. The governors refused to support the proposal by Governor Wright calling for a third-party movement. Instead they charged a committee to study matters and recommend a course of action. Chaired by Thurmond, the committee included Laney, R. Gregg Cherry of North Carolina, Beauford H. Jester of Texas, and William M. Tuck of Virginia. With the exception of the relatively moderate Cherry, none of the members made a secret of their hostility to Truman and the policies of the national Democrats. [20]

The committee formulated the strategy of the Dixiecrats. Among its activities, Thurmond's committee met with J. Howard McGrath, the chairman of the national Democratic party. The meeting yielded little beyond antagonism. According to Laney, "We were told to go back home and behave, that the nat[ional] party knew what they were doing, and that we were entirely out

[19] Charles Wallace Collins, *Whither Solid South? A Study in Politics and Race Relations* (New Orleans, 1947), 258, 260; Charles Wallace Collins to Merritt H. Gibson, November 8, 1948, Frank M. Dixon to Charles Wallace Collins, July 14, 1948, both in Dixon Papers.

[20] John N. Popham in New York *Times*, February 8, 1948; Ethridge, "Mississippi's Role in the Dixiecrat Movement," 44–54.

of our place and would be glad to get back in the party in [the] November election." In March, 1948, the committee offered its report at a special meeting of the Southern Governors' Conference in Washington, D.C. "Our inquiry," Thurmond and his associates stated, "has satisfied us that the virtually unanimous will of the people of the southern states is to take every possible effective action within their power, not only to prevent the enactment of the proposed legislation but also to defeat those who have proposed it and any others advocating it." They recommended, consequently, that the southern states oppose the renomination of Truman and insist on a state rights plank in the Democratic party platform. If repulsed, the southern Democratic parties should instruct their electors to vote against the national party candidates. Seven southern governors—in the case of Virginia through the governor's authorized representative—endorsed the report, although several explained that they were not legally entitled to commit their state parties.[21]

State rights advocates met in Jackson, Mississippi, in May to plan their move toward southern political independence. Anyone who wished to attend was welcome, but the enthusiastic crowd—mostly white Mississippians—was little more than window dressing. Dixiecrat insiders had firm control over decision making. The leadership created a States' Rights Democratic campaign committee chaired by Governor Laney. The Jackson conference granted the Democratic party executive committee in each of the eleven former Confederate states the right to appoint two members to serve on the committee, although Laney was authorized to select members from the states until the executive committees acted, as well as in the event that any failed to act.

The Dixiecrat strategy was to oppose Truman and his program at the Democratic convention. If the States' Rights movement did not prevail there, delegates appointed by southern state executive committees were to meet at a conference in Birmingham to choose a States' Rights presidential ticket to "recommend" to the

[21] "Transcript of Conference of Southern Governors with Senator J. Howard McGrath," February 23, 1948, Ben Laney's Untitled Memoirs of the States' Rights Campaign, unpaginated, n.d., "Committee Report to Southern Governors Conference," March 13, 1948, all in Laney Papers; Edward T. Folliard in Washington *Post*, March 14, 1948.

state parties. The state organizations could then make the Dixie-crat candidate the candidate of the Democratic party throughout the region. In the solidly Democratic South, a Democratic vote would be a vote for the Dixiecrat choice, whereas Truman—if he appeared on the ballot at all—would be there as a third-party possibility. Thus the Dixiecrat strategy was to win the allegiance of state party officials rather than voters, and though the campaign committee issued campaign buttons and attempted to kindle pop-ular enthusiasm, it was first of all a lobbying body with the aim of garnering the support of party elites. After a session of the cam-paign committee in June, Laney explained to the media, "The national party organization is merely an association of the various state party organizations, and the plan of action outlined herein serves to return the party to the people and to the principles on which it was founded." [22]

Frustrated at the Democratic national convention in July, the Dixiecrats held their conference in Birmingham. Although long planned, the conference was a confused affair. The leadership offered the presidential recommendation to Senator Richard Rus-sell, who declined it. The Dixiecrats turned to Ben Laney, who refused to be a candidate. Governor Thurmond was willing, and Governor Wright agreed to be the vice-presidential candidate. Many of the Dixiecrats found little about the South Carolina gov-ernor to admire beyond his energy and enthusiasm. After all, as one of them sniffed in delivering the ultimate put-down within States' Rights circles, Thurmond had never even read Collins' *Whither Solid South?* The well-attended sessions in Birmingham were raucous. Unlike previous Dixiecrat gatherings, this one gave the podium to some none too carefully screened orators who at times veered into racist diatribes. Apparently caught up in the mood, the normally restrained Frank Dixon, who delivered the keynote address, damned civil rights as a program "to reduce us to the status of a mongrel, inferior race, mixed in blood, our Anglo-Saxon heritage a mockery." [23]

[22] "Minutes" and "Declaration of Principles" of Conference of States' Rights Democrats, May 10, 1948, in Laney Papers; *States' Righter,* May, 1948; "Complete Campaign Organi-zation," n.d., Ben Laney, "Press Release," June 8, 1948, both in Laney Papers.

[23] Gilbert C. Fite, *Richard B. Russell, Jr., Senator from Georgia* (Chapel Hill, N.C., 1991),

The Birmingham conference recast Dixiecrat strategy. Prior to July, 1948, the Dixiecrats had behaved as facilitators of a movement within the southern state Democratic parties, and they confined their campaign to the eleven states of the former Confederacy. The campaign committee functioned as a holding company for eleven independent state parties. By the time of Birmingham, the bankruptcy of that approach was evident. In May, only five state Democratic parties—those in Alabama, Arkansas, Georgia, Mississippi, and South Carolina—had sent authorized delegations to the meeting in Jackson, and the contingent from Georgia refused to commit the state organization it represented to the Dixiecrats' program of promoting anti-Truman presidential electors. The Georgians remained at the conference but chose not to participate in the proceedings. At the June meeting of the campaign committee, chairman Laney acknowledged "that the South's anti-Truman fight is cooling off." [24]

Only in July did Dixiecrat strategists officially acknowledge that the southern Democratic parties were not rallying to the movement. Dixiecrat regulars still hoped that the state parties would embrace the Thurmond-Wright ticket, but realists were aware that a general revolt was no longer a feasible prospect. In order to continue, the movement had to become a third party. Such a strategic shift was by no means easy for believers in a solid Democratic South to accept.

Ben Laney at first rejected a third-party approach, refusing to be considered as a presidential contender and boycotting the Birmingham conference by retiring to a hotel room for its duration. The only feasible response to the national Democratic party, Laney held, was through the "official Democratic organizations in each respective state." Any other course would divide southern white people at the very moment that political unity was vital. At all events, Laney contended, a third-party effort "was doomed for

---

239–41; Talbot Field, Jr., to Frank M. Dixon, December 1, 1948, Frank M. Dixon, "Keynote Address," July 17, 1948, both in Dixon Papers; McLaurin, "The Role of the Dixiecrats," 168–91; Ethridge, "Mississippi's Role in the Dixiecrat Movement," 162–92.

[24] "Statement of James S. Peters," May 10, 1948, "Minutes of States' Rights Democratic Campaign Committee," June 8, 1948, both in Laney Papers. Peters was the party chairman for Georgia.

failure, because of a lack of money, time and organization." Ultimately Laney and his followers relented. Laney retained the Dixiecrat chair. With the decision to launch a third-party campaign and "to enter the ticket in most of the states in the union," the States' Rights Democrats went on to hold a convention in Houston, at which they nominated the Thurmond-Wright ticket. In the end, Thurmond lamented, only "four of the southern states—South Carolina, Mississippi, Alabama, and Louisiana—carried out the program chartered by the Southern Governors' Conference" when it met in Washington. Only in those states did Thurmond appear on the ballot as the candidate of the Democratic party, and only in those states was his campaign successful.[25]

Through most of the South, the Dixiecrat movement created conflict within state Democratic parties. All the former Confederate states possessed their state rights and loyalist factions. The Mississippi party was the most united, with Governor Wright, Senator Eastland, and virtually everyone else with influence favoring the States' Rights cause. Wright was the first to champion southern political independence and, together with Eastland, helped make *Whither Solid South?* the handbook of the movement by mailing copies to States' Rights sympathizers throughout the region. The Mississippi state party played host to the first conference of "true Democrats" and welcomed the establishment of Dixiecrat headquarters in Jackson. In South Carolina, Governor Thurmond and his States' Rights allies remained firmly in control of party affairs. Elsewhere the struggle between loyalists and Dixiecrats was more intense.[26]

In the other states of the Deep South, the governors—James E. Folsom in Alabama, Earl K. Long in Louisiana, and Melvin E. Thompson in Georgia—favored loyalty to the national party. In

[25] Ben Laney, "Statement," July 17, 1948, Ben Laney, Untitled Memoirs of the States' Rights Campaign, n.d., both in Laney Papers; G. C. Long, Jr., in Montgomery *Advertiser*, July 19, 1948; Frank M. Dixon to Robert A. Watson, August 3, 1948, in Dixon Papers; J. Strom Thurmond to Ben Laney, November 8, 1948, in Laney Papers.

[26] Ethridge, "Mississippi's Role in the Dixiecrat Movement," 1–126; Helen Fuller, "The New Confederacy," *New Republic*, CXIX (1948), 10–14; Frank M. Dixon to Wallace W. Wright, August 18, 1948, in Dixon Papers; Banks, "Strom Thurmond and the Revolt Against Modernity," 99–214; Robert McC. Figg, Jr., to Frank M. Dixon, May 25, 1948, in Dixon Papers.

all three states, state righters were powerful within the Democratic parties. In Alabama, the state party chairman, Gessner T. Mc-Corvey, and his associates settled matters by successfully running unpledged electors in the spring Democratic primaries. In the November presidential election, the Thurmond-Wright ticket appeared under the Democratic label; Truman's name was not on the ballot.[27]

In Louisiana, the Dixiecrat faithful created a statewide organization in July, 1948, after which the campaign gained momentum. The state central committee voted in September to make Thurmond and Wright the Democratic party's candidates. By then, according to one study, "Earl Long stood virtually alone among leading politicians in defending the right of Harry Truman to be put on the ballot as the national Democratic party nominee, which he obviously was." Long had to call a special session of the legislature to get Truman's name on the ballot at all.[28]

The Dixiecrats suffered a significant setback in Georgia, the only state of the Deep South to remain loyal to the national party. The conservative Talmadge faction—led by Herman after the death of his father, Eugene, in 1946—controlled the state party organization. The Talmadge forces had long been at odds with the national organization, and the Dixiecrat inner circle clearly expected Georgia to join the crusade. After James S. Peters, the state party chairman, told the States' Rights Democrats in Jackson that Georgia would not participate officially in the Dixiecrat effort, the Georgia Democrats drifted away from the movement. Even after Herman Talmadge defeated Governor Thompson in the September state primary election—which solidified the Talmadge faction's political control of the state—the party in Georgia did not join the States' Rights camp. A hodgepodge of conservative Democrats did venture a third-party effort in behalf of Thurmond, but it won only 20 percent of the vote.[29]

[27] William D. Barnard, *Dixiecrats and Democrats: Alabama Politics, 1942–1950* (University, Ala., 1974), 103–10.

[28] Michael L. Kurtz and Morgan D. Peoples, *Earl K. Long: The Saga of Uncle Earl and Louisiana Politics* (Baton Rouge, 1990), 152; Jeansonne, *Leander Perez*, 165–81.

[29] William Anderson, *The Wild Man from Sugar Creek: The Political Career of Eugene Talmadge* (Baton Rouge, 1975), 82–233; "Statement of James S. Peters," May 10, 1948, in Laney Papers; James S. Peters to Frank M. Dixon, May 20, 1948, in Dixon Papers.

Also disappointing to the Dixiecrats were political developments in Virginia, Arkansas, and Texas. The Virginia Democratic
party was initially a leader in the States' Rights movement. Senator
Byrd, Governor Tuck, and other organizational stalwarts denounced Truman's program, and Tuck was an enthusiastic member of the committee of the Southern Governors' Conference that
Thurmond chaired. In February Tuck introduced a bill in the
Virginia general assembly empowering the state Democratic central committee to determine who the state's Democratic electors
would support. The bill, fraught with antidemocratic features,
touched off a storm of controversy that forced changes. The law
that passed the legislature still permitted the state party convention to choose the Democratic party candidates. Byrd explained
that the "Truman people will have to petition to get on the ballot,"
and even then Truman would not be the "official Democratic
candidate." Yet the strength of the opposition sobered Byrd and
the organization forces. The urban press, citizens groups, antiorganization Democrats, and state Republicans condemned the new
law. Governor Tuck was noticeably absent from the May meeting
of the States' Righters. "We thought it best not to participate in
the Jackson Convention," he explained, "even though we are in
thorough sympathy with the objectives." Virginia Democrats, like
their counterparts in Georgia, ended by divorcing themselves
from the Dixiecrats; the Democratic central committee officially
announced a position of neutrality in the election.[30]

For a time, the Arkansas Democratic party seemed to be committed to the movement. Governor Laney and the Arkansas Free
Enterprise Association led the States' Rights effort. By late May,
however, Lamar Williamson, the president of the association, was
complaining that "the left wing new deal Democrats of Arkansas
are of course working desperately to undermine the program of
our Arkansas States' Rights Democrats." In August, Sidney S.
McMath won the Democratic gubernatorial primary and gained
control of the Democratic party machinery. McMath supported

[30] Harry F. Byrd to Ben Laney, March 8, 1948, William M. Tuck to Ben Laney, March 9,
1948, both in Laney Papers; William M. Tuck to Frank M. Dixon, May 21, 1958, in Dixon
Papers; William Bryan Crawley, Jr., *Bill Tuck: A Political Life in Harry Byrd's Virginia* (Charlottesville, Va., 1978), 154–79.

the national party, and the Dixiecrat movement gradually declined.[31]

In Texas, Governor Jester opposed Truman's civil rights program and seemed to favor the Dixiecrat cause. The Texas Regulars, presumably having benefited from their campaign experience in 1944, remained a force in the party and assumed
leadership of the battle against Truman. At the state Democratic
party convention in May, the conservatives held the upper hand
and selected presidential electors of dubious loyalty to the national party. By that time, however, Jester had concluded that "the
South can gain nothing by imitating Henry Wallace and forming
another party." The congenial governor added, "I want to be a
party builder—not a party bolter." Robert W. Calvert, the state
party chairman, was openly hostile to the States' Rights advocates,
deploring the "negative attitude they have harbored so long." The
Dixiecrat leadership sought to enthuse Texas conservatives by
holding their national nominating convention in Houston in August, but at the state Democratic convention in September the
loyalists were firmly in command, replacing the presidential electors chosen in May and requiring them to take a loyalty pledge.[32]

The States' Rights Democrats received organizational support
in Tennessee and Florida. In Memphis, the Democratic boss, Edward H. Crump, attempted to align the state with the Dixiecrats,
but by 1948 his organization was in decline. Despite a great deal
of tactical maneuvering among party factions, loyalists held most
of the elective offices and consigned the Dixiecrats to third-party
status. Infighting in Florida produced a similar result. Frank D.
Upchurch, an influential member of the state party executive
committee, with the assistance of Associated Industries of Florida,
came close to engineering a Democratic electoral slate that was at

[31] Lamar Williamson to Frank M. Dixon, May 24, 1948, John L. Daggett to Frank M.
Dixon, May 28, 1948, both in Dixon Papers; Lamar Williamson to Ben Laney, September
27, 1948, Marvin B. Norfleet to Ben Laney, October 1, 1948, both in Laney Papers.

[32] Copy of "Address" delivered in Fort Worth by Beauford H. Jester, April 20, 1948,
Beauford H. Jester to Ben Laney, April 26, 1948, R. W. Calvert, "Response to a Poll of
Southern Leaders," n.d., all in Laney Papers; George Norris Green, *The Establishment in
Texas Politics: The Primitive Years, 1938–1957* (Westport, Conn., 1979), 101–13.

least in part committed to the States' Rights movement, but eventually loyalist forces purged the anti-Truman electors.[33]

All the Democratic political interests in North Carolina, Kentucky, and Oklahoma remained with the national party, and the States' Rights movement amounted to little. In each of those states the existence of a legitimate—or at least semilegitimate—Republican opposition encouraged party loyalty. The Dixiecrats attempted to mount a campaign in North Carolina, but for the most part they ignored Kentucky and Oklahoma. The choice of Senator Alben W. Barkley as Truman's running mate ensured the national party's success in Kentucky, Barkley's home state. Owing to the difficult filing requirements in Oklahoma, the candidates of neither the States' Rights nor the Progressive party appeared on the ballot.[34]

As V. O. Key and Alexander Heard have documented, the Thurmond-Wright ticket fared best in plantation counties with relatively large numbers of nonvoting blacks. The Dixiecrat slate won substantial popular majorities as the Democratic ticket in Alabama, Mississippi, and South Carolina and a comfortable plurality in Louisiana. These states—along with one errant elector from Tennessee—gave Thurmond thirty-nine electoral votes, not nearly enough to influence the outcome. As third-party candidates, Thurmond and Wright made their best showing in Georgia, where they received 20 percent of the presidential vote. Their weakest performances in the former Confederacy were in North Carolina and Texas, where they won less than 10 percent.[35]

Although the Dixiecrat ticket received more than a million votes, the States' Rights cause enjoyed far stronger support in Democratic party councils than among the electorate. In Virginia, Texas, Florida, and Tennessee, the movement's popular base failed to match the enthusiasm in certain party circles. Even after appropriating the Democratic rooster emblem on the ballot in

[33] McLaurin, "The Role of the Dixiecrats," 244–52; Key, *Southern Politics*, 329–44; Garson, *The Democratic Party and the Politics of Sectionalism*, 293–314.

[34] Key, *Southern Politics*, 329–44; Garson, *The Democratic Party and the Politics of Sectionalism*, 293–314; James R. Scales and Danney Goble, *Oklahoma Politics: A History* (Norman, Okla., 1982), 256–59.

[35] Heard, *A Two-Party South?* 20–36, 251–78; Key, *Southern Politics*, 329–44.

Louisiana, the States' Righters fell short of winning half the votes. Throughout the region, they were well in advance of grass-roots sentiment. The Dixiecrats clearly represented not the racism of poor whites and the white working class, but the animosities of one wing of the southern conservative establishment.

The Dixiecrats were peculiarly ill suited for leading a popular revolt. Ben Laney had been right at Birmingham; the Dixiecrats could not function effectively as a mass movement. The leadership did not believe in broad political participation. No matter how much Frank Dixon talked of "crossroads democracy," the States' Rights partisans were defenders of disfranchisement. They favored local control of local affairs by a local elite. Given such an outlook, the Dixiecrats seemed torn between their desire to arouse support from the white hoi polloi through racial demagoguery and their distaste for involving the masses in questions of policy. Similarly, the Dixiecrats found themselves in the awkward position of attempting to save the solid Democratic South by undoing it. They supported the one-party system in state politics while opposing the Democratic nominee for President, a position that was difficult to translate into effective political action.

Southern liberals and moderates denounced the Dixiecrats. The metropolitan press was in the main antagonistic toward the States' Rights campaign, and such journalists as Jonathan Daniels, Jennings Perry, Harry M. Ayers, and Ralph McGill delivered a steady stream of criticism. According to Daniels, there was "no real southern revolt," just the noisy machinations of "some reactionary southern politicians" who are "increasingly regarded as out of date even in the South." The Nashville *Tennessean* editorialized that "the revolting Southerners have so strengthened President Truman's popularity among liberal elements elsewhere in the country that he may get millions of more votes where they will do him the most good." Politicians sympathetic to the New Deal, like Lister Hill of Alabama and Olin D. Johnston of South Carolina, reminded citizens of the benefits they received from federal economic programs. Labor leaders warned that the civil rights issue was a smoke screen and that the real Dixiecrat target was the New Deal. Through most of the South, metropolitan business and professional people demonstrated little interest in a movement that threatened to embarrass their quest for northern capital and industrial development.[36]

Most of all, the Dixiecrats failed to rally southern conservatives in the numbers they expected. Despite widespread discontent with Truman and his policies, much of the old-guard leadership remained with the national party. There were federal subsidies, patronage, congressional chairmanships, and the like to be mindful of, and southern political leaders were preponderantly lifelong and deeply committed Democrats. The Dixiecrat demand for partisan independence had the virtue of logical consistency, but it also contradicted the nationalizing forces of the era. Senator Russell railed against Truman's program as a "crime against our civilization and a sin against nature's God," but he also waged battle within the Democratic party. Other staunchly conservative Democrats agreed.[37]

The conservative regulars mapped their resistance in the halls of Congress. Shortly after Truman's civil rights message, twenty-one of the twenty-two senators from the former Confederate states—Claude Pepper was the exception—organized the opposition under the "generalship" of Senator Russell. In the House of Representatives, southern Democrats created a twelve-member "strategy committee," with a Dixiecrat, Congressman William Colmer of Mississippi, as its chairman. "We submit," Russell explained, "that the white people of the South, though widely misunderstood and oft maligned, have some few rights as American citizens."[38]

In any immediate sense, Russell need not have worried. The coalition of conservative Republicans and southern Democrats controlled Congress, and President Truman, having won the election, demonstrated a diminished ardor for minority rights. Even while trumpeting its Fair Deal program, the Truman administra-

[36] Jonathan Daniels in St. Louis *Star Times*, March 3, 1948; Nashville *Tennessean*, July 20, 1948; Frank Watts Ashley, "Selected Southern Liberal Editors and the States' Rights Movement of 1948" (Ph.D. dissertation, University of South Carolina, 1959).

[37] Richard B. Russell, "National Radio Broadcast," March 23, 1948, in *Congressional Record*, 80th Cong., 2nd Sess., Vol. 94, Appendix A, A1865.

[38] Fite, *Richard B. Russell*, 232; Ethridge, "Mississippi's Role in the Dixiecrat Movement," 71–72; New York *Times*, March 7, 1948, February 22, 1948; Russell, "National Radio Broadcast," A1864.

tion attempted to accommodate the southern conservatives. When Republicans held a congressional majority during 1947 and 1948, the administration had followed a strategy of confrontation. Facing a hostile Congress, Truman had sought not the enactment of reform legislation but clearly defined conflict with Congress over "major issues" that were "carefully selected solely on the basis of the quantity of public support." By battling Congress over the Taft-Hartley Act, civil rights, and the like, the administration constructed a campaign platform. The maneuver alienated southern conservatives, but as Clark Clifford noted, the "reactionary domination exercised over the Democratic Party by the congressional Southerners" cost the Democratic party African-American and white liberal votes. Distancing the Truman administration from the "reactionary" southerners was good presidential politics.[39]

In the 1948 election, the Democrats regained their majority in Congress, and the southern Democrats reclaimed their committee chairmanships. The Truman administration found it politically expedient to appease the southern conservatives. On most issues pertaining to foreign affairs and national defense, as in routine party matters, the southern Democrats generally supported the administration. The national party made only pro forma efforts to discipline Dixiecrat bolters, with Senator Eastland allowed to assume the chairmanship of the Senate judiciary subcommittee on civil rights and Congressman Colmer taken on as a member of the powerful House Rules Committee.[40]

Truman continued to declaim the merits of his civil rights program and to press Congress to take action, especially on his fair employment practices bill. By placing that legislation at the top of the civil rights agenda, the White House virtually assured that the conservative coalition would triumph. Many Republican congress members favored laws against poll taxes and lynching but were suspicious of one governing fairness in the workplace. A Re-

[39]James Rowe, Jr., "The President's Relationship with an Opposition Congress," n.d., Clark Clifford, Memorandum for the President, November 19, 1947, pp. 7, 18–19, both in Clifford Papers, Political File, Truman Library.

[40]Charles S. Murphy, Memorandum for the President, February 17, 1949, in Charles S. Murphy Papers, White House File, Truman Library; Berman, The Politics of Civil Rights, 160–63.

publican senator called the fair employment practices proposal the "one civil rights bill that they know will be hardest to pass." By giving priority to it, Truman managed to support minority rights and thereby to appease black and white liberals while at the same time antagonizing southern conservatives as little as possible by not actually accomplishing anything. With the rise of McCarthyism and the beginning of the Korean War, the Truman administration capitulated to the southern conservatives. In 1950 the president privately agreed not to sponsor additional civil rights legislation, and he tendered to Senator Russell the position of Senate majority leader.[41]

If Truman's retreat gladdened southern conservatives, it did not restore harmony in the Democratic party. The administration continued to enunciate its commitment to civil rights, oversaw the gradual dismantling of segregation in the armed services, appointed occasional blacks to prominent government positions, and remained uneasy about what racial problems were doing to the nation's image abroad. The federal courts expanded the interpretation of the Fourteenth Amendment, and desegregation made inroads in higher education and in other limited spheres in the South. Black voter participation, confined in most states to urban areas, slowly grew. Northern liberals persisted in criticizing southern white racism, and African Americans campaigned for racial progress. All of these matters gave southern conservatives cause for concern.

The tidelands oil controversy helped move conservative dissent beyond civil rights. During the 1930s the federal government had asserted claim to the mineral rights in submerged areas off the coast of the United States, in what seemed to the states most affected—Texas, Louisiana, Mississippi, Florida, and California—a trespass. In 1946 Congress passed legislation affirming state ownership of the tidelands; Truman vetoed the bill. In 1947 and again in 1950 the Supreme Court ruled in favor of the federal claim to the underwater minerals.

[41] Senator Kenneth Wherry of Nebraska quoted in *The Politics of Civil Rights*, by Berman, 163; Alonzo L. Hamby, *Beyond the New Deal: Harry S. Truman and American Liberalism* (New York, 1973), 442. Senator Russell did not accept the appointment the president offered.

As offshore drilling increased, so too did the attendant tax bonanza. The oil companies usually lobbied for the principle of state ownership, inasmuch as the federal government assessed a 37.5 percent royalty whereas the state of Texas collected 12.5 percent. State rights sentiment, the power of oil companies, and resistance to the idea of the federal government expropriating property for anything but defense purposes broadened support for the oil states' position, and in 1952 Congress again endorsed state ownership. Again Truman vetoed the bill. With several southern states committed to local ownership and the Truman administration advocating federal control, the tidelands oil issue exacerbated sectional strife within the Democratic party.[42]

The former Dixiecrats failed to turn the ongoing intraparty discord to political profit. In 1950 Democratic regulars regained control of the party organizations in Alabama, Louisiana, and South Carolina. Thurmond failed in his campaign to unseat Senator Johnston in 1950, and Laney finished a distant second in his effort to regain the Arkansas governorship. The Dixiecrats tried to keep their movement alive by establishing the National States' Rights Committee in 1949 and opening a national bureau in Washington. They never regained momentum, however, and in 1952 the Washington bureau closed.[43]

Despite the decline of the Dixiecrats, southern state politics gave comfort to the conservatives. Senators Claude Pepper and Frank Graham lost their seats to conservative challengers in Florida and North Carolina. The 1950 elections made James F. Byrnes governor of South Carolina and Allan Shivers governor of Texas. Herman Talmadge, after winning a special gubernatorial contest in Georgia in 1948, won a full four-year term in 1950. The Byrd organization continued to steer policy in Virginia when it elected John S. Battle to the governorship in 1949. In 1951 one rabid conservative succeeded another as Hugh L. White replaced Gov-

[42] Robert A. Calvert and Arnoldo De Leon, *The History of Texas* (Arlington Heights, Tex., 1990), 369–72; Earnest R. Bartley, *The Texas Tidelands Controversy: A Legal and Historical Analysis* (Austin, Tex., 1953); Glen Jeansonne, *Leander Perez*, 164–68, 195.

[43] Heard, *A Two-Party South?* 164–65; National States' Rights Committee, "Constitution and Declaration of Principles," 1949, in Laney Papers. Leander Perez served as national director and head of the Washington office. See Jeansonne, *Leander Perez*, 185–88.

ernor Wright in the Mississippi statehouse. In early 1952 Robert F. Kennon, a leader of the anti-Long faction, followed Earl Long as governor of Louisiana. Each of these transfers of office confirmed conservative strength.[44]

The Democratic national convention of 1952 demonstrated the resurgence of southern influence in party affairs. A bevy of southern Democrats competed for the presidential nomination. Senator Estes Kefauver of Tennessee, who had established a national reputation by chairing a Senate committee that conducted a televised investigation of organized crime, became the first twentieth-century southerner to conduct a fully national campaign. Kefauver accelerated Truman's return to private life by beating the president in the New Hampshire primary, and he went on to win most of the Democratic primary contests. In the South, only Florida held a primary, which Kefauver lost to Richard Russell. Kefauver campaigned as a liberal, slightly to the left of the Democratic center, and his support was national rather than southern. He arrived at the convention as the nominal front-runner.

Senator Russell carried the banner of the southern conservatives. In attempting to broaden his following, Russell went so far as to suggest superseding the Taft-Hartley Act with new legislation, but he remained distinctly a southern candidate. Vice-President Barkley was considered a credible contender until liberal and labor concern about his being seventy-four years old and having affinities with Senate colleagues from farther southward than Kentucky led him to withdraw. Senator Robert S. Kerr of Oklahoma conducted a national campaign that failed to discover a following outside his home state. The only other plausible announced candidate was Averell Harriman of New York.[45]

[44] Dewey W. Grantham, *The Life and Death of the Solid South: A Political History* (Lexington, Ky., 1988), 125–34.

[45] Charles L. Fontenay, *Estes Kefauver: A Biography* (Knoxville, Tenn., 1980), 187–209; Joseph Bruce Gorman, *Kefauver: A Political Biography* (New York, 1971), 50–159; Fite, *Richard B. Russell*, 271–300; Anne Hodges Morgan, *Robert S. Kerr: The Senate Years* (Norman, Okla., 1977), 138–141; Richard L. Strout in *Christian Science Monitor*, July 23, 1952. This brief account of the 1952 convention is based primarily on *The National Story* and *The South*, Vols. I and III of *Presidential Nominating Politics in 1952*, by Paul T. David, Malcolm Moos, and Ralph M. Goldman (5 vols.; Baltimore, 1954); on Allan P. Sindler's "The Unsolid South: A Challenge to the Democratic National Party," in *The Uses of Power: Seven Cases in*

Complicating the convention was the threat of a southern revolt. Officials in six southern states—Georgia, Louisiana, Mississippi, South Carolina, Texas, and Virginia—had made arrangements to hold state party gatherings after the national selection
of a candidate, for the purpose of settling on whom the state parties would list on the Democratic line of the ballot. Loyalist Democrats in Texas and Mississippi sent competing delegations to vie
for the convention's recognition, and Georgia's delegates were
intent on promoting Russell's candidacy. As a result, the most outspoken state rights delegations were those from Louisiana, South
Carolina, and Virginia, all three of which adamantly refused to
sign a pledge of loyalty. "We're just going to sit here," Senator
Byrd taunted, "and maybe they'll have to throw us out." [46]

Some liberals, led by the Americans for Democratic Action,
were ready to defy the southern conservatives. Walter Reuther, a
leader in both the CIO and the ADA, explained, "We do not believe the South will bolt, but if it so chooses, let this happen. Let
the realignment of the parties proceed." The strategists for Kefauver and Harriman viewed a sharply defined and largely sectional conflict over the loyalty pledge as a method to polarize the
convention and thereby to combat the efforts of the party managers to draft the enigmatic Governor Adlai E. Stevenson of Illinois as a compromise candidate. When the convention imposed
a loyalty requirement, the Louisiana, South Carolina, and Virginia
delegations stood by their refusal to sign it.[47]

The Truman administration chose to appease the southern
conservatives. The president put his influence behind the movement to draft Stevenson. The convention managers and the administration forces gained control, and they permitted the Louisiana, South Carolina, and Virginia delegations to vote without
complying with the requirements the convention had laid down.
Truman persuaded the indecisive Harriman to withdraw in favor

American Politics, ed. Alan F. Westin (New York, 1962), 230–83; and on Democratic National Committee Papers, Newspaper Clipping File, Subject File, Truman Library.

[46] Thomas L. Stokes in Washington *Star,* July 23, 1952; Byrd quoted in *The National Story,*
by David, Moos, and Goldman, 134.

[47] Gould Lincoln in Washington *Star,* July 25, 1952; Reuther quoted in "The Unsolid
South," by Sindler, 233.

of Stevenson. Most of the southern delegates remained with Russell until Kefauver conceded. The nomination—unlike that of 1948—was made unanimous.[48]

In contrast to 1948, the national party establishment in 1952 went to considerable pains to accommodate the southern conservatives. Next to Russell, Stevenson was the candidate most acceptable to southern conservatives, and after winning the nomination, the Illinois governor chose Senator John Sparkman of Alabama as his running mate. "To Adlai Stevenson," Bayard Rustin observed bluntly, "the struggle against racial discrimination was more a potential liability than an opportunity for moving the party forward." Apart from approving a toned-down civil rights plank, the convention largely ignored the issue. Yet the South was no longer solid, at least in presidential politics. Stevenson supported civil rights, even if not especially enthusiastically, and he endorsed Truman's position on the federal title to tidelands oil.[49]

Dwight D. Eisenhower, the Republican nominee, became the first Republican ever to campaign in the South and seriously to pursue southern voters. During the months leading up to November, he visited most of the southern states, and in Columbia, South Carolina, when the band played "Dixie," he rose to tell the audience, "I always stand up when they play that song." Eisenhower was a war hero and a Texas native who accepted the Republican party's timid stance on civil rights; he was a business-oriented moderate who promised to reject the centralizing philosophy of the left and who favored state control of offshore oil. Both angry Bourbon conservatives and restive urban moderates found much to admire in the popular Eisenhower.[50]

In the 1952 presidential election, prominent southern Democrats again worked to defeat the Democratic candidate for president. This time, rather than supporting a southern "true" Democrat, the bolting Democrats championed a Republican. Gov-

[48] Willard Edwards in Washington *Times Herald,* July 26, 1952; James I. Loeb, Oral History Interview, June 27, 1970, Charles S. Murphy, Oral History Interview, July 15, 1969, both in Truman Library.

[49] Bayard Rustin, *Strategies for Freedom: The Changing Patterns of Black Protest* (New York, 1976), 32.

[50] Eisenhower quoted in *The Disruption of the Solid South,* by George Brown Tindall (Athens, Ga., 1972), 51; Samuel Lubell, *Revolt of the Moderates* (New York, 1956), 180–205.

ernor Shivers of Texas, Governor Kennon of Louisiana, and Governor Byrnes of South Carolina were notable among the phalanx of Democrats and former Dixiecrats who promoted the Democrats for Eisenhower, Citizens for Eisenhower, and Americans for Eisenhower that flourished through the region. The Texas Democratic party convention resolved, "Every Democrat in Texas [should] vote and work for the election of Dwight D. Eisenhower for President and Richard Nixon for Vice President." The Byrd organization in Virginia again adopted a haughty neutrality.[51]

The election helped clarify political trends in the South. Eisenhower carried five states—Florida, Oklahoma, Tennessee, Texas, and Virginia—and came very close to winning several others. The Eisenhower candidacy fared extremely well in traditionally Republican mountain counties, where partisan preferences dated from the Civil War era. More significant, it attracted strong support from the rising urban and suburban middle class, which became a crucial factor in regional politics for the first time. In Oklahoma and Texas, the Republican ticket swept upper-income metropolitan neighborhoods to swell Eisenhower's majorities. Republican ballots from the cities of south Florida overwhelmed the Democratic votes from north Florida. Affluent urbanites joined with mountain Republicans to produce victories in Tennessee and Virginia and only narrowly missed doing so in Kentucky. Through most of the region, business and professional urbanites—the "better element," as they had already become known in Georgia— made their numbers felt.

Joining the suburbanites were voters residing in plantation counties with a high percentage of nonvoting blacks. Throughout the Deep South there was a close correlation between county support for the Dixiecrats in 1948 and enthusiasm for Eisenhower in 1952. Not in twenty years had a Republican presidential candidate won 5 percent of South Carolina's ballots; Eisenhower won almost 50 percent. Similarly, by appealing to suburban and plantation-

---

[51] Resolution quoted in *Texas Presidential Politics in 1952,* by O. Douglas Weeks (Austin, Tex., 1953), 88; L. Vaughan Howard and David R. Deener, *Presidential Politics in Louisiana* (New Orleans, 1954); James F. Byrnes, *All in One Lifetime* (New York, 1958), 98–205; J. Harvie Wilkinson III, *Harry Byrd and the Changing Face of Virginia Politics, 1945–1966* (Charlottesville, Va., 1968), 80–88.

county whites, the Republican ticket came close to carrying Louisiana and even received 40 percent of the vote cast in Mississippi. "If we act in concert with other southern states on these questions and let the leaders of both political parties know we are no longer 'in the bag' of any political party," Governor Byrnes had informed the South Carolina Democratic convention, "we will no longer be ignored." Clearly the southern electorate was no longer exclusively in the Democratic bag.[52]

Southern liberals had endeavored to unite the South with the nation on a program of economic development leading toward political and industrial democracy. Basing their campaign on an appeal to the masses of workers and farmers, they tried to enlist change-oriented middle-class whites as well. Their movement failed.

States' Rights Democrats had charted a route toward sectional independence in social and partisan matters. Largely untempted by modernizing forces, the Dixiecrats appealed to county-seat elites, especially those in plantation regions, and to old-guard conservatives generally. Their strike for political autonomy also failed. Although third-party movements continued to appear in the South during the postwar years, the Dixiecrat defeat was decisive.

By rejecting both the popular-front left and the independent right, politically active southerners tacitly accepted the historical imperatives of the New Deal and World War II. The presidential politics of 1952 demonstrated the extent to which southern influence in national politics had grown since the region's forlorn isolation in 1948. In the election, substantial numbers of whites residing in the suburbs, the plantation counties, and the mountains joined hands in support of Eisenhower. The electoral alliance in presidential politics between the advocates of modernization and

[52] Donald S. Strong, "The Presidential Election in the South, 1952," *Journal of Politics,* XVII (1955), 343–89; Donald S. Strong, *The 1952 Presidential Election in the South* (University, Ala., 1956); Numan V. Bartley, *The Rise of Massive Resistance: Race and Politics in the South During the 1950s* (Baton Rouge, 1969), 47–57; Byrnes quoted in New York *Times,* April 17, 1952.

the defenders of tradition suggested that modernization in the South was apt to follow a more conservative path than that trod by an earlier generation of northerners. Southern Democratic solidarity in presidential politics had been broken, but the power of Bourbon conservatives remained intact.

CHAPTER IV

THE MAKING OF
THE MODERN SOUTH

W
RITING in the early 1950s, William T. Polk, a North
Carolina journalist, analyzed the South and found it to
be a divided region. It had been "rural, agrarian, easy-
going, poor and proud of its distinctive way of life. Now it is becoming urban, industrial, hard-working, comparatively prosperous and relatively standardized." Part of the South had adopted
the new way of life; the other part resisted it. As a result, there
were "two Souths which exist side by side in each Southern state,
but are as different as Chicago and Bangkok." The New South
flourished in cities; it tended to be upland, to be oriented toward
manufacturing, and to be materialistic in its values. The Old South
survived in the towns; it tended to be lowland, to be oriented
toward agriculture, and to place emphasis on nonmaterial values.
Symbolizing the New South were such signs of progress as the
"H-bomb plant rising in the Savannah River basin"; representative
of the Old South were the statues of Confederate soldiers that
graced virtually every county-courthouse lawn. Polk's depiction of
the two Souths may have been simplistic, but his *Southern Accent*
explained a great deal about the region.[1]

Towns were the centers of the "southern way of life." The
twelve hundred or so southern towns—those nonmetropolitan
communities with at least the 2,500 people necessary to qualify as
urban—enjoyed relatively flush times during the 1940s. "The
county seat has never fared better in its history," Jasper Berry
Shannon wrote in the late 1940s. As agricultural marketing cen-

[1] William T. Polk, *Southern Accent: From Uncle Remus to Oak Ridge* (New York, 1953), 227,
19, 23.

ters, towns profited from the lofty prices of farm products during World War II, the high federal price supports during the late forties, and the burst of demand during the Korean war. Such town-oriented industries as textiles, apparel, and lumber also did well during the period.

Consequently, southern towns grew significantly in the 1940s. The approximately five million people living in urban communities outside the metropolitan districts made up 13 percent of the southern population in 1940; in 1950 some seven million townspeople constituted 16 percent of the population. During the 1950s, however, population growth in the towns stagnated. Agricultural prices went into a relative decline, as did the fortunes of textiles, apparel, timber, and coal mining. In 1960 approximately seven million town residents made up 14 percent of the South's population. The more materially and demographically expansive towns became metropolitan areas, and some others were absorbed by metropolitan areas, but in general towns languished as economic and population growth, and ultimately political power, shifted toward the large cities.[2]

Southern towns were the traditional sources of political authority in the region and the nucleus of William Polk's Old South, but as Polk pointed out, the Old South rested on an agricultural foundation. Historically, southern towns had functioned as market, service, and government centers for surrounding agricultural areas, and to a residual degree, many continued to do so in the postwar era. Novelist Harper Lee described an Alabama county seat in which the "proportion of professional people ran high: one went there to have his teeth pulled, his wagon fixed, his heart listened to, his money deposited, his soul saved, his mules vetted."

[2] Kenneth Weiher, "The Cotton Industry and Southern Urbanization, 1880–1930," *Explorations in Economic History*, XIV (1977), 120–40; T. Lynn Smith, "The Emergence of Cities," in *The Urban South*, ed. Rupert B. Vance and Nicholas J. Demerath (Chapel Hill, N.C., 1954), 24–37; John M. Maclachlan and Joe S. Floyd, Jr., *This Changing South* (Gainesville, Fla., 1956), 36–42; Jasper Berry Shannon, *Toward a New Politics in the South* (Knoxville, Tenn., 1949), 51; Calvin B. Hoover and B. U. Ratchford, *Economic Resources and Policies of the South* (New York, 1951), 146–48. Unless otherwise noted, all statistics in this chapter are from the United States Bureau of the Census. The bureau changed its definition of *urban* in 1950, and therefore the figures are not strictly comparable. Throughout this chapter, statistics for 1940 and 1950 are based on the earlier definition; figures for 1960 are based on the new definition.

Lee also wrote of the "grubbiness of most Alabama towns," but during the early postwar years such communities remained at the heart of southern life.[3]

Saturday was shopping day, and rural people flocked in not only to buy but to gossip and socialize. A black farmer in Georgia explained that "there would be so many people in town you couldn't hardly walk either of the streets on Saturday." People from the farms came into William Faulkner's fictional town of Jefferson "to do a week's shopping for staples and delicacies like bananas and twenty-five-cent sardines and machine-made cakes and pies and clothes and stockings and feed and fertilizer and plow-gear." Towns also pressed the cotton, milled the cottonseed, shipped the lumber, and repaired the machinery.[4]

Nonmetropolitan areas shared in the industrial growth in the region. During the decade following the war, the number of factories that employed at least twenty-five workers increased by one-third. The new industrial establishments manufactured a wide range of goods, but the majority of the new plants were traditional low-wage, usually labor-intensive operations producing textiles, apparel, furniture, lumber, tobacco, and food products. Many engaged in the first-stage transformation of raw materials from southern farms, forests, and mines and located in and around the towns where the materials were at hand and the labor was cheap and abundant. Thus from the midforties to the midfifties, industry expanded impressively while the value added per employee declined relative to the national average. Southern industrial development included a range of "new industries" that became increasingly important, but sophisticated, capital-intensive, high-value-added concerns gravitated toward the skilled labor, centralized transportation, and subsidiary services the metropolitan areas offered. As southern towns became more dependent on manufacturing, their reliance on a low-wage labor market persisted.[5]

[3] Harper Lee, *To Kill a Mockingbird* (New York, 1960), 133.

[4] Jane Maguire, comp., *On Shares: Ed Brown's Story* (New York, 1975), 220; William Faulkner, *Intruder in the Dust* (New York, 1948), 151.

[5] Hammer and Company, *Post-War Industrial Development in the South* (Atlanta, 1956) 1–52; *Selected Materials on the Economy of the South: Report of the Committee on Banking and Currency,* U.S. Senate, 84th Cong., 2nd Sess., 10–31; Research Department, Federal Reserve Bank

The cotton-textile belt stretching through the southeastern piedmont from Virginia into Alabama was the regional industrial belt, and it was also the setting of the classic southern industrial town. In *Lower Piedmont Country,* H. C. Nixon described a "typical industrial town of the hill country," with its easily recognizable Uptown, Milltown, and Niggertown sections. Churches, lodges, social clubs, and almost all the doings in the town sorted themselves according to these divisions, just as gender defined social roles within each group. In one sense, Niggertown or Colored Town or Black Bottom, or whatever name the local white terminology gave it, was simply an inchoate ghetto that lacked the social disorganization and density of the massive black communities in the developing metropolitan areas. Similarly Uptown or The Town or The Community was an embryonic form of the more insulated upper-status enclaves that spread through suburban counties. Milltown was in some ways a more socially knit imitation of a tenement district in a northern industrial city. Yet the piedmont industrial towns also had much in common with the agricultural marketing centers. In both, class, caste, and gender relations sprang from traditional assumptions about the natural order of things.[6]

of Atlanta, *Statistics on the Developing South* (Atlanta, 1968); Joseph J. Spengler, "Demographic and Economic Change in the South, 1940–1960," in *Change in the Contemporary South,* ed. Allan P. Sindler (Durham, N.C., 1963), 26–63; Joseph J. Spengler, "Southern Economic Trends and Prospects," in *The South in Continuity and Change,* ed. John C. McKinney and Edgar T. Thompson (Durham, N.C., 1965), 101–31; Edgar S. Dunn, Jr., *Recent Southern Economic Development As Revealed by the Changing Structure of Employment* (Gainesville, Fla., 1962); Harvey S. Perloff *et al., Regions, Resources, and Economic Growth* (Baltimore, 1960), 467–551; Howard G. Shaller, "Income of the South: Structure, Sources, Potentials," in *Raising the Income and Productivity of the South* (Frankfort, Ky., 1961), 1–5; Albert W. Niemi, Jr., *Gross State Product and Productivity in the Southeast* (Chapel Hill, N.C., 1975); Gavin Wright, *Old South, New South: Revolutions in the Southern Economy Since the Civil War* (New York, 1986), 239–72. In 1947, 34 percent of southern production workers participated in the manufacture of textiles and apparel, 18.5 percent in lumber and furniture, 10 percent in food products, and 3 percent in tobacco. See Hoover and Ratchford, *Economic Resources and Policies of the South,* 126–28.

[6] H. C. Nixon, *Lower Piedmont Country: The Uplands of the Deep South* (University, Ala., 1946), 74–80; H. C. Nixon, *Possum Trot: Rural Community, South* (Norman, Okla., 1941); H. C. Nixon, "Farewell to 'Possum Trot'?" in *The Urban South,* ed. Vance and Demerath, 6–23; Rudolf Heberle, "The Mainsprings of Southern Urbanization," in *The Urban South,*

Family roots and social place regulated town affairs. Everyone knew that "No Crawford Minds His Own Business" and "All the Bufords Walk Like That." To whites, blacks were "our Nigras" so long as they remained in their "place." To ensure that they did, white society taught the observance of proper "race etiquette" with the same sobriety that it fostered time-tested models of gender behavior. "Southerntown," John Dollard once observed, "is a veritable Cheka in its vigilance on caste matters." A character in one of Faulkner's novels described a white storekeeper who tolerated minor pilfering by black customers: "All he requires is that they act like niggers." Because so many black women worked as domestics in uptown homes, the white milltown families were in some ways the most isolated group. Liston Pope remarked in his study of a North Carolina mill community, "It would be as unthinkable in most uptown homes to invite a 'common millhand' to dinner as it would be to invite a Negro." Not all southern boroughs possessed clearly defined milltowns or other industrial communities, though working-class residential areas were common in towns throughout the region. Well-behaved, "respectable" workers were "good common people," whereas less tractable laborers were apt to occupy a social stratum not unlike that of the sharecroppers in the surrounding countryside.[7]

Uptown elites demonstrated the greatest reverence for family lineage and the strongest devotion to the southern past and to Lost Cause mythology. "If they get mad with you," an informant explained, "they don't just get mad with you—they go back as far as they can—telling stories on each other's ancestors." *Judge* and *Colonel* were frequent forms of address, and as Shannon noted,

283–92; David L. Carlton, *Mill and Town in South Carolina, 1880–1920* (Baton Rouge, 1982); Anthony M. Tang, *Economic Development in the Southern Piedmont, 1860–1950: Its Impact on Agriculture* (Chapel Hill, N.C., 1958); Catherine H. C. Seaman, "Kinship and Land Tenure in a Piedmont County: A Diachronic Study of a Heterogeneous Community in the South" (Ph.D. dissertation, University of Virginia, 1969); Jackson M. McClain and Robert B. Highsaw, *Dixie City Acts: A Study in Decision-Making* (University, Ala., 1962); Melton A. McLaurin, *Separate Pasts: Growing Up White in the Segregated South* (Athens, Ga., 1987).

[7] Lee, *To Kill a Mockingbird*, 134; John Dollard, *Caste and Class in a Southern Town* (3rd ed.; Garden City, N.Y., 1957), 48; Faulkner, *Intruder in the Dust*, 33; Liston Pope, *Millhands and Preachers: A Study of Gastonia* (New Haven, 1942), 68.

the wives of the county-seat elite buttressed "their social ascendancy by industriously preoccupying themselves with their ancestors of the American Revolution or the War between the States."[8]

In a revealing study of an Alabama piedmont county-seat town conducted during the early 1950s, two investigators found that within the uptown "community" of the established elite "the family system and associated values are interwoven into every aspect of community life, individual behavior, and response to events within and outside the community." Permeating the "community" was an "ancestor-oriented" belief system according to which "qualities are hereditary and . . . education, brains, success, moral character, and good taste run in the family line." It was little wonder that county-seat political leaders tended to be a trifle backward looking.[9]

The piedmont county seat had been a "conservative old Southern town." Since 1940 it had added more than thirty new industries, many of them small but in the aggregate greatly altering the town's economic foundation and expanding its middle class. During the war and in the early postwar years, numerous other southern boroughs experienced similar developments. Business and industrial growth, along with federal mortgage-guarantee programs, created, in Faulkner's somewhat condescending portrait of a fictional Mississippi town, the "neat small new one-story houses designed in Florida and California set with matching garages in their neat plots of clipped grass and tedious flowerbeds . . . where the prosperous young married couples lived with two children each and (as soon as they could afford it) an automobile each and the memberships in . . . the junior rotary and chamber of commerce and the patented electric gadgets for cooking and freezing and cleaning and the neat trim colored maids in frilled caps to run them . . . while the wives in sandals and pants and painted toenails puffed lipstick-stained cigarettes over shopping bags in the chain groceries and drugstores." Such residential de-

---

[8] Allison Davis, Burleigh B. Gardner, and Mary R. Gardner, *Deep South: A Social Anthropological Study of Caste and Class* (Chicago, 1941), 85–86; Shannon, *Toward a New Politics in the South,* 47.

[9] Solon T. Kimball and Marion Pearsall, *The Talladega Story: A Study in Community Process* (University, Ala., 1954), 11, 45–46.

velopments paled when compared with the rabid expansion of metropolitan suburbs, but they did symbolize the growth of a middle class in the more prosperous towns.[10]

The most successful real-estate dealers, small businessmen, and industrialists—"strainers" or "climbers," in regional terminology—accumulated sufficient property to vie for a voice in uptown affairs. The corporations establishing branch plants in the South normally brought with them their own—frequently nonsouthern—executives and managers. Thriving local businessmen often based their claims for power and preferment on wealth rather than ancestry and were perhaps not entirely unlike an earlier generation of northern capitalists in their views toward labor organization and social reform. Many of the northern managers resided in the South only because their corporations had sought to escape northern unions and pay packages. From an uptown perspective, such parvenus were "pushy" and lacked the proper respect for family lineage and traditional mythology.

Yet uptown families had their own economic interests to promote, and on most questions bearing on commerce and industry they differed little from those they saw as their social inferiors. Local strainers, executives from afar, and uptown elites shared a respect for the rights of property and an aversion to union organization and independent action by the southern working class. Town leaders continued to offer formidable incentives to industrialists, or at least to industrialists who did not offend social decency by accepting labor unions or corrupting blacks and women with equal opportunities or upsetting wage scales by exceeding the local norm. But if the opening of leadership opportunities carried with it little in the way of new economic attitudes, it did gradually attenuate traditional paternal class relationships and give scope to market forces. In this regard, Faulkner's chronicle of the Snopes clan was prescient sociology.

Cotton-mill workers were the largest category of industrial employees in the South, and they concentrated in and around the towns rather than in the metropolitan areas. On the eve of World War II, the research director for the Textile Workers Union of

[10] *Ibid.*, 8; Faulkner, *Intruder in the Dust*, 79.

America toured southern textile mills in composing a report on problems connected with organizing southern workers. The New York–based researcher perceived the southern textile worker to be a "small-town, suspicious individual, who is extremely provincial, petty, gossip-mongering." Textile workers were clannish, he stated, and preferred "to be left alone and isolated." Apt to be "most suspicious of every outsider," they possessed "no incentive for higher standards." During the war, George Baldanzi, vice-president of the Textile Workers Union, made his own survey of southern workers. He concurred that "Southerners are not a cosmopolitan group," but beyond that his report was quite different from the earlier one. Among southern workers, Baldanzi concluded, there "is a much greater appreciation of human values than is found in the North; they are by nature kindly, react to human tragedy with a sort of calm fatalism, and are strongly religious." He found it refreshing that southern workers were less cynical and less materialistic than those in the North. The two reports may have revealed more about their authors than about southern textile workers, but neither was entirely inaccurate.[11]

Academic studies usually emphasized the cultural isolation of mill villages. Although the plantation style of industrial organization, with the company owning the houses, community center, churches, and commissary, had declined in milltowns by the mid-forties, more than six out of ten cotton-mill workers still lived in company-owned houses. In a South Carolina milltown, the workers seemed "in many respects actually more segregated than the Negro elements of Kent society." The "folk culture" that "encapsulated" workers reinforced a sense of the fixity of social position and subverted ambition. So too did the paternal labor relations. Mill hands, so owners and managers continued to insist, were "like irresponsible children—they have to be cared for and the employer is the one best fitted for the job." Labor unions, the argument ran, would only disrupt the milltown's family harmony. As more southern factories came to have absentee owners and as more managers came to be college-educated outsiders trained in

[11] Solomon Barkin to Emil Rieve, October 25, 1939, George Baldanzi to Emil Rieve *et al.*, April 8, 1942, both in Textile Workers Union of America Papers, Series A, File 1A, State Historical Society of Wisconsin, Madison.

business-school efficiency, the comparison with a family rang increasingly hollow. Yet the residents of milltowns themselves often felt the force of the image: "It was kind of one big family, and we hung together and survived." [12]

Because in abandoning the mill village the company usually sold the houses to the workers, the disruption of mill communities was a gradual process. Mill families continued to labor in the mill; their children frequently moved away. The evidence suggested that mill youngsters paid a heavy price in leaving the familiar milltown society to compete in the increasingly dynamic southern labor market. Most remained in blue-collar jobs or married blue-collar workers. Girls were somewhat more likely to finish high school and to seek office employment. Boys searching for broader horizons often joined the armed services. The decline of the mill villages, as well as the mining towns, lumber camps, and other company communities, not only severed work from community life but contributed to the conversion of labor into a free-flowing commodity. [13]

The depopulating of southern agriculture cast into the cities vast numbers not only from the farms but also from the hamlets that depended on farmers as customers and clients. Their trek to factory and service jobs often meant—as it did for the people leaving the milltowns—a wrenching readjustment. A workday set by time clocks and factory whistles was a far cry from one guided by the progress of the sun across the sky. The unrelenting industrial pace yielded no slack seasons for fishing, hunting, and loafing. Even though factory work was often less toilsome than farm labor and even though air conditioning had become relatively common in postwar factories, the work was still indoors. As Ben

[12] John K. Morland, *Millways of Kent* (Chapel Hill, N.C., 1958), ix; Herbert J. Lahne, *The Cotton Mill Worker* (New York, 1944), 36, 66; Jacquelyn Dowd Hall *et al.*, *Like a Family: The Making of a Southern Cotton Mill World* (Chapel Hill, N.C., 1987), xi.

[13] Morland, *Millways of Kent;* Harriet L. Herring, *Passing of the Mill Village: Revolution in a Southern Institution* (Chapel Hill, N.C., 1949); Lahne, *The Cotton Mill Worker;* Hall *et al.*, *Like a Family;* Jacquelyn Dowd Hall, Robert Korstad, and James Leloudis, "Cotton Mill People: Work, Community, and Protest in the Textile South, 1880–1940," *American Historical Review,* XCI (1986), 245–86; J. Kenneth Morland, "Kent Revisited: Blue-Collar Aspirations and Achievements," in *Blue-Collar World: Studies of the American Worker,* ed. Arthur B. Shostak and William Gomberg (Englewood Cliffs, N.J., 1964), 134–43.

Robertson once remarked, "I had never spent all of a day in any house in my life."[14]

William Faulkner's "Shingles for the Lord" depicted the gradual transformation of regional attitudes toward labor. In the short story, Pap, one of the three men who had agreed to gather early one morning to reroof the local church, was two hours late. Solon Bookwright, who had been employed by the New Deal's Works Progress Administration, explained that the two hours were "three man-hour units a hour, multiplied by two hours . . . a total of six work units," which Pap owed for his tardiness. Pap defended the old-fashioned view: "I didn't know there was but one idea about work—until it is done, it ain't done, and when it is done, it is." He continued that, anyway, the Lord "ain't interested in time, nohow." To Solon Boatwright, such attitudes were passé: "You don't seem to kept up with these modern ideas about work that's been flooding and uplifting the country in the last few years." Modern timework discipline was nothing new in the South, but during World War II and afterward it affected far more people than in the past.[15]

Large numbers of white women worked in textiles, and during the war years women employees were common in defense industries. Wartime necessity did not, however, go far toward changing "attitudes about women's work in general or about their primary role as homemakers," Mary Martha Thomas concluded from a study of Alabama. Women, Thomas observed, continued to regard "their work as a job rather than a career," and men—at least those who could afford it—continued to expect wives to be full-time homemakers. As the postwar years progressed, young women increasingly aspired to careers, but among blue-collar teenagers, one study reported, realism limited expectations. During the early postwar years, the southern work force was predominantly male.[16]

[14] Ben Robertson, *Red Hills and Cotton: An Upcountry Memory* (Columbia, S.C., 1942), 274.
[15] William Faulkner, "Shingles for the Lord," in *The Faulkner Reader: Selections from the Works of William Faulkner* (New York, 1954), 576–77.
[16] Mary Martha Thomas, *Riveting and Rationing in Dixie: Alabama Women and the Second World War* (Tuscaloosa, Ala., 1987), 121; Ethelyn Davis, "Careers as Concerns of Blue-Collar Girls," in *Blue-Collar World*, ed. Shostak and Gomberg, 154–64; Dolores E. Janiewski, *Sisterhood Denied: Race, Gender, and Class in a New South Community* (Philadelphia, 1985), 152–78.

The factory paid better than the farm, and many families raised their standard of living. Their expectations and their expenses also rose, and southern families often gained relatively little in the way of economic security. A huge pool of unemployed and underemployed workers awaited steady jobs. When an Ohio-based firm occupied a factory building the taxpayers in Kosciusko, Mississippi, had financed, it received five thousand applications for the four hundred jobs it announced. In Tennessee, a garment company moved into a publicly financed factory and employed three hundred white women only after the town of Dresden guaranteed a labor pool of a thousand from which the firm could draw. A corporation headquartered in St. Louis made its acceptance, at "nominal rent," of a factory built by Tupelo, Mississippi, contingent on the city's satisfying it that white males were available in abundance to man the production lines. The disproportion of five thousand workers to four hundred openings was newsworthy because it was unusual, but throughout the region workers often newly arrived from farms and hamlets discovered that the industrializing South was considerably more solicitous of the well-being of outside corporation executives than of native employees.[17]

The factory in Tennessee that employed only white women as production workers was not unusual, but more common was the hiring of white males for factory work and black males for janitoring, as at the firm in Tupelo. Much less frequent was the employment of white males, black males, and white females in roughly equal numbers, as at the plant in Kosciusko. Noticeably absent were black women, and it was by no means rare for those who made the decisions in southern towns to assume that black women properly occupied their time as domestics in white households. The white male supremacy policies that survived in southern politics and culture applied with equal force to commerce and industry. The ineffectiveness of the wartime fair employment practices commission and the abject failure of the federal and state governments to protect black access in the South to training benefits under the GI Bill prefigured postwar employment prac-

[17]B. M. Wofford and T. A. Kelly, *Mississippi Workers: Where They Come from and How They Perform* (University, Ala., 1955), 14–49; William H. Baker, "The Economics of a Small Southern Town" (Ph.D. dissertation, University of Alabama, 1963), 127–31.

tices. Blacks normally held only those factory jobs that were particularly strenuous and dirty. Historian Jacqueline Jones has written of black women that "their occupational structure remained intact during and after World War II." Much the same was true of black southerners generally.[18]

The magnitude of southern black poverty made the living standards of whites appear prosperous by comparison. Gunnar Myrdal reported that "the majority of the Negro population suffers from severe malnutrition. This is true at least about the South." A journalist affirmed that in the "most neglected regions of Central America" he had "never beheld anything to equal" the black district of a Louisiana town. Mississippian David L. Cohn described a black residential area in Greenville, where "long rows of crazy hovels perched uncertainly on cement blocks along creeks or drainage ditches" and where most dwellings were "without toilet facilities except for a multi-family privy, lacking screens, running water, or access to a fire plug." An intensive study in the late 1940s of a black community in a South Carolina piedmont town reported that nine out of ten homes lacked flush toilets and stood on unpaved streets and that eight out of nine were "badly in need of major repairs." Nine out of ten of the employed blacks in the community held positions as unskilled workers or laborers. In such a world black men had a "hard road to travel when looking for employment," Anne Moody reflected. "A Negro woman, however, could always go out and earn a dollar a day because whites always needed a cook, a baby-sitter, or someone to do housecleaning."[19]

A black bourgeoisie composed of undertakers, store owners, teachers, clergymen, and the like, virtually all serving a black cli-

[18] Wofford and Kelly, *Mississippi Workers*, 34–60; Baker, "The Economics of a Small Southern Town," 127–46; David H. Onkst, "Black World War Two Veterans and the GI Bill of Rights in Georgia, Alabama, and Mississippi, 1944–1947" (M.A. thesis, University of Georgia, 1990); Jacqueline Jones, *Labor of Love, Labor of Sorrow: Black Women, Work, and the Family from Slavery to the Present* (New York, 1985), 234.

[19] Gunnar Myrdal, *An American Dilemma: The Negro Problem and Modern Democracy* (New York, 1944), 375; Agnes E. Meyer, *Journey Through Chaos* (New York, 1943), 192; David L. Cohn, *Where I Was Born and Raised* (Boston, 1948), 239; Hylan Lewis, *Blackways of Kent* (Chapel Hill, N.C., 1955), 25–45, 230–35; Anne Moody, *Coming of Age in Mississippi* (New York, 1968), 112.

entele, existed in the towns of the South. Its numbers were so small, however, that the basic social division in black areas was often between the "respectable" and the "nonrespectable." Among all-black institutions, the churches and the taverns were the most prominent, and they symbolized the orientations of respectable and nonrespectable people. The relatively more affluent tended to be respectable—to put a premium on family stability, to participate in church activities, and to look down on those blacks who turned to alcohol, sexual promiscuity, and rowdyism for solace. A light skin color and "white" hair added to social status and respectability. Social divisions based on the observances of propriety were not unique to the black community, but such distinctions were of considerably greater practical relevance within black neighborhoods.[20]

Like mill villages, black residential areas were usually communities. "We didn't feel deprived," a black woman explained. "It was only when you left the community that it hit you." Many—doubtless most—southern towns were "good" towns. "When the blacks called Denmark a good Southern town," a young black man from South Carolina explained, "they meant that the police 'minded their own business,' that the Ku Klux Klan was not active, and that the local whites did not maliciously flaunt their power." The same observer, who had grown up in Denmark, added, "I know a great deal, almost everything, about black Denmark." The sharing and closeness within such communities helped to alleviate the trials of southern black life. As in the mill villages, however, the sense of community declined during the postwar years.[21]

Although black domestics sometimes took pride in the material well-being of "their" white families, the social distance between whites and blacks widened. Reminiscing about growing up in a town in southern Arkansas, Maya Angelou explained that white

[20] Lewis, *Blackways of Kent,* 225–35; John Dollard, *Caste and Class in a Southern Town;* Davis, Gardner, and Gardner, *Deep South;* Hortense Powdermaker, *After Freedom: A Cultural Study in the Deep South* (New York, 1939).

[21] Louise Washington quoted in *Sammy Younge, Jr.: The First Black College Student to Die in the Black Liberation Movement,* by James Forman (New York, 1968), 38; Cleveland Sellers, *The River of No Return: The Autobiography of a Black Militant and the Life and Death of SNCC* (New York, 1973), 16, 3; Molly Crocker Dougherty, *Becoming a Woman in Rural Black Culture* (New York, 1978).

people were "to be dreaded, and in that dread was included the hostility of the powerless against the powerful, the poor against the rich, the worker against the worked for and the ragged against the well dressed." Historian Elizabeth Rauh Bethel described the changed atmosphere in Promiseland, South Carolina, in the late 1940s: "Traditionally, superficially at least, guided by the reciprocal principles of paternalism and obsequiousness, . . . interracial interchanges now took on a new tension." The widespread impression was that "the younger generation of Negroes is sharply at odds with their elders." Anne Moody wrote, "I got a feeling that there existed some kind of sympathetic relationship between the older Negroes and whites that the younger people didn't quite get or understand." [22]

Disgruntled black youngsters left the rural and small-town South at an even greater rate than did their white counterparts, and their exodus probably involved more pain. The distance between the South they knew and the impersonality of the metropolitan ghetto was vast. The sorry state of segregated black schools, the unavailability of on-the-job training, and all the other hindrances that beset blacks left them at a disadvantage even if they found employers in southern or northern metropolitan areas who were prepared to consider their qualifications rather than their skin color. The sheer size of the black exodus assured social disorganization in the metropolitan ghettos and conflicts over turf and housing with abutting white working-class and ethnic neighborhoods. Nevertheless, the migrating blacks contributed to the transformation of a relatively static caste-based society into a depersonalized and dynamic one.

Southern towns of course varied enormously. Such larger towns as Decatur and Florence in Alabama and Kingsport, Bristol, and Maryville in Tennessee had access to low-cost power from the Tennessee Valley Authority and established diversified economies that included relatively high paying manufacturing. Oak Ridge, Tennessee, was a special case. During World War II, the federal government constructed the secret city as a research and production

[22] Maya Angelou, *I Know Why the Caged Bird Sings* (New York, 1969), 25; Elizabeth Rauh Bethel, *Promiseland: A Century of Life in a Negro Community* (Philadelphia, 1981), 229; Moody, *Coming of Age in Mississippi*, 109.

site for fissionable material needed for atomic bombs. Thereafter the Atomic Energy Commission assumed control, and Oak Ridge became a center for nuclear research and ultimately a part of the Knoxville metropolitan statistical area.

Huntsville, Alabama, which was a quiet town of cotton brokers and textile mills in 1940, became the home of the Redstone Arsenal during World War II. Built to manufacture poison gas and other ordnance, the arsenal went from nineteen thousand employees to two hundred when the war was over. At that point the army converted the arsenal into a missile facility, and in 1958 the National Aeronautics and Space Administration established the Marshall Space Flight Center in the city. The 1950 census counted a few more than sixteen thousand people living in Huntsville; by 1960 the population had risen to more than seventy-two thousand. Similar booms came to Brevard County, Florida, with the development of the John F. Kennedy Space Center, and Orlando, Florida, the home of Disney World.[23]

Between town and farm stretched a substantial rural nonfarm population. In 1940 more than 8.5 million people, 23 percent of the South's population, lived in nonurban areas but were not engaged in agriculture. By 1950 their number had increased to 12.5 million, or 30 percent of the population. During the fifties, their number, like that of the South's townspeople, remained—at least statistically—relatively stable. In 1960 rural nonfarmers came to just under 13.5 million, or 27 percent of the population. On the fringes of metropolitan areas, around the towns, along the growing number of paved roads, and in innumerable hamlets and hollows, the rural nonfarm population included the families of commuters, of workers in nonurban mill villages, of Appalachian coal miners, of employees of oil-drilling operations in Texas and the Southwest, and of the hands in lumber and naval-stores camps scattered across the region. Many rural nonfarm people had been displaced from agriculture and survived as laborers or seasonal workers or depended, in whole or in part, on the meager dole of

[23] Charles W. Johnson and Charles O. Jackson, *City Behind a Fence: Oak Ridge, Tennessee 1942–1946* (Knoxville, Tenn., 1981); Neal R. Peirce, *The Deep South States of America: People, Politics, and Power in the Seven Deep South States* (New York, 1974), 271–76; Charlton W. Tebeau, *A History of Florida* (Coral Gables, Fla., 1971).

southern welfare programs. For many, rural nonfarm subsistence was a stopover on the way from farm to metropolis.[24]

The most concentrated rural nonfarm population in the nation resided in the Appalachian highlands. If as Harper Lee commented, many southern towns were grubby, the Appalachian coal-mining camps were among the grubbiest of them all. A journalist referred to the "extreme squalor prevailing in most of the camps"; Harry M. Caudill described them as "a few solid, well-planned towns and . . . many scabrous camps that were hideous slums from the beginning." But no matter how repugnant middle-class observers found conditions, mining towns—like mill villages—normally had community cohesion. "I really liked it in the coal-mining camps," a miner's wife remembered. "It was just one big family. All the houses were sort of close together. Everybody knew each other." The coal-mining companies normally owned the towns, and living standards were more or less comparable to those in company-owned mill villages.[25]

The Appalachian coal industry was both different from and illustrative of broader southern economic trends. Nowhere else in the South did outsiders own such a preponderant proportion of the material resources. "The region and its people," Caudill wrote, "had been and were being exploited in a manner that might have reddened the cheeks of Attila the Hun." Absentee ownership and extractive industry made the southern upland coal-mining region stretching from Kentucky and Virginia into Alabama an exaggerated version of southern industrial development generally.[26]

During the early postwar years miners fared relatively well economically. Because the United Mine Workers had emerged vic-

[24]William H. Nicholls, "The South as a Developing Area," *Journal of Politics*, XXVI (1964), 22–40; John Maclachlan and Joe S. Floyd, Jr., *This Changing South* (Gainesville, Fla., 1956); George Thomas, *Poverty in the Nonmetropolitan South: A Causal Analysis* (Lexington, Ky., 1972).

[25]Selden Menefee, *Assignment, U.S.A.* (New York, 1943), 212; Harry M. Caudill, *Theirs Be the Power: The Moguls of Eastern Kentucky* (Urbana, Ill., 1983), 5; Crandall A. Shifflett, *Coal Towns: Life, Work, and Culture in Company Towns of Southern Appalachia, 1880–1960* (Knoxville, Tenn., 1991), 153.

[26]Caudill, *Theirs Be the Power*, 3; Harry M. Caudill, *Night Comes to the Cumberlands: A Biography of a Depressed Area* (Boston, 1963); John Gaventa, *Power and Powerlessness: Quiescence and Rebellion in an Appalachian Valley* (Urbana, Ill., 1980).

torious from earlier labor wars, mine workers were among the highest-paid blue-collar workers in the South. Working and living conditions were harsh, but the wages were good. The biracial unionism John L. Lewis and the UMW had forged did not eliminate racial discrimination, but it offered far more equitable employment conditions for blacks than they received virtually anywhere else in the region. To a black coal miner's daughter who had been reared in the rural South, the experience of living in a house painted "on all four sides" and appointed with wallpaper and running water "was like I had gone to heaven, you know." [27]

Coal mining flourished during the 1940s and into the 1950s, but the growing preference for petroleum as a source of energy helped bring the boom to an end. During the late 1940s, the mining corporations, following the example of the textile companies, began to sell their workers the houses in which they lived. The companies also invested heavily in mechanization. The continuous miner, introduced in the early 1950s, decimated the labor force by eliminating much of the arduous manual labor in the mines. Mechanized mining also made the work more dangerous and greatly increased the incidence of black lung disease by stirring up coal dust. The move away from shaft mining to strip mining accelerated the substitution of machinery for labor. In western Kentucky, the terrain allowed strip mining to take over even more rapidly than in Appalachia, and the results were similar. By the end of the 1950s, there were approximately half as many coal miners in both areas as at the beginning of the decade. The UMW had effectively collapsed, and erstwhile coal miners had joined the declining Appalachian small farmers in the exodus from the highlands. [28]

Petroleum workers, like coal miners, received relatively high pay. Yet in the oil country, "the sudden swirling influx of a heterogeneous crowd of aggressive rootless people, the feverish speculation, intense competition, and social disorder, left behind shallow-rooted, fragile communities, lacking in stability and cohesion." Nor did the discovery of oil necessarily produce general

[27] Shifflett, *Coal Towns*, 147; Ronald L. Lewis, *Black Coal Miners in America: Race, Class, and Community Conflict, 1780–1980* (Lexington, Ky., 1987).

[28] Shifflett, *Coal Towns*, 199–212; Lewis, *Black Coal Miners in America*, 168–93.

prosperity. In Texas, the oil-producing counties were not significantly more prosperous than others. Refining, and the manufacturing that went with petrochemicals, generated wealth in metropolitan areas, but the economic benefits to people near where the oil was extracted appear to have been slight.[29]

During World War II timber camps flourished over wide areas of the South. Intended to be temporary, the timber and naval-stores encampments were the most sordid of all company towns. As historian C. Calvin Smith has noted, during the war the timber industry in Arkansas became the largest employer in the state and also the "most feudal in the nation." Employment in timber, like that in coal mining, declined rapidly during the 1950s.[30]

In mill villages, women worked beside the men. In mining camps and petroleum boomtowns, women were normally full-time wives and mothers and the keepers of community culture. A coal miner's wife reminisced, "We helped each other. And played with each other. And cried with each other." Oil settlements—often nothing more than house trailers—were more transient, but as one worker's wife explained, "Oil-field people are friendly, clannish. They stick together, and they help their own." Because work crews often remained intact from one job to the next, women created what a scholar has termed a "sisterhood of the oil fields." The segregation of most leisure activity by gender presumably encouraged both sisterhood and brotherhood. As Crandall A. Shifflett observed in his study of mining towns, males "engaged in certain forms of activity," like drinking and athletics, "females in others," like church socials and quilting bees.[31]

The decimation of the farm population during the postwar years disrupted both town and country life. As a black Georgia farmer observed, "Things in Abbeville and Wilcox County kept shrinkin' down. People you seen on the street today would be

[29] D. W. Meinig, *Imperial Texas: An Interpretive Essay in Cultural Geography* (Austin, Tex., 1969), 80; Francis Benton Burdine, "Regional Economic Effects of Petroleum Industry Development in Texas, 1900–1970" (Ph.D. dissertation, University of Texas, 1976).

[30] C. Calvin Smith, *War and Wartime Changes: The Transformation of Arkansas, 1940–1945* (Fayetteville, Ark., 1986), 116.

[31] Shifflett, *Coal Towns*, 152, 175; Anna C. Walsh, "They's Just Like Sisters to Me: Informal Support Networks in the Oil Patch," in *Women in the South: An Anthropological Perspective*, ed. Holly F. Mathews (Athens, Ga., 1989), 92, 94.

gone tomorrow." Indeed, the observer himself soon boarded a bus bound for the city. "I had a job waiting for me in Atlanta and four one-dollar bills. I thought if I had to, I could walk back." Agriculture may have lain at the base of William Polk's Old South, but what impressed Polk most was the expansion of New South cities and factories. The massive depopulation of southern farms attracted relatively little attention during the postwar period; the remarkable feature was "how quietly rural people melted away." In 1940 the southern farm population numbered almost sixteen million, or 42 percent of the general southern population. During the tumultuous war years the farm population dropped by more than four million. Returning servicemen and workers released by war industries created a short-lived movement back to the farm. The farm boom was a temporary phenomenon, however, and the migration off the land promptly resumed. By 1950 only eleven million people lived on farms, and by 1960 farm residents came to but seven million, 15 percent of the region's people.[32]

The changes "in the mode of production, in social organiza-tion, and in the nature of rural life," historian Pete Daniel has written, "proved the most revolutionary in southern history." His-torian Gilbert C. Fite has described the "years from about 1935 to 1945" as the "crucial turning point in the history of southern farming." The "revolution" in southern agriculture reached cul-mination during the forties and fifties. The South, historian Jack Temple Kirby has concluded, "was modern and developed by about 1960."[33]

The disruption of rural folk cultures was one of the prices paid for modernization. "What one could mourn was the passing of the underpinnings of the old culture—the families that were bro-ken and dispersed to the cities, the communities that wilted, the small rural churches that had bonded such communities, and the neighborliness that allowed such deprived people to endure even

[32] Maguire, comp., *On Shares*, 220, 224; Pete Daniel, *Breaking the Land: The Transformation of Cotton, Tobacco, and Rice Cultures Since 1880* (Urbana, Ill., 1985), xv; Hoover and Ratch-ford, *Economic Resources and Policies of the South*, 89–92; James H. Street, *The New Revolution in the Cotton Economy: Mechanization and Its Consequences* (Chapel Hill, N.C., 1957).

[33] Daniel, *Breaking the Land*, 239; Gilbert C. Fite, *Cotton Fields No More: Southern Agriculture, 1865–1980* (Lexington, Ky., 1984), 173–74; Jack Temple Kirby, *Rural Worlds Lost: The American South, 1920–1960* (Baton Rouge, 1987), 117.

the vicissitudes of sharecropping." The traditional southern rural virtues that revolved around family, clan, church, and community, as well as the familiar sense of roots and place, yielded to the juggernaut of progress. Ben Robertson, who grew up on a large South Carolina farm and like many other southerners left the region to seek his fortune elsewhere, could in 1942 still find reassurance in the knowledge that "someone is always keeping the home place": "It is a great comfort to a rambling people to know that somewhere there is a permanent home—perhaps it is the most final of the comforts they ever really know." But even when Robertson wrote, the days of the homeplace were numbered.[34]

Southerners left the land for a variety of reasons. Many did not do so voluntarily. The bleak choice confronting farm residents was, as Arthur M. Ford has phrased it, to "stay and starve or migrate and hope to do better." Most preferred not to starve. Some—particularly young people—welcomed the opportunity to search for economic advancement and a more fulfilling life. Their attitude might well have been the one Anne Moody expressed: "I knew if I got involved in farming, I'd be just like Momma and the rest of them." As Moody saw it, that would have meant having no chance to travel or to be somebody.[35]

During the 1950s some 5.5 million farm people left the land and almost 1.5 million whites and nearly 2 million blacks migrated out of the region. Well over 10 million southerners by birth—the equivalent of more than 20 percent of the South's population—lived outside the region in 1960. The people from the farms bound for Houston or Nashville, Chicago or Newark, tended most of all to be young. During the 1940s an estimated 75 percent of farm youngsters reaching maturity left agriculture, and the trend continued during the years that followed. Typically, migrants were

[34] Pete Daniel, *Standing at the Crossroads: Southern Life Since 1900* (New York, 1986), 123; Robertson, *Red Hills and Cotton*, 20; Pete Daniel, "Transformation of the Rural South, 1930 to the Present," *Agricultural History*, LV (1981), 231–48; Jack Temple Kirby, "The Transformation of Southern Plantations, c. 1920–1960," *Agricultural History*, LVII (1983), 257–76.

[35] Arthur M. Ford, *Political Economics of Rural Poverty in the South* (Cambridge, Mass., 1973), 34; Moody, *Coming of Age in Mississippi*, 89.

more skilled and better educated than their neighborhood peers, and they were more apt to be male than female.[36]

African Americans were in the vanguard of the flight from the land. The economic conditions of black farmers were disastrous even before agricultural modernization inordinately disrupted their lives. African Americans were much more likely to be tenants; seven out of ten white farmers were landowners in 1950, but only three in ten black farmers owned the land they worked. Blacks who were owners customarily held small acreages of relatively poor ground. The burden of poverty, along with institutionalized racism, persuaded many blacks to abandon the South entirely. African Americans, whose labor had once been crucial to southern agriculture, gradually lost their place in farming.[37]

The conclusions drawn from a study of a western Tennessee agricultural county applied to much of the rural South. William H. Baker found that during the 1950s a total of 432 whites and 33 blacks graduated from the segregated high schools in the county. Of those, 149 whites (56 males and 93 females) and 7 blacks (1 male and 6 females) remained in the county, though some of them were not planning to stay. Almost two-thirds of the white graduates and more than three quarters of the black had already left the county. A majority of the departing whites and all the departing blacks had moved outside Tennessee. Yet a majority of those who lived outside the county and who could be located said that they would return if it were economically feasible.[38]

Federal farm programs established during the 1930s hastened the shift from plantation agriculture to large-scale capital-intensive farming. The Department of Agriculture and its allies in Congress championed what Kirby has referred to as the "federal road to rural development," which emphasized "economics of scale,

[36] James M. Henderson, "Some General Aspects of Recent Regional Development," in *Essays in Southern Economic Development*, ed. Melvin L. Greenhut and W. Tate Whitman (Chapel Hill, N.C., 1964), 176; C. Horace Hamilton, "Continuity and Change in Southern Migration," in *The South in Continuity and Change*, ed. John C. McKinney and Edgar T. Thompson (Durham, N.C., 1965), 57; Homer L. Hitt, "Peopling the City: Migration," in *The Urban South*, ed. Vance and Demerath, 54–77; Neil David Fligstein, *Going North: Migration of Blacks and Whites from the South, 1900–1950* (New York, 1981).

[37] Kirby, *Rural Worlds Lost*, 237; Fite, *Cotton Fields No More*, 208–209.

[38] Baker, "The Economics of a Small Southern Town," 263–308.

industrial organization, and generous governmental assistance."
In the federal endeavor to regulate the production of staple crops
and to stabilize commodity prices, sharecroppers and marginal
farmers were obstacles to be cleared away. In 1945 Congress eliminated the Farm Security Administration, the last surviving agency
concerned with the interests of landless farmers, and thereafter
the drive to replace labor with capital and scientific efficiency continued without interruption. Federal farm programs encouraged
planters to replace sharecroppers with hired laborers and then
through subsidies provided the capital for mechanization, eliminating the need for much of the labor.[39]

The mechanization of southern agriculture not only doomed
the region's tenant population but also drastically changed the
geography of cotton planting. Innovations like mechanical cotton
pickers and chemical weed killers made cotton farming more labor efficient. Around 1950 when mechanical pickers first appeared in significant numbers, some forty-one thousand tenants
lived in seventeen Mississippi River lowland counties in Arkansas.
In 1959 the counties contained 3,254 cotton harvesters and fourteen thousand tenants. Yet within the old cotton belt, mechanical
pickers came into general use only in the Mississippi Delta area
of Mississippi, Arkansas, and Louisiana. Elsewhere mechanical ad-
vancements led to a curtailment of cotton growing rather than
making it more efficient. Tractors encouraged agricultural diversification and stimulated the propagation of soybeans, grains, pea-
nuts, and livestock. By 1960 the long-cherished vision of a diversified agricultural economy had by and large become a reality.[40]

[39] Kirby, *Rural Worlds Lost*, 15; Ford, *Political Economics of Rural Poverty*, 35–37; Grant
McConnell, *The Decline of Agrarian Democracy* (Berkeley and Los Angeles, 1953); Christiana
McFadyen Campbell, *The Farm Bureau and the New Deal: A Study of the Making of National
Farm Policy, 1933–1940* (Urbana, Ill., 1962); Anna Rochester, *Why Farmers Are Poor: The
Agricultural Crisis in the United States* (New York, 1940).

[40] Harry C. Dillingham and David F. Sly, "The Mechanical Cotton-Picker, Negro Migration, and the Integration Movement," *Human Organization*, XXV (1966), 344–51; Richard
H. Day, "The Economics of Technological Change and the Demise of the Sharecroppers,"
American Economic Review, LVII (1967), 427–49; Charles R. Sayre, "Cotton Mechanization
Since World War II," *Agricultural History*, LIII (1979), 105–24; Gilbert C. Fite, "Mechanization of Cotton Production Since World War II," *Agricultural History*, LIV (1980), 190–
207.

Cotton, along with federal cotton allotments, increasingly moved west. In 1949 Texas, Oklahoma, New Mexico, Arizona, and California grew more than half of America's cotton. The new cotton belt that pushed from western Texas into central California was highly capitalized, relying on machines to produce crops on irrigated land. Unlike the croppers and hands on southern plantations, labor for western agriculture was mainly itinerant. Cotton cultivation in the West and abroad increasingly dwarfed the southern production that had once dominated the world market. Filament yarn, especially rayon, had become less expensive than cotton and by 1950 was replacing cotton in important markets, including the manufacture of automobile tires. Outside the Mississippi Delta cotton went the way of tenant farmers and mules. In 1959 cotton was the principal crop in only eleven counties in the old cotton belt.[41]

The sugar plantations, concentrated in southern Louisiana, were similar in their labor practices to cotton plantations. The planters broke a general strike by Louisiana cane workers in 1953 by evicting the strikers' families from company housing, prohibiting trade at company stores, deputizing plantation foremen, bringing in strikebreakers, and calling on the state courts for assistance. The disgruntled workers were only one of the problems besetting the labor-intensive sugar plantations, and the center of sugarcane production ultimately shifted to better-capitalized farms in Florida.[42]

Rice growing was the most highly mechanized sector of southern agriculture. The rice growers who cultivated large acreages in southern Louisiana and southern Texas and in the Mississippi River lowlands of Arkansas and Mississippi relied upon machines rather than plantation laborers. Like sugar planters, they often suffered from the inconsistencies in federal policy. Typically, "as the government reduced [rice] allotments to keep down produc-

[41] Hoover and Ratchford, *Economic Resources and Policies of the South*, 314–15; Street, *The New Revolution in the Cotton Economy*, 49–80; Kirby, *Rural Worlds Lost*, 73.

[42] J. Carlyle Sitterson, *Sugar Country: The Cane Sugar Industry in the South, 1753–1950* (Lexington, Ky., 1953), 379–95; J. R. Dempsey, *The Operation of the Right-to-Work Laws* (Milwaukee, 1961), 16–20.

tion, it promoted research to produce higher yields per acre," Daniel has written. "Boom and bust in the rice culture" became a "cycle," and rice planters operated "almost like poker players."[43]

The traditional paternalistic obligations of planters to their tenants and hands had limited observable effect on their rush to modernize. W. J. Cash had earlier observed that "the feeling which had lain at the heart of the old notion of paternalistic duty was fast dwindling, leaving only the shell—at the same time that the notion of paternalistic privilege was remaining as strongly entrenched as ever, and even perhaps being expanded." A plantation supervisor in Alabama remarked, "Them mechanical cotton pickers out west won't come around here for a long time. We got all the labor we need—it's cheaper for us and the cotton's lots cleaner. Besides, we're raising more cattle every year, and when cotton out west gets too tough for us to match we'll just stay with the cattle. Don't know what'll happen to all the niggers then. Guess they'll have to go north." Such callous attitudes seem close to the norm, even if planters and their county-seat and mill-owner peers frequently boasted of their solicitude.[44] Tenant farming declined rapidly. In absolute numbers tenancy reached its peak in the mid-1930s, when a substantial majority of all southern farmers were tenants. By 1945 almost six in ten southern farmers were owners, and by 1950 almost two-thirds were. By the end of the 1950s the Bureau of the Census had stopped counting the dwindling sharecropper population as a separate group. To the degree that farm labor was still needed, year-round and seasonal hired workers took the place of tenants. In the early 1960s a civil rights worker in southern Georgia could watch the "truckloads of cotton pickers . . . passing on the road that curls clumsily through the hamlet of Sasser, past Mt. Olive, . . . past the slouching cotton gin, past the faded town."[45]

Well before its demise, southern tenant farming had fallen into disrepute. The nation's discovery of southern sharecroppers dur-

[43] Daniel, *Breaking the Land,* 287–88.

[44] W. J. Cash, *The Mind of the South* (New York, 1941), 276; Morton Rubin, *Plantation County* (Chapel Hill, N.C., 1951), 20.

[45] Hoover and Ratchford, *Economic Resources and Policies of the South,* 107; Kirby, *Rural Worlds Lost,* 67–75; Jack Chatfield to Wiley Branton, December 11, 1962, in Voter Education Project Files, Box 6, Atlanta University Center.

ing the 1930s had occasioned a spate of frequently sympathetic but usually unflattering, and sometimes stereotyped, depictions of tenant life. In fact, various levels of tenancy existed, and some tenants lived comfortably. On the whole, though, poverty, dietary inadequacy, and unmet medical and dental needs were the givens of day-to-day life. Too often tenants worked small plots of land with implements that "would not seem strange to Moses and Hammurabi." In the late 1940s the bulk of black tenant families in the southeastern states lived in unpainted houses that lacked indoor plumbing and window screens. Nine out of ten had only single-year oral contracts with landowners.[46]

Insecurity and discouragement were inevitable. A black tenant farmer in one of Alice Walker's novels moved his family "about from shack to shack, where ever he could get work. When cotton declined in Georgia and dairying rose, he tried dairying. They lived somehow." For both black and white landless farmers, social mobility was limited; tenants seemed "to be born into tenancy, to marry into tenancy, and to die in tenancy." A former white sharecropper recalled, "We were not ignorant, but time and circumstances had not worked in our favor for real progress. We were just plodding along, hoping but not really expecting very much from life."[47]

Federal acreage allotments were a particular hardship for small-scale cotton farmers. The allotment formula favored the larger operators, and after the Korean War small farmers felt acutely the reimplementation of stringent acreage controls that had been relaxed during the conflict. The allotments to small cotton farmers were often minuscule. Four out of five allotments in North Carolina were for six acres or less, and because farmers with such circumscribed plantings were unlikely to possess tractors, their disadvantage relative to their neighbors with large farms became insuperable. A Georgian complained: "Thousands of farmers

[46] J. Wayne Flynt, *Dixie's Forgotten People: The South's Poor Whites* (Bloomington, Ind., 1979), 74–78; Arthur F. Raper and Ira De A. Reid, *Sharecroppers All* (Chapel Hill, N.C., 1941), 21; Ralph A. Felton, *These My Brethren: A Study of 570 Negro Churches and 1542 Negro Homes in the Rural South* (Madison, N.J., 1950).

[47] Alice Walker, *The Third Life of Grange Copeland* (New York, 1970), 55; Robertson, *Red Hills and Cotton*, 288; Roy G. Taylor, *Sharecroppers: The Way We Really Were* (Winston, N.C., 1984), 225; Maguire, comp., *On Shares*.

have had to leave their farms and seek other work because under the present law they can not have enough acreage to make a living."[48]

Tobacco farmers, most numerous in the Upper South and particularly in Kentucky, North Carolina, and Virginia, fared somewhat better. The Tobacco Section of the Agricultural Adjustment Administration was protective of small landowners and even of tenants. The many small tobacco allotments and the fact that tobacco was the most labor intensive of all southern crops hampered large-scale enterprise and thereby retarded mechanization. Tobacco growers, as Pete Daniel has concluded, "survived and prospered under federal control." When mechanization finally came in the sixties, the concurrent industrial expansion permitted farmers to move gradually to other employment, often without physical dislocation.[49]

The already diversified dairy-, livestock-, and grain-producing areas in Tennessee, Virginia, and Kentucky and the fruit-growing and truck-gardening region in Florida presented the most favorable conditions in the South for the survival of family farms. Tenant farming was rare in much of central Florida, through the Shenandoah Valley in Virginia, in the middle third of Tennessee and in parts of the eastern third of the state, and in scattered areas of Kentucky. Sizable family farms served urban markets and more closely resembled the farms elsewhere in the nation than they did the southern model of agriculture. The diversified family farmers lived in a world of cash, commerce, and checking accounts and were better positioned than most rural southerners to weather the upheavals that swept over the region.[50]

The South's most impoverished white landowners resided in the Appalachian highlands and in the smaller Ozark and Ouachita mountain areas of Arkansas and Oklahoma. During the early postwar years, highland farm families continued practicing a form of agricultural self-sufficiency, with the income they earned coming from small plots of tobacco and sometimes from the manufacture and transportation of illegal whiskey. Hunting was for food, not

[48] Fite, *Cotton Fields No More*, 180–209, p. 194 quoted.
[49] Daniel, *Breaking the Land*, 110.
[50] Kirby, *Rural Worlds Lost*, 40–45, 153–54.

for sport. Men often augmented family incomes by hiring out, especially during the winter months, to do "public work" within the area or in the northern industrial cities. During the 1940s and 1950s highland counties gradually became less isolated as paved roads, automobiles, and modern marketing practices penetrated into the mountains. By the early 1960s, mountain families had largely "abandoned their gardens, hen houses, and pigpens" to "live out of bags" from the chain grocery stores, as Kirby has put it. With the decline of coal mining, lumbering, and agriculture, many people moved away. Much of the land reverted to forest, and those who remained "lived by cash, the pickup truck, and the Piggly Wiggly."[51]

Even after mechanization, crop diversification, and land consolidation were well under way, southern farms remained smaller and less prosperous than those elsewhere in the nation. A decade after World War II, only some 18,000 southern farm operators produced a crop with a value in excess of $25,000, whereas almost 650,000 produced a crop that sold for less than $2,500. The statistics during the postwar era understated rural poverty, since the small farmers, rural laborers, and rural families who had given up trying to make their farms yield a livelihood were impoverished and often underemployed but did not appear on unemployment or welfare lists. As the rural population turned to industry and business for employment, it in practical effect if not statistically became a part of nearby towns and cities. Some living in the country managed to commute to wage-paying jobs while continuing modest farming operations, especially in raising poultry. Those who continued living outside the towns benefited from the federally sponsored rural electrification and rural telephone programs that spread during the early postwar years. To an appreciable degree, however, the convulsion in southern agriculture moved the region's rural poverty into the cities.[52]

[51] *Ibid.*, 115, 122; Marion Pearsall, *Little Smoky Ridge: The Natural History of a Southern Appalachian Neighborhood* (University, Ala., 1959); Thomas R. Ford, ed., *The Southern Appalachian Region: A Survey* (Lexington, Ky., 1962).

[52] *Selected Materials on the Economy of the South,* 14–19; Deward Clayton Brown, "Rural Electrification in the South, 1920–1955" (Ph.D. dissertation, University of California at Los Angeles, 1970).

Postwar metropolitan prosperity offered economic opportunities, and many expatriate farmers took advantage of them. A white North Carolinian who was economically successful after migrating from the land mused, "Many of us were able to have modern homes of our own with all the conveniences. . . . Somehow, it failed to bring that happiness, that feeling of security we had hoped for." Despite the prosperity, he judged that people were "more selfish today, busier, more unsure of ourselves or our world." A clergyman in a working-class district of Atlanta reminisced in a Sunday sermon, "A long time ago you could hear the horses biting corn out of the trough, and see the firelight in the stove in the kitchen. . . . And smell the cornbread cooking. Many things happened on the farm, you know. . . . My it's so beautiful out there." A successful black woman who grew up in a sharecropper family explained that she was nostalgic not "for lost poverty" but "for the solidarity and sharing a modest existence can sometimes bring." [53]

The demographic upheavals that accompanied the passing of the mill villages and mining camps and the depopulation of the farms cast huge numbers of southerners adrift. Folk cultures declined as uprooted people endeavored to adjust to a market society wherein labor was a free-flowing commodity and social fragmentation replaced community. Storytelling fell by the wayside; even conversation as "passing the time of day" ceded ground to television and other entertainment that did not presuppose a sense of community. Young men who had once driven white lightning down "thunder road" from Appalachian stills to city markets turned to stock car racing as spectator sports became more important. Women had to find their way with withering support from community and kin.

Southern folk music captured the transformation of southern society. Since the early twentieth century, blues had communicated the alienation and dissatisfaction and the anguish and heart-

<hr />

[53] Taylor, *Sharecroppers*, 235; Harry Groff Lefever, "Ghetto Religion: A Study of the Religious Structures and Styles of a Poor White Community in Atlanta, Georgia" (Ph.D. dissertation, Emory University, 1971), 55; Alice Walker, "The Black Writer and the Southern Experience," *New South*, Fall, 1970, p. 24; Floyd C. Watkins and Charles Hubert Watkins, *Yesterday in the Hills* (Athens, Ga., 1963).

ache of southern African Americans, as well as a hedonistic, rambling, and individualistic outlook. To many blues musicians, "Rock is my pillow and cold ground is my bed. The highway is my home, Lord I might as well be dead." Although blues music was much more sexually explicit than contemporaneous white music, its vocalists sang of predicaments that were hardly exclusive to blacks—as when bluesmen asked, "Have you ever loved somebody that don't love you?" During the urbanization of African Americans after World War II, blues became "rhythm and blues," an amplified music with greater commercial potential.[54]

The white counterpart to blues was the honky-tonk country sound. Growing from western swing and influenced by the blues, honky-tonk music, which became the predominant white folk music during the decade after the war, expressed the alienation, loneliness, and dislocation of an uprooted people in an urban and industrial world. "Never before," Bill C. Malone has written, "has a form of music so effectively mirrored the concerns of the southern working class." It was beer-drinking music that emerged from the oil fields of Louisiana, Oklahoma, and Texas and reverberated through the southern taverns where "honky-tonk angels" and men "born to lose" went for solace and where more than one drinker might have described himself as "so lonesome I could cry." Both blues and country honky-tonk caught the ambivalence of ordinary southerners of the period, in that both manifested a fascination with "moving on" at the same time that they showed a desire for permanence and place.[55]

Rhythm and blues and country fused in rock 'n' roll in the midfifties. Until then, segregated clubs and bars, and record companies that marketed black music to black audiences, had kept the two forms essentially distinct. By the midfifties, both were becoming more commercialized, and young people had become the target consumer group for recordings. Rock 'n' roll completed the transformation of southern music into a commodity to be

[54] William Ferris, *Blues from the Delta* (Garden City, N.Y., 1979), 29, 73; Lawrence W. Levine, *Black Culture and Black Consciousness: Afro-American Folk Thought from Slavery to Freedom* (New York, 1977), 217–39.

[55] Bill C. Malone, "Honky-Tonk Music," in *Encyclopedia of Southern Culture*, ed. Charles Reagan Wilson and William Ferris (Chapel Hill, N.C., 1989), 1015.

marketed nationally by record shops and television and radio stations. Most successful rock 'n' roll musicians were southerners, and of them Elvis A. Presley was the one who was pivotal. "Never before," James C. Cobb has written, "had the musical culture of blacks and lower-class whites been so closely conjoined as they were in the early stylings of Presley." Presley's audience was young and national, and his influence was to make southern music more packaged, more homogenized, and less southern.[56]

Fed by the influx of rural and town southerners, metropolitan areas boomed during the postwar years. In 1940 some eight million southerners—little more than two in ten people—lived in metropolitan districts. At an accelerating pace during the next two decades, the cities virtually exploded. By 1960 approximately twenty-one million people—43.5 percent of the region's people—resided in metropolitan areas. Texas and Florida, the most rapidly urbanizing of the southern states, had populations that were approximately two-thirds metropolitan in 1960. Three southern urban conglomerations—Houston, Dallas, and Atlanta—counted more than a million people each, and each of a dozen metropolitan areas numbered more than a half million souls.[57]

In 1940 New Orleans and Houston were the only metropolitan districts to contain as many as 500,000 people. Although a dozen southern metropolises exceeded 200,000 in 1940, most regional cities more closely resembled towns than great urban centers. Neighborhoods within the cities often delineated day-to-day life. The neighborhoods differed mainly in diversity and complexity

[56] James C. Cobb, *The Most Southern Place on Earth: The Mississippi Delta and the Roots of Regional Identity* (New York, 1992), 300; Bill C. Malone, *Southern Music, American Music* (Lexington, Ky., 1979).

[57] Significant studies of southern urbanization include David R. Goldfield's *Cotton Fields and Skyscrapers: Southern City and Region, 1607–1980* (Baton Rouge, 1982); *The Rise of the Sunbelt Cities,* ed. David C. Perry and Alfred J. Watkins (Beverly Hills, Calif., 1977); Carl Abbott's *The New Urban America: Growth and Politics in Sunbelt Cities* (Rev. ed.; Chapel Hill, N.C., 1987); *Sunbelt Cities: Politics and Growth Since World War II,* ed. Richard M. Bernard and Bradley R. Rice (Austin, Tex., 1983); *Searching for the Sunbelt: Historical Perspectives on a Region,* ed. Raymond A. Mohl (Knoxville, Tenn., 1990); Raymond A. Mohl *et al.'s Essays on Sunbelt Cities and Recent Urban America* (College Station, Tex., 1990); Bernard L. Weinstein and Robert E. Firestine's *Regional Growth and Decline in the United States: The Rise of the Sunbelt and the Decline of the Northeast* (New York, 1978); and Bruce J. Schulman's *From Cotton Belt to Sunbelt: Federal Policy, Economic Development, and the Transformation of the South, 1938–1980* (New York, 1991).

from town communities. "As late as the 1940s," urbanist Christopher Silver has explained in his study of Virginia's state capital, "Richmond still claimed nearly a score of distinct and discernible inner-city residential 'communities' differentiated by features like architecture, ethnicity, class, economic function, race, spatial location, and tradition." Government, especially in the smaller cities, was frequently of a caretaker type that maintained traditional services, limited expenditures and new programs, and dealt with neighborhood problems by personal response and sometimes through patronage and favors. Political machines such as the Old Regulars in New Orleans, the Crump machine in Memphis, the Cracker Party in Augusta, Georgia, and the ethnic-based organizations in San Antonio and Tampa were among the better-known practitioners of caretaker government, but it existed in many other southern cities. As Don H. Doyle has written about Nashville, the dominant political organization was "based in the neighborhoods where common people . . . looked to it for benefits in exchange for their votes." [58]

The upheavals of World War II, the GI revolts, and the expansion of metropolitan economies touched off a wave of urban reform. In reaction to the perceived inefficiency and corruption of the caretaker regimes, prospering uptown business groups, rising middle-class business and professional people, and upwardly mobile GIs rallied beneath the banner of progress. Chambers of commerce, good government leagues, and independent citizens associations launched political crusades throughout the region. The campaigns sought to throw the entrenched rascals out and to replace them with governments committed to efficient, rationalized procedures, centralized planning, and a symbiotic relationship between private enterprise and public policy.

Most of all, the demand was for governments that sponsored and promoted rapid economic development. As urbanist Carl Ab-

[58] Christopher Silver, *Twentieth-Century Richmond: Planning, Politics, and Race* (Knoxville, Tenn., 1984), 98–99; Oliver P. Williams and Charles R. Adrian, *Four Cities: A Study in Comparative Policy Making* (Philadelphia, 1963), 11–47; Don H. Doyle, *Nashville Since the 1920s* (Knoxville, Tenn., 1985), 64; Douglas L. Smith, *The New Deal in the Urban South* (Baton Rouge, 1988); Philip J. Funigiello, *The Challenge to Urban Liberalism: Federal-City Relations During World War II* (Knoxville, Tenn., 1978); David M. Tucker, *Memphis Since Crump: Bossism, Blacks, and Civic Reformers, 1948–1968* (Knoxville, Tenn., 1980).

bott has pointed out, the two decades after World War II were a "golden age for the planners, housing experts, public health specialists, and redevelopment officials." The newly constituted governments worked to strengthen the authority of planning commissions and professional city managers, to replace ward-based city council elections with citywide contests, to annex the taxable properties and middle-class electorates of neighboring suburbs, and to construct the expressways for funneling customers and employees in and out of the central business districts.[59]

Neither urban economic boosterism nor the quest for more efficient public services was new. Much of postwar urban reform was "in the old-fashioned good-government tradition organized to get policies back on track." The extent of government change and the emphasis in public policy varied from city to city, but like the innovations of an earlier progressive movement, the new reforms augmented the power of business elites at the expense of less prominent residents. A study of San Antonio has reported that the electoral success of the Good Government League "signaled an end to lower-class ethnic influence in local politics." Uptown business interests had the strongest hand in framing the good-government agenda, and a central impulse of postwar reform was "its tendency to cater unquestioningly to the predispositions of the local elite." Historian Richard M. Bernard has concluded in his study of Oklahoma City, "It was, in fact, the Chamber of Commerce, backed by elected officials, that would control the city's, and indeed the region's, postwar maturity."[60]

Among southern cities, the two great regional metropolises were Atlanta and Dallas. Rupert B. Vance and Sara Smith, in their pathbreaking study "Metropolitan Dominance and Integration," ranked southern cities according to wholesale and retail sales, business-services income, bank clearings, number of corporate branch offices, and value added by manufacturing. On these criteria, Atlanta and Dallas were significantly ahead of other south-

[59] Abbott, *The New Urban America*, 247.

[60] Richard M. Bernard and Bradley R. Rice, "Introduction," in *Sunbelt Cities*, ed. Bernard and Rice, 21; David R. Johnson, "San Antonio: The Vicissitudes of Boosterism," *ibid.*, 239; Silver, *Twentieth-Century Richmond*, 9; Richard M. Bernard, "Oklahoma City: Booming Sooner," in *Sunbelt Cities*, 213.

ern metropolises. The two cities had much earlier established their positions as the commercial centers of the Southeast and Southwest, and they strengthened those positions after the war. Both were regional headquarters of the Federal Reserve Bank, and both were transportation centers, first as railroad hubs and later as junctions for expressways and transfer points for air travel. In the South, it was said, "Whether you're going to heaven or hell, you'll have to change planes in Atlanta." As centers of commerce, transportation, distribution, finance, insurance, and services, Atlanta and Dallas had much in common.[61]

The two cities also had their differences. Located strategically in relation to Texas oil fields, Dallas performed administrative, financial, and service functions for the petroleum industry, an activity that declined as Houston gradually usurped the role. More than most southern metropolises, Dallas was a manufacturing center, specializing in light industry and the production of aircraft, oil machinery, and apparel, the last of which gave the city a position in fashion circles. By the early 1950s about a third of the labor force in the Dallas metropolitan area was in manufacturing. Although metropolitan Atlanta also had light industry and aircraft and automobile assembly plants, manufacturing was less important to the economy, employing in 1950 fewer than two in ten workers.[62]

Both Dallas and Atlanta exemplified "power elite" politics. Organized in 1937, the Dallas Citizens Council dominated decision making and provided the city with what one scholar termed an "elitist, business-oriented leadership." The Citizens Council limited its membership to corporation chief-executive officers. The critic who described the council as a "collection of dollars represented by men" was not far wide of the mark. More is known about the Atlanta political establishment. Floyd Hunter made the Atlanta "power structure" the subject of a classic "study of decision

[61] Rupert B. Vance and Sara Smith, "Metropolitan Dominance and Integration," in *The Urban South,* ed. Vance and Demerath, 114–35.

[62] Otis Dudley Duncan *et al., Metropolis and Region* (Baltimore, 1960), 368–75; Truman A. Hartshorn, *Metropolis in Georgia: Atlanta's Rise as a Major Transaction Center* (Cambridge, Mass., 1976); Bradley R. Rice, "If Dixie Were Atlanta," in *Sunbelt Cities,* ed. Bernard and Rice, 31–57; Martin V. Melosi, "Dallas–Fort Worth: Marketing the Metroplex," in *Sunbelt Cities,* 162–95.

makers," and Ivan Allen, Jr., a member of the establishment, president of the chamber of commerce, and eventually the mayor of the city, was remarkably candid in his memoirs.[63]

According to Hunter, forty people—thirty-nine men and one woman—were Atlanta's decision makers. The power elite included eleven executives of major companies, seven directors of banking or investment firms, five executives of manufacturing concerns, and five corporation lawyers. The list included two labor leaders, one dentist, and five social and civic leaders, four of them men and one a woman. Because establishment decision making frequently involved public policy, it was reassuring that Hunter's power structure encompassed four people in government positions. A large majority of the forty inherited wealth and position; only fifteen were self-made men.[64]

"We were," Mayor Allen wrote, "the presidents of the five major banks, the heads of the Atlanta-headquartered industries like Coca-Cola, the presidents of the three big utilities, the heads of the three or four top retail establishments, the managers of the leading national-firm branches for the Southeast, the man in charge of the city transit system, the heads of the larger local businesses such as the Ivan Allen Company and the Haverty Furniture Company, and the leading realtors. When you talked about the 'power structure' or the 'establishment' in Atlanta, you were really talking about the leaders of the top fifty or so businesses in the city." Allen's list did not include elected officials, labor leaders, a dentist, or a lady and gentlemen of leisure, but otherwise it was generally compatible with Hunter's findings. Allen explained what Atlanta's leadership had in common: "We were white, Anglo-Saxon, Protestant, Atlantan, business-oriented, nonpolitical, moderate, well-bred, well-educated, pragmatic, and dedicated to the betterment of Atlanta." Much the same summary would have

[63] Melosi, "Dallas–Fort Worth," 176; Carol Estes Thometz, *The Decision-Makers: The Power Structure of Dallas* (Dallas, 1963); William J. Brophy, "Active Acceptance—Active Containment: The Dallas Story," in *Southern Businessmen and Desegregation*, ed. Elizabeth Jacoway and David R. Colburn (Baton Rouge, 1982); Warren Leslie, *Dallas Public and Private: Aspects of an American City* (New York, 1964); Floyd Hunter, *Community Power Structure: A Study of Decision Makers* (Chapel Hill, N.C., 1953); Ivan Allen, Jr., *Mayor: Notes on the Sixties* (New York, 1971).

[64] Hunter, *Community Power Structure*, 12–29.

served for the membership of the Citizens Council in Dallas and for the decision makers in a host of southern cities.[65]

In Atlanta, as elsewhere, a black establishment formed alongside the white one. According to Hunter, professional people—mainly social workers, clerics, and educators—predominated in the African-American leadership, and most of the remaining black leaders were businessmen. In the main, those in the group were middle-class rather than wealthy, and they based their influence among whites on the increase in the number of black registered voters. Economic power in the cities continued to be wielded by whites. The three largest black-owned business operations in the South at the beginning of the sixties were insurance companies in Durham, Atlanta, and Memphis. There were ten African-American banks, all with limited deposits, and many more small savings and loan associations. Black-owned manufacturing firms were relatively rare. The largest of those produced cosmetics for the African-American market. Restaurants, inns, mortuaries, and other businesses catering to local segregated black markets were common in metropolitan areas. Next to the white enterprises headquartered in New York, or even in Dallas, Houston, or Atlanta, the businesses that blacks owned were minuscule. Samuel Lubell could write in 1952, "One of the more striking features of the economic revolution sweeping Dixie today is the degree to which the South has been able to transfer its traditional, agrarian-rooted racial attitudes to the new emerging industrial society." [66]

By 1950 Houston was the largest metropolitan area in the South. In 1947 John Gunther reported that the "region between Houston and Beaumont seems, in fact, to be a single throbbing factory." The petrochemical complex of which Houston was the nucleus came to stretch along the Gulf Coast from Corpus Christi to Lake Charles, Louisiana. Houston was the chief port and storage area of the region as well as a center for oil refining and

[65] Allen, *Mayor*, 30–31.

[66] Hunter, *Community Power Structure*, 116–17; August Meier and David Lewis, "History of the Negro Upper Class in Atlanta, Georgia, 1890–1958," *Journal of Negro Education*, XXVIII (1959), 128–39; Harding B. Young and James M. Hund, "Negro Entrepreneurship in Southern Economic Development," in *Essays in Southern Economic Development*, ed. Greenhut and Whitman, 112–57; Samuel Lubell, *The Future of American Politics* (Garden City, N.Y., 1952), 128.

chemical manufacturing. If journalistic accounts were to be believed, it was also, "with the possible exception of Tulsa, Oklahoma, the most reactionary community in the United States." Houston's leadership, unlike that of most other southern metropolises, had little patience with planning, zoning, and federally supported urban projects. The decision makers were known as the 8F group, since they often met in Suite 8F of a center-city hotel. They were people of the same prominence as those who formed the establishments in Dallas and Atlanta, and according to one scholar, they "did not draw a fine line between their private interests and the interests of the city."[67]

Urban demographers and social scientists often placed Houston among the "regional capitals" that played the same role for more limited hinterlands that Atlanta and Dallas did for larger areas. Southern cities had evolved as a part of the colonial economy; they collected the products of southern farms, forests, and mines for shipment north, marketed nonsouthern manufactured goods as well as insurance and financial and other services, and were the seat of traditional regional industries. They grew in size and complexity, but far more so than in other parts of the nation, regional capitals remained indispensable to the southern economy. Regional capitals as varied as Oklahoma City, Fort Worth, Memphis, Nashville, Louisville, and Richmond, as well as rising centers like Little Rock and Charlotte, set the main trends in southern metropolitan development.[68]

These cities were generally considered "progressive." During the forties and early fifties all of them maintained, established, or revitalized political regimes with outlooks that the chambers of commerce shared, vigorously promoting programs of economic growth and urban development. Most of them experienced population growth well above the national average. Their work forces had a higher proportion of white-collar employees than did met-

[67] John Gunther, *Inside U.S.A.* (New York, 1947), 827–28; George Norris Green, *The Establishment in Texas Politics: The Primitive Years, 1938–1957* (Westport, Conn., 1979), 121–34; Barry J. Kaplan, "Houston: The Golden Buckle on the Sunbelt," in *Sunbelt Cities,* ed. Bernard and Rice, 203; Meinig, *Imperial Texas,* 96–111.

[68] Duncan *et al., Metropolis and Region,* 381–442; Vance and Smith, "Metropolitan Dominance and Integration"; Abbott, *The New Urban America,* 36–145. Of the thirteen regional capitals identified nationally by Duncan and his associates, nine were located in the South.

ropolitan areas generally, and most of the governing elites made at least modest efforts to accommodate black elites. Compared with other American cities, their governments functioned with minimum corruption and commendable efficiency. At the same time, the inclinations of their civic leaders were conservative, and progress was measured by factories, office buildings, and express-ways. Houston, Dallas, and especially Atlanta served as the met-ropolitan ideals most worthy of emulation.[69]

New Orleans and Jacksonville also qualified as regional capitals, but compared with their more aggressive sister cities, they re-tained a stronger commitment to traditional practices. Mayor deLesseps Morrison, who had come to power in New Orleans on a reform ticket in 1946, mounted a number of innovative pro-grams, but his administration failed to reorient public policy and stayed in office by adopting many of the ways of the machine it had overturned. To the economic elite in New Orleans, a "pleas-ant and gracious" life-style mattered most. It greeted "new ideas and new values" with a studied aloofness and had "only a mild interest in such matters as economic development." Wealth in New Orleans, historically the South's largest city, tended to be old wealth. One study has commented, "In no other American city does birth, as opposed to achievement, count for so much." In both New Orleans and Jacksonville, "progressive" politicians dis-covered the limits of electoral government when opposed by con-solidated economic power.[70]

Even more traditional were the older and smaller cities of Charleston and Savannah, both of which were southern towns that happened to be home to a lot of people. Alfred O. Hero, Jr., has asserted of Charleston's leaders that "their consciousness of the past, resistance to change and to compromise with industrialism and modernism, elitist view of mass participation in public affairs,

---

[69] Abbott, *The New Urban America*, 36–59; Duncan *et al.*, *Metropolis and Region*, 381–442; Robert L. Crain, *The Politics of School Desegregation: Comparative Case Studies of Community Structure and Policy-Making* (Chicago, 1968).

[70] Edward F. Haas, *DeLesseps S. Morrison and the Image of Reform: New Orleans Politics, 1946–1961* (Baton Rouge, 1974); Robert L. Crain and Morton Inger, *School Desegregation in New Orleans: A Comparative Study of the Failure of Social Control* (Chicago, 1966), 103–27; Arnold R. Hirsch, "New Orleans: Sunbelt in the Swamp," in *Sunbelt Cities,* ed. Bernard and Rice, 118.

and strong class consciousness were remarkable in the light of national, and even Southern, developments." The voice for the Charleston gentry was the *News and Courier,* which as Robert Coles once commented, seemed "to look upon the twentieth century as one giant conspiracy." Charleston may have been in a class by itself, but many of the smaller southern cities were under the sway of traditional values. The attitude toward the brashness and boost-erism of Atlanta and Houston was apt to be derisive rather than admiring.[71]

Expanding towns sometimes found they had become metro-politan areas. In the transition small businessmen prospered and discovered that they were members of a metropolitan elite. Often they were "self-made, rugged, free enterprisers" who benefited from change but also distrusted it. The leadership in such cities as Albany, Georgia, Jackson, Mississippi, Shreveport and Monroe, Louisiana, and Tyler, Texas, combined an acquisitive capitalism with southern traditionalism. The establishment in these cities had much in common with that in the large piedmont towns.[72]

Several metropolitan areas at the fringe of the South were spe-cial cases. Miami and the other burgeoning cities of south Florida relied heavily on income produced by tourists and retirees, al-though as the postwar era wore on the southern Florida economy became increasingly diversified and complex. Virtually all south-ern cities contained military bases, but the San Antonio and Norfolk-Portsmouth metropolitan areas were great armed out-posts saved by the Cold War from the ravages of peace. The Knox-ville metropolitan area, which included both Oak Ridge and the headquarters of the Tennessee Valley Authority, and the Virginia suburbs of Washington, D.C., were also oriented toward the fed-eral government. Although considered one of the regional capi-tals, Birmingham was the South's premier industrial city, and it sometimes seemed to weave together the worst features of Amer-ican industrialism, Appalachian absentee ownership, and south-

[71] Alfred O. Hero, Jr., *The Southerner and World Affairs* (Baton Rouge, 1965), 35–36; Rob-ert Coles, *Farewell to the South* (Boston, 1972), 93.

[72] Hero, *The Southerner and World Affairs,* 302–309; Daniel J. Elazar, *American Federalism: A View from the States* (2nd ed.; New York, 1972), 106–107.

ern racism. Such special cases were the least southern of all the South's cities.[73]

The development of "new" industries was crucial to the remarkable growth of metropolitan areas. A third or so of the factories employing at least twenty-five workers that opened in the decade following World War II were in "new type" industries—including chemicals, transportation equipment, paper, machinery, and fabricated metals—rather than in the industries that were the South's traditional employers. The arriving industries paid relatively high wages and manufactured high-value-added products. Since they usually located in metropolitan areas, they invigorated the urban markets in construction and services.[74]

The metropolitan economies were a mix of the old and the new during the forties and fifties, but increasingly thereafter, Gavin Wright has observed, "a new Southern economy prevailed, located in the same geographic space as the old one, but encompassing a very different package of labor, capital, natural resources, and entrepreneurship: not an advanced version of the old economy, but a new economy." During the transitional period, the South acquired the economic infrastructure and established the policies and practices that created the new metropolitan economy.[75]

The federal government played a significant role in the promotion of southern growth. The Roosevelt administration's *Report on Economic Conditions of the South* signaled a basic shift in federal policy. During the postwar era the region supped heartily from the public trough. Texas was the South's premier beneficiary of federal largess, but a study of the southern states that excluded Texas and Oklahoma found that in 1940 the region earned 13 percent of the nation's personal income, paid more than 17 percent of the nation's taxes, and absorbed something more than 16 percent of federal outlays, whereas in 1960 it earned almost 16

---

[73] Duncan *et al., Metropolis and Region*, 517–50.

[74] Hammer and Company, *Post-War Industrial Development in the South; Selected Materials on the Economy of the South;* Albert W. Niemi, Jr., *Gross State Product and Productivity in the Southeast* (Chapel Hill, N.C., 1975).

[75] Gavin Wright, *Old South, New South*, 241.

percent of the nation's personal income, paid 12 percent of the nation's taxes, and absorbed 25 percent of federal outlays. A study of the census South calculated that in 1952 it received $1.50 in federal funds for every dollar it paid in taxes. Another study estimated that in 1955 one of every ten dollars of personal income in the region was wages and salaries the federal government directly disbursed to military and civilian employees. Still, given that 27 percent of the nation's population lived in the South, federal spending showed little consistent per capita bias.[76]

National intervention in southern affairs went considerably beyond the expenditures of the federal government. For the cities to a greater extent than the towns, the campaign to sell the South succeeded; external capital fueled metropolitan growth. A study from the late forties identified fifty firms that had constructed eighty-eight new factories in the region during the immediate postwar years. "It is interesting to note," the authors commented, "that, although this was a study of the South, almost all the interviewing was done in the North." That was because the new factories were branch plants of northern firms. Branch plants produced about 70 percent, by value, of the goods manufactured in the South, and virtually all the heavily capitalized "new type" industries were owned outside the region. Similarly the South produced 60 percent of the nation's petroleum and quartered 40 percent of its refineries. About 15 percent of American manufacturing and mining was southern, but the region's banks in the early 1950s held only 8 percent of the deposits of the nation's manufacturing and mining firms.[77]

Arthur F. Raper and Ira De A. Reid in 1941 described Atlanta, Dallas, Memphis, and New Orleans as "branch-house" cities dominated by executives employed by northern corporations. They classified most of the other major southern cities as "subregional

[76] Werner Hochwald, "Interregional Income Flows and the South," in *Essays in Southern Economic Development*, ed. Greenhut and Whitman, 338; Timothy G. O'Rourke, "The Demographic and Economic Setting of Southern Politics," in *Contemporary Southern Politics*, ed. James F. Lea (Baton Rouge, 1988), 22; *Selected Materials on the Economy of the South*, 10.

[77] Glenn E. McLaughlin and Stefan Robock, *Why Industry Moves South: A Study of Factors Influencing the Recent Location of Manufacturing Plants in the South* (Washington, D.C., 1949), 3–20, 129–94; C. Addison Hickman, "The Entrepreneurial Function: The South as a Case Study," in *Essays in Southern Economic Development*, ed. Greenhut and Whitman, 69–111.

headquarters" for national firms. Atlanta was the home of numerous branch firms led by "itinerant and overseer executives," most from nonsouthern backgrounds and with "non-Southern interests to protect." To Raper and Reid, the corporate invasion of the South just marked another phase in the region's economic colonization. Two decades later, Ralph W. McGill took an altogether more sanguine view of it, celebrating the "thousands of new plants" that had arrived and taking satisfaction in the way "most were organized and managed by outside corporations." Because, in his opinion, "Southern merchants and managers" had largely "gone to seed," the "makers of the New South" had to be the "executives, young and old, who poured into the South to direct the new assembly and production plants and the burgeoning retail business." Raper and Reid and McGill were in agreement about who owned and ran the South, but they differed on how salutary outside ownership was.[78]

The relationship between outside ownership and socioeconomic development is unclear. Economists and planners have often seen little reason to care whether development came from outside or inside: economic growth was economic growth. For ordinary people it doubtless made little immediate difference whether the owning class lived on a hill outside their city or on a hill outside some other city. Other scholars, however, have insisted that an imported "industrial revolution" is fundamentally different from a homemade one. "Development cannot be given," urbanist Jane Jacobs has written. "It has to be *done*. It is a process, not a collection of capital goods." [79]

What is indisputable is that the material standard of living in the South rose dramatically. People were eating better, living longer, and consuming more than before. Per capita income increased more rapidly in the South than nationally. In 1940 southerners made do with incomes that were 60 percent of the national

[78] Raper and Reid, *Sharecroppers All*, 202–205; Ralph W. McGill, *The South and the Southerner* (Boston, 1963), 208–209.

[79] Jane Jacobs, *Cities and the Wealth of Nations: Principles of Economic Life* (New York, 1984), 119; Joseph Persky, "Regional Colonialism and the Southern Economy," *Review of Radical Political Economics*, IV (1972), 73; Robert B. Cohen, "Multinational Corporations, International Finance, and the Sunbelt," in *The Rise of the Sunbelt Cities*, ed. Perry and Watkins, 211–26.

average; in 1960 per capita income in the South was 76 percent of that in the nation. Rising incomes permitted the consumer economy to reach significant numbers of southerners it had previously bypassed. The expanding economy also broadened economic opportunity. Not since the early nineteenth century had southerners enjoyed such a favorable climate for occupational and material advancement.[80]

By 1960 the South possessed a modern economy. The extent of modernization varied from state to state, but the region as a whole had become predominantly urban and the metropolitan population was soon to be in the majority. Industry and commerce dwarfed agriculture, with the southern people by and large gaining their livelihood from manufacturing, trade, and services. The colonial economy of the sort described in President Roosevelt's *Report on the Economic Conditions of the South* was a memory, and a modern economic infrastructure was its successor. Modernization also debased southern culture and community and created a more individualized and more competitive society. Labor, no longer bound to tenancy and company towns, became a commodity in the marketplace. The transformation took place within a social order dominated by white males, based on de jure white supremacy, and led politically by an old-guard county-seat elite.

[80] Thomas H. Naylor and James Clotfelter, *Strategies for Change in the South* (Chapel Hill, N.C., 1975), 10–12.

CHAPTER V

RACE AND REFORM

S OUTHERN state governments responded to the socioeconomic upheavals in the region with a variety of programs. Economic growth increased tax revenues, and modernizing administrators plotted improvements in education, transportation, and other public services. When the federal courts required that separate but equal facilities be equal in more than name, their mandate gave impetus to public-school reform. The southern states recorded notable accomplishments in education and other areas, but the "road toward governmental adjustment to urbanization and metropolitan development," as academicians were prone to describe it, was by no means a smooth one.[1]

At the end of World War II, southern political leaders normally put the maintenance of social stability—and most particularly the perpetuation of racial segregation—at the top of their political agenda. Disfranchisement, legislative malapportionment, and one-party politics buttressed the political and social status quo. The region's long-standing poverty and its low level of public expenditures had left it with festering problems, and conflicting views about the ends of social reform complicated the search for ameliorative solutions. Nonetheless, by 1945 all the southern states except Florida and Texas had enacted personal and corporate income taxes, and six states had adopted general sales taxes as well. Compared with the rest of the nation, however, the South not only had less to tax but collected public levies at a somewhat lower rate even when measured by capacity to pay. Tax rates were

[1] Robert H. Connery and Richard H. Leach, "Southern Metropolis: Challenge to Government," *Journal of Politics,* XXVI (1964), 81.

lowest in Harry Flood Byrd's Virginia, and they were highest in Earl K. Long's Louisiana.[2]

Roads and schools made the largest drafts on state treasuries. The South maintained a rough parity in transportation. With 28 percent of the nation's acreage, the South possessed 28 percent of its railroad mileage and 29 percent of its paved highways. In 1947 the region accounted for approximately a third of all funds allocated in the United States to road construction and maintenance. As a consequence the central debate revolved not so much around whether to build roads but around what kind of transportation facilities to construct. Rurally oriented politicians called for farm-to-market roads to get farmers "out of the mud," advocates of development supported a centralized transportation infrastructure that included port facilities and airports, and uptown business groups in the cities sought rationalized and metropolitan-centered highway systems as well as other projects that might benefit their own cities. The Long forces in Louisiana liked to gibe that the New Orleans *Times-Picayune,* in opposing their road-building programs, was simply declaring a preference for bad roads, but the editorial opposition also had to do with the kind of roads the populist-leaning Long faction chose to construct.[3]

More pressing was the plight of public education. At the end of World War II, the southern states had one-third of the nation's public-school enrollment but earned less than one-fifth of the country's income. Expenditures per pupil in the region were

[2] Department of Education and Research, Congress of Industrial Organizations, *A Handbook on State and Local Taxes* (Washington, D.C., 1955), 42–69, 85–104; James W. Martin and Glenn D. Morrow, *Taxation of Manufacturing in the South* (University, Ala., 1948), 104–105; Edward W. Reed, *Comparative Analysis of the Arkansas Tax System* (Fayetteville, Ark., 1950), 4–145; B. U. Ratchford, "Recent Economic Developments in the South," *Journal of Politics,* X (1948), 259–81; Calvin B. Hoover and B. U. Ratchford, *Economic Resources and Policies of the South* (New York, 1951), 199–207.

[3] Hoover and Ratchford, *Economic Resources and Policies of the South,* 16–18; A. J. Liebling, *The Earl of Louisiana* (New York, 1961), 27. Among numerous studies of the relationship between politics, economics, and development, informative are Ira Sharkansky's *Public Administration: Agencies, Policies, and Politics* (San Francisco, 1982), esp. 261–88; Bruce J. Schulman's *From Cotton Belt to Sunbelt: Federal Policy, Economic Development, and the Transformation of the South, 1938–1980* (New York, 1991); and Peter A. Lupsha and William J. Siembieda's "The Poverty of Public Services in the Land of Plenty: An Analysis and Interpretation," in *The Rise of the Sunbelt Cities,* ed. David C. Perry and Alfred J. Watkins (Beverly Hills, Calif., 1977), 169–90.

about half the nonsouthern average. Educational accomplishments were even less than such a figure might imply because of the high dropout rate. A study conducted during the early 1950s discovered that of every hundred children who had entered the first grade scarcely more than ten graduated from high school. Through much of the South, a public-school system hardly existed. The funding disparity between urban and rural schools and between white and black schools created great unevenness. White metropolitan schools were often adequately financed; the condition of black rural schools staggered visiting journalists: "This thing is a school, this dilapidated, sagging old shack, leaning and lopsided as its makeshift foundations crumble." Southern state governments had long attempted to provide "equalization" appropriations to bring all schools to a minimum level of funding, but their success was limited.[4]

During the postwar years all the southern states launched public-school reform programs. The legislatures in Florida and Tennessee adopted minimum foundation programs in 1947. Within a decade the other states either enacted new comprehensive minimum-funding legislation or strengthened earlier equalization laws. In 1949 the legislatures of Georgia and Texas created minimum foundation programs. Oklahoma, the state that had most nearly achieved equalization, substantially increased public-school funding, as did North Carolina. Kentucky revised and expanded its plan. The most influential of the postwar measures was the Texas Gilmer-Aikin Foundation School Program, which served as a model for southern school reform. Such programs established or strengthened uniform standards and minimum salaries for teachers, twelve-year graduation programs with nine-month school years, school consolidation and construction, and centralized authority and planning.[5]

[4] Hoover and Ratchford, *Economic Resources and Policies of the South*, 31; Truman M. Pierce *et al., White and Negro Schools in the South: An Analysis of Biracial Education* (Englewood Cliffs, N.J., 1955), 240; Ray Springle, *In the Land of Jim Crow* (New York, 1949), p. 50 quoted; Rupert B. Vance, *All These People: The Nation's Human Resources in the South* (Chapel Hill, N.C., 1945), 436–43; Harry S. Ashmore, *The Negro and the Schools* (Chapel Hill, N.C., 1954); Ernest W. Swanson and John A. Griffin, *Public Education in the South, Today and Tomorrow* (Westport, Conn., 1955).

[5] Tennessee Department of Education, *Annual Statistical Report for the Scholastic Year Ending*

Southern state governments financed their foundation programs primarily through consumer taxes. By the end of 1951 Tennessee, Florida, Georgia, and South Carolina had enacted general
sales taxes—leaving only Kentucky, Texas, and Virginia without
them—and Alabama had increased its levies. Other states raised
sales taxes on selected products, often gasoline or cigarettes, and
several approved sizable bond issues for school construction. Min-
eral-rich states—especially Oklahoma, Louisiana, and Texas—received revenue in the form of royalties, leases, and severance
taxes. Texas and Louisiana in particular gained financially when
President Dwight D. Eisenhower signed the Submerged Lands Act
of 1953, which returned to the states the mineral rights to the
tidelands. By the mid-1950s Texas and Louisiana derived from
minerals more than one-third of the total revenue they collected.
The South's rising prosperity and increasingly consumer-targeting
taxation permitted an impressive infusion of funds into education.[6]

The school-reform measures narrowed—although they never
closed—the expenditure gaps. The sudden influx of money into
rural and black schools could not in any immediate sense overcome long decades of neglect. The new programs also permitted

---

June 30, 1948 (Nashville, 1948); Lee Seifert Greene, David H. Grubbs, and Victor C. Hob-
day, *Government in Tennessee* (4th ed.; Knoxville, Tenn., 1982), 299–305; Amicus Curiae
Brief of the Attorney General of Florida, 185–98, Amicus Curiae Brief of the Attorney
General of North Carolina, 25–44, both in U.S. Supreme Court Records, Briefs, *Brown* v.
Board of Education of Topeka, 349 U.S. 294 (1955); Thomas D. Bailey (Florida state superintendent of public instruction) in Miami *Herald*, May 12, 1959; David R. Colburn and
Richard K. Scher, *Florida's Gubernatorial Politics in the Twentieth Century* (Tallahassee, Fla.,
1980), 237–58; Georgia Minimum Foundation Law, in *States' Laws on Race and Color*, ed.
Pauli Murray (Cincinnati, 1950), 96–109; Texas Education Agency, *Public School Law Bulletin, 1952* (Austin, Tex., 1952), 8–14, 408–27; Ashmore, *The Negro and the Schools*, 153–
55. The Fund for the Advancement of Education sponsored a comprehensive investigation
of southern education in the early 1950s that resulted in the publication of Ashmore's *The
Negro and the Schools*, of Swanson and Griffin's *Public Education in the South*, and of *White and
Negro Schools in the South*, by Pierce *et al.* Southern educational developments during the
1950s are surveyed in the essays prepared by the staff and associates of the Southern
Education Reporting Service for *Southern Schools: Progress and Problems*, ed. Patrick McCauley
and Edward D. Ball (Nashville, 1959).

[6] Ashmore, *The Negro and the Schools*, 114, 152; Swanson and Griffin, *Public Education in
the South*, 77; Council of State Governments, *State Government*, XXVIII (1955), 53; Department of Education and Research, CIO, *A Handbook on State and Local Taxes*, 42–104.

local districts to impose additional taxes, and the more affluent increasingly did so, thus ensuring greater resources for suburban schools than for their rural and black counterparts. The foundation school reforms, along with rising per capita income, laid the basis for conspicuous improvements in public education or at least in the quality of physical plants and in the preparation and pay of teachers.

Relative to the rest of the nation, however, the South made only halting progress in education. In 1950 the state governments of the South spent 3.3 percent of the region's total personal income on schools, as compared with an expenditure of 2.7 percent of total personal income outside the South. At the same time, local communities in the region spent less in support of education than did communities elsewhere, and total expenditures per pupil as a percentage of purchasing power differed little from national norms. In the United States, spending for public schools increased by approximately a billion dollars per year during the fifties. The pace made it difficult for a disadvantaged region to improve its position relative to the nation as a whole.[7]

Financial support for education also varied widely from one southern state to another. During the 1949–1950 school year, students in Mississippi got by on one-third the amount spent per pupil nationally. Total outlays per student in Alabama and Kentucky were about half the national average, and expenditures in Arkansas, Georgia, and South Carolina were less than 60 percent of it. Funding per student in Louisiana, on the other hand, matched the national average, and Florida, Oklahoma, and Texas were not far behind it. The remaining southern states—North Carolina, Tennessee, and Virginia—spent two-thirds to three-quarters of what the nation as a whole did per student. Ten years later, Mississippi had greatly increased expenditures per student. According to figures of the National Education Association, students in Mississippi were better funded during the 1959–1960 school year than those in Alabama, Arkansas, Georgia, Kentucky, or South Carolina. Louisiana continued to match national norms;

[7] Ashmore, *The Negro and the Schools,* 114–16; Tom Flake, "Expenditures: Dollars on a Treadmill," in *Southern Schools,* ed. McCauley and Ball, 31–39, 93; Department of Health, Education, and Welfare, *Digest of Educational Statistics, 1963 Edition* (1963).

the other southern states ranged from Tennessee, at 61 percent of the national average, to Florida, at 86 percent.[8]

Although the state governments in the South traditionally made more generous appropriations for higher education than for elementary and secondary schooling, regional expenditures for colleges and universities lagged behind national averages. Because a majority of the postsecondary students in the Northeast attended private institutions, public southern outlays for higher education did not suffer by comparison with the appropriations there. The states of the West and Midwest allocated approximately 13 percent of their budgets to higher education, however, whereas the southern states spent around 9 percent. Nevertheless, expenditures per student in the South were similar to those at midlevel universities in the rest of the nation, because fewer southerners continued their education beyond high school.[9]

More than tight budgets circumscribed higher education in the South. J. Frank Dobie remarked in 1945, "To achieve tranquillity at the University of Texas, put your mind to sleep. . . . Perfect yourself in the cunning of circumlocution, and prove to farmers on forty-acre patches that their best friend has always been Wall Street and their worst enemy organized labor." As the topic of school desegregation began to command greater attention, the Fund for the Advancement of Education offered in early 1954 to finance a study of the region's dual school system. No educational institution would accept the money; "the subject was considered too hot for any southern university to handle," according to Harry S. Ashmore, editor of the *Arkansas Gazette*. Ashmore became project director, and a number of southern scholars participated as individuals.[10]

During the late fifties and early sixties, academic freedom in the South came under considerable pressure from segregationists.

[8] National Education Association, Special Project on School Finance, *Financing the Public Schools* (National Education Association, 1962), 131–49; American Commission on Intergovernmental Relations, *Measures of State and Local Fiscal Capacity and Tax Effort* (1962).

[9] Vance, *All These People*, 440–43; Allan M. Cartter, "Qualitative Aspects of Southern University Education," *Southern Economic Journal*, XXXII (1965), 36–69; Allan M. Cartter, "The Role of Higher Education in the Changing South," in *The South in Continuity and Change*, ed. John C. McKinney and Edgar T. Thompson (Durham, N.C., 1965), 277–97.

[10] Dobie quoted in *Southern Patriot*, March, 1945; Harry S. Ashmore, *An Epitaph for Dixie* (New York, 1958), 161.

In Florida, the Legislative Investigation Committee conducted an extensive and often bizarre search for integrationists, homosexuals, and Communists—on the apparent theory that the three were essentially the same. In 1961 the committee claimed credit for forcing the dismissal of thirty-nine public-school teachers and fifteen members of the faculty and staff at the University of Florida. During the early 1960s, the fact that black colleges were hotbeds of civil rights protest often provoked the fury of segregationist officials. When in 1960 the State Board of Education ordered the president of Alabama State College for Negroes to fire an integrationist faculty member "before sundown tonight," some wryly asked whether the board's decision left time for due process. Outrages like this notwithstanding, overt violations of academic freedom were relatively infrequent in the postwar era. More significant were the subtle pressures to conform to regional norms.[11]

Under such circumstances, modernizing university presidents and administrators struggled with some success to improve higher education in the region. Southern institutions received a boon from the Servicemen's Readjustment Act of 1944. Scores of thousands of former GIs flooded into the colleges and universities, conferring on the schools not only their numbers and grant money but also the serious and mature attitudes they often brought along. The GI Bill opened opportunities for many southerners, but at the same time, as Clarence L. Mohr has pointed out, it helped remasculinize higher education and it reemphasized the primacy of career training for men. To make room for veterans, some universities established maximum quotas for enrollment by women, who in any event were tacitly expected to pursue marriage partners rather than careers. The GI Bill also exposed the gulf separating southern universities from the better nonsouthern institutions and spurred a drive toward improvement.[12]

During and after the fifties, the universities of the South moved steadily in the direction of becoming research institutions with

[11] *Report of the Florida Legislative Investigation Committee to the 1961 Session of the Legislature* (Tallahassee, Fla., 1961); Montgomery *Advertiser,* June 15, 1960.

[12] Clarence L. Mohr, "Postwar Visions and Cold War Realities: The Metamorphosis of Southern Higher Education, 1945–1965" (Paper presented at Porter L. Fortune, Jr., History Symposium, University of Mississippi, October 7, 1992), 1–6.

national reputations. The number of schools offering Ph.D.s and the number of students receiving them increased impressively. Research scholars competed for the grant money that flowed from foundations and especially the federal government. The pursuit of federal research and development dollars and foundation funds, like the creation of respectable graduate programs, forced southern universities to adopt national standards of research and scholarship. Much of the research that the federal government supported sprang from the Cold War, and as Mohr has stated, "Military influence came to permeate those southern universities that aspired to national status."[13]

Both the GI Bill and the decisions of the United States Supreme Court laid bare the stunted estate of higher education for southern African Americans. Black veterans received the same federal benefits as whites, but the black colleges were small and ill favored. Graduate and professional schools hardly existed for blacks. When in 1938 the Supreme Court ruled in *Gaines* v. *Canada* that separate educational facilities had also to be equal, Virginia State College and Prairie View Agricultural and Mechanical College in Texas were the only black institutions in the South that offered graduate training. Black plaintiffs soon brought suit to gain admission to graduate and professional schools in most of the southern states on the grounds that it was illegal for the state to support graduate, law, or medical programs for white students when no comparable programs were open to blacks. Throughout the region, the prospect of litigation led to the hasty creation of graduate and professional programs for African Americans. The result, in greater or lesser degree, was often like the one-student, three-instructor law school established in Oklahoma in a corner of the state capitol.[14]

The subterfuges failed to halt desegregation. Makeshift graduate and professional schools were not equal, and the federal courts refused to accept out-of-state tuition payments to African Americans when whites had access to the same programs at home.

[13] *Ibid.*, 20; Cartter, "Qualitative Aspects of Southern University Education"; Bernard Berelson, *Graduate Education in the United States* (New York, 1960).

[14] George Brown Tindall, *The Emergence of the New South, 1913–1945* (Baton Rouge, 1967), 561–64; United States Commission on Civil Rights, *Equal Protection of the Laws in Public Higher Education* (1960), 17–39.

The reality was that the already hard-pressed southern states could not possibly support two respectable university systems. In 1948 the University of Arkansas voluntarily began to accept black applicants in programs not otherwise available in the state.[15]

The University of Oklahoma, which admitted a black graduate student under court order, adopted an approach that had been tried but promptly abandoned in Arkansas. The Board of Regents and the state legislature required George W. McLaurin, a graduate student in the School of Education, to attend classes in an anteroom separate from but equal to the schoolroom of his white classmates, eat at a separate table in the school cafeteria, study at a separate table in the library, and use separate toilet facilities. In Texas, Heman Sweatt, a black letter carrier, sued to study law at the University of Texas. In response, state officials created a segregated facility in Austin staffed by faculty of the University of Texas and supported by the resources of the state law library.

Lawyers for the National Association for the Advancement of Colored People brought action on behalf of both McLaurin and Sweatt. In both cases, the separate facilities provided were as materially equal as segregated programs were apt to be. The Supreme Court ruled in June, 1950, that McLaurin and Sweatt were being denied equal protection of the laws. Relying on intangible factors, the justices held that the segregated arrangements for McLaurin deprived him of advantages such as intellectual exchange with classmates and that the law school provided for Sweatt lacked tradition, prestige, and the other "qualities which are incapable of objective measurement but which make for greatness in a law school." *McLaurin* and *Sweatt* did not overturn segregation, but they left the concept of separate but equal with only a tenuous legality. "After 1950," as one study has stated, "every careful student of constitutional law knew that, given the climate of judicial—as well as national—opinion, the 'separate but equal' formula was doomed."[16]

[15] Commission on Civil Rights, *Equal Protection of the Laws in Public Higher Education*, 28–30.

[16] James R. Scales and Danney Goble, *Oklahoma Politics: A History* (Norman, Okla., 1982), 262–66; George Lynn Cross, *Blacks in White Colleges: Oklahoma's Landmark Cases* (Norman, Okla., 1975); Mark V. Tushnet, *The NAACP's Legal Strategy Against Segregated Education,*

As southern education was being reconstructed, so too was regional health care. Medical reform, unlike the improvements in schooling, owed more to federal than to state initiatives. Southerners who served in the military during World War II experienced regular medical and dental care, and the Emergency Maternal and Infant Care program rendered services for their wives. The wartime experience, Edward H. Beardsley has concluded, created a "new hospital consciousness" in the South. In 1946 Senator Lister Hill of Alabama and Representative Harold H. Burton of Ohio successfully sponsored the Hospital Survey and Construction Act, which provided federal matching funds for the construction of hospitals and public health centers. The matching formula favored nonmetropolitan areas in poorer, less developed states and thereby ensured that the South was one of its prime beneficiaries. Over the following two decades, Hill-Burton facilities appeared through much of the region.[17]

The Hill-Burton Act left administration of the facilities to the states and specifically recognized the legitimacy of racial separation. As a result, according to Virginia V. Hamilton, "free care for the poor was almost completely ignored," and black patients received treatment in separate although generally equal wards. The white medical fraternity was adamant about keeping black doctors and interns off Hill-Burton staffs. The improved health centers and hospitals benefited the middle strata of rural and town society most. The massive health problems of the southern rural poor were ultimately ameliorated not by doctors but by the depopulation of the rural South. Nevertheless, because of the Hill-Burton Act and the paucity of private hospitals, per capita public health expenditures in the South were normally higher than those elsewhere in the nation.[18]

1925–1950 (Chapel Hill, N.C., 1987), 105–37; *McLaurin* v. *Board of Regents,* 399 U.S. 637 (1950); *Sweatt* v. *Painter,* 39 U.S. 634 (1950); Walter F. Murphy, *Congress and the Court: A Case Study in the American Political Process* (Chicago, 1962), 80.

[17] Edward H. Beardsley, *A History of Neglect: Health Care for Blacks and Mill Workers in the Twentieth-Century South* (Knoxville, Tenn. 1987), 172–85, p. 174 quoted.

[18] *Ibid.;* Virginia Van der Veer Hamilton, *Lister Hill, Statesman from the South* (Chapel Hill, N.C., 1987), 135–41, p. 139 quoted; Allan Crimm, *Access by the Poor to Health Care in Southern Hill-Burton Hospitals* (Southern Regional Council, 1974).

The southern states constructed highways, schools, and hospitals and neglected most other public services. Public-welfare payments in the region lagged far behind national norms and were frequently more restrictive. Such laws as Alabama's Relatives Responsibility Act, which denied welfare payments to people whose families were capable of supporting them, were by no means uncommon. Apart from a declining number of neopopulist liberals, few southern officials doubted the soundness of low welfare expenditures. Normally, only the old-age assistance program was politically controversial. Old-age payments went most often to whites, frequently to whites who voted and who formed a relatively attentive issue-conscious constituency. Liberals dependent on the rural vote and some pragmatic office seekers favored raising old-age pensions; conservatives united to forestall such extravagance. In the South as a whole, old-age payments were usually quite modest. Timothy G. O'Rourke has observed, "Although the pattern in the [southern] states of low taxes, limited services, and meager welfare spending may not be ideal public policy, it *is* conducive to economic growth." The pattern also encouraged social stability.[19]

The forces of change and the forces of tradition coalesced to support policies that extended well beyond education, transportation, health, and welfare. While determinedly defending state rights, the southern congressional delegation pursued federal funds with mounting ardor, especially those related to defense, development, or the pork barrel. State bureaucracies protected by the merit system expanded. In 1954 Louisiana and Georgia replaced their traditional biennial legislative sessions with annual meetings, and, along with South Carolina which had earlier adopted annual sessions, initiated a trend that was ultimately to become general. Legislators throughout the region continued to ignore urban growth when they considered legislative apportionment.[20]

[19] Fred Taylor in Atlanta *Sunday Journal-Constitution*, March 21, 1954; Timothy G. O'Rourke, "The Demographic and Economic Setting of Southern Politics," in *Contemporary Southern Politics*, ed. James F. Lea (Baton Rouge, 1988), 29.

[20] Gavin Wright, *Old South, New South: Revolutions in the Southern Economy Since the Civil War* (New York, 1986), 261; Council of State Governments, *State Government*, XXVIII (1955), 76.

By imposing consumer taxes, the southern states limited the burden on business, industry, and property owners. "Between 1950 and 1978," it has been calculated, "the average state corporate income tax rate in the South declined from 185 percent above, to 13 percent below, the average in all states." Nevertheless, total state tax revenues were relatively high. Throughout the 1950s, most states in the region collected more than the national average as a percentage of personal income. On the other hand, local taxes—particularly property taxes—were substantially lower than the national norm. By 1960 all the southern states except Texas and Virginia collected higher taxes relative to personal income than did the average state outside the region, and every southern state trailed national norms in local tax receipts. The low property taxes were partly due to the proliferation of tax exemptions for new industries, but they also reflected the disinclination of county elites to bother themselves with public requisitions. As the postwar years progressed, southern tax levies lagged farther behind national norms, and the South solidified its general position as a low-tax region, particularly in the realm of income and property taxes.[21]

Public vocational and technical schools increased in number, as did right-to-work laws. During 1954 and 1955, four states— Alabama, Mississippi, South Carolina, and Texas—enacted such measures; at the end of 1955, all the southern states save Kentucky and Oklahoma enforced right-to-work policies. Southern political leaders subsidized industry with increasing ingenuity at the same time that they deplored giveaway programs having to do with public welfare. They continued their inflexible opposition to racial integregation even as national forces chipped away at segregation and the Supreme Court moved toward a reversal of *Plessy* v. *Ferguson*.[22]

By the time of *Sweatt* and *McLaurin*, the NAACP had launched a direct attack on segregation in education. In cases that origi-

[21] Robert J. Newman, *Growth in the American South: Changing Regional Employment and Wage Patterns in the 1960s and 1970s* (New York, 1984), 3; Council of State Governments, *State Government*, XXVIII (1955), 53.

[22] J. R. Dempsey, *The Operation of the Right-to-Work Laws* (Milwaukee, 1961), 24–27; James C. Cobb, *The Selling of the South: The Southern Crusade for Industrial Development, 1936–1980* (Baton Rouge, 1982).

nated in Clarendon County, South Carolina, and Prince Edward County, Virginia, lawyers for the organization argued that segregation per se was a denial of equal protection. These two cases, combined with three others, went before the Supreme Court in December, 1952. Six months later the Court requested further debate on specific issues. By that time the cases were fixtures in the southern press. Ralph W. McGill warned his readers that "one of these days it will be Monday" and the Court would declare separate but equal an unconstitutional doctrine.[23]

The long series of federal decisions involving higher education and culminating in *Brown* v. *Board of Education* placed southern schools in the vanguard of social change. The Supreme Court, after addressing southern disfranchisement in *Smith* v. *Allwright,* turned from voting rights, which were explicitly guaranteed by the Fifteenth Amendment. Even some southern Bourbons saw the futility of trying to find grounds that would legitimate withholding the right to vote, but they could and did insist that the federal courts had no constitutional authority over the admissions policies of state-financed public schools. The justices also shied from issues related to fair employment and desegregated housing, two objectives from which the federal government itself departed by supporting segregation through its hiring practices and its home loan guarantee programs. Instead, the Court chose education as the "yardstick by which racial progress would be judged." The priority the Court accorded education was of course a mark of the times. Access to white schools would presumably broaden opportunities for blacks, while encountering blacks on equal terms would wean whites from their racial prejudices. Also in keeping with the times, school desegregation provided an outlet for upper-middle-class reform impulses while raising no disconcerting questions about the distribution of wealth and income, no disturbing doubts about the righteousness of national institutions, and no nagging thoughts about the need for jobs—perhaps publicly funded jobs— and social reforms. With the bulk of black southerners disfranchised, the state legislatures grossly malapportioned, the housing

[23] Walter White, *How Far the Promised Land?* (New York, 1955), 36–38; Tushnet, *The NAACP's Legal Strategy,* 115–66; Ralph W. McGill, *The South and the Southerner* (Boston, 1959), 22.

of the cities ever more segregated, and the opportunities in the South for black employment declining, the Supreme Court directed its attention to education.[24]

Black Monday, as segregationists were quick to label it, turned out to be May 17, 1954. In *Brown* v. *Board of Education*, the Supreme Court posed the question "Does segregation of the children in public schools solely on the basis of race, even though the physical facilities and other 'tangible' factors may be equal, deprive the children of the minority group of equal educational opportunities?" The justices unanimously answered in the affirmative. "Separate education facilities," they declared, "are inherently unequal." But "because of the wide applicability of this decision, and because of the great variety of local conditions," the Court asked for further argument on the best method for implementing its decree. One year later, in May, 1955, the justices issued their implementation order mandating public-school desegregation "with all deliberate speed." [25]

By the time of the decision, a vocal minority of southern officials were declaiming their inalterable resistance to desegregation. The most defiant was Governor Herman Talmadge, whom a reporter for the New York *Times* described as "the South's foremost spokesman of 'white supremacy.' " The Georgia governor was the first southern chief executive to take concrete steps against the gradual integration of higher education. After *McLaurin* and *Sweatt,* the Talmadge forces in the state legislature included in the appropriations act of 1951 a provision denying state funds to any institution that desegregated. "As long as I am governor," Talmadge vowed, "Negroes will not be admitted to white schools." [26]

Georgia soon advanced to more vigorous measures in fulfillment of Talmadge's pledge. In 1953 the legislature authorized submission to the electorate of a constitutional amendment elim-

[24] J. Harvie Wilkinson III, *From Brown to Bakke: The Supreme Court and School Integration, 1954–1978* (New York, 1979), 45.

[25] *Brown* v. *Board of Education* (1954), *Brown* v. *Board of Education* (1955), both in *Race Relations Law Reporter*, I, 8–9, 11–12.

[26] John N. Popham in New York *Times*, September 9, 1954; Talmadge quoted in *New South*, July, 1951, p. 8.

inating the state's obligation to maintain public schools and allowing the state government to pay "tuition grants" to parents for educating their children. The legislature also created the Georgia Education Commission, a segregationist strategy committee comprising administration officials, legislators, and prominent private citizens. The first task of the commission was to promote the "private school amendment," which the electorate ratified by a relatively close margin in 1954. The south Georgia plantation counties voted heavily in favor of the amendment, while metropolitan areas and the predominantly white north Georgia counties opposed it.[27]

While seizing leadership of the old order, Talmadge was by no means a prisoner of the past. His faction had overseen the enactment of Georgia's minimum foundation program, and in 1951 it pushed through the legislature a 3 percent sales tax to support school reform and other developmental projects. Eugene Talmadge had as governor been the scourge of the cities, trivializing public education because "it ain't never taught a man to plant cotton" and inviting rural male audiences, "Come see me at the mansion. We'll sit on the front porch and piss over the rail on those city bastards." In 1946 the Atlanta *Journal* damned him as "this blatant demagogue, this fomenter of strife, this panderer to the passions of the ignorant and to the fears of the timid, [who should be] exposed for what he is, that is, a blatherskite, a cheap fraud and a menace to the security and the welfare of us all." [28]

Herman Talmadge's approach was different. Unlike his father, he was an able administrator whose agenda of improving state services with money from consumer taxation appealed to suburbanites as well as county leaders. The hostility of the metropolitan newspapers faded as the Talmadge faction consolidated its domination of Georgia politics. In 1954 the voters chose a Talmadge

[27] *New South,* December, 1953; *Southern School News,* September, 1954; Act 653, Georgia Legislative Acts, 1953 Sess., in *Facts on Film* (Southern Education Reporting Service), reel 3; Numan V. Bartley and Hugh D. Graham, comps., *Southern Elections: County and Precinct Data, 1950–1972* (Baton Rouge, 1978), 116–19.

[28] Talmadge quoted in *The Wild Man from Sugar Creek: The Political Career of Eugene Talmadge,* by William Anderson (Baton Rouge, 1978), 103, 209; Atlanta *Journal,* June 9, 1946.

lieutenant as governor, in 1956 they overwhelmingly elected Talmadge to the United States Senate, and in 1958 they endorsed another Talmadge associate as chief executive.[29]

Governor Talmadge yoked his defense of the social status quo with support for economic modernization. He and his immediate successors—Governors Marvin Griffin and Ernest Vandiver—pursued policies that propitiated business, courted outside investors, promoted educational reforms, opposed labor organization, and demeaned black people. The program won support from the downstate plantation counties and from metropolitan business groups while retaining that of lower-status white voters. It was a formula for political success that was to be emulated in other states.[30]

In South Carolina, Governor James F. Byrnes charted a similar course. During his long career in national politics, Byrnes had served as congressman, senator, Supreme Court justice, top-level White House aide, and secretary of state. Historian Ernest M. Lander has called him "probably the most influential South Carolina political leader in Washington since John C. Calhoun." After breaking with President Truman over civil rights and other matters, he returned home, in Howard H. Quint's words, "to vent his frustration against the national government and the Democratic Party." In 1950 he sought and easily won election as governor.[31]

Byrnes said in his inaugural address, "It is our duty to provide for the races substantial equality in school facilities. We should do it because it is right. For me, that is sufficient reason. If any person wants an additional reason, I say it is wise." The new governor shepherded through the legislature a school funding program, a substantial bond issue to begin it, and a 3 percent sales tax to

[29] Joseph L. Bernd, *Grass Roots Politics in Georgia* (Atlanta, 1960); Roger N. Pajari, "Herman E. Talmadge and the Politics of Power," in *Georgia Governors in an Age of Change: From Ellis Arnall to George Busbee,* ed. Harold P. Henderson and Gary L. Roberts (Athens, Ga., 1988), 75–92; Herman E. Talmadge, "Reflections on the Gubernatorial Years," in *Georgia Governors in an Age of Change,* 93–97; George McMillan, "Talmadge—The Best Southern Governor?" *Harper's Magazine,* CCIX (1954), 34–40.

[30] Numan V. Bartley, *The Creation of Modern Georgia* (2nd ed.; Athens, Ga., 1990), 179–207.

[31] Ernest M. Lander, *A History of South Carolina, 1865–1960* (Chapel Hill, N.C., 1960), 80; Howard H. Quint, *Profile in Black and White: A Frank Portrait of South Carolina* (Washington, D.C., 1959), 15.

support it. During the same session in 1951, the legislature created a segregationist strategy committee headed by state senator L. Marion Gressette and broadened the authority of local officials to set school enrollment policies. Gressette's committee recommended, as a "preparedness measure," a constitutional amendment permitting the state to abolish the public-school system. In 1952 the voters approved the amendment by a two-to-one majority.[32]

The Byrnes administration laid the groundwork for a modern school system in South Carolina at the same time that it made arrangements to eliminate it. The governor's tenure brought an improvement of hospital and university facilities and an upgrading of state services. It also included higher university tuition fees, a right-to-work law, and belligerent opposition to changes in racial practices. In the village of Promiseland, a modern, consolidated brick elementary school replaced the sagging one-teacher schoolhouse for black children. "Now, so long ignored and neglected by the official world," Elizabeth R. Bethel has written, "these children had the best the county could afford. They were not expected to demand any more." As Governor Byrnes observed in a radio address in 1951, "Education, tolerance, and time will bring about better understanding between the races."[33]

Some public officials responded more constructively to the *Brown* decision. The border region—the District of Columbia, Delaware, Maryland, Missouri, West Virginia—promptly began school desegregation. Governor Lawrence Wetherby announced that "Kentucky will do whatever is necessary to comply with the law." His declaration, as historian Steven A. Channing has observed, "may have been tokenism by later standards, but measured by the climate of the day, it was an act of courage." Governor Johnston Murray of Oklahoma flirted with resistance. "I don't believe in forcing people to do something they don't want to do," he avowed, and in November, 1954, he joined with several other

[32] James F. Byrnes, *All in One Lifetime* (New York, 1958), 407; New York *Times*, May 27, 1951; *New South*, February, 1953; *Southern School News*, September, 1954.

[33] W. D. Workman in Charleston *News and Courier*, December 19, 1954, January 2, 1955; Elizabeth Rauh Bethel, *Promiseland: A Century of Life in a Negro Community* (Philadelphia, 1981), 233; Byrnes quoted in Charleston *News and Courier*, May 12, 1951.

southern governors in signing a statement that called for a defense of state rights. By that time, however, Raymond D. Gary had been elected governor, and Gary, much like Wetherby in Kentucky, eased Oklahoma into compliance with the court ruling.[34]

No other southern governors acceded to the Court's decision. Governor William B. Umstead of North Carolina professed himself "terribly disappointed" with it. Governor Thomas Stanley of Virginia pledged to "use every means at my command to continue segregated schools in Virginia" and recommended repeal of the Virginia constitutional provision requiring a public-school system. The Texas Democratic party convention, abetted by Governor Allan Shivers, accepted a platform plank urging "every legal means to continue our public schools as they are, on a separate but equal basis." All three governors—Umstead, Stanley, and Shivers—created strategy committees to plan the response of their states to *Brown*.[35]

In a speech in early 1954, John N. Popham, southern correspondent for the New York *Times,* explained that the reality of southern politics made it "impractical" for "any sizable white Southern leadership to give forthright support" to desegregation. Local leaders in the former Confederate states demonstrated little inclination to accept desegregation. A survey undertaken in Florida just after the decision of 1954 found that three-fourths of whites deemed to be in leadership positions opposed *Brown* and that more than 30 percent opposed it contentiously. More than 40 percent opposed desegregation and thought that their communities shared their opposition, but they indicated no irrevocable commitment to segregation.[36]

[34] Don Shoemaker, ed., *With All Deliberate Speed: Segregation-Desegregation in Southern Schools* (New York, 1957), esp. Robert Lasch, "Along the Border: Desegregation at the Fringes," 56–70; Steven A. Channing, *Kentucky: A Bicentennial History* (New York, 1977), 204; *Southern School News,* September, 1954, October, 1954, December, 1954; Murray quoted in *The Ordeal of Desegregation: The First Decade,* by Reed Sarratt (New York, 1966), 3.

[35] Umstead quoted in New York *Times,* May 18, 1954; Stanley quoted *ibid.,* June 26, 1954, Platform Plank, *ibid.,* September 19, 1954.

[36] Popham quoted in New York *Times,* April 17, 1954; Amicus Curiae Brief of the Attorney General of Florida. Just after the *Brown* decision of 1954, Richard W. Ervin, the attorney general of Florida, commissioned a group of academics to look into leadership opinion in

The findings in Florida supported other more impressionistic evidence. In late 1953 Governor Gordon Persons of Alabama elicited an extensive correspondence when he wrote several hundred educators, government officials, and media representatives asking for their "views and suggestions" about the course the state should follow in the event that the Supreme Court ruled against segregation. Most white respondents balked at desegregation, some of them to the point of belligerence, but beyond that their opinions varied widely. In both Alabama and Florida, militant segregationists were most likely to be found in rural and small-town counties. Sentiment was particularly strong in the old plantation regions of southern Alabama and northern Florida.

To a south Alabama legislator, segregation was sacred: "God Almighty did not intend for the races to mix. The fowls of the air do not mix, neither do the beasts of the fields or the fishes of the sea." To a school superintendent in a north Alabama city the problem seemed not especially pressing: "We have only one negro student in our city who is 12 years old and lives with his mother who keeps house for a Cullman family. We check out a set of books to his mother's employer and she teaches him during the year and turns in the books in the Spring after having promoted him to the next grade. Therefore, we really have no local problem unless we should have a demand to admit this student to our schools." [37]

None of this dictated a harshly racist reaction to the *Brown* decision. A large majority of the Florida white leadership, having grown up with, or at least having become accustomed to, the southern caste system, approved of it, but only a minority were unyielding segregationists. Black leaders in Florida overwhelmingly welcomed the Court's decision, about a quarter of the whites accepted it at least in principle, and a majority of the segregation-

the state. Coordinated by Lewis M. Killian, a sociologist at Florida State University, the investigation included a substantial mail survey and, later, extensive interviews. Ervin's brief reports the results.

[37] Birmingham *World*, December 25, 1963; Fred Taylor in Atlanta *Journal and Constitution*, December 27, 1953; J. W. Brassell to Gordon Persons, December 22, 1953, L. W. Yates to Gordon Persons, December 29, 1953, both in Persons Executive Papers, File 319, Alabama Department of Archives and History, Montgomery.

ists were not inclined to oppose it actively. Many of Governor Persons' correspondents from north Alabama seemed to regard desegregation as a south Alabama concern and expressed resentment about being "called upon to pull the Black Belt's chestnuts out of the fire." [38]

Nevertheless, bitter-end segregationists had a huge political advantage. Few white southerners had any particular reason to support desegregation or anything concrete to gain from it. The popular-front liberals had held an ideological commitment to racial change, but their demise left no viable liberal counterweight to the policies of racial extremism. The small number of white neo-populists who continued to win elections during the 1950s favored enfranchisement and broad citizenship rights for the disadvantaged, both white and black, but the growing preoccupation with issues of race divided their amorphous and disorganized following. Black southerners opposed segregationist fanaticism, but few of them could vote, and black elites were divided, politically anemic, and not always resolute. Neither populists nor African Americans in the 1950s offered effective resistance to the tide rising against desegregation.

Opposition to racial extremism fell largely to business-oriented southern moderates. In late 1953 Governor Frank G. Clement stated, "The public schools of Tennessee have been operating since the first flat boat came in, and the public schools will continue to operate for the benefit of all the people." The New York Times quoted Clement's statement as evidence of southern "moderation." In the wake of the Brown decision, some predominantly white school districts in western Texas and two districts in western Arkansas voluntarily desegregated, but in the main anything short of rabid resistance came to count as moderate. As a result, racial conservatives structured the debate and set the direction of policy.[39]

Uncompromising segregationists were also strategically situated in southern politics. The study in Florida disclosed that, of

[38] J. L. Meeks, Jr., et al. to Gordon Persons, December 24, 1953, in Persons Executive Papers, File 319.

[39] Clement quoted in New York Times, December 14, 1953; New South, April–May, 1954, June–July, 1954; Southern School News, September, 1954, October, 1954.

the groups polled, law-enforcement officials felt the strongest allegiance to white supremacy and harbored the direst expectations
of violence if desegregation were attempted in their communities.
A survey of county sheriffs and police chiefs in North Carolina
revealed similar attitudes and apprehensions. State legislatures
tended to include a disproportionate number of hard-line segregationists. As an Alabama legislator informed Governor Persons,
"I will never agree to or accept any breakdown in segregation."[40]

In part, the sentiment in favor of white supremacy reigned in
state legislatures because of the overrepresentation of rural areas,
particularly the plantation counties. In Florida a majority of the
legislature represented one-eighth of the population, and in Alabama, Georgia, Oklahoma, and Tennessee, Malcolm E. Jewell has
calculated, a "majority of the legislators could be elected by about
one-fourth of the population." The least imbalanced general assemblies met in Arkansas, Kentucky, and Virginia, where rural
dwellers had only twice the representation of urbanites. "In these
legislative bear pits," Harry S. Ashmore of the *Arkansas Gazette*
observed, "the Southern political system has reached its lowest
ebb."[41]

The minimum foundation programs for school districts—ar-
guably the most important modernizing projects of the era—were
also bulwarks against desegregation. They tempted black leaders
to accept separation in exchange for equal facilities. Through
most of the region, both black and rural white students increasingly found themselves being bused to consolidated schools with
indoor toilets, drinking fountains, cafeterias, gymnasiums, and
specially equipped classrooms for science, agriculture, and home
economics. Teachers were being better trained and more adequately paid. As in Promiseland, why should blacks or indeed the
masses in general want more?

Governor Robert F. Kennon of Louisiana ventured the opinion
in 1954 that "building equal facilities for both races largely will

[40] Amicus Curiae Brief of the Attorney General of Florida, 28; *Southern School News*, December, 1954; Amicus Curiae Brief of the Attorney General of North Carolina; J. W.
Springer, Sr., to Gordon Persons, January 5, 1954, in Persons Executive Papers, File 319.

[41] Malcolm E. Jewell, "State Legislatures in Southern Politics," *Journal of Politics*, XXVI
(1964), 178; Ashmore, *An Epitaph for Dixie*, 111.

solve problems brought about by the Supreme Court decision." Governor Luther H. Hodges of North Carolina championed a "dual system of schools in which the children of each race voluntarily attend separate schools." Perhaps because minimum foundation programs brought increased funding to the schools, white educators were especially optimistic about voluntary arrangements. "If equal facilities are provided, based on careful districting," a county school superintendent informed Governor Persons, "there will be very little trouble maintaining separate schools." The veiled threat was that desegregation would provoke antiblack violence and encourage whites to abandon the public schools altogether.[42]

The enthusiasm for voluntary plans was consistent with the social perception of much of the white leadership. "White leaders believe Negroes to be much more satisfied with segregation than Negroes are," the leadership study in Florida reported, "and Negro leaders believe that whites are much more willing to accept desegregation gracefully than whites proved to be." Historian William H. Chafe was also no doubt correct when he suggested that North Carolina's voluntary plan rested at bottom on the "larger truth that whites could not conceive of any blacks questioning a white view of reality." Improved public facilities did damp black demands for desegregation, but black leaders consistently refused to accept the principle of voluntarism. When Governor Stanley privately convened a meeting of black leaders in Virginia in the spring of 1954, they smartly rebuffed his appeal for a continuation of public-school segregation along voluntary lines.[43]

Voluntarism was most directly tested in Mississippi. Shortly after the Court's decision in 1954, Governor Hugh L. White called a biracial conference, to which he invited almost a hundred African-American leaders. In preparation, officials in White's administration conferred with some of the participating blacks, offering full implementation of the state's school-equalization program in ex-

[42] Kennon and Hodges quoted in *The Ordeal of Desegregation*, by Sarratt, 5–6; O. C. Weaver to Gordon Persons, December 22, 1953, in Persons Executive Papers, File 319.

[43] Amicus Curiae Brief of the Attorney General of Florida, 111; William H. Chafe, *Civilities and Civil Rights: Greensboro, North Carolina, and the Black Struggle for Freedom* (New York, 1981), 54; New York *Times*, June 26, 1954.

change for a voluntary acceptance of segregation. A number of accommodationists were receptive to the bargain. Prior to the conference, however, more militant blacks led a drive to reject the agreement. When the meeting took place in July, T. R. M. Howard, the president of the Regional Council of Negro Leadership, spoke for most of the other black participants when he insisted on "strict observance of the Supreme Court's integration order." An embarrassed Hugh White, mumbling about the untrustworthiness of modern Negroes, called a special legislative session to prepare the way for a constitutional amendment that would let the state eliminate its public-school system.[44]

The biracial conference in Mississippi compressed the general trend in the evolution of black leadership during the decade and a half after World War II. The old-style conservatives whose influence rested on their talent for wringing modest concessions from the white power structure in exchange for accommodating it declined throughout the region, although next to the precipitous collapse of the labor militants their decline seemed gradual. The rising expectations of black southerners were hospitable to a more diverse leadership.[45]

The NAACP was by far the best known and most prestigious of black organizations, and certainly it was the one most despised by white southern segregationists. The association's judicial victories

[44] Howard quoted in *Southern School News*, September, 1954; James W. Silver, *Mississippi: The Closed Society* (Rev. ed., New York, 1966), 88–89.

[45] Helpful works on southern black leadership and strategy include Daniel C. Thompson's *The Negro Leadership Class* (Englewood Cliffs, N.J., 1963); Everett Carll Ladd, Jr.'s *Negro Political Leadership in the South* (Ithaca, N.Y., 1966); William R. Keech's *The Impact of Negro Voting: The Role of the Vote in the Quest for Equality* (Chicago, 1968); Harry Holloway's *The Politics of the Southern Negro: From Exclusion to Big City Organization* (New York, 1969); M. Elaine Burgess' *Negro Leadership in a Southern City* (Chapel Hill, N.C., 1962); Donald R. Matthews and James W. Prothro's *Negroes and the New Southern Politics* (New York, 1966); Louis E. Lomax' *The Negro Revolt* (New York, 1963); James Q. Wilson's *Negro Politics: The Search for Leadership* (Glencoe, Ill., 1960); Jacquelyne Johnson Clarke's *These Rights They Seek: A Comparison of the Goals and Techniques of Local Civil Rights Organizations* (Washington, D.C., 1962); Hugh D. Price's *The Negro and Southern Politics: A Chapter of Florida History* (New York, 1957); Doug McAdam's *Political Process and the Development of Black Insurgency, 1930–1970* (Chicago, 1982); Chafe's *Civilities and Civil Rights; Martin Luther King, Jr.: Civil Rights Leader, Theologian, Orator*, ed. David J. Garrow (3 vols.; Brooklyn, 1989); and Aldon D. Morris' *The Origins of the Civil Rights Movement: Black Communities Organizing for Change* (New York, 1984).

in cases involving voting, public transportation, and education had undermined—at least in the abstract—much of the legal foundation for de jure segregation. After *Brown*, the state governments in the South waged a sustained attack on the organization. "The other side is stopping at nothing," Roy Wilkins, the executive secretary of the NAACP, complained. During the late fifties, the NAACP had to invest considerable time and effort simply in protecting itself from state harassment.[46]

The *Brown* decision focused the NAACP's attention on school desegregation. "The principal task before any community," Roy Wilkins stated, "is the abolition of segregated schools." To a growing body of critics, the NAACP's preoccupation was both "too legal" and too narrow. "School desegregation does not involve the Negro masses," Louis E. Lomax objected, lamenting the way a concentration upon it "suggests that relief for those Negroes not attending school is to be delayed or less emphasized as of now." The NAACP's executive corps struck Lillian E. Smith as simply too bourgeois. It was as if the most "urgent question" before NAACP officials was, as she put it, "How soon can we get every Negro into a gray flannel suit and traveling down the middle of the road shoulder to shoulder with all the other gray flannel suits?"[47]

To moderate black community leaders, the commitment of the NAACP's headquarters to desegregation was too inflexible. Many of these leaders favored desegregation, but they usually chose to negotiate with rather than to confront the local white establishment, and desegregation was not necessarily their most urgent objective. Even if the NAACP and its liberal allies tended to rank school desegregation above all else, many blacks in the South were more intent on improved government services, better job opportunities, fairer law enforcement, and the like. As a critic of the NAACP's orientation stated, "It does not matter where a person is to sit on a train if he is not going anywhere. It does not matter

[46] Roy Wilkins to E. Frederick Morrow, December 2, 1955, in E. Frederick Morrow Papers, Dwight D. Eisenhower Library, Abilene, Kans.; Numan V. Bartley, *The Rise of Massive Resistance: Race and Politics in the South During the 1950s* (Baton Rouge, 1969), 190–236.

[47] Lomax, *The Negro Revolt*, 112–32, p. 123, Wilkins quoted, p. 126 quoted; Lillian E. Smith, "Negroes in Gray Flannel Suits," *Progressive*, February, 1956, p. 34.

what high school a person is to attend if he is going to drop out anyway." [48]

The hostility of white officialdom and the perceived narrowness of the NAACP's strategy combined with internal restraints to encumber the organization. The hierarchical and bureaucratic structure that served the association well when implementing national desegregation strategy also contributed to its inflexibility when attending to local problems. Headed nationally by lawyers, oriented toward the federal courts, and committed to a program of civil rights and particularly public-school desegregation, the NAACP was ill constituted to respond to the problems closest to black communities in a rapidly changing region. In the early 1950s, a majority of the NAACP's local branches and almost half its membership was southern. Thereafter the organization's regional presence deteriorated. [49]

The gradual expansion of the black electorate augmented the influence of politically-oriented leaders. With the decision in *Smith* v. *Allwright* in 1944, voting by African Americans surged. The Southern Regional Council estimated that almost 600,000 blacks were registered to vote in the former Confederate states in 1947, and more than 1 million in 1952. Its estimates, however, were nothing more than that. Record keeping and registration procedures varied from community to community. In 1949 Governor James E. Folsom, who wished to expand black voter participation, had little success in determining the number of blacks already registered in Alabama. With governors in the dark about the composition of their state's electorates, agencies—whether private, like the Southern Regional Council, or public, like the United States Commission on Civil Rights—could do little but make informed guesses. The evidence suggests that the council exaggerated black registration. Even those African Americans who managed to get their names on the registration rolls often did not vote

[48] John P. Frank, "Legal Developments in Race Relations, 1945–1962," in *Change in the Contemporary South*, ed. Allan P. Sindler (Durham, N.C., 1963), 85; Matthews and Prothro, *Negroes and the New Southern Politics*, 175–200; Amicus Curiae Brief of the Attorney General of Florida.

[49] Morris, *The Origins of the Civil Rights Movement*, 33–34, 120–27; Lomax, *The Negro Revolt*, 112–32.

regularly, and after 1952 the growth of black registration slowed. The Southern Regional Council estimated that African-American registration grew from approximately 1 million in 1952 to 1.4 million, or 28 percent of the potential black electorate, in 1960.[50]

Nowhere in the region did black voting have a decisive impact in state politics prior to the 1960s. In a typical southern state, blacks amounted to less than 10 percent of the registered electorate, and the black turnout was probably still less. Six states— Arkansas, Florida, Georgia, Louisiana, South Carolina, and Virginia—compiled "official" voter-registration figures that showed black registration in 1958 ranging from 9 percent of the total in Florida to 14 percent in Louisiana. In the presidential elections of 1952, 1956, and 1960, black voters cast 6 percent of the southern ballots. African Americans were beginning to hold local offices, but black elected officials were unknown at the state level.[51]

Nine of the thirteen southern states continued to enforce disfranchisement laws, and all five of the states of the Deep South enacted new ones to suppress black voting. As a prominent state legislator explained, there was a dangerous "trend in Alabama at the present time toward turning government over to the masses." At the end of the fifties, Alabama, Georgia, Louisiana, Mississippi, North Carolina, South Carolina, and Virginia all required literacy tests for registration, and Alabama, Arkansas, Mississippi, Texas, and Virginia collected poll taxes. Florida, Kentucky, Oklahoma, and Tennessee offered no official impediments to registration.[52]

Local conditions also strongly influenced the nature and extent

[50] Margaret Price, *The Negro Voter in the South* (Southern Regional Council, 1957); Margaret Price, *The Negro and the Ballot in the South* (Southern Regional Council, 1959); "1960 Voter Registration Statistics," in Southern Regional Council Papers, Atlanta University Center; Vernon J. Parenton and Roland J. Pellegrin, "Social Structure and Leadership Factor in a Negro Community," *Phylon*, XVII (1956), 74–78; "Survey Results," in Governor James E. Folsom Executive Papers, File 248, Alabama Department of Archives and History.

[51] *Report of the United States Commission on Civil Rights, 1959*, 19–146; Price, *The Negro and the Ballot;* Earl Black and Merle Black, *The Vital South: How Presidents Are Elected* (Cambridge, Mass., 1992), 191, 215.

[52] Pat Watters and Reese Cleghorn, *Climbing Jacob's Ladder: The Arrival of Negroes in Southern Politics* (New York, 1967), 121–24; Matthews and Prothro, *Negroes and the New Southern Politics*, 152–56; *Report of the United States Commission on Civil Rights, 1959*, 19–146; *Voting: 1961 Commission on Civil Rights Report;* W. C. Givhan to G. T. McCorvey, February 24, 1949, in Frank Murray Dixon Papers, Alabama Department of Archives and History.

of black political participation. Gunnar Myrdal had written in 1944 that "the disfranchisement of Negroes is losing its entire legal foundation and now depends mainly on illegal measures." Myrdal's observation gained greater validity in the postwar years. African Americans in plantation counties were unlikely to vote, while blacks in many southern cities participated in electoral politics with little overt interference. Despite the notable efforts by Georgia's politicians to safeguard the voting booths, African Americans in Atlanta cast ballots without apparent difficulty.[53]

In numerous cities, the black vote mattered and there were often effective black political organizations. The Atlanta Negro Voters League provided essential support for Mayor William B. Hartsfield and helped elect, and almost reelect, Helen Douglas Mankin, a white liberal, to the United States House of Representatives. The Durham Committee on Negro Affairs, the Greensboro Citizens Committee, and the Houston Council of Organizations could not be ignored in their cities. Black voters were indispensable for the election of Mayor Edmund Orgill in Memphis, the election and reelection of Mayor Ben West in Nashville, and the reelection of Mayor Marshall Kurfees in Winston-Salem. In these and other cities the black vote was a significant factor in urban public affairs.[54]

Elsewhere potential black voters faced formidable obstacles. In some cities, black activists struggled simply to get black citizens on the registration rolls. Particularly in smaller cities and towns, the white leadership sometimes co-opted the emerging black electorate. "Hell," a Florida county judge told investigators, "the federals are interested only when you try to keep the colored from voting, and we're voting them to the hilt." The fact that black political

[53] Gunnar Myrdal, *An American Dilemma: The Negro Problem and Modern Democracy* (New York, 1944), 518.

[54] Jack L. Walker, "Protest and Negotiation: A Study of Political Leaders in a Southern City" (Ph.D. dissertation, State University of Iowa, 1963), 40–58; Lorraine Nelson Spritzer, *The Belle of Ashby Street: A Political Biography of Helen Douglas Mankin* (Athens, Ga., 1982), 64–130; Keech, *The Impact of Negro Voting,* 24–39; Chafe, *Civilities and Civil Rights,* 20–28; Holloway, *The Politics of the Southern Negro,* 188–309; David M. Tucker, *Memphis Since Crump: Bossism, Blacks, and Civic Reformers, 1948–1968* (Knoxville, Tenn., 1980), 61–78; Don H. Doyle, *Nashville Since the 1920s* (Knoxville, Tenn., 1985), 222–30; Ladd, *Negro Political Leadership in the South,* 65–110.

organizations often insisted on receiving campaign "expense money" before endorsing a white candidate furthered the influence of well-endowed white political factions.[55]

Such widely varied local conditions facilitated the rise of black political leaders who might best be termed "racial diplomats." Normally pragmatic in decision making and moderate in policy, these politicians specialized in mobilizing and organizing black voters and in negotiating with white elites. Unlike the Uncle Tom accommodationists, racial diplomats did not accept segregation—at least in principle. Unlike the popular-front labor liberals, they were oriented toward the black business and professional middle class. Unlike the NAACP's central leadership, they were flexible in welcoming improved even if segregated facilities. During the forties and fifties, the racial diplomats not infrequently endorsed local bond issues to upgrade education, health, and social services—which usually meant allying with whites who wanted to equalize separate facilities.[56]

In more socially conservative areas, the results of racial diplomacy were modest. Even when black voter turnout was high, a "manipulated Negro vote" did little more than reinforce existing political power structures in exchange for fairer, less hostile law enforcement and a degree of respect—at least, as an Arkansas journalist wrote, "in the private places where campaign strategy is plotted." Mannerly deputy sheriffs were not a gain to be made light of, and the very existence of a significant black electorate discouraged the more outrageous gestures of racial supremacy. In a manipulated Texas county, a candidate for sheriff campaigned on the taunt that he did not want the "nigger vote"; he did not get it, and he did not win.[57]

[55] Alfred Clubok, John DeGrove, and Charles Farris, "The Manipulated Negro Vote: Some Preconditions and Consequences" in *The American South in the 1960s*, ed. Avery Leiserson (New York, 1964), 112–29, p. 117 quoted; James R. Soukup, Clifton McCleskey, and Harry Holloway, *Party and Factional Division in Texas* (Austin, Tex., 1964), 108–26; Thomas W. Madron, "Some Notes on the Negro as a Voter in a Small Southern City," *Public Opinion Quarterly*, XXX (1966), 279–84; Watters and Cleghorn, *Climbing Jacob's Ladder*, 331–58.

[56] The term *racial diplomat* is from Thompson's *The Negro Leadership Class*, esp. 68–70.

[57] Ashmore, *An Epitaph for Dixie*, 23; Clubok, DeGrove, and Farris, "The Manipulated Negro Vote"; Holloway, *The Politics of the Southern Negro*, 119–51; Watters and Cleghorn, *Climbing Jacob's Ladder*, 331–58.

In more progressive southern cities, black political participation frequently produced discernible if still limited rewards. Blacks joined southern police departments, though the new officers patrolled only black neighborhoods and were usually not empowered to arrest whites. In 1947 the Southern Regional Council counted 221 black policemen and 7 black policewomen in 41 cities in 10 southern states. By 1954, it could tally a thousand black officers in 150 cities and 22 counties. The desegregation of municipal golf courses, parks, and other peripheral public facilities was well under way by the midfifties, and 24 cities no longer required segregated seating on urban buses. Occasionally medical, bar, and other professional organizations admitted black members.[58]

Black voters in city after city elected the first African American to hold public office in the twentieth century. John N. Popham reported that at the time of the *Brown* decision in 1954 African Americans served on eleven city councils in the South and on fifteen boards of education. The appointment of African Americans to official commissions, committees, and panels was almost a commonplace where blacks held significant political power. After *Brown* the flaring of racial antagonisms put a brake on both the election and the appointment of blacks to office.[59]

The emergence of a substantial black electorate resulted in a broader range of voting coalitions. Most frequently, black racial diplomats entered into alliances with the central-city business leadership, thereby joining the poorest people, the inner-city blacks, with the most affluent people, the business and professional white urbanites. This coalition encouraged racial moderation by the white establishment, but everywhere blacks were the junior partners in the coalition.

Black voters had less leverage in state politics. Malapportionment limited metropolitan influence, and state candidates, even

[58] "Negro Police in Southern Cities," *New South*, October, 1947, pp. 1–6; Elliott M. Rudwick, *The Unequal Badge: Negro Policement in the South* (Southern Regional Council, 1962); John N. Popham, "The Southern Negro: Change and Paradox," *New York Times Magazine*, December 1, 1957, 27ff. From 1954 on, such developments can best be followed in *Southern School News*, published monthly by the Southern Education Reporting Service.

[59] Popham, "The Southern Negro," 27ff.

175

those of relatively progressive inclinations, usually chose to protect their right flank. A white candidate who did well in black precincts during a first primary faced the risk of being labeled the "bloc vote" candidate or worse in the runoff. The black political leadership sometimes found itself endeavoring to divide the African-American vote in the first election and then to unite it behind a favored candidate in the second primary.[60]

The racial diplomats who negotiated these treacherous currents often demonstrated considerable political skill, but their goals were usually modest. Their solicitude for the needs of the black middle class facilitated alliances between inner-city ghettos and outlying enclaves of wealth and smoothed relationships with central-city business interests, but it also circumscribed their political agenda. It was not entirely a coincidence that as a rule one of the first public facilities in a city to desegregate was the municipal golf course. As Daniel C. Thompson has noted, racial diplomacy mainly served to accomplish "racial uplift in the framework of a biracial system." During the fifties the per capita income of black southerners declined relative to that of whites. Central-city development programs, especially expressway and slum-clearance projects, fractured neighborhoods already under strain from the influx of rural blacks. In day-to-day texture, the lives of ordinary black people changed relatively little, except perhaps for the worse. Martin Luther King, Sr., who had been active in the Atlanta Voters' League, reminisced about the 1950s: "The battles of the Negro middle class had separated from those of the poor, and the groups seemed to be drifting in different directions."[61]

The bus boycotts of the mid-1950s attracted broader support. In Baton Rouge, Montgomery, Tallahassee, and Rock Hill, South Carolina, black communities refused to patronize city transit systems. All the boycotts took place in the lower South in midsized (Baton Rouge and Montgomery) or small (Tallahassee and Rock

[60] Numan V. Bartley and Hugh D. Graham, *Southern Politics and the Second Reconstruction* (Baltimore, 1975), 24–80.

[61] Thompson, *The Negro Leadership Class*, 69; Martin Luther King, Sr., *Daddy King: An Autobiography* (New York, 1980), 135; Vivian W. Henderson, *The Economic Status of Negroes: In the Nation and in the South* (Southern Regional Council, n.d.); James D. Cowhig and Calvin L. Beale, "Relative Socioeconomic Status of Whites and Nonwhites, 1950 and 1960," *Southwestern Social Science Quarterly*, XLV (1964), 113–24.

Hill) cities. They were not in any direct sense protests against the slow pace of desegregation. Blacks initially demanded not integration but fair treatment on the bus lines. A Montgomery Women's Political Council leaflet explained that even within a segregated society "Negroes have rights, too." In every case black communities resisted the humiliating treatment that was routine for black passengers. In Montgomery, Tallahassee, and Rock Hill, the spark that lit the indignation was a bus driver's requiring a black woman to stand so that a white could occupy her bus seat.[62]

The boycotts elevated new people into leadership. In all four cities, black voter registration was low, black political influence limited, and the existing black leadership accommodationist or at any rate undemanding. To unify blacks and orchestrate their action, boycott leaders formed umbrella organizations that included diverse segments of the black communities. As Lewis Killian and Charles Grigg have remarked, the boycott in Tallahassee brought about "a change, not a split, in leadership" by replacing accommodationists with protest leaders. Black ministers were particularly prominent in the new leadership, and black churches served as the organizing centers for protest.[63]

The first of the boycotts occurred in Baton Rouge in June, 1953. As in other southern cities, black citizens were tired, Theodore J. Jemison explained, of being "molested and insulted and intimidated" on the buses. In the spring of 1953, some African Americans petitioned the city council to establish a first-come-first-seated principle, with blacks taking seats from the back of the bus and whites from the front. Wedded to economic growth, Baton Rouge's city government had already demonstrated less rigidity in racial matters than was typical for the region, and it consented to the petition. When the bus drivers declared a strike over the council's decision, however, Louisiana officials insisted that state seg-

---

[62] David J. Garrow, ed., *The Montgomery Bus Boycott and the Women Who Started It: The Memoir of Jo Ann Gibson Robinson* (Knoxville, Tenn., 1987), 45; August Meier and Elliott Rudwick, "The Origins of Nonviolent Direct Action in Afro-American Protest: A Note on Historical Discontinuities," in *Along the Color Line: Explorations in the Black Experience,* by August Meier and Elliott Rudwick (Urbana, Ill., 1976), 307–404; Morris, *The Origins of the Civil Rights Movement,* 17–76.

[63] Lewis Killian and Charles Grigg, *Racial Crisis in America: Leadership in Conflict* (Englewood Cliffs, N.J., 1964), 86.

regation laws be enforced. At that point, the black community began a boycott.[64]

The protest lasted only a week, but it set a pattern for other boycotts. The United Defense League, led by Theodore Jemison, brought together representatives from divers black groups. The church served as the link between leaders and followers, mass church meetings helped build morale, and church collections raised money for the protest. Jemison, who was pastor of the large Mount Zion Baptist Church, and his associates organized a free transportation service that picked up passengers at designated street corners. The boycott ended when the negotiators satisfied state segregation laws by reserving the back row of seats for blacks and the frontmost seats for whites. "The Baton Rouge boycott," Aldon D. Morris has written, "was a mass, church-based, direct-action movement guided by a new organization of organizations."[65]

Vastly more publicized were the events in Montgomery between December, 1955, and December, 1956. Rosa Parks, a seamstress and an active member of the NAACP, refused to surrender her seat to a white passenger as a bus driver had commanded. Parks's arrest for violating a segregation ordinance brought to a head a long series of incidents on the bus line. Edgar D. Nixon, who was head of the Montgomery Brotherhood of Sleeping Car Porters and a longtime proponent of black rights, and Jo Ann Robinson, a leader of the Women's Political Council, began independent preparations for a boycott of the buses. They joined forces with the formation of the Montgomery Improvement Association, under the guidance of Martin Luther King, Jr. The Montgomery Improvement Association implemented on a larger scale the tactics the United Defense League had employed in Baton Rouge. Mass meetings at black churches sustained morale, collected money for car lifts, and coordinated community action.[66]

[64] Morris, *The Origins of the Civil Rights Movement,* 17–25, p. 17 Jemison quoted.
[65] Ibid., 24.
[66] Helpful works dealing with the Montgomery boycott include *The Montgomery Bus Boycott and the Women Who Started It: The Memoir of Jo Ann Gibson Robinson;* Martin Luther King, Jr.'s *Stride Toward Freedom: The Montgomery Story* (New York, 1958); L. D. Reddick's "The Bus Boycott in Montgomery," *Dissent,* III (1956), 107–17; J. Mills Thornton III's "Challenge

The discipline and dignity of blacks, the nonviolent philosophy that King developed and articulated during the protest, and King's charismatic leadership captured the imagination of journalists and national liberals. The sometimes devious, sometimes bullying, and always inept white leadership in Montgomery lent contrast and drama. Alone among boycott organizations, the Montgomery Improvement Association received major financial contributions from outside the region as liberal and religious groups in northern and western cities raised money to support the movement.[67]

Montgomery blacks vowed to continue the boycott until city officials agreed to three conditions. The protesters wanted courteous treatment from drivers, the employment of black drivers on predominantly black routes, and the "right, under segregation, to seat ourselves from the rear forward on a first come, first served basis," with no one having to give up seats to new passengers. Montgomery's elected leadership—Mayor William A. Gayle and two commissioners—at first chose to negotiate. The bus company, headquartered in Chicago, refused to modify its policies or to hire black drivers, and city officials were reluctant to appear lacking in segregationist sentiment. The negotiations went nowhere.[68]

In January, Gayle and his commissioners met secretly with three old-line African-American accommodationists who were amenable to an agreement that left most of the company's policies intact. The Montgomery Improvement Association repudiated the pact, and the three black clergymen, feeling the ire of the black community, maintained that they had been tricked into signing, thereby accusing white city officials of deception if not outright fraud. Gayle and the commissioners broke off negotiations, joined the segregationist Citizens' Council, and set about to break the

---

and Response in the Montgomery Bus Boycott of 1955–1956," *Alabama Review*, XXXIII (1980), 165–235; Norman W. Walton's "The Walking City: A History of the Montgomery Bus Boycott," *Negro History Bulletin*, XX (1956–57), 17–21, 27–33, 102–104, 147–52; *The Walking City: The Montgomery Bus Boycott, 1955–1956*, ed. David J. Garrow (Brooklyn, 1989).

[67] Richard Lentz, *Symbols, the News Magazines, and Martin Luther King* (Baton Rouge, 1990), 21–41; David J. Garrow, *Bearing the Cross: Martin Luther King, Jr., and the Southern Christian Leadership Conference* (New York, 1986), 11–82.

[68] Martin Luther King, Jr., "Our Struggle," *Liberation*, April, 1956, p. 4.

boycott. Their get-tough policy continued through most of 1956. The city police attempted to destroy the car lift service by what one observer described as a campaign of "wholesale arrests and harassment." In February a county grand jury indicted leaders of the boycott for conspiracy, and eighty-nine were arrested, although only Martin Luther King was taken to trial. Some whites turned to violence, bombing King's home and perpetrating other incidents. The Montgomery Improvement Association struck back by turning from its original goal of fair treatment "under segregation" to mount a challenge in federal district court against the constitutionality of bus segregation. A three-judge panel ruled against Jim Crow seating arrangements, and in November, 1956, the United States Supreme Court upheld the district court's ruling. Shortly afterward the boycott ended and the buses desegregated.[69]

Some six months after Rosa Parks decided not to surrender her seat, two black women who were students at the Florida Agricultural and Mechanical University were similarly defiant on a crowded bus in Tallahassee. Upon their arrest, their fellow students undertook not to ride the buses for the remainder of the academic year. Immediately afterward the Tallahassee black community organized the Inter Civic Council, headed by Charles K. Steele. The white Tallahassee leadership met with a group of less militant African Americans and agreed to the conditions that the boycott leaders in Montgomery had originally set as their goal: courtesy on the part of bus drivers, the employment of black drivers on predominantly black routes, and seating arrangements on a first-come basis with a few seats at the front reserved for whites. The Inter Civic Council rejected the agreement and called for nothing less than complete desegregation. The police, like those in Montgomery, attempted to shut down the car lift and arrested the boycott leaders as well as a number of drivers.

The Supreme Court's decision invalidating bus segregation in Montgomery seemed to resolve the issue. The Inter Civic Council announced that blacks would resume riding the buses, and the

[69] Reddick, "The Bus Boycott in Montgomery," 115; *Browder* v. *Gayle*, in *Race Relations Law Reporter*, I, 678.

city transit company readily agreed to integrated seating. The city government, however, refused to capitulate. Mayor John Y. Humpress and the city commission suspended the transit company's franchise, and police arrested nine bus drivers for permitting mixed seating. In early 1957 the commissioners passed an ordinance requiring drivers to assign bus seats to protect the "health, safety and welfare" of passengers. When several black and white college students tested the new ordinance, they were arrested. Gradually the parties to the conflict arrived at a tacit compromise according to which the buses on predominantly white routes remained segregated and those on predominantly black routes were desegregated. The boycott continued sporadically until the spring of 1958.[70]

The Rock Hill boycott began in July, 1957. C. A. Ivory, a Presbyterian minister, led the campaign. The transit company responded by dropping the routes through the black sections and attempting to operate with white patronage alone. The tactic failed, and in January, 1958, the bus company ceased operations. Occurring during the school desegregation crisis in Little Rock, the trouble in Rock Hill attracted little outside attention. Similarly, large-scale boycotts of white businesses in Orangeburg, South Carolina, and Tuskegee, Alabama, created hardships for marginal enterprises but had a limited impact on civic leaders.[71]

The boycotts of the mid-1950s constituted a transitional stage in the black struggle for equality. In some ways, the bus boycotts represented a final resurgence of the old order rather than the inauguration of a new one. The campaigns were passive, not requiring blacks to confront whites but simply requiring them not to ride buses. They presupposed cohesive black communities, something increasingly rare in the mushrooming black ghettos. It was perhaps unsurprising that the one bus boycott attempted in a major southern metropolis—Birmingham, in 1958—was unsuc-

[70] Tom R. Wagy, *Governor LeRoy Collins of Florida, Spokesman of the New South* (University, Ala., 1985), 78; Charles U. Smith and Lewis M. Killian, *The Tallahassee Bus Boycott* (New York, 1958); Lewis M. Killian and Charles U. Smith, "Negro Protest Leaders in a Southern Community," *Social Forces,* XXXVIII (1960), 253–62.

[71] *Southern School News,* July, 1957, January, 1958; Meier and Rudwick, "The Origins of Nonviolent Direct Action in Afro-American Protest," 363–70.

cessful. The boycotts united members of black communities across class lines more effectively than any other protests of the era, and in every case black communities resisted putatively unwarranted white incursions. Rather than being revolts against the system, the boycotts initially had to do with fair treatment within a segregated society. Rather than deliberately rejecting the NAACP's gradualist policies, the leaders of the protests created new umbrella organizations in part to distance themselves from the association's "radicalism."[72]

At the same time the boycotts did broach a new black militancy. August Meier and Elliott Rudwick have written that the Montgomery "campaign itself—and, more important, the charismatic leader it produced—made an extraordinary impression on Afro-Americans around the country." Martin Luther King declared that the boycott demonstrated a "revolutionary change in the Negro's evaluation of himself." The boycotts elevated clergymen, whose all-black churches were beyond white control, and hastened the decline of educators and other blacks who were dependent on the goodwill of whites. They focused attention on southern racial practices; a study of Gallup poll data found that the civil rights issue "was virtually unrecognized as a problem area" prior to the bus boycott in Montgomery. Journalist Pat Watters observed that "all over the South Negroes were forming organizations in imitation of the Montgomery Improvement Association."[73]

The Southern Christian Leadership Conference united many of the black protest organizations. King and Steele, along with Fred L. Shuttlesworth of the Birmingham-based Alabama Christian Movement for Human Rights, issued "A Call to Attend a Southwide Conference on Discrimination in Transportation." Bayard Rustin, Ella J. Baker, and Stanley D. Levison, all New Yorkers who had formed In Friendship to raise money for and proffer

[72] Adam Fairclough, "The Preachers and the People: The Origins and Early Years of the Southern Christian Leadership Conference, 1955–1959," *Journal of Southern History*, LII (1986), 401–40.

[73] Meier and Rudwick, "The Origins of Nonviolent Direct Action in Afro-American Protest," 367; King quoted in *Bearing the Cross*, by Garrow, 81; Tom W. Smith, "America's Most Important Problem—A Trend Analysis, 1946–1976," *Public Opinion Quarterly*, XLIV (1980), 170; Pat Watters, *Down to Now: Reflections on the the Southern Civil Rights Movement* (New York, 1971), 50.

advice to King and the Montgomery movement, originated the idea for a conference. The object, in Rustin's words, was to form an "indigenous, black-led organization" that might fill the "need for a small disciplined group of non-violent volunteers" who could "inspire" community protest and encourage black voter registration. About sixty of the hundred or so people invited attended the conference held in January, 1957, in Atlanta. A larger meeting the following month in New Orleans created a permanent organization and elected King president. The group's first convention, in August, 1957, adopted the name Southern Christian Leadership Conference.[74]

The SCLC was a federation of protest groups. In addition to the organizations in Baton Rouge, Montgomery, Tallahassee, and Birmingham, SCLC affiliates included such others as the Nashville Christian Leadership Council, the Shreveport United Christian Movement, the Petersburg Improvement Association, the Louisville Non-Partisan Registration Committee, and the Western Christian Leadership of Los Angeles. The group in Los Angeles, the only nonsouthern affiliate, served as a fund-raising agency. Baptist ministers dominated the board of directors, which included one white—a cleric from Montgomery—and one woman, who was the federation's financial secretary. "Like the black church, the structure of SCLC was autocratic," Rustin explained. "I don't remember any time," Steele was to recall, "that Dr. King made a proposal that we did not accept."[75]

King had achieved international recognition while serving as president of the Montgomery Improvement Association. His oratorical blend of civil rights and biblical Christianity inspired both his followers and visiting journalists. King called for a "militant . . . mass movement" based on a philosophy of nonviolence. "We will meet your physical force with soul force," King promised whites. "In winning our freedom we will win you in the process."

[74] "Working Papers, Southern Negro Leaders Converence," January 10–11, 1957, in Southern Christian Leadership Conference Papers, Box 34, Martin Luther King, Jr., Center for Social Change, Atlanta; Adam Fairclough, *To Redeem the Soul of America: The Southern Christian Leadership Conference and Martin Luther King, Jr.* (Athens, Ga., 1987), 11–55.

[75] Bayard Rustin, *Strategies for Freedom: The Changing Patterns of Black Protest* (New York, 1976), 39; Steele quoted in *The Origins of the Civil Rights Movement*, by Morris, 93.

Race relations were "not a political but a moral issue"; much like Gunnar Myrdal in *An American Dilemma,* King pointed to the nation's "schizophrenic personality on the question of race." America "has been torn between selves—a self in which she has proudly professed democracy and a self in which she has sadly practiced the antithesis of democracy." Nonviolent resistance was a means to force a confrontation between those two selves and to awaken the "moral consciousness . . . of white Americans concerning segregation." The conflict was "between justice and injustice," King wrote in 1958, not "Negroes set against whites," and the goal was not "to defeat or humiliate the opponent, but to win his friendship and understanding."[76]

As Richard Lentz has observed, King "promised not race war but reconciliation, not hatred but love, and not revolution but reform achieved at a measured pace." It was little wonder that King appeared on the cover of *Time* magazine in February, 1957, and that he held appeal for many white northern liberals. At the same time, he was sufficiently militant to maintain his standing among blacks. At the Washington "prayer pilgrimage" in May, 1957, on the third anniversary of the *Brown* decision, King shared the rostrum with A. Philip Randolph and Roy Wilkins, thereby confirming his leadership status.[77]

Despite King's prestige, the SCLC's early years were lean ones. The bus boycotts had created hardships for blacks while accomplishing relatively little desegregation. Only in Montgomery did a boycott achieve an unambiguous victory, and there the federal courts rather than black resistance integrated the buses. Three months after the boycott ended, the Montgomery commissioners passed an ordinance making it "unlawful for white and colored persons to play together . . . in any game of cards, dice, dominoes, checkers, pool, billiards, softball, basketball, baseball, football, golf, track, and at swimming pools, beaches, lakes or ponds, or any other games." Desegregation of the buses had only exacerbated the segregationist sentiments of Montgomery's politicians. As King focused on the SCLC and in 1960 moved to Atlanta, the

[76] King, *Stride Toward Freedom: The Montgomery Story,* 102, 190, 205, 214, 217, 220.
[77] Lentz, *Symbols, the News Magazines, and Martin Luther King,* 37–38; August Meier, "On the Role of Martin Luther King" in *Martin Luther King, Jr.,* ed. Garrow, 635–42.

black leadership in Montgomery, one study has concluded, "returned, if not to its old perspective of pre-protest days, to something closely resembling it." The SCLC leadership's initial enthusiasm for a boycott movement waned.[78]

Instead, the SCLC turned to voter registration. Ella Baker of In Friendship set up the SCLC headquarters in Atlanta and launched the voter-registration "crusade for citizenship" in early 1958. Soon afterward, John L. Tilly, a Baltimore preacher with experience in such drives, became executive secretary, but his tenure was not successful, and Baker again assumed direction of the campaign. The crusade accomplished little. Inadequate funding and the organization's unwieldy structure as a federation hampered SCLC's activities, as did a growing rift between Baker and King. To Baker, King's celebrity status and his willingness to augment it induced a "cult of personality" that undermined efforts to build self-sustaining local-action groups. Relations between SCLC and the NAACP became frigid. One of the reasons King and his associates had established a federation rather than a membership organization was to avoid competition with the association. Nevertheless, the NAACP's position was that "we need only one national organization to speak for Negroes," and it announced a rival voter-registration drive. The overall result was what one scholar has referred to as the general "aimlessness" of the SCLC in the late 1950s.[79]

The inchoate spirit of protest behind both the boycott movement and the formation of the SCLC also influenced politics. Black activists demonstrated an increasing impatience with the ways of the racial diplomats. During 1957 restless African Americans in Atlanta created the Committee for Cooperative Action, which pointedly limited its membership to people under forty, to press for more rapid racial change. In Houston, the Council of Organizations, a black group, abandoned its alliance with white

[78] Ordinance No. 15–57, *Race Relations Law Reporter*, II, 714; Ralph H. Hines and James E. Pierce, "Negro Leadership After the Social Crisis: An Analysis of Leadership Changes in Montgomery, Alabama," *Phylon*, XXVI (1965), 172.

[79] Fairclough, "The Preachers and the People," 432–40; Garrow, *Bearing the Cross*, p. 98 quoted; Eugene Pierce Walker, "A History of the Southern Christian Leadership Conference, 1955–1965: The Evolution of a Southern Strategy for Social Change" (Ph.D. dissertation, Duke University, 1978), 63.

business leaders to join a coalition of labor, minority, and liberal activists. In Memphis, Russell Sugarman, Jr., Benjamin Hooks, and other prominent young African Americans denounced the coalition politics that allied blacks with "well-meaning" but "ineffectual" white civic reformers. They ran an all-black slate of candidates for the local elections in 1959. The Memphis civic reformers and their Citizens Association joined with remnants of the Crump machine to support a "white unity" ticket that won the election. The political protest evidenced the disenchantment of more militant and often younger blacks with the slow pace of social change, but as in Memphis, the revolts were normally unsuccessful.[80]

The *Brown* decision, historian Adam Fairclough has observed, "mobilized southern whites behind segregation far more effectively than it did southern blacks behind integration." Clergymen became protest leaders, but most black preachers continued to minister to their flocks much as they had always done. Politically inclined blacks registered displeasure with the racial diplomats, but the large majority of southern African Americans did not vote. The NAACP continued its struggle in the courts, but southern state governments commanded far greater resources than the NAACP, and in 1956 the former Confederate states initiated a formidable campaign to destroy the association in the region. White segregationists commanded public affairs, and they were more militant than black southerners. They termed their program "massive resistance," and it charted the direction of public affairs in the region during the second half of the 1950s.[81]

[80] Jack L. Walker, "Protest and Negotiation," 62–68; Holloway, *The Politics of the Southern Negro,* 229–309; Chandler Davidson, *Biracial Politics: Conflict and Coalition in the Metropolitan South* (Baton Rouge, 1972); Tucker, *Memphis Since Crump,* 100–117, p. 101 quoted.

[81] Fairclough, "The Preachers and the People," 418.

CHAPTER VI

RACE AND REACTION

DURING the second half of the 1950s, southern state governments truculently resisted implementation of *Brown* v. *Board of Education*. Much of the region's political leadership, and most particularly its formidable Bourbon contingent, intensified the defense of social stability. "Although the whites of the black belts are few in number," V. O. Key, Jr., had earlier written, "their unity and their political skill have enabled them to run a shoestring into decisive power at critical junctures in southern political history." The *Brown* decision presented another critical juncture, and plantation-county whites once again responded to the challenge. The absence of a politically viable liberal alternative, the irresolution of regional moderates, and the reluctant national commitment to equality strengthened the position of the segregationist extremists.[1]

Even before the *Brown* decision, the governments of several states of the lower South had taken measures adamantly hostile to school desegregation, and elsewhere in the region public officials greeted the prospect of integration with apprehension. Nevertheless, when Governor Thomas Stanley of Virginia chaired a meeting of representatives from fifteen states where segregation was public policy, unity proved elusive. Although delegates from twelve of the states voiced disagreement with the Court's decision, the conference arrived at no general plan of action. Indeed, the Richmond *News Leader* editorialized that the meeting demonstrated the impossibility of a "united approach." The Southern Governors' Conference later in the year seemed to confirm the newspaper's conclusion. The governors or governors-elect from

[1] V. O. Key, Jr., *Southern Politics in State and Nation* (New York, 1949), 6.

eight states pledged to defend state control of public schools, but representatives from Alabama, Arkansas, Kentucky, and Tennessee declined. The Court's decision in 1955 enunciating a piecemeal and gradualist implementation "with all deliberate speed" appeared to strengthen the position of the southern moderates and further to sunder regional unity.[2]

Such was the situation in November, 1955, when the Richmond *News Leader* proposed editorially "to recur to fundamental principles for guidance." *Brown* v. *Board of Education,* editor James J. Kilpatrick insisted, was not an interpretation of the Constitution. It was an illicit amendment of the document in which "nine men arrogated unto themselves powers vested by the Constitution in the people" of the states. Given "this rape of the Constitution," the *News Leader* asked, "does not Virginia have a right and a duty to interpose its sovereignty in a valiant effort to halt the evil?" In a three-month campaign for "interposition now," the *News Leader* reprinted such pre–Civil War guides "to fundamental principles" as the Kentucky and Virginia Resolutions, explained in excruciating detail the compact theory of the Union, defined interposition as the "basic right of a State to assert its sovereignty against Federal encroachments," and argued that Virginia and the rest of the South had a "duty" to interpose state sovereignty between the federal government and the people of their states. "What concerns us here," the newspaper proclaimed, "is the preservation of the constitutional structure of our Union."[3]

As constitutional doctrine, interposition was hoary. As a strategy of state action, it was of enormous consequence. It afforded a conceptual basis for total state opposition to the enforcement of the *Brown* decision. If the former Confederate states centralized authority over school enrollment in state governments and refused to comply with the desegregation decision, the thinking went, the Supreme Court would be forced to abandon its "abominable decision." *Brown* would suffer a fate similar to the prohi-

[2] Richmond *News Leader,* June 11, 1954; New York *Times,* June 11, 1954, November 14, 1954; *Southern School News,* December, 1954.

[3] Richmond *News Leader,* November 21, 1955, November 23, 1955, November 29, 1955, January 19, 1956, February 2, 1956.

bition experiment, which failed because of popular unwillingness to conform to the Eighteenth Amendment and the Volstead Act.[4]

The moderate program aimed to delay, limit, and in the main, evade the effect of the Court's decision without denying its legitimacy. During the period when it seemed that interpositionists might face down the Court, the moderate position was a crucial factor in keeping the principle of the *Brown* decision alive. The sometimes subtle distinctions between the two strategies came out in Virginia, where a sizable number of whites accepted the ruling, if reluctantly, as the "law of the land." Such views were most common in the predominantly white northern and western portions of the state and in metropolitan areas. Among antiorganization Democrats, educators, ministerial and church groups, state-level labor-union officials, and women's associations, the *Brown* decision did not always provoke hostility.[5]

Other Virginians viewed the Supreme Court ruling with antagonism. Senator Harry Flood Byrd declared his disappointment with an edict that created for Virginia a "crisis of the first magnitude," and prominent members of the Democratic organization voiced similar sentiments. "No child of any race," Attorney General J. Lindsay Almond vowed, "is going to be compelled to attend a mixed school." Former governor and southside congressman William Tuck equated a moderate "middle-of-the-roader" with a "double-crosser." The League of Virginia Counties unanimously resolved that its members were "unalterably opposed to integration in public schools," and other politically potent groups took similar actions. Governor Stanley professed his own opposition to desegregation and in August, 1954, appointed a commission on public education headed by southside state senator Garland Gray to formulate a state policy.[6]

[4] *Ibid.*, November 29, 1955.

[5] New York *Times*, May 18, 1954. Competent studies of the response by Virginia to the *Brown* decision include Benjamin Muse's *Virginia's Massive Resistance* (Bloomington, Ind., 1961); Robbins L. Gates's *The Making of Massive Resistance: Virginia's Politics of Public School Desegregation, 1954–1956* (Chapel Hill, N.C., 1964); J. Harvie Wilkinson III's *Harry Byrd and the Changing Face of Virginia Politics, 1945–1966* (Charlottesville, Va., 1968); and James W. Ely, Jr.'s *The Crisis of Conservative Virginia: The Byrd Organization and the Politics of Massive Resistance* (Knoxville, Tenn., 1976). See also Numan V. Bartley, *The Rise of Massive Resistance: Race and Politics in the South During the 1950s* (Baton Rouge, 1969).

[6] Byrd quoted by James Latimer in Richmond *Times-Dispatch*, May 18, 1954; Almond

The dynamics of Virginia politics augmented the influence of die-hard conservatives. Nowhere else in the region were county elites so fully incorporated into a Democratic party faction. As V. O. Key had noted in 1949, "The leading citizens of each community—the banker, the preacher, the lawyer, the doctor, the merchants and often the newspaper owners— . . . follow the Senator in his pursuit of New Dealers, Communists, the CIO-PAC." As events made clear, they were also to stalk *Brown v. Board of Education.* A Washington newspaper explained that in Virginia "a community's social elite is in many cases indistinguishable from its political leadership." [7]

In Key's words, Virginia was a "political museum piece." A critic lamented that "Byrd and his closest friends and advisors are Tories in the 18th century meaning of the word." The organization's "government of the gentry" favored rural areas. It gave precedence to farm-to-market roads over city streets and preferred taxes that fell hardest on affluent urban and suburban residents. Much of its leadership came from rural and particularly black belt backgrounds. A Virginia newspaper moralized, "A majority of Virginia voters favor fiscal conservatism, balanced budgets, right to work laws, Constitutional government, the rights of the States and localities to determine their educational destinies, and so on." [8]

In such matters ordinary people, whether black or white, had virtually no voice. Virginia was the least democratic state in the Union. Little more than one in ten adult citizens cast ballots in the all-important Democratic primaries. A house painter—a white—condensed the deferential nature of Virginia politics when he explained, "Colonel, you know I don't belong to the folks who vote." The folks who did vote, and those who ruled, came disproportionately from the heavily agricultural southside black belt counties. [9]

---

quoted in *Southern School News,* September, 1954; Tuck quoted in Norfolk *Virginian Pilot,* November 4, 1954; Resolution quoted in Washington *Evening Star,* October 27, 1954.

[7] Key, *Southern Politics,* 33–34; Washington *Post,* July 18, 1965.

[8] Key, *Southern Politics,* 19; Francis Pickens Miller, *Man from the Valley: Memoirs of a Twentieth-Century Virginian* (Chapel Hill, N.C., 1971), 170; William Bryan Crawley, Jr., *Bill Tuck: A Political Life in Harry Byrd's Virginia* (Charlottesville, Va., 1978), 13; Lynchburg *Daily Advance* quoted in *The Crisis of Conservative Virginia,* by Ely, 12–13.

[9] Numan V. Bartley and Hugh D. Graham, comps., *Southern Elections: County and Precinct*

At the apex of the Democratic organization was Senator Byrd. Elected governor in 1925 and appointed senator in 1933, Byrd, like many other American politicians, became more rigid in his political philosophy the longer he served. He despaired of the ever-growing power of the federal government: "Another twenty-five-year period of profligate public spending and unbelievable waste—of piling up new debts and increasing taxes, of cheapening our dollar, of continuing to destroy states' rights and concentrate greater and greater power in Washington—our country, as great as it is, can be seriously injured." Such policies, he held, diminished "self-discipline not only by the people themselves but by local and state governments," and the worst offender—the "greatest menace to free government that we have"—was the United States Supreme Court. The *Brown* decision not only made the NAACP a "fourth branch of the federal government" but created the "greatest crisis since the War Between the States." And, a Virginia journalist added, "In ordering an end to a time-honored practice in Virginia, the Supreme Court had intruded, not merely upon the rights of states, but upon the personal domain of Harry Byrd." [10]

The Gray Commission delivered its recommendations to Governor Stanley in November, 1955. Its report endorsed the main features of the local-option policy that was becoming the moderate position in the South. The Gray plan tacitly assumed the inevitability of token desegregation and placed the control of social change in the hands of local officials. At the center of its recommendations was a pupil-assignment bill that enjoined local school boards to assign individual students to schools on a "nonracial" basis that took into account the availability of transportation and classroom facilities, the academic progress, aptitude, and health of each student, and "the welfare of the particular child as well as

Data, 1950–1972 (Baton Rouge, 1978), 325–27; Miller, *Man from the Valley*, p. 169 quoted. Gates's *The Making of Massive Resistance* and Wilkinson's *Harry Byrd* are particularly good on the nature of the Byrd organization. Ely's *The Crisis of Conservative Virginia* is a perceptive analysis of the outlook and strategy of organization insiders.

[10] Byrd quoted in Richmond *Times-Dispatch*, May 3, 1958, August 31, 1958, in Washington *Post*, September 1, 1957, and in Washington *Evening Star*, October 12, 1957; Muse, *Virginia's Massive Resistance*, 26.

the welfare and best interests of all other pupils attending a particular school." The report specified that there was to be no general reassignment of pupils from segregated schools, and it fashioned an exhausting and time-consuming system of appeals for parents who objected to a child's assignment. To ensure that no children were coerced into attending desegregated schools over parental objections, the plan called for modifying compulsory attendance laws and awarding "tuition grants" when parents wished to send their children to private academies. The latter provision required an amendment to the state constitution.[11]

Hardly had the Gray Commission delivered its report when the *News Leader* launched its turn "to fundamental principles for guidance." Kilpatrick and Byrd were close friends, and the *News Leader* was a potent voice in the state. "Most of the newspapers," a small-town publisher explained, "more or less followed Kilpatrick's lead." The Byrd organization joined the *News Leader* in supporting the amendment of the state constitution to permit implementation of the Gray plan, but many within the organization clearly preferred a more militant and encompassing policy. Congressman Howard W. Smith privately lamented that the Gray plan was the "best that can be done at the present in the light of public opinion in the state." Byrd referred to the constitutional amendment as "merely a first step" on a "long and rocky" road in the "battle to preserve our public-school system," and he called for "some degree of coalition between the eleven southern states which will strengthen the position of the individual states."[12]

In January, 1956, the Virginia electorate by a two-to-one majority authorized a limited constitutional convention to amend the portion of the constitution that was an obstacle to tuition grants. Many white moderates supported the amendment as a workable means of limiting social change while complying with the Supreme Court's mandate for desegregation "with all deliberate

[11] "Report of the Commission on Public Education," in *Race Relations Law Reporter*, I, 241–47.

[12] Barrye Wall, publisher of the Farmville *Herald*, and Smith quoted in *The Crisis of Conservative Virginia*, by Ely, 14, 38; Byrd quoted in Washington *Evening Star*, December 18, 1955.

speed." The strongest opposition came from black precincts and the northern Virginia suburbs of Washington, D.C.[13]

The election returns had scarcely been counted, however, before the Richmond *News Leader* announced that the voters' approval of a constitutional convention was an endorsement of interposition. Senator Byrd viewed it as an expression of the "opposition of the people to integration." By the time the convention met in early March, the legislature had passed an interposition resolution, Byrd had issued a call for "massive resistance" to desegregation, and an all-out defense of white supremacy had become the dominant theme of Virginia politics.[14]

The Virginia general assembly overwhelmingly approved an interposition resolution in early February, 1956. State legislators pledged their "firm intention to take all appropriate measures honorably, legally and constitutionally available to us, to resist this illegal encroachment upon our sovereign powers." They also urged "upon our sister States ... their prompt and deliberate efforts to check this and further encroachment by the Supreme Court, through judicial legislation, upon the reserved powers of the States." Senator Byrd explained, "If we can organize the southern states for massive resistance to this order, I think that in time the rest of the country will realize racial integration is not going to be accepted in the South." The senator added, "In interposition the South has a perfectly legal means of appeal from the Supreme Court's order."[15]

The practical import of interposition became apparent in late summer. In July, 1956, top-level members of the organization met in Byrd's office in Washington to map strategy. Agreeing that "hardening public sentiment over the state would now support the sterner line," the participants decided that Governor Stanley should call a special legislative session and recommend a program of massive resistance. Stanley, who had originally supported the Gray plan and its acquiescence to token desegregation, soon an-

[13] Gates, *The Making of Massive Resistance,* 73–99.

[14] Richmond *News Leader,* January 10, 1956.

[15] Interposition Resolution, in *Race Relations Law Reporter,* I, 445–47; Byrd quoted in New York *Times,* February 26, 1956.

nounced, "I cannot endorse or recommend any legislation, or action, which accepts the principle of integration of the races in the public schools." The Gray Commission, rent with internal dissension, chose to retract its recommendation of local option in order to bring its proposals into alignment with the governor's position.[16]

The Virginia general assembly held a special session on massive resistance during August and September, 1956. The legislature decreed that the state would assume "direct responsibility for the control of any school, elementary or secondary, in the Commonwealth to which children of both races are assigned and enrolled by any school authorities acting voluntarily or under compulsion of any court order." In such a case, the school would close until the governor could reestablish segregation under the police powers of the state. The reasoning was that this would make the state the defendant in any suits contesting the reinstitution of segregation. Because constitutionally a state could not be sued without its consent, segregated schools would be legally protected. The special session put on record that "the Commonwealth hereby declines and refuses . . . to be subject to such a suit." The general assembly created a state-level board with the authority to assign pupils to schools and voted to terminate state funding to any school that desegregated. It also enacted the non-local-option measures recommended by the Gray Commission and laid the legislative basis for a concerted attack on the National Association for the Advancement of Colored People. By the time the special session adjourned, the issue of school desegregation pitted the sovereignty of the commonwealth against the authority of the federal judiciary. "The attempted and illegal federal dictation is the most drastic since Reconstruction," Senator Byrd orated, "and it has therefore to be resisted as drastically."[17]

The doctrine of interposition spread through the former Confederacy. During early 1956 legislatures in five other states— Alabama, Georgia, Louisiana, Mississippi, and South Carolina—

[16] Stanley quoted in Richmond *Times-Dispatch*, July 24, 1956; Muse, *Virginia's Massive Resistance*, 28; Washington *Evening Star*, August 23, 1956.

[17] *Race Relations Law Reporter*, I, 1091–1113, pp. 1104, 1106 quoted, II, 1015–26; Byrd quoted in Richmond *News Leader*, September 26, 1956.

approved interposition resolutions. Members of the general assemblies in Alabama, Georgia, and Mississippi, later joined by those in Florida, carried the doctrine to its logical conclusion by pronouncing *Brown* null and void. The legislators of Mississippi not only declared the federal judiciary's "usurpation of power" to be "unconstitutional, invalid and of no lawful effect within the confines of the State of Mississippi" but in "An Act to Give Effect to the Resolution of Interposition" commanded public employees at both the state and local levels "to prohibit . . . the implementation or the compliance with the Integration Decision."[18]

In July, 1956, lawmakers in North Carolina denounced the Court's "tyrannical usurpation of power." Democrats in the July primary elections in Texas overwhelmingly voted to make interposition a part of the party platform, and in the November general elections the voters of Arkansas approved an interposition amendment to the state constitution. In early 1957 the legislature in Tennessee adopted a "manifesto of protest" promising to do everything "honorably and legally" possible to combat "illegal encroachments" on state rights. By mid-1957 eight states had approved interposition measures, the Democrats of Texas had endorsed the doctrine, and the legislators of North Carolina and Tennessee had approved resolutions that stopped just short of interposition.[19]

During 1956 events seemed to corroborate the might of interposition. In February a federal court ordered the admission of Autherine J. Lucy, a black student, to the University of Alabama. On her second day of classes, a mob, composed mainly of university students, succeeded in driving her from campus. The university's board of trustees suspended Lucy "for her own safety," and after Lucy and her attorney from the NAACP charged university officials with "intentionally permitting the demonstrations to create an atmosphere of mob rule," it made her expulsion permanent.[20]

[18] *Race Relations Law Reporter*, I, 442, II, 480.

[19] *Southern School News*, August, 1956; *Race Relations Law Reporter*, II, 230, 481–83; Bartley, *The Rise of Massive Resistance*, 126–49.

[20] *Southern School News*, March, 1956, quoted; Thomas J. Gilliam, "The Second Folsom Administration: The Destruction of Alabama Liberalism, 1954–1958" (Ph.D. dissertation, Auburn University, 1975), 273–307.

In the fall of 1956 whites in Texas opposed the court-ordered enrollment of black students at Mansfield High School and at Texarkana Junior College. In both cases Governor Allan Shivers dispatched Texas Rangers "to maintain order and keep down violence." The mobs prevented desegregation, the Rangers prevented violence, and both schools remained segregated. Governor Shivers suggested that, should such "actions be construed as contempt of the federal court," the charges were to be laid "against the governor and not the local people."[21]

In Tennessee, Governor Frank G. Clement courageously refused to permit white opposition to thwart the court-decreed desegregation of Clinton High School. Clement sent the state police and units of the National Guard to the eastern Tennessee town to maintain public order. Clinton High School desegregated while the National Guard occupied the streets, but the highly publicized event at Clinton did not further the cause of moderation. "The pictures of tanks in an American town at Clinton caused national revulsion," a journalist pointed out, "and a strong rise in segregationist sentiment." Louisville and some other school districts in Kentucky desegregated without notable incidents, but the summoning of the National Guard to two towns in the state during the fall of 1956 strengthened the impression that the white South would not desegregate peacefully.[22]

Throughout the region, state legislatures bombarded statute books with a bewildering variety of laws protecting segregation. The new enactments snarled the enforcement of the *Brown* decision and did indeed, as a segregationist in Alabama asserted, "serve notice on the rest of the nation that Alabama and the South

[21] Shivers quoted in New York *Times,* September 11, 1956, and in Birmingham *News,* September 13, 1956; *Southern School News,* September, 1956; John Howard Griffin and Theodore Freedman, *Mansfield, Texas: A Report on the Crisis Situation Resulting from Efforts to Desegregate the School System* (Anti-Defamation League, 1957); Charles Alan Wright, "School Integration: An Almost Lost Cause," *Progressive,* August, 1958, pp. 7–10.

[22] John Bartlow Martin, *The Deep South Says, Never* (New York, 1957), p. 172 quoted; Anna Holden, Bonita Valien, Preston Valien, and Francis Manis, *Clinton, Tennessee: A Tentative Description and Analysis of the School Desegregation Crisis* (Anti-Defamation League, 1957); Roscoe Griffin, *Sturgis, Kentucky: A Tentative Description and Analysis of the School Desegregation Crisis* (Anti-Defamation League, 1958); Wallace Westfeldt, "Communities in Strife," in *With All Deliberate Speed: Segregation-Desegregation in Southern Schools,* ed. Don Shoemaker (New York, 1957), 36–55.

will not accept integration." Kilpatrick and a good many other southern segregationists reasoned that if they could "hold out 10 years from the date of the Supreme Court decision" they "could yet win the war." [23]

Ultimately, however, massive resistance rested on a willingness to close the public schools. Even before interposition became popular, four states of the lower South had prepared for such an eventuality, and eventually a majority of the southern states adopted legislation permitting the discontinuance of public education. Not infrequently, advocates of massive resistance pronounced the abandonment of public education to be a positive good. A prominent Georgia segregationist was hardly unique when he declared that a return to private academies "would contribute twenty years to the advancement of education in this state" and "get Karl Marx and John Dewey out of the schools," to boot. [24]

As a last resort, bitter-end segregationists expected their governors to defy the federal courts to the point of being jailed for contempt. In Virginia, Byrd and Kilpatrick privately urged J. Lindsay Almond, who became governor in 1958, to adopt such a course. By following a policy "of contemptuous defiance," the governor could create an "incident" that, Kilpatrick argued, would have a "powerful effect on the whole country in dramatizing the depth of the South's resistance." It would also, Senator Byrd assured Almond, bring glory, since "the people will lionize you." Almond was unconvinced, and so too were the other southern governors who heard such appeals. Perhaps they—like Governor Marvin Griffin of Georgia—concluded that "bein' in jail kind of crimps a governor's style." [25]

During the midfifties the champions of massive resistance sought to unify the political South behind the principle of state interposition. Such a quest required suppressing dissent. When moderates in Virginia showed signs of wavering, Congressman

[23] Samuel M. Engelhardt quoted in Memphis *Commercial Appeal,* January 20, 1956; Richmond *News Leader,* October 26, 1957.

[24] R. Carter Pittman quoted in Atlanta *Constitution,* January 9, 1959.

[25] Kilpatrick and Byrd quoted in *The Crisis of Conservative Virginia,* by Ely, 125; Griffin quoted in *Gothic Politics in the Deep South: Stars of the New Confederacy,* by Robert Sherrill (New York, 1968), 3.

Tuck proclaimed, "We cannot allow Norfolk or Arlington to integrate. If they won't stand with us, I say make them." In the name of constitutional government, conservatives promoted state rights; in the name of state rights, they restricted individual dissent and local option. At the same time, they worked for regional unity. As Governor Griffin explained, "If we in the South band together and present a united front, they'll never get to us. If we get scattered, they'll pick us off one at a time." [26]

As enthusiasm for massive resistance swelled, the southern congressional delegation dramatically issued its "Declaration of Constitutional Principles" in March, 1956. Signed by 19 of the former Confederacy's 22 senators and 82 of its 106 representatives, the Southern Manifesto condemned the Supreme Court's "unwarranted exercise" of "naked judicial power" and commended the "motives of those States which have declared the intention to resist forced integration by any lawful means." Initiated by Senator J. Strom Thurmond and Senator Byrd, the manifesto originally endorsed interposition and labeled the *Brown* decision unconstitutional. Congressional moderates, who did not want their names left off a segregationist proclamation but also objected to its more bellicose language, insisted on revisions. After several rewritings, the document was still a spirited attack on the Supreme Court. It declared *Brown* "contrary to the Constitution" and pledged every effort to bring about a reversal.[27]

The delegations from seven states—Alabama, Arkansas, Georgia, Louisiana, Mississippi, South Carolina, and Virginia—unanimously supported the declaration, as did most of the members from Florida and North Carolina. The greater number of the nonsigners were from Texas, the home of Sam Rayburn, the House majority leader, who was less than enthusiastic about such a starkly sectional approach. The legislators from Tennessee divided, with both Senator Estes Kefauver and Senator Albert Gore declining to sign. Lyndon Johnson, the Senate majority leader, was not asked for support. Senator Byrd gloated that the manifesto was "part of

[26] Tuck quoted in Richmond *Times-Dispatch*, November 15, 1958; Griffin quoted in Atlanta *Journal*, May 8, 1957.
[27] "Declaration of Constitutional Principles," *Southern School News*, April, 1956.

the plan of massive resistance we've been working on, and I hope and believe it will be an effective action." [28]

The expanding resistance to desegregation coincided with the founding of the Citizens' Councils. In July, 1954, whites organized the first council in Indianola, Mississippi. Within a year councils proliferated through Mississippi and the South. When chapters of the NAACP filed desegregation petitions with school boards in some sixty southern communities, many whites responded by joining the organized resistance. By the time of the Montgomery bus boycott, the councils had become a formidable force. Organizers had their greatest success in Alabama, Louisiana, Mississippi, South Carolina, and Virginia. In Virginia, the groups went by the less commonplace name of Defenders of State Sovereignty and Individual Liberties. Within the former Confederacy, the movement was least effective in Florida, Georgia, and Tennessee. At the peak, Citizens' Councils and allied bodies enrolled as many as a quarter million white southerners. [29]

Council leaders created an interstate organization at a meeting in New Orleans in April, 1956. The delegates adopted a four-point

[28] Byrd quoted in Richmond *News Leader*, March 12, 1956. Among numerous journalistic accounts of the making of the Southern Manifesto are Doris Fleeson's in Charleston *Gazette*, March 16, 1956; Elizabeth Carpenter's in *Arkansas Gazette* (Little Rock), March 18, 1956; Joe Hatcher's in Atlanta *Journal*, March 18, 1956; and Bruce Jolly's in Greensboro *Daily News*, July 13, 1956.

[29] The best study of the Citizens' Council movement is Neil R. McMillen's *The Citizens' Council: Organized Resistance to the Second Reconstruction, 1954–1964* (Urbana, Ill., 1971). Other helpful works include Martin's *The Deep South Says, Never;* James W. Vander Zanden's "The Southern White Resistance Movement to Integration" (Ph.D. dissertation, University of North Carolina, 1958); Hodding Carter III's *The South Strikes Back* (Garden City, N.Y., 1959); Carl T. Rowan's *Go South to Sorrow* (New York, 1957); Dan Wakefield's *Revolt in the South* (New York, 1960); James Graham Cook's *The Segregationists* (New York, 1962); David Halberstam's "The White Citizens' Councils: Respectable Means for Unrespectable Ends," *Commentary*, XXII (1956), 293–302; and James W. Vander Zanden's "The Citizens' Councils," *Alpha Kappa Deltan*, XXIX (1959), 3–9. The Citizens' Councils published a voluminous literature, a substantial sample of which is collected in Southern Regional Council Papers, Atlanta University Center. The Southern Regional Council also conducted its own surveys of segregationist groups, most of which are unpublished. See, however, Southern Regional Council, *Special Report: Pro-Segregation Groups in the South* (Atlanta, 1956); Frederick B. Routh and Paul Anthony, "Southern Resistance Forces," *Phylon*, XVIII (1957), 50–58; and Harold C. Fleming, "Resistance Movements and Racial Desegregation," *Annals of the American Academy of Political and Social Science*, CCCIV (1956), 44–52.

program that called for interposition, an attack on the NAACP, a national propaganda campaign, and renewed membership drives. Designed to serve as a "coordinating and planning agency for the several state associations," the Citizens' Councils of America established headquarters in Greenwood, Mississippi, with Robert B. Patterson, one of the charterers of the original council, as executive secretary. Its official publication was the *Citizens' Council,* edited by William J. Simmons in Jackson, Mississippi. For the most part, however, the state associations continued to operate independently.[30]

The councils thrived in the lowland towns of the black belt stretching from southside Virginia into east Texas. There paternalism defined relations between employer and employee, black workers were a large part of the labor force, and segregation was the foundation of the social order. Even whites without a robust ideological commitment to caste might well feel misgivings about the practical problems that would attend the integration of huge numbers of poor black children with comparatively advantaged white students. The whites of the old plantation counties had historically been the mainstay of the Bourbon order, and many of them once again rallied to the defense of white supremacy.

The racism of the Citizens' Councils was less the psychological racism Gunnar Myrdal had described than an ideological commitment to traditional white values. In an age of declining community, the councils reaffirmed white folk culture. Much as black communities in Montgomery and elsewhere united to resist encroachments from whites, white townspeople combined to defend time-honored prerogatives. The council program was reactionary, and its members based their defense of community practices on white supremacy. In this regard, they had something in common with their northern liberal adversaries, who also tended to reduce broad issues to simple questions of racism.

The organizers of the original Citizens' Council in Indianola were business and political leaders. "If they did not represent the wealthiest, most aristocratic families of the Mississippi Delta," a

[30] *The Citizens' Councils of America,* November, 1956, quoted; *The Citizens' Council,* May, 1956; New Orleans *Times-Picayune,* April 8, 1956; Martin, *The Deep South Says, Never,* 137–43; Carter, *The South Strikes Back,* 70–73.

journalist has observed, "they did represent the active middle and upper class of businessmen." As the councils multiplied, they continued to attract "respectable" segregationists. An FBI investigation caused J. Edgar Hoover to wax enthusiastic: "The membership of these organizations reflects bankers, lawyers, doctors, state legislators and industrialists. In short, their membership includes some of the leading citizens of the South." Recruiters for the councils spoke before the Rotary, Lions, Civitans, and Kiwanis, and the councils' officers worked closely with such patriotic groups as the Daughters of the American Revolution and the American Legion. The councils rejected violence, presented their movement as a "responsible" alternative to the Ku Klux Klan, and attempted to attract a "respectable" membership.[31]

"The Citizens' Council," a widely circulated promotional pamphlet explained, "is the modern version of the old-time town meeting called to meet any crisis by expressing the will of the people." Theoretically, all "patriotic white citizens" were eligible for membership, but in practice the movement was overwhelmingly male. As defenders of white "racial purity" and guardians against the evils of "miscegenation," council members viewed themselves as fighting a battle to which women should not be exposed. One Alabama organizer did not hedge on the point in late 1954: "Women will not be allowed to join, because we feel that it is a job for men." The councils in Alabama, like those elsewhere, did eventually accept women members and claimed to have enrolled "some of the best women in the state." But true to the paternal order they defended, their rolls were always preponderantly male.[32]

Council leaders and other massive-resistance spokesmen harangued ceaselessly about the dangers of "intermarriage," "miscegenation," and "mongrelization." Since many of the same white men who were apprehensive of "interbreeding" also held the con-

[31] Martin, *The Deep South Says, Never*, 3; J. Edgar Hoover, "Racial Tensions and Civil Rights," March 1, 1956, p. 16 quoted, in Cabinet Series, Dwight D. Eisenhower Library, Abilene, Kans.; Carter, *The South Strikes Back*, 205–206; McMillen, *The Citizens' Council*, 20–28.

[32] *The Citizens' Council* (Pamphlet, 1956); Alston Keith quoted in Nashville *Tennessean*, November 28, 1954; Paul Anthony, "A Survey of Resistance Groups of Alabama," 8, in Southern Regional Council Papers; *The Citizens' Council*, June, 1956.

viction that blacks were biologically, or at least culturally, inferior to whites, it was not altogether clear what appeal black men had against which white women were expected to be without resistance. Some council members feared intermarriage. Others might have agreed with the Alabama Council leader who stated, "Intermarriage isn't what we fear. It's sex relations. Desegregating the schools will lead to rape!" For generations, white men had taken sexual advantage of black women. Somehow, in very different social circumstances, black men and white women might even the score. Lillian E. Smith referred to the "race-sex-sin spiral," and council oratory suggested pangs of sexual insecurity. It also indicated an awareness of the close association between white supremacy and white male supremacy.[33]

Though based in the old plantation belt, the most successful state federations of Citizens' Councils had well-placed allies in the cities. In Mississippi, the state council organization absorbed the Jackson States' Rights Association, which was headed by the president of the capital city's chamber of commerce. Among association members, William J. Simmons, scion of a socially prominent banking family, became administrator of the state organization of Citizens' Councils as well as editor of the *Citizens' Council*. The South Carolina Committee of Fifty-Two, which included a former governor and the president of the state bar association, coalesced with South Carolina's council federation and claimed credit for "guiding" its development. The Society for the Preservation of State Government and Racial Integrity of New Orleans and the American States' Rights Association of Birmingham, both enrolling what a journalist described as a "substantial number of prominent and wealthy people," worked closely with the councils in Louisiana and Alabama. Such affiliations broadened the movement's sweep and provided linkages with reactionary allies outside the black belt.[34]

[33] Samuel M. Engelhardt quoted in *The Southern Temper*, by William Peters (New York, 1959), 208; Lillian E. Smith, *Killers of the Dream* (New York, 1949).

[34] McMillen, *The Citizens' Council*, esp. 29–30; Paul Anthony, "The Resistance Groups of South Carolina," Anthony, "A Survey of Resistance Groups of Alabama," and Paul Anthony, "The Resistance Groups of Louisiana," all in Southern Regional Council Papers; Louisville *Courier-Journal*, November 21, 1954, quoted.

The spread of the councils into metropolitan areas also created problems. In the cities, membership drives drew mainly from the lower-status, less "respectable" part of the population. The alliance of middle-class black belt whites and metropolitan working-class whites was logical enough: they were the two white social groups that would in practice do most of the integrating. The differences were also substantial. Most notably in Alabama and Louisiana, the middle-class propriety of the councils in the plantation county towns conflicted with the common-man style of the workers in Birmingham and New Orleans, a schism described by a journalist as "part of the old feud between the Bourbon and the Red Neck." [35]

In early 1956 the North Alabama Citizens' Council, led by Asa Carter, a radio announcer, broke with the Citizens' Councils of Alabama. To Carter and his Birmingham associates, a bunch of "political big shots" dominated the state association. The North Alabama council crusaded against rock 'n' roll on the grounds that the music was a black assault on white culture. It organized a physical attack on black singer Nat King Cole, provided a forum for tirades against African Americans that bordered on advocating violence against them, and showed clear tendencies toward anti-Semitism. [36]

Officials of the state association denounced their erstwhile colleagues to the north as "budding bullies," "prisoners of hate," and "spreaders of poison for their own personal gain." One leader solemnly affirmed that there was "no place for prejudice" in the councils. Similar social dynamics in Louisiana created a smoldering and debilitating division between the plantation-district councils and the powerful Greater New Orleans Citizens' Council, which also demonstrated a propensity toward violence and anti-Semitism. The state association managed to hold the movement together by mediating between its two warring wings. [37]

[35] Douglas Cater, "Civil War in Alabama's Citizens' Councils," *Reporter,* May 17, 1956, pp. 19–21, p. 20 quoted; John N. Popham in New York *Times,* December 2, 1956; Robert S. Bird in St. Louis *Post Dispatch,* February 28, 1956; Ed Townsend in *Christian Science Monitor,* May 17, 1956.

[36] Martin, *The Deep South Says, Never,* p. 108 quoted; Cater, "Civil War in Alabama's Citizens' Councils," 19–21.

[37] "Statement" of Citizens' Councils of Alabama, Louisville *Courier-Journal,* March 11,

Asa Carter, after being hounded from the Alabama council movement, became an adviser to one of the numerous Ku Klux Klan groups scattered through the southern and particularly the southeastern states. The Klan continued to exercise a powerful appeal on certain common-folk segregationists. Fragmented, denigrated by "respectable" whites, limited in membership and financial resources, and in the main burdened by ineffective leadership, the Klan was less a social movement than a psychological palliative. It stirred primarily men in marginal and frequently declining lower-middle-class and working-class occupations who vented their frustration and insecurity in ritual and violence. The Klan offered an image of virtue, a sense of community and purpose, and enemies—and its members were often profoundly loyal.

Klansmen bore a not undeserved reputation for violence. As a journalist commented in 1957, "The robe-and-hooded tradition has a prevailing power of its own even without 'organization' and 'leadership.' " The Klan posed a very real threat to blacks, and to whites who openly deviated from racial orthodoxy. By distending the right edge of the political and social spectrum, it also permitted segregationist politicians and even spokesmen for the Citizens' Councils to portray themselves as moderates who stood squarely between the extremism of the Ku Klux Klan and the NAACP.[38]

The Citizens' Councils systematically attempted to suppress dissent at home. From the start, they employed economic intimidation as a form of suasion when African Americans supported desegregation, voted, or otherwise forgot their place. A council leader in Alabama was blunt: "We intend to make it difficult, if not impossible, for a Negro who advocates desegregation to find and hold a job, get credit, or renew a mortgage." When black parents petitioned for desegregated schools during the summer

---

1956; Alston Keith quoted in Birmingham *Post-Herald*, March 1, 1956; McMillen, *The Citizens' Council*, 41–72.

[38] New York *Herald Tribune*, April 23, 1957, quoted; James W. Vander Zanden, "The Klan Revival," *American Journal of Sociology*, LXV (1960), 456–62; David Chalmers, "The Ku Klux Klan and the Radical Right" (Paper delivered at the Sixth Annual Intergroup Relations Conference at the University of Houston, March 27, 1965), in Southern Regional Council Papers; *Intimidation, Reprisal, and Violence in the South's Racial Crisis* (Southern Regional Council, 1959). The article in the *Herald Tribune* was part of a series of thirteen by Robert S. Bird that ran from April 14, 1957, to April 28, 1957.

of 1955, the councils published the names of petitioners and encouraged an employers' blacklist. Although effective, the reprisals commanded critical media coverage, and blacks fought back with their own economic boycotts. After the midfifties, the pronouncements of council officers became more guarded. "We do not recommend economic pressure," Robert Patterson, the executive secretary of Citizens' Councils of America, told a journalist. "That's false propaganda from the press. But of course we don't denounce 'freedom of choice' in business arrangements. If employers fire their help, that's their business." [39]

Speakers before the councils constantly took to task the "misguided" ministers, "spineless" politicians, and "carpetbaggers and scalawags" who kept the white South from unanimity on racial questions. The message was that such miscreants deserved to be socially and economically ostracized. Herman Talmadge, the former governor of Georgia, exhorted a council audience, "Don't let him eat at your table, don't let him trade at your filling station, and don't let him trade at your store." The councils called for total war on "atheism, communism, and mongrelization" and insisted that compromise was treason. "The self-styled moderates," Congressman John Bell Williams of Mississippi warned, "are simply saying they believe in a little bit of pregnancy." Paul Anthony of the Southern Regional Council concluded in 1956 that the councils, "by effectively drawing a line over which they [would] not allow the white community to step," were exercising a "subtle power more effective, if less dramatic, than their public demonstrations." [40]

The movement, according to the *Citizens' Council,* was "nonpartisan in nature." The journal added, "But there is a vast difference between being non-partisan and being non-political." Political candidates and incumbents came to expect the councils to call upon them to "state openly, frankly and fearlessly what, if anything, they have to propose, and whether they can be relied

[39] Alston Keith quoted in *Southern School News,* January, 1955; Patterson quoted in *Revolt in the South,* by Wakefield, 45.

[40] Talmadge quoted by Fred Taylor in Birmingham *News,* June 23, 1955; *The Citizens' Council* (Pamphlet, 1956); Williams quoted in *Delta Democrat-Times* (Greenville, Miss.), February 29, 1956; Anthony, "A Survey of Resistance Groups of Alabama," 30.

upon to give their full support to a program that will prevent integration." Well before the Richmond *News Leader* began retailing interposition, the Defenders of State Sovereignty and Individual Liberties promoted a "plan for Virginia" that called for all-out resistance to desegregation. The Patriots of North Carolina led campaigns in the Democratic primaries of 1956 that defeated two of the three congressmen who had been unwilling to sign the Southern Manifesto. In Arkansas, the Citizens' Councils sponsored successfully a nullification amendment to the state constitution and agitated for state intervention in the planned desegregation of Central High School in Little Rock. The councils in Mississippi aggrandized power until, in one critic's estimation, the state had a "Soviet-style government, with the Citizens' Councils paralleling the state machine in emulation of a successful Communist Party." Over much of the South, what one journalist described as a "dynamic and contagious grass-roots force" had forged an alliance with powerful political elements to determine the direction of state policy during the late 1950s.[41]

The crusade to unite whites behind a policy of social reaction provoked widespread political conflict. In the Deep South, neo-populists—whose class-based assumptions dictated racial moderation—provided the principal opposition to massive resistance. James E. Folsom, who was reelected governor of Alabama in 1954, and Earl K. Long, who was reelected governor of Louisiana in 1956, remained discernibly aloof from the Citizens' Councils. Folsom gibed, "I favor the White Citizens' Council, Black Citizens' Council, Yellow Citizens' Council, and any other color you might mention." Folsom enunciated the traditional liberal position: "As long as Negroes are held down by privation and lack of opportunity, the other poor people will be held down alongside them." Long considered race a bogus issue: "There are a lot of fakers trying to make themselves politically by using that issue to befuddle the people."[42]

[41] *The Citizens' Council,* September, 1960; "Plan for Virginia," Richmond *Times-Dispatch,* June 9, 1955, quoted; *Southern School News,* June, 1956; McMillen, *The Citizens' Council,* 92–115; Bartley, *The Rise of Massive Resistance,* 82–107; Leslie W. Dunbar, "The Changing Mind of the South: The Exposed Nerve," *Journal of Politics,* XXVI (1964), p. 20 quoted; Muse, *Virginia's Massive Resistance,* p. 8 quoted.

[42] Folsom quoted in Montgomery *Advertiser,* March 8, 1959; Atlanta *World,* December 27,

Folsom and Long sometimes seemed perplexed by the depth of the hostility white supremacists displayed toward black people. "If they had been making a living for me like they have for the black belt," Folsom scoffed, "I'd be proud of them instead of cussing and kicking them all the time." Long joked that one day soon William M. Rainach, a state senator and Citizens' Council leader, would go home, "get up on his front porch, take off his shoes, wash his feet, look at the moon, and get close to God." Turning to Rainach in the senate chamber, Long concluded, "And when you do, you got to recognize that niggers is human beings!"[43]

Neither governor espoused integration. "I don't intend to make the good colored people of Alabama go to school with us white folks," Folsom explained. Both, however, supported political rights for blacks. "If these colored people helped build this country, if they could fight in its army," Long reflected, "then I'm for giving them the vote." The receptivity of Long and Folsom to black suffrage was not entirely free of expediency, for the newly enfranchised were likely to cast ballots for the politicians who had worked to give them the vote. At the same time, both governors made a serious effort to treat blacks fairly in the allocation of state services, public-welfare benefits, and the like. "I could never get all excited about our colored brothers," Folsom commented. "I find them to be good citizens."[44]

Both governors rejected much of the mythology and practice of white supremacy. The statue of the Confederate soldier on the

---

1949; Long quoted in New Orleans *Times-Picayune*, May 4, 1956. Valuable on Folsom are Carl Grafton and Anne Permaloff's *Big Mules and Branchheads: James E. Folsom and Political Power in Alabama* (Athens, Ga., 1985); George E. Sims's *The Little Man's Big Friend: James E. Folsom in Alabama Politics, 1946–1958* (University, Ala., 1985); William D. Barnard's *Dixiecrats and Democrats: Alabama Politics, 1942–1950* (University, Ala., 1974); and Gilliam's "The Second Folsom Administration." Among the more helpful of numerous works on Long and Louisiana politics are Michael L. Kurtz and Morgan D. Peoples' *Earl K. Long: The Saga of Uncle Earl and Louisiana Politics* (Baton Rouge, 1990); A. J. Liebling's *The Earl of Louisiana* (New York, 1961); Stan Opotowsky's *The Longs of Louisiana* (New York, 1960); Thomas Martin's *Dynasty: The Longs of Louisiana* (New York, 1960); Allan P. Sindler's *Huey Long's Louisiana: State Politics, 1920–1952* (Baltimore, 1956); and Perry H. Howard's *Political Tendencies in Louisiana* (Rev. ed.; Baton Rouge, 1971).

[43] Folsom quoted in Birmingham *World*, June 1, 1955; Long quoted in *The Earl of Louisiana*, by Liebling, 29–30.

[44] Folsom quoted in *Southern School News*, September, 1955; Long quoted in *The Longs of Louisiana*, by Opotowsky, 159.

lawn of the state capitol, Folsom once suggested, "should be moved to the Confederate Cemetery where it belongs." Although Long often deplored the flood of measures stiffening segregation that poured from the Louisiana legislature, he signed the bills into law to avoid being tarred as an integrationist. When in 1958 his administration fulfilled a campaign promise to open a branch of Louisiana State University in New Orleans, it also provided for the construction nearby of a branch of Southern University, a black institution. Nevertheless, Long did nothing to abet segregation at either of the schools, and LSU–New Orleans enrolled approximately a thousand whites and two hundred blacks, making it the only educational institution in the South to be integrated—as opposed to desegregated in token form.[45]

Folsom confronted the issue directly. He vetoed a number of bills buttressing segregation and derided the legislature's interposition resolution as akin to "a hound dog baying at the moon and claiming it's got the moon treed." Folsom's willingness to confront white-supremacy practices produced a political disaster when congenially he invited Congressman Adam Clayton Powell to have a drink in the governor's mansion. The black New Yorker rode from the airport in the executive limousine, entered the mansion through the front door, sipped a drink with the governor, and in a speech that night quoted his host as having said, "Integration is inevitable. It is here now." Such an open breach of the etiquette of segregation gave the news media a field day. "Hell, I wouldn't run for dogcatcher today," Folsom remarked soon afterward. "I'd get the hell beat out of me." [46]

The destruction of Folsomism and Longism resulted directly from the politics of massive resistance, but from a long-term perspective their ruin was perhaps inevitable. The national redefinition of liberalism stressing the moral imperative of individual civil rights for African Americans increasingly isolated politicians who focused on economics and class. Demographics decimated their

[45] Folsom quoted in Atlanta *Journal*, January 24, 1970; New Orleans *Times-Picayune*, September 14, 1958; Kurtz and Peoples, *Earl K. Long*, 198–202.

[46] Folsom quoted in Montgomery *Advertiser*, January 26, 1956, January 16, 1956; Powell quoted in Nashville *Tennessean*, November 4, 1955; *Southern School News*, December, 1955, January, 1956.

rural electoral base, and an urbanizing and modernizing South lost its tolerance for the antics, personal failings, and hell-of-a-fellow flamboyance that were hallmarks of their careers. Folsom, who stood six foot eight and weighed 260 pounds, drank excessively, faced a highly publicized and politically damaging paternity suit during his first term, and was consistently careless in administrative procedure. Long was more effective as a government leader, but toward the end of the 1950s he too began to drink heavily, separated from his wife, Blanche, and romanced striptease performers, notably Blaze Starr of New Orleans. Neither Folsom nor Long was able to transfer his grass-roots popular appeal from the hustings to the ever more decisive campaign medium of television. Long once acknowledged that television "makes me look like a monkey on a stick." [47]

In the developing South, the "buccaneering liberalism" both governors practiced was out of tune with the times. Folsom and Long were spoils politicians who distrusted middle-class-oriented state bureaucracies and resented civil service standards. In 1948 the Long forces succeeded in repealing Louisiana's civil service law, although a later anti-Long administration restored it. Folsom and Long disdained such "good government" innovations as centralized purchasing and competitive bidding, statewide rationalized administrative procedures, and ethics oversight. In answer to journalists who criticized his administration for conflicts of interest, Folsom once groused, "I don't know why others should get the gravy. I'm governor." [48]

The metropolitan press in Alabama and Louisiana ceaselessly alleged government corruption, and clearly the charges had some foundation. Public corruption was the only arsenal Folsom and Long possessed for combating the reactionary political forces in their states. Disfranchisement, malapportionment, and one-party rule consolidated the power of cotton and steel in Alabama and cotton and commerce in Louisiana. The Big Mules of Birmingham and their corporate counterparts in New Orleans had the wherewithal to reward the faithful, most frequently by paying re-

[47] Long quoted in *Dynasty*, by Martin, 198.
[48] Folsom quoted in *Gothic Politics in the Deep South*, by Sherrill, 274. The term *buccaneering liberalism* is Sindler's, in *Huey Long's Louisiana*, 209.

tainers to legislators and to law firms with political access. Their allies in the metropolitan news media tirelessly insisted that upstart insurgents were irresponsible and unrespectable. The county elite held the political leverage to sustain their friends. To counter such entrenched power, Long and Folsom relied on patronage, bribery, and pork barrels.[49]

Folsom and Long conducted their freebooting in the name of the "people." In style and substance, their claims were not without validity. After winning the governorship in 1948, Long invited the entire state to attend his inauguration in the football stadium at Louisiana State University. The people who came consumed 240,000 soft drinks, 16,000 gallons of buttermilk, and 200,000 hot dogs. At Long's reelection, the legislature prevented a repeat performance by capping inauguration expenses. In 1956 Folsom held two inaugural balls, one for whites at the Agricultural Coliseum in Montgomery, and the second for blacks at Alabama State College for Negroes. Separate, the galas were equal, and the arrangement afforded black people greater public recognition than they were apt to receive anywhere else in the nation at the time.[50]

The programs of the two governors sought to deliver services to the people who needed them most. In Louisiana, Earl Long's older brother, Huey, had as governor successfully challenged the established system. Consequently Uncle Earl inherited a functioning organization capable of delivering on his campaign promises. Louisiana's per capita public-school expenditures were the highest in the South and matched the national average, and its funding for public hospitals and welfare—most especially for old-age pensions—led the region. In 1956 the Long forces repealed the state's right-to-work law, and even though the legislature restored it for agricultural workers, Louisiana was alone among the former Confederate states in exempting most of its workers from right-to-work coverage.[51]

[49] This point is discussed by T. Harry Williams in "The Politics of the Longs," in *Romance and Realism in Southern Politics,* ed. T. Harry Williams (Athens, Ga., 1961), 65–84; and by Grafton and Permaloff, in *Big Mules and Branchheads,* 87–98.

[50] Opotowsky, *The Longs of Louisiana,* 149–52; *Southern School News,* February, 1955.

[51] New York *Times,* July 13, 1956; William C. Havard and Robert F. Steamer, "Louisiana Secedes: Collapse of a Compromise," *Massachusetts Review,* I (1959), 134–46.

Folsom tried to create a comparable political faction in Alabama, but he failed to achieve lasting results. When he became governor, Folsom had never held elective office, and he was unable to gain influence over the legislature. By his second term, he was a more effective governor. The general assembly substantially increased spending for farm-to-market roads and old-age payments, it repealed the Relatives Responsibility Act, and it authorized constitutional amendments providing for a graduated income tax to fund education, for a state bond issue to enable school construction, and for legislative reapportionment.[52]

Increasingly, however, racial issues dominated political and legislative debate. Folsom complained that every time there was an attempt to pass progressive legislation, "they bring up the race issue." Bills expanding the franchise, permitting women to serve on juries, and repealing the right-to-work law failed in the legislature, and the electorate defeated the income-tax, school-bond, and reapportionment amendments. The voters approved amendments allowing the state to dispose of public parks, public housing, public schools, and the like. Folsom struggled to stem the tide by convening editors and publishers and persuading them to create a state-level biracial commission, and by launching a speaking tour in which he made a "report to the people" that decried racist "mobocracy" and defended his "democratic" program. All was for naught. "Apparently," he lamented, "a great majority of the people are for segregation, period."[53]

In the Alabama gubernatorial election of 1958, the principal candidates all rejected "Folsomism." Attorney General John Patterson defeated Judge George C. Wallace in the Democratic runoff with a bitterly racist campaign. Wallace explained his defeat: "John Patterson out-nigguhed me. And boys, I'm not goin' to be out-nigguhed again." Patterson had promised to maintain segregation, and consonant with his vow, he invited no blacks to attend

[52] Murray Clark Havens, *City Versus Farm? Urban-Rural Conflict in the Alabama Legislature* (Tuscaloosa, Ala., 1957); Sims, *The Little Man's Big Friend*, 140–60.
[53] Folsom quoted in New York *Times*, June 21, 1955; Montgomery *Advertiser*, January 13, 1957; Gilliam, "The Second Folsom Administration."

his inauguration, not even the bands from black colleges that had traditionally taken part in inaugural parades.[54]

Long became enmeshed in the politics of race after the Citizens' Councils began a purge of African Americans from the voter registration rolls. When Rainach and the segregationists introduced legislation to facilitate the purges, Long countered with a bill to protect registrants. In the fierce legislative conflict that followed, Long suffered a much publicized breakdown. The Long family placed him under psychiatric care, and during the next weeks he was in and out of three mental institutions before regaining the governorship. He was unable, however, to regain control of the legislature or of the direction of Louisiana politics.[55]

Jimmie H. Davis, a previous governor and an anti-Long stalwart, became Long's successor in the statehouse. Davis' fame rested not so much on his lackluster performance as governor during the midforties as on his authorship of such songs as "You Are My Sunshine" and "Bed Bug Blues." One longtime observer of the Louisiana political scene described Davis as a man who "almost never demonstrated definite convictions about anything." Long needled that Davis wanted to win office only to steal: "Jimmie Davis loves money like a hog loves slop." Davis' campaign was extremely well financed, and later when asked about the source of his campaign funds, he answered, "I don't know nothing about nothing and especially about that." In any event, he entered into an alliance with Rainach and the Citizens' Councils and purported to be "1,000 percent" for segregation. His aides assured reporters that he would go to jail rather than relent on the question.[56]

The fire storm of massive resistance suffocated the racial moderation associated with neopopulist liberalism. A student of Alabama politics has subtitled his dissertation on Folsom's second administration "The Destruction of Alabama Liberalism." Perry

---

[54] Wallace quoted in *Wallace,* by Marshall Frady (New York, 1968), 127; Birmingham *News,* December 27, 1958; Montgomery *Advertiser,* January 20, 1959.

[55] Kurtz and Peoples, *Earl K. Long,* 194–256.

[56] Harnett T. Kane, "Dilemma of a Crooner-Governor," *New York Times Magazine,* January 1, 1961, p. 10 quoted; Long quoted in *The Earl of Louisiana,* by Liebling, 146; Davis quoted in *Leander Perez: Boss of the Delta,* by Glen Jeansonne (Baton Rouge, 1977), 214; New Orleans *Times-Picayune,* November 4, 1959; William C. Havard, Rudolf Herberle, and Perry H. Howard, *The Louisiana Elections of 1960* (Baton Rouge, 1963).

H. Howard has concluded that the contest in 1960 between Davis and deLesseps S. Morrison left Louisiana with a "cleavage which pitted North against South, Protestant against Catholic, and rendered race the primary issue in the place of economic realities." Long received some vindication in 1960 when he won a seat in the United States House of Representatives, but he died before being sworn in. His death marked the final disintegration of the Long faction. As the politics of the Cold War had destroyed popular-front liberalism a decade earlier, the politics of massive resistance completed the devastation of southern rural liberalism.[57]

Business-oriented moderates continued to be the leading opponents of massive resistance. In states on the periphery of the Deep South—Florida, North Carolina, Arkansas, Tennessee, and after former senator Price Daniel replaced Allan Shivers in the statehouse in 1957, Texas—public officials often supported local-option arrangements reminiscent of the Gray Commission's original plan for Virginia. In 1955 Senator James O. Eastland of Mississippi grumbled, "I'm ashamed that we have three southern governors who howl that it is a local matter and feel no obligation to the people of their states." Eastland was referring to LeRoy Collins of Florida, Luther H. Hodges of North Carolina, and Orval E. Faubus of Arkansas. All three were moderates on race, giving priority to the cultivation of an image attractive to outside investors and conducive to business development.[58]

The three governors entered politics as members of the progressive wings of their state parties. Collins, a state senator from Tallahassee and one of the framers of the state's minimum foundation program for education, was an ally of Governor Daniel T. McCarty, who was elected in 1952 but died shortly after inauguration. Under Florida's constitution, Charley E. Johns, president of the state senate, became acting governor. Johns was a prominent member of the rural Pork Chop Gang, which seemed to resist all changes in rapidly changing Florida. Johns replaced many of McCarty's appointees and reversed much of his program. Collins made the restoration of McCarty's policies his issue in a

[57] Gilliam, "The Second Folsom Administration"; Howard, *Political Tendencies in Louisiana*, 355.

[58] Eastland quoted in Jackson *Daily News*, October 5, 1955.

successful run for the governorship in the 1954 special election. He won reelection in 1956.[59]

During the 1930s, Hodges held appointive office in the Democratic faction in North Carolina that V. O. Key described as an "economic oligarchy." Thereafter, Hodges lived outside the state. Upon retiring from a vice-presidency at Marshall Field in Chicago, he returned to North Carolina, where in 1952 he ran for lieutenant governor. By that time, W. Kerr Scott, elected governor in 1948 and senator in 1954, had established a more liberal and rurally oriented faction to compete against the regular organization. Hodges ran as an independent, building on personal contacts from his years as a businessman and a Rotarian, and he achieved an upset. In the same election, William B. Umstead won the governorship. Hodges, who inherited the statehouse at Umstead's death in 1954, was still a relative unknown quantity, but as James R. Spence has remarked, the establishment regulars soon found that, although he "was a strong man, he was one of their own."[60]

Born in the Ozark Mountains, Faubus joined the state government of Arkansas as one of Governor Sidney S. McMath's appointees. At first part of the loosely structured progressive crowd around McMath, Faubus veered off on his own as the result of what Key described as the "confusion and paralysis of disorganized factional politics" that in Arkansas encouraged the ambi-

[59] Significant works dealing with the Collins administration include Tom R. Wagy's *Governor LeRoy Collins of Florida, Spokesman of the New South* (University, Ala., 1985); Thomas Howard Akerman's "The Triumph of Moderation in Florida Thought and Politics: A Study of the Race Issue from 1954–1960" (Ph.D. dissertation, American University, 1967); Joseph Aaron Tomberlin's "The Negro and Florida's System of Education: The Aftermath of the *Brown* Case" (Ph.D. dissertation, Florida State University, 1967); Douglas Price's *The Negro and Southern Politics: A Chapter of Florida History* (New York, 1957); William C. Havard and Loren P. Beth's *The Politics of Mis-Representation: Rural-Urban Conflict in the Florida Legislature* (Baton Rouge, 1962); V. M. Newton, Jr.'s *Crusade for Democracy* (Ames, Iowa, 1961); and David R. Colburn and Richard K. Scher's *Florida's Gubernatorial Politics in the Twentieth Century* (Tallahassee, Fla., 1980).

[60] Key, *Southern Politics*, 211; James R. Spence, *The Making of a Governor: The Moore-Preyer-Lake Primaries of 1964* (Winston-Salem, N.C., 1968), 22. Hodges' memoirs, *Businessman in the Statehouse: Six Years as Governor of North Carolina* (Chapel Hill, N.C., 1962), provide the best account of his governorship. Other helpful works include Jack D. Fleer's *North Carolina Politics: An Introduction* (Chapel Hill, N.C., 1968), and William Bagwell's *Desegregation in the Carolinas* (Columbia, S.C., 1972).

tious to pursue their own advantage. McMath was later to sigh, "I brought Orval down out of the hills, and every night ask forgiveness." Faubus proved to be an astute "politician of the courthouse-trading variety," and in 1954 he challenged and defeated incumbent governor Francis Cherry. In that election, Faubus' strongest backing came from rural voters and from his mountaineer neighbors. When he won reelection in 1956, he carried majorities in Little Rock's affluent white districts and in black precincts.[61]

The administrations of Collins, Hodges, and Faubus were the South's most devoted suitors of new industry. Governor Collins created a development credit corporation to make loans to new enterprises and an industrial services division to tender assistance to new industries, in addition to a state advertising commission and a nuclear development commission. He constituted the Florida Development Commission to coordinate the various state agencies devoted to the attraction of investors and tourists, and an international trade department to carry the courtship abroad. Governor Hodges strengthened his state's Department of Conservation and Development and lowered taxes on corporations.[62]

The most innovative and successful of these projects was the Research Triangle. Because North Carolina's existing industry was mainly of the traditional low-wage variety, Hodges inaugurated an ambitious program to attract technologically sophisticated and research-driven operations. The points of the triangle were the University of North Carolina at Chapel Hill, Duke University at Durham, and North Carolina State University at Raleigh, and its heart was the Research Triangle Institute. Hodges nursed the privately funded, state-supported research park through its difficult early years, and by 1959 he could take satisfaction that "the Research Triangle, the Research Triangle Park, and the Research Triangle Institute had become realities." After serving as secretary

[61] Key, *Southern Politics*, 184; McMath quoted in *Gothic Politics in the Deep South*, by Sherrill, 76; David W. Hacker in Louisville *Courier-Journal*, September 5, 1957; Bartley and Graham, comps., *Southern Elections*, 34–38, 352. Although a considerable literature deals with the desegregation crisis in Little Rock, there is relatively little of consequence about Faubus and his administration. The best source is Faubus' own *Down from the Hills* (Little Rock, Ark., 1980) and *Down from the Hills–II* (Little Rock, Ark., 1986).
[62] Charlton W. Tebeau, *A History of Florida* (Coral Gables, Fla., 1971), 439–40; Wagy, *Governor LeRoy Collins of Florida*, 54–58.

of commerce for President John F. Kennedy, Hodges in 1963 became chairman of the Triangle Foundation. "By the early seventies," historian James C. Cobb has written, "the Research Triangle Park was the site of some of the most impressive research being conducted in the entire nation." With both corporate and government laboratories, the project was the South's most successful high-technology venture.[63]

Collins and Hodges spent much of their time wooing industrial prospects in the North and abroad. One of Collins' campaign songs of 1956 exulted, "He went travlin' North, met the V.I.P.s / And he brought back millions in new industries." A symbiosis between the private and the public sectors had clearly become a reality.[64]

Governor Faubus' initiatives were more modest. His administration pushed through a bill establishing the Arkansas Industrial Development Commission, and he won approval for a constitutional amendment that permitted local governments to assist employers and prospective employers within their jurisdictions by buying land and constructing plants for them. Faubus chose Winthrop Rockefeller to head the development commission. A grandson of John D. Rockefeller and a socially prominent New Yorker before moving to Arkansas, Rockefeller paired family and state funds to make his industry-recruiting agency one of the most visible in the region. Although Faubus often boasted of all he had done to bring in jobs and industry, he left most of the task to Rockefeller and his well-heeled staff.[65]

All three chief executives were exponents of "good government," and at least in comparison with the precedents in their states, they were reasonably successful. Collins was the most aggressive champion of rationalized administrative procedures, the merit system, and the like, and he fought a continuous but always losing battle for legislative reapportionment. "The most meaning-

[63] Hodges, *Businessman in the Statehouse*, 29–56, p. 215 quoted; James C. Cobb, *The Selling of the South: The Southern Crusade for Industrial Development, 1936–1980* (Baton Rouge, 1982), 175.

[64] Wagy, *Governor LeRoy Collins of Florida*, 71.

[65] John L. Ward, *The Arkansas Rockefeller* (Baton Rouge, 1987), 1–20; Kathy Kunzinger Urwin, *Agenda for Reform: Winthrop Rockefeller as Governor of Arkansas, 1967–1971* (Fayetteville, Ark., 1991), 1–26; Faubus, *Down from the Hills*, 71–179.

ful thing we can do to assure the exercise of states' rights," Collins insisted, "is to improve state competence." In his memoirs, Hodges pointed to a "pet theory of mine that the sound principles of good business could and should apply to government." Faubus, who had to balance the interests of a diverse and amorphous voting coalition, was a less enthusiastic government reformer, but he did manage to initiate more rational administrative and spending procedures.[66]

A business-pleasing agenda entailed improving state infrastructures for transportation, education, and public services, and all three governors favored at least modest tax increases to that end. In early 1957 the Faubus administration increased sales, income, and severance taxes, with much of the new revenue destined for the public schools. The business-friendly agenda did not require more generous welfare appropriations. In 1959 the Hodges administration sponsored a record budget that cut appropriations for some welfare programs. "I was," Hodges remembered, "accused of taking away funds for poor people and sick people." Business progressivism often benefited working people. Indeed, North Carolina enacted a state minimum wage—though it exempted such predominantly black occupational categories as agricultural workers and domestic servants. But when textile workers struck the Harriet-Henderson Mills, Hodges dispatched state police and National Guardsmen to help break the strike, and eight unionists served prison sentences for destroying company property.[67]

During the mid-1950s Collins, Hodges, and Faubus were the former Confederacy's most notable business-oriented moderates. Collins explained his outlook: "Nothing will turn investors away quicker than the prospect of finding communities . . . seething under the tension and turmoil of race hatred." All three governors called themselves segregationists, but only Hodges appeared to hold a serious personal commitment to Jim Crow. All three agreed with Governor Faubus that desegregation "is a local prob-

[66] Collins quoted in St. Petersburg *Times*, May 31, 1958; Hodges, *Businessman in the Statehouse*, 5; Diane P. Blair, *Arkansas Politics and Government* (Lincoln, Nebr., 1988), 249–50.

[67] Faubus, *Down from the Hills*, 157–78; Hodges, *Businessman in the Statehouse*, 159, 224–50; Boyd Payton, *Scapegoat: Prejudice-Politics-Prison* (Philadelphia, 1970).

THE NEW SOUTH

lem and can best be solved on the local level," and Florida and
North Carolina in 1955 and Arkansas in 1956 approved locally
administered pupil-assignment laws that, in the language of the
North Carolina act, gave "full and complete" authority over
school enrollment to local school boards. Collins pronounced interposition to be "demagoguery," Hodges viewed it as "protest,"
and Faubus did not seem to consider anything so abstract to be
of more than academic significance.[68]

All three did regard desegregation as a treacherous political
issue. In 1956 General Sumter Lowery, a leader of the Florida
Federation for Constitutional Government, conducted a vigorously racist campaign against Collins, and James D. Johnson, a
former state senator and a spokesman for the Arkansas Citizens'
Councils, took on Faubus. Both Collins and Faubus protected
their flanks against the challengers in the primaries by adopting
more conspicuously segregationist policies. At Collins' behest, the
Florida legislature enacted a more sophisticated pupil-placement
measure and broadened the governor's authority to regulate the
use of public facilities and to employ military force in emergen-
cies. The Faubus administration promoted initiative referenda on
a pupil-placement law and an interposition resolution. During the
campaign, Faubus underlined that "no school district will be
forced to mix the races." Collins and Faubus won primary victories
without runoffs, but they owed the overriding issue of their campaigns to their opponents.[69]

Hodges headed off serious segregationist opposition by co-opt-
ing the race issue. On the one hand, he championed "voluntary
segregation" and reproached such "selfish and militant" extremists as the NAACP, and on the other, he pushed through the general assembly a package of legislation permitting local districts to
close the public schools by majority vote, and providing for tuition

[68] Collins quoted in Miami *Herald*, February 8, 1956; St. Petersburg *Times*, January 9,
1957; Faubus quoted in *Arkansas Gazette* (Little Rock), March 23, 1956; North Carolina
Placement Law, in *Race Relations Law Reporter*, I, 240–41; Hodges quoted in Raleigh *News
and Observer*, February 3, 1956.
[69] The campaigns are covered in *Southern School News* of April to August, 1956. For the
Florida laws, see *Race Relations Law Reporter*, I, 924–53. For the Arkansas laws, see *Race
Relations Law Reporter*, I, 579–81, 1116–18.

218

grants for private schools. The voters approved the constitutional amendments authorizing the program in September, 1956. These measures cleared the path to easy reelection and, in Hodges' words, did what was necessary "to save our schools and our traditions." [70]

Collins, Hodges, and Faubus had greater latitude than Folsom and Long in addressing problems of race. Florida's diverse and metropolitan electorate was far different from that of the Citizens' Council–ridden counties of Alabama. In North Carolina and Arkansas, the black belt leadership seemed content to accept local option on the assurance that school desegregation would not be coerced. A committee headed by Thomas Pearsall of the eastern black belt designed the program in North Carolina, and a similar committee of five members, all of whom lived within fifty miles of the Mississippi, drafted the legislation in Arkansas. Neither committee endorsed massive resistance. When the Arkansas Citizens' Councils planned a segregationist rally in the Mississippi Delta, the sheriff of Lincoln County refused to grant a permit. "We're getting along fine," the sheriff said, "without anybody stirring up trouble." [71]

Collins, once he was reelected and after the bus boycotts in Montgomery and Tallahassee subsided, became, in one national journalist's opinion, the "No. 1 exponent of the 'moderate' viewpoint among political leaders of his region." Repudiating the proposition that "the South should wrap itself in a Confederate blanket and consume itself in racial furor," Collins stated, "The inevitable tide of human progress moves against racial discrimination. . . . We must abandon the defiant attitude of never." In practice Florida's schools remained segregated, as did those in North Carolina below the university level. Only Arkansas made token progress toward desegregation. There eight public-school

[70] Hodges quoted in Greensboro *Daily News*, August 9, 1956, and in Charlotte *News*, June 24, 1955. For the laws, see *Race Relations Law Reporter*, I, 928–34. See also *Southern School News*, August, 1956, October, 1956.

[71] *Arkansas Gazette* (Little Rock), June 10, 1956; North Carolina Committee Report, in *Race Relations Law Reporter*, I, 582–84; Arkansas Committee Report, in *Race Relations Law Reporter*, I, 717–28; Tebo Cogbill quoted in *Arkansas Gazette* (Little Rock), October 14, 1955.

districts, higher education, and most public transportation had abandoned Jim Crow. "My only child," Faubus pointed out, "is now attending classes in a state-supported integrated college." [72]

To give their states' pupil-placement acts credibility with federal authorities, both Collins and Hodges began to encourage some local communities to desegregate. Attorney General Richard Ervin explained, "Either there must be some integration of pupils assigned on nonracial grounds according to the [pupil-placement] act, or the act will be declared unconstitutional." In the fall of 1957 Charlotte, Winston-Salem, and Greensboro accepted a few black students into formerly white schools, and Hodges issued a statement proclaiming that "no lawlessness or violence" would be permitted to disrupt their attendance. [73]

In comparison with the policies of massive resistance, the moderates' program appeared enlightened, and the national press accorded it generally favorable attention. Nonetheless, southern states erected ever more barriers to integration. During the first half of 1957, the legislatures in Arkansas and Florida added to their segregationist battery of laws. The governments of Tennessee and Texas for the first time approved legislative packages to combat *Brown*. Governor Clement and the Tennessee legislature endorsed a pupil-assignment law and other lesser measures. The Texas general assembly passed a pupil-placement bill and a law prohibiting public-school desegregation unless 20 percent of a district's voters petitioned for it and a majority approved it in a referendum. Prior to 1957 most of the desegregation in the former Confederacy had been in western and central Texas. The law requiring a referendum halted school desegregation in Texas and thereby brought regional compliance with the *Brown* decision to a standstill. By the late 1950s it was sometimes difficult to tell the difference between states committed to massive resistance and states choosing moderation. [74]

[72] Henry Lesenne in *Christian Science Monitor*, October 30, 1957; Collins quoted in St. Petersburg *Times*, September 24, 1957; Miami *Herald*, February 4, 1958; Faubus quoted in *Arkansas Gazette* (Little Rock), September 27, 1957; *Southern School News*, October, 1957.

[73] Ervin quoted in Miami *Herald*, November 8, 1958; Charlotte *News*, August 29, 1957.

[74] For the Arkansas laws, see *Race Relations Law Reporter*, II, 493–96. For the Florida laws,

During the decade following the *Brown* decision of 1954, legislatures in the former Confederate states enacted some 450 segregationist laws and resolutions. All eleven states approved pupil-placement laws, most authorized closing schools to avoid desegregating them, and all but North Carolina passed or strengthened laws designed to hobble the NAACP. A number of states, including North Carolina, limited the NAACP's action by enforcing older laws having to do with foreign corporations or, in some cases, with the Ku Klux Klan.

Eight states set up investigative committees, most of which searched for Communists and inevitably found integrationists. Groups like the Louisiana Joint Legislative Committee on Un-American Activities produced grist for six-column headlines: "Louisiana Probers Conclude Reds behind Racial Tensions in South." The Florida Legislative Investigation Committee added some much needed but rather bizarre novelty by concluding that homosexuals were Communists and energetically combing the state for its homosexual integrationist Communists. When not enacting new laws and conducting investigations, legislators often whiled away their time approving resolutions such as one originating in Mississippi that commended the "determined stand of the government of the Union of South Africa in maintaining its firm segregation policy." [75]

The racial moderation of the business progressives aimed to achieve social stability and economic growth. It severely limited desegregation while promoting a nationally acceptable public image. Like national liberalism, it treated civil rights as an individual issue and permitted carefully screened black students to attend "white" schools, thereby placing the burden of racial change entirely on African Americans. The moderate course—the middle

---

see *ibid.*, 707–12, 843–44. For the Tennessee laws, see *ibid.*, 215–19, 497–501. For the Texas laws, see *ibid.*, 693–96.

[75] Charleston *News and Courier,* March 10, 1957; Louisiana Joint Legislative Committee, *Subversion in Racial Unrest* (Baton Rouge, 1957); *Report of the Florida Legislative Committee* (Tallahassee, Fla., 1961); Resolution quoted in *Southern School News,* May, 1960. On southern legislative action, see Southern Education Reporting Service, *Statistical Summary* (Nashville, 1962), and *Southern School News,* May 17, 1964 ("Ten Years in Review").

way, as it was known in North Carolina—tried to thread between the extremes of massive resistance and rapid desegregation. As such, moderation inherently lacked stability, but at the same time it was the only effective political alternative to massive resistance.[76]

[76] Good critiques of moderate policies are David R. Colburn's "Florida's Governors Confront the *Brown* Decision: A Case Study of the Constitutional Politics of School Desegregation, 1954–1970," in *An Uncertain Tradition: Constitutionalism and the History of the South,* ed. Kermit L. Hall and James W. Ely, Jr. (Athens, Ga., 1989), 326–55; and William H. Chafe's *Civilities and Civil Rights: Greensboro, North Carolina, and the Black Struggle for Freedom* (New York, 1981), 42–70.

CHAPTER VII

INTERPOSITION, MODERATION, AND THE FEDERAL GOVERNMENT

T HE desegregation crisis in Little Rock was the crucible for racial politics. It exposed the untenable position of southern moderates and compelled them to ponder the implications of racial turmoil, closed schools, and the scorched earth policies of massive resistance. It forced the Eisenhower administration to confront school desegregation. Federal intervention in Little Rock saved the federal courts from potential defeat, enraged but also sobered the bitter-end segregationists, and heartened black advocates of desegregation. The upheavals in Little Rock between 1957 and 1959 encouraged the proponents of massive resistance, the practitioners of moderation, and the partisans of desegregation to reevaluate their strategies.

Only days after the *Brown* decision of 1954 the school board in Little Rock announced that the city would comply with the ruling. One year later, in May, 1955, Virgil T. Blossom, the superintendent of schools, made public the Little Rock Phase Program. The plan called for the selection of a few black students to attend one white high school in 1957, with the extension of desegregation in succeeding years to the junior high schools and by the fall of 1963 to the elementary schools. So gradual and so token was the program that black parents brought suit in a federal court to compel more rapid compliance with the Supreme Court's mandate of "all deliberate speed." The federal district and circuit courts approved the phase program.[1]

The plan delayed desegregation until the fall of 1957 to permit the completion of a new high school. By the 1957–1958 academic

---

[1] *Aaron v. Cooper*, in *Race Relations Law Reporter*, I, 851–60.

year, Little Rock had four senior highs. The largest, and the one
to be desegregated, was Central High School, which drew white
students from a wide social stratum of working-class, middle-class,
and lower-middle-class families. Technical High School, which was
to desegregate next, was the trade school. Horace Mann High
School was for the foreseeable future to remain an all-black institution. The new Hall High School, located in the affluent and lily-
white Heights section of the city, would be the upper-status and
all-white high school. Thus the Little Rock Phase Program envisioned desegregation for the white common folk and segregation
for most blacks and for affluent whites.[2]

Superintendent Blossom undertook a busy speaking schedule
to explain the desegregation plan to the people of Little Rock.
He addressed with disproportionate frequency civic, church, educational, and women's groups, much of the membership of
which resided in the attendance area of Hall High School. Blossom consistently defended the Little Rock Phase Program by arguing that desegregation was inevitable and that the plan maintained local control of developments while providing the least
desegregation spread over the longest transitional period possi-

[2] *Ibid.* Helpful studies of the Little Rock crisis include Corinne Silverman's *The Little Rock
Story* (Rev. ed.; University, Ala., 1959); Ernest Q. Campbell and Thomas F. Pettigrew's
Christians in Racial Crisis: A Study of Little Rock's Ministry (Washington, D.C., 1959); *Little
Rock, U.S.A.: Materials for Analysis*, ed. Wilson Record and Jane Cassels Record (San Fran-
cisco, 1960); Henry M. Alexander's *The Little Rock Recall Election* (Eagleton Institute, 1960);
David E. Wallace's "The Little Rock Central Desegregation Crisis of 1957" (Ph.D. disser-
tation, University of Missouri at Columbia, 1977); Irving J. Spitzberg, Jr.'s *Racial Politics in
Little Rock, 1954–1964* (New York, 1987); Anthony Freyer's *The Little Rock Crisis: A Consti-
tutional Interpretation* (Westport, Conn., 1984); Colbert S. Cartwright's "Lesson from Little
Rock," *Christian Century*, LXXIV (1957), 1193–94, and "The Improbable Demagogue of
Little Rock, Ark.," *Reporter*, October 17, 1957, pp. 23–25; and Elizabeth Jacoway's "Taken
by Surprise: Little Rock Business Leaders and Desegregation," in *Southern Businessmen and
Desegregation*, ed. Elizabeth Jacoway and David R. Colburn (Baton Rouge, 1982), 15–41.
Significant memoirs include Virgil T. Blossom's *It Has Happened Here* (New York, 1959);
Robert R. Brown's *Bigger Than Little Rock* (Greenwich, Conn., 1958); Daisy Bates's *The Long
Shadow of Little Rock: A Memoir* (New York, 1962); Brooks Hays's *A Southern Moderate Speaks*
(Chapel Hill, N.C., 1959); Dale Alford and L'Moore Alford's *The Case of the Sleeping People
(Finally Awakened by Little Rock School Frustrations)* (Little Rock, Ark., 1959); Woodrow Wilson
Mann in New York *Herald-Tribune,* January 19, 1958–January 31, 1958; "The Story of Little
Rock—As Governor Faubus Tells It," *U.S. News and World Report,* June 20, 1958, pp. 101–
106; and Orval Eugene Faubus' *Down from the Hills* (Little Rock, Ark., 1980) and *Down from
the Hills–II* (Little Rock, Ark., 1986). This discussion also borrows from Numan V. Bartley's
"Looking Back at Little Rock," *Arkansas Historical Quarterly*, XXV (1966), 101–16.

ble. "Many Negro parents," Daisy Bates, a leader of the National Association for the Advancement of Colored People in Little Rock, observed, "became convinced that Superintendent Blossom was more interested in appeasing the segregationists by advocating that only a limited number of Negroes be admitted than in complying with the Supreme Court decision."[3]

Through all this, Blossom, the school board, and virtually everyone else treated desegregation as a problem in school administration. They devised a plan without seriously consulting the people it would most affect. Blossom worked hard to win the accord of the groups educators normally looked to for support, and he sought to appease influential whites by exempting many of their children from at least the early stages of desegregation. Otherwise school authorities sought no active community involvement. When an occasional white group—such as the city ministerial association—offered to endorse the plan publicly, Blossom discouraged the action.

Few whites demonstrated any desire to become involved in an unpopular social innovation. Although Little Rock business and civic leaders were an active and effective force in community affairs, they listened politely to Blossom and otherwise tried to ignore the issue. Black citizens had no opportunity to contribute except by bringing suit in opposition to the plan. Ordinary whites either evinced apathy or became more hostile to the whole idea of desegregation. The city government left the matter to the educators, partly by default, since a change in city government was taking place.

During 1957 the Good Government Committee, composed of Little Rock civic leaders, successfully sponsored a manager-commissioner form of government to replace the neighborhood-based mayor-alderman system. The voters of Little Rock approved the change in the spring. With elections to fill the newly created offices scheduled for November, Mayor Woodrow Wilson Mann headed a lame-duck administration that had been discredited at the polls. Mann and the city government, along with the officials of Pulaski County, seemed indifferent to the developing contro-

[3] Bates, *The Long Shadow of Little Rock*, 51–52.

versy over school desegregation. Mann's administration made belated plans to maintain public order, but it issued no statement offering assurances on the point. Like a large majority of the aldermen, both city police chief Marvin H. Potts and county sheriff Tom Gulley were avowed segregationists who showed little interest in supporting school desegregation.[4]

Ordinary whites increasingly turned to the Capital Citizens' Council for guidance. Based mainly in working-class neighborhoods and ably led, the council demanded an end to the experiment with the city's children. The council, later joined by the Mothers' League of Central High School, decried the desegregation plan as an alien program inflicted on ordinary whites by rich people. By the summer of 1957, the Council was holding frequent rallies—sometimes with imported speakers such as Governor Marvin Griffin of Georgia—and packing school-board meetings with antagonistic and clamorous audiences. Council leaders implored Governor Orval Faubus to keep his promise to prevent "forced" desegregation.[5]

As segregationist pressure mounted, Superintendent Blossom and the members of the school board became increasingly alarmed. Blossom and the school board, a federal official reported, were "greatly concerned about the possibility of violence when schools start in September." Blossom wrote in his memoirs, "The integration of Central High School was no longer a local, school administrative problem." He and the school board concluded that the interests of public safety required that Governor Faubus intervene to ensure peaceful desegregation.[6]

During the weeks before the schools opened, both the opponents and the proponents of desegregation insisted that Faubus take action. Segregationists argued that if Governor Allan Shivers of Texas could block court-sanctioned desegregation, so too could the governor of Arkansas. Blossom and the school-board members

[4] Good critiques of Little Rock's preparations for desegregation include Cartwright's "Lesson from Little Rock"; Brown's *Bigger Than Little Rock;* Wallace's "The Little Rock Central Desegregation Crisis of 1957"; and Spitzberg's *Racial Politics in Little Rock,* 31–81.

[5] *Southern School News,* June, 1957–October, 1957; Neil R. McMillen, *The Citizens' Council: Organized Resistance to the Second Reconstruction, 1954–1964* (Urbana, Ill., 1971), 267–76.

[6] Arthur B. Caldwell to Warren Olney III, July 24, 1957, in Arthur B. Caldwell Papers, University of Arkansas Libraries; Blossom, *It Has Happened Here,* 48.

met often with Faubus, relaying on several occasions rumors of impending violence. The educators entreated Faubus to release a statement similar to the one Governor Luther H. Hodges of North Carolina had issued, warning that the state would not permit disruptions and violence. "The more the tension mounted late in August," Blossom explained, "the more anxious the school board was to persuade Governor Faubus to issue a formal statement." [7]

Faubus did not wish to become involved. He had consistently pledged that "no school board will be forced to mix the races in schools while I am governor." In practice he had left local communities to work out their own salvation. Little Rock disrupted the state government's laissez-faire policy. Both segregationists and desegregationists insisted that the situation in Little Rock required state intervention. Faubus indicated no desire to defy the federal courts. "Everyone knows," he pointed out, "that state laws can't supersede federal laws." At the same time, the governor displayed no inclination to commit what he deemed to be "political suicide" by employing state power to "force" an unwilling community to desegregate. During the days prior to the opening of the schools in early September, 1957, Faubus maneuvered frantically to avoid taking a stand in Little Rock. [8]

The governor first asked the Eisenhower administration to assume responsibility. In response to the governor's request, the Justice Department sent Arthur B. Caldwell of the civil rights section to confer with Faubus. The governor's primary concern was "to find out what, if anything, could be expected from the federal government in the way of assistance if disorder occurred." Caldwell answered that the federal executive branch did not wish to become involved. In Faubus' view, the national government was

---

[7] Blossom, *It Has Happened Here*, 49; Wayne Upton Interview, New Orleans *Times-Picayune*, January 29, 1959; "The Story of Little Rock—As Governor Faubus Tells It"; Faubus, *Down from the Hills*, 174–204. Wayne Upton was a member of Little Rock's school board. After the event, Faubus consistently maintained that it was the information Blossom and the school board supplied that convinced him that violence was imminent and state action necessary.

[8] Faubus quoted in *Southern School News*, July, 1956, and in *Arkansas Gazette* (Little Rock), July 18, 1957; Orval Faubus Interview, June 14, 1974, in Southern Oral History Program, Bass-DeVries Southern Politics Series, 1947–1974, Southern Historical Collection, University of North Carolina at Chapel Hill.

"cramming integration down our throats" but refusing "to help keep order." Federal authorities, he complained, "intended for me to do their dirty work for them." [9]

Faubus next looked to the state judiciary. In late August Faubus helped initiate and testified in support of a suit by the Mothers' League seeking to enjoin school authorities from imposing their plan. Relying heavily on the governor's testimony, the chancery court judge pointed to the "threat of violence, riots and bloodshed" in issuing the injunction. On the following day, August 30, the federal district court voided the state court's ruling, ordered school officials to carry out their desegregation plan, and enjoined others from obstructing its implementation. [10]

At this point Faubus had run out of politically acceptable options. As Congressman Brooks Hays recalled, "the Governor was sincere in his fear of the outbreak of violence." Faubus also feared that the exercise of state force to achieve desegregation would result in political disaster. On September 2 he called out the National Guard to prevent desegregation when the schools opened the following day. "You are directed," Faubus instructed his adjutant general, "to place off limits to white students those schools for colored students and to place off limits to colored students those schools heretofore operated and recently set up for white students." In a television address that night and in later statements, the governor reiterated that the role of the guardsmen was not to act as "segregationists or integrationists" but "to maintain or restore order and to protect the lives and property of citizens." The nine black teenagers who were to attend Central High School remained home on the first day of classes, but on September 4 they attempted to attend school and were turned away by the guardsmen. A politically-oriented governor who saw himself as "sitting on a keg of dynamite" blocked the desegregation that a

[9] Faubus quoted in New York *Times*, August 31, 1957; Faubus, *Down from the Hills*, p. 198 quoted. See also Arthur B. Caldwell to Warren Olney III, "Memorandum: Conference with the Governor of Arkansas on 28 August 1957," August 30, 1957, Warren Olney III, "A Government Lawyer Looks at Little Rock," October 3, 1957, both in Caldwell Papers.

[10] Court orders and other documents related to the crisis may be found in *Race Relations Law Reporter*, II, 929–83.

federal court had ordered and directly, if largely unintentionally, put to the test the viability of interposition.[11]

The school board returned to the federal district court for a delay in desegregation because of rising racial tensions. Judge Ronald Davies denied the petition and soon afterward directed the Eisenhower administration to enter the case as friends of the court. At the court's request, the Justice Department asked for an injunction restraining Faubus and the National Guard commanders from impeding desegregation. Federal attorneys averted an immediate confrontation by seeking a preliminary injunction rather than an immediate restraining order, and Judge Davies scheduled a hearing on the federal petition for September 20. During the interim, Congressman Hays, whose district included Little Rock, arranged a meeting between Faubus and Eisenhower that ended inconclusively. The National Guardsmen lounged around Central High School, watching the crowds that gathered to watch them. At the scheduled hearing, Judge Davies ordered Arkansas officials to cease interfering with the desegregation of Central High School. Immediately afterward Faubus removed the guard.[12]

Central High School desegregated on Monday, September 23. By that time, Mayor Mann's authority had collapsed. The city police chief, according to Mann, sought "to get out from under his responsibility," and the fire chief would not provide hoses for crowd control. A mob of a thousand or so whites demanded that the black students be removed from the school. As the demonstration became more obstreperous, state police evacuated the newcomers. Mann requested assistance from the federal government, and on the following day President Eisenhower federalized the Arkansas National Guard and sent in regular army units to

[11] Hays, *A Southern Moderate Speaks*, 154; Faubus quoted in *Race Relations Law Reporter*, II, 960, in *Southern School News*, October, 1957, and in *Racial Politics in Little Rock*, by Spitzberg, 64; Arthur B. Caldwell to Warren Olney III, September 3, 1957, J. Edgar Hoover to attorney general, "Segregation in Public Schools, State of Arkansas," September 9, 1957, Warren Olney III to attorney general, "Summary of FBI Report in Little Rock," September 13, 1957, all in Caldwell Papers.

[12] *Race Relations Law Reporter*, II, 958–63; Hays, *A Southern Moderate Speaks*, 132–71; Olney, "A Government Lawyer Looks at Little Rock."

restore peace in the city. Like Faubus, Eisenhower maintained that "the troops are not there as a part of the segregation problem" but to uphold constitutional government. Central High School remained desegregated for the remainder of the 1957–1958 school year. The National Guard patrolled the school, the black students faced organized harassment by some of the white students, and teachers tried to conduct classes in virtually impossible circumstances.[13]

The desegregation crisis in Little Rock betrayed the general lack of white commitment to desegregation. The city's leadership was willing to accept desegregation so long as it was limited and Blossom and the school board took care of it. The Faubus administration was willing to accept desegregation so long as the governor did not have to assume any responsibility for it. The Eisenhower administration was willing to accept desegregation so long as the president could remain aloof from it. Such a complete vacuum of leadership invited demagoguery and irresponsibility, and Faubus ultimately supplied it. Irresponsible stewardship was in evidence everywhere, but the irresolution of the federal government determined in large measure the extent and duration of the crisis.

The Eisenhower administration had from the beginning shown doubt and ambivalence toward *Brown* v. *Board of Education*. A true conservative, Eisenhower had little confidence that prejudice would "succumb to compulsion." As he observed in 1953, "Improvement in race relations is one of those things that will be healthy and sound only if it starts locally." From the president's perspective, "progress toward equality had to be achieved finally in the hearts of men rather than in legislative halls." At a press conference in 1954, he referred to the "deep-seated emotions" that *Brown* touched. He plainly believed that "these great emotional strains and the practical problems" were important considerations.[14]

[13] Mann in New York *Herald-Tribune,* January 27, 1958, January 29, 1958; Hays, *A Southern Moderate Speaks,* 166–73; Press Conference Series, October 3, 1957, Herbert Brownell, Jr., to President Eisenhower, Memorandum for the Record, Administrative Series, n.d. [October, 1957], both in Dwight D. Eisenhower Library, Abilene, Kans.

[14] Dwight David Eisenhower Diary Series, July 20, 1953, Press Conference Series, November 23, 1954, both in Eisenhower Library. Helpful on the Eisenhower administration are

Most of Eisenhower's advisers agreed. When in 1953 the Supreme Court invited the new administration to follow Truman's example in filing a brief in the case as a friend of the court, officials at the Justice Department recoiled. The "prevailing attitude," one of their number recounted, "was expressed by [assistant attorney general William P.] Rogers, who said in effect, 'Jesus, do we really have to file a brief? Aren't we better off staying out of it?' " The Justice Department did decide to participate, and in the proceedings about implementation it argued for flexible and gradual compliance.[15]

President Eisenhower never publicly endorsed the *Brown* decision, and as southern resistance spread, he voiced reservations. "I personally think," he once told a staff member, "that the decision was wrong." The president did accept the "general principle" of equality before the law, Sherman Adams, Eisenhower's chief of staff, has emphasized. In areas directly under federal control—including the armed forces and the public schools in Washington, D.C.—the administration acted with considerable dispatch to promote desegregation. But in relation to the *Brown* decision, the president, according to another aide, worried more about "social disintegration" than about "school integration." Eisenhower once remarked privately, "I am convinced that the Supreme Court decision set back progress in the South at least fifteen years." By 1958 "Eisenhower's own private, abiding dissent from the Supreme Court action" had become common knowledge among White House journalists, one of whom inquired about it at a press conference. Eisenhower responded that "it might have been that I said something about 'slower' " regarding implementation of the *Brown* decision.[16]

Robert F. Burk's *Symbolic Equality: The Eisenhower Administration and Black Civil Rights, 1953–1961* (Knoxville, Tenn., 1984) and James C. Duram's *A Moderate Among Extremists: Dwight D. Eisenhower and the School Desegregation Crisis* (Chicago, 1981).

[15] Richard Kluger, *Simple Justice: The History of Brown v. Board of Education and Black America's Struggle for Equality* (New York, 1975), 650. Philip Elman is the quoted official from the Justice Department.

[16] Arthur Larson, *Eisenhower: The President Nobody Knew* (New York, 1968), 124; Sherman Adams, *Firsthand Report: The Story of the Eisenhower Administration* (New York, 1961), 332; Emmet John Hughes, *The Ordeal of Power: A Political Memoir of the Eisenhower Years* (New York, 1961), 201, 242; Press Conference Series, August 27, 1958, in Eisenhower Library.

Eisenhower had little tolerance for the impatience of blacks. National African-American leaders frequently asked to meet with the president, and E. Frederic Morrow, the self-described "black man in the White House," made the case to the president that he should consent. Eisenhower invited Martin Luther King, Jr., Lester Granger, A. Philip Randolph, and Roy Wilkins to the oval office in June, 1958. The president's guests called attention to the slow pace of civil rights progress and to the growing frustration felt by black Americans. According to an aide's notes on the meeting, Eisenhower responded that "after five and a half years of effort and action in this field these gentlemen were saying that bitterness on the part of the Negro people was at its height. He wondered if further constructive action in this field would not only result in more bitterness." [17]

National political equations reinforced the administration's torpor in racial matters. Eisenhower Democrats such as Governor Shivers of Texas had been instrumental to Eisenhower's electoral success in the South. Republican strategists hoped to expand their beachhead in the region and consulted their newfound allies on patronage and other matters. Eisenhower rebuked a Texas Republican who did "not realize that Democrats in the state elected the administration," and he appointed Oveta Culp Hobby of Houston to his cabinet and Robert B. Anderson of Fort Worth as secretary of the navy.[18]

The Eisenhower administration sponsored two modest civil rights bills, which Congress enacted in 1957 and 1960. Both concerned voting rights, which Eisenhower favored. The administration's support for each of the laws came only after the president overruled a number of his advisers. Cabinet members demonstrated considerably greater sympathy for J. Edgar Hoover's warnings about the danger of Communist influence in civil rights affairs. Hoover briefed the cabinet in March, 1957, on provocations "by some overzealous but ill-advised leaders of the NAACP and by

[17] E. Frederic Morrow, *Black Man in the White House: A Diary of the Eisenhower Years by the Administrative Officer for Special Projects, The White House, 1955–1961* (New York, 1963), 51– 233; "Memorandum for the Files," Official File, June 24, 1958, in Eisenhower Library.

[18] New York *Times*, December 19, 1952; Dwight David Eisenhower Diary Series, Telephone Calls (Sid Richardson *re* Jack Porter), August 5, 1953, in Eisenhower Library.

the Communist party, which seeks to use incidents to further the so-called class struggle." Sherman Adams ominously observed that the "Communist influence" in civil rights matters "was tremendous."[19]

In early 1957 the Justice Department restated its guiding principle: "The primary responsibility for the maintenance of law and order is lodged in state and local authorities." That summer Eisenhower asserted at a press conference, "I can't imagine any set of circumstances that would ever induce me to send federal troops ... into any area to enforce the orders of a federal court, because I believe that the common sense of Americans will never require it." Just after Faubus called out the National Guard, Eisenhower stressed at a press conference the "very strong emotions on the other side, people that see a picture of the mongrelization of the race, as they call it." On September 6, the president's press secretary assured reporters that the administration remained opposed to the use of federal force in desegregation.[20]

The Eisenhower administration resisted making federal marshals available to help keep the peace in Little Rock. After Faubus called out the National Guard, the administration rejected the simple expedient of nationalizing the guardsmen and changing their orders. After the Justice Department was forced to enter the judicial proceedings, it did not seek an immediate order restraining the governor and his generals but welcomed a cooling-off period. When Eisenhower finally did federalize the guard and send in regular soldiers, he had already passed up ample opportunity to minimize the crisis.

Officials serving under Eisenhower often argued that their policy permitted southern whites a necessary period to adjust to a

[19]"Minutes," March 9, 1956, March 23, 1956, J. Edgar Hoover, "Racial Tension and Civil Rights" (Presentation to cabinet, March 9, 1956), March 1, 1956, p. 24 quoted; Hoover, "Briefing on Internal Security," November 6, 1958, all Cabinet Series, in Eisenhower Library; Adams quoted in Morrow, *Black Man in the White House*, 52; J. W. Anderson, *Eisenhower, Brownell, and the Congress: The Tangled Origins of the Civil Rights Bill of 1956–1957* (University, Ala., 1964); Daniel M. Berman, *A Bill Becomes a Law: Congress Enacts Civil Rights Legislation* (2nd ed.; New York, 1966).

[20]Assistant Attorney General Warren Olney III quoted in *Southern School News*, March, 1957; Press Conference Series, July 17, 1957, September 3, 1957, both in Eisenhower Library; Chattanooga *Times*, September 7, 1957.

new social order. In 1958 Rogers, then the attorney general, explained that the administration's approach granted time for "southern public opinion . . . to be brought to accept the inevitability of racially mixed schools." However reasonable that approach, Eisenhower combined it with an insistence that "I do not believe it is the function or indeed it is desirable for a president to express his approval or disapproval of any Supreme Court decision." By not speaking in favor of *Brown*, or at least the principle behind it, Eisenhower undermined the strategy his administration claimed to be pursuing. Chief Justice Earl Warren had a point when he ventured the opinion that "much of our racial strife could have been avoided if President Eisenhower had at least observed that our country is dedicated to the principle" of desegregation and civic equality.[21]

Eisenhower's detachment undermined the southern moderates, whose position essentially rested on popular acceptance of the inevitability of desegregation. Approximately eight out of ten southern whites consistently disapproved of the verdict in *Brown* throughout the second half of the 1950s. About 20 percent of white southerners were adamant segregationists who were willing to oppose integration with force. Another 20 percent accepted or even approved of the decision. That left a majority of white southerners—six in ten—"strict segregationists" who would not condone violence to maintain racial castes. If desegregation were inevitable, such behavior was irrational. In early 1956, according to pollsters, a majority of white southerners—55 percent—did think the day would come when whites and blacks shared the same public facilities. Most blacks—seven out of ten—agreed. One-third of southern whites disagreed, and 12 percent professed uncertainty. By the summer of 1957, however, massive resistance and the Eisenhower administration's laconic demeanor contributed to a sizable shift in popular convictions. By then, only 43 percent of southern whites believed that desegregation was inevitable; the majority either expected segregation to continue or admitted they were unsure. Little Rock restored popular acceptance of the prop-

---

[21] Rogers quoted in Richmond *Times-Dispatch*, September 21, 1958; Eisenhower quoted in *Race Relations Law Reporter*, IV, 5; *The Memoirs of Earl Warren* (Garden City, N.Y., 1977), 291.

osition that changes in racial practices were unavoidable. By the fall of 1958, a majority of white southerners again accepted desegregation as a certainty. By early 1961, three-quarters of all southerners—black and white—believed desegregation was inevitable.[22]

For six of Eisenhower's eight years in office, the Democratic party controlled Congress, with the southern delegation dominating the committees of both chambers through seniority. Republicans needed southern Democratic support to pass the administration's programs, and that dependence provided both a reason and a rationalization for the Republican leadership to counsel patience concerning civil rights.

The two civil rights laws Congress enacted during the Eisenhower years impressed some as important legislative accomplishments. It would be equally possible to describe them as monuments to congressional cynicism. The bills were calculated to improve the image of the Eisenhower administration and such nationally ambitious southerners as Lyndon B. Johnson, the Senate majority leader. They permitted northern liberals to boast of their triumphs and permitted southern conservatives to explain that the laws did not mean anything. When Senator J. Strom Thurmond violated southern caucus policy by resorting to a twenty-four-hour filibuster against the civil rights bill of 1957, his southern colleagues roundly castigated him as an irresponsible maverick. That five senators from former Confederate states—Johnson and Ralph W. Yarborough of Texas, Estes Kefauver and Albert Gore of Tennessee, and George A. Smathers of Florida—cast ballots in favor of civil rights legislation during the period did suggest, though, a new flexibility within southern congressional ranks.[23]

[22] George Gallup in Nashville *Tennessean*, February 29, 1956, October 15, 1958, February 12, 1961; Melvin M. Tumin *et al.*, *Desegregation: Resistance and Readiness* (Princeton, 1958); Helen Gaudet Erskine, "The Polls: Race Relations," *Public Opinion Quarterly*, XXVI (1962), 137–48.

[23] James MacGregor Burns, *The Deadlock of Democracy: Four-Party Politics in America* (Englewood Cliffs, N.J., 1963); Robert Dallek, *Lone Star Rising: Lyndon Johnson and His Times, 1908–1960* (New York, 1991), 509–91; Robert Edward Hayes, "Senatorial Voting Behavior with Regard to the 'Southern Interest'" (Ph.D. dissertation, University of Colorado, 1964), 177–255; Michael Gerald Rakow, "Southern Politics in the United States Senate, 1948–1972" (Ph.D. dissertation, Arizona State University, 1973); W. Wayne Shannon, *Party,*

On the whole, Congress devoted considerably more time to battling the Supreme Court than to legislating in behalf of civil rights. Between 1954 and 1958, it debated a plethora of anti-Court bills, the most significant of which did not pertain directly to black civil rights but did aim to limit the jurisdiction of the Court. Of more immediate moment for the South were the proceedings of several congressional committees, including the House Committee on Un-American Activities, the Senate Internal Security Subcommittee, and the House Committee on the District of Columbia. The Senate subcommittee held hearings in New Orleans in 1954 and discovered that the Southern Conference Education Fund was a Communist front. Between 1956 and 1958 the congressional custodians of domestic patriotism held hearings in Georgia, Louisiana, North Carolina, and Tennessee, ceaselessly searching for Communists and confusing them with integrationists. The House Committee on the District of Columbia chipped in with a damning report on the desegregation of Washington's schools, and predictably a majority recommended "that racially separate public schools be reestablished." Most significant of all was the day-to-day policies of the congressional committees and bureaucratic agencies that tended the interests of suburban developers, large agriculturists, and such.[24]

The congressional investigating committees became models for state bodies in the South. The Arkansas legislature created a committee to probe the causes of the crisis in Little Rock. The committee imported professional witnesses who normally testified before congressional committees and whose epic fantasies seemed

Constituency, and Congressional Voting: A Study of Legislative Behavior in the United States House of Representatives (Baton Rouge, 1968).

[24] Walter F. Murphy, *Congress and the Court* (Chicago, 1962), 182–212; *Investigation of Public School Conditions: Report of the Subcommittee to Investigate Public School Standards and Conditions and Juvenile Delinquency in the District of Columbia,* 84th Cong., 2nd Sess., 47; Numan V. Bartley, *The Rise of Massive Resistance: Race and Politics During the 1950s* (Baton Rouge, 1969), 170–89. Among numerous studies of congressional anticommunism, particularly relevant to the South are Anne Braden's *House Un-American Activities Committee: Bulwark of Segregation* (Los Angeles, 1963) and Wayne Addison Clark's "An Analysis of the Relationship Between Anti-Communism and Segregationist Thought in the Deep South, 1948–1964" (Ph.D. dissertation, University of North Carolina, 1976). After the hearing in Atlanta in 1958, Anne Braden's husband, Carl, served a year in prison for contempt of Congress.

to shake the Arkansas lawmakers, and doubtless some viewers of the televised hearings. Nevertheless, the members of the committee rose to the occasion and delivered a report that found the "international Communist conspiracy of world domination squarely behind the entire shocking episode."[25]

As a group, southern congressional Democrats were considerably to the right of southern politicians generally, particularly on racial questions. John Dos Passos once observed that the seniority system elevated to power an "oligarchy of oldtimers" whose "real contacts with real people and things had been made fifteen or twenty years ago." Some southern members, according to journalists, were "acutely conscious of the ultimate futility of deadend resistance," but they supported the old guard anyway, explaining in private "that they can't help themselves, that they have nowhere else to go." Mississippi congressman Frank E. Smith reported that "talking Negro" was by no means exclusively a southern Democratic proclivity; liberal members "went out of their way" to tell him that "they agreed with the Southern position but couldn't vote for it." At any rate, the southern congressional delegation constituted a minority of congressional Democrats, not to mention of all members of Congress. National legislators could have modified or eliminated the seniority system in any session in which they had the will to do so. Only because of their inaction did the Dixieland congressional band retain its remarkable unity and influence.[26]

The limits of southern congressional power became evident in 1960. Johnson, the Senate majority leader, and Sam Rayburn, the speaker of the House, attempted to exploit their positions of influence in Congress to advance Johnson's bid for the Democratic presidential nomination. Their plan was to forgo the presidential primaries and instead to prevail on their congressional colleagues to sway convention delegations. Johnson and Rayburn "thought

---

[25] Quoted in *Arkansas Gazette* (Little Rock), January 17, 1959.

[26] John Dos Passos, *State of the Nation* (Boston, 1944), 195; Harry S. Ashmore, *An Epitaph for Dixie* (New York, 1958), 31; Frank E. Smith, *Congressman from Mississippi* (New York, 1964), 104; W. Wayne Shannon, "Revolt in Washington: The South in Congress," in *The Changing Politics of the South*, ed. William C. Havard (Baton Rouge, 1972), 637–87. See also Ralph W. McGill, "Southern Moderates Are Still There," *New York Times Magazine*, September 21, 1958, pp. 13ff.

they could reach the state power centers through friendly members of Congress," one study has concluded, but what they discovered was that many of their congressional allies were "grossly out of touch with political realities in their states." At the convention, Johnson proved to be a sectional candidate, winning most of the southern votes but losing decisively outside the region. Senator John F. Kennedy won the nomination on the first ballot.[27]

Kennedy chose Johnson as the vice-presidential candidate. From an electoral perspective the choice was quite logical. The Protestant, southern Johnson balanced a ticket headed by a northeastern Catholic. Johnson, eager to achieve national standing, agreed to campaign on a platform with the strongest civil rights plank in the history of the party. Johnson also protected himself against a possible defeat of the national ticket by concurrently running for, and winning, his Texas Senate seat.

In Congress, Senator Kennedy had established a reputation as a moderate and had cultivated southern support. In his successful presidential campaign, however, he made clear that he placed greater weight on symbolic equality than either Eisenhower or the Republican presidential candidate, Richard M. Nixon. America's standing abroad, Kennedy often pointed out, required racial progress at home. He promised to restore the nation's leadership of the free world, to make the presidency a "symbol of the moral imperative upon which a free society is based," and to place at the top of the administration's domestic agenda the "great moral issue" of civil rights.[28]

As it turned out, an incident involving Martin Luther King, Jr., gave Kennedy an opportunity to make an emblematic racial gesture that helped him among black voters. When King was arrested on questionable grounds in DeKalb County, a part of the Atlanta

[27] D. B. Hardeman and Donald C. Bacon, *Rayburn: A Biography* (Austin, Tex., 1987), 389–445, p. 435 quoted; Dallek, *Lone Star Rising,* 544–91; Harry McPherson Oral History Interview, December 5, 1968, in Lyndon Baines Johnson Library, Austin, Tex.

[28] Kennedy quoted in *John F. Kennedy and the Second Reconstruction,* by Carl M. Brauer (New York, 1977), 44, and in *Southern School News,* October, 1960. See also Guy Paul Land, "John F. Kennedy's Southern Strategy, 1956–1960," *North Carolina Historical Review,* LVI (1979), 41–63; Theodore H. White, *The Making of the President, 1960* (New York, 1961); Dallek, *Lone Star Rising,* 571–91; and Pierre Salinger, *With Kennedy* (Garden City, N.Y., 1966), 29–48.

metropolitan area, and placed in the state penitentiary in the south Georgia town of Reidsville, Kennedy phoned King's wife, Coretta Scott King, to show solidarity, and the candidate's brother Robert F. Kennedy lodged a complaint with the county judge. Still, Nixon carried the black precincts in Atlanta.[29]

Johnson focused his campaign on the South. With his help, the Democratic ticket won in Arkansas, Georgia, Louisiana, North Carolina, South Carolina, and Texas. Nixon carried Florida, Kentucky, Oklahoma, Tennessee, and Virginia. State righters ran strong campaigns in Mississippi, Alabama, and Louisiana, carrying Mississippi and in Alabama winning six of the eleven seats in the electoral college, the other five going to electors who were for Kennedy. The state rights campaign was an attempt to extend massive resistance into national politics.[30]

Facing the fury of massive resistance, the antipathy of Congress, and usually the detachment of the executive branch, the Supreme Court became conspicuously restrained. During the late 1950s and well into the 1960s, federal judges accepted "tokenism," at least in those cases, one scholar has explained, "where the local authorities were prepared to symbolize their acceptance of the principle of desegregation by the actual physical introduction of Negro pupils into white schools." In early 1958 the Supreme Court's ruling in *Shuttlesworth* v. *Birmingham Board of Education* upheld the Alabama pupil-placement law. The opinion, in Ralph W. McGill's words, was "really an astounding decision." The Court had, McGill stated, "in a very real sense taken itself off the hook" by accepting a law that gave the "state an almost rigid control of its school system."[31]

Most of the legal action relating to desegregation fell to federal district-court and federal circuit-court judges. Studies of the "fifty-eight lonely men" who occupied district judgeships in the former

[29] Harris Wofford, *Of Kennedys and Kings: Making Sense of the Sixties* (New York, 1980), 11–28.

[30] Land, "John F. Kennedy's Southern Strategy"; *Southern School News*, August, 1960–December, 1960.

[31] Alexander M. Bickel, "The Decade of School Desegregation: Progress and Prospects," *Columbia Law Review*, LXIV (1964), 205; J. W. Peltason, *Fifty-Eight Lonely Men* (New York, 1961), 56–92; McGill quoted in Atlanta *Constitution*, February 17, 1959; *Shuttlesworth* v. *Birmingham Board of Education*, in *Race Relations Law Reporter*, III, 425–34.

Confederacy have consistently awarded the judges high marks for upholding the basic principle of *Brown* under difficult conditions. Most of the judges favored segregation personally, and some betrayed a consistent state rights bias in their decisions. Only two, the successive occupants of the Northern District Court of Texas, actually challenged the Supreme Court's authority regarding desegregation. Still, the district courts, like the Supreme Court, became less disposed toward black plaintiffs. Kenneth N. Vines has calculated that whereas district judges in the midfifties delivered "pro-Negro" opinions in a majority of their racial cases, by the late fifties the majority of their rulings in such cases were against the blacks who had brought suit.[32]

Despite its strategic retreat, the Supreme Court acted decisively during the Little Rock crisis. While Central High School limped through its first year of desegregation, the school board petitioned the federal district court for permission to restore segregation for two and a half years in order to allow the abatement of racial animosities. The Supreme Court, in hearing the appeal, had to decide whether popular hostility to integration justified segregation. In September, 1958, the Court ruled that it did not. "The constitutional rights of respondents," it said in *Cooper* v. *Aaron*, "are not to be sacrificed or yielded to the violence and disorder which have followed upon the actions of the Governor and Legislature." The resounding reaffirmation of the principle of *Brown* did not, however, result in the continued desegregation of Central High. A few hours after the decision was announced, Governor Faubus issued a proclamation closing the four public high schools in Little Rock.[33]

During the year that separated the armed confrontation in Little Rock in September, 1957, and the judicial determination in *Cooper* v. *Aaron* in September, 1958, Governor Faubus had developed a latent talent for demagoguery. The governor charged that

[32] Peltason, *Fifty-Eight Lonely Men;* Kenneth N. Vines, "Federal District Judges and Race Relations Cases in the South," *Journal of Politics,* XXVI (1964), 337–57; Jack Bass, *Unlikely Heroes* (New York, 1981); Frank T. Read and Lucy S. McGough, *Let Them Be Judged: The Judicial Integration of the Deep South* (Metuchen, N.J., 1978).

[33] *Cooper* v. *Aaron,* in *Race Relations Law Reporter,* III, 855–67; *Arkansas Gazette* (Little Rock), September 13, 1958.

FBI agents were holding Central High School female students incommunicado for long periods, that federal troops were entering the girls' dressing rooms, and that federal agents had tapped his telephone lines. Riding a wave of popular adulation, Faubus vowed to continue defending the "right of states and communities to govern their own affairs on a local level." The Arkansas County Judges Association and other politically powerful groups acclaimed the governor's stand, and in the summer of 1958 he handily won nomination for a third term as governor. The delegates to the state Democratic convention were there mainly as his cheering section. By that time he was arguing that school desegregation was a Communist plot and that the Little Rock school board should either reimpose segregation or resign and make way for a board with the backbone to do it.[34]

In August, 1958, Faubus convened a special session of the legislature. The governor submitted a segregationist legislative package and Bruce Bennett, the state attorney general, offered a host of bills aimed at the NAACP as a part of his Southern Plan for Peace. Altogether the legislature enacted fourteen laws, the most far-reaching of which authorized the governor to close any school threatened by violence or integration. On the same day that Faubus shut down the high schools in Little Rock, Governor J. Lindsay Almond closed Warren County High School in Virginia to block desegregation. Soon afterward he did the same with six schools in Norfolk and two in Charlottesville.[35]

The Arkansas law provided for a referendum, and in late September, citizens of Little Rock voted almost three-to-one in favor of closed schools. The wording on the ballot proffered the unappealing alternative of "racial integration of all schools within the school district," but notwithstanding the leading language, the returns demonstrated impressive support for the governor's position. In early November, Dale Alford, a segregationist and a

[34] *Southern School News*, November, 1957, December, 1957; Faubus quoted in Louisville *Courier-Journal*, July 31, 1958; John Robert Starr, *Yellow Dogs and Dark Horses: Thirty Years on the Campaign Beat* (Little Rock, Ark., 1987), 9–41. The governor's changing views are traced in *Arkansas Gazette* (Little Rock), September 7, 1958.

[35] *Race Relations Law Reporter*, III, 869, 1037–52; *Southern School News*, September, 1958, October, 1958.

member of the school board, ousted veteran congressman Brooks Hays through a write-in campaign. A moderate, Hays had earned the wrath of Faubus and the resistance by trying to mediate the school conflict. The only issue in Alford's campaign was segregation. Soon afterward, the other members of the school board resigned, citing the "utter hopelessness, helplessness and frustration" of their position. They bought out Blossom's contract to spare him further humiliation. In December, 1958, Little Rock elected a new school board. Because of a split in the ranks of the Citizens' Council, two moderates won with pluralities, and the election resulted in a deadlocked school board composed of three moderates and three segregationists.[36]

In Virginia, Governor Almond enunciated a considerably more rigid commitment to massive resistance. Almond proclaimed that Virginia would "not abandon or compromise with principle to have it lost, never to be regained." To the governor and the Byrd organization, a journalist wrote, "to allow one Negro student to enter a Virginia public school under federal court orders would be an admission of the legality of the Supreme Court's ruling." At the same time that Hays was being defeated in Arkansas, Senator Harry Flood Byrd was winning reelection by his usual landslide. In Norfolk, the city council put the question of school closure to the voters in a referendum, and six out of ten favored shuttering the schools over acceding to integration. As in Little Rock, the wording of the question was not neutral.[37]

While the politicians orated, thirteen southern schools remained idle. In Little Rock, more than nine out of ten of the white students managed to enroll in other districts or to attend private schools. About half the black high-school students simply did not go to school during the 1958–1959 academic year. In Virginia, Almond closed only white schools subject to court-ordered desegregation; black students—except for the seventeen scheduled to enroll in desegregated schools—continued to attend classes. Seg-

[36] *Arkansas Gazette* (Little Rock), September 28, 1958; School-board statement in *Southern School News*, December, 1958.

[37] Almond Radio-Television Address, Richmond *Times-Dispatch,* January 21, 1959; Robert E. Baskin in Dallas *Morning News,* September 1, 1958; Ernest Q. Campbell, *When a City Closes Its Schools* (Chapel Hill, N.C., 1960), 13–14, 51–54.

regationists in Warren County and Charlottesville created viable private-school programs, and most students, aided by state tuition grants, remained in school. The greatest chaos was in Norfolk, where parents of ten thousand displaced students scrambled frantically, and frequently unsuccessfully, for educational facilities. The white parents in Norfolk, like those in Little Rock, nevertheless accepted with good grace short-term dislocations that were in the interest of segregation. "Parents of children closed out of public schools in Norfolk," a careful study determined, "did not constitute a distinctly more vigorous body of opponents to the school closings." [38]

Shortly after Faubus swept the 1958 gubernatorial primary, the *Arkansas Gazette* editorialized, "The moderate position formerly espoused by many Southern political leaders, and by this newspaper as a matter of principle, has been rejected by the mass of voters in this Upper Southern state and is now clearly untenable for any man in public life anywhere in the region." In the fall of 1958 the accuracy of the *Gazette*'s position appeared obvious. Insofar as the Supreme Court expected that "all deliberate speed" conceded time for southern whites to adjust to desegregation, it had underestimated the fixity of existing attitudes. Insofar as national liberals assumed that the American Creed would win the hearts and minds of white southerners to racial equity, they had overestimated the power of the abstract against the quotidian. Few white southerners saw anything particularly immoral about segregation, and virtually none had anything to gain by the coming of integration. [39]

Closed schools, however, were a different matter. Many "strict segregationists" also supported public education. A survey of white citizens undertaken several months after the schools had shut down in Norfolk found that 25 percent were "unyielding" segregationists who preferred locked schools to integration and that 15 percent supported the proposition "Desegregation in the

[38] Spitzberg, *Racial Politics in Little Rock,* 99–100; Benjamin Muse, *Virginia's Massive Resistance* (Bloomington, Ind., 1961), 111–14; *Southern School News,* November, 1960, December, 1960; Campbell, *When a City Closes Its Schools,* p. 65 quoted. See also Bob Smith, *They Closed Their Schools: Prince Edward County, Virginia, 1951–1964* (Chapel Hill, N.C., 1965).

[39] *Arkansas Gazette* (Little Rock), July 21, 1958.

public schools is the right thing." The remaining 60 percent of respondents were "practical" segregationists who "would prefer segregation but not if it means closing the schools." The dialectic had been rephrased in a fashion that benefited the southern moderates.[40]

James v. *Almond* further strengthened the moderate position. In a case initiated by white citizens associated with the Norfolk Committee for Public Schools, a three-judge federal court held that closing some schools while continuing to operate a public-school system denied the displaced students equality before the law. In *Cooper* v. *Aaron* the Supreme Court had ruled that "State support of segregated schools through any arrangement, management, funds or property cannot be squared with the command of the Fourteenth Amendment that no State shall deny to any person within its jurisdiction the equal protection of the laws." In *James* v. *Almond* a lower court ruled that a state could not operate some public schools and close others. Together, *Cooper* v. *Aaron* and *James* v. *Almond* left southern state governments with a stark choice: they could end public education entirely, or they could accept some desegregation.[41]

For the first time a popular moderate movement emerged in the South. Save-the-schools campaigns demanded that public education continue. First appearing in Arlington and the other Virginia suburbs of Washington, D.C., the Virginia Committee for Public Schools had by early 1959 grown into a formidable statewide movement. Help Our Public Education, chartered in Atlanta in November, 1958, soon claimed thirty thousand members. The Women's Emergency Committee, constituted in Little Rock to support open schools in the referendum of September, 1958, was the city's first effective moderate organization. These and other local groups challenged the influence of the Citizens' Councils and provided a "respectable" alternative to massive resistance. Refusing to debate the question of segregation and desegregation, they argued that the real issue was open schools or closed schools.

The moderate movement was metropolitan, white, affluent, and especially in its early development predominantly female. The

[40] Campbell, *When a City Closes Its Schools*, 56–57.
[41] *James* v. *Almond,* in *Race Relations Law Reporter,* IV, 45–54; *Cooper* v. *Aaron, ibid.,* III, 856.

typical member of the Women's Emergency Committee in Little Rock had a college education, a husband with a college degree who was employed in business or a profession, a residence in a good neighborhood, and two children of school age. Most of the members were homemakers and political amateurs, but they had the time, energy, and education to constitute a powerful political force. The men who participated in the movement tended to be young, affluent, upwardly mobile executives and professionals. In some cases, snob appeal appears to have contributed to the attractiveness of the moderate organizations. A moderate businessman in Little Rock disdainfully mentioned that Citizens' Councils did not attract the city's leadership and that "successful people didn't want to be identified with them." Some in the movement to save the public schools favored desegregation on its merits, but their organizations usually maintained unity and curried the goodwill of whites by barring blacks and laying stress on the indispensability of public schools to economic development.[42]

The region's established metropolitan business leadership moved gradually from acquiescence to moderation. Most businessmen, the evidence suggests, preferred segregation, and during the midfifties they for the most part took studious care not to become involved in the fray over the schools. But the financiers, merchants, publishers, and industrialists also had a substantial stake in economic growth and dreaded the economic impact of closed schools. As a study of Tampa concluded, closed schools and racial strife simply "did not make good dollars and cents" to the guardians of the city's financial interests.[43]

During the winter of 1958–1959, the Norfolk Committee of One Hundred, the Charlottesville Independent Citizens, and the chambers of commerce in Little Rock and, later, Atlanta were among establishment groups demanding open schools. Metro-

[42] Spitzberg, *Racial Politics in Little Rock*, 153–54; Jacoway, "Taken by Surprise," p. 36 quoted; Muse, *Virginia's Massive Resistance*, 56–162; Paul E. Mertz, "Hope, Inc., and School Desegregation in Georgia" (Paper delivered to Southern Historical Association, November, 1988).

[43] Richard Cramer, "School Desegregation and New Industry: The Southern Community Leader's Viewpoint," *Social Forces*, XLI (1963), 384–89; Steven F. Lawson, "From Sit-In to Race Riot: Businessmen, Blacks, and the Pursuit of Moderation in Tampa, 1960–1967," in *Southern Businessmen and Desegregation*, ed. Jacoway and Colburn, 280.

politan newspapers became increasingly hostile to closed schools. In late 1958 James J. Kilpatrick and the Richmond *News Leader*—along with other metropolitan dailies including the Richmond *Times-Dispatch*—dropped their support of massive resistance and came out for a flexible policy that could keep the schools open. Soon afterward, twenty-nine of the state's most consequential bankers, industrialists, and businessmen met with Almond to encourage an end to massive resistance. In 1960 Ivan Allen, Jr., the president of the Atlanta chamber of commerce, insisted, "Atlanta's public schools must stay open, and the chamber should provide its share of vigorous leadership in seeing that they do." [44]

The rise of a strong moderate movement emboldened educators. From the beginning, black teacher associations had supported the *Brown* decision even though it was widely believed that desegregation would result in a loss of jobs for some of their members. The organizations for white educators inclined to circumspection, given that the state and local officials who controlled their livelihoods wanted to preserve segregation at all costs. Normally these groups remained silent or threw their weight behind massive resistance. Only in Florida and North Carolina were white education organizations noticeably willing to risk giving offense. As popular sentiment swung to saving the public schools, however, state education associations and parent-teacher associations began coming out on the side of racial moderation. State education associations in Arkansas, Georgia, and Virginia, passed resolutions in favor of keeping the public schools open. Actions by education associations that often held the largest adult conventions in their states had an effect, as did the increasing involvement of church groups and the League of Women Voters. [45]

The massive-resistance front soon began to disintegrate. In late January, 1959, Almond informed a special session of the Virginia general assembly, "The time has arrived to take a new, thorough,

[44] Allen quoted in Atlanta *Constitution*, November 29, 1960; *Southern School News*, December, 1958; Muse, *Virginia's Massive Resistance*, 106–10. See the essays in *Southern Businessmen and Desegregation*, ed. Jacoway and Colburn.

[45] Reed Sarratt, *The Ordeal of Desegregation: The First Decade* (New York, 1966), 75–123; Bartley, *The Rise of Massive Resistance*, 315–19; William Peters, *The Southern Temper* (Garden City, N.Y., 1959).

and long look at the situation which confronts us." Almond had consistently exhorted resistance, but he had not acted on the state law that would have let him seize desegregating schools in order to reestablish segregation in defiance of the federal courts. "I know of nothing more futile," Almond told the legislature, "than a penal sentence that contributes to nothing but the ridiculous." The governor appointed a legislative commission under the chairmanship of Mosby G. Perrow, Jr., to restudy the school desegregation problem. On February 2, the schools in Norfolk reopened, and the governing bodies in Arlington and Norfolk admitted twenty-one black students to formerly all-white schools.[46]

The Perrow Commission's recommendations resembled those of the Gray Commission three and a half years earlier. The new report, issued by a commission made up mostly of moderates, proposed a local-option policy capable of holding desegregation to token levels while granting white students maximum "freedom of choice" about the schools they attended. It suggested a locally administered pupil-assignment law, along with safeguards for whites that included the continuation of tuition grants. The governor called another special session in April, 1959, to enact the report. According to him, the proposals dealt "with fact—not fiction, a condition and not abstract theory, reality not surmise and wishful thinking." By the time of the session, the champions of massive resistance had recovered from the shock of Almond's "betrayal," and the deliberations were confrontational and bitterly divisive. The general assembly enacted the Perrow recommendations by narrow majorities. State action was the heart of interposition; with the adoption of a local-option policy, as James W. Ely, Jr., has observed, "the state government withdrew from meaningful participation in the school issue."[47]

The decisive conflict in Little Rock occurred in May, 1959. The Little Rock school board, hopelessly divided between three mod-

[46]Almond's Address, Richmond *News-Leader,* January 28, 1959; Benjamin Muse in Washington *Post,* February 15, 1959; J. Harvie Wilkinson III, *Harry Byrd and the Changing Face of Virginia Politics, 1945–1966* (Charlottesville, Va., 1968), 139–54.

[47]"Report of the Perrow Commission," in *Race Relations Law Reporter,* IV, 392–409; New Virginia Laws, *ibid.,* 411–39; Almond's Address, Richmond *Times-Dispatch,* April 7, 1959; James W. Ely, Jr., *The Crisis of Conservative Virginia: The Byrd Organization and the Politics of Massive Resistance* (Knoxville, Tenn., 1976), 135.

erates and three extreme segregationists, met to consider the renewal of teacher contracts. After a fruitless morning, the three moderates announced that they were "withdrawing from this meeting and declaring that no quorum exists upon our withdrawal." Undeterred, the three remaining members voted not to renew the contracts of forty-four teachers and administrators. The employees to be dismissed, according to one of the board participants, were mostly "integrationist or they collaborated with integrationists." The Women's Emergency Council, joined by the city's PTA council, the chamber of commerce, the ministerial association, and other agents of Little Rock respectability, organized Stop This Outrageous Purge and began a campaign to recall the three offending board members. The Citizens' Council and the Mothers' League countered with the Committee to Retain Our Segregated Schools and a campaign to recall the three moderates. Governor Faubus joined the battle, warning the "good, hardworking, honest people out there" that STOP carried the banner for the "charge of the Cadillac brigade, with many good, honest, hardworking Negroes in the front as shock troops." [48]

STOP won a narrow but conclusive victory. The three moderates retained their seats on the school board, and the voters recalled the three segregationists. The county commissioners then appointed three moderates to fill the seats vacated. During June the new school board announced its intention to reopen the high schools on a desegregated basis, and a three-judge federal court ruled that the school-closing laws were unconstitutional. Faubus, with only fitful grumbling, withdrew from the affairs of Little Rock, and in August six black students desegregated Central High and Hall High. Local authorities firmly quieted a dispirited segregationist protest demonstration. [49]

An acceptance of token desegregation became the norm in cities through most of the region. In the fall of 1959, a Miami school district admitted black pupils to a formerly all-white school, and in the fall of 1960 a ruling by the Texas attorney general

[48] Alexander, *The Little Rock Recall Election*, 12, 13; Faubus quoted in *Arkansas Gazette*, May 23, 1959; *Southern School News*, June, 1959.

[49] Alexander, *The Little Rock Recall Election*, 31; *Aaron v. McKinley*, in *Race Relations Law Reporter*, IV, 543–50; *Southern School News*, July 1959–September, 1959.

permitted Houston to desegregate without the loss of state funds. In Texas, as elsewhere, state governments increasingly withdrew from the controversy over desegregation, leaving local authorities and the courts to work matters out, as the Supreme Court had assumed they would in the *Brown* decision of 1955. Only in the Deep South—in Alabama, Georgia, Louisiana, Mississippi, and South Carolina—were public school systems entirely segregated and interpositionist policies still alive, and both Atlanta and New Orleans were under court order to desegregate.[50]

In Atlanta the open-schools forces dominated the public forum. Mayor William B. Hartsfield described Atlanta as a city "too busy to hate" and demanded that the city be permitted to desegregate without state interference. Hartsfield, the Atlanta business community, the daily newspapers, education groups, most professional associations, the city's black leadership, Help Our Public Education, and the proponents of progress generally insisted that the city's public image required peaceful and orderly desegregation. "If we behave like a banana republic," a prominent banker explained to a Rotary Club, "we shall get and deserve the economic rewards characteristic of a banana republic."[51]

State and county political leaders denounced the open schools campaign. The Georgia Association of County Commissioners passed a resolution opposing "any race mixing in any Georgia schools anywhere, at any time, under any circumstances." Governor Ernest Vandiver declared, "I have no patience with those who are now coming out in the open and demanding that the races be mixed in the classrooms in the schools of Georgia, contrary to the laws and constitution of this state." Yet Atlanta was a formidable economic and demographic entity, and the costs of doctrinaire resistance became evident in early 1959 when Ellis G. Arnall, a former governor, arose from a long political slumber to champion Atlanta's cause. Should the schools be closed, Arnall threat-

[50] *Southern School News*, September, 1959, October, 1959, September, 1960, October, 1960.

[51] Hartsfield quoted in *William Berry Hartsfield: Mayor of Atlanta*, by Harold H. Martin (Athens, Ga., 1978), 142; Malcolm Bryan, president of the Federal Reserve Bank of Atlanta, quoted in *The Selling of the South: The Southern Crusade for Industrial Development, 1936–1980*, by James C. Cobb (Baton Rouge, 1982), 130.

ened, "I will be candidate for governor in 1962, and I will be elected." [52]

The prospect of Arnall's reentry into Georgia politics put further pressure on the Talmadge-led Democratic leadership. Governor Vandiver continued publicly to shout defiance and to condemn Atlanta moderates for running up the "flag of surrender over our capital city," but privately he hinted that desegregation was inevitable. In early 1960 Vandiver and the legislature created a committee on schools to restudy the issue. Fittingly, the chairman of the committee was John A. Sibley, a prominent lawyer, businessman, and banker and a leading member of the Atlanta establishment. Like the Perrow commission in Virginia, the Sibley committee delivered a report recommending a policy of local option that permitted communities to respond to desegregation in the manner they chose. While the issue was being debated, federal district judge Frank A. Hooper permitted Atlanta to delay desegregation until 1961 to provide time for the Georgia legislature to reevaluate its massive-resistance policy.[53]

While the Georgia state government reluctantly retreated from interposition, officials in Louisiana made a determined attempt to implement the doctrine. Under court order to desegregate, New Orleans in 1960 had done little to prepare for the event. The civic leadership, with a greater interest in defending the values of the old families of the city than in promoting the commercially expedient, felt little practical imperative to press for desegregation, and Mayor deLesseps S. Morrison took the position that "if those SOBs aren't going to do anything, I'll be damned if I'm going to stick my neck out." After thirteen years in the mayor's office, Morrison yearned for the statehouse and jealously guarded his segregationist credentials. The moderate save-the-schools coalition that dominated public affairs in Atlanta was inchoate and hesitant in New Orleans.[54]

[52] Resolution in Atlanta *Constitution,* March 30, 1960; Vandiver quoted in Atlanta *Journal,* December 15, 1958; Arnall quoted in Atlanta *Journal,* April 19, 1959.

[53] Vandiver quoted in Atlanta *Constitution,* February 9, 1960; "Education Committee Report," *Race Relations Law Reporter,* V, 509–20.

[54] Morrison quoted in *DeLesseps S. Morrison and the Image of Reform: New Orleans Politics, 1946–1961,* by Edward F. Haas (Baton Rouge, 1974), 262. Good studies of the New Or-

The New Orleans school board was in the end no more courageous than the mayor. In the spring of 1960 the board polled the parents of public-school children to see whether they preferred closing the schools or keeping them open with token desegregation. Although the wording of the ballot prompted a choice to continue public education, white parents expressed a preference for closing the schools by a five-to-one margin. Black parents favored open schools by an even greater margin, and the overall result was a narrow victory for public education with token desegregation. The school board, like Mayor Morrison and most other officials, paid far more attention to white preferences than those of blacks. As one study summarized the state of affairs, "With the white parents seemingly eager to close down the schools, and with the mayor and the business elite offering the board no support, the beleaguered board members found themselves even more stranded when the expected moral example of the Catholic Church never materialized." The school board turned to the state government, requesting that the governor protect the city through interposition.[55]

Beginning in the summer of 1960, the state government made a determined effort to implement interposition. A state district court ruled that federal district judge J. Skelly Wright had acted unconstitutionally and directed the school board to continue segregation. Governor Jimmie H. Davis took over the city's schools. The federal judiciary issued restraining orders against both Davis and the board and held state attorney general Jack P. F. Gremillion in contempt of court. Shortly before the imposition of desegregation in November, Davis called the first of a series of special

leans school crisis include *The New Orleans School Crisis: Report to the United States Commission on Civil Rights,* by Louisiana State Advisory Committee (New Orleans, 1961); Robert L. Crain and Morton Inger's *School Desegregation in New Orleans: A Comparative Study of the Failure of Social Control* (Chicago, 1966); Earlean Mary McCarrick's "Louisiana's Official Resistance to Desegregation" (Ph.D. dissertation, Vanderbilt University, 1964); Morton Inger's *Politics and Reality in an American City: The New Orleans School Crisis of 1960* (New York, 1969); and Edward L. Pinney and Robert S. Friedman's *Political Leadership and the School Desegregation Crisis in New Orleans* (New York, 1963).

[55] Louisiana State Advisory Committee, *The New Orleans School Crisis,* 5–6; Crain and Inger, *School Desegregation in New Orleans,* p. 30 quoted; *Southern School News,* July, 1960, August, 1960.

legislative sessions. A legislative committee took control of the New Orleans schools and was thwarted with a restraining order; the legislature took control of the schools and was issued a restraining order; a board appointed by the legislature took control of the schools, and it too was issued a restraining order. The legislature froze the school board's financial assets, appointed new school boards, urged whites to boycott the schools, and enacted almost every other impediment to desegregation that ingenuity proposed.[56]

Within New Orleans, the powerful Greater New Orleans Citizens' Council led the resistance to desegregation. As in Little Rock, working and lower-middle-class whites bulked largest in council membership. When the school board finally agreed to prepare a desegregation plan, it chose two white schools in a working-class area. In conformity with the Louisiana pupil-placement act, it assigned four African-American girls to attend first grade in the two schools. The council led a highly successful white boycott of the two schools and harassed the few white parents whose children crossed the picket lines. Although there was frequent violence during the early period of desegregation, the Eisenhower administration prevented attacks on the black students by introducing federal marshals as escorts. "New Orleans provided," James C. Cobb has written, "an epic-length drama more shocking than Little Rock in the intensity of hate it portrayed."[57]

The school boycotts lasted through the 1960–1961 academic year, but the resistance gradually subsided. The legislature lost some of its fire in late December, 1960, when Governor Davis asked for an increase in the state sales tax to finance the battle against the federal government and to enable tuition grants for students displaced by any school closings. The legislature denied the governor his request. The federal judiciary stood firm, and the Supreme Court ruled directly on interposition: "The conclusion is clear that interposition is not a constitutional doctrine. If taken seriously, it is illegal defiance of constitutional authority." In New Orleans, the influence of the Citizens' Council abated as

[56] *Southern School News,* June, 1960–June, 1961.

[57] McMillen, *The Citizens' Council,* 285–96; Claude Sitton in New York *Times,* November 27, 1960; Cobb, *The Selling of the South,* 133.

growing numbers of moderates called for a restoration of law and order.[58]

Classroom desegregation came to Georgia not in Atlanta, as expected, but at the University of Georgia in January, 1961. Acting under court order, the university in Athens enrolled two black students. A riot, orchestrated by law students, patterned on the anti-Lucy riots at the University of Alabama, and scheduled to follow a basketball game, ensued, and officials at the university suspended the two black students. Federal district judge William A. Bootle promptly voided the suspension. The two students returned to campus, the legislature adopted the recommendations of the Sibley Committee, and in the fall of 1961 Atlanta's public schools desegregated without incident. Two years later Clemson University in South Carolina desegregated calmly, and public-school desegregation followed in Charleston in the fall of 1963.[59]

By the time Governor Ross R. Barnett attempted to interpose the sovereignty of Mississippi between the federal government and the state university, interposition was passé. Nevertheless, impelled by the Citizens' Councils, Barnett and the state political leadership deployed every resource they could muster to prevent the enrollment of James H. Meredith at the University of Mississippi. The "insurrection against the armed forces of the United States at the University of Mississippi on September 30–October 1, 1962," as James W. Silver described the upheaval, resulted in two deaths, the wounding of twenty-eight federal marshals by gunfire, hundreds of injuries, and some three hundred arrests. The Kennedy administration, which had assigned federal marshals to assure order, had to rescue them by federalizing the Mississippi National Guard and dispatching regular army units. In the fall of 1964, four Mississippi towns enrolled black students in formerly all-white public schools.[60]

[58] New Orleans *Times-Picayune*, December 30, 1960; *United States* v. *Louisiana*, in *Race Relations Law Reporter*, V, 1008.

[59] Calvin Trillin, *An Education in Georgia: Charlayne Hunter, Hamilton Holmes, and the Integration of the University of Georgia* (1964; rpr. Athens, Ga., 1991), 50–78; Sarratt, *The Ordeal of Desegregation*, 124–35; *Southern School News*, February, 1961.

[60] James W. Silver, *Mississippi: The Closed Society* (New York, 1966), 3; Brauer, *John F. Kennedy and the Second Reconstruction*, 180–204.

Governor George C. Wallace gained considerable notoriety through his "stand in the schoolhouse door" at the University of Alabama. "I'm gonna make 'em bring troops into this state," Wallace vowed, and the Kennedy administration did federalize the Alabama National Guard. The university desegregated without violence in June, 1963. That fall, Wallace brought out the state police and the National Guard in an effort to prevent desegregation of the public schools. The Kennedy administration again federalized the guardsmen, and the federal district courts put the governor and the state police under restraining orders. The gesture by Governor Wallace achieved little. By the time of the last-ditch resistance by segregationists in Louisiana, Mississippi, and Alabama, the metropolitan areas in the region had largely accepted the necessity of token desegregation.[61]

The great struggle over the future of the public schools broadly pitted metropolitan against black belt county-seat elites. The federal judiciary, sometimes supported by the federal executive branch, forced the region to choose between social custom and economic development. For the first time in history, southern cities successfully challenged county-seat leadership, and thereafter metropolitan moderates increasingly dictated the direction of state policy. In 1962 the United States Supreme Court ratified the new arrangement by declaring legislative malapportionment unconstitutional.[62]

The moderate triumph had profound implications. At the same time, southern moderates operated within the context of traditional southern political and social practices, and they still had to come to terms with entrenched defenders of the old regime. Throughout the region the exponents of massive resistance accepted defeat with ill-concealed hostility. The Richmond *News Leader* snarled, "Virginia does not submit in obedience to what we conceive to be law; Virginia submits only in recognition of superior force." In such a setting, the meaning of moderation was sometimes ambiguous.[63]

[61] Wallace quoted in *Southern School News*, May, 1962, and in *Wallace*, by Marshall Frady (New York, 1968), 141; Benjamin Muse, *Ten Years of Prelude: The Story of Integration Since the Supreme Court's 1954 Decision* (New York, 1964), 242–65.

[62] *Baker* v. *Carr*, 369 U.S. 186 (1962).

[63] Richmond *News Leader*, February 2, 1959.

In Mississippi, moderation was a distinctly minority view. V. O. Key had earlier remarked, "Northerners, provincials that they are, regard the South as one large Mississippi. Southerners, with their eye for distinction, place Mississippi in a class by itself." A civil rights worker wrote of the state's uniqueness in 1964: "When you're not in Mississippi, it's not real and when you're there the rest of the world isn't real." White Mississippians, James Silver ventured in the midsixties, were prone to see black civil rights progress "not as a legitimate outcome of classic American values but as a criminal conspiracy against sanctified institutions." Not until late in the decade were moderates accorded a hearing in the state's politics.[64]

In Alabama and Louisiana, metropolitan leaders had long before joined with the plantation-county establishment in opposition to liberal factions headed by James Folsom and Lister Hill and by Huey Long and Earl Long. Even as liberalism collapsed in both states, the long-standing black belt–big-mule coalition remained intact. The economic power holders in Birmingham often resided in Pittsburgh and New York and were happy to accept the black belt ethos of low wages, low taxes, and white supremacy. In Louisiana, deLesseps Morrison and the moderates of New Orleans found the Citizens' Councils more congenial allies than the Long forces, and having enlisted under the anti-Long banner, they were never able to chart an independent course. Alabama, Louisiana, and Mississippi lagged behind the emerging moderate consensus.

Georgia's political evolution was more typical of the region. By the end of the 1950s, it had become clear to the state leadership that closing schools posed greater political risk than accepting token desegregation. In December, 1959, James S. Peters, the acknowledged patriarch of the Talmadge forces, explained that if the schools were closed, Arnall would "be difficult indeed to defeat and Herman could very well go down with him." In a private letter that became public, Peters reasoned that the Talmadge camp could "lose control of the government and entrench Ellis Arnall and the integrationists in the control of the government

[64] V. O. Key, Jr., *Southern Politics in State and Nation* (New York, 1949), 229; Robert Moses quoted in *Letters from Mississippi*, ed. Elizabeth Sutherland (New York, 1965), 15; Silver, *Mississippi*, 3.

for decades to come." He continued, "some form of integration is inevitable, and the only question left unanswered today is whether this integration will be under the control of the friends of segregation or the proponents of integration." Clearly, according to Peters, desegregation would work best if it were guided by people who did not want it to succeed.[65]

Governor Vandiver led the strategic shift away from massive resistance. Disencumbered of the defense of segregation, he became one of the region's most enthusiastic industrial promoters. The governor spent much of his remaining tenure recruiting northern investment. "If you send an industrial representative to these places," Vandiver explained, "he talks to his counterpart in the business, but a governor—any governor—gets to the president and chairman of the board where the final decisions are made." Two decades before, Governor Arnall and the southern liberals had worried about corporate lobbyists unduly influencing state officials. During the 1960s southern governors spent much of their time attempting to gain influence with corporations.[66]

In 1963 Carl E. Sanders replaced Vandiver, who like the governors in most of the southern states was ineligible to succeed himself. Although Sanders was unaligned in Georgia's decaying factional politics, he was acceptable to Talmadge loyalists. "It shall be my purpose," Sanders proclaimed, "to unify our people for economic growth and progress—not to divide them in stagnation." The new governor informed a reporter, "In my case, 'moderate' means that I am a segregationist but not a damned fool. . . . I am determined that during my administration this state will move ahead—fast." Georgia remained a Deep South state, and in 1966 segregationists elected Lester G. Maddox governor. But even under the fiery Maddox, policy—although not gubernatorial rhetoric—remained for the most part moderate.[67]

The Byrd organization in Virginia similarly extricated itself from its exposed massive-resistance position. Senator Byrd made

[65] James S. Peters to Roy V. Harris, December 30, 1959, in Atlanta *Journal and Constitution*, January 17, 1960.

[66] Vandiver quoted in Atlanta *Constitution*, June 2, 1961.

[67] Sanders quoted in "Campaign Platform," in Carl E. Sanders Collection, University of Georgia Libraries, and in "Progress Goes Marching Through Georgia," by Ben Hibbs, *Saturday Evening Post*, February 16, 1963, p. 70.

clear that he was not happy with Governor Almond's acceptance of desegregation. "I stand now as I stood when I first urged massive resistance," the senator affirmed. "I have no apologies for what I have done." Sniping between hard-liners and the Almond moderates continued for the remainder of the governor's tenure. In the 1961 gubernatorial primary, the moderates rallied behind Attorney General A. E. S. Stephens, a collaborator in Almond's policies. The Byrd organization supported Albertis S. Harrison, who during four hectic years as lieutenant governor had managed not to take a stand in favor of anything more controversial than low taxes and state rights. After Harrison won the election, he did his best to ignore racial controversies while spending his time promoting industrial development. In 1965 Harry Flood Byrd retired from the Senate, and Harrison appointed Harry Flood Byrd, Jr., his successor. In the same year, Mills E. Godwin, a onetime champion of massive resistance and a close associate of Senator Byrd, won the statehouse.[68]

In neither Georgia nor Virginia did the ascendance of the moderate viewpoint bring a political sea change, but it did reorient state policy. In both states, vocational and technical schools and community colleges increasingly dotted the landscape, and schemes for industrial development peppered the statute books. Governor Sanders undertook ambitious educational reforms, particularly in higher education. Governor Godwin pushed through the Virginia legislature a general sales tax that greatly increased funding for public schools and highways. J. Harvie Wilkinson III has explained the reorientation of state policy in Virginia: "The major difference was that the state's political arm was . . . beginning to augment its economic progress instead of ignoring or actively working against it."[69]

Governor Faubus made the transition from defiance to moderation with no less political dexterity than he had shown in going from moderation to defiance. In 1960 he supported a constitutional amendment permitting communities to close their public

[68] Byrd quoted in Washington *Post*, August 30, 1959; Ely, *The Crisis of Conservative Virginia*, 165–83; Wilkinson, *Harry Byrd*, 238–304.

[69] Numan V. Bartley, *The Creation of Modern Georgia* (2nd ed.; Athens, Ga., 1990), 222–29; Wilkinson, *Harry Byrd*, 243.

schools. This time, the Arkansas Education Association and other open-school groups conducted a vigorous opposition campaign. The electorate defeated the amendment by a large majority. It was the only time during the era that southern voters defeated a segregationist measure. The state's citizenry had come to terms with token desegregation. Governor Faubus lost no time in appealing for black political support, claiming to be the representative of "all the people." Rehearsing the accomplishments of his administration, he intoned, "These things we did by working together, not by fighting, not by yielding to the agitators of whatever race or creed." Wrapping himself in the mantle of "industrial and state progress," he continued to be reelected with monotonous regularity.[70]

In North Carolina's 1960 gubernatorial primary election, Governor Hodges endorsed Attorney General Malcolm B. Seawell. Senator W. Kerr Scott died prior to the campaign, and Terry Sanford, his campaign manager, ran for governor as the bearer of the reform mantle. The new force in the election was I. Beverly Lake, once a law professor at Wake Forest College and an avid segregationist. Lake promised to "create a widespread awareness of the NAACP and its allies, and a climate of unyielding opposition to it and to them." Seawell, Sanford, and the metropolitan press excoriated Lake for stirring racial animosities, but the law professor finished second behind Sanford in the Democratic voting. In the runoff, Hodges and the establishment forces—convinced that Lake's election would be a disaster for the state—moved behind Sanford. Sanford won the election and proved to be a progressive governor committed to public education and economic growth. A standard history of North Carolina saluted his achievements: "The 1961 General Assembly enacted more far-reaching legislation than any similar body in the twentieth century."[71]

---

[70] *Southern School News*, December, 1960; Faubus quoted in *Arkansas Gazette* (Little Rock), May 23, 1960; Faubus, *Down from the Hills–II*, 94.

[71] Lake quoted in Greensboro *Daily News*, May 6, 1960; Hugh Talmadge Lefler and Albert Ray Newsome, *North Carolina: The History of a Southern State* (Rev. ed.; Chapel Hill, N.C., 1963), 656; James R. Spence, *The Making of a Governor: The Moore-Preyer-Lake Primaries of 1964* (Winston-Salem, N.C., 1968), 8–32.

In Oklahoma, the administration of J. Howard Edmondson from 1959 to 1963 marked the appearance of what two historians of the state's politics have termed "new men, new forces and new issues." Although Edmondson spent much of his four years locked in acrimonious combat with a legislature under rural domination, he succeeded in establishing a state merit system and a central purchasing procedure, not to mention in repealing prohibition. "By the early 1960s," the same two historians have written, "one era of state politics had come to a sudden and surprising close." Governor Bert T. Combs brought comparable vigor to Kentucky's government during the four years from 1959 to 1963. He successfully promoted a 3 percent sales tax that permitted substantial improvements in education and other services.[72]

Moderation also carried political risk. In Florida the 1960 gubernatorial primary resulted in a runoff between C. Farris Bryant, who took a strongly conservative line, and Doyle Carlton, Jr., who identified with the moderate policies of Governor LeRoy Collins. To Bryant, Carlton stood "for moderate integration. I am a firm believer in segregation." Governor Collins energetically supported Carlton. The voters chose Bryant by a large majority. As a south Florida editor groused, "The three candidates supported by the 'Pork Chop Gang' for Governor, Secretary of State and Commissioner of Agriculture scored easy victories, although they were opposed by the editorial page of every big newspaper in south Florida." Four years later the even more socially conservative Haydon Burns became governor.[73]

Despite the state-to-state variations, the demise of massive resistance and the emergence of the moderates did reanimate the drive for new industry and government reform. By 1964 Leslie W. Dunbar of the Southern Regional Council could write, "Southern governors have become the *de facto* executive directors of the state chambers of commerce and spend their time competing with each

[72] James R. Scales and Danney Goble, *Oklahoma Politics: A History* (Norman, Okla., 1982), 307; John Ed Pearce, *Divide and Dissent: Kentucky Politics, 1930–1963* (Lexington, Ky., 1987).

[73] Bryant quoted in St. Petersburg *Times*, May 10, 1960; V. M. Newton, Jr., *Crusade for Democracy* (Ames, Iowa, 1961), 133.

other as supplicants for new plants. We have talked of state socialism and state capitalism, but what do we call governments whose chief affair it is to entice and propitiate business?"[74]

The triumph of the business ethic in politics possessed an element of irony. In 1940 the South was poor. Huge numbers of people lived marginal lives. By 1960 the South was relatively affluent. Per capita income was 76 percent of that of the rest of the nation, and by almost any human standard relating to diet, housing, health, and education, the resources existed for people to live comfortable lives. The problem had become not so much additional economic growth, additional exploitation of natural resources, additional devastation of the environment, and the like, but more effective utilization and fairer distribution of existing affluence. At that very time, the southern leadership became ever more infatuated with rapid economic growth as the cure for social ills and ever more hostile to broadly based social reform that could redistribute material abundance.

Massive resistance offered nothing in the way of solutions to southern problems, but it did prevent anyone else from dealing constructively with them. The movement effectively stultified social change during a period of economic and demographic transition. The politics of massive resistance oriented the regional spectrum far to the right. Even the most progressively oriented moderates usually felt compelled to avow their devotion to segregation before timidly suggesting token alternatives.

Metropolitan elites emerged as the arbiters of the regional political agenda, and their victory marked the triumph of modernizing elites in southern public policy. The establishment of the new order did not go uncontested. Entrenched old-guard conservatives continued to fight a rearguard action. On the left, a new generation of black southerners who had come of age after *Brown* found little in the moderate program to applaud. On the right, huge numbers of ordinary whites were unreconciled to the latest version of New South progress.

[74] Leslie W. Dunbar, "The Changing Mind of the South: The Exposed Nerve," *Journal of Politics*, XXVI (1964), 20.

CHAPTER VIII

GOD AND SOCIETY IN THE MODERNIZING SOUTH

W HITE metropolitan moderates gained the initiative in
southern politics. They defined the public-school crisis
as a conflict over the future of the southern economy,
they defended public education, not desegregation, and they
looked to further economic growth as the nostrum that would
ameliorate regional social traumas. The moderates envisioned a
competitive and individualized society oriented toward material
advancement. Such an agenda clashed with traditional folk values
and forced southerners to adapt to a changed ideological imperative.

The emergent orthodoxy received its clearest statement in
Southern Tradition and Regional Progress, written by William H. Nicholls, a Vanderbilt University economist, and published in 1960. In
the early 1950s William T. Polk had depicted "two Souths which
are as different as Chicago and Bangkok." Nicholls too described
a deeply rent region. The two Souths Nicholls identified, however,
did not abide in uneasy coexistence; they were locked in mortal
combat. On the one side was a tradition-bound and backward-
looking rural population wedded to a static and "gangrenous"
social system based on segregation. On the other was a dynamic
urban public that represented economic growth and a fluid social
structure. By 1960 the conflict between the "two Souths" was beyond compromise. "It has become my firm conviction," Nicholls
wrote in the introduction to his work, "that the South must choose
between tradition and progress." His solution "was an even more
rapid rate of regional industrial-urban development," with the dynamic "new urban middle class" providing the leadership. In this

regard, Nicholls was hopeful: "With increasing urbanization, the South is at last giving its vigorous and hard-working middle class an opportunity to emerge from the subordinate position it held in the hidebound rural society." [1]

Nicholls was not alone in his views. Leonard Reissman placed the "new middle class" on the cutting edge of southern change. According to him, the very existence of middle-class values undermined "aristocratic domination," for "land as a source of wealth and power is challenged by money; ascribed status is challenged by status through achievement; and traditionalism is challenged by pragmatism." The revolt of a modernizing bourgeoisie against the old order was inescapable, since the "future power and prestige" of a powerful and expanding social group required the redistribution of social and political authority. Samuel Lubell in a series of books and articles proclaimed the "new middle-class elements—lawyers, doctors, clerks, engineers"—to be the "real political rebels in the South today." The "southern way of life" had long been an impediment to economic progress; by 1960 a formidable segment of southern society provided the base for challenging the old regime. [2]

By the time Nicholls presented his analysis, the South had become an urban region, and the changing balance of economic forces further strengthened the moderate cause. In 1960 a substantial majority of the people in the thirteen southern states lived in urban communities, and approaching half—43.5 percent of the population—resided in metropolitan areas. Thereafter a majority of the people in the thirteen southern states were metropolitan residents. With urban expansion came a vast increase in the labor force employed in retail and wholesale trade, insurance, finance, government, the professions, and similar predominantly

[1] William T. Polk, *Southern Accent: From Uncle Remus to Oak Ridge* (New York, 1953), 19; William H. Nicholls, *Southern Tradition and Regional Progress* (Chapel Hill, N.C., 1960), x, 55, 57, 68.

[2] Leonard Reissman, "Social Development and the American South," *Journal of Social Issues,* XXII (1966), 105–106; Samuel Lubell, *The Future of American Politics* (Rev. ed.; Garden City, N.Y., 1956), 119; Samuel Lubell, *White and Black: Test of a Nation* (New York, 1964), 69; Samuel Lubell, *Revolt of the Moderates* (New York, 1956); Samuel Lubell, *The Hidden Crisis in American Politics* (New York, 1970). Unless otherwise noted, statistics here and elsewhere in this chapter are from the United States Bureau of the Census.

white-collar occupations. Together, these fields composed the fastest growing sector of the southern labor market, and the relentless quest for customers and clients was the central force underlying the growth ethos. In 1940 these occupations employed one in four southern workers. In 1960 they engaged the services of four in ten employed people, and in 1980 more than half. Such enterprises clustered in metropolitan areas and fed both urban growth and the insatiable appetite for further growth.

The southern white-collar legions were a rising force in society and politics. Despite the frequent references to a "new middle class," its membership, aside from being overwhelmingly white in racial composition, was a more diverse aggregation than some contemporary accounts implied. Almost two in ten workers—18 percent of the southern labor force in 1960—pursued occupations normally associated with middle-class status. Most were white males. By the mid-1960s approximately one-fourth of employed white men held managerial, professional, or technical jobs, as compared with fewer than one in ten employed white women. The accountants, engineers, clergymen, teachers, nurses, and lawyers, the businessmen, executives, administrators, and department heads, and all the others who held professional, technical, proprietary, and managerial positions were in the aggregate the most lucratively recompensed people in the region. They were better educated and more widely informed on public issues than southerners generally and, according to opinion polls, were more tolerant on racial matters. Their families were in the vanguard of the stampede to suburbia and of the introduction of far-reaching changes in southern life-styles. They formed the base for the open-schools movement and for the moderate position in southern politics.[3]

Another two in ten employed southerners held sales, clerical, and kindred positions. The insurance and real estate agents and other salespeople often fared relatively well financially and joined

---

[3] Ray Marshall and Virgil L. Christian, Jr., "Some South and Non-South Comparisons," in *Employment of Blacks in the South: A Perspective on the 1960s,* ed. Ray Marshall and Virgil L. Christian, Jr. (Austin, Tex., 1978), 196–99; Vivian W. Henderson, *The Economic Status of Negroes: In the Nation and in the South* (Southern Regional Council, n.d.), 17; Alfred O. Hero, Jr., *The Southerner and World Affairs* (Baton Rouge, 1965), 336–40, 369–73.

their business and professional peers in the more comfortable reaches of suburbia. The much larger number of salesgirls, secretaries, receptionists, file clerks, and bookkeepers earned less. Arthur F. Raper and Ira De A. Reid once explained that they held "white collar status without white collar pay, and so their white collars [were] frequently frayed." The clerical and counter sales workers formed an overwhelmingly Caucasian white-collar proletariat that was heavily female. The salaries of women office workers were less than the wages of blue-collar operatives and decidedly less than the incomes of skilled blue-collar workers. Many of its members came from, socialized with, and married into blue-collar households. Their numbers swelled the white-collar ranks and their workplace experiences doubtless affected their social and political attitudes, but their bourgeois status rested on a quite generous definition of the term middle class.[4]

Some academics and progressives bemoaned the materialism and shallowness of urban middle-class life. Robert J. Steamer wrote in 1963 that a typical member was a "rootless nomad whose primary, and sometimes, only loyalty is to business. His political ideas are substantively barren, because at bottom, materialism is his life philosophy, but translating his thought into political maxims we get free enterprise, fiscal sanity, balanced budgets," and certainly it was true that the South's uptown business leadership frequently equated sensible social policy with what best served the exigencies of the real estate market. Chafing at white middle-class caution during the conflict over the public schools, Wilma Dykeman deplored the "middle-of-the-road man" who draped himself in "his gray flannel sheet" and permitted racial extremists to usurp policy.[5]

The ultimate triumph of the moderates did not signify acceptance of racial equality but simply the realization that further resistance was futile and unprofitable. Moderation, Steven F. Lawson concluded in his study of Tampa, "provided a practical tool wielded by civic elites pushing for economic modernization with

[4] Arthur F. Raper and Ira De A. Reid, *Sharecroppers All* (Chapel Hill, N.C., 1941), 189.
[5] Robert J. Steamer, "Southern Disaffection with the National Democratic Party," in *Change in the Contemporary South*, ed. Allan P. Sindler (Durham, N.C., 1963), 153; Wilma Dykeman, "The Man in the Gray Flannel Sheet," *Progressive*, February, 1959, pp. 8–9.

a minimum of political and social disruption." Norfolk desegregated its public facilities after experimenting with closed schools, but, as one study concluded, "Black residents retained the status of guests whose living space was subject to constant amendment by the Norfolk Redevelopment and Housing Authority." The same commitment to economic growth that dictated acquiescence to desegregation assured that public resources would fund development, not social reform. Convention centers and trade marts, expressways and airport terminals, stadiums and tourist attractions, Forward Atlanta and Richmond Forward promotion projects were the proper beneficiaries of taxpayer largess.[6]

The people Lubell described as the "real political rebels in the South today" did not get their reputation through the promulgation of left-leaning policies, and various studies questioned the extent to which education and affluence actually undermined prejudice. Education taught people the "proper" responses to pollsters and encouraged them to place discourse within intellectually acceptable parameters. It did not necessarily make them tolerant. Charles H. Stember explained that "on many issues, the educated show as much prejudice as the less educated, and on some issues more." A South Carolina observer remarked about moderates, "I don't think they take the Negroes seriously as people. . . . They look at it as something . . . that doesn't really have much to do with them." Middle-class metropolitan southerners threatened the paternal order because of their commitment to atomistic individualism, consumer materialism, upward mobility, and unfettered economic development.[7]

In *The Hamlet*, William Faulkner described Flem Snopes as a man "who answered Yes and No to direct questions and who apparently never looked directly or long enough at any face to remember the name which went with it, yet who never made mis-

[6] Steven F. Lawson, "From Sit-In to Race Riot: Businessmen, Blacks, and the Pursuit of Moderation in Tampa, 1960–1967," in *Southern Businessmen and Desegregation*, ed. Elizabeth Jacoway and David R. Colburn (Baton Rouge, 1982), 281; Paul S. Lofton, Jr., "The Norfolk Business Community: The Crisis of Massive Resistance," *ibid.*, 118.

[7] Charles H. Stember, *Education and Attitude Change: The Effect of Schooling on Prejudice Against Minority Groups* (New York, 1961), 168; Judith Caditz, *White Liberals in Transition: Current Dilemmas of Ethnic Integration* (New York, 1976); William H. Barnwell, *In Richard's World: The Battle of Charleston, 1966* (Boston, 1968), 46.

takes in any matter pertaining to money." By 1960 an impersonal and bureaucratic world based on formal contracts, legal procedures, and money transactions was approaching maturity. Even though wide diversity existed within white-collar ranks, the "new middle class" relentlessly undermined the paternal foundations of the old social order. The sense of roots, place, and stability that had for so long been central to the southern value system retreated before new ideological currents emanating from the metropolitan areas.[8]

In the 1940s Ben Robertson had found "great comfort" in knowing that someone "is always keeping the home place." By the 1960s middle-class houses were no longer homeplaces; they were capital investments. Men struggled to "get ahead" in an increasingly competitive society where time was money and traditional forms of leisure were passé and unremunerative. Women endeavored with declining success to maintain family and society. The feminine mystique and the suburban ideal influenced southern women, probably more so than their peers outside the region. Motherhood and homemaking in a nice house in a suburb with good schools, convenient shopping centers, and low crime rates was the socially proper goal for middle-class and upwardly mobile women. Responding to the prevailing values of the day, many middle-class women looked to family life for fulfillment in a society that became ever more individualist and work-oriented.[9]

The alienation and malaise that accompanied such an individualized world view was a theme of Walker Percy's novel *The Moviegoer*, published in 1960. In Percy's middle-class universe, a person lived without values, measured success by money, and alleviated boredom with periodic sexual conquests. Romance and involvement were things one found in movies, or on television. It was a prosperous world: "A beautiful boulevard, ten thousand handsome cars, fifty thousand handsome, well-fed and kind-hearted people, and the malaise settles on us like a fallout." The malaise was not hard to understand. It "is the pain of loss. The world is lost to you, the world and the people in it, and there

---

[8] William Faulkner, *The Hamlet* (New York, 1940), 56.
[9] Ben Robertson, *Red Hills and Cotton: An Upcountry Memory* (Columbia, S.C., 1842), 20.

remains only you and the world and you no more able to be in the world than Banquo's ghost." In shedding the values of an older South, the New South had become a place where credit cards defined an individual's identity. Like the cinema in *The Moviegoer* "about a man who lost his memory in an accident," a person "found himself a stranger in a strange city." [10]

Percy's treatment of existential alienation in an impersonal southern world was evidence of the maturation of the modernist impulse in the region's literature. Modernism arrived in the South much earlier; by the time that Robert Penn Warren's *All the King's Men* appeared in 1946 it was an increasingly dominant influence in southern thought. Modernists, as Daniel Joseph Singal has distilled their ideas, held "that man was the human animal, that the universe was inherently irrational, that morality was embedded in history and not in immutable natural law," and that unpredictability and uncertainty were inevitable human conditions. In the brave new existentialist world of southern thought, people searched for individual identity amid the ruins of community disintegration and ethical chaos.[11]

The triumph of modernism brought to an end the distinctively southern literary renaissance. Walter Sullivan, a critic of modernist incursions into literature, has argued, "The South joined the modern world, assumed the modern world's values, and deteriorated as a culture to the point that it could no longer support the production of serious art." Other observers pointed out that with the adoption of existentialist themes, southern writing became part of the universal literature. Writers continued to produce works about the South, often works with great insight, but family, community, the weight of southern history, and the brooding presence of the region itself were less and less integral to the story. The Southern gradually disappeared, as did the literature that, in Flannery O'Connor's words, "conjures up an image of Gothic monstrosities and the idea of a preoccupation with everything deformed and grotesque." [12]

---

[10] Walker Percy, *The Moviegoer* (New York, 1960), 133, 99, 12.

[11] Daniel Joseph Singal, *The War Within: From Victorian to Modernist Thought in the South, 1919–1945* (Chapel Hill, N.C., 1982), 261.

[12] Walter Sullivan, *A Requiem for the Renascence: The State of Fiction in the Modern South*

The modernist assumptions that increasingly permeated southern thought created a host of ethical and social dilemmas. "We are told," Sullivan complained, "that human nature is ameliorable, that weakness is strength, that license is freedom, that morality is negotiable." The extreme individualism, relativism, and pragmatism that undergirded the modernist ethos left little room for a social ethic. In an increasingly bureaucratic region, money and achievement measured success, and an impractical commitment to ethics was superfluous for, if not deleterious to, proper administrative procedure.[13]

Social reform became even more intellectually unfashionable. As Richard H. King has observed in his study of southern thought, contemporary society "lacks any compelling vision to unite its members beyond the dictates of self-interest. . . . There is no public realm in the normative sense, no notion of the common good, whether religiously or politically defined." In the 1930s Erskine Caldwell had written about the grotesque inhabitants of Tobacco Road and attributed their condition to a social system that could be redeemed through political and economic reform. Two decades later, Flannery O'Connor wrote about more or less the same people and attributed the condition of each to an unfulfilled longing for God's grace, which made social reform rather beside the point.[14]

(Athens, Ga., 1976), 23; Walter Sullivan, *Death by Melancholy: Essays on Modern Southern Fiction* (Baton Rouge, 1972); Floyd C. Watkins, *The Death of Art: Black and White in Recent Southern Novels* (Athens, Ga., 1970); Floyd C. Watkins, *In Time and Place: Some Origins of American Fiction* (Athens, Ga., 1977); Louis D. Rubin, Jr., "Is the Southern Renascence Over? A Sort of Cautionary Epistle," in *The Rising South: Changes and Issues*, ed. Donald R. Noble and Joab L. Thomas (University, Ala., 1976), 72–91; John M. Bradbury, *Renaissance in the South: A Critical History of the Literature, 1920–1960* (Chapel Hill, N.C., 1963); Allen Tate, "The New Provincialism," *Virginia Quarterly Review*, XXI (1945), 262–72; C. Vann Woodward, "Why the Southern Renaissance?" *Virginia Quarterly Review*, LI (1975), 222–39; Flannery O'Connor, "The Fiction Writer and His Country," in *The Living Novel: A Symposium*, ed. Granville Hicks (New York, 1957), 189.

[13] Sullivan, *A Requiem for the Renascence*, 22.

[14] Richard H. King, *A Southern Renaissance: The Cultural Awakening of the American South, 1930–1955* (New York, 1980), 291; Erskine Caldwell, *Tobacco Road* (New York, 1932); Flannery O'Connor, *A Good Man Is Hard to Find* (New York, 1955); Flannery O'Connor, *Everything That Rises Must Converge* (New York, 1965); C. Hugh Holman, *The Roots of Southern Writing: Essays on the Literature of the American South* (Athens, Ga., 1972), 96–107; C. Hugh Holman, *The Immoderate Past: The Southern Writer and History* (Athens, Ga., 1977).

The new intellectual currents harmonized with social developments in the South. The decline of traditional communities and their folk cultures, the expansion of the metropolitan middle class and its commitment to individual material success, the absence of any form of mass organization that might have knit ordinary people to common social objectives, and the growing influence of a national commitment to civil rights individualism and Cold War morality contributed to a practical acceptance of the tenets of modernism. So too did the changing life-style in the South. In particular, modern values expanded comfortably in prospering suburbia.

Throughout the South an increasing number of families—along with their mortgage companies—owned their own homes, and a growing number of the newly constructed dwellings contained central heating, air conditioning, and other amenities. In 1940 only four in ten occupied dwellings in Texas housed their owners, and one-third possessed indoor plumbing. More than six in ten residents had access to electricity and owned a radio, but none had a television set and virtually none an air-conditioner. In 1960 two-thirds of the households in Texas owned their dwellings, eight out of ten had indoor plumbing and television, and three in ten lived in air-conditioned comfort, through the use of either window or central units.

Other states exhibited similar trends, although often at a slower pace. In 1940 three in ten households in Georgia owned their own residences and hardly more than that had indoor plumbing. In 1960 a majority owned their own dwellings, more than six in ten enjoyed indoor plumbing, and eight in ten found a place for a TV set, although hardly more than one in ten had acquired an air-conditioner. In Kentucky, almost half the households owned their dwellings in 1940, but only one in three had bathrooms. Two decades later, two-thirds of the households were owners, and six out of ten had plumbing and eight out of ten TV sets. As in Georgia, only slightly more than one out of ten had air conditioning.[15]

[15] The development and significance of air conditioning is examined by Raymond Arsenault in "The End of the Long Hot Summer: The Air Conditioner and Southern Cul-

Urban, and especially suburban, areas contained most of the new housing construction, and they led in the acquisition of modern amenities. By 1970 historian Raymond Arsenault has reported, 60 percent of urban households had air conditioning, as compared with 33 percent of rural households. White southerners not surprisingly occupied most of these dwellings; only two in ten black households were air-conditioned. In 1963 an academic at the University of Georgia attempted to recapture the cultural values of his youth by investigating the community where he had grown up, in a predominantly rural county that later became part of the Atlanta metropolitan area. "We can no more go back to [that] culture than we can become a medieval peasant," he decided. "A brick house with a bath and a half is also a state of mind." [16]

The new state of mind touched virtually every aspect of life and thought, including religion. An advice columnist in one of O'Connor's novels suggested, "Perhaps you ought to re-examine your religious values to see if they meet your needs in life. A religious experience can be a beautiful addition to living if you put it in the proper perspective and do not let it warf you." Many southerners, and most especially affluent metropolitan southerners, did alter their religious practices if not their core religious values. After all, O'Connor's advice columnist explained, the problem was "one of adjustment to the modern world." [17]

Metropolitan churches appealing to an affluent clientele prospered apparently unwarfed in the modern South. Such churches became plants with large staffs, investment committees, and endowment funds. Virtually all the clergy held college degrees, and many had received postgraduate training. Paid assistant ministers, choir and recreational leaders, soloists, and secretaries aided the minister in the performance of his myriad duties. Social halls, wedding chapels, church-school wings, and of course acres of parking lots were part of the plant. The more grandiose churches,

---

ture," in *Searching for the Sunbelt: Historical Perspectives on a Region*, ed. Raymond A. Mohl (Knoxville, Tenn., 1990), 176–211.

[16] Arsenault, "The End of the Long Hot Summer," 186; Floyd C. Watkins and Charles Hubert Watkins, *Yesterday in the Hills* (Athens, Ga., 1963), xi.

[17] Flannery O'Connor, *Wise Blood* (New York, 1952), 119.

Orville W. Taylor has noted, included "gymnasiums, jogging tracks, arts and crafts and game rooms, reducing salons, and snack bars." Activities specifically for youth, senior citizens, business-men, and women were common in the larger churches, some of which sponsored radio and television ministries. As a North Caro-lina Baptist minister told a visitor, "It takes good business judg-ment to operate a church like the First in these days and times." [18]

The largest church in the South was the First Baptist Church of Dallas. By the late 1970s First Baptist spread over five city blocks and included a kindergarten, a Christian academy, a Bible college, and a recreational building complete with bowling alley, skating rink, and gymnasium. Dr. W. A. Criswell, the church's longtime minister, conducted radio and television programs. The entire op-eration required more than a hundred full-time and well over a hundred part-time employees, including the people working in the ten missions sponsored by the church.[19]

In the mid-1960s Erskine Caldwell, who had grown up the son of a southern minister, returned to the South and found the ways of the "go-getter modernist church" appalling. In Atlanta, Cald-well attended the "Sunday morning fashion parade" at a large and affluent church and listened to the "unoffending platitudes" that assured "another week of salvation." He talked with a thor-oughly secular young stockbroker, who explained that the "churches in this part of town" were the "best place of all to get acquainted with rich stock-buying prospects." Caldwell concluded in sorrow that "modernist religion in its most advanced form is comparable to the 'boosterism' of such businessmen's civic orga-nizations as Kiwanis, Rotary, and the Junior Chamber of Com-merce." [20]

Nevertheless, the southern religious pattern that one historian has described as "denominational diversity and religious homo-geneity" changed relatively little. In the early 1960s almost 90

[18] Orville W. Taylor, "Arkansas," in *Religion in the Southern States: A Historical Study*, ed. Samuel S. Hill, Jr. (Macon, Ga., 1983), 52; Erskine Caldwell, *Deep South: Memory and Obser-vation* (New York, 1969), 65.

[19] Gene McLean Adams, "An Analytical Study of Southern Religion of the 1970s as Based on Samuel Hill, Jr.'s Southern Culture-Religion Thesis" (Ph.D. dissertation, Florida State University, 1980), 127–82.

[20] Caldwell, *Deep South*, 61, 96, 97.

percent of all white southerners were Protestants. Of these, about five in ten were Baptists, two in ten Methodists, and one in ten Presbyterians, with the remaining two in ten scattered across a variety of denominations and sects. Most Protestants—80 to 90 percent of them—endorsed at least nominally such basic biblical propositions as life after death, the existence of a devil, and the return of Jesus Christ. Flannery O'Connor was probably correct when she observed, "While the South is hardly Christ-centered, it is most certainly Christ-haunted." [21]

Catholics and Jews were distinct minorities. The homeland of regional Catholicism had historically been the Acadian parishes of southern Louisiana. During the postwar years, an influx of Latins, particularly in Texas and Florida, swelled Catholic ranks. Jews were most numerous in the Miami metropolitan area, but elsewhere their prominence in business, especially retailing, made them influential. In most southern cities, they were members of the uptown leadership. Outside southern Texas, southern Louisiana, and southern Florida, however, Protestantism set the tone of regional religious life.

The institutional church changed more than did southern theology. In some respects, the increasingly secular religion of the metropolitan white middle class coexisted relatively comfortably with modernism. Both theology and modernism stressed individualism, even if their agreement did not go much beyond that. Personal salvation lay at the heart of a Protestantism that blended fundamentalism and evangelism. The purpose of the gospel was to offer salvation to the sinner and, in the more fashionable churches, to do so with a minimum of discomfort. A preacher expecting to rise in the church hierarchy "does not wish . . . to damn his listeners to Hell unless somehow he gets them back in time to attend service each Sunday," a study of the churches in Little Rock noted.[22]

[21] Fred J. Hood, "Kentucky," in *Religion in the Southern States*, ed. Hill, 120; John Shelton Reed, *The Enduring South: Subcultural Persistence in Mass Society* (Lexington, Mass., 1972), 57–81; Flannery O'Connor, "Some Aspects of the Grotesque in Southern Fiction," in *Mystery and Manners*, ed. Sally Fitzgerald and Robert Fitzgerald (New York, 1961), 44.

[22] Ernest Q. Campbell and Thomas F. Pettigrew, *Christians in Racial Crisis: A Study of Little Rock's Ministry* (Washington, D.C., 1959), 90.

Southern Protestantism, like ideological modernism, contained little in the way of a social ethic. Ministers opposed individual sins such as consumption of the demon rum, and they frequently collected alms for poor individuals, but they rarely demonstrated theological interest in the broader problems of society. As Samuel S. Hill has pointed out, "the concern for personal salvation and assurance has colored and conditioned the entire outlook of popular religion in the South," and as a result, the "effective neglect of social ethics" was a "primary and distinguishing feature of popular southern religion." Metropolitan middle-class churches became larger and more diverse but for the most part retained their time-honored focus on born-again salvation. Many materially successful urbanites had been raised in fundamentalist households, and in suburbia they often continued to espouse if not to practice much of the traditional theology.[23]

During the controversies over desegregation in the 1950s and 1960s, all the mainline denominations approved statements endorsing racial desegregation at least in principle. A number of white southern clerics braved public censure to uphold equality in the sight of God, and some lost their pulpits as a result. More often than not, metropolitan ministerial associations could be counted on to support moderate policies. Occasionally women's groups, most notably the United Church Women, boldly upheld equality. For the most part, though, the southern religious establishment managed to affect a vague neutrality and, like one Mississippi minister, to "look beyond the chaos which is around us today" by preaching the sacred rather than the social gospel. The minister of a large plant in North Carolina explained to Erskine Caldwell, "The church in the South has to play it safe."[24]

[23] Samuel S. Hill, Jr., *Southern Churches in Crisis* (New York, 1967), 89, 112. Other relevant works by Hill include Samuel S. Hill, Jr., ed., *Religion in the Southern States;* Samuel S. Hill, Jr., *The South and the North in American Religion* (Athens, Ga., 1980); Samuel S. Hill, Jr., and Robert G. Torbet, *Baptists North and South* (Valley Forge, Pa., 1964); and Samuel S. Hill, Jr., *et al., Religion and the Solid South* (Nashville, 1972). See also Kenneth K. Bailey, *Southern White Protestantism in the Twentieth Century* (New York, 1964); David M. Reimers, *White Protestantism and the Negro* (New York, 1965); Andrew Michael Manis, *Southern Civil Religions in Conflict: Black and White Baptists and Civil Rights, 1947–1957* (Athens, Ga., 1987); and John Lee Eighmy, *Churches in Cultural Captivity: A History of the Social Attitudes of Southern Baptists* (Rev. ed.; Knoxville, Tenn., 1987).

[24] Nicholas Von Hoffman, *Mississippi Notebook* (New York, 1964), 48; Caldwell, *Deep South,*

No one better personified metropolitan white middle-class southern religion than Billy Graham. Born the son of a modestly successful dairy farmer in North Carolina, Graham grew up a Presbyterian. He became a Southern Baptist while preaching at a Baptist church in Florida in the late 1930s. His theology changed relatively little. "If by fundamentalism," he acknowledged, "you mean a person who accepts the authority of Scriptures, the virgin birth of Christ, the atoning death of Christ, His bodily resurrection, His second coming, and personal salvation by faith through grace, then I am a fundamentalist."[25]

In 1945 Graham became a full-time organizer for Youth for Christ, a movement that sought to combat juvenile delinquency and Communism. Graham proved to be an able evangelist and soon began to conduct his own revivals. By the late 1940s he had become one of a score or more of proselytizers with a claim to a national reputation. In 1949 his attacks on Communism and his defense of traditional values at a revival in Los Angeles led William Randolph Hearst to instruct his publishing empire to promote the young evangelist. "Until that time," Graham recalled, "our crusade had never attracted any press coverage. When I arrived at the tent that night, I found the place swarming with reporters and photographers." Soon afterward, at a rally in Columbia, South Carolina, Henry Luce met with Graham and "pledged the cooperation of his magazines to support all the subsequent Graham campaigns in other cities." The backing of Hearst, an avid domestic anticommunist, and Luce, the original promoter of "American Century" Cold War policies, assured Graham national prominence. It was also an important event in the marriage of southern fundamentalism and northern anticommunism that was so powerfully to influence postwar developments.[26]

As Graham's stature grew, so did his national acceptance. In 1957 Graham held a crusade in New York City sponsored by the

---

66. See also Samuel S. Hill, Jr., "Southern Protestantism and Racial Integration," *Religion in Life*, XXXIII (1964), 421–29; William Peters, *The Southern Temper* (New York, 1959).

[25] Graham quoted in *Billy Graham: Revivalist in a Secular Age*, by William G. McLoughlin, Jr. (New York, 1960), 70.

[26] Billy Graham, "God Is My Witness, Part II," *McCalls*, May, 1964, p. 179; McLoughlin, *Billy Graham*, 56.

city's Protestant Council of Churches. Before that, his sectarian support had come almost exclusively from denominations belonging to the National Association of Evangelical Churches. By 1957 mainstream denominations even in Gotham City welcomed the revivalist. Southern fundamentalism was gaining increasing national support. The New York crusade was also the first Graham rally to be televised. Graham had conducted a television ministry previously, but the televising of the crusade proved to be immensely popular and became a regular part of his revivalism. By 1964 Graham could state, "I probably have preached before more millions on more continents than anyone ever." [27]

Graham was, as his most perceptive biographer has noted, an "evangelist to an affluent society" who appealed to "predominantly middle-class white-collar audiences." Chambers of commerce, Rotary, Lions, and similar local business and service groups normally rallied behind Graham's crusades. In Graham's theology, there was little conflict between God and mammon. "Thousands of businessmen have discovered the satisfaction of having God as a working partner," Graham stated. "The plant that prays together profits together." Indeed, Graham once described the Garden of Eden as a place where there were "no labor unions, no snakes, no disease." Communists were the agents of Satan, and the struggle between Communism and capitalism was a "battle to the death" between "Christ and anti-Christ." A critic remarked, "It's all for a Baptist uneasy in his buick of a Sunday." [28]

The mission of Graham's crusades was "to bear witness to Jesus Christ," and like southern Protestantism generally, he distrusted a social gospel. "Social sins, after all, are merely a large-scale projection of individual sins and need to be repented of by the offending segment of society." Crime was not a result of poverty. "There was no rioting, looting, or killing of police officers in depression days when people were much poorer." The answer to

[27] Billy Graham, "God Is My Witness, Part I," *McCalls,* April, 1964, p. 122; Marshall Frady, *Billy Graham: A Parable of American Righteousness* (Boston, 1979), 289–318.
[28] McLoughlin, *Billy Graham,* 83, 100; Billy Graham, "God Before Gold," *Nation's Business,* September, 1954, pp. 34, 35; William G. McLoughlin, Jr., *Revivals, Awakenings, and Reform: An Essay on Religion and Social Change in America, 1607–1977* (Chicago, 1978), 189; Billy Graham, "Satan's Religion," *American Mercury,* LXXIX (1954), 41; Frady, *Billy Graham,* 215.

national problems was each individual's "moral and spiritual renewal," not social reform. "The one great answer to our racial problem is for men and women to be converted to Christ." In the meantime, Graham wrote to President Eisenhower, "If the Supreme Court will go slowly and the extremists on both sides will quiet down, we can have a peaceful social readjustment over the next ten-year period." During the 1950s Graham increasingly insisted on desegregating his rallies, but except for that he consistently came down on the side of gradualism.[29]

Ideological modernism and religious fundamentalism were of course ultimately incompatible. "Many of our educational leaders," Graham lamented, "sneer at the old-fashioned idea of God and a moral code." They hold, Graham observed, "that morality is relative—that there is no norm or absolute standard"—and they scorn religion by advancing a secular humanism for which scientific, material, and social progress take the place of the biblical God. Like other southern churchmen, Graham worried about moral relativism and human arrogance without being able to combat them except by appeal to the authenticity of the Scripture, the importance of salvation, and the soundness of traditional family values. "A nation is only as strong as her homes," Graham reiterated, and he warned listeners that satanic Communism toiled unremittingly to destroy American families. He warned parents that children must be taught discipline and obedience, and he reminded women, "Wives submit yourselves unto your husbands, as it is fit in the Lord." His strictures were to little avail. Church attendance increased, but so too did secular and relativist values.[30]

The white-collar metropolitan middle class absorbed much of the South's postwar prosperity and exercised an increasingly im-

[29] Billy Graham, *World Aflame* (New York, 1965), 9; Billy Graham, "What Ten Years Have Taught Me," *Christian Century*, LXXVII (1960), 189; Graham quoted in *Religion and the New Majority: Billy Graham, Middle America, and the Politics of the Seventies,* by Lowell D. Streiker and Gerald S. Strober (New York, 1972), 57; McLoughlin, *Billy Graham,* 48; Billy Graham, "The Answer to Corruption," *Nation's Business,* September, 1969, p. 48; Billy Graham to president, June 4, 1956, in Name Series (Graham), Dwight D. Eisenhower Library, Abilene, Kans.

[30] Graham quoted in *Billy Graham,* by McLoughlin, 85, 213–14; Graham, "Satan's Religion," 41–46; Graham, "The Answer to Corruption," 46–49.

portant role in public life. Broadly, its members championed moderation in race relations, Republicanism in presidential politics, and economic development in public policy. Northern industries opening southern branch plants often brought their managerial people with them, and rising southern prosperity attracted other skilled and educated immigrants. In the midfifties three out of four immigrants from the North held white-collar status. An Atlanta real estate agent, according to Flannery O'Connor, could promise a Wisconsin family, "You'll like this neighborhood. There's not a southerner for two miles." [31]

The influx of corporate employees made the southern metropolitan middle class more diverse, but it also hampered economic mobility for native residents. Historian Bruce J. Schulman has asserted that "the new businesses recruited their best-paid workers from outside the South and hired locals for manual and custodial positions." In fact, material opportunities did expand for native southerners—at least for white males—but the approximately one in ten members of the southern population in 1960 who were born outside the South, and the two in ten in 1980, held the better jobs of the region far out of proportion to their numbers. The southern working class, modestly paid in comparison with their peers elsewhere and scorned by liberals as the moral villains in race relations, harbored growing resentments.[32]

In 1960 blue-collar workers constituted 48 percent of the southern labor force. Factory workers, the largest contingent and the most strategically placed, amounted to more than 22 percent of the work force. Most of the other blue-collar employees were in construction, communications, transportation, and service occupations. Eight out of ten of the manufacturing, construction, transportation, and communications workers were male, and 85 percent of them were white. Blue-collar services, the lowest-paying category, was approximately 50 percent black and two-thirds fe-

---

[31] Philip E. Converse, "A Major Political Realignment in the South?" in *Change in the Contemporary South*, ed. Sindler, 210; Flannery O'Connor, "The Regional Writer," in *Mystery and Manners*, ed. Fitzgerald and Fitzgerald, 57.

[32] Bruce J. Schulman, *From Cotton Belt to Sunbelt: Federal Policy, Economic Development, and the Transformation of the South, 1938–1980* (New York, 1991), 159; Earl Black and Merle Black, *Politics and Society in the South* (Cambridge, Mass., 1987), 15–22.

male. As a proportion of total southern employment, blue-collar workers were at their zenith in the early 1960s. Thereafter their numbers declined relative to white-collar employees. In 1970 blue-collar and white-collar numbers were approximately equal. By 1980 blue-collar workers made up 44 percent of the southern labor force, while white-collar workers were 51 percent.

Blue-collar employment encompassed a wide range of occupations. In the midsixties almost one-quarter of employed white males and about one in twenty white females were foremen, craftsmen, and the like. In the aggregate, the foremen, electricians, plumbers, carpenters, bakers, mechanics, and locomotive engineers were relatively well compensated. They ranked behind only the business and professional middle class in income. Operatives probably best fit the blue-collar stereotype. They included workers in textile, tobacco, and chemical factories as well as construction and refinery workers and truck drivers, and came to about 18 percent of the regional work force. Laborers and blue-collar service workers—maids, cooks, janitors, garbage men, waitresses, unskilled workers—made up another 18 percent.

Surveys regularly found racial intolerance to be greatest among whites with lower education, income, and social standing. During the 1950s and 1960s working-class whites fulfilled Gunnar Myrdal's prophecy by becoming increasingly hostile to social change. Their opposition to desegregation went well beyond a psychological commitment to white supremacy. Doubtless a belief in black inferiority did contribute to segregationist sentiment, as did an apprehensiveness about black competition for jobs and advancement and a concern over the direct impact that might be felt from school and housing integration. Yet the racial prejudice of the white proletariat was often not the "bigoted, working-class, redneck" mindlessness that many well-educated members of the middle class ascribed to them. During the 1960s black southerners won their battle for civil rights, and middle-class southerners gained further affluence and political power. Working-class and lower-middle-class whites remained powerless, and they became increasingly frustrated, angry, and alienated. As a New Orleans carpenter explained to Robert Coles, "While the rich invent clever schemes to get out of paying taxes, and while the colored come running into a city like this one, expecting money from the city every week, the rest of us have big deductions taken out every week from our paychecks, and there isn't a thing we can do about it." [33]

The southern working class had ample grievances. The consumer-based taxes of the southern states, on top of a federal tax system that was skewed toward levies on wage income, hit workers especially hard. The shortage of lower-cost housing and affordable medical care, the relative unavailability of public services for the lower-middle class, and the low pay scales in the region hurt both the white and the black working class. Relatively few southern workers could plan on meaningful retirement pensions, and southern labor legislation was the most regressive in the nation. "I've worked all my life," a retired truck driver said. "I never made nothing. I'm still poor, and there is nothing I can do about it." [34]

About half the working white women in the South held blue-collar jobs. "Being a working-class woman means being stepped on, pushed around, degraded, overworked and underpaid," Kathy Kahn fumed. "More than that, it means you have little hope that you will do anything more in life than a lot of hard work. If you have talent and ability it goes unrecognized. I gradually built up a deep anger inside me at the conditions of myself and other working people." [35]

A central tragedy was that many lower-income whites blamed blacks rather than the system. A North Carolina factory worker was hardly alone in fretting, "The government will help the niggers, but they don't give us nothing." As David H. Tabb concluded, "The race issue has often served as a symbolic equivalent of a class issue." Although southern workers frequently exhibited class consciousness and often seemed to discern that they had more in common with working-class blacks than with affluent whites, they rarely carried—or had much opportunity to carry—that realiza-

[33] Robert Emil Botsch, *We Shall Not Overcome: Populism and Southern Blue-Collar Workers* (Chapel Hill, N.C., 1980), 159; Robert Coles, *Farewell to the South* (Boston, 1963), 372.

[34] David Hirsh Tabb, "Attitudes Toward Economic Equality in the South: A Study of the Political Ideology of the Poor" (Ph.D. dissertation, University of North Carolina, 1969), 142.

[35] Kathy Kahn, ed., *Hillbilly Women* (New York, 1973), 21.

tion into the political arena. The failure of labor unions and popular-front liberalism in the 1930s and 1940s helped to explain
working-class political behavior in the 1950s and 1960s.[36]

By the 1970s the southern lower-middle class was the most alienated of the nation's statistically surveyed social groups. The
Harris Poll found that the South was the "most disenchanted part
of the country" and that its "lower-middle-income and blue collar
types" felt the most "left out of the mainstream of American life
and taken advantage of by people with power." Disorganized and
socially isolated, many white workers clung to church, family, and
neighborhood. "The attributes they value," Robert Emil Botsch
has observed, "were private morality, church attendance, giving
to charities, being a good neighbor, and other, mostly private,
individual activities." According to Tabb, "Most often the church
was the only social life outside the workplace that interested these
men."[37]

A substantial majority of workers were Baptists and Methodists,
like almost everybody else. At the same time, there were differences between working-class and upper-middle-class Protestantism. A working-class church was inevitably smaller, and it was often, as Erskine Caldwell noted, a "home-folksy meeting place with
an atmosphere of informal sociability and entertainment where
at the same time sin can be shed and souls saved." Robert Botsch
has related the experience of a worker in a furniture factory who
attended services at a fashionable metropolitan church: "I got
stared at the whole time I was there. I tried to be friendly and
nice, but the people just acted like they didn't want to have
nothin' to do with me cause I wasn't in their class. Which I reckon

[36]Tabb, "Attitudes Toward Economic Equality in the South," 108; Botsch, *We Shall Not Overcome;* Mimi Conway, *Rise Gonna Rise: A Portrait of Southern Textile Workers* (New York, 1979); Marc S. Miller, ed., *Working Lives: The "Southern Exposure" History of Labor in the South* (New York, 1980); Arthur B. Shostak and William Gomberg, eds., *Blue Collar World: Studies of the American Worker* (Englewood Cliffs, N.J., 1964); John Kenneth Morland, *Millways of Kent* (Chapel Hill, N.C., 1958); Lee Rainwater, Richard Coleman, and Gerald Handel, *Workingman's Wife* (New York, 1959).

[37]Louis Harris in Atlanta *Constitution,* September 20, 1976; Botsch, *We Shall Not Overcome,* 178; Tabb, "Attitudes Toward Economic Equality in the South," 43; James Clotfelter and William R. Hamilton, "Beyond Race Politics: Electing Southern Populists in the 1970s," in *You Can't Eat Magnolias,* ed. H. Brandt Ayers and Thomas H. Naylor (New York, 1972), 136–59.

they could look at me and tell that I wasn't. Course I really didn't care. I just went to be going one time to see what it was like in a fancy church." [38]

The most dynamic working-class religious movement grew out of pentecostalism. A variety of sects, the largest of which were the Pentecostal Holiness, Pentecostal Church of God, Church of God, and Assemblies of God, subscribed to the "full gospel," to "entire sanctification," to revivalism, and most of all, to the "baptism of the Holy Spirit." Laborers, factory workers, clerks, and filling station attendants, as well as mountaineers and the rural and small-town poor, joined the congregations, which gathered in the small churches located in urban low-rent districts and along country roads. The sects engaged their faithful in ways that went beyond the intellectual, and healing and the speaking in tongues were part of their services. Pentecostals believed that the Holy Spirit descended on them in glossolalia and miracle working just as it had descended on the apostles at Pentecost, or Whitsunday. The preachers were usually men of limited education, and it was not unusual for them to hold weekday jobs to make ends meet. Fashionable middle-class southerners normally denigrated the antics of the unwashed, but the sects, both the clergy and the laity, approached doctrinal matters much more seriously than the mainstream denominations. As to indecorum, Francis Butler Simkins had a point when he observed, "The shouting, screaming, and jumping in which Primitivists indulge is no more irrational than the shouting, screaming, and jumping in which people of high rank indulge at football games." [39]

---

[38] Caldwell, *Deep South*, 35; Botsch, *We Shall Not Overcome*, 107.

[39] Francis Butler Simkins, "The Rising Tide of Faith," in *The Everlasting South* (Baton Rouge, 1963), 79; David Edwin Harrell, Jr., *White Sects and Black Men in the Recent South* (Nashville, 1971); David Edwin Harrell, Jr., *All Things Are Possible: The Healing and Charismatic Revivals in Modern America* (Bloomington, Ind., 1975); Charles Hudson, "The Structure of a Fundamentalist Christian Belief-System," in *Religion and the Solid South*, by Hill *et al.*, 122–42; C. Dwight Dorough, *The Bible Belt Mystique* (Philadelphia, 1974); Harry Groff Lefever, "Ghetto Religion: A Study of the Religious Structures and Styles of a Poor White Community in Atlanta, Georgia" (Ph.D. dissertation, Emory University, 1971); Ronald Graydon Hicks, "The Protestant Ethic and the Generation Gap in the Modern Urban Southern Family" (Ph.D. dissertation, Louisiana State University, 1970); Howard Dorgan, *Giving Glory to God in Appalachia: Worship Practices of Six Baptist Subdenominations* (Knoxville, Tenn., 1987).

Flannery O'Connor, who found backwoods prophets and fundamentalist excess arresting, often depicted sect figures as grotesques. Still, she saw much to admire in them. "When you write about backwoods prophets, it is very difficult to get across to the modern reader that you take these people seriously," O'Connor once explained, "that you are not making fun of them, but that their concerns are your own and, in your judgment, central to human life." In an increasingly modern and secular South, O'Connor lamented, "I hate to think that in twenty years Southern writers too may be writing about men in gray-flannel suits and may have lost their ability to see that these gentlemen are even greater freaks than what we are writing about now." [40]

The healing revival that lasted from the late 1940s to the late 1950s laid the foundation for a broader charismatic movement. Talented and often colorful, the healing evangelists employed tent revivals, radio, and television to propagate their message. Most were southern-born white males from poor and pentecostal backgrounds. Historian David Edwin Harrell, Jr., has remarked, "The healing revival was clearly outside the boundaries of respectable religion in America. It bore the raggedy image of shoddy pentecostal buildings and holy roller services." Religious healers faced the prospect of being charged with practicing medicine without a license, of using the mails to defraud, and of operating a business without a permit. Accusations of quackery came from both medical and religious sources. Some of the healers did seem to have an unbecoming interest in personal gain, and some were susceptible to the temptations of alcohol and riotous living. In spite of it all, the healing revival became a powerful southern, national, and international movement. [41]

Most of the sect churches unabashedly defended racial segregation, agreeing with the American Council of Christian Churches that integration "does violence to the true gospel of Jesus Christ." Yet the sect churches were the most likely to practice biracial worship. The Church of God of Prophecy was apparently the region's

---

[40] Flannery O'Connor, "The Catholic Novelist in the Protestant South," in *Mystery and Manners*, ed. Fitzgerald and Fitzgerald, 204; Flannery O'Connor, "Some Aspects of the Grotesque in Southern Fiction," *ibid.*, 50.

[41] Harrell, *All Things Are Possible*, 95

first fully desegregated modern church, and the healing revivalists welcomed black worshipers, often in separate sections of the tent but sometimes with integrated seating. The tension between segregationism and biracialism in the sect churches was true to the complexity of lower-class white attitudes toward racial questions.[42]

Granville Oral Roberts was the most successful of the healing revivalists. He claimed to have laid hands on more than a million sufferers. In 1955 Roberts began to televise his healing revivals, and by the end of the fifties he directed a huge television and radio ministry, had constructed a seven-story Abundant Life office building in Tulsa, and employed more than six hundred people. Apart only from Billy Graham, he was the nation's best-known revivalist.[43]

The son of a pentecostal minister in Oklahoma, Roberts grew up in near poverty. At seventeen, he was diagnosed as having tuberculosis. An itinerant pentecostal evangelist "healed" him of his disabling ailment, at the same time curing him of a stutter. He went on to serve twelve years as a pentecostal minister in several southern states before returning to Oklahoma, where, by his account, he received instructions from God to "heal the sick and cast out devils by my power." In 1947 he began his healing ministry at a Pentecostal Holiness church in the town of Enid. The following year he purchased a tent and hit the sawdust trail. In his crusades, he blended evangelism and millennialism with his healing.[44]

Roberts held relatively conventional social views. "He had always been a chest-thumping Oklahoman," his biographer has written, "a flag-waving American, an outspoken defender of the 'free enterprise system,' and a critic of Communism." At the same time, his social vision extended beyond that of Billy Graham. Roberts equated racial harmony with "individual men and women of every race . . . giving of themselves," but he also called for "more equitable laws." From the beginning, Roberts refused "to accept the

[42] *The State*, May 1, 1958; Campbell and Pettigrew, *Christians in Racial Crisis*, 41–59; Harrell, *White Sects and Black Men in the Recent South*.

[43] Oral Roberts, *The Call: An Autobiography* (New York, 1972), 14, 180–85.

[44] *Oral Roberts' Life Story As Told by Himself* (Tulsa, 1952), 90; Oral Roberts, *Best Sermons and Stories* (Tulsa, 1956), 37.

limitation of a whites-only ministry," and though he acceded to officially "forced segregated seating," he refused to accept segregated salvation and healing lines, defying "any person in this service or any official of this city to try and force the altar of God to be segregated."[45]

By the end of the 1950s tent revivals and healing lines had begun to seem remnants of an earlier era. Worshipers, Roberts noted, "had become used to cushioned chairs and air-conditioning and to watching television." More important, the charismatic movement gained adherents in the mainstream churches. "Thousands of people in the traditional churches had become interested in the charismatic message," David Harrell has written; "hundreds of thousands of religious Americans were dissatisfied with their own lethargic denominations and were searching for a more dynamic experience." Roberts and other pentecostal evangelists adjusted by deemphasizing healing and accentuating salvation and the supernatural gifts of the Holy Spirit. The once ridiculed faith of the southern poor achieved respectability. Although the southern lower-middle class remained the bedrock audience for televised services, the charismatic movement, in Harrell's words, "contributed to the remarkable growth of the pentecostal denominations, an explosion of independent charismatic churches throughout the country, and the continued formation of independent charismatic fellowships within most mainstream churches and the Catholic Church."[46]

Oral Roberts exemplified the transformation. In 1965 he abandoned his older television format for prime-time specials that matched Billy Graham's productions in their technological sophistication. At the World Congress on Evangelism in 1967, Graham went out of his way to extol Roberts' contributions to revivalism and, according to Roberts, "to open my eyes to the mainstream of Christianity." The following year Roberts left the Pentecostal Holiness church to become a Methodist and a member of the fashionable Boston Avenue Methodist Church in Tulsa. By that time Oral Roberts University was in operation as an insti-

[45] David Edwin Harrell, Jr., *Oral Roberts: An American Life* (Bloomington, Ind., 1985), 448; Roberts, *The Call*, 112, 103.

[46] Roberts, *The Call*, 122; Harrell, *All Things Are Possible*, 7; Harrell, *Oral Roberts*, 422.

tution for training charismatic ministers, and a hospital complex opened in the 1970s. As a Methodist, Roberts continued to speak in tongues and to pray for the healing of the afflicted, but such practices were no longer confined to the southern underclass.[47]

Roberts proclaimed television the "most powerful means the world has ever known for spreading the gospel," and others apparently agreed. From 1970 to 1975 the number of syndicated religious programs increased from thirty-eight to sixty-six, and the estimated viewing audience grew from ten million to well over twenty million, with half residing in the South and many others southern-born residents living elsewhere. "Not surprising given its theological complexion," an English social scientist commented, "the electronic church is still a largely southern phenomenon." Jerry Falwell and Pat Robertson of Virginia, Jimmy Swaggart of Louisiana, James Robison and Kenneth Copeland of Texas, and Jim and Tammy Bakker of North Carolina appealed most to older, female, lower-status, nonmetropolitan southerners.[48]

In his brief for southern progress, William Nicholls regretted the "static society" and "conservative, paternalistic, and backward-looking" traditionalism of the rural areas and small towns. Nicholls mused, "It is a paradox that the South, which by every objective standard is the most religious region in America, could be so blind to the practical implications of Christianity." He was by no means alone in identifying southern Protestantism—the region's "civil religion" or "culture religion," as academics were prone to label it—with traditional values and an otherworldly detachment from social imperatives. Erskine Caldwell, while traveling through the Appalachian area of Tennessee and Kentucky, concluded, "In such an environment of unyielding traditions and steadfast fundamentalism, it is to be expected that the social and political changes that have been commonplace elsewhere in the United States in recent years should be resisted in the Cumberlands." As

---

[47] Roberts, *The Call*, 122; Harrell, *Oral Roberts*, 196–209.

[48] Roberts, *Best Sermons and Stories*, 50; Steve Bruce, *Pray TV: Televangelism in America* (London, 1990), 110; Jeffrey K. Hadden and Charles E. Swann, *Prime Time Preachers: The Rising Power of Televangelism* (Reading, Mass., 1981); Peter G. Horsfield, *Religious Television: The American Experience* (New York, 1984); Peter G. Horsfield et al., "The Mediated Ministry," *Journal of Communication*, XXXV (1985), 89–156.

Samuel Hill has concluded, the religion of the historic agricultural South "is dominantly a conservative or reinforcing agent for the traditional values held by white southern society." [49]

To be sure, agriculture itself employed a precipitously declining share of southern workers. In 1960 agriculture, forestry, and mining—the enterprises that had once been the foundation for a colonial economy—employed only 12.6 percent of the southern labor force, and by 1980 that proportion had declined to 5 percent. The change reflected the dwindling number of farmers. In 1960 some 15 percent of the southern population lived on farms; in 1980 hardly more than 3 percent did. Agriculture, forestry, and mining retained a pivotal role in the economy, largely because they supplied the raw materials for basic southern industries, but the number of farmers grew ever smaller. In rural areas, most households were not situated on farms. During the 1960s and 1970s rural nonfarm dwellers constituted 25 to 30 percent of the total southern population, and a substantial majority of those who were employed worked in blue-collar occupations.

The decline of the farm population attracted surprisingly little attention while it was happening. In 1957 James H. Street, in a notable study of the mechanization of cotton production, observed that for farmers displaced by machines, "the means of population mobility in this country are great and the avenues of escape numerous." Nicholls declared that a "Southern enclosure movement" had "failed to materialize" because farmers moved to "better economic opportunities elsewhere." During the 1960s, however, an awareness grew of the "southern roots of the urban crisis." The irony was apparent to one scholar: "The federal government . . . caused the transformation of southern agriculture at the expense of poor whites and blacks. Then, in the 1960s, the federal government found these same people and promptly declared them 'poverty-stricken.' " [50]

[49] Nicholls, *Southern Tradition and Regional Progress*, 63, 27, 163; Caldwell, *Deep South*, 25; Hill, "The South's Two Cultures," in *Religion and the Solid South*, by Hill *et al.*, 36. See also Charles Reagan Wilson, "God's Project: The Southern Civil Religion, 1920–1980," in *Religion and the Life of the Nation*, ed. Roland A. Sherrill (Urbana, Ill., 1990), 65–83; and Adams, "An Analytical Study of Southern Religion."

[50] James H. Street, *The New Revolution in the Cotton Economy: Mechanization and Its Conse-*

During the 1950s and 1960s farmers for the most part experienced relatively difficult times. Beginning in 1972 the Soviet Union began to purchase American crops in large volume. Southern farmers joined the rest of the nation's agriculturists in a period of prosperity. The United States government lifted most acreage restrictions, and productivity soared. But later in the decade a new wave of hostility toward the Soviet Union and a concern over inflation of domestic food prices led to limits on food exports. The era of farm prosperity was as short as it had been unexpected.

Reacting to the return of economic hard times, farmers created the American Agricultural Movement. The organization spread over much of the South. Participants in the movement urged farmers to strike—to refuse to plant crops until the federal government guaranteed higher price supports. They dramatized their cause with tractor parades, one in Atlanta in 1977 that included five thousand tractors, and two more in 1978 and 1979 in Washington. Federal policy did not change, however, and the strike never materialized.[51]

Southern towns continued to decline relative to the metropolitan areas, and the county-seat establishment surrendered its domination over state politics. The decisive victory of metropolitan elites in the struggle over school desegregation, the court-ordered reapportionment of the legislatures, and the rising influence of black voters sapped the authority of the counties. No longer able to command state affairs, county leaders remained formidable on the local level, and they were the most determined opponents of the black civil rights movement of the 1960s.

When the South participated in the Sunbelt boom of the late 1970s, relatively few nonmetropolitan counties shared in the eco-

---

quences (Chapel Hill, N.C., 1957), 247; Nicholls, *Southern Tradition and Regional Progress*, 61; Roger Beardwood, "The Southern Roots of the Urban Crisis," *Fortune*, August, 1968, pp. 8off.; Neil D. Fligstein, "Migration from Counties of the South, 1900–1950: A Social, Historical, and Demographic Account" (Ph.D. dissertation, University of Wisconsin, 1978), 416; David Ray James, "The Transformation of Local and State Class Structure and Resistance to the Civil Rights Movement in the South" (Ph.D. dissertation, University of Wisconsin, 1981).

[51] Gilbert C. Fite, *Cotton Fields No More: Southern Agriculture, 1865–1980* (Lexington, Ky., 1984), 226–31.

nomic growth and prosperity. Travelers often remarked on the more isolated southern towns, with their old-fashioned court-houses, Confederate monuments, and sleepy tempo. A journalist mercilessly caught the feel of a county seat in south Georgia: "The center of town had remained a paltry collection of brick and stone buildings inscribed with dedication dates from the turn of the century, all of them long since weathered to the drab uncolor of snuff or dead leaves or the earth itself, and along its idle streets, there weighed some abiding lassitude of brute tedium."[52]

Nevertheless, southern towns and their hinterlands were not immune to the material and cultural forces emanating from the metropolitan areas. In the mid-1970s a study of southern change described a town in southern Arkansas that had six factories, five with owners outside the state. Three nonsouthern paper compa-nies owned about half the county's acreage. Of several department stores, just one was locally owned. In Alabama, Erskine Caldwell spoke to the proprietor of a general store, the last in town as shoppers flocked to chain stores. The proprietor's three children had left to search for better opportunities elsewhere. David E. Whisnant, a student of Appalachian culture, sighed in 1970 about the "fifteen miles between Asheville and Canton, North Carolina: a virtually unbroken strip of junkyards, franchised fast-food eat-eries, ugly motels and gasoline stations, and tawdry roadside 'tour-ist attractions.' " When an Atlanta suburbanite sought calm by moving to a southern town, he found the "same eager, hectic clutter of pancake houses and shopping centers, merely a dupli-cate in microcosm of what he had fled." In these communities, the day of the furnishing merchant and of Saturday shopping and socializing had passed.[53]

Most employed black southerners held blue-collar jobs. In 1940 blacks made up 25 percent of the South's population and 28 percent of its labor force. By 1960 they constituted 21 percent of the population and less than 20 percent of the labor force. In 1980 they came to slightly more than 18 percent of the population

[52] Marshall Frady, *Southerners: A Journalist's Odyssey* (New York, 1980), 229.

[53] Thomas H. Naylor and James Clotfelter, *Strategies for Change in the South* (Chapel Hill, N.C., 1975), 37–38; Caldwell, *Deep South*, 110–11; David E. Whisnant, "Finding New Mod-els for Appalachian Development," *New South*, Fall, 1970, p. 71; Frady, *Southerners*, 284.

but only 15 percent of the labor force. The migration of working-age blacks out of the region and the influx of whites largely accounted for the declines, but so too did the fact that African Americans had simply been denied entry into the emerging southern economy. In the nonmetropolitan portions of six Lower South states, white workers gained 287,000 jobs during the sixties, while black workers lost 97,000. In the midsixties more than nine out of ten employed black men held blue-collar jobs, but fewer than one in ten was a skilled craftsman and fewer than a third were operatives. The majority—almost 60 percent—were laborers and blue-collar service workers. Approximately 85 percent of employed black women held blue-collar jobs, and well over half were laborers and service workers. In the larger white economy, black employees were the janitors, maids, laborers, and garbage men when they were not unemployed.[54]

The average income of southern black families was well below the poverty line in 1960. "If one assumes that a family income of $3,000 a year is required to buy the basic necessities of life," one study calculated, "then over 70 per cent of all southern Negro families are poverty-stricken." In the late sixties the Citizens' Board of Inquiry into Hunger and Malnutrition found that substantial numbers of citizens in most nonmetropolitan southern counties and in many metropolitan areas suffered not only from poverty and malnutrition but from "serious" or "emergency" hunger. Low living standards were nothing unusual in the South, especially among African Americans, but the vitality that had come to the southern marketplace and the improved material well-being of so many whites made black poverty glaringly obvious.[55]

[54] James Louis Walker, "Economic Development, Black Employment, and Black Migration in the Nonmetropolitan Deep South" (Ph.D dissertation, University of Texas, 1974), 15; Henderson, *The Economic Status of Negroes;* H. M. Douty, "Wage Differentials: Forces and Counterforces," *Monthly Labor Review,* XCI (1968), 74–81; James D. Cowhig and Calvin L. Beale, "Relative Socioeconomic Status of Southern Whites and Nonwhites, 1950 and 1960," *Southwestern Social Science Quarterly,* XLV (1964), 113–24; Louis Cleveland Green, "Economics of a Separatist State: U.S. Blacks in Five Southern States" (Ph.D. dissertation, University of California at Berkeley, 1975); Marshall and Christian, eds., *Employment of Blacks in the South.*

[55] Donald R. Matthews and James W. Prothro, *Negroes and the New Southern Politics* (New York, 1966), 285; *Hunger, U.S.A.: A Report by the Citizens' Board of Inquiry into Hunger and Malnutrition in the United States* (Washington, D.C., 1968); *Hunger U.S.A. Revisited: A Report*

Only slightly less in the burgeoning metropolitan ghettos of the South than in those of the North, the black "underclass" became ever more alienated from the broader society. Probably it was at least as alienated as the white working class the pollsters had identified. James Weldon Johnson once referred to the "desperate class" of poor blacks who "cherish a sullen hatred for all white men, and they value life as cheap." Referring to inner-city Birmingham, David L. Lewis noted the many "young adult males (periodically or only barely employed) for whom the black church and [Martin Luther King, Jr.'s] vision of brotherhood were contemptible irrelevancies." The women of the ghetto remained more closely identified with the black church, but in practice they too rejected many of the values associated with New South progress. The prevalence of single-parent households and of crime was symptomatic of the mounting social problems of ghetto blacks.[56]

In 1960 fewer than a third of African-American adults had a high-school education, itself usually the product of an inadequate segregated school. Many blacks suffered psychological scars from their long experience with white supremacy. Survey research revealed that African Americans were poorly informed, resistant to change, authoritarian in personality, and intolerant of freedom of speech for nonconformists, which to only a slightly lesser degree were the shortcomings ascribed to white blue-collar workers and farmers. Blacks were more racially tolerant than whites, and they held whites in higher regard than whites did them. Overall, Alfred O. Hero, Jr., was probably justified in concluding that "the Southern Negro, even more than the white, has been unlettered, poor, close to the soil, insulated from events and ideas beyond the community, and convinced that only God could change his fate."[57]

Black churches functioned as sanctuaries in a difficult and often antagonistic world, even if their influence declined as African

---

by the *Citizens' Board of Inquiry into Hunger and Malnutrition in the United States* (Southern Regional Council, 1972); George Thomas, *Poverty in the Nonmetropolitan South: A Causal Analysis* (Lexington, Ky., 1972).

[56] David L. Lewis, *King: A Critical Biography* (New York, 1970), p. 202 Johnson quoted.

[57] Hero, *The Southerner and World Affairs,* 504–43, p. 504 quoted; Matthews and Prothro, *Negroes and the New Southern Politics,* 265–312.

Americans settled in the cities. As historian Clayborn Carson has written, civil rights workers discovered during the 1960s that "there were no black institutions in cities comparable to the rural black church which served as a cohesive force . . . capable of reaching large segments of the black population." Black theology tended to be fundamentalist, otherworldly, and fatalist; it offered an escape from the travails of this world and the promise of a better life to come. At the same time, African-American religion affirmed the equality, dignity, and worth of the worshipers and served as a base for social dissent and protest. Some theologians maintained that what Joseph R. Washington has termed "Negro folk religion" possessed a "soul" or "genius" uniquely different from that of white Protestantism. In any event, the legacy of black churches was paradoxically both conservative and—at least germinally—reformist, depending on circumstances and leadership.[58]

More than nine out of ten black southerners were Protestant. At least six out of ten were Baptists, and as many as two out of ten were Methodists. Among lower-class blacks, pentecostalism thrived, as did a spiritual movement that blended African antecedents with American materialism. A New York resident born in South Carolina, Frederick J. Eikerenkoetter II—the Reverend Ike—illustrated one thread of spiritualism with his televised admonition that "the lack of money is the root of all evil." In the turbulent metropolitan areas, the institutional church possessed less social authority than it had commanded in the past, but as E. Franklin Frazier pointed out, "For the masses of Negroes, the Negro church continue[d] to be a refuge, though increasingly less of a refuge, in a hostile white world." [59]

[58] Clayborne Carson, *In Struggle: SNCC and the Black Awakening of the 1960s* (Cambridge, Mass., 1981), 168; Joseph R. Washington, Jr., *Black Religion: The Negro and Christianity in the United States* (Boston, 1964), 296; E. Franklin Frazier, *The Negro Church in America* (1963; rpr. New York, 1973); Gayraud S. Wilmore, *Black Religion and Black Radicalism: An Interpretation of the Religious History of the Afro-American People* (2nd ed., Maryknoll, N.Y., 1983); Ruby Funchess Johnson, *The Religion of the Negro Protestants: Changing Religious Attitudes and Practice* (New York, 1956); Hart M. Nelsen, Raytha L. Yokley, and Anne K. Nelsen, eds., *The Black Church in America* (New York, 1971); Hart M. Nelsen and Anne K. Nelsen, *Black Church in the Sixties* (Lexington, Ky., 1975).

[59] Reverend Ike quoted in *All Things Are Possible*, by Harrell, 235; Frazier, *The Negro Church,*

Black ministers exercised far more influence over their flocks than did white pastors. "In the eyes of my people," a black clergyman stated, "I am qualified to carry out these functions: race and civic leader, moral instructor, preacher, church builder, labor arbitrator, organization official, promoter of business, social and welfare agent, denominational spokesman and educator." Prominent clerics often exercised authoritarian control over their congregations and were frequently the recognized leaders of black communities in political and other matters.[60]

Critics described the black preacher as a "most devoted 'Uncle Tom,' the transmitter of white wishes, the admonisher of obedience to the caste system." Wyatt T. Walker of the Southern Christian Leadership Conference estimated that no more than one in ten black ministers participated actively in the civil rights movement, and in the climactic demonstrations of 1963 in Birmingham only about 20 of the city's 250 black preachers were involved. As Martin Luther King, Jr., maintained, "The church has not been true to its social mission on the question of racial justice. In this area, it has failed Christ miserably."[61]

King spearheaded a major effort to reorient church policy in the early 1960s by trying to replace Joseph H. Jackson as president of the National Baptist Convention, U.S.A., the nation's largest black religious body. According to one of King's biographers, Jackson believed "the role of the preacher was to bring the good news of the Gospel to his flock, to save the members of his flock for Jesus, and to effect change by exemplary conduct." After contentious but futile floor fights at the 1960 and 1961 conventions, the civil rights forces abandoned their effort to unseat Jackson, seceded from the convention, and formed the liberal Progressive Baptist Convention.[62]

85; Joseph R. Washington, Jr., *Black Sects and Cults* (Garden City, N.Y., 1972); Hans A. Baer, *The Black Spiritual Movement: A Religious Response to Racism* (Knoxville, Tenn., 1984).

[60] Washington, *Black Religion,* 91; Charles V. Hamilton, *The Black Preacher in America* (New York, 1972).

[61] James H. Cone, *Black Theology and Black Power* (New York, 1969), 106; William Brink and Louis Harris, *The Negro Revolution in America* (New York, 1964), 108; Martin Luther King, Jr., *Strength to Love* (Philadelphia, 1963), 101.

[62] Lewis, *King: A Critical Biography,* 158; Hamilton, *The Black Preacher,* 148–70.

Middle-class African Americans became more important in church affairs. Black professionals, particularly educators and clergymen serving black congregations and student bodies, black businessmen, who were usually undercapitalized and dependent on black customers, and the supporting sales and clerical workers increased in number along with the black urban population. Although in 1960 fewer than one in ten blacks worked in a white-collar capacity, the black middle class, by Frazier's calculation, encompassed about 12 percent of the black population in the South. In 1970 almost 15 percent of the black population of the region resided in suburban areas; that figure—even taking into account the vast disparity between suburbs—was a general indication of the size of the black bourgeoisie.[63]

The black "new middle class" occupied a difficult and ambiguous position in the social structure of the South and of the nation. Having gained affluence and often education, middle-class African Americans took pains to distance themselves from the black masses. As Frazier put it, they "reject[ed] the folk heritage and [sought] to slough off any reminders of their folk inheritance." Growing residential segregation made standoffishness difficult. Metropolitan housing patterns typically not only divided the white middle class from the white working class but also divided whites from blacks. In 1940 metropolitan residential areas were less segregated in the South than elsewhere; by 1960 they were more segregated. Black businessmen and professionals were also dependent on ordinary blacks for customers and clients. As a result, Martin Luther King, Jr., complained, "Negroes in the middle class who, because of a degree of academic and economic security, and because at points they profit by segregation, have unconsciously become insensitive to the problems of the masses."[64]

One of the effects of the growing influence of the black middle class was that the black churches in mainstream denominations

---

[63] Frazier, *The Negro Church*, 80; Marshall and Christian, "Some South and Non-South Comparisons," in *Employment of Blacks in the South*, ed. Marshall and Christian, 183.

[64] Frazier, *The Negro Church*, 81; Karl E. Taeuber and Alma F. Taeuber, *Negroes in Cities: Residential Segregation and Neighborhood Change* (Chicago, 1965), 70; Martin Luther King, Jr., "Letter from Birmingham City Jail," in *A Testament of Hope: The Essential Writings of Martin Luther King, Jr.*, ed. James Melvin Washington (San Francisco, 1986), 296.

became more secular, more decorous, and according to critics, more directionless. Like many white churches, they broadened their outreach programs. In Joseph Washington's description, they "assumed the burden of being the community center for the people—replete with amusements, politics, fellowship, leadership, and emotional release." These churches were also apt to become more conscious of status. Civil rights leaders, including King, often indicted the church that had "developed a class system and boast[ed] of its dignity, its membership of professional people, and its exclusiveness." The black bourgeoisie, Frazier judged, had "no cultural roots in either the Negro or the white world," and consequently had lost its way.[65]

Foremost among black churchmen was Martin Luther King, Jr. In keeping with the spirit of the times, King rested his theology not on social-gospel assumptions but on personalism—which, as King once explained, is the theory that "the meaning of ultimate reality is found in personality." Institutions and concepts were to be evaluated by assessing their impact on persons. In personalist theory, life was sacred, and all people were God's children; therefore, any system that diminished human personality was immoral. Traditionally an individualist and conservative philosophy, personalism became in King's rendering of it a compelling justification for civic reform.[66]

Segregation, according to King, was evil because it "scars the soul and degrades the personality." The legislation that decreed Jim Crow deprived the oppressed of self-respect and a sense of "somebodiness" and empowered the oppressor with a destructive sense of superiority. "Any law that uplifts human personality is just," King preached. "Any law that degrades human personality

---

[65] Joseph R. Washington, Jr., *Black Religion*, 129; King, *Strength to Love*, 63; E. Franklin Frazier, *Black Bourgeoisie* (Glencoe, Ill., 1957), 112; Gibson Winter, *The Suburban Captivity of the Churches* (New York, 1962), 132–39.

[66] Martin Luther King, Jr., *Stride Toward Freedom: The Montgomery Story* (New York, 1958), 100. Works by King, besides *Stride Toward Freedom* and *Strength to Love*, include *The Measure of a Man* (Philadelphia, 1959), *Why We Can't Wait* (New York, 1964), *Where Do We Go from Here: Chaos or Community?* (New York, 1967), *The Trumpet of Conscience* (New York, 1967), and numerous shorter pieces, many of them collected in *A Testament of Hope*, ed. James Melvin Washington. Among many studies of King's thought and theology, especially helpful are the materials reprinted in *Martin Luther King, Jr.: Civil Rights Leader, Theologian, Orator*, ed. David J. Garrow (3 vols.; Brooklyn, 1989).

is unjust. All segregation statutes are unjust because segregation distorts the soul and damages the personality." King's constant principle was the "recognition of the sacredness of human personality." [67]

King's most significant contribution to personalist thought, as Warren E. Steinkraus has pointed out, was his insistence on the moral imperative of direct nonviolent action. Although King himself credited Mohandas Gandhi with inspiring his thinking on nonviolence, the philosophy also grew directly from his own metaphysics. Because segregation was "morally wrong and sinful," King reasoned, it offended the "law of God," and an individual had "as much a moral obligation to refuse to cooperate with evil as . . . to cooperate with good." Therefore, a person had "not only a legal but a moral responsibility to disobey unjust laws." Civil disobedience had to be undertaken lovingly and nonviolently, inasmuch as the purpose was not "to defeat or humiliate the opponent, but to win his friendship and understanding." Love, King insisted, "is the most durable power in the world," whereas "hate scars the soul and distorts the personality." [68]

Like other preachers, King inveighed against relativist morality and the "tragic breakdown of moral standards." He deplored an impersonal world "rife with sexual promiscuity and gone wild with a philosophy of self-expression." He rejected the scientific humanism that was "sweeping the modern world like a plague" and attempting "to substitute a man-centred universe for a God-centred universe." He often lectured his listeners on the importance of hard work, thrift, self-help, and religious faith. "The richer we have become materially," he rued, "the poorer we have become morally and spiritually." Here only King's eloquence dis-

[67] King, *Strength to Love,* 142; King, "Letter from Birmingham City Jail," 293; Martin Luther King, Jr., "The Ethical Demands for Integration," in *A Testament of Hope,* ed. James Melvin Washington, 118.

[68] Warren E. Steinkraus, "Martin Luther King's Personalism and Nonviolence," in *Martin Luther King, Jr.,* ed. Garrow, III, 891–905; Warren E. Steinkraus, "Martin Luther King's Contributions to Personalism," *ibid.,* 907–19; Warren E. Steinkraus, "The Dangerous Ideas of Martin Luther King," *ibid.,* 921–30; King, "Letter from Birmingham City Jail," 289–302; Martin Luther King, Jr., "Love, Law, and Civil Disobedience," in *A Testament of Hope,* ed. James Melvin Washington, 43–53; King, *Stride Toward Freedom,* 102; King, *Strength to Love,* 51, 55.

tinguished him from most of the rest of his white and black Baptist peers.[69]

Until the midsixties King's individualist program was generally compatible with the aims of national Cold War liberals. Indeed, James Forman once referred to King as the "darling of the U.S. State Department" because his commitment to peaceful change within the system was an example of how people in other developing lands were supposed to behave. "His ultimate vision was the integration of the Negro into the existing structure of society," Adam Fairclough has written, and he "had given little consideration either to the economic hardship which afflicted most blacks or to the complex forces which created and perpetuated the ghetto."[70]

Nevertheless, poverty and war debased the human personality, and all along King enunciated a position to the left of his white allies. He criticized any religion that occupied itself with the "souls of men" but ignored the slums and social conditions "that damn them." He condemned a "world gone mad with arms buildups, chauvinistic passions, and imperialist exploitation" and called upon the church to be the "conscience of the state." Eventually he broadened his critique and became more radical in his outlook. By the time of his death in 1968, he had moved far to the left of the "vital center" so cherished by Cold War liberals. In the final analysis, his thinking had an enormous impact on the civil rights movement, but it had little effect on southern religious life.[71]

The modernizing South remained largely segregated, but by 1960 intellectual currents had eroded the arguments for Jim Crow. Whatever its social and ethical limitations, modernist thought with its emphasis on individualism was a liberating philosophy that undermined past justifications for civic inequality. As Gunnar Myrdal had earlier pointed out, the paternal ideology assigned African Americans and women their places in the social

[69] King, *Strength to Love*, 58, 18, 106, 128; King, *Where Do We Go from Here*, 171.

[70] James Forman, *The Making of Black Revolutionaries* (New York, 1972), 219; Adam Fairclough, *To Redeem the Soul of America: The Southern Christian Leadership Conference and Martin Luther King, Jr.* (Athens, Ga., 1987), 199, 197.

[71] King, *Stride Toward Freedom*, 28; King, *Strength to Love*, 61–62.

system on much the same grounds: "The study of women's intelligence and personality has had broadly the same history as the one . . . for Negroes." Economic opportunities for both, Myrdal continued, "are regularly in the low salary bracket and do not offer much of a career." By 1960 little ideological justification for such practices remained.[72]

The problem was particularly acute for restive black southerners. Modernist thought supported a market-society ideology that encouraged individuals to seek their identities in the marketplace. The black church became more secular. The minimum foundation programs for funding the public schools and the upgrading of black colleges—both in part designed to buttress segregation—had improved black educational facilities. The victory of metropolitan elites over the county seats abated opposition from state governments to black progress. Young, educated, and ambitious African Americans could view segregation as the principal barrier to wider economic opportunity in the expanding southern economy. Under such conditions, a new generation of southern African Americans, many born during World War II, launched a determined campaign to overturn the southern caste system.

[72] Gunnar Myrdal, *An American Dilemma: The Negro Problem and Modern Democracy* (New York, 1944), 1077.

CHAPTER IX

THE CIVIL RIGHTS MOVEMENT

T HE revolt against segregation began on February 1, 1960. Four eighteen-year-old freshmen at North Carolina Agricultural and Technical State College sat down at a lunch counter restricted to whites at a Woolworth's in Greensboro. The four students had for some time been considering an overt defiance of segregation, and the Woolworth's variety store, which served black customers in all departments except the lunch counter, seemed an appropriate target. On the last night of January, they decided, as one of them put it, "Let's just go down to Woolworth's tomorrow and ask for service, and the tactic is going to be simply this: we'll just stay there." The store refused to serve the students, but because the manager was reluctant to press trespass charges, they were not arrested. They simply sat at the counter until the store closed. "I felt as though I had gained my manhood, so to speak," one of them later recalled, "and not only gained it, but had developed quite a lot of respect for it."[1]

At its inception, the Greensboro sit-in was by no means unique. Blacks had staged sit-ins or other demonstrations in Oklahoma City, Austin, Miami, Nashville, and a dozen other southern cities. Those protests had been brief and attracted only local attention. The Greensboro sit-in immediately gained widespread campus support. Soon hundreds of demonstrators became involved. The protest continued for a week and spread to other variety stores. "It was like a fever," a student at the college explained. "Everyone wanted to go. We were so happy." White hecklers harassed the participating students, and according to police reports, the situ-

[1] Howell Raines, *My Soul Is Rested: Movement Days in the Deep South Remembered* (New York, 1977), 75, 78.

ation "became immediately explosive" when three white girls from a nearby women's college joined the "colored group." Law-enforcement officials, however, maintained a reasonable degree of order, and there was no serious violence.[2]

The Greensboro demonstrations received national press coverage, and within days black college students in other North Carolina cities began sit-ins. On February 10 the movement spread into Virginia, and on February 12 into South Carolina and Florida. Northern students organized sympathy demonstrations. On February 12 police in Raleigh, North Carolina, arrested forty-one black students, the first of a host to be charged in the actions. In mid-February black high-school students began sit-ins in High Point, North Carolina, a city without a black college. The movement was spontaneous and contagious. During the spring of 1960 approximately fifty thousand people participated in protests in some hundred cities in all thirteen southern states. Law-enforcement officials arrested at least two thousand demonstrators, and officials at black colleges expelled more than a hundred students and fired at least a dozen faculty members.[3]

The campaign marked a new phase in southern race relations that was ideally exemplified by a white woman in Nashville. Attempting to shop at a store where blacks sat in at the lunch counter, she walked into the rest room for white women to find two black girls standing before the lavatories. "Oh! Nigras everywhere," she exclaimed. Of course, there had been "Nigras everywhere" all along, but they were no longer invisible to whites. It was indicative of the new mood that the black students did not fear the woman's indignation. "Just as the Supreme Court decision was the legal turning point," Harold C. Fleming of the

[2] Miles Wolff, *Lunch at the Five and Ten: The Greensboro Sit-Ins* (New York, 1970), 41, 44.

[3] Among the most informative of numerous accounts of the sit-in movement are *We Shall Overcome: The Civil Rights Movement in the United States in the 1950s and 1960s,* ed. David J. Garrow (3 vols.; Brooklyn, 1989); James H. Laue's *Direct Action and Desegregation, 1960–1962: Toward a Theory of the Rationalization of Protest,* ed. David J. Garrow (Brooklyn, 1989); Martin Oppenheimer's "The Genesis of the Southern Negro Student Movement (Sit-In Movement): A Study in Contemporary Negro Protest" (Ph.D. dissertation, University of Pennsylvania, 1963); Clayborne Carson's *In Struggle: SNCC and the Black Awakening of the 1960s* (Cambridge, Mass., 1981); Howard Zinn's *SNCC: The New Abolitionists* (Boston, 1964); Jack Newfield's *A Prophetic Minority* (New York, 1966); and August Meier and Elliott Rudwick's *CORE: A Study in the Civil Rights Movement, 1942–1968* (New York, 1973).

Southern Regional Council observed, "the sit-ins were the psychological turning point in race relations in the South."[4]

The sit-in movement was basically different from the bus boycotts of the mid-1950s. Whereas the boycotts had been community protests, the sit-ins were individualist efforts to break out of the black community into the white economic system. The demonstrators, according to one study, "only wanted their share of the middle-class American dream—success, prestige, and money." When Virginia Foster Durr in Montgomery asked a black lad if he had ever "heard about the big struggle for desegregation of the buses," he replied, "Mrs. Durr, who wants to ride on a bus? I want a car of my own." The sit-ins appealed to the young, the educated, and the upwardly mobile. The most likely participants were black students from high-status families attending high-prestige black colleges. Pat Watters and Reese Cleghorn of the Southern Regional Council aptly termed the movement a "libertarian revolution."[5]

The demonstrators had little quarrel with mainstream American values. Clayborne Carson has pointed out that "most student protesters aspired to middle-class status and did not basically object to American society or its dominant political institutions. They protested against the pace rather than the direction of change." As an activist in Columbia, South Carolina, explained to newsmen, "What we are aiming for is a better South Carolina, a better America, [with] freedom for all." On a cold March day in nearby Or-

[4] Diane Nash, "Inside the Sit-Ins and Freedom Rides: Testimony of a Southern Student," in *We Shall Overcome*, ed. Garrow, 48; Fleming quoted in *A Prophetic Minority*, by Newfield, 55.

[5] Newfield, *A Prophetic Minority*, 21; *Outside the Magic Circle: The Autobiography of Virginia Foster Durr*, ed. Hollinger F. Barnard (University, Ala., 1985), 330; John M. Orbell, "Protest Participation Among Southern Negro College Students," *American Political Science Review*, LXI (1967), 446–56; Pat Watters and Reese Cleghorn, *Climbing Jacob's Ladder: The Arrival of Negroes in Southern Politics* (New York, 1967), 339. Suggestive works on the changing outlook of black southerners include Leslie Gerard Carr's "Class, Activism, and Acquiescence: Aspects of the Civil Rights Movement in the American South" (Ph.D. dissertation, University of North Carolina, 1973); Ronald Cecil Semone's "The Negro Middle Class in the South: A Study of Race, Class, and Political Behavior" (Ph.D. dissertation, University of North Carolina, 1969); Kathleen Marie Handy's "Determinants of Race Consciousness and Class Consciousness Among Blacks in a Southern City" (Ph.D. dissertation, Louisiana State University, 1979); *The New Negro*, ed. Mathew H. Ahmann (New York, 1969); and Samuel D. Proctor's *The Young Negro in America, 1960–1980* (New York, 1966).

angeburg, law-enforcement authorities, after filling the jails, confined some 350 demonstrators within a wire-enclosed, open-air pen, where—much to the annoyance of the constabulary—they passed their time singing "God Bless America."[6]

Most of the participants in the sit-ins were religious, and they subscribed to the nonviolent philosophy counseled by Martin Luther King, Jr., and, within the movement, by James Lawson and other Nashville activists. At the same time, the college campuses, not the churches, were the staging grounds. "Though they sing spirituals . . . and pray before the oppressor," Joseph R. Washington commented, "this is a way of fortifying their nonviolence, not an affirmation of their faith in Christian love." Some students, according to one of their number, even resented the "quasi-religious orientation of the movement." Another remarked, "We have been singing and praying for three hundred years. Now is the time we should do something for ourselves." The sit-in campaign was a middle-class crusade led by young blacks who wanted access to the American system and to the South's newfound prosperity. The movement corresponded closely to the central ideological tenets of the era.[7]

National elites welcomed the sit-ins. A movement in the errant South that espoused patriotic, middle-class, individualistic values was assured a sympathetic hearing, particularly among northern liberals. Former president Harry S. Truman denounced the sit-ins as a Communist-inspired assault against private property, but few prominent national figures publicly agreed with him. The Southern Regional Council in a series of celebratory reports helped set the tone for the national news media. Even James J. Kilpatrick of the Richmond *News Leader* observed in a widely quoted editorial, "Here were the colored students, in coats, white shirts, ties, and one of them was reading Goethe and one was taking notes from a biology text. And here, on the sidewalk out-

[6] Carson, *In Struggle*, 14; *Southern School News*, January, 1961; New York *Times*, March 15, 1960.

[7] Joseph R. Washington, Jr., *Black Religion: The Negro and Christianity in the United States* (Boston, 1964), 46; Cleveland Sellers, *The River of No Return: The Autobiography of a Black Militant and the Life and Death of SNCC* (New York, 1973), 38; H. Haywood Burns, *The Voices of Negro Protest* (New York, 1963), 46.

side, was a gang of white boys come to heckle, a ragtail rabble, slack-jawed, black-jacketed, grinning fit to kill. . . . It gives one pause." National church and youth groups passed resolutions supporting the sit-ins, as did a number of metropolitan ministerial associations in the South.[8]

Southern public officials frequently condemned the campaign. The official response in Alabama, Louisiana, and Mississippi was draconian, as was that of local governments through much of the region. States and localities enacted new trespass legislation on the model of two laws the Arkansas legislature approved in the late fifties after a flurry of demonstrations in Oklahoma. Particularly to black people, the southern legal system appeared awesome. Julian Bond remarked after being arrested in Atlanta, "I was indicted on enough charges to put me away for ninety-nine years, and you think I wasn't scared." In such massive demonstrations as that in Louisville in early 1961, police arrested some seven hundred participants. That the movement continued unabated testified to its strength.[9]

One of the most extreme examples of official intimidation, and certainly the most publicized, was the sentencing of Martin Luther King in October, 1960, to four months at hard labor in a maximum-security prison. Earlier, King, while driving Lillian E. Smith to a hospital appointment, had been stopped and cited for not transferring his driver's license from Alabama to Georgia when he moved from Montgomery to Atlanta. The county judge, after levying a small fine, placed King on probation. In October, students in Atlanta persuaded King to practice what he preached and join them in a sit-in demonstration. Police arrested him and a number of students, though soon afterward they released all the demonstrators except King. At that point county authorities seized King, and the judge sentenced him to the state prison at Reidsville for violating the terms of his probation. "They are going to kill

[8] Truman quoted in New York *Times*, April 18, 1960; Southern Regional Council, *The Student Protest Movement, Winter, 1960* (Atlanta, 1960); Southern Regional Council, *The Student Protest Movement: A Recapitulation* (Atlanta, 1961); "Direct Action in the South," *New South*, October–November, 1963; Richmond *News Leader*, February 22, 1960; Oppenheimer, "The Genesis of the Southern Negro Student Movement," 121–28.

[9] *Southern School News*, April, 1960, March, 1961; Bond quoted in *My Soul Is Rested*, by Raines, 87.

him," Coretta Scott King predicted, "I know they are going to kill him." Presidential candidate John F. Kennedy exploited the occasion to call Coretta in what the New York *Times* termed the "most important single campaign move" of the election, and Robert Kennedy called the judge who rendered the sentence. Governor Ernest Vandiver, apparently bending to national pressure and perhaps recognizing the basis for Coretta King's fear, assured aides in the Kennedy retinue that King would be released, and the next morning the judge granted bail.[10]

The white segregationist mobs that often confronted the demonstrators felt no allegiance to a philosophy of nonviolence. Police maintained rudimentary law and order, not infrequently by arresting the victims of mob violence. Blacks occasionally responded to violence with violence. Chattanooga, Jacksonville, and Greenville, South Carolina, were among the cities in which black and white gangs battled in the streets. The Chattanooga *Times* referred to the conflict in that city as the "most massive racial clash in the history of Chattanooga." Nevertheless, in a region with a reputed propensity to violence, surprisingly few serious casualties resulted from the sit-ins.[11]

The movement was an assault on segregation, and it was also a rejection of the racial diplomats and the NAACP. King commented in April, 1960, "The sit-in movement is a revolt against those Negroes in the middle class who have indulged themselves in big cars and ranch-style homes, rather than joining in the movement for freedom." Jack L. Walker noticed that in Atlanta "student leaders talked, and frequently acted, as if adult Negro leaders were as much their enemies as the segregationist whites." Cleveland Sellers expressed a widely shared sentiment when he condemned the NAACP for failures that included being "too slow, too courteous, too deferential and too ineffectual." To militant students, the older, established leadership overvalued patience,

---

[10] Coretta King quoted in *Bearing the Cross: Martin Luther King, Jr., and the Southern Christian Leadership Conference,* by David J. Garrow (New York, 1988), 146; Harris Wofford, *Of Kennedys and Kings: Making Sense of the Sixties* (New York, 1980), 13–27; New York *Times,* November 27, 1960.

[11] Chattanooga *Times,* February 24, 1960; *Southern School News,* August, 1960, September, 1960, October, 1960.

with its steady cautions that "you young people are trying to go too fast." [12]

The public pronouncements of old-guard black leaders frequently fit the students' stereotype. The editor of the Charlotte *Post*, a black newspaper, lamented, "Bitterness between the races will be increased manifold unless something is done immediately to clarify the atmosphere and restore sanity to the minds of those who are caught up in the fire and fury of this ill-advised movement." The students' skepticism, however, was reciprocated even by the less hidebound. Roy Wilkins of the NAACP found it difficult to work with the students: "They don't take orders from anybody. They don't consult anybody. They operate in a kind of vacuum: parade, protest, sit-in." [13]

The compelling appeal of the sit-in movement swept most objectors aside. College students, high-school students, young adults, and particularly in the Upper South, a considerable number of white students participated. Because boycotts against local stores often accompanied the sit-ins, scores of thousands of people indirectly supported the movement. Virtually every major southern city experienced demonstrations. By late 1961 at least some facilities in ninety southern cities had desegregated, and many cities and three states—Florida, Kentucky, and Oklahoma—had established biracial committees to negotiate settlements. [14]

In April, 1960, Ella J. Baker, acting executive director of the Southern Christian Leadership Conference, organized a meeting of student protest leaders. Some 120 activists from fifty-six colleges and high schools attended. Much of the SCLC leadership assumed that the student movement would become a youth wing of SCLC, but Baker, deeply frustrated by her experiences with King and his ministerial allies, worked tirelessly to ensure that the organization

[12] King quoted in *A Prophetic Minority*, by Newfield, 61; Jack L. Walker, "Protest and Negotiation: A Study of Political Leaders in a Southern City" (Ph.D. dissertation, State University of Iowa, 1963), 145; Sellers, *The River of No Return*, 19, 26; Watters and Cleghorn, *Climbing Jacob's Ladder*, 96–101.

[13] Charlotte *Post* quoted in "The Genesis of the Southern Negro Student Movement," by Oppenheimer, 176; Wilkins quoted in *Time*, January 12, 1962, p. 15.

[14] Southern Regional Council, *The Student Protest Movement: A Recapitulation;* Oppenheimer, "The Genesis of the Southern Negro Student Movement"; Laue, *Direct Action and Desegregation.*

she directed could not thwart the students as it had thwarted her. At Baker's prompting, the students created their own Temporary Student Nonviolent Coordinating Committee and adopted a "statement of purpose" that affirmed the "philosophical or religious ideal of nonviolence as the foundation of our purpose, the presupposition of our faith, and the manner of our action." The committee established an office in Atlanta, soon began publication of the *Student Voice,* and attempted to serve as the communications and coordination hub for the sit-in movement.[15]

As it turned out, the Student Nonviolent Coordinating Committee—SNCC—had rather little to do. The spontaneous and dynamic nature of the movement did not lend itself to direction. During the summer of 1960, people associated with SNCC talked of "shaping the student movement" rather than coordinating it, but they accomplished little. In October, another conference of student protest leaders established SNCC as a permanent organization, chose Charles McDew of South Carolina State College as chairman, decided upon employing an administrative secretary, and appointed Edward King of Kentucky to the position. Even while electing officers, SNCC members demonstrated a clear distrust of authority. They declared that each member of the group would have "equal status and shall be equally considered a spokesman for the movement," that local chapters would remain "autonomous," and that the goal of the movement would be "individual freedom and personhood."[16]

In early 1961 several SNCC members and volunteers traveled to Rock Hill, South Carolina, to take part in a "jail-in." The protesters refused bond after being arrested, out of both an unwillingness to compromise with evil and the expectation that by filling the jails they could bring financial and moral pressure to bear. The officials in Rock Hill stood firm, and the jail-ins were unsuc-

[15] Ella Baker Interview, September 9, 1974, in Southern Oral History Program, Southern Women Series, File G-7, Southern Historical Collection, University of North Carolina at Chapel Hill; "Statement of Purpose," "Findings and Recommendations," April 17, 1960, both in Student Nonviolent Coordinating Committee Papers, 1959–1972, Series I, reel 1 (Microfilming Corporation of America); Carson, *In Struggle,* 19–25.

[16] "Student Non-Violent Coordinating Committee" (Memorandum), "Recommendations Passed . . . October 14–16, 1960," "Constitution," October, 1960, all in SNCC Papers, Series V, reel 11.

cessful. As sit-ins, kneel-ins, swim-ins, and even occasional stand-ins raged across the region, SNCC drifted without apparent purpose.

The freedom rides shifted the direction of southern protest and provided SNCC with a mission. The Congress of Racial Equality, a northern-based civil rights organization that had pioneered direct-action techniques, announced in the spring of 1961 that it would send an integrated team of bus riders from Washington to New Orleans. In 1947 CORE had sponsored a "journey of reconciliation" after the Supreme Court banned segregated seating on transit vehicles in interstate operation. That trip through the Upper South resulted in several confrontations, twelve arrests, and in North Carolina, the sentencing of three of the riders to twenty-two-day prison terms. Later, both the Interstate Commerce Commission and the Supreme Court extended the prohibition of segregation from vehicles to terminals and other facilities serving interstate travel. The bus riders of 1961 tested southern compliance with the more recent rulings.[17]

During May, 1961, the participants journeyed ever deeper into the southern heartland. The trip through Virginia and North Carolina was relatively uneventful. There were some violence and several arrests at two stops in South Carolina, but no one was seriously injured and police did not detain the riders. The trek through Georgia proceeded without hindrance, and after pausing in Atlanta, the riders headed to Alabama in two buses. There the situation was entirely different. Moderates controlled the seaboard states. For the most part, they permitted the freedom riders "to integrate to their hearts' content." When the bus left for the next town, race relations returned to normal. The moderates were, as Calvin Trillin explained, smart segregationists. On the other hand, Alabama was, "it was generally agreed, ... the world headquarters for dumb segs." Moderates there received little hearing, and Governor John Patterson made no secret of how he felt about outside agitators.[18]

[17] James Peck, *Freedom Ride* (New York, 1962), 14–27; Meier and Rudwick, *CORE,* 34–39; Catherine A. Barnes, *Journey from Jim Crow: The Desegregation of Southern Transit* (New York, 1983), 44–161.

[18] Calvin Trillin, "Reflections: Remembrance of Moderates Past," *New Yorker,* March 21, 1977, p. 86.

The first bus arrived in Anniston, on May 14. A white mob attacked it, breaking windows and slashing tires, but local police managed to control the crowd sufficiently for the bus to escape the station. A few miles along the road to Birmingham, the slashed tires went flat, and pursuing whites resumed their attack. A fire bomb that sailed through a broken window set the bus afire. A plainclothes Alabama policeman who had joined the riders in Atlanta and a passing highway patrolman held back the mob with their pistols, and the riders escaped further injury, although several required hospitalization because of smoke inhalation. Fred L. Shuttlesworth of SCLC led an automobile caravan that drove the riders to Birmingham.

The second bus arrived in Anniston shortly afterward. Whites rushed aboard, beat several riders, and tried to compel Jim Crow seating. The bus managed to proceed to Birmingham. There a mob that included Klansmen mauled the riders, a few seriously. It later came out that Eugene "Bull" Connor, Birmingham's police commissioner, had conceded the Klan fifteen minutes to teach the riders a lesson before his men intervened. When journalists questioned him about the delay, he explained earnestly that it was Mother's Day and policemen had been spending time with their families. The commissioner blamed "out-of-town meddlers," both "the ones who got whipped and the ones who did the whipping." The battered freedom riders, unable to find a driver who would conduct their bus to Montgomery, flew to New Orleans.[19]

In Nashville, members of SNCC decided that the freedom rides should continue. Canceling them, Diane Nash, John Lewis, and other SNCC partisans reasoned, would encourage white violence by rewarding it. Ten members of SNCC took a bus to Birmingham in order to continue the freedom rides. The police in Birmingham promptly placed all ten in protective custody and late at night hauled them to the Tennessee state line. Nash, who had remained in Nashville, made arrangements for cars to take the dumped ac-

[19] Connor quoted in Birmingham *News*, May 15, 1961; Wofford, *Of Kennedys and Kings*, 151–54; Peck, *Freedom Ride*, 114–31; William A. Nunnelley, *Bull Connor* (Tuscaloosa, Ala., 1991), 86–111; Gary Thomas Rowe, Jr., *My Undercover Years with the Ku Klux Klan* (New York, 1976), 38–50.

tivists back to Birmingham. They attempted with considerable difficulty to arrange for bus transportation to Montgomery. As a realistic bus driver explained, "I have only one life to give, and I'm not going to give it to CORE or the NAACP." Governor Patterson showed his annoyance at a press conference: "The state of Alabama can't guarantee the safety of fools, and that's what they are." [20]

Finally, negotiations between federal and state authorities enabled SNCC members to board a bus bound for Montgomery on May 20. Birmingham police escorted the vehicle to the city limits, and state police escorted it to Montgomery. At that point, police protection ended. Governor Patterson, sobered by the international attention accorded the events in his state, expected the police in Montgomery to take over, but they did not. Instead, a white mob met the bus at the station and proceeded to maul the riders. With wives and girlfriends acting as cheerleaders as well as accessories, the mob was the largest and fiercest the freedom riders had encountered. Not only riders but a representative from the Justice Department and several newsmen suffered beatings. [21]

The next night, more than a thousand of Montgomery's black residents gathered at the First Baptist Church, where Ralph D. Abernathy was pastor, to honor the freedom riders and to hear speeches by King and others. Newly arrived federal marshals endeavored to maintain order, but the riotous whites teeming around the church intimidated the marshals. Along with a great many ordinary people inside the church was much of the leadership of SCLC, SNCC, and CORE. Outside, an emboldened mob threatened to set the packed church aflame. The night of May 21, 1961, was the night a profound tragedy failed to happen. At virtually the last moment, Governor Patterson declared "qualified martial law," and the Alabama National Guard restored a semblance of order. Not until the next morning did the guard's com-

[20] Raines, *My Soul Is Rested* 119; Patterson quoted in Montgomery *Advertiser,* May 18, 1961.
[21] Helen Fuller, "We, the People of Alabama," *New Republic,* CXLIV (1961), 21–23; Burke Marshall Oral History Interview, May 29, 1964, in John Fitzgerald Kennedy Library, Boston; Barnes, *Journey from Jim Crow,* 160–64.

mander pronounce it safe for the massed audience to leave the church under armed protection.[22]

To the Kennedy administration, the white reaction to the freedom rides was a major diplomatic embarrassment. Attorney General Robert F. Kennedy, the administration's "quarterback for civil rights" according to admiring biographers, called for a "cooling-off period," a plea civil rights leaders rejected. Instead, representatives of SCLC, CORE, and SNCC vowed to continue the rides into Mississippi and Louisiana, and new volunteers arrived in Montgomery. Such intractability was "too much" for the Kennedy administration. "I wonder whether they have the best interest of their country at heart," Robert Kennedy reflected aloud to an associate. "Do you know that one of them is against the atom bomb—yes, he even picketed against it in jail! The president is going abroad, and this is all embarrassing him." [23]

As the attorney general's remark suggested, the Kennedy administration not only placed its primary emphasis on foreign affairs but tended to evaluate civil rights through the prism of international relations. "The prevailing official United States attitude, both under the Republicans and Democrats," one freedom rider complained, "has been that public protest against segregation, rather than segregation itself, constitutes the greatest obstacle for the United States in winning favorable world opinion." The president and his advisers had no comprehensive plan for responding to the southern civil rights movement but instead dealt with developments pragmatically case by case, crisis by crisis. During the 1960 presidential campaign, Kennedy had assured several southern governors that he would not use federal force in the South—a promise he kept except for being unable to avoid using federal marshals in Montgomery and employing military units to uphold federal court orders regarding school desegregation in Mississippi and Alabama. As president, Kennedy tried not to antagonize further the southern bloc in Congress. The administration did work for voting rights, and in 1962 Congress ap-

[22] Raines, *My Soul Is Rested*, 122–29, 304–11; Wofford, *Of Kennedys and Kings*, 154–55; United States Commission on Civil Rights, *Report, 1961, Justice*, 29–33.

[23] Lester David and Irene David, *Bobby Kennedy: The Making of a Folk Hero* (Toronto, 1986), 192; Robert Kennedy quoted in *Of Kennedys and Kings*, by Wofford, 156.

proved a measure against poll taxes that eventually became the Twenty-Fourth Amendment to the United States Constitution.[24]

The Kennedy administration did, of course, have a civil rights strategy. Designed to satisfy middle-class and most especially northern middle-class African Americans, it rested squarely on symbolic equality. "It didn't matter what you did for the Negro," Robert Kennedy explained, "so long as you had the outward manifestations of being interested." Consequently, President Kennedy appointed numerous African Americans to government positions. A leader in the Americans for Democratic Action, recalling the alleged New Deal proclivity to "spend and spend and elect and elect," described Kennedy's approach as "appoint and appoint and elect and elect." The administration also created a civil rights subcabinet to foster and monitor "affirmative action" in hiring, by which was meant that "the test for employment should be individual merit not class quotas." A presidential executive order at least in theory extended "affirmative action" to federal contractors and subcontractors. These efforts accomplished little. Two years after President Kennedy's death, officials in the Johnson administration were noting the dearth of African Americans in positions of "substantive responsibility." The Kennedy administration's largely symbolic gestures included the desegregation of the White House press corps, the refusal to provide speakers from the executive branch for segregated audiences, and the readiness of the president to talk with civil rights leaders.[25]

[24] Peck, *Freedom Ride,* 156; S. Ernest Vandiver Oral History Interview, May 22, 1967, Harris Wofford Oral History Interview, November 29, 1965, both in Kennedy Library. Helpful on the Kennedy administration's civil rights policies are Carl M. Brauer's *John F. Kennedy and the Second Reconstruction* (New York, 1977); Bruce Miroff's *Pragmatic Illusions: The Presidential Politics of John F. Kennedy* (New York, 1976); Victor S. Navasky's *Kennedy Justice* (New York, 1971); Edwin Guthman's *We Band of Brothers* (New York, 1971); and Wofford's *Of Kennedys and Kings.*

[25] Robert F. Kennedy Oral History Interview, February 29, 1964, p. 91, Joseph L. Rauh, Jr., Oral History Interview, December 23, 1965, p. 107, both in Kennedy Library; Robert F. Kennedy, "Notes," Harris Wofford, Jr., to President-Elect Kennedy, December 30, 1960, both in Robert F. Kennedy Papers, Attorney General's Personal Correspondence, Kennedy Library; Executive Order 10925, March 7, 1961, Robert F. Kennedy to president, "A Report on the Progress in the Field of Civil Rights," January 24, 1963, both in Lee White Civil Rights Files, Kennedy Library; Clifford L. Alexander, Jr., to Harry C. McPherson *et al.,* December 14, 1965, Office Files of Harry McPherson (Civil Rights), Lyndon Baines Johnson Library, Austin, Tex.

In the short term, these policies were for the most part politically productive. Civil rights spokespeople often publicly criticized the administration for "moving too slowly," but they also applauded its initiatives. The northern-based Leadership Conference on Civil Rights observed in its "Proposals for Executive Action" that "the Kennedy administration has been more active in defense of civil rights than any previous administration in a comparable period." Kennedy did grant greater recognition to black aspirations than Eisenhower had conceded, and both public-opinion polls and the private remarks of civil rights leaders testified to the appeal of the administration's actions to African Americans. The problem was the civil rights movement in the South, which demanded more than symbolic gestures.[26]

The exigencies of symbolic equality required ending highly publicized racial violence. Attorney General Kennedy found a solution through the good offices of Senator James O. Eastland of Mississippi. Governor Ross R. Barnett agreed that there would be no violence in Mississippi; the riders would simply be arrested and jailed. Arthur M. Schlesinger, Jr., has written, "Plainly the Riders were within their constitutional rights. Plainly the federal government had an obligation to protect travel in interstate commerce." Even more plainly, the Kennedy administration had an image of American moral superiority to promote. The attorney general agreed not to contest the denial of constitutional rights to the riders if Mississippi kept the peace and avoided publicity. In September, 1961, members of SNCC and CORE began sit-ins at the Department of Justice.[27]

On May 24, two buses filled with freedom riders departed from Montgomery for Jackson, Mississippi. Alabama guardsmen gave protection as far as the Mississippi state line, from where a larger contingent of Mississippi troopers escorted the riders to Jackson. There police herded the riders into jail cells. Other civil rights

---

[26] Leadership Conference on Civil Rights to president, "Proposals for Executive Action to End Federally Supported Segregation," August 29, 1961, in Lee White Civil Rights Files, Kennedy Library; Richard Scammon, "Memorandum on Polls," in Robert F. Kennedy Papers, Attorney General's Personal Correspondence.

[27] Barnes, *Journey from Jim Crow*, 164–67; Arthur M. Schlesinger, Jr., *Robert Kennedy and His Times* (New York, 1978), 317; Robert F. Kennedy and Burke Marshall Oral History Interview, December 4, 1964, p. 387, in Kennedy Library.

activists joined the procession. Altogether more than 350 riders traveled to confinement by way of interstate commerce, most of them in Mississippi. The greater number of the riders declined bond and spent at least part of their summer in Parchman Penitentiary or in county jail. According to Carl M. Brauer, the Kennedy administration was "pleased with its handling of the crisis."[28]

The freedom rides and the Mississippi imprisonment, Clayborne Carson has pointed out, "contributed to the development of a self-consciously radical southern student movement" and helped mold the movement's leadership. SNCC soon completed its transformation from an alliance of students who spent their spare time demonstrating into a cadre of full-time organizers. The rides catapulted CORE to prominence among civil rights groups and redirected much of its program toward the South. The events in Alabama and Mississippi shifted the focus of the movement from North Carolina and the Upper South to the Deep South, and from large metropolitan areas like Atlanta and Nashville to the countryside and to towns and smaller cities.[29]

The Kennedy administration responded to the freedom rides by promoting black voter registration. From the administration viewpoint, the channeling of black protest into voter registration promised to curtail embarrassing incidents, to bring pressure on southern congressional Bourbons to moderate their opposition to Kennedy's policies, and quite probably to yield votes for the Democrats in the next presidential election. In June, 1961, officials of the Justice Department invited leaders of the major civil rights organizations to Washington, where Attorney General Kennedy announced that private foundations would provide adequate financing for a registration project and pledged that the Justice Department and the FBI would protect field workers. Although many SNCC, CORE, and SCLC members were suspicious of a federal project that shifted attention from direct action, they agreed to participate.

[28] Brauer, *John F. Kennedy and the Second Reconstruction*, 109.

[29] Carson, *In Struggle*, 37; Meier and Rudwick, *CORE*, 135–70; James Forman, *The Making of Black Revolutionaries* (New York, 1972), 145–57; James Farmer, *Lay Bare the Heart: An Autobiography of the Civil Rights Movement* (New York, 1985), 195–214.

The result was the Voter Education Project, which began in the spring of 1962. Administered by the Southern Regional Council, the project was a tax-exempt research program that sought to uncover explanations for the low rate of voter participation in the South by encouraging voter registration. As such, the acceptance of VEP funds sharply restricted direct action and other forms of protest. The Kennedy administration reneged on its commitments: VEP funding was never as generous as the attorney general had implied, and the Justice Department quickly abandoned any pretense of offering protection to registration workers. Nevertheless, VEP financing was a significant factor in directing black protest into the Deep South and the southern hinterlands.[30]

Well before VEP funds became available, SNCC had begun the shift away from direct action to voter registration and from cities to smaller communities. In August, 1961, Robert P. Moses, a New Yorker who journeyed south to work with SNCC, began a voter registration drive in Pike County in southern Mississippi. He was the first SNCC worker to attempt to organize a community by living in it and becoming part of it. Soon afterward, Charles Sherrod, a student at Virginia Union University who was SNCC's first paid field secretary, established a project in southwest Georgia. In September, 1961, James Forman, a public-school teacher from Chicago, became executive secretary of the organization. Forman brought a modicum of structural stability, and he soon had a fund-raising network in place that alleviated, although it never solved, SNCC's chronic financial shortfalls. Other field secretaries joined SNCC's staff and began projects in numerous southeastern counties and smaller cities.[31]

SNCC staffers targeted the county-seat heartland of white racism and southern poverty. There was a certain logic to the strategy.

[30] Watters and Cleghorn, *Climbing Jacob's Ladder*, 44–55; Meier and Rudwick, *CORE*, 169–81; Brauer, *John F. Kennedy and the Second Reconstruction*, 110–25; Frederick M. Wirt, *Politics of Southern Equality: Law and Social Change in a Mississippi County* (Chicago, 1970), 72–116; Neil R. McMillen, "Black Enfranchisement in Mississippi: Federal Enforcement and Black Protest in the 1960s," *Journal of Southern History*, XLIII (1977), 351–72; Michal R. Belknap, *Federal Law and Southern Order: Racial Violence and Constitutional Conflict in the Post-Brown South* (Athens, Ga., 1987), 106–27.

[31] Carson, *In Struggle*, 37–82.

At least in the beginning, SNCC's membership accepted the basic validity of the American success story and optimistically endeavored to bring the deviant South into conformity with national norms. "If we can knock out Mississippi," James Forman stated in the summer of 1961, "Illinois will be a mopping up action." SNCC staffers envisioned their assault on the heart of southern racism as inspiriting long-suppressed blacks and through voter registration driving a wedge into the base of Bourbon power. "Our ultimate goal," a field secretary explained, "was the destruction of the awesome power of the Dixiecrats." Anyway, Robert Moses reflected, "You can't be in the position of turning down the tough areas, because the people would simply lose confidence in you."[32]

As more people dropped out of college to work full time, SNCC members achieved the élan that made them the model for the baby boom generation's conception of involved youth. "Our staff workers live with the people," Charles McDew explained. "We live where we work because we don't think you can get people registered in the South by sending down orders from New York or Atlanta." The pay of full-time field workers was consistent with the organization's position that they should live within the black community. In the beginning, they received forty dollars a week, but as the staff increased, that declined to ten to twenty dollars for single employees and somewhat more for married staffers. Howard Zinn, an academic closely associated with SNCC, described field workers: "They are young, they are Negro, they come from the South, their families are poor and of the working class, but they have been to college." Whites made up about 20 percent of the staff in 1963, but William W. Hansen, the director of the Arkansas project, was the only white to occupy a prominent leadership position.[33]

A substantial majority of staff members were male, although in the beginning women occupied influential positions. Besides Ella Baker and Diane Nash, Jane Stembridge, a white theology student, handled administrative matters, and Constance Curry, the direc-

[32] Forman, *The Making of Black Revolutionaries*, 138; Sellers, *The River of No Return*, 108, Moses quoted p. 49.

[33] Charles McDew, "SNCC Story," April 27, 1963, in Howard Zinn Papers, Box 1, State Historical Society of Wisconsin, Madison; Zinn, *SNCC*, 10.

tor of the National Student Association's southern programs, was a member of SNCC's executive council. As the size of the organization and the confidence of its staff grew, men took over. Ruby Doris Robinson, who was Forman's administrative assistant and later executive secretary, was the chief exception. During the mid-sixties SNCC increasingly recruited indigenous people from local communities. Among them, Fannie Lou Hamer of Sunflower County, Mississippi, became a legend rivaling Moses.

While SNCC's field workers were predominantly male, local volunteers were disproportionately black women. Black women tended to be more emboldened by their religious faith, they were more likely than men to attend meetings of any kind, including civil rights meetings, and they were often influenced by the people they knew, sometimes young relatives, to become involved. Civil rights protest probably gave black women a sense of empowerment, but it did not signify a revolt against male authority. The object of the movement, Hamer cautioned, was "not to fight to liberate ourselves from the men—this is another trick to get us fighting among ourselves—but to work together with black men." As Anne Standley has concluded, there was a contradiction between the vigor with which black women protested against oppression and their readiness to accept the "authority of the black male clergy." The reason that black women joined the voter registration movement in large numbers was, a white female volunteer in Mississippi concluded, "that women seem to have the calm courage necessary for a nonviolent campaign." [34]

The size of SNCC's field staff grew more or less steadily during the first half of the 1960s. It was largest during the summer months, when students could participate without dropping out of school. In the summer of 1962 there were 40 full-time staffers; by late fall the number had ebbed to 28. In the spring of 1963 SNCC deployed 55 full-time workers; that summer the staff included 12

[34] Hamer quoted in "Women as Culture Carriers in the Civil Rights Movement: Fannie Lou Hamer," by Bernice Johnson Reagon, in *Women in the Civil Rights Movement: Trailblazers and Torchbearers, 1941–1965*, ed. Vicki L. Crawford *et al.* (Brooklyn, 1990), 214; Anne Standley, "The Role of Black Women in the Civil Rights Movement," *ibid.*, 187; Elizabeth Sutherland, ed., *Letters from Mississippi* (New York, 1965), 61. See also Charles Payne, "Men Led, but Women Organized," in *Women in the Civil Rights Movement*, 1–11; and Sally Belfrage, *Freedom Summer* (New York, 1965), esp. 76.

office workers, 60 field secretaries, 121 full-time volunteers, and
a host of local part-time volunteers. On the eve of Mississippi Freedom Summer in 1964, the paid full-time staff numbered 130, and
in the spring of 1965 it reached 230. Although Mississippi remained SNCC's primary focus, the organization sponsored ambitious projects in Alabama, Arkansas, the Carolinas, Georgia, and
Virginia.[35]

SNCC had greater difficulty raising funds than any of the other
principal civil rights groups. The organization never received an
equitable share of VEP allocations. SNCC's insistence on working
in hard-core areas ensured that the numbers it added to the registration rolls were unimpressive, its record keeping was often woe-
fully casual, and SNCC staffers sometimes seemed to go out of
their way to disparage the civil rights establishment, especially the
NAACP, all of which contributed to the group's problems with
VEP, foundations, and other sources of liberal largess. Field workers were always short of money for transportation, bail bonds, and
daily expenses. An organizer in southwest Georgia regretted that
"some of us will have to get a job to support the others, as we did
this summer." Another wrote, "We are broke and hungry, going
day by day with no more than one meal, and sometimes nothing."
A field worker plaintively explained, "I could be more efficient if
I had a top coat and a pair of shoes."[36]

James Forman and his staff vigorously pursued northern dollars. A few black entertainers, notably singer Harry Belafonte,
raised funds, and SNCC pried donations from unions, religious
sodalities, foundations, and student associations. SNCC also established its own extensive network. By the midsixties it operated
offices in six northern and western cities and sponsored twenty
Friends of SNCC auxiliaries, mainly on or near the campuses of

[35] James Forman to Wiley Branton, October 31, 1962, in Voter Education Project Files,
Box 4, Atlanta University Center, hereinafter VEP Files; McDew, "SNCC Story"; John Lewis
to William Shawn, April 22, 1965, in Martin Luther King, Jr., Papers, Box 23, Martin Luther
King, Jr., Center for Social Change, Atlanta; Emily Schottenfeld Stoper, "The Student
Nonviolent Co-ordinating Committee: The Growth of Radicalism in a Civil Rights Orga-
nization" (Ph.D. dissertation, Harvard University, 1968), 114; Carson, *In Struggle*, 71.

[36] Charles Sherrod to Wiley Branton, November 9, 1962, in VEP Files, Box 6; Willie Ricks,
"Field Report," March 15, 1964, in VEP Files, Box 18; Carver Neblett to SNCC, Atlanta,
January 10, 1963, in VEP Files, Box 6.

large universities outside the South. The result was an expanding budget of more than $100,000 in 1962, more than $300,000 in 1963, and $650,000 in 1964. After that, SNCC became more radical, and its income diminished.[37]

SNCC's "guerrilla fighters" served as the shock troops of the civil rights movement. Above all the others, one study reported, they had the "magic to inspire blind loyalty and epic myth." They lived, or at least on occasion claimed to live, "on the three C's of health, well, at least our health—crackers, cucumbers, and collards"—and they mobilized strong community movements in unlikely places. "Those SNCC boys," a black college student in Jackson, Mississippi, recalled, "had friends everywhere, among the Negroes, that is. Most whites were just waiting for the chance to kill them all off." Howard Zinn, writing in 1964, described them as the "most serious social force in the nation today."[38]

SNCC's closest ally was the southern branch of the Congress of Racial Equality. Referring to the period following the freedom rides, James Farmer, CORE's national director, could write, "Rarely has any organization in the nation's history experienced in one brief year such mushrooming growth and impact as has CORE in the year 1961." CORE's staff multiplied and became more southern as the organization promoted civil disobedience and instituted voter registration projects in the Carolinas, Florida, Mississippi, and Louisiana, the last absorbing the greatest attention. In addition to assigning two-thirds of its field secretaries to the South, CORE recruited task-force members who worked for twenty-five dollars a week. In the spring of 1963 CORE employed 49 full-time staffers, in the spring of 1964 the staff numbered more than 90, and in early 1965 it came to 117, although by then hardly more than half worked in the South. CORE's income swelled during the early 1960s, reaching almost $850,000 in 1964. Yet, like SNCC, the organization was always pressed for funds, and

[37] "Friends of SNCC Groups and Key Fund-Raising Contacts," October, 1964, in Lucile Montgomery Papers, State Historical Society of Wisconsin; Doug McAdam, *Political Process and the Development of Black Insurgency, 1930–1970* (Chicago, 1982), 208–18, 253.

[38] Newfield, *A Prophetic Minority*, 99; Charles Sherrod to Wiley Branton, September 20, 1962, in VEP Files, Box 6; Anne Moody, *Coming of Age in Mississippi* (New York, 1968), 242; Zinn, *SNCC*, 5.

the wages of task-force workers, the larger portion of the full-time field staff in the South, were reduced by half. CORE adopted increasingly radical policies in the midsixties and watched its income decline.[39]

SNCC and CORE personnel worked closely together and indeed often went to jail together. Anne Moody commented that in Mississippi, SNCC and CORE "could draw teen-agers into the Movement as no other organization could." They shared a similar élan, and members of CORE came to adopt SNCC's freewheeling ways. The southern wing of CORE also became more independent of the national office. David J. Dennis, regional program director, and his field staff frequently clashed with national executives, at one point accusing them of acting like an "absentee landlord." CORE set up regional headquarters in New Orleans, but tension between the southern wing and national officials continued.[40]

Although only SNCC and CORE worked regularly in the most recalcitrant parts of the South, the Southern Christian Leadership Conference, the NAACP, and a number of other organizations and local groups sponsored voter registration projects. SCLC promoted registration programs in a half dozen southeastern states. The NAACP was particularly active in Texas and Tennessee. All the major civil rights organizations sponsored substantial summer projects staffed with college and high-school students. The largest was SNCC's Mississippi Freedom Summer, but others included the SCLC's Summer Community Organization and Political Education project in 1965, a series of initiatives by CORE in Louisiana, and SNCC's summer campaigns in Mississippi in 1963 and in Arkansas and Mississippi in 1965.[41]

The relations between civil rights organizations were often less than cordial. SNCC workers mocked Martin Luther King, Jr., as "De Lawd" and resented his highly publicized but often short-

[39] James Farmer, "Staff Report by the National Director," February 11, 1962, Richard Haley, "CORE in the South," January, 1963, in Congress of Racial Equality Papers, Southern Regional Office, Box 3, State Historical Society of Wisconsin; Meier and Rudwick, *CORE*, 152, 225, 337.

[40] Moody, *Coming of Age in Mississippi*, 242; Meier and Rudwick, *CORE*, esp. 259–61.

[41] Martin Luther King, Jr., "Report to the Administrative Committee," November 12, 1965, in Southern Christian Leadership Conference Papers, Box 28, Martin Luther King, Jr., Center for Social Change; Watters and Cleghorn, *Climbing Jacob's Ladder*, esp. 143.

lived campaigns. "King & Co.," a field secretary for CORE grumbled, "are stealing the show without producing—even in South Carolina, where CORE has done all the work." The NAACP, regarding itself as the premier civil rights organization, objected to any equal billing or "joint listing" that might "imply equality" with other civil rights groups. "The way I see this whole thing," a field secretary for SNCC confided, "is the NAACP thinks that SNCC wants to take something from them." The differences between civil rights groups eventually proved destructive, but in the early 1960s they paled in comparison with the fury of the white resistance to black civil rights.[42]

"People have been shot, Mass Meetings have been raided, churches blown up, and SNCC headquarters shot into many, many times and ultimately blown up in December 1963," one of SNCC's field secretaries reported from a southwest Georgia county, but otherwise things were going pretty well and the county was a "place of much hope." Such reports appeared with monotonous frequency. In Arkansas, authorities arrested two SNCC workers for "planning to breach the peace." In Mississippi, a fifteen-year-old high-school girl who joined a sit-in received a one-year jail sentence for delinquency. Police beat another young black woman because she refused to say, "Yes, sir," to an officer, and they arrested a young black man for "parading without a permit" because he wore a T-shirt bearing the words CORE and Freedom Now. At one point, sixty-two of the sixty-seven field secretaries and volunteers SNCC had in Mississippi were in jail. It was not unusual for voter registrars to attack field workers, although in only one case did a voter registrar's wife attack a CORE staff member with her shoe, after which police arrested the worker for disturbing the peace.[43]

[42] David L. Lewis, *King: A Critical Biography* (New York, 1970), 152; Meier and Rudwick, *CORE*, 164; Roy Wilkins to Leslie Dunbar, October 17, 1961, in VEP Files, Box 1; James Robinson, "Field Report for January 6–12, 1963," in VEP Files, Box 6; "CORE-VEP Field Report: North Louisiana, Feb. 1–March 14," in VEP Files, Box 18.

[43] Don Harris, "Field Report," March 27, 1964, in VEP Files, Box 18; *Arkansas Gazette* (Little Rock), October 8, 1963; Sellers, *The River of No Return*, 49–50; Watters and Cleghorn, *Climbing Jacob's Ladder*, 363; SNCC, "Mississippi: A Chronology of Violence and Intimidation in Mississippi Since 1961" (Mimeographed flyer, 1964); Stoper, "The Student Nonviolent Co-ordinating Committee," 28; "CORE Field Report from Louisiana," September 12, 1963, in VEP Files, Box 18.

Leslie W. Dunbar of the Southern Regional Council estimated that between 1955 and 1965 "as many as eighty-four killings in the South have been connected with the civil-rights drive." Only one of the perpetrators, a white man who in 1964 shot a black woman during civil rights demonstrations in Jacksonville, Florida, was convicted and imprisoned. Attorney General Kennedy reflected that in Alabama, Louisiana, and Mississippi, "lawless activities . . . have the sanction of local law enforcement agencies, political officials, and a substantial segment of the white population." That observation held equally for many rural and small-town counties in other states. Just "staying alive" in a die-hard Louisiana parish, a staffer explained, "was a major project of CORE workers." [44]

The violence that whites—individuals, groups, and law enforcement agents—visited upon civil rights workers and those who cooperated with them generated bitterness and conflict. The Justice Department promised protection for voter registrants, yet in the face of escalating white violence, the Kennedy administration abandoned its commitment. Officials in the Justice Department ended up telling imperiled civil rights workers that, as Pat Watters and Reese Cleghorn have put it, "the original pledge had not meant what it seemed to say." Such mendacity sparked wider criticism of federal behavior. Local whites "had an excuse for behaving the way they did," two civil rights workers conceded, but not "those mealy-mouth bastards from Washington who said they were going to do something and who were concerned about civil rights." [45]

The Justice Department retreated into legalities. The federal government's warrant was only to investigate civil rights violations; it had no authority to protect individuals or punish violent behav-

[44] Leslie W. Dunbar, *A Republic of Equals* (Ann Arbor, Mich., 1966), 114; Belknap, *Federal Law and Southern Order*, 121; Robert F. Kennedy, "Memorandum for the President," June 5, 1964, in White House Central Files, Name File, Johnson Library; Edward Hollander, "Louisiana Summer 65 Brief Summary," n.d., in CORE Papers, Southern Regional Office, Box 2.

[45] McMillen, "Black Enfranchisement in Mississippi," 359–63; John Dittmer, "The Politics of the Mississippi Movement, 1954–1964," in *The Civil Rights Movement in America*, ed. Charles W. Eagles (Jackson, Miss., 1986), 78–79; Meier and Rudwick, *CORE*, 173–74; Watters and Cleghorn, *Climbing Jacob's Ladder*, 58; Wirt, *Politics of Southern Equality*, 128.

ior. Law enforcement, the department reiterated, was a responsibility of state and local government. The federal government could prosecute cases under Reconstruction legislation that prohibited people from conspiring to deprive individuals of their civil rights. In 1945 a divided Supreme Court construed one of the provisions of that legislation narrowly, requiring the prosecution to prove that the conspirators intended to deprive victims of their civil rights. The ruling made prosecution difficult, and the Justice Department consistently argued thereafter that the federal government had no jurisdiction to act on violence against blacks. "There is no federal police force," a Justice Department official explained. "The responsibility for protection is that of the local police." [46]

The Justice Department's arguments were largely specious. President Harry S. Truman's Civil Rights Committee had earlier concluded that vigorous prosecution of civil rights violations— whether or not they ended in convictions—would have a "sobering influence upon local attitudes and practices." Federal marshals and the FBI could have made "probable cause arrests" even if attaining convictions proved impossible. In any event, the federal courts had changed considerably since 1945, and during the 1950s they had taken a less restrained view of the Reconstruction provisions. When the Johnson administration eventually did pursue convictions for southern civil rights violations, it met with success. As Attorney General Nicholas Katzenbach told President Johnson, "The problem of using large numbers of federal civilian law enforcement personnel [was] more practical than legal." [47]

The Kennedy administration feared southern power in Congress. Some presidential advisers were less than enthusiastic about rescuing civil rights workers who had deliberately placed themselves in jeopardy by moving into the most dangerous areas of the

[46] *Screws* v. *United States*, 325 U.S. 91 (1945); John Doar quoted in *The Summer That Didn't End*, by Len Holt (London, 1966), 50. See also Belknap, *Federal Law and Southern Order*.

[47] *To Secure These Rights: The Report of the President's Committee on Civil Rights* (New York, 1947), 128; Administrative History of the Department of Justice Civil Rights Division, VII, 88–100, in Johnson Library; Nicholas Katzenbach, "Memorandum for the President," July 1, 1964, in White House Central Files, Name File (Lee White), Johnson Library; Nicholas Katzenbach Oral History Interviews, November 12, 1968, November 23, 1968, both in Johnson Library.

South. The FBI showed an open antipathy to the civil rights movement. Attorney General Kennedy explained that there was a "reluctance to start down the path that would lead inevitably to the creation of a national police force." Yet federal authorities routinely provided protection for visiting civil rights dignitaries. A bemused civil rights worker in Mississippi observed, "Dr. King arrived accompanied by four cars of FBI men, whose function was unclear since they were not, of course, a police force and could not, of course, protect anyone."[48]

Most of all, the national Democratic party's approach to civil rights fettered vigorous enforcement. Symbolic equality was a matter of individual rights, not social change. Burke Marshall, the head of the Civil Rights Division in the Justice Department, stated the matter clearly: "The most fundamental, primary notion, of course, is that the constitutional rights involved are individual and personal, to be asserted by private citizens as they choose, in court, speaking through their chosen counsel." The poor blacks with whom SNCC and CORE worked could contribute little to an image of civic progress, and the rural and small-town South only occasionally commanded national and international headlines. The federal government provided protection for newsworthy figures and otherwise tried to ignore the travails of the southern countryside.[49]

In the beginning SNCC and CORE workers shared some of the assumptions that underlay federal policy. They too favored individual rights and material progress. "We feel that we are engaged in a psychological battle for the minds of the enslaved," Charles Sherrod wrote in 1962. "Our criterion for success is not how many people we register, but how many people we can get to begin initiating decisions solely on the basis of their personal opinion." In short order, however, the poverty and racism of the rural and small-town South changed civil rights workers to a greater extent than the civil rights workers were ever able to change the rural

[48] Belknap, *Federal Law and Southern Order*, 106–82; Kenneth O'Reilly, *Racial Matters: The FBI's Secret File on Black America, 1960–1972* (New York, 1989), 1–155; Meier and Rudwick, *CORE*, 180; Robert F. Kennedy, "Foreword," in *Federalism and Civil Rights*, by Burke Marshall (New York, 1964), ix; Belfrage, *Freedom Summer*, 164.

[49] Marshall, *Federalism and Civil Rights*, 50.

and small-town South. Civic reforms that made sense to urban black college students had little relevance in the southern backwoods. The federal government's "betrayal" of the movement also hastened a reevaluation of aims within the ranks of SNCC and CORE.[50]

Soon after Robert Moses and his co-workers began their voter registration project in southern Mississippi in 1961, a local white politician murdered a local black who had tried to register. White witnesses supported the assailant's plea of self-defense, but Moses located three black witnesses, and one, Louis Allen, agreed to testify if he was given federal protection. The Justice Department refused to provide the protection, and the FBI informed county lawmen of his request. Shortly afterward a deputy sheriff beat the black witness, who under the circumstances decided to testify in support of the politician's plea of self-defense. Still, in early 1964, Allen was murdered by unknown assailants. Thereafter, the antagonism between SNCC and the federal government intensified.[51]

Aside from the lack of national support, civil rights workers faced the problems of "apathy, Uncle Tom leadership, [and] limited community support" from blacks. Acquiescence by blacks to local norms was often because of the "fear being put into them by public officials." Whites controlled jobs and credit—after all, "if you can afford to vote you don't need a loan"—and, as a SNCC worker in southwest Georgia observed, blacks who sought the vote risked "their lives, homes, families, churches." Civil rights workers, one of their number pointed out, were also confronting a black person and "demanding a confession that his life up until now had been lived upside down."[52]

In particular, blacks who were better off financially were likely to be "ultra-conservative" and to stress "past progress." To them, a frustrated activist in CORE burlesqued, "Our school is as good

[50] Sherrod quoted in *Climbing Jacob's Ladder*, by Watters and Cleghorn, 7.

[51] Robert Moses, "Report Concerning the Louis Allen Case," n.d., in Lucile Montgomery Papers; Carson, *In Struggle*, 46–50.

[52] Ronnie M. Moore to Barbara I. Whitaker, May 21, 1964, in CORE Papers, Southern Regional Office, Box 1; Major Johns, "Field Report," June, 1963, in VEP Files, Box 6; Frank Smith to Wiley Branton, December 13, 1962, in VEP Files, Box 11; Penny Patch to Wiley Branton, December 8, 1962, Jack Chatfield to Wiley Branton, December 11, 1962, both in VEP Files, Box 6.

as theirs and white folks love Negroes and everybody is happy."
Many within the voter registration movement shared Sherrod's
impression of black educators as careerists "who refuse to think
further than a new car, a bulging refrigerator, and an insatiable
lust for more than enough of everything we call leisure." Increasingly, as one scholar has written, members of SNCC came "to
identify with the poorer elements of the community and to distrust black middle class motives." Civil rights workers who had
started out as patriotic proponents of middle-class civic individualism grew ever more estranged from the United States government, from bourgeois values, and from national concepts of virtue
and progress.[53]

The Southwest Georgia Project was one of SNCC's more substantial enterprises. Although focusing on the rural counties of
the area, organizers could hardly ignore the city of Albany, which
Sherrod referred to as the Crossroads of Civilization in Southwest
Georgia. "All that happens in Albany," he explained, "is news and
house gossip in the surrounding counties." Moreover, the presence of all-black Albany State College provided a ready source of
recruits. In November, 1961, SNCC workers created the Albany
Movement, an umbrella organization similar to those formed to
direct the bus boycotts of the mid-1950s. The Albany Movement
issued a miscellany of demands, including fair employment and
the desegregation of the city's public transportation and its municipal facilities, and resorted to mass protests to achieve them.
Within a month the city police had arrested 500 demonstrators,
and Governor Vandiver had dispatched 150 state troopers to assist
in maintaining "law and order."[54]

[53] Roy Shields, "Field Report," July 23, 1964, Mike Lesser to Ronnie Moore, May 4, 1964,
both in VEP Files, Box 18; Sherrod quoted in *SNCC*, by Zinn, 126; Stoper, "The Student
Nonviolent Co-ordinating Committee," 46.

[54] Charles M. Sherrod to Wiley Branton, October 9, 1962, in VEP Files, Box 6. Perceptive
discussions of the Albany Movement include Howard Zinn's *Albany: A Study in National
Responsibility* (Atlanta, 1962) and *The Southern Mystique* (New York, 1964), 149–213; Lewis'
King, 140–70; Garrow's *Bearing the Cross*, 173–230; Adam Fairclough's *To Redeem the Soul of
America: The Southern Christian Leadership Conference and Martin Luther King, Jr.* (Athens, Ga.,
1987), 85–110; Eugene Pierce Walker's "A History of the Southern Christian Leadership
Conference, 1955–1965: The Evolution of a Southern Strategy for Social Change" (Ph.D.
dissertation, Duke University, 1978), 108–30; John A. Ricks III's " 'De Lawd' Descends
and Is Crucified: Martin Luther King, Jr., in Albany, Georgia," *Journal of Southwest Georgia*

At that point William Anderson, the group's president, decided to invite Martin Luther King to the city. A local osteopath, Anderson felt the oppressive responsibilities of leading a highly divisive campaign that had triggered death threats against his family. Some members of the Albany Movement, including SNCC staffers on the left and local black moderates on the right, opposed issuing the invitation, but Anderson proceeded anyway. On December 15 King and several aides arrived in Albany. Intending only to make an appearance, King, according to one of his biographers, "had no intention of getting involved in Albany." Certainly he and his staff made no advance preparations for joining the protests. That night King addressed a mass rally, and the following day he agreed to participate in a demonstration. Police arrested King, Ralph Abernathy, and more than two hundred other blacks. King declined bond and announced that he would spend "Christmas in jail." He added, "I hope thousands will join me." [55]

King's arrest temporarily reinvigorated the Albany Movement, but thereafter growing dissension within the leadership undermined the campaign. State and national NAACP executives and some members of the local middle-class black establishment condemned the movement. King's involvement and arrest brought international publicity and made SCLC officials, particularly the imperious Wyatt T. Walker, spokesmen for the protest, which in turn led SNCC staffers to accuse Walker and SCLC of usurping the authority of the local Albany Movement leadership. Ella Baker, who was an adviser to SNCC, arrived in Albany to continue her vendetta against King and the pastors. The press reported a widening chasm between SNCC and SCLC. Some local blacks in the Albany Movement, concerned over the harsh treatment being meted out to the demonstrators in jail and doubtless mindful of the fact that they would have to live in the city after the adventurers departed, sought to defuse the crisis and reached a truce with city officials.[56]

History, II (1984), 3–14; and Paul Douglas Bolster's "Civil Rights Movements in Twentieth Century Georgia" (Ph.D. dissertation, University of Georgia, 1972), 255–84.

[55] Stephen B. Oates, *Let the Trumpet Sound: The Life of Martin Luther King, Jr.* (New York, 1982), 189; King quoted in *King*, by Lewis, 149.

[56] Atlanta *Constitution*, December 18, 1961–December 22, 1961.

The truce freed King and seven hundred other demonstrators from jail, but otherwise the hasty oral concord achieved nothing. King later regretted accepting bail, explaining that "I thought that the victory had been won." The agreement and the release of the demonstrators sapped the strength of the movement. The earlier "community enthusiasm," David J. Garrow has remarked, was "transformed into a feeling of defeat." King and his aides departed, segregation remained as firmly entrenched as ever, and Attorney General Kennedy telephoned congratulations to Albany's mayor for settling the crisis. Sporadic but ineffective protests continued, along with boycotts of the city's larger stores and its public transportation.[57]

The Albany Movement regained momentum in July, 1962. Having been convicted of parading without a permit and disorderly conduct, King returned to Albany for sentencing. When a local judge gave King and Abernathy the choice of paying a fine or serving forty-five days at hard labor, they chose imprisonment. Their confinement revitalized the Albany Movement. "As much as we may disagree with MLK about the way he and SCLC do things," SNCC's William Hansen commented, "one has to admit that he can cause more hell to be raised by being in jail one night than anyone else could if they bombed city hall." The point was not lost on Albany's white leadership, which arranged for an unidentified and slightly mysterious stranger to pay King's bond without his consent. The authorities released King and Abernathy, prompting the latter sardonically to remark, "I've been thrown out of lots of places in my day, but never before have I been thrown out of jail."[58]

Massive protests continued for a week after King's release. Then, later in July, a federal district judge, one appointed by President Kennedy, enjoined further demonstrations. King chose not to disobey the court order, and although people not named in the injunction kept the Albany Movement alive, the court's action sharply curtailed public protest. Several days later a higher court overturned the injunction, and a few days after that, in early Au-

[57] King quoted in *King*, by Lewis, 154; Garrow, *Bearing the Cross*, 189.
[58] Hansen quoted in *To Redeem the Soul of America*, by Fairclough, 103–104; Abernathy quoted in *King*, by Lewis, 159.

gust, 1962, the district judge blithely issued another. Meantime, King returned to jail, after being arrested for leading a prayer meeting in front of city hall. By early August more than a thousand demonstrators languished in jail, and on August 10, the day that King was released from jail yet again, the Albany Movement suspended its demonstrations. The long-suffering blacks of Albany had made serious sacrifices but had gained nothing from the intransigent city government and had experienced little reaction from the federal government beyond the active hostility of the FBI.[59]

The Albany Movement collapsed, in large measure owing to the dexterity of city officials and particularly the police chief, Laurie Prichett. Law-enforcement officers avoided public violence and arrested demonstrators not for violating segregation laws but for offenses like parading without a permit and disorderly conduct. Local authorities claimed that with "firm but fair law enforcement they had 'broken the back' of the Albany movement." Black "onlookers," who as King pointed out "were not a part of our movement," occasionally threw rocks and bottles at the police. The Albany Movement sought to pressure the local government by the sheer magnitude of the demonstrations, but Chief Prichett countered by "farming out" prisoners to county jails throughout southeast Georgia. "We were naïve enough to think we could fill up the jails," Hansen ruminated. "We ran out of people before [Pritchett] ran out of jails." Ruby Hurley of the NAACP sniffed, "Albany was successful only if the goal was to go to jail."[60]

What happened in Albany had a powerful impact on the Southern Christian Leadership Conference. It provided the organization with a raison d'être. Prior to Albany, SCLC had conducted programs in voter registration and leadership training and had supported the sit-in movement. In none of these endeavors was its role of crucial significance. The events in Albany suggested to King and the people around him the possibility of implement-

---

[59] "Albany Manifesto," July 15, 1962, Martin Luther King, Jr., and W. G. Anderson, "Joint Statement," July 22, 1962, Martin Luther King, Jr., "Why Albany," August 8, 1962, all in King Papers, Box 1.

[60] Ricks, " 'De Lawd' Descends," 11; King quoted in *Bearing the Cross*, by Garrow, 209; Hansen quoted in *In Struggle*, by Carson, 61; Hurley quoted in *King*, by Lewis, 169.

ing a broader strategy and, indeed, of taking civil rights protest into a new phase. In the beginning, according to Wyatt Walker, there had been the bus boycotts, following them were the sit-ins, and then came the freedom rides. Albany constituted a fourth stage, a new "kind of blanket protest and sacrifice." Walker pointed out, "That was the first instance where we had a community mobilized and organized to the point . . . they were willing to go to jail in large numbers." Martin Luther King observed that in Albany "approximately 5% of the total Negro population went willingly to jail." [61]

The Albany Movement failed for a variety of largely controllable reasons. Among them were the lack of advance planning, the constant squabbling within the leadership, the nebulous goals of desegregation and fair employment, and the decision to make government officials the target of protest rather than pressuring businessmen. A campaign that was better planned and organized offered the opportunity to tear away the veil of "legality" that cloaked the underlying brutality and unconstitutionality of the Jim Crow system and to focus the attention of the news media and the federal government. It also promised to restore SCLC's tattered prestige. SCLC could, a staff member commented, "profit by and build on the Albany experience." Thereafter, King and his SCLC associates focused much of their energy on mobilizing campaigns in Birmingham, St. Augustine, Selma, and elsewhere. [62]

After the collapse of the Albany Movement, King turned his efforts to expanding the SCLC's staff, to improving the organization's finances, and to attracting local groups to affiliate with it. In the South, King conducted "people-to-people" tours to build support for civil rights and for SCLC. Outside the South SCLC revamped its fund-raising apparatus. In 1962 SCLC's budget was approximately $400,000, in 1963 it was almost $900,000, and in

[61] Wyatt T. Walker, "The Deep South in Social Revolution," November 10, 1961, Wyatt T. Walker, "The American Dilemma in Miniature: Albany, Georgia," March 26, 1963, both in King Papers, Box 1; Fairclough, *To Redeem the Soul of America*, 107; Martin Luther King, Jr., *Why We Can't Wait* (New York, 1964), 36.

[62] Minutes of Executive Staff Meeting, January 23, 1963, in King Papers, Box 1; "*Playboy* Interview," January, 1965, in *A Testament of Hope: The Essential Writings of Martin Luther King, Jr.*, ed. James Melvin Washington (San Francisco, 1986), 340–77; Garrow, *Bearing the Cross*, 218–35.

1965 it reached a high of $1.5 million. King's staff also began planning for Project X, a direct-action campaign in Birmingham, Alabama.[63]

The Alabama Christian Movement for Human Rights, headed by Fred L. Shuttlesworth, was SCLC's affiliate in Birmingham. Although Shuttlesworth became pastor of a church in another state in 1961, he remained active in Birmingham, and the congregations of his former church and the churches of two close ministerial allies made up much of the affiliate's membership. In the main, members of the ACMHR were strongly religious in outlook and lower-middle class in social composition. Although their broad goals were mainstream civic and economic equality of opportunity, Shuttlesworth and his allies also demanded a reallocation of political power within the black community and an equitable voice for blacks in making and implementing city policy. As a result, both black and white leaders in Birmingham considered ACMHR to be a radical organization. Up until 1963, however, it had accomplished relatively little.[64]

To many observers, Birmingham was the "toughest city in the South," the "most segregated city in America," and perhaps even the "world's most race-conscious city." In the spring of 1960, Harrison E. Salisbury wrote, "Every channel of communication, every medium of mutual interest, every reasoned approach, every inch of middle ground has been fragmented by the emotional dynamite of racism, reinforced by the whip, the razor, the gun, the bomb, the torch, the club, the knife, the mob, the police and many branches of the state's apparatus." Birmingham earned its reputation not because of a peculiar malice in the white population but because of the structural determinants of the city's behavior. Birmingham exaggerated the social dynamics pervading the metropolitan South.[65]

[63] Fairclough, *To Redeem the Soul of America*, 91–100; Minutes of Executive Staff Meeting, January 23, 1963; Wyatt T. Walker, "Tentative Schedule for Project X," n.d., in King Papers, Box 1.

[64] Glenn T. Eskew, "The Alabama Christian Movement for Human Rights and the Birmingham Struggle for Civil Rights, 1956–1963," in *Birmingham, Alabama, 1956–1963: The Black Struggle for Civil Rights*, ed. David J. Garrow (Brooklyn, 1989), 3–114.

[65] "Birmingham: Integration's Hottest Crucible," *Time*, December 15, 1958, p. 16; King, *Why We Can't Wait*, 43; Carl T. Rowan, *South of Freedom* (New York, 1952), 158; Harrison

Birmingham's established leadership—the Big Mules in local parlance—took its instructions from New York and Pittsburgh. An audit of the metropolitan area released in 1960 pointed out the extent to which the men setting Birmingham's course were non-natives who ranked their own success and that of their corporations above the interests of the city. A prominent Birmingham attorney explained to an investigator for the Southern Regional Council that those who wished to sway public policy in the city "could talk to half a dozen people outside of Alabama with possibly far-reaching results." The corporate owners of Birmingham's industry, communications, and much else and their local minions cooperated with black belt planters in supporting low wages and low taxes, but as attorney Charles Morgan remarked, they "really did not give a damn whether Tweedledee or Tweedledum occupied office space in City Hall."[66]

Relatively few of Birmingham's white business and professional middle class lived in the city. The smog and grime that settled into Jones Valley disposed economically comfortable whites to reside "over the mountain," in Homewood, Mountain Brook, and Vestavia Hills. Middle-class whites occupied the Highland Park and Forest Park sections of the city, but their limited numbers gave them little voice in civic affairs. About 40 percent of Birmingham's population was black, but the black electorate was considerably smaller. A rigorous board of registrars endeavored with some success to keep the franchise limited. Neither blacks nor low-income whites enjoyed unfettered access to the polls. In 1963 African

E. Salisbury in New York *Times,* April 12, 1960. Important works on the Birmingham campaign include Glenn T. Eskew's "But for Birmingham: The Local and National Movements in the Civil Rights Struggle" (Ph.D. dissertation, University of Georgia, 1993); Robert Gaines Corley's "The Quest for Racial Harmony: Race Relations in Birmingham, Alabama, 1947–1963" (Ph.D. dissertation, University of Virginia, 1979); *Birmingham, Alabama, 1956–1963,* ed. Garrow; Lee Edmundson Bains, Jr.'s "Birmingham, 1963: Confrontation over Civil Rights" (Honors thesis, Harvard University, 1977); William A. Nunnelley's *Bull Connor* (Tuscaloosa, Ala., 1991); King, *Why We Can't Wait;* and Charles Morgan, Jr.'s *A Time to Speak* (New York, 1964).

[66] "Birmingham: Integration's Hottest Crucible," 16; Corley, "The Quest for Racial Harmony," 194–205; Benjamin Muse, "Confidential Memorandum: Visit to North Alabama, Birmingham, and Tuscaloosa," July 13, 1961, in Southern Regional Council Papers, Atlanta University Center; Morgan, *A Time To Speak,* 89; "Alabama Notebook," in Robert F. Kennedy Papers.

Americans amounted to under 20 percent of the voting population.

Consequently, the white working class and lower-middle class controlled Birmingham's politics during the 1950s and into the 1960s. Skilled workers, artisans, small-business people, city-government employees, and the like held greater political power in the city than they did elsewhere. They had nothing to gain with the coming of racial equality, and they had a great deal to lose. Integration threatened to increase the competition for jobs and end the "race wage" that conceded whites higher pay and access to the most coveted jobs. An influx of educationally deprived blacks imperiled public-school standards and the integrity of neighborhood schools. Traditional white lower-middle-class Birmingham communities—East Lake, Ensley, Woodlawn, Wylam, Inglenook—were already in decline as better-paid and younger workers moved outside the city. Equal opportunities for blacks augured further decline. It was little wonder that many lower-status whites staunchly supported segregation. They perceived that metropolitan black progress would be largely at their expense.[67]

The political dynamics of Birmingham favored politicians like Bull Connor, the city's police commissioner. When students at Miles College, a historically black school, conducted a brief flurry of sit-ins in Birmingham, Connor's cops quickly arrested them. When freedom riders arrived, Connor collaborated with the Ku Klux Klan to enable the Mother's Day violence. While the city earned the sobriquet of Bombingham, Connor's police failed to come up with a single suspect, apart from the occasional black they deemed to have dynamited himself. When a federal court ordered the desegregation of public facilities in Birmingham, Connor and his fellow commissioners closed the city's parks, playgrounds, golf courses—whatever the court order covered. When blacks organized boycotts of the larger Birmingham stores, the city commission halted the surplus food program that mainly ben-

[67] The best social and political analysis of Birmingham is Eskew's "But for Birmingham." The discussion here is also based on precinct returns and census data. See Numan V. Bartley and Hugh D. Graham, *Southern Politics and the Second Reconstruction* (Baltimore, 1975), esp. 201–12.

efited the black poor. Eventually, Connor's crudity and brutality undermined his support among the white lower-middle class upon whom he was politically dependent.[68]

Gradually moderate forces emerged in Birmingham. During the postwar years, the city's industrial economy had declined relative to the expanding consumer and service sectors. Real estate agents, retailers, and other proponents of economic development timidly began to advance the idea that the escalating racial crisis had some bearing on the city's sluggish economic performance. During 1962 the chamber of commerce organized the Senior Citizens Committee to open negotiations with black leaders. Headed by Sidney W. Smyer, a prominent real estate agent and the outgoing president of the chamber of commerce, the committee included Birmingham's principal employers. In the same year, Citizens for Progress, mostly younger white businessmen and attorneys, circulated a petition to change Birmingham's form of government and implicitly to rid the city of Bull Connor. The campaign to install a mayor-council system succeeded, and in March, 1963, Albert Boutwell defeated Connor in the runoff for mayor. Connor and the other commissioners refused to accept the election results, insisting that they had the right to complete the final two years of their terms. Thus Birmingham limped along with two governments, one run by the commissioners and the other headed by Boutwell, a segregationist but also an advocate of economic development. Both Smyer of the Senior Citizens Committee and Boutwell were former massive-resistance leaders who concluded that the price of defiance was too high. Grudgingly, they moved to the side of moderation.[69]

By the time King embarked on Project X in early April, 1963, Birmingham's reluctant moderates had in place a structure for negotiating with demonstration leaders. The problem was the divisions within the white economic elite. The basic rift was between the iron aristocracy, which identified segregation with low wages and a docile work force, and service-sector businessmen, whose goals were economic growth and the maximizing of real estate

[68] Nunnelley, *Bull Connor*, 68–128.

[69] Corley, "The Quest for Racial Harmony," 191–249; Benjamin Muse, "Dangerous Situation in Birmingham," January 11, 1962, in Southern Regional Council Papers.

values. Burke Marshall later explained that the city's merchants would not agree to an accommodation with black leaders without the consent of the Big Mules, who refused to compromise.[70]

The Southern Christian Leadership Conference and the Alabama Christian Movement for Human Rights launched Project X on April 3. The hope of promoting demonstrations the size of those in Albany was quickly deflated. In droves, Birmingham's blacks failed to rally to the cause. Throughout April leaders of the project struggled to marshal followers, and the whole undertaking teetered on the brink of failure.

The disappointing response related closely to the deep divisions between Birmingham's blacks. A sizable black middle class lived in the city, but few of its members welcomed demonstrations. The Birmingham *World,* a black newspaper, editorialized, "This direct action seems to be both wasteful and worthless." Soon the SCLC leadership was denouncing, in Abernathy's description, "the elite, the bourgeoisie, the class in Birmingham who are now living on the hill, learning to talk proper." King attempted to heal the breach by creating a central advisory committee dominated by the black establishment, but the feuding continued. Although the state of Alabama had succeeded in banishing the NAACP, former officials of that organization were prominent among the SCLC's critics.[71]

Constrained by Birmingham's repressive social atmosphere and by the anemic political strength of blacks, the black establishment had learned caution. During the early 1960s, however, the white leadership had evinced a willingness at least to discuss common problems, and Boutwell's election had inaugurated what the Birmingham *News* hailed with the headline "New Day Dawns for Birmingham." Few establishment African Americans were willing to put recent gains at risk by offending whites with disruptive demonstrations led by outside agitators and by Fred Shuttlesworth. To the black leadership, the religiously inspired Shuttlesworth appeared dictatorial, self-righteous, and uncompromising. His con-

[70] Eskew, "But for Birmingham," 238–40; Burke Marshall Oral History Interview, June 20, 1964, pp. 99–101, in Kennedy Library.

[71] *World* and Abernathy quoted in "But for Birmingham," by Eskew, 303, 313; Garrow, *Bearing the Cross,* 231–47.

frontational tactics threatened the gradually blossoming rapport between whites and the black middle class. Just as bad, should the demonstrations prove successful, Shuttlesworth might emerge as the leader of black Birmingham. From the perspective of the black establishment, greater peril than promise attended Project X.[72]

Birmingham's substantial population of unemployed and underemployed blacks did not participate in the demonstrations, but many gathered to watch, and often to cheer, the protests. The onlookers, who throughout the month of April far outnumbered the marchers, contributed to the impression that the movement was larger than it was. Connor and the police dealt with the demonstrators by making wholesale arrests, which frequently drew taunts from the onlookers. On April 7 law-enforcement officials used police dogs on the spectators. It was the only time during the month that the police resorted to such tactics. Nevertheless, as Glenn T. Eskew has underlined, the police brutality portrayed in the media gave the movement a boost during a difficult period and led Wyatt Walker to reevaluate SCLC's posture. Soon afterward, Walker replaced Project X with Project C, for confrontation. The rising animosity between the police and the alienated onlookers helped convince many in Birmingham and in Washington that a negotiated settlement was a necessity.[73]

On April 10 an Alabama state court issued an injunction against demonstrations. King, Abernathy, and other activists promptly disobeyed the court order and were placed under arrest. While interned, King penned the classic "Letter from Birmingham City Jail," a powerful and persuasive justification for the black civil rights movement. Apart from occasioning his letter, however, his imprisonment did little to revive the protest. The lower-middle-class constituency of the movement held employment that rarely accommodated lengthy penal absences. By the end of April, the Birmingham campaign teetered on the verge of defeat. "We had

[72] Birmingham *News*, April 3, 1963; Bains, "Birmingham, 1963," 91–122; Garrow, *Bearing the Cross*, 237–41.

[73] Wyatt T. Walker to Martin Luther King, Jr., and Ralph Abernathy, "Project C," in King Papers, Box 1; Eskew, "But for Birmingham," 262–349.

run out of troops," Walker stated. King—out of jail on bail—added that the media was losing interest in the campaign.[74]

Some SCLC staffers led by James Bevel, a former member of SNCC, argued that the key to revitalizing the movement lay in recruiting high-school students. The teenagers had less to lose than adults and indeed might jump at an honorable excuse for playing hooky. More fundamentally, as Bevel put it, "The black community as a whole did not have that kind of cohesion or camaraderie. But the students, they had a community they'd been in since elementary school, so they had bonded quite well." The more ambitious among the students also had a momentous stake in the outcome of the movement. King was ambivalent about bringing untrained teenagers into such a volatile situation, and the members of the black establishment on the central advisory committee were disgusted by the idea. Bevel and his associates acted anyway, apparently without clear authorization.[75]

On May 2 SCLC launched the Children's Crusade. Wave upon wave of black protesters, most of them students, marched toward the central business district. The police made hundreds of arrests, but the continuing flow of demonstrators strained the city's law-enforcement apparatus and inundated the jails. The next day, a harried and distraught Bull Connor ordered the use of high-pressure water hoses and police dogs to dam the flood of marchers. The brutality toward teenagers and sometimes younger children enraged blacks on the sidelines. Spectators hurled rocks and bottles at police, who in turn employed further force to disperse the crowds. Police filled the jails and housed the overflow of prisoners in an open-air stockade. The fire hoses injured but did not halt the demonstrators, but their use spurred more conflict between police and onlookers. By May 7 the police had all but capitulated. Out of jail space and unable to contain the escalating demonstrations, Bull Connor watched helplessly as marchers streamed downtown.

[74] "Letter from Birmingham City Jail," in *A Testament of Hope*, ed. James Melvin Washington, 289–302; Walker quoted in *Bearing the Cross*, by Garrow, 247.
[75] Bevel quoted in *Voices of Freedom: An Oral History of the Civil Rights Movement from the 1950s Through the 1980s*, by Henry Hampton and Steve Fayer (New York, 1990), 131.

The fire hoses and police dogs made Birmingham an international byword. The Kennedy administration, which had been cool to demonstrations and had aligned itself with the black establishment's prescription of voter registration and patience, exerted pressure on corporations to encourage their Alabama executives to support a settlement. The Senior Citizens Committee, meeting in downtown Birmingham on May 7, watched the collapse of public order and adjusted to the inevitable. That night, white and black representatives reached an agreement, and SCLC halted the demonstrations. "Birmingham," King, Abernathy, and Shuttlesworth could declare two days later, "has reached an accord with its conscience." [76]

The Birmingham protests illustrated many of the contradictions, dilemmas, and conflicts that permeated the black civil rights movement and the white resistance. The settlement illustrated them as well. The confrontation accelerated a basic change in Birmingham's white leadership; it had little effect on the city's black leadership. Within the white elite, representatives of the service and consumer economy won a decisive victory over the titans of industry. Interestingly, individuals from the private sector conducted all the negotiations. The matters were too critical to entrust to politicians. As King explained, "The political power structure always responds to the economic power structure." [77]

The black negotiators came from the black bourgeoisie and from SCLC. They were willing to accept considerably less than Shuttlesworth would have preferred. The black establishment won concessions, maintained its relationship with the city's white power brokers, and solidified its hold over black Birmingham. King and his allies achieved the aims of the national civil rights movement. They made it a matter of international consequence, compelled huge numbers of Americans to confront the issue, energized the national government, and enhanced the prestige of

[76] Michael Dorman, *We Shall Overcome* (New York, 1964), 143–87; Vincent Harding, "A Beginning in Birmingham," *Reporter,* June 6, 1963, pp. 13–19; Corley, "The Quest for Racial Harmony," 258–88; Eskew, "But for Birmingham," 350–99; Charles H. Levine, *Racial Conflict and the American Mayor: Power, Polarization, and Performance* (Lexington, Mass., 1974), 85–108; Birmingham *News,* May 10, 1963, quoted.
[77] King quoted in Birmingham *Post-Herald,* May 11, 1963.

the Southern Christian Leadership Conference and of Martin Luther King, Jr.

Out in the cold were Shuttlesworth and the Alabama Christian Movement for Human Rights. At the announcement of an agreement, Shuttlesworth, who had sustained an injury in the demonstrations, rushed from his hospital bed to dissociate himself from King and the settlement, which met few of the local movement's original demands and left the traditional black leadership in charge. Ultimately, under great pressure from the Kennedy administration and from his movement allies and unable to resist basking in the glow of victory, Shuttlesworth joined King in supporting the agreement. The conflict did clearly reveal, as staffers at SNCC had frequently noted, that the national and local movements often gave precedence to different objectives.[78]

Bitter-end segregationists attempted to sabotage the agreement. Connor's forces arrested King and Abernathy and refused to release jailed demonstrators without bond. School authorities expelled the students who had missed classes. Vigilantes bombed the home of A. D. King, Martin Luther King's brother, and the Gaston Motel, King's headquarters. The bombings touched off a major riot in the black area adjacent to the motel. Most tragically, well after the issue had been settled, dynamite exploded on a Sunday morning at the Sixteenth Street Baptist Church, the staging center for the demonstrations, and killed four girls attending Sunday school. None of these outrages altered the course of events. The Alabama Supreme Court declared the Boutwell administration the city's legal government, the elected city council repealed Birmingham's segregation ordinances, and the parks and public facilities reopened. Hesitantly, sometimes violently, moderation arrived in Birmingham.[79]

Birmingham was the civil rights movement's most important victory. All over the nation demonstrators took to the streets in support—and in opposition to Jim Crow. The hundreds of demonstrations in the South during 1963, some of them massive, resulted in the arrest of more than twenty thousand people. Civil

[78] Raines, *My Soul Is Rested,* 154–61; Ralph David Abernathy, *And the Walls Came Tumbling Down* (New York, 1989), 263–70; Eskew, "But for Birmingham," 385–99.
[79] Nunnelley, *Bull Connor,* 157–68; Corley, "The Quest for Racial Harmony," 273–87.

rights leaders sought to build on Birmingham by organizing a "march on Washington" in support of equal opportunities and the passage of federal civil rights legislation. The culmination of the huge march, held on August 28, 1963, was King's oration "I Have a Dream," probably his most famous speech.[80]

Birmingham and the national revulsion against southern segregation left the Kennedy administration and the federal government unable to evade the issue. A Justice Department official acknowledged, "We cannot continue a City by City battle without intolerable risks." Attorney General Kennedy and Burke Marshall agreed that "it was going to get worse and worse and worse and had to be dealt with." President Kennedy observed, "Clear evidence exists that the problem is being exploited abroad and has serious implications in our international relations."[81]

In a national television and radio address on June 11, 1963, President Kennedy asked Congress to enact sweeping civil rights legislation. "We are confronted primarily with a moral issue," Kennedy told his countrymen. "It is as old as the Scriptures and as clear as the American constitution." The president added, "The events in Birmingham and elsewhere have so increased the cries for equality that no city or state or legislative body can prudently choose to ignore them." By the measure of one student of the civil rights movement, Kennedy "committed the presidency to the preservation of the nation's social fabric and in theory, at least, recognized the moral injustice of racial discrimination."[82]

The growing national consensus on the necessity of racial reform in the benighted South permeated even the halls of Congress. The events in Alabama "changed the atmosphere of the country as a whole," Theodore C. Sorensen affirmed. The man-

[80] Southern Regional Council, "Civil Rights: Year-End Summary," December 31, 1963, in Southern Regional Council Papers; Garrow, *Bearing the Cross*, 265–86; Martin Luther King, Jr., "I Have a Dream," in *A Testament of Hope*, ed. James Melvin Washington, 217–20.

[81] Ramsey Clark to Robert F. Kennedy, May 15, 1963, in Robert F. Kennedy Papers; Burke Marshall Oral History Interview, June 20, 1964, p. 105, in Kennedy Library; "Report of Business Council Meeting with the President," July 17, 1963, in Lee White Civil Rights Files, Kennedy Library.

[82] "Remarks of the President on Nationwide Radio and Television," June 11, 1963, in Robert F. Kennedy Papers; Eugene Pierce Walker, "A History of the Southern Christian Leadership Conference," 151.

agers of both parties had to respond, because, in Sorensen's words, "a national crisis required it." As Congress debated, the undiminishing upheavals in the South made the magnitude of the crisis ever more evident. "It is being argued in a nervous Congress that the need for civil rights legislation was not to advance the Negro cause but to control and contain it," Harry S. Ashmore commented.[83]

The legislative deliberation continued into the summer of 1964. After President Kennedy's assassination, civil rights legislation offered itself as a monument to the fallen leader. President Lyndon B. Johnson wielded his considerable political skills in corralling votes for a strong and comprehensive measure. Senator Richard B. Russell of Georgia held together a hard-core bloc of twenty senators from the former Confederate states to oppose the bill, but overwhelmingly the rest of the senators chose to support civil rights. On June 10 the Senate voted to terminate debate and end the southern filibuster. As Gilbert C. Fite has noted, "The power of the Southern Bloc, which had held back any comprehensive civil rights legislation for nearly a quarter of a century, had been broken." In early July President Johnson signed the 1964 Civil Rights Act, which erased the White and Colored signs across the South.[84]

The Voting Rights Act of 1965 followed. During civil rights demonstrations in Selma earlier in the year, the brutality of Sheriff James G. Clark surpassed that of Bull Connor. The march from Selma to Montgomery that climaxed the campaign marked the apex of the national consensus that the de jure segregation Connor and Clark enforced was no longer tolerable. By the time Congress began serious consideration of voting legislation, Senator Russell was hospitalized with emphysema and the southern congressional forces were in disarray. In the House of Representatives, defections abounded. On the final vote, 31 of the 106 members

[83] Theodore C. Sorensen Oral History Interview, March 26, 1964, pp. 124, 133, in Kennedy Library; Sorensen, *Kennedy* (New York, 1965), 475–501; Harry S. Ashmore, "The Desegregation Decision: Ten Years After," *Saturday Review*, May 16, 1964, p. 69.

[84] Gilbert C. Fite, *Richard B. Russell, Jr., Senator from Georgia* (Chapel Hill, N.C., 1991), 413; Charles Whalen and Barbara Whalen, *The Longest Debate: A Legislative History of the 1964 Civil Rights Act* (Washington, D.C., 1985).

from former Confederate states supported the bill. The civil rights movement had succeeded in discrediting Jim Crow segregation.[85]

[85] Watters and Cleghorn, *Climbing Jacob's Ladder,* 33–35; David J. Garrow, *Protest at Selma: Martin Luther King, Jr., and the Voting Rights Act of 1965* (New Haven, 1978).

CHAPTER X

CONFLICT, CONSENSUS, AND CIVIL RIGHTS

THE civil rights victories of the mid-1960s achieved the original aims of the movement. At the same time, as Martin Luther King, Jr., observed, "These victories did very little to penetrate the lower depths of Negro deprivation, particularly in the North." Less than a week after President Lyndon B. Johnson signed the Voting Rights Act, the Watts section of Los Angeles exploded in a massive riot. Thereafter, civil rights issues became more national in scope and more divisive in nature. "Everyone underestimated," King reflected, "the amount of rage Negroes were suppressing and the amount of bigotry the white majority was disguising." Civil rights organizations, the Johnson administration, and the federal courts attempted to deal with the radically altered situation. The destruction of segregation was an enormous accomplishment that created a "crisis of victory."[1]

The National Association for the Advancement of Colored People, along with the Urban League and most white northern liberals, refused to compromise with changing circumstances. To them, the "Negro problem" remained a white problem. The strategy of "pro-Negro" groups, as Gunnar Myrdal had long before observed, was to focus "attention on the suppressed moral conflict" and to exploit the "moral dilemma" and the resulting guilt of well-meaning white Americans. To consider seriously the internal reformation of ghettos was anathema. The Supreme Court

[1] "Dr. King's Speech, Frogmore," November 14, 1966, in Southern Christian Leadership Conference Papers, Box 49, Martin Luther King, Jr., Center for Social Change, Atlanta; Martin Luther King, Jr., "The State of the Movement" (Staff speech), November 28, 1967, in SCLC Papers, Box 28; August Meier and Elliott Rudwick, *CORE: A Study in the Civil Rights Movement, 1942–1968* (New York, 1973), 329.

341

had pontificated in 1954 that separate facilities were "inherently unequal." The object of civil rights activity was to move African Americans out of segregated facilities into white ones. "Negro leaders," as Charles E. Silberman described the NAACP and its allies, "were trapped in a rhetoric and a logic whose premise was that any all-Negro institution is per se degrading." [2]

To the NAACP leadership and that of other establishment "pro-Negro" groups, the accomplishments of the civil rights movement were imposing. August Meier and Elliott Rudwick observed that "the right wing of the protest movement, which included a substantial group in the NAACP, was impressed by the changes which had occurred and came to view its role as exercising influence within established institutions rather than fighting from the outside." African Americans gained greater political influence, particularly within the Democratic party, and wider opportunity to promote their program of desegregation and middle-class progress. Further assimilation promised to expand the black middle class and ultimately to eradicate the "Negro problem." [3]

Such an approach had limited relevance to the majority of black people. Prior to the victories of the midsixties, critics had often attacked the NAACP for being too conservative. Thereafter, the organization's strategy, by remaining consistent, became more conservative. It provided opportunities, Andrew Young of the Southern Christian Leadership Conference observed, for "Negroes to try to be middle class" without raising troublesome questions about the values of white middle-class culture. To the Student Nonviolent Coordinating Committee's Stokely Carmichael, the assimilationist agenda rested "on the assumption that there was nothing of value in the Negro community, so the thing to do was to siphon off the 'acceptable' Negroes into the surrounding middle-class white community." Whatever the validity of the criticisms, the distance between the NAACP-oriented black leadership and the black masses widened. [4]

[2] Gunnar Myrdal, *An American Dilemma: The Negro Problem and Modern Democracy* (New York, 1944), lxvii–lxix; *Brown v. Board of Education* (1954), in *Race Relations Law Reporter*, I, 9; Charles E. Silberman, "Beware the Day They Change Their Minds," *Fortune*, November, 1965, p. 152.

[3] Meier and Rudwick, *CORE*, 374.

[4] Andrew Young Oral History Interview, June 18, 1970, in Lyndon Baines Johnson Li-

SNCC and the Congress of Racial Equality moved rapidly toward a black-power position. SNCC and CORE staffers agreed that whites had created the racial problem but blacks themselves would have to provide the solution. "The posture of the civil rights movement was that of the dependent, the suppliant," who pandered to the federal government and to middle-class whites, Carmichael stated. The changed conditions inaugurated by civil rights legislation permitted a turn "to the Ghetto to organize these communities to control themselves." In early 1966 the SNCC central committee approved a statement calling "upon all black Americans to begin building independent political, economic, and cultural institutions that they will control and use as instruments of social change in this country." As Carmichael elaborated, blacks should take command of the "institutions within the black community," including those relating to law enforcement, education, welfare, and public housing.[5]

The black-power program was considerably more relevant than its critics acknowledged. It rejected the prevailing ideology by insisting on social solutions to social problems. It identified institutional racism as the main impediment to black progress, rather than the individual racism that Myrdal had seen as the white American's moral dilemma. It combated the psychological damage inflicted by slavery and segregation by proclaiming that "black people must redefine themselves" and indeed retitle themselves because the word *Negro* was the "invention of our oppressor." It offered a serious critique of integrationist strategy, which according to Carmichael, simply drained "skills and energies from the ghetto into white neighborhoods." It grappled with the enormous economic problems confronting black Americans by offering a colonial analogy that depicted ghettos as internal colonies exploited for their labor. "Negroes will in the next three decades control the heart of our great cities," two SNCC staffers explained

brary, Austin, Tex.; "Stokely Carmichael Speaks to the Howard University School of Law," October 14, 1966, in Howard Zinn Papers, Box 2, State Historical Society of Wisconsin, Madison.

[5] "Stokely Carmichael Speaks"; "Statement," May 23, 1966, in Zinn Papers, Box 2; Stokely Carmichael, "Report from the Chairman," May 5, 1967, in Student Nonviolent Coordinating Committee Papers, Box 7, Martin Luther King, Jr., Center for Social Change.

in a 1966 position paper. "These areas can become either concentration camps with a bitter and volatile population whose only power is the power to destroy, or organized and powerful communities able to make a constructive contribution to the total community. . . . This is the choice the country will have to make."[6]

Critics of "black power for black people" were legion. Because SNCC rejected the dogma codified by Myrdal, black and white organizations and individuals assaulted the doctrine from a variety of perspectives. From the beginning, one scholar has written, "the media, politicians, and civil libertarians across the country expressed absolute horror and outrage at the idea of aggressive black separatism." There were thoughtful critiques of black power, but as Richard Lentz has suggested, the national media seized upon the more extreme features and described its advocates as "hypermilitants" practicing a "politics of racial hostility," demagoguery, "black Jacobinism," and treason.[7]

SNCC and CORE staffers contributed to their own public-relations problems. The excesses of their rhetoric and romanticism provided a ready target for opponents. With the adoption of black power, civil rights militants also opted for self-defense rather than nonviolence, a decision that grew from their experiences in the rural, small-town South. Having for so long been the victims of white violence, they eventually concluded that the time to turn the other cheek had passed. All along, SNCC had gamely borne a reputation as a maverick organization with a pronounced proclivity for baiting the establishment. The redefinition of goals in the midsixties increased the organization's divergence from the mainstream civil rights movement.

SNCC and the southern wing of CORE initiated their most audacious project in 1964 with Mississippi Freedom Summer.

[6] Stokely Carmichael and Charles V. Hamilton, *Black Power: The Politics of Liberation in America* (New York, 1967), 37; Carmichael, "Power and Racism," in *Stokely Speaks: Black Power Back to Pan-Africanism* (New York, 1971), 23; Mike Thelwell and Courtland Cox quoted in *Memories of the Southern Civil Rights Movement,* by Danny Lyon (Chapel Hill, N.C., 1992), 184.

[7] Mary Aickin Rothschild, *A Case of Black and White: Northern Volunteers and the Southern Freedom Summers, 1964–1965* (Westport, Conn., 1982), 178; Richard Lentz, *Symbols, the News Magazines, and Martin Luther King* (Baton Rouge, 1990), esp. 202, 216, 241 (quoting from *Newsweek, Time,* and *U.S. News and World Report*).

Frustrated by their inability to accomplish significant change in Mississippi, SNCC staffers searched for a method to break the stalemate. Robert Moses and his associates decided in 1963 to hold a "mock election" outside the official Mississippi "democratic" process. More than a hundred Stanford and Yale students came to Mississippi to help conduct the election. SNCC-supported candidates "ran" for the major state offices in the November general election, and some eighty thousand blacks voted. The extent of black voter participation led Moses and other staffers to propose a larger project that would bring hundreds of volunteers into Mississippi during the summer of 1964. The campaign would promote grass-roots community organization in Mississippi while appealing for "the massive aid of the country as a whole, backed by the power and authority of the federal government."[8]

The decision to launch Mississippi Freedom Summer was not an easy one to reach. Some SNCC field workers objected to introducing large numbers of whites into a predominantly black movement. The volunteers of 1963, according to the critics, popped into Mississippi, often assumed leadership positions, garnered favorable national publicity, and left. Bringing in more Tarzans and Janes to work among the natives was not sound policy. After lengthy debate, project advocates ultimately carried the issue. Fanny Lou Hamer, a black woman who emerged from a sharecropper's shack to demonstrate impressive leadership abilities, argued, "If we're trying to break down this barrier of segregation, we can't segregate ourselves." Having made the decision, SNCC set about to recruit a thousand or so volunteers who would spend all or part of their summer in Mississippi while paying their own

[8] "Prospectus for the Mississippi Freedom Summer," in *The Summer That Didn't End*, by Len Holt (London, 1966), 197. Accounts of Mississippi Freedom Summer include Rothschild's *A Case of Black and White;* Holt's *The Summer That Didn't End;* Doug McAdam's *Freedom Summer* (New York, 1988); William McCord's *Mississippi: The Long, Hot Summer* (New York, 1965); Sally Belfrage's *Freedom Summer* (New York, 1965); *Letters from Mississippi*, ed. Elizabeth Sutherland (New York, 1965); Tracy Sugarman's *Stranger at the Gates: A Summer in Mississippi* (New York, 1966); Nicholas Von Hoffman's *Mississippi Notebook* (New York, 1964); and Nicolaus Mills's *Like a Holy Crusade: Mississippi, 1964—The Turning of the Civil Rights Movement in America* (Chicago, 1992).

travel and living expenses and having access to a minimum of five hundred dollars for bail money.[9]

The Council of Federated Organizations sponsored Mississippi Freedom Summer, but COFO was largely a creature of SNCC. Because the national leadership insisted that its southern wing maintain a separate identity, CORE assumed responsibility for one Mississippi congressional district, while SNCC organized the other four. Aaron E. Henry, president of the Mississippi NAACP, was the Freedom Democratic candidate for governor, but the NAACP's national office was largely hostile. SCLC lent moral support. Robert Moses of SNCC served as director of the project, and David J. Dennis of CORE was assistant director. Two thousand or so people participated. About half were northern volunteers, mostly white college students along with a significant number of teachers. Some 650 were clergymen, lawyers, doctors, and other professionals. The remainder included SNCC and CORE field workers and full-time black volunteers from within Mississippi.

The project included a number of often innovative programs. Northern volunteers staffed the freedom schools that spread over the state. As SNCC planners visualized them, the schools would awaken the social consciousness of high-school students and produce a new cohort of civil rights activists. In practice the northern students and teachers often gave the schools more of an academic cast. Other volunteers set up community centers, designed to provide recreational, educational, and social services, but first of all to "form a dynamic focus for the development of community organization." Southern whites created the white folk's project, an effort, in SNCC's Sam Shirah's words, "to reach the great number of white people in the South who have felt that this movement is their enemy." Most important, SNCC founded the Freedom Democratic party. Not only would the party put up candidates for another mock election, it would lay the foundation for challenging delegates of the regular Mississippi Democratic party at the Democratic national convention.[10]

[9] Hamer quoted in *SNCC: The New Abolitionists*, by Howard Zinn (Boston, 1964), 188; "Staff Meeting Minutes," June 9, 1964–June 11, 1964, in Zinn Papers, Box 2.

[10] "Prospectus for the Mississippi Freedom Summer," 202; Shirah quote in *In Struggle: SNCC and the Black Awakening of the 1960s*, by Clayborne Carson (Cambridge, Mass., 1981), 102; McAdam, *Freedom Summer*, 76–77, 154–57; Rothschild, *A Case of Black and White*.

Mississippi Freedom Summer, a CORE prospectus explained, "was a grass-roots movement" that sought to "by-pass the established leadership" and maintain its independence. It was, the report continued, "one of the few creative movements that the conservative elements in the civil rights movement had no control over." Aaron Henry added, "The Mississippi project was started without permission of any national organization. Nobody could fire us, because nobody had hired us." As a local "grass-roots movement," the project was "almost invulnerable to any type of threat of compromise offer from seemingly 'big' people or the established leadership." SNCC and southern CORE staffers wanted northern liberals to cooperate with the project without attempting to dominate it.[11]

The Johnson administration took the position that the federal government had "no authority" to protect the civil rights of citizens. Privately administration sources expressed hostility toward the Mississippi project. A White House aide informed the president that it was "nearly incredible that those people who are voluntarily sticking their head into the lion's mouth would ask for somebody to come down and shoot the lion." The federal government responded vigorously when whites murdered three civil rights workers in Neshoba County. According to civil rights workers, the fact that two of the three murder victims were white accounted for the government's reaction. Otherwise the Johnson administration attempted to ignore the Mississippi drama. According to statistics compiled by Pat Watters and Reese Cleghorn, the summer's violence resulted in six murders, including the three in Neshoba County; three gunshot wounds in thirty-five shooting incidents; thirty bombings and the burning of thirty-five churches; and eighty beatings. The cases of police harassment went uncounted.[12]

[11] "Proposed Plan of Action for CORE," in Congress of Racial Equality Papers, Southern Regional Office, Box 3, State Historical Society of Wisconsin; Aaron E. Henry Oral History Interview, September 2, 1970, in Johnson Library.

[12] Burke Marshall, "Speech" [delivered by John Doar to volunteers in Oxford, Ohio], in Burke Marshall Special Correspondence, John F. Kennedy Library, Boston; Lee White, Memorandum for the President, June 17, 1964, in White House Central Files (Human Rights), Johnson Library; Michal R. Belknap, *Federal Law and Southern Order: Racial Violence and Constitutional Conflict in the Post-Brown South* (Athens, Ga., 1987), 128–58; William Brad-

The Freedom Democratic party registered voters, conducted precinct meetings, nominated candidates, selected a delegation of sixty-four blacks and four whites, and called upon the national party to recognize the Freedom Democratic party "as the true representative of Mississippi Democrats." The regular Mississippi Democratic party performed as expected. At their all-white state convention, the participants approved resolutions supporting segregation and condemning both major parties. The regular Democrats stood for disfranchisement, white supremacy, and opposition to national Democratic policies. The Freedom Democratic party, in contrast, aligned itself with the national party, accepted both blacks and whites into its ranks, and chose candidates of both races. The party picked Joseph Rauh, an Americans for Democratic Action vice-president and general counsel for the United Automobile Workers, to represent it at the national convention, and the Americans for Democratic Action, along with some state parties and numerous individual delegates, endorsed its challenge.[13]

For a time the Freedom Democratic party's prospects appeared favorable. Then in July, the Republicans nominated Barry M. Goldwater, a conservative senator from Arizona, as their presidential candidate, thus freeing Lyndon Johnson from the need to protect his left electoral flank. When the Democrats met in August, much of the southern political establishment supported the Mississippi regulars, and seven southern state delegations talked of walking out should the Mississippi regulars be ousted. Ultimately, most of the Alabama and Mississippi delegates did stomp out of the convention. Under such circumstances, party managers calculated that "an all-black [sic] delegation going on the floor to replace the white one is going to add to the backlash" and strengthen Goldwater's candidacy. The Johnson administration mobilized against the Freedom Democratic party. The FBI, receiving an assignment to its liking, contributed a team of fifty agents and a great deal of electronic surveillance equipment to

ford Huie, *Three Lives for Mississippi* (New York, 1965); Pat Watters and Reese Cleghorn, *Climbing Jacob's Ladder: The Arrival of Negroes in Southern Politics* (New York, 1967), 139.

[13] Aaron Henry to John M. Bailey, July 17, 1964, in White House Central Files (Mississippi), Johnson Library; Holt, *The Summer That Didn't End*, 149–83.

eavesdrop on the Freedom delegates, and Senator Hubert H. Humphrey, who was soon to become the Democratic vice-presidential candidate, accepted the assignment of herding the Americans for Democratic Action and the northern liberals into line.[14]

The Freedom delegates made a favorable impression at the convention and received generally sympathetic press coverage. Before the credentials committee, Fannie Lou Hamer gave a moving account of her travails while trying to register as a voter in Mississippi. National television networks carried most of her talk, before the coverage could be interrupted by a hastily called presidential press conference. Party managers sought to defuse the issue by recognizing the regular Mississippi Democratic party, awarding two at-large seats to Freedom delegates, permitting the remaining Freedom delegates to be guests at the convention, and offering assurances that future conventions would not recognize delegations that accepted disfranchisement. The liberal establishment—Rauh, the Americans for Democratic Action, the NAACP, even Martin Luther King—lined up behind the compromise.

The Freedom delegates might have accepted the arrangement except for one crucial provision. Fearful that the SNCC-oriented delegates might choose unacceptable people for the two at-large seats, the compromise stipulated that the positions would be filled by Aaron Henry and Edwin King, one of whom was black, one of whom was white, and both of whom were middle-class professional people. As Hubert Humphrey explained, "The president has said that he will not let that illiterate woman [Hamer] speak on the floor of the Democratic convention." To many of the delegates, it was just another instance of the liberal establishment choosing the leadership of the movement. The Freedom Democratic party rejected the compromise.[15]

The failed challenge proved to be a deeply disillusioning experience for SNCC workers and their allies. The Freedom Dem-

---

[14] Walter Reuther quoted in Joseph Rauh Oral History Interview, August 8, 1969, p. 14, in Johnson Library; Catha D. DeLoach to William D. Moyers, September 10, 1964, in White House Central Files, Name File (DeLoach), Johnson Library; Theodore H. White, *The Making of the President, 1964* (New York, 1965), 292–350.

[15] Humphrey quoted in Edwin King Interview, in Anne Romaine Papers, State Historical Society of Wisconsin. Anne Romaine and Howard Romaine interviewed most of the Freedom delegates soon after the convention.

ocrats had observed the rules of the political game, courted and relied on northern liberals, and assumed that right and social justice would triumph. In practice, the liberals reneged on their promises, and justice had rather little to do with a Democratic convention. The Freedom Democratic party carried through its planned challenge to the seating of the regular Democratic congressional delegation, but this time the challengers expected to lose. Congress promptly seated the white-supremacy regulars. The experiences of the Freedom Democrats discredited the strategy of relying on liberals and counting on the goodwill of whites. Pat Watters and Reese Cleghorn have concluded that these developments marked the "turning point for the young radicals away from the hope of gaining their ends through the mainstream."[16]

After Mississippi Freedom Summer and the convention challenge, the SNCC staff engaged in a long period of reevaluation and soul-searching. In part the growing dissension within the organization was the result of internal problems. In Mississippi SNCC had recruited indigenous activists such as Hamer who were older than previous staffers and who in the main were poor and—at least in a formal sense—uneducated. Of more immediate significance, some two hundred northern volunteers elected to remain in Mississippi after the summer project, and eighty-five of them secured staff positions. Most of the northerners were from urban and middle-class backgrounds, and many were white. They lacked SNCC's traditional constraints and, according to their critics, "floated" from one project to another. The "floaters" were central to a lengthy debate over strategy.

James Forman, Cleveland Sellers, and Ruby Doris Robinson were leaders of the "hardliners." They wanted to take advantage of the publicity and prestige that SNCC had earned with Mississippi Freedom Summer to expand the organization's membership and influence. To do so, the hardliners insisted on centralized authority, staff discipline, and limitations on "individualism." The floaters, joined by some SNCC veterans including Robert Moses, formed the opposition to Forman's centralizing reforms. Despite

[16]Watters and Cleghorn, *Climbing Jacob's Ladder,* 289.

a great deal of debilitating controversy, the issue was never really resolved.[17]

The influx of white volunteers during Mississippi Freedom Summer and the expanded number of whites on the staff thereafter prompted growing concern about the role of whites in SNCC. Female staff members questioned the "women's role"— which usually included cooking, laundry, and cleaning—and called "for serious discussion of [the] question of women in [the] movement." Many of the summer volunteers had been white women, and the unprecedented social proximity of black men and white women at SNCC freedom houses had generated sexual tensions and sometimes conflict. During the seemingly endless debates, black staffers increasingly stressed the development of race consciousness as an approach to organizing black communities.[18]

The march from Selma to Montgomery illustrated SNCC's increasing alienation from the mainstream civil rights movement. SNCC staffers organized the Selma movement, and then, as in Albany three years earlier, King and SCLC arrived to take charge of the campaign. According to Cleveland Sellers, it was just another occasion when "SCLC would submit a list of demands to the local power structure, win minor concessions, proclaim a great moral victory and leave town." SNCC officially chose not to participate in the march, viewing it as a sham climax to events in Selma, although a number of members acting as individuals joined the campaign. As the staff of the SNCC freedom center in Chicago summarized the march, it was the "modern counterpart

[17] James Forman, *The Making of Black Revolutionaries: A Personal Account* (New York, 1972), 408–27; Cleveland Sellers, *The River of No Return: The Autobiography of a Black Militant and the Life and Death of SNCC* (New York, 1973), 130–41; Emily S. Stoper, "The Student Non-violent Co-ordinating Committee: The Growth of Radicalism in a Civil Rights Organization" (Ph.D. dissertation, Harvard University, 1968), 114–51.

[18] Waveland Retreat "Minutes," November 7, 1964, in Student Nonviolent Coordinating Committee Papers, 1959–1972, Series V, reel 11 (Microfilming Corporation of America); Alvin F. Poussaint, "The Stresses of the White Female Worker in the Civil Rights Movement" (Copy of paper delivered to American Psychiatric Association, May 13, 1966), in SCLC Papers, Box 45; Rothschild, *A Case of Black and White*, 127–49; Sara Evans, *Personal Politics: The Roots of Women's Liberation in the Civil Rights Movement and the New Left* (New York, 1979), esp. 69–87, 233–35.

of that historic opiate of the people in Roman times, the Circus, complete with Christian martyrs."[19]

The Watts riot of the summer of 1965 greatly accelerated the reorientation of SNCC and CORE from the southern countryside to the inner cities of the nation. CORE's James Farmer observed that none of the civil rights organizations "had any roots in the ghetto." To remedy that situation, SNCC and CORE staffers increasingly turned to black consciousness as a strategy for appealing to ghetto blacks. In January, 1966, Farmer retired as national director of CORE, and Floyd McKissick replaced him. McKissick closed CORE's southern regional office and moved the national headquarters to Harlem. At the organization's convention in 1966, the delegates endorsed a black-power strategy, rejected nonviolence, and resolved opposition to the war in Vietnam.[20]

SNCC moved along a parallel course. In 1965 SNCC's Julian Bond ran successfully for the Georgia legislature from a predominantly black district in Atlanta. In January, 1966, SNCC denounced United States involvement in Vietnam, and Bond endorsed the statement. Georgia legislators, who had been opposing national policies for more than a decade, suddenly decided that Bond's dissent from national policy precluded him from assuming a seat in the legislature. Bond's electoral victory encouraged SNCC staffers to begin political organizing campaigns in other cities, and his debarment from the legislature represented another example of the futility of working within the system.

To support Bond's claim to a legislative seat, a group of SNCC staff members organized the Atlanta Project, which quickly became a center of black-power propaganda. In May, 1966, a fateful staff meeting at Kingston Springs, Tennessee, elected Stokely Carmichael president of SNCC and chose Ruby Doris Robinson as executive secretary. Carmichael promptly made clear that in terms of SNCC policy liberalism was an "extension of paternalism" and

[19] Sellers, *The River of No Return*, 117; "Report of the Staff of the Chicago Freedom Center," May, 1965, in Student Nonviolent Coordinating Committee Papers, State Historical Society of Wisconsin.

[20] Farmer quoted in "Beware the Day They Change Their Minds," by Silberman, 262; Meier and Rudwick, *CORE*, 390–415.

integration was "irrelevant." In his judgment, "political and economic power is what black people have to have." Later in the month, the SNCC central committee issued a manifesto disdaining participation in a White House conference on civil rights and exhorting black people to seize control of their own institutions and to develop their own bases of power. The committee vowed to place greater emphasis on creating offices in northern cities and on organizing black communities by developing black consciousness.[21]

SNCC's black-power strategy addressed poorer blacks in the nation's cities, but it also had a more directly southern objective. SNCC aimed to break the moderate alliance between middle-class whites and middle-class blacks that dominated most southern states and particularly southern cities. The conflict between middle-class moderates and SNCC radicals was sharpest in Mississippi and Georgia.

In early 1965 the Mississippi NAACP withdrew from the Council of Federated Organizations and began a campaign to organize a moderate coalition. Rejecting both the white-supremacy Democratic regulars and the Freedom Democratic party radicals, the moderates formed the Mississippi Democratic Conference. It included Aaron Henry, who had wanted to accept a delegate-at-large seat at the Democratic convention in 1964; Charles Evers, a capable and opportunistic black politician who, according to his biographer, "wanted folks to look to the established black middle class" for leadership; numerous urban middle-class African Americans; such white moderates as Hodding Carter III, editor of the *Delta Democrat-Times;* and state AFL-CIO officials. Senator James O. Eastland and other members of the Mississippi congressional delegation quietly supported the conference as a means of protecting their congressional seniority.[22]

[21] "Prospectus for an Atlanta Project," "Atlanta Project Paper," both in Atlanta Project Papers, State Historical Society of Wisconsin; Carmichael quoted in New York *Times,* May 23, 1966; "Minutes of SNCC Central Committee," May 17, 1966–May 19, 1966, in SNCC Papers, Box 6, Martin Luther King, Jr., Center for Social Change.

[22] Aaron E. Henry Oral History Interview, September 12, 1970, in Johnson Library; Evers quoted in *Amazing Grace: With Charles Evers in Mississippi,* by Jason Berry (New York, 1973),

To middle-class African Americans, the emergence of indigenous black leaders was a particular threat. As Moses explained, "Jackson Negroes are embarrassed that Mrs. Hamer is representing them—she is too much a representative of the masses." The Freedom Democratic party's Edwin King commented, "The old Negro leadership class refused to work with the Freedom party." In his estimation, it was a case of a "displaced leadership class [seeking] to restore itself and take leadership from a new class of leaders." Joined by moderate—or at least realistic—whites and supported by northern liberals and the Johnson administration, the Mississippi Democratic Conference set out to replace the regular Democrats and to break the power of SNCC in the state.[23]

During Mississippi Freedom Summer, SNCC workers had organized not only the Freedom Democratic party but also the Freedom Labor Union, the Poor People's Corporation, farmers cooperatives, and other projects. Closely allied with SNCC was the Delta Ministry, sponsored by the National Council of Churches. To the Mississippi Democratic Conference's Hodding Carter III, the Delta Ministry represented the "whole SNCC bit: The hell with politics as winning elections. We're in for politics as forming a vision around which people can coalesce so that someday they'll bring about the kind of society we need." Hampered by internal dissension, the withdrawal of a growing number of organization veterans, and the shift in emphasis from the countryside to the cities, SNCC was unable to withstand the moderate counterattack. In the summer of 1965, SNCC once again brought in northern volunteers—some three hundred of them—but they were unable to restore the organization's flagging projects. The Mississippi Democratic Conference forces—now terming themselves Loyal Democrats—won control of federal patronage and poverty funds and in 1968 recognition at the Democratic national convention

34; John Dittmer, "The Politics of the Mississippi Movement, 1954–1964," in *The Civil Rights Movement in America*, ed. Charles W. Eagles (Jackson, Miss., 1986), 65–93.

[23] Moses quoted in "Staff Meeting Notes," June 9, 1964–June 11, 1964, in Zinn Papers, Box 2; King quoted in "The Politics of the Mississippi Movement," by Dittmer, 89–90. See also John R. Salter, Jr., *Jackson, Mississippi: An American Chronicle of Struggle and Schism* (Malabar, Fla., 1987).

as the state's Democratic party. Mississippi state government grad-ually joined the trend toward southern moderation.[24]

In early 1966 SNCC endeavored to disrupt the moderate coa-lition that dominated Atlanta. Emphasizing black consciousness in an effort to polarize Atlanta politics along racial lines, James Forman denounced Georgia's nine black legislators as Uncle Toms. "The established Negro leadership in Atlanta are all of the middle class," SNCC charged, adding that such people had little concern for the problems of poor blacks. The targeted black lead-ers vowed to thwart the SNCC campaign. "We do not intend," one of their number declared, "to let them come in and take over Atlanta." Unable to defeat the moderate coalition, frustrated SNCC staffers ultimately tried to further racial divisions by en-couraging a riot in the city. None of SNCC's efforts proved suc-cessful. As elsewhere, moderates remained ascendant.[25]

Black power entered the popular lexicon during the Meredith march in June, 1966. James Meredith, who in 1962 had deseg-regated the University of Mississippi, announced that he would undertake a "walk against fear" from Memphis to Jackson. Hardly had he crossed the Mississippi state line when a would-be assassin wounded him with a shotgun blast. Representatives of the leading civil rights organizations gathered in Memphis to lay plans for continuing the walk, but by mid-1966 the chasm between the NAACP and the Urban League on the right and SNCC and CORE on the left was too vast to be bridged. As a participant later related, SNCC staffers told "Roy Wilkins what people in our organization had been wanting to say for so long—that is, retire, to teach in a college and write a book about his earlier days." The NAACP and the Urban League withdrew; SNCC, CORE, and SCLC sponsored the march. As the marchers progressed from one Mississippi town to the next, Carmichael, McKissick, and others began to promote

[24]Hodding Carter Interview, April 1, 1974, in Southern Oral History Program, Bass-DeVries Southern Politics Series, 1947–1974, Southern Historical Collection, University of North Carolina at Chapel Hill; Delta Ministry Commission, "Confidential Working Pa-pers," May 6, 1966, in SCLC Papers, Box 43; Dittmer, "The Politics of the Mississippi Movement"; Bruce Hilton, *The Delta Ministry* (Toronto, 1969).

[25]Atlanta *Journal,* January 18, 1966, quoted; Carson, *In Struggle,* 224–26.

the slogan Black Power. "What do you want?" SNCC staffers would shout, and back from the local black crowds would come, "Black Power." Martin Luther King and his associates countered with Freedom Now. Both slogans won popular approval at the rallies on the march route, but journalists found Black Power to be the more novel and newsworthy. By the time the march ended, SNCC and CORE had become firmly identified with black-power rhetoric.[26]

Shortly afterward, Martin Luther King characterized black power as "a slogan, not a program." King's criticism was not entirely fair. SNCC and CORE staffers had been debating the policy implications of black consciousness for at least two years prior to the Meredith march. Nevertheless, there was a point to King's observation. SNCC members employed black-power rhetoric in Mississippi well before they attempted to explain the term's meaning. James Forman later regretted that SNCC, by popularizing a term rather than a strategy, permitted "opportunists to define the term in any manner they chose." King labeled the phrase a "cry of pain," but more so than most critics, he also recognized the constructive psychological, political, and economic aspects of black power. Its greatest failing, according to King, was its endorsement of separation and potential violence.[27]

While SNCC and CORE turned to black power, King and SCLC promoted voter registration, leadership training, and nonviolent direct action. During 1964 King became deeply and largely unsuccessfully involved in a long series of demonstrations in St. Augustine, Florida. "This is," King wrote, "the most lawless community in which we have ever worked." Despite the limited accomplishments of the St. Augustine campaign, King maintained his position as the recognized leader of nonviolent black protest. In late 1964 he traveled to Oslo to accept the Nobel Prize for Peace.[28]

[26] Carson, *In Struggle*, 207. Carson is quoting Stanley Wise.

[27] "Dr. King's Speech, Frogmore," November 14, 1966; Forman, *The Making of Black Revolutionaries*, 459.

[28] Martin Luther King, Jr., to Israel S. Dresner, June 12, 1964, in Martin Luther King, Jr., Papers, Box 8, Martin Luther King, Jr., Center for Social Change; David R. Colburn, *Racial Change and Community Crisis: St. Augustine, Florida, 1877–1980* (New York, 1985).

The culmination of King's national prestige and indeed of that of the civil rights movement followed the Selma demonstrations. SCLC moved into Selma in January, 1965, to support a campaign of nonviolent action that came to a head on Bloody Sunday, March 7, 1965. Although King was in Atlanta on that fateful Sunday, Hosea Williams of SCLC and John Lewis of SNCC led more than five hundred protestors across the Pettus Bridge. There Alabama state troopers under the command of Albert J. Lingo and a posse organized by sheriff James G. Clark brutally attacked the marchers. The assault, Pat Watters and Reese Cleghorn have written, produced "television's best showing of racism's brutishness in a fast few minutes of film footage."[29]

Later in the month, demonstrators trod the fifty-eight miles from Selma to Montgomery in behalf of the right to vote. From all over the nation, civil rights advocates flocked to Alabama to join the protest, and some Alabama whites, for the first time ever, joined the demonstrators. President Johnson federalized the Alabama National Guard and provided regular army units to protect the marchers. Standing on the steps of the Alabama State Capitol on March 25, 1965, Martin Luther King proclaimed, "I stand before you today with the conviction that segregation is on its deathbed, and the only thing uncertain about it is how costly the segregationists will make the funeral."[30]

Soon after the march, Stanley D. Levison, one of King's shrewdest advisers, evaluated the impact of the campaign. Selma, Levison concluded, "was bigger than Birmingham though it was smaller in scope because for the first time whites and Negroes from all over the nation physically joined the struggle in a pilgrimage to the deep South." The events in Selma and Montgomery, Levison wrote to King, "made you one of the most powerful figures in the country—a leader now not merely of Negroes, but of millions of whites." Levison continued, "The movement you lead is the single movement in the nation at this time which arouses the finer democratic instincts of the nation . . . , that presents itself as clean,

[29] Watters and Cleghorn, *Climbing Jacob's Ladder*, 57; David J. Garrow, *Protest at Selma: Martin Luther King, Jr., and the Voting Rights Act of 1965* (New Haven 1978); Charles E. Fager, *Selma, 1965* (New York, 1974).

[30] "Address by Dr. Martin Luther King, Jr.," March 25, 1965, in SCLC Papers, Box 27.

honest, idealistic and as an enemy to violence, selfishness and narrow-mindedness." [31]

The problem was that the "crisis of victory" and the subsequent urban rioting undermined King's position at the center of the civil rights movement. The NAACP and its Cold War liberal allies became relatively more conservative, SNCC and CORE became more radical, and the problems facing the civil rights movement became more intractable. "King found it more difficult, and finally impossible," August Meier and Elliott Rudwick have written, "to maintain the symbolic role he had once played so effectively—serving . . . as a bridge between the movement's radical and conservative wings." Increasingly, King came to view the restructuring of national society as the only tenable design for achieving social justice. [32]

At first, King tried to carry the southern nonviolent direct-action campaign to the North. During the summer of 1965, SCLC opened offices in Chicago, and in January, 1966, King arrived to take command. During the months that followed, King and his staff attempted to direct ghetto anger into nonviolent protest. In some ways, King's Chicago campaign was his finest hour; his ability to communicate with street-gang members, street people, and the poor and disinherited generally was impressive. The movement's demand for open housing, however, frightened the residents of white ethnic and working-class neighborhoods and evoked massive defiance. "I've never seen anything like it," King remarked after a particularly disruptive march in early August. "I've been in many demonstrations all across the South, but I can say that I have never seen—even in Mississippi and Alabama—mobs as hostile and hate-filled as I've seen in Chicago." In late August, 1966, King and his associates reached a largely meaningless agreement with city officials that allowed SCLC to retreat gracefully. The campaign in Chicago was basically a failure. [33]

---

[31] Stanley D. Levison to Martin Luther King, Jr., April 7, 1965, in King Papers, Box 14.

[32] Meier and Rudwick, CORE, 375; Meier, "On the Role of Martin Luther King," in Martin Luther King, Jr.: Civil Rights Leader, Theologian, Orator, ed. David J. Garrow (3 vols.; Brooklyn, 1989), 635–42.

[33] David J. Garrow, Bearing the Cross: Martin Luther King, Jr., and the Southern Christian Leadership Conference (New York, 1988); King quoted in Let the Trumpet Sound: The Life of Martin Luther King, Jr., by Stephen B. Oates (New York, 1982), 413.

The Meredith march interrupted King's effort in Chicago. The march further divided the civil rights movement, just as Chicago called into question the viability of the southern movement as a strategy for combating the intransigent institutional racism of northern cities. The great civil rights victories in the South, King concluded, produced "at best surface changes, they were not really substantive changes." They benefited "mainly the Negro middle class" and "did not cost the nation one penny." As the middle ground occupied by King grew dangerously narrow, he reminded his SCLC colleagues that they faced a "long, hard struggle."[34]

As exponents of black power shouted about the primacy of race, King placed increasing emphasis on class analysis. He talked more and more of redistributing wealth and power in the nation and of providing jobs and income for the dispossessed. The persistence of widespread poverty in an era of unparalleled affluence led King to question whether "something is wrong with the economic system of our nation" and "with capitalism" itself. As one scholar has written, "His solution, emerging more fully with each eruption of rioting, was to embrace the cause of the urban underclass, but as a radical critic of capitalism rather than a black nationalist." Like SNCC and CORE, King moved beyond a preoccupation with the moral dilemma of individual whites to confront issues of class, social structure, and economic institutions.[35]

Even while battling in the South for access to public accommodations and the vote, King had often called attention to the desperate economic plight of so many black Americans. In 1964 he began to talk of an economic bill of rights—a Marshall Plan or GI Bill for the disadvantaged of all races. In an interview published in early 1965, he argued, "If America can afford to underwrite its allies and ex-enemies, it can certainly afford—and has a much greater obligation as I see it—to do at least as well by its own no-less-needy countrymen." As conditions changed, King's analysis became more trenchant. Not only was it foolish to "talk about solving the economic problems of the Negro without talking about billions of dollars," he stated in 1966, but the situation

[34] "Dr. King's Speech, Frogmore," November 14, 1966.

[35] *Ibid.*; Robert Weisbrot, *Freedom Bound: A History of America's Civil Rights Movement* (New York, 1990), 267.

demanded a "restructuring of the very architecture of American society."[36]

At a staff retreat in late 1967, King and his associates formulated plans for a poor people's campaign. The project envisioned bringing legions of the poor to the nation's capital to participate in "mass civil disobedience." As King explained, the campaign would adapt nonviolence "to urban conditions and urban moods" and would "transmute the deep anger of the ghetto into a creative force." The purpose would be to force the federal government to deal with the problems of the nation's poor. Specifically, according to King, the campaign would demand either a public-employment program that would provide jobs for the needy or a guaranteed annual income, as well as federal assistance for the "demolition of slums and [their] rebuilding by the population that live in them." Additionally, the campaign would serve as a focus for community organizing in cities throughout the nation in a "massive move toward self-determination and the shaping of our own destinies." Its goals included the political mobilization of the ghettos and the retirement of "many of the white racists" in Congress. "To dislocate the functioning of a city without destroying it," King observed, "can be more effective than a riot." It would also be more morally acceptable than violence and more difficult for the government to quell by superior force. King's southern movement had become a national crusade.[37]

The obstacles to the success of the poor people's campaign were formidable. "The decade of 1955 to 1965, with its constructive elements, misled us," King acknowledged. "The short era of widespread goodwill evaporated rapidly." The movement could "not count on government goodwill," particularly in a campaign that called for national social justice rather than southern desegregation. White policy makers created discrimination and slums, and "they perpetuate unemployment and poverty." Therefore "unwilling authorities," King insisted, must be compelled "to yield

---

[36] "*Playboy* Interview," January, 1965, in *A Testament of Hope: The Essential Writings of Martin Luther King, Jr.*, ed. James Melvin Washington (San Francisco, 1986), 367; "Dr. King's Speech, Frogmore," November 14, 1966.

[37] King, "The State of the Movement," November 27, 1967.

to the mandates of justice." As King stated several days later when the SCLC made the poor people's campaign public, "The immediate responsibility for removing the injustices can be laid directly at the door of the federal government."[38]

With the poor people's campaign scheduled to begin in the spring of 1968, SCLC staffers set about recruiting a "first wave" of three thousand poor people to be trained as marshals. The "succeeding waves" of less trained and disciplined people would include African Americans, Native Americans, Puerto Ricans, Mexican Americans, and poor white people, as well as volunteers "from all walks of life" recruited through the resources of "people of goodwill, the churches, labor, liberals, intellectuals, [and] students." King affirmed that "we still believe in black and white together. . . . We are struggling for something now, that will really filter down to the lower depths of black deprivation, and poor people generally." As Myles Horton of the Highlander Folk School reported from Atlanta, the campaign had the "making of a bottom-up coalition."[39]

On April 4, 1968, Martin Luther King was assassinated in Memphis. The developments after King's death tended to confirm the criticisms often voiced by SNCC staffers: SCLC was too dependent on the leadership and prestige of a single individual. Ralph D. Abernathy, King's successor, was a competent aide but not Martin Luther King. The poor people's campaign died aborning. In May, 1968, participants erected Resurrection City in Washington, D.C., but thereafter the campaign floundered. King had envisioned Resurrection City as the base for massive demonstrations that would "dislocate the city's functioning if necessary." As events turned out, the campaign never proceeded much beyond the creation of a shantytown. Congress did enact a civil rights bill in 1968, an action taken more as a memorial to King than as a result of the

[38] *Ibid.;* "Statement by Dr. King," December 4, 1967, in SCLC Papers, Box 177.

[39] James R. McGraw, "An Interview with Andrew J. Young," *Christianity and Crisis,* January 22, 1968, p. 4; "Poor People's Campaign," in SCLC Papers, Box 177; Martin Luther King, Jr., "Showdown for Nonviolence," in *A Testament of Hope,* ed. James Melvin Washington, 66; Martin Luther King, Jr., "Pre-Washington Campaign" (Training speech, Miami), February 23, 1968, in SCLC Papers, Box 28; Myles Horton to Andrew J. Young, April 5, 1968, in SCLC Papers, Box 177.

poor people's campaign. In June, 1968, the federal government closed Resurrection City, and in the following month the campaign came to an end.[40]

Both SCLC's poor people's campaign and SNCC's black-power strategy failed to accomplish their broader objectives. The explanations were manifold. The massive urban rioting that rocked the nation during the sixties engendered a white backlash and an escalating concern for law and order. The first of the riots took place in Birmingham in 1963, but not until the great Watts riot of 1965 did the issue become a primary concern. Thereafter, ghetto riots became increasingly common, reaching their zenith in the summer of 1967 and in the period immediately following the death of Martin Luther King in the spring of 1968. King's death ignited what historian Robert Weisbrot has called the "most concentrated week of racial violence Americans had ever known." After 1968 ghetto rioting declined. Although there were significant upheavals in Atlanta, Augusta, Houston, Nashville, Tampa, and elsewhere in the South, the bulk of the rioting took place in the North and on the West Coast. One of the more violent disturbances occurred in Washington shortly before the arrival of the poor people's campaign. Federal officials and indeed huge numbers of Americans generally evidenced a growing concern for social order rather than reform.[41]

Against such a backdrop, the violent rhetoric of Stokely Carmichael and his successor, Hubert "Rap" Brown, and the provocative pronouncements of Black Panthers and members of other, mainly nonsouthern, radicals fueled white resentment and federal repression. "The media yielded to a monopoly of Stokely Carmichael, Floyd McKissick, H. Rap Brown, and burning cities," a critic observed. "The news delectated over every lugubrious pronouncement of the Black Power militants." In 1968 Congress en-

[40] Adam Fairclough, *To Redeem the Soul of America: The Southern Christian Leadership Conference and Martin Luther King, Jr.* (Athens, Ga., 1987), 357–91; Garrow, *Bearing the Cross,* 575–624; King quoted in "Washington, D.C., Poor People's Campaign" (Staff paper), January, 1968, in SCLC Papers, Box 49; Charles Fager, *Uncertain Resurrection: The Poor People's Washington Campaign* (Grand Rapids, 1969).

[41] Weisbrot, *Freedom Bound,* 270; *Report of the National Advisory Commission on Civil Disorders* (1968).

acted an antiriot provision that strengthened federal authority to prosecute black radicals.[42]

From the beginning, J. Edgar Hoover and the FBI equated "civil rights activism with un-American activity." In the wake of the march on Washington in 1963, historian Kenneth O'Reilly has written, they launched a "frontal assault on Dr. King and the movement he helped to lead." With the advent of black power, the campaign became a crusade. The FBI eavesdropped electronically on King and other civil rights leaders, planted informants and agents provocateurs in their ranks, fabricated evidence, news releases, and rumors to denigrate or disrupt the civil rights movement, pressed foundations and other agencies to deny financial contributions, and joined with local police in a general assault on radicals.[43]

The war in Vietnam poisoned the popular atmosphere and absorbed the funds that King had hoped would finance domestic reform. SNCC and CORE, already under harsh attack for Communist proclivities, adopted antiwar positions during 1966. The NAACP leadership supported federal policy, judging that it was impolitic to break with the Johnson administration and that the war was not relevant to civil rights. King and others in SCLC recognized that war, racism, reform, and nonviolence were inseparably bonded, but they muted their criticisms until King finally concluded that his conscience would no longer permit him to remain silent. During early 1967 he began to speak against American intervention, and on April 4 of that year he delivered his widely publicized address at New York City's Riverside Church. According to King, the Johnson administration's war in Vietnam was immoral, it beggared the poverty program and domestic reform, it cruelly manipulated the poor, and it made the United States government the "greatest purveyor of violence in the world today."[44]

---

[42] David L. Lewis, *King: A Critical Biography* (New York, 1970), 356.

[43] Kenneth O'Reilly, *Racial Matters: The FBI's Secret File on Black America, 1960–1972* (New York, 1989), 40, 126; David J. Garrow, *The FBI and Martin Luther King, Jr.* (New York, 1981).

[44] Carson, *In Struggle*, 105–62; Garrow, *Bearing the Cross*, 527–74; Martin Luther King, Jr., "A Time to Break Silence," in *A Testament of Hope*, ed. James Melvin Washington, 233.

King's Riverside speech, a White House aide informed President Johnson on the following day, demonstrated that he had "thrown in with the Commies." J. Edgar Hoover predictably detected sedition: "Based on King's activities and public utterances, it is clear that he is an instrument in the hands of subversive forces seeking to undermine our nation." White House staffers encouraged journalists to attack both King and Arkansas senator J. William Fulbright, the two most formidable opponents of the war. Most mainstream journalists needed no encouragement to criticize dissenters. Like many other southern moderates, Ralph W. McGill had little patience with King's defection, accusing the civil rights leader of stepping over a "line of demarcation between loyal, patriotic dissent *and* the advocacy of near-treasonable action." As black columnist Carl T. Rowan explained in the *Reader's Digest,* King's egotism, and possibly Communist influence, led him to his ill-considered and "tragic" meddling in foreign affairs. The Johnson administration worried not so much about King's being a Communist as—like Henry A. Wallace before him—his being manipulated by the Communists.[45]

King periodically pointed out that there were "as many Communists in the freedom movement as there are Eskimos in Florida," and he continued to criticize the war. According to King, Vietnam had "made the Great Society a myth and replaced it with the troubled and confused society." The antagonism between King and Johnson escalated. "We always had a kind of split attitude toward the federal government in SCLC," Andrew Young reminisced. "We . . . lost faith in President Johnson altogether." King and his associates became ever more hostile toward Lyndon Johnson, his war, and his reelection in 1968.[46]

[45] John P. Roche to Lyndon B. Johnson, April 5, 1967, in White House Central Files, Confidential File (Human Rights 2), Johnson Library; Hoover quoted in *Bearing the Cross,* by Garrow, 555; George Christian to Lyndon B. Johnson, April 8, 1967, in White House Central Files, Name File (King), Johnson Library; John P. Roche to Lyndon B. Johnson, September 1, 1967, in White House Central Files, Confidential File (Human Rights 2), Johnson Library; Richard Lentz, *Symbols, the News Magazines, and Martin Luther King* (Baton Rouge, 1990), 236–62; Bernice McGill and Ralph W. McGill to Martin Luther King, Jr., May 1, 1967, in King Papers, Box 15; Carl T. Rowan, "Martin Luther King's Tragic Decision," *Reader's Digest,* September, 1967, pp. 37–42.

[46] "*Playboy* Interview," 362; Martin Luther King, Jr., "The Domestic Impact of the War

Lyndon Baines Johnson was the first southern resident to be president of the United States in more than a century. During his years as congressman, Senate majority leader, and vice-president, Johnson had established a reputation as a masterly politician, but there was a clear duality in Johnson's approach to public issues. In domestic affairs, he was effective, flexible, and pragmatic. In foreign policy, he was dogmatic, insecure, and blindly ideological, as were his mostly Kennedy-appointed foreign policy advisers. Even in domestic matters, Johnson's forte was his ability to accomplish immediate legislative objectives and to deal with pressing problems. Rarely did he deviate from the mainstream values of the Cold War consensus or question the rectitude of national institutions.[47]

During the midsixties when civil rights idealism was at its apex, Johnson pushed through Congress an impressive array of reform measures. In addition to the Civil Rights Act, legislation enacted in 1964 included two major economic initiatives. To Johnson, "the basic Negro problem was an economic problem," and "the salvation for the South lay through economic progress for everybody." The two new laws, both originally proposed by Kennedy, were an economic stimulus act that cut taxes primarily on corporations and affluent individuals and an economic opportunity bill that launched a "war on poverty." The tax-reduction law was sufficiently regressive to lead some scholars to argue that the "Kennedy-Johnson tax cut" marked "the abandonment of the traditional liberal-labor program and the acceptance of the substantive proposals of old-fashioned conservatives." While the tax program offered benefits to the most affluent members of society, the

---

in America" (Speech in Chicago), November 11, 1967, in SCLC Papers, Box 28; Andrew Young Oral History Interview, June 18, 1970, pp. 2, 19, in Johnson Library; Garrow, *Bearing the Cross*, esp. 575, 604.

[47] Studies examining President Johnson from various perspectives include Robert Dallek's *Lone Star Rising: Lyndon Johnson and His Times, 1908–1960* (New York, 1991); Robert A. Caro's *The Years of Lyndon Johnson: The Path to Power* (New York, 1982) and *The Years of Lyndon Johnson: Means of Ascent* (New York, 1992); Ronnie Dugger's *The Politician: The Life and Times of Lyndon Johnson* (New York, 1982); Paul K. Conkin's *Big Daddy from the Pedernales: Lyndon B. Johnson* (Boston, 1986); and Eric F. Goldman's *The Tragedy of Lyndon Johnson* (New York, 1969).

poverty program attempted to improve the lot of the poorest members.[48]

The juxtaposition of the two programs meant that poverty had to be defined as a fixed rather than a relative condition. A poor family was not one that, for example, earned less than 50 percent of the average national family income, it was a family that subsisted on less than three thousand dollars a year. Such an approach precluded wealth redistribution. "Taken together," Allen J. Matusow has concluded, "the programs spawned by these two strategies did little to diminish inequality and therefore, by definition, failed measurably to reduce poverty." In President Johnson's Great Society, the mighty American economy would simply make the rich richer and the poor richer without anyone having to sacrifice anything.[49]

In 1965 the Johnson administration recorded another banner year of legislative accomplishments. Some of the programs, such as the Job Corps, Neighborhood Youth Corps, and Work Experience Program, aimed to make poor people more employable but predictably did not provide new jobs for graduates to fill. For practical reasons, such programs usually prepared participants for low-skill occupations; most "nineteen-year-old dropouts," as Matusow has noted, "lacked the educational background for advanced technical training."[50]

While providing no general jobs program, the war on poverty did employ poor people to aid other poor people, which was one of its most significant accomplishments. SNCC and CORE staffers,

[48] Johnson quoted in Burke Marshall Oral History Interview, October 28, 1968, p. 7, and in Harry McPherson Oral History Interview, December 5, 1968, p. 14, both in Johnson Library; Marvin E. Gettleman and David Mermelstein, eds., *The Great Society Reader: The Failure of American Liberalism* (New York, 1967), 48.

[49] Allen J. Matusow, *The Unraveling of America: A History of Liberalism in the 1960s* (New York, 1984), 220. Helpful among numerous works examining the Great Society are *The Great Society Reader*, ed. Gettleman and Mermelstein; James L. Sundquist's *On Fighting Poverty: Perspectives from Experience* (New York, 1969); Francis Fox Piven and Richard A. Cloward's *Regulating the Poor: The Functions of Public Welfare* (New York, 1971); Henry J. Aaron's *Politics and the Professors: The Great Society in Perspective* (Washington, D.C., 1978); David Zarefsky's *President Johnson's War on Poverty: Rhetoric and History* (New York, 1986); and Michael B. Katz's *The Undeserving Poor: From the War on Poverty to the War on Welfare* (New York, 1989).

[50] Matusow, *The Unraveling of America*, 105.

long accustomed to less than poverty wages, suddenly found themselves in demand at much higher pay as community organizers for government-sponsored projects. As Meier and Rudwick have written, "One of the first results of the initial anti-poverty programs was to siphon off much of the ablest leadership—particularly in the more militant organizations." Some CORE staffers held that "Johnson's War on Poverty killed CORE as much as anything." One of several reasons for the rapid decline of the civil rights movement in the South after the midsixties was the co-optation of activists in SNCC, CORE, and local groups that were often affiliated with SCLC.[51]

Relying heavily on the findings of academic investigators, federal officials usually defined the problems of the poor in psychological rather than material terms. The "subculture of poverty" helped to explain why indigent people did not escape their plight. The antipoverty program, William H. Chafe has observed, "involved an effort to change the *attitudes* of the poor, in Sargent Shriver's words, 'to move those in poverty from indifference to interest, ignorance to awareness, resignation to ambition, and an attitude of withdrawal to one of participation.' " To combat what was seen as the poor's unfortunate inclination toward fatalism and despair, the war on poverty included such programs as VISTA, Head Start, and Upward Bound.[52]

None of these programs had a substantial impact on the South. The various educational and training programs permitted some economically deprived individuals to take advantage of expanding regional prosperity. At the same time the South harbored 44 percent of the nation's poor people and received 20 percent of the antipoverty program's expenditures. Most funding went to the nation's major cities, which placed the South at a disadvantage. Often southern officials did not vigorously compete for federal dol-

[51] August Meier and Elliott Rudwick, "Negro Protest and Urban Unrest," *Social Science Quarterly,* IL (1968), 441; Meier and Rudwick, *CORE,* 364; Carson, *In Struggle,* esp. 65, 233.

[52] William H. Chafe, "The End of One Struggle, the Beginning of Another," in *The Civil Rights Movement in America,* ed. Eagles, 133; Economic Opportunity Act of 1964 (Copy), in Southern Regional Council Papers, Atlanta University Center; Granville J. Foster, "Southern Congressmen and Welfare Policy in the 1960s: A Case Study of Redistribution Politics" (Ph.D. dissertation, University of Southern California, 1972), 335–57; U.S. Department of Health, Education, and Welfare, *Low Income Life Styles* (1965).

lars designated for reform rather than development. In southern cities, moderate leaders normally managed to control community-action and related programs. When federal investigators examined the community-action agency in Atlanta, they concluded that it had "developed into a large, cumbersome bureaucracy whose major achievement to date appears to have been the attraction of federal money into the city." [53]

Similarly, the Appalachian Regional Commission, initiated by Kennedy and awarded congressional sanction in 1965, mainly served those already in power. Covering thirteen states stretching from Mississippi to New York, the commission in theory promoted regional development and combated regional poverty. In practice, the thirteen governors dominated it, and as Neal R. Peirce has pointed out, they "thought of the ARC as 'theirs,' a happy hunting ground in which they could logroll to their hearts' content in the bargaining for federal aid." Most federal funds went into road building on the grounds that modern highways would break down isolation, promote tourism, and encourage economic development. Only a minor portion of federal largess went to local community agencies for job training, education, and similar activities, and the federal government, according to critics, insisted on "channeling its assistance through the very forces, political and economic, which are considered responsible for the region's plight in the first place." Although highway contractors usually brought skilled workers in from the outside, the road-building program still provided a considerable number of local jobs.[54]

In Mississippi, Great Society programs sometimes became embroiled in the struggles between competing Democratic factions. The dominant regular Democrats demonstrated a noticeable reluctance to promote federally funded reform, while the moderates and militants fought for control of the projects that did exist. The Delta Ministry sponsored the Child Development Group of Mississippi, which was surely the nation's best-known Head Start

[53] Watters and Cleghorn, *Climbing Jacob's Ladder,* 305; Matusow, *The Unraveling of America,* pp. 285–86 quoted.

[54] Neal R. Peirce, *The Border States: People, Politics, and Power in the Five Border South States* (New York, 1975), 25; York (Pa.) *Gazette and Daily,* June 30, 1965, quoted; New York *Times,* June 22, 1970, November 29, 1970.

project. According to moderate critics, "these ministry profession-als" used the program to create community organizations de-signed to instigate "revolutionary change." Senator John H. Sten-nis and other regular Democrats joined the attack on the Child Development Group, and their criticisms prompted some north-ern liberals to come to the group's defense.[55]

In the midst of the controversy, striking plantation laborers and other dispossessed blacks seized a deactivated air force base out-side Greenville, Mississippi, in order to find shelter and to dram-atize the need for, well, an antipoverty program. The incident, which occurred in early 1966, embarrassed the Johnson admin-istration. Attorney General Nicholas Katzenbach explained to the president that "acute discontent" was being "exploited by Leftist elements of the civil rights movement" and that there was a "real possibility that Mississippi [would] be the Selma, Alabama of 1966." As things turned out, the affair had no lasting repercus-sions, although it did lead Robert Coles to remark, "No historian a few centuries hence will be able to say that this great nation turned inward on itself and worried selfishly about its own hungry people."[56]

Southern education benefited significantly from the Johnson administration's Aid to Education Act of 1965. Because the law allocated federal funds on the basis of the number of poor people in a school district, the region received a substantial share of the allotments. As with other Great Society programs, aid went to school districts, and local school officials normally used the funds in a traditional manner. Even if federal money did not go directly toward the education of poor people, it doubtless improved facil-ities and instruction in poor districts. The new funds also provided

[55] Nicholas Von Hoffman in Chicago *Daily News*, July 28, 1965; "Confidential Working Papers, Delta Ministry Commission," May 6, 1966, in SCLC Papers, Box 43; Polly Green-berg, *The Devil Has Slippery Shoes: A Biased Biography of the Child Development Group of Missis-sippi* (New York, 1969). In the Chicago *Daily News*, Von Hoffman cited the *Delta Democrat-Times* (Greenville, Miss.).

[56] Memorandum, attorney general to president, February 14, 1966, in White House Cen-tral Files (Human Rights 2/State 24), Johnson Library; Robert Coles, *Farewell to the South* (Boston, 1972), 62; James C. Cobb, "Somebody Done Nailed Us on the Cross: Federal Farm and Welfare Policy and the Civil Rights Movement in the Mississippi Delta," *Journal of American History*, LXXVII (1990), 912–36.

the federal government with greater leverage for enforcing school desegregation.

As elsewhere, lawyers, social workers, consultants, teachers, doctors and other medical professionals, construction contractors, and bankers profited from reform. Medicare and Medicaid, along with various transfer payments, helped to account for the fact that children gradually replaced old people as the South's most economically disadvantaged age group. Individual poor people were able to take advantage of government initiatives to improve their economic standing, but as a war on poverty, the program, Meier and Rudwick have noted, "increased the frustration and discontent of the slumdwellers by further escalating their expectations but failing to deliver anything substantial."[57]

While most antipoverty programs had limited measurable impact on southern society, the Great Society's civil rights legislation was of enormous consequence. Unlike the laws that were a part of the war on poverty, the civil rights acts raised no disturbing questions about wealth redistribution nor did they question national economic institutions and practices. As Martin Luther King had observed, they cost the nation very little in terms of financial resources, and they were directed toward the South, which augmented the support of northern liberals. The most encompassing of the civil rights measures was of course the 1964 Civil Rights Act. At least in regard to the South, it was clearly the most important domestic enactment of the post–World War II era.

In addition to opening public accommodations to black people, the act decreed equal economic opportunity. Despite the discrepancy between mandate and practice, the law for the most part eliminated the race wage—the practice of paying whites more for the same work—and opened the way for blacks to gain employment in occupations previously reserved for whites. The result was a substantial improvement in the economic status of black southerners. Since World War II black people had gained economically by moving to cities. Even the lowliest urban job paid more than sharecropping and domestic service. Yet, the black economic progress that resulted from urbanization during the first two de-

[57] Meier and Rudwick, *CORE*, 375.

cades after the war was to a considerable degree a statistical phe-nomenon; it also cost more to live in cities, and in any event such gains were overwhelmingly nonsouthern. The 1964 Civil Rights Act broadened opportunities in the South and permitted blacks to record real advances in income relative to whites. One careful study concluded, "Southern blacks experienced sharp relative wage gains over the decade 1965–1975, with virtual stagnation thereafter."[58]

The provisions of the act prohibited discrimination in federally assisted programs and protected equal employment opportunity. The purpose of both stipulations was to forbid the overt discrim-ination practiced in the South. Title VI of the law banned discrim-ination in any activity assisted by federal grants, loans, or contracts. Its goal, Hugh D. Graham has written, "was to use the power of the purse to stop, rather than subsidize, segregated programs in the South." Title VII created the Equal Employment Opportunity Commission to police businesses, labor unions, and the like and to ensure fair practices. Its stated purpose was the promotion of a color-blind marketplace. It specifically prohibited racial prefer-ences and quotas that might prove inconvenient if applied to non-southern economic practices.[59]

The equal economic opportunity section of the act made it unlawful "to discriminate against any individual because of his race, color, religion, sex, or national origin." The inclusion of the word *sex* was primarily the result of failed southern conservative legerdemain. Virginia Congressman Howard W. Smith, an arch-conservative even by southern congressional standards, intro-duced the "sex" amendment, and a coalition of southern Dem-ocrats and northern Republicans approved it. As Carl M. Brauer has concluded, Smith's motives seem to have been mixed. He feared passage of the bill without his amendment might result in protection for blacks and discrimination for white women. The

[58] John J. Donohue III and James Heckman, "Continuous Versus Episodic Change: The Impact of the Civil Rights Policy on the Economic Status of Blacks," *Journal of Economic Literature*, XXIX (1991), 1610.

[59] Hugh D. Graham, "The Origins of Affirmative Action: Civil Rights and the Regulatory State," *Annals*, DXXIII (September, 1992), 56; Hugh D. Graham, *The Civil Rights Era: Origins and Development of National Policy, 1960–1972* (New York, 1990), esp. 145–49.

amendment offered a method to attack the liberal-labor preference for social feminism that protected women in the workplace. Most of all, adding a gender provision to the bill afforded another reason to oppose it. When Congress adopted Smith's amendment, the Johnson administration and the Democratic leadership chose to accept it rather than to delay the bill's passage. The inclusion of the amendment in the 1964 Civil Rights Act was a milestone in the emergence of a women's movement that was ultimately to have profound repercussions in the South as elsewhere in the nation.[60]

Title VI, which related to federally assisted programs, transformed the debate over southern school desegregation. By 1964 token desegregation had spread through the moderate South, particularly in the cities, but the vast majority of black and white children attended segregated schools. In late 1964 the Office of Education announced that in order to continue receiving federal assistance, school districts would be required to submit acceptable desegregation plans. In early 1965 the Office of Education issued the first of a series of "guidelines" establishing minimum requirements for acceptable desegregation programs.

The guidelines made school desegregation an administrative matter. Bureaucrats in the Office of Education had the unenviable task of overseeing desegregation in the hundreds of school districts that spread across the South. Because the education section—Title IV of the Civil Rights Act—prohibited busing to achieve racial balance, the Office of Education directed its attention to the towns and small cities of the South, where residential patterns made desegregation without busing a feasible prospect. To enforce its guidelines, the Office of Education could halt the flow of funds to noncomplying districts, an option it exercised on numerous occasions, even though cutting off financial aid only punished students and teachers for the failings of white school administrators and boards of education. Despite such handicaps, the federal bureaucrats administered the guidelines with considerable competence.

[60] Public Law 88-352 (Copy), in Burke Marshall Papers, Kennedy Library; Carl M. Brauer, "Women Activists, Southern Conservatives, and the Prohibition of Sex Discrimination in Title VII of the 1964 Civil Rights Act," *Journal of Southern History*, IL (1983), 37–56.

The collapse of massive resistance left George C. Wallace's Alabama as the only state government that consistently attempted to combat guideline requirements. Elsewhere state governments largely left school-district officials to solve their own problems. Their solution was "freedom of choice." Local authorities assigned students to the schools they had attended in the past, which were normally segregated schools. All students had the freedom of choice to request transfer to another school. The result of such arrangements was to limit the extent of desegregation. Many youngsters preferred to remain in their own schools, and because whites were not apt to request transfer to black schools, the entire burden of desegregation fell on individual black families. Integrationists routinely condemned the Office of Education's tolerance of freedom of choice. Nevertheless, the relentless pressure of the federal bureaucracy steadily undermined segregation. For the first time, school desegregation expanded beyond token levels.[61]

The Civil Rights Act emboldened federal judges. After having steadily retreated from the school desegregation controversy for more than a decade, the federal courts evidenced increasing impatience with the Office of Education's modest progress and with the often manipulative freedom-of-choice plans. Federal judges, particularly those in the fifth judicial circuit, upheld and expanded the requirements of the guidelines. As circuit judge John Minor Wisdom proclaimed in an influential opinion, past injustices required that school authorities "take affirmative action to reorganize their schools into a unitary, nonracial system." In a second decision concerning the same case, the court of appeals decided that school officials had the "affirmative duty under the Fourteenth Amendment to bring about an integrated, unitary sys-

---

[61] Gary Orfield, *The Reconstruction of Southern Education: The Schools and the 1964 Civil Rights Act* (New York, 1969); George R. Metcalf, *From Little Rock to Boston: The History of School Desegregation* (Westport, Conn., 1983), 3–81. The Southern Regional Council closely monitored and reported on the guidelines and the performance of federal authorities. As the titles of its reports suggest, it was highly critical of the pace of school desegregation: *The Continuing Crisis: An Assessment of New Racial Tensions in the South* (1966); *School Desegregation: The Slow Undoing* (1966); *Lawlessness and Disorder: Fourteen Years of Failure in Southern School Desegregation* (1968); *The Federal Retreat in School Desegregation* (1969); and *The South and Her Children: School Desegregation, 1970–1971* (1971).

tem in which there are no Negro schools and no white schools—just schools." [62]

The Supreme Court endorsed the lower court's logic in *Green v. County School Board of New Kent County,* decided in 1968. Rejecting "all deliberate speed," the Supreme Court ruled, "The burden on a school board today is to come forward with a plan that promises realistically to work and promises realistically to work *now.*" School authorities, according to the Court, had the "affirmative duty to take whatever steps might be necessary to convert to a unitary system in which racial discrimination would be eliminated root and branch." With both the federal bureaucracy and the federal judiciary demanding integration, local white resistance gradually declined.[63]

During the late 1960s and early 1970s, the rural and small-city South made the transition to desegregated public-school systems. White violence punctuated social change, but ultimately whites more or less accepted integration. At the beginning of the 1960s a decisive majority of southern whites called themselves strict segregationists. By 1972 only a quarter did—which was approximately the same proportion that approved of desegregation. About half the white respondents favored "something in-between." In 1972 the federal government announced that 44 percent of black students in the states of the former Confederacy attended majority-white schools, which was a substantially higher percentage than that in the border states and far higher than in the North and West.[64]

The 1964 Civil Rights Act brought the civil rights movement under federal management. The existence of such agencies as the Equal Employment Opportunity Commission and the Office of Federal Contract Compliance encouraged aggrieved individuals to press their claims before administrative agencies or courts

[62] *United States* v. *Jefferson County Board of Education,* 372 F.2d.847 (1966), 380 F.2d.389 (1967).

[63] *Green* v. *County School Board of New Kent County, Virginia,* 391 U.S. 437–39 (1968).

[64] Earl Black and Merle Black, *Politics and Society in the South* (Cambridge, Mass., 1987), 195–212; U.S. Department of Health, Education, and Welfare, "News Release," January 13, 1972, in Southern Regional Council Papers.

rather than taking to the streets, and to rely on the advice of lawyers rather than civil rights staffers. The antipoverty program brought militants into the fold by employing them to promote reform under government direction. The structure of the war on poverty widened the cleavages between grass-roots organizations by putting them in competition for federal grants.

Similarly, the 1965 Voting Rights Act induced a shift from protest to politics which the federal government had consistently favored. The law assigned to the federal government substantial authority over voter registration in all or a major part of six southern states. Caught between black militancy and white backlash, the Johnson administration counted on black voting to divert civil rights activities onto familiar political terrain. "Surely," White House aide Harry C. McPherson commented, "the next generation of Negro leadership does not have to be dominated by Stokely Carmichael and Willie Ricks." [65]

SNCC and CORE failed to afflict the next generation, at least in terms of strategy. Both movements declined rapidly. Unable to rally the ghetto masses behind a black-power program, officials in both organizations increasingly turned to fiery public rhetoric. The SNCC leadership was especially prone to self-destructive harangues. Carmichael and Ricks called for retaliatory violence and guerrilla warfare, and condemned whites and in particular President Johnson, whom Ricks labeled a "white honky cracker, an outlaw from Texas." Such pronouncements lent a surface credibility to black psychiatrist Alvin F. Poussaint's analysis of black power as a "sense of psychological emancipation from racism through self-assertion and a release of aggressive angry feelings." SNCC held its last staff meeting in June, 1967, and thereafter faded into oblivion. CORE continued nominally to exist but no longer as a significant organization.[66]

[65] Harry C. McPherson to Nicholas Katzenbach, September 20, 1966, in McPherson Files, Johnson Library; Voting Rights Act of 1965, in *Political Participation,* by United States Commission on Civil Rights (1968), 202–11.

[66] Carson, *In Struggle,* 229–86, p. 256 Ricks quoted; Alvin F. Poussaint, "A Negro Psychiatrist Explains the Negro Psyche," *New York Times Magazine,* August 20, 1967, p. 76; Julius Lester, *Look Out, Whitey: Black Power's Gon' Get Your Mama* (New York, 1968). On the decline

The collapse of SNCC and CORE and the death of Martin Luther King ended efforts to organize the residents of ghettos, to rebuild slum areas, and to apply social solutions to social problems. Black power, often with a "black is beautiful" emphasis, came to be associated with affluent African Americans. As Rap Brown commented, black consciousness had been "diluted and prostituted to the point where even the most conservative negroes are now for Black Power." Shorn of its radicalism and its mass orientation, black consciousness exercised a formidable influence on economically prosperous metropolitan black people.[67]

Black churchmen were particularly prompt to appropriate the concept of black power. Little more than a month after the slogan gained currency in Mississippi, the hastily formed National Conference of Black Churchmen issued a Black Power Statement. Black ministers in predominantly white denominations were the driving force behind religious militancy. Long ignored and disparaged, minority preachers occupied a marginal position in white-majority denominations. Through much of the 1950s and 1960s and into the 1970s, members of the United Methodist Church had engaged in a divisive battle to assimilate the segregated black central jurisdiction into the church's regular white organizational structure. Southern segregationists created various assemblies beginning with the Association of Methodist Ministers and Laymen to combat the integrationist scheme, and similar though less antagonistic conflicts occurred within other Protestant denominations. Black power provided a philosophical position for black churchmen to fight back. By late 1968 black caucuses existed in the major Protestant churches, the Catholic church, and the National Council of Churches.[68]

In its more extreme form, black theology divined, in Clifton F. Brown's words, "a black messiah, the concept of a black nation as

of the civil rights movement, see John Herbers, *The Lost Priority: What Happened to the Civil Rights Movement in America?* (New York, 1970).

[67] Brown quoted in *In Struggle,* by Carson, 76.

[68] "Black Power Statement," New York *Times,* July 31, 1966; James H. Cone, *For My People: Black Theology and the Black Church* (Maryknoll, N.Y., 1984); Clifton F. Brown, "Black Religion, 1968," in *The Black Church in America,* ed. Hart M. Nelsen, Raytha L. Yokley, and Anne K. Nelsen (New York, 1971), 17–28; Joseph C. Hough, *Black Power and White Protestants: A Christian Response to the New Negro Pluralism* (New York, 1968).

a chosen people and the recapture of the revolutionary imperative in Christianity." In its more moderate form, black theology
was an assertion of cultural diversity and an effort to theorize from
within the African-American experience rather than the white Eu-
ropean or white North American tradition. Although not without
influence, it failed to convert the black church. The major black
denominations endeavored to ignore black-power religious protest, as did Martin Luther King and most of the established black
ministry.[69]

Isolated within predominantly white denominations, the exponents of black theology focused on awakening the guilt and
exploiting the moral dilemma of white church people. "We spent
entirely too much of our time writing protest documents to
whites," James H. Cone has reminisced, and relied "too much
upon moral suasion and too little upon the tools of social analysis." Black theology remained a distinctly minority movement
championed by black ministers in predominantly white denominations and associated with the higher status blacks who were
likely to be members of the same denominations.[70]

Other black-power initiatives produced similar results. Nationally prominent African Americans held black-power conferences
in New Jersey in 1967 and in Philadelphia in 1968. The first conference was split between those who associated black power with
black capitalism and those who called for radical alteration of
American capitalism. Moderates dominated the second conference and identified black power with "ownership of apartments,
ownership of homes, ownership of businesses, as well as equitable
treatment for all people." Conference participants called upon
African Americans to "buy black" and emphasized the importance
of black economic development and the role of businessmen as
the prime agents for achieving black power. Floyd McKissick and
Roy Innis, successive national directors of CORE, became outspoken champions of black capitalism.[71]

[69] Brown, "Black Religion, 1968"; Gayraud S. Wilmore, *Black Religion and Black Radicalism: An Interpretation of the Religious History of the Afro-American People* (2nd ed.; Maryknoll,
N.Y., 1983); James H. Cone, *Black Theology and Black Power* (New York, 1969).
[70] Cone, *For My People*, 88, 113.
[71] Robert L. Allen, *Black Awakening in Capitalist America: An Analytic History* (New York,

Even while conducting its ambiguous war on poverty, the Johnson administration continued to promote the interests of middle-class blacks and those who aspired to be middle-class. The open-housing provisions of the 1968 Civil Rights Act, the last of such measures during the civil rights era, maintained established federal policy by easing the escape of affluent African Americans from ghettos. The federal courts strengthened the trend by endorsing "affirmative action," a compensatory approach to fair economic practices federal agency officials formulated in reaction to urban rioting and the failure of the Great Society. Affirmative action mainly benefited educated African Americans who sought entry into graduate and professional schools, employment and promotion in the public and corporate sectors, and contracts for minority business firms.[72]

While campaigning for the presidency in 1968, Richard M. Nixon endorsed black power. Denouncing Great Society "welfare" programs, Nixon called for government policies "oriented towards more black ownership, black pride, black jobs, black opportunity, and yes, black power." Nixon's preference for dismantling parts of the Great Society and for privatizing federal aid to minorities was a program for black bourgeois progress and represented little break with the goals of federal authorities under Democratic administrations.[73]

Black nationalists and integrationists remained divided, although the vigor of the debate declined along with the civil rights movement itself. The NAACP reclaimed its position at the forefront of civil rights activities and continued to promote integration. Black nationalists maintained that the real issue was not "exposure to Whites in and of itself" but was a question of who controlled a school or other institution and "in whose best interest it is controlled." The National Urban League adopted a compromise position by advocating desegregation and black power through black capitalism. Integrationists charged that black na-

---

1969), 138; Nathan Wright, Jr., *Black Power and Urban Unrest: Creative Possibilities* (New York, 1967); Earl Ofari, *The Myth of Black Capitalism* (New York, 1970); Harold Cruse, *Rebellion or Revolution?* (New York, 1968), 193–258.

[72] Graham, *The Civil Rights Era,* 186–277, 377–92.

[73] Nixon quoted in New York *Times,* April 26, 1968.

tionalists were afraid to compete in an open market with whites, while nationalists responded that integrationists were too impressed with white culture and too inclined toward self-hatred.[74]

Black theology and black capitalism reached their peak in the late sixties and early seventies. They served a significant function as the vehicles by which leadership of civil rights activities was transferred from the South back to the North. Southern black protest did accomplish the original aims of the sit-in movement. As the civil rights campaign progressed, however, southern black participants expanded their demands and extended them outside the South. Doug McAdam has calculated that between 1961 and 1965, more than seven of every ten "movement initiated" protests took place in the South. Between 1966 and 1970 two-thirds of such protests occurred outside the region. Growing northern protest and urban rioting combined with what became a northern-dominated black-power movement to shift leadership northward.[75]

The imagery and trappings of black power had a profound psychological impact on African Americans. As Manning Marable has noted, ordinary black people in the South as elsewhere in the nation "were addressing each other as 'brother' when they passed in the streets; 'soul food' restaurants became a matter of community pride; 'black history' the all-consuming topic, Malcolm X the authoritative source." Marable also pointed out, "Black Power quickly became the cornerstone of conservative forces." "Buy black" appealed to African-American business people servicing black customers, but increasingly black consciousness became a psychological lenitive that reinforced the self-esteem of affluent African Americans who earned their livelihood as "outsiders" in a predominantly white economic world. Multiculturalism gained currency among black and white elites, and black consciousness became sufficiently conservative and elitist to be accepted as

[74] Congress of Racial Equality, "A Proposal for Community School Districts," in *The Great School Bus Controversy*, ed. Nicholaus Mills (New York, 1973), 312; Charles V. Hamilton, "The Nationalist vs. the Integrationist," *ibid.*, 297–310; Guichard Parris and Lester Brooks, *Blacks in the City: A History of the National Urban League* (Boston, 1971), 463–71.

[75] Doug McAdam, *Political Process and the Development of Black Insurgency, 1930–1970* (Chicago, 1982), 190.

"politically correct" by faculty and administrators at the nation's universities.[76]

Critics have charged that the Second Reconstruction represented progress without change, an effort to "bourgeoisify" enough black people to legitimate the American system. Such criticism, while not entirely inaccurate as an evaluation of the results of the era, was not justified. The civil rights movement recorded substantial accomplishments, and the most important were in the South. There the movement restructured regional social practices. It expanded the commodification of labor and created a more dynamic society. It broadened economic opportunities for substantial numbers of black people. Because the South had essentially accomplished economic modernization before the civil rights movement achieved success, the long-term gains for ordinary black people were limited. Desegregation most benefited those African Americans who were sufficiently educated, ambitious, and psychologically prepared to enter the mainstream white economy. Such changes affected huge numbers of white people and produced political conflict sufficiently intense to challenge the domination of the moderate Democrats.[77]

[76] Manning Marable, *Race, Reform, and Rebellion: The Second Reconstruction in Black America, 1945–1982* (Jackson, Miss., 1984), 110, 106; Lois Benjamin, *The Black Elite: Facing the Color Line in the Twilight of the Twentieth Century* (Chicago, 1991).

[77] Alan D. Freeman, "Antidiscrimination Law: A Critical Review," in *The Politics of Law: A Progressive Critique*, ed. David Kairys (New York, 1982), 110.

CHAPTER XI

POLITICS, PROTEST, AND PALLIATIVE

T HE direct-action crusade, the 1964 Civil Rights Act, and the federal guidelines brought home to ordinary white southerners the extent of the social convulsion taking place in the region. Urban rioting, rising crime rates, and the spread of the movement outside the South fed a white backlash in the North. While southern voters struggled to come to terms with their changed social environment, both Republican conservatives and regional segregationists looked to the southern bloc of electoral-college votes as the foundation for a national movement championing social and cultural conservatism. They insisted that the American political-party system had arrived at an impasse, and they demanded a realignment of national politics.

To Governor George C. Wallace of Alabama, the national parties were Tweedledee and Tweedledum: "There's not ten cents' worth of difference between them." To Republican political strategist F. Clifton White, the major parties were "at best two factions, erroneously labeled Republican and Democrat, going through the motions of fighting a rubber-stamp election every four years for control of an all-powerful government." Upper-middle-class northern liberals, safely ensconced in their lily-white and largely crime-free suburbs, allegedly dominated both parties and endeavored to impose their cultural values on the rest of America. "They," Wallace declaimed, "have looked down their noses at the average man on the street too long." Republican Patrick J. Buchanan explained that "socially and culturally" the basic division was between "traditional America" and the "liberal elite." Republican conservatives and Wallaceites set out to rally the common white folk against an insulated and unrepresentative elite centered in New York and Washington. Their goals, however, were quite different from those of the popular-front liberals who had attempted a similar strategy two decades before.[1]

Even while running for governor in 1962, Wallace made no secret of his national ambitions. The South, Wallace stated, "can become the strongest and most effective minority bloc in the nation." He vowed to "fight the federals in the arena of an increasingly sympathetic national public opinion." In his inaugural address, he appealed to the white South's "sons and daughters who have moved north and west throughout the nation." During 1963 and into 1964 Wallace promoted an independent-elector strategy designed to deny either major party a majority in the electoral college, much as J. Strom Thurmond and the Dixiecrats had attempted to do in 1948. Wallace also undertook speaking tours to carry his message to the North and West.[2]

As governor, Wallace doggedly fought the "federals," whether in Birmingham, Selma, or Tuscaloosa. At his inauguration, he had exhorted, "Segregation now, segregation tomorrow, segregation forever." When reproached for violating the law, he replied that if Martin Luther King, Jr., had a "right to disobey an unjust law," so too did the governor of Alabama. In any event, Wallace added, "Nobody knows what the law is anymore with the present court system we have got, because they write the law as they go along."

[1] Wallace quoted in "George Wallace Tells His Plans: Interview with a Candidate," *U.S. News and World Report,* June 17, 1968, p. 59, and in *George C. Wallace and the Politics of Powerlessness: The Wallace Campaigns for the Presidency, 1964–1976,* by Jody Carlson (New Brunswick, N.J., 1981), 6; F. Clifton White, *Suite 3505: The Story of the Draft Goldwater Movement* (New Rochelle, N.Y., 1967), 40; Patrick J. Buchanan, *The New Majority: President Nixon at Mid-Passage* (N.p., 1973), 57.

[2] Wallace quoted in *The Wallace Story,* by Bill Jones (Northport, Ala., 1966), 41, 58; "Inaugural Address," Birmingham *News,* January 14, 1963. Helpful works on Wallace include Carlson's *George C. Wallace and the Politics of Powerlessness;* Jones, *The Wallace Story;* Wayne Greenhaw's *Watch Out for George Wallace* (Englewood Cliffs, N.J., 1976); James Lewis Canfield's *A Case of Third Party Activism: The George Wallace Campaign Worker and the American Independent Party* (Latham, Md., 1984); John J. Synon's *George Wallace: Profile of a Presidential Candidate* (Kilmarnock, Va., 1968); Harold G. Grasmick's "Social Change and the Wallace Movement in the South" (Ph.D. dissertation, University of North Carolina, 1973); Forrest H. Armstrong's "George C. Wallace: Insurgent on the Right" (Ph.D. dissertation, University of Michigan, 1970); Philip Crass's *The Wallace Factor* (New York, 1976); and Marshall Frady's *Wallace* (New York, 1968).

As an aide remarked, the "social revolution" that "swept the nation under the guise of civil rights" was "ready-made" for Wallace.[3]

In the spring of 1964 Wallace entered the Democratic presidential primaries in three states north of the Potomac. Running against stand-ins for President Johnson, Wallace garnered 34 percent of the vote in Wisconsin, 30 percent in Indiana, and 43 percent in Maryland. Because politicians and journalists associated racism with the white South and dismissed the Alabamian's poorly organized and underfinanced campaign as quixotic, his showing at the voting booths had a stunning impact. The Indianapolis *Star* editorialized, "If any responsible official had suggested six months ago that a segregationist from the Deep South could poll such a vote in Indiana, he would have been hooted into silence and shuffled quietly into obscurity." The splash Wallace made in presidential politics established him as the nation's leading proponent of social reaction. After the election in Maryland, he abandoned the presidential primaries to concentrate on his third-party initiative.[4]

The Republican nomination of Senator Barry M. Goldwater of Arizona disrupted Wallace's plans. Although the differences between Wallace and Goldwater were considerably greater than their similarities, both championed state rights and both opposed the 1964 Civil Rights Act. Many of Wallace's political allies and financial backers diverted their support to the Republican nominee. Wallace's aides concluded that a third-party campaign would simply produce a three-way race in the South that would divide the state-rights vote and would likely result in pluralities for Lyndon B. Johnson. In July, 1964, Wallace bowed to the inevitable and withdrew from the presidential race. He did not formally endorse Goldwater.[5]

The draft-Goldwater movement in the Republican party produced important consequences in the South as elsewhere. Po-

[3] "Inaugural Address"; Transcript of Conversation Between Attorney General Robert F. Kennedy and Governor Wallace, Montgomery, April 25, 1963, in Robert F. Kennedy Papers, Attorney General's Personal Correspondence, John F. Kennedy Library, Boston; Jones, *The Wallace Story*, 33.

[4] Indianapolis *Star* quoted in *The Wallace Factor*, by Crass, 81.

[5] Reese Cleghorn, "Aftermath in Alabama," *Reporter*, December 3, 1964, pp. 34–35; Glen Jeansonne, *Leander Perez, Boss of the Delta* (Baton Rouge, 1977), 330–32; Jones, *The Wallace Story*, 323–38; Robert G. Sherrill, "Wallace and the Future of Dixie," *Nation*, ICC (1964), 266–72.

litical scientists Earl Black and Merle Black have observed that Goldwater's nomination "represented a shift of power from northeastern Republicans—progressives or moderates or liberals, as they chose to refer to themselves—to the Republicans of the South and West—conservatives as they thought of themselves." Southern Republicans helped engineer Goldwater's nomination, and at the Republican national convention they overwhelmingly supported the Arizonan. In the 1964 general election, five of the six states that gave their electoral votes to the Republican candidate were southern.[6]

For years national Republican strategists had been conscious of what the Republican National Committee described as the "strong dependence on the South of the Democrats for their majorities." During the 1950s the Republicans had established a relatively well financed Operation Dixie to build a viable partisan alternative in the region, but the results were limited. The same rural, small-town, and working-class white folk who voted for state and local candidates who vowed to defy national Democratic policies also voted for the candidates of the national Democratic party. So too did a growing number of black voters. As members of the Republican National Committee lamented, the Democrats won in the South by securing the "support of an unnatural coalition—Negroes demanding change in the pattern of race relations and those most strongly opposed to departure from the pattern." To break that coalition was a central aim of the movement to draft Goldwater.[7]

[6] Earl Black and Merle Black, *The Vital South: How Presidents Are Elected* (Cambridge, Mass., 1992), 127; Jerald Ter Horst, "The Grenier Plan for the G.O.P.," *Reporter,* October 8, 1964, pp. 24–26; Bernard Cosman, *The Case of the Goldwater Delegates* (University, Ala., 1966); Harry S. Dent, *The Prodigal South Returns to Power* (New York, 1978), 59–70.

[7] Republican National Committee, *The 1962 Election: A Summary Report with Supporting Tables* (Washington, D.C., 1963), 7, 38. Works helpful on southern Republicanism include V. O. Key, Jr.'s *Southern Politics in State and Nation* (New York, 1949), 277–97; Alexander Heard's *A Two-Party South?* (Chapel Hill, N.C., 1952); Bernard Cosman's *Five States for Goldwater: Continuity and Change in Southern Presidential Voting Patterns* (University, Ala., 1966); Wayne Greenhaw's *Elephants in the Cottonfields: Ronald Reagan and the New Republican South* (New York, 1982); Alexander P. Lamis' *The Two-Party South* (New York, 1984); *Election 1964: A Ripon Society Report* (Cambridge, Mass., 1965); John C. Topping, Jr., John R. Lazarek, and William H. Linder's *Southern Republicanism and the New South* (Cambridge, Mass., 1966); Michael S. Lottman's *The GOP and the South* (Cambridge, Mass., 1970); *The 1968*

By uniting the white common folk with white suburbanites, Goldwater's backers sought to turn the South into the base for a Republican majority. The first pamphlet composed by the draft-Goldwater committee stated, "Barry Goldwater will take all 128 electoral votes of the eleven Southern States! . . . This is the key to Republican success!" Political scientist Bernard Cosman has observed that "Senator Goldwater became the first Republican presidential candidate to make victory in the South a major factor in his strategy for victory in the nation." At an Atlanta press conference in 1961, Goldwater summarized the Republican approach: "We're not going to get the Negro vote as a bloc in 1964 or 1966, so we ought to go hunting where the ducks are." The ducks were white and southern, and when combined with votes from the West and elsewhere, they represented a potential national electoral majority.[8]

In the South, Republicans possessed little in the way of ideological unity. The region's mountain Republicanism rested more heavily on a historical legacy dating back to the Civil War and to Reconstruction than on political philosophy. Party leaders, especially the lawyers among them, not infrequently lusted after federal patronage, but mountain Republicanism was essentially provincial, preoccupied with elections to local offices and with local policies and patronage. Much of the Republican county-seat leadership was conservative and often cooperated with the ruling Democrats. Only in the Upper South was the party a factor in state politics, and especially in Kentucky and Virginia, Republicans often advocated reformist policies.

General Dwight D. Eisenhower's campaign in 1952 brought to southern Republicanism a wave of suburban conservatives. Most

---

Elections: A Summary Report with Supporting Tables, by Republican National Committee (Washington, D.C., 1969); Donald S. Strong's *Issue Voting and Party Realignment* (University, Ala., 1977); Donald T. Wolfe's "Southern Strategy: Race, Religion, and Republican Presidential Politics, 1964 and 1968" (Ph.D. dissertation, Johns Hopkins University, 1974); O. Douglas Weeks's "The South in National Politics," *Journal of Politics*, XXVI (1964), 221–40; Donald S. Strong's "Further Reflections on Southern Politics," *Journal of Politics*, XXXIII (1971), 239–56; Black and Black's *The Vital South;* and Dent's *The Prodigal South Returns to Power.*

[8] Robert D. Novak, *The Agony of the G.O.P., 1964* (New York, 1965), 136; Cosman, *Five States for Goldwater*, 40; Goldwater quoted in *Election 1964*, 17; White, *Suite 3505*, 97–98, 135, 174–75; Ralph de Toledano, *The Winning Side: The Case for Goldwater Republicanism* (New York, 1963), esp. 100–116.

remained Democrats in state and local politics, but those who converted normally aligned themselves with the national party. Reacting to the perceived corruption and backwardness of the southern Democrats, Eisenhower Republicans often fitted A. J. Liebling's description: "Like the Parsees in India and the Mozabites in Algeria, they have won respect as clean, sober and industrious people." From their ranks came Eisenhower's highly acclaimed appointments to the federal judiciary.[9]

The Goldwater campaign brought into the party a host of arch-conservatives who both strengthened and further divided southern Republicanism. Having switched to the Republicans out of disaffection from the philosophical orientation of the national Democratic party, the newcomers, a Republican party official in Alabama observed, often made a fetish of "ideological purity." A Tennessee Republican explained that southern Republicans "usually are converted to Republicanism . . . by national issues, so they run for tax assessor, arguing about the gold standard, and for the legislature, talking about the unbalanced federal budget, when most people care more about the sewers, jobs, better schools, health care of the children down the block."[10]

Unlike the mountain Republicans, Goldwater Republicans were often personally affluent, and they frequently treasured free-market economics above all else. In Tennessee the new Republican leadership centered in Memphis, Nashville, and Chattanooga reached what one study described as a "consensus on the necessity to reconstitute the Republican party as a lily-white, solidly conservative, business-oriented organization prepared to challenge the Democrats for office at all levels." The Republican party in Texas was, according to another study, based on "middle- and upper-class elements in the urban communities, spearheaded by conservative or sometimes reactionary business and professional groups," that had "virtually written off that one-fourth of the electorate composed of Negroes and Latin Americans." Not wholly surprisingly, the Republican party won more than grudging respect from conservative Democrats. As a Democratic party official

[9] A. J. Liebling, *The Earl of Louisiana* (New York, 1961), 48.
[10] Lamis, *The Two-Party South*, 84, 177. Quoted are Bill Harris, chairman of the Republican party in Alabama, and Governor Lamar Alexander of Tennessee.

in Mississippi acknowledged, "If it weren't for the Democratic congressional delegation from Mississippi, I'd rather be a Republican." [11]

Prior to the Goldwater campaign, southern Republicans had managed modest advances. Most prominent Republicans were moderately conservative, cultivating either an independent image that seemed to appeal to their upland constituents or an ardor for economic growth that differed little from suburban Democrats. Serious Republican contenders appeared only on the southern fringe—in the Upper South, in western and metropolitan Texas, and in southern Florida.

Republicanism was most successful in Kentucky. In 1956 Kentucky voters elected Republican Thruston B. Morton to the Senate, and in 1960 it awarded a full Senate term to John Sherman Cooper, who had three times been chosen to fill unexpired terms. Republicans in North Carolina made their first serious postwar effort to compete for the governorship by running Robert L. Gavin in 1960. Gavin won 45 percent of the ballots and thereby gave Republicanism credibility in the state's politics. In 1962 voters in Oklahoma elected Henry Bellmon the state's first Republican governor. These campaigns, along with occasional congressional victories, encouraged Republican strategists but left the South still a Democratic enclave.[12]

More representative of emerging trends in southern Republicanism was Texan John G. Tower's election to the Senate. In 1960 Lyndon Johnson had taken the precaution of running for his Senate seat at the same time he was seeking the vice-presidency as John F. Kennedy's running mate. In the senatorial election, Tower won more than 40 percent of the popular vote. After Johnson

[11] Norman L. Parks, "Tennessee Politics Since Kefauver and Reece: A 'Generalist' View," *Journal of Politics*, XXVIII (1966), 153; Clifton McCleskey, *The Government and Politics of Texas* (2nd ed.; Boston, 1966), 102–103; "Which Mississippi?" *New Republic*, CLXVI (1972), 10. The Democratic official in Mississippi was Leon Bramlett, the executive committee chairman.

[12] For a review of the politics of the period, see William C. Havard, ed., *The Changing Politics of the South* (Baton Rouge, 1972); Numan V. Bartley and Hugh D. Graham, *Southern Politics and the Second Reconstruction* (Baltimore, 1975); Jack Bass and Walter DeVries, *The Transformation of Southern Politics: Social Change and Political Consequence Since 1945* (New York, 1976); and Lamis, *The Two-Party South*.

became vice-president, Tower won the special election to fill the vacant Senate seat. A political scientist at a west Texas college, Tower was staunchly conservative. He was the first Republican after World War II to win a statewide election in the former Confederacy, and for Goldwater Republicans he served as an example of the gains a conservative southern strategy could reap.[13]

During 1962 and 1963 conservative Republicans challenged Democrats through most of the lower South. In Alabama, James D. Martin, a Republican businessman, opposed Senator Lister Hill. Martin called for a "return to the spirit of '61—1861, when our fathers formed a new nation"—and came within a few thousand votes of defeating Hill. In South Carolina, William D. Workman, a journalist and a friend to the Citizens' Councils, commanded 43 percent of the ballots in a vigorous campaign against Olin D. Johnston, like Hill a onetime New Dealer and Senate veteran. The Goldwater Republicans who entered Senate races in Arkansas, Florida, Louisiana, and North Carolina fared less well, but Jack Cox, an erstwhile conservative Democrat, drew 46 percent of the votes in the Texas gubernatorial election and Republican conservatives won four new congressional seats in Florida, North Carolina, Tennessee, and Texas. In 1963 Republican candidates captured just under four in ten votes in gubernatorial elections in Louisiana and Mississippi. The Republicans lost all the statewide elections, but their campaigns demonstrated that victory in the Democratic primaries was no longer tantamount to election.[14]

The 1964 presidential election massively disrupted normal partisan voting alignments in the South. Goldwater fared best in the old plantation counties and in rural and small-town areas. He captured the five states of the Deep South: Alabama, Georgia, Louisiana, Mississippi, and South Carolina. In Mississippi the Goldwater ticket won almost nine out of ten of the ballots, leading one wag to remark that "Mississippi believes in the two-party system; it just believes in having them one at a time." Goldwater appears to

---

[13] Paul Casdorph, *A History of the Republican Party in Texas, 1865–1965* (Austin, Tex., 1965), 217–24.

[14] Martin quoted in "The Alabama Senatorial Election of 1962: Return of Inter-Party Competition," by Walter Dean Burnham, *Journal of Politics*, XXVI (1964), 810.

have won a majority of the votes cast by whites in all the southern states except Kentucky and Texas, but by "hunting where the ducks are," he surrendered virtually the entire black vote to President Johnson. Goldwater lost all of the peripheral states, most of which had voted more or less consistently for Republican candidates in the previous three presidential elections. His appeal to metropolitan voters outside the Deep South was particularly feeble.[15]

Senator Thurmond of South Carolina, abandoning the Democrats once again, shifted to the Republican party in order to support Goldwater. A South Carolina congressman joined Thurmond in switching parties, and the Republicans also won five congressional elections in Alabama and one each in Georgia and Mississippi, while losing three seats in Texas and Kentucky. Republican congressional gains would have been larger had the party fielded more candidates in the Deep South. Outside Alabama, state Republicans seemed loath to contest congressional elections in the traditionally Democratic lowlands and thus to antagonize county-seat Democrats who were supporting Goldwater. The Republicans failed in 1964 to win any statewide elections in the South, although their candidates ran strong races in a half dozen states. In 1966 and 1967, however, Republican candidates won election to the statehouses in Arkansas, Florida, Kentucky, and Oklahoma. Howard H. Baker, Jr., was also victorious in his Senate campaign in Tennessee, and Senator Cooper was reelected in Kentucky.

Such impressive gains reflected the deteriorating position of the Democratic party in the South. While the Goldwater campaign cemented the Democratic loyalty of black southerners, the proportion of white southerners calling themselves Democrats took another sharp drop. In 1952 three-quarters of southern whites identified with the Democratic party. In 1964 approximately two-thirds did. By 1968 only half the white respondents referred to themselves as Democrats. The Republican party benefited relatively little from the partisan dealignment. Throughout the 1960s

[15] Bartley and Graham, *Southern Politics and the Second Reconstruction*, 106–107; Southern Regional Council, "What Happened in the South?" November 15, 1964, in Southern Regional Council Papers, Atlanta University Center.

and 1970s, only about 20 percent of the white electorate identified with the Republican party. As the proportion of Democrats declined—sinking to one-third of white voters by the mid-1980s—and the proportion of Republicans remained steady, the ranks of white independents swelled.[16]

The decimation of the yellow-dog Democrats—those Democrats who would vote for a yellow dog if the party ran one—coincided not only with the civil rights movement and reapportionment but also with the liberation of the southern political agenda from the grip of county elites. As power shifted to metropolitan offices and boardrooms and the federal government enacted black-oriented Great Society reforms, huge numbers of white southerners found themselves adrift. They had, one study phrased it, "sacrificed much of the old paternal security in exchange for a rather small 'mess of pottage.' " Right-wing Republicans sought to win them over by displaying a solid conservativism and continuing to hunt where the ducks were. Nevertheless, the Goldwater campaign, despite making the party in the South more conservative, did not unify whites behind the Republican standard, nor did it achieve the ideological purity that some Republicans desired. Moderate Republicans continued to gain prominence, mainly in the Upper South, and conservative Republicans faced the formidable competition offered by George C. Wallace and other like-minded Democrats.[17]

Because Alabama's constitution prohibited a governor from serving consecutive terms, Wallace supported his wife's candidacy for the statehouse in 1966. Although ill and lacking personal political ambition, Lurleen Wallace dutifully entered the race, promising to make George her number-one assistant. "Bedfellows make

[16] Earl Black and Merle Black, *Politics and Society in the South* (Cambridge, Mass., 1987), 232–56; Everett Carll Ladd, Jr., and Charles D. Hadley, *Transformations of the American Party System: Political Coalitions from the New Deal to the 1970s* (New York, 1975), 129–77; Carol Ann Cassel, "A Longitudinal Analysis of Components of Political Change in the American South" (Ph.D. dissertation, Florida State University, 1975), 60–65; Denis G. Stadther, "The Rise of Southern Republicanism, 1956–1976" (Ph.D. dissertation, University of Pittsburgh, 1981), 161–75.

[17] James Clotfelter and William R. Hamilton, "Beyond Race Politics: Electing Southern Populists in the 1970s," in *You Can't Eat Magnolias,* ed. H. Brandt Ayers and Thomas H. Naylor (New York, 1972), 145.

strange politics," or so it was said in Alabama as Lurleen faced nine opponents in the Democratic primary. James Martin, the Republican who had almost defeated Senator Hill in 1962 and who had won a congressional seat in 1964, announced his availability for the governorship, and the Republicans for the first time put up candidates in most of the state legislative districts. Against such an array of opponents, the Wallaces were invincible. Lurleen Wallace swamped her Democratic rivals, winning a majority in the primary election, and then defeated Martin by a two-to-one landslide in the general election. Although the Republicans salvaged three congressional seats, most of their candidates succumbed to the Wallace onslaught.[18]

The Wallaces' victory was the most dramatic of a series of similar electoral contests that challenged both the Republicans' southern strategy and the policies of the moderate Democrats. Lester G. Maddox survived the political wars of 1966 to become governor of Georgia. A resolute segregationist, Maddox had closed his Atlanta restaurant rather then serve black customers. In the Democratic primary, Maddox faced a galaxy of impressive opponents, including former governor Ellis G. Arnall, as well as the Democratic establishment's favorite, Garland T. Byrd, and an attractive newcomer, Jimmy Carter. Lacking organization and funding, Maddox rambled through Georgia tacking up This Is Maddox Country signs and venting his spleen at integration, the Great Society, and a great deal more. Maddox finished second in the balloting and then, to the astonishment of those editors and publishers who, in Harry S. Ashmore's words, "are prone to stand in the bar of the country club and assume they are listening to the voice of the people," defeated Arnall in the runoff to win the Democratic nomination.[19]

Sensing victory, Georgia Republicans nominated Congressman Howard H. Callaway, a Goldwater Republican, and for the first

---

[18] Topping, Lazarek, and Linder, *Southern Republicanism and the New South*, 31; Winton Blount Interview, John Grenier Interview, both in Southern Oral History Program, Bass-DeVries Southern Politics Series, 1947–1974, Southern Historical Collection, University of North Carolina at Chapel Hill.

[19] Harry S. Ashmore, *An Epitaph for Dixie* (New York, 1958), 164; Bruce Galphin, *The Riddle of Lester Maddox* (Atlanta, 1968); Numan V. Bartley, *From Thurmond to Wallace: Political Tendencies in Georgia, 1948–1968* (Baltimore, 1970), 67–82.

time since Reconstruction seriously contested a statewide election. Faced with a choice between Maddox and Callaway, liberals organized a write-in campaign in behalf of Arnall, which appealed mainly to black voters. In the election, Maddox overpowered the opposition in rural and small-town areas and in white working-class urban districts. Callaway swept the affluent metropolitan neighborhoods, and urban black voters divided their ballots between Callaway and Arnall. Callaway won a slight plurality, but because no candidate achieved a majority, the Democratic legislature selected Maddox as governor.

The Georgia election pitted a poor-folk segregationist—Maddox had dropped out of high school to help support his family—against a rich-folk segregationist—Callaway was heir to a textile fortune. It countered the Republican southern strategy by rallying ordinary whites under the Democratic banner. It offered black voters the option of supporting a right-wing Republican, a common-man segregationist, or a hopeless write-in candidate. It challenged the rule of the moderates. Mayor Ivan Allen, Jr., of Atlanta aptly depicted Maddox: "His heart was in the small Southern Baptist churches out in the flat stretches of segregated south Georgia rather than in the board rooms of Atlanta corporations." The disruptions might have been greater had more ordinary people voted. Only three in ten Georgia adults appeared at the polls for the primaries that gave Maddox the Democratic nomination, and fewer than four in ten voted in the general election.[20]

Maddox's tenure in the Georgia statehouse exposed the bankruptcy of a purely negative program. He had vowed to repel the Communist onslaught on Georgia's social traditions, but in office there was little he could do. No longer did the federal government or Georgia blacks or a consensus of whites accept segregation and the "southern way of life." No longer was it possible to spurn secular modernist values and social change without also spurning economic progress. Moderates in Atlanta remarked with evident relief that Maddox was not as bad a governor as he had promised to be. Yet an alienated and disdained white common folk looked to the Wallaces and Maddoxes for deliverance.[21]

[20] Ivan Allen, Jr., *Mayor: Notes on the Sixties* (New York, 1971), 140–41.
[21] Galphin, *The Riddle of Lester Maddox,* 168–218.

A "politics of turmoil" characterized southern electoral competition during the mid- and late 1960s. Goldwater Republicans like Claude R. Kirk, Jr., elected governor of Florida in 1966, endeavored to solidify white voters, while occasional moderate Republicans like Winthrop Rockefeller, elected governor of Arkansas in 1966, reached out from their bases in the mountains and suburbs in an effort to appeal to the expanding black electorate. Common-white-folk segregationists like Wallace, Maddox, and John J. McKeithen, elected governor of Louisiana in 1964 and reelected in 1967, scrambled to hold the loyalty of common whites. An aging phalanx of old-guard Democrats, having failed to turn back social change with their program of massive resistance, struggled to maintain as much of the traditional order as possible. Metropolitan Democratic moderates, buffeted on all sides, tried to keep the southern political agenda focused on economic development. Throughout the region, Republicans denounced the policies of the Johnson administration, and Democrats either joined the attack or at least attempted to keep their own campaigns divorced from national developments. Both national Republicans and George C. Wallace gazed southward as they plotted strategy for the 1968 presidential election.[22]

In the South the 1968 election was a three-party race that divided the electorate in a relatively logical fashion. Threatened by new and uncertain political currents, the Democrats and Republicans nominated old party war-horses as their presidential candidates in an attempt to hold together customary voter alignments. The national Democrats nominated Vice-President Hubert H. Humphrey at a divisive convention in Chicago while police battled antiwar demonstrators in the streets. The Republicans chose former Vice-President Richard M. Nixon, another Cold War stalwart. The nominations lent some plausibility to George Wallace's jibe that the United States did not have two parties but faked giving voters a choice with a "Tweedledee and Tweedledum system." Wallace launched his campaign as the candidate of the American Independent party.[23]

[22] Bartley and Graham, *Southern Politics and the Second Reconstruction*, 111–35; Lamis, *The Two-Party South*, 20–37.

[23] Wallace quoted in *George C. Wallace and the Politics of Powerlessness*, by Carlson, 131.

Wallace spoke against the "Democratic-Republican Establishment Party," offered himself as the candidate of the "average American," and waxed indignant at bearded bureaucrats and other "overeducated, ivory-tower folks with pointed heads looking down their noses at us." As a perceptive journalist noted, his campaign "expose[d] some of the realities of American political life which the bland, banal rhetoric of Hubert Humphrey . . . serve[d] only to conceal. The politics of democracy really has failed to develop leadership and provide representation for the excluded people of the society, the 'invisible' ordinary people whose lives, Wright Mills once said, 'seem nowadays to be a series of traps!' " Both Wallace and Nixon sought to take advantage of the troubles of the Johnson administration, but as survey research revealed, "Republicans and Wallaceites are different kinds of people—they belong to different kinds of clubs and churches, go different places on Saturday night and Sunday morning, and respond differently to 'bigness.' "[24]

Wallace appealed most to the alienated, to people who felt powerless and had lost confidence in the basic integrity of the national government. In the South, such a reaction was apt to be associated with a negative attitude "to the *culture* of urban, industrial society." One study found that Wallace's supporters tended to express a "commitment to rigid sex roles, attachment to kin, [and] attachment to local community." They frequently agreed with the proposition that "material progress in the South won't be worth much if it means giving up the Southern way of life." In social terms, rural, small-town, and blue-collar whites were most likely to favor the Wallace candidacy, and Wallace won a majority of the votes cast by white southern manual workers. Outside the South, Wallace fared best with whites who had moved from the South and with disaffected blue-collar workers fearful of rioting, crime, and the deterioration of urban life. Racism, whether expressed directly or indirectly, was central to the Wallace appeal. Martin Luther

[24] Wallace quoted by Margaret Shannon in *Atlanta Journal and Constitution Magazine*, November 3, 1968, and in Birmingham *Post-Herald*, September 4, 1968; Andrew Kopkin, "The Real Significance of Wallace," *New Statesman*, LXXVI (1968), 132; Clotfelter and Hamilton, "Beyond Race Politics," 155.

King had earlier declared him "perhaps the most dangerous racist in America today."[25]

Southern Republicans, who had given their hearts to Goldwater in 1964, learned their lesson from the candidate's failed campaign. In 1968 they turned to Richard Nixon and played a crucial role in engineering his nomination. Early in the year the Southern State Republican Chairman's Association, which included all the southern states except Oklahoma, adopted a strategy of "hanging loose but hanging together." Meeting with Nixon in Atlanta in May, the southern chairmen responded favorably to the candidate's "sympathetic" understanding of white southern problems, his opposition to forced busing, and his unbending posture on national defense. Reassured, they gravitated toward the Nixon camp. Earl Black and Merle Black have written, "To a large extent, Nixon owed his narrow first-ballot victory at Miami to the size and cohesion of the southern delegations."[26]

Nixon was Wallace's chief competitor for the votes of white southerners. Combining economic conservatism and a law-and-order commitment to social stability, Nixon was the candidate of the "new middle class." He won a majority of the votes cast by whites in white-collar occupations. Recognizing the nature of Wallace's appeal, Nixon effectively conceded all the Deep South save Thurmond's South Carolina. Elsewhere in the region, Republican campaigners such as Barry Goldwater maintained that a vote for Wallace went "right down a rat-hole." The most realistic choice for conservatives, it was said, was Richard Nixon.[27]

The Democratic party was in even more disarray than usual. Lyndon Johnson, with a failing war in Vietnam and a failing Great Society at home, abandoned his quest for the Democratic nomi-

[25] Grasmick, "Social Change and the Wallace Movement," 159, 160, 146; Carlson, *George C. Wallace and the Politics of Powerlessness*, 85–126; Canfield, *A Case of Third Party Activism*, 47–56; "*Playboy* Interview," January, 1965, in *A Testament of Hope: The Essential Writings of Martin Luther King, Jr.*, ed. James Melvin Washington (San Francisco, 1986), 373.

[26] Lewis Chester, Godfrey Hodgson, and Bruce Page, *An American Melodrama: The Presidential Campaign of 1968* (New York, 1968), 439; Black and Black, *The Vital South*, 132.

[27] Bartley and Graham, *Southern Politics and the Second Reconstruction*, 126–35; Barry Goldwater, "Don't Waste a Vote on Wallace," *National Review*, XX (1968), 1060; James J. Kilpatrick, "What Makes Wallace Run?" *National Review*, XIX (1967), 400–409.

nation rather than face humiliating defeats in the presidential primaries. But, as journalists from England who were covering the campaign noted, "Johnson might be a lame-duck President, but he was not . . . a lame-duck party leader." Johnson had "invested his massive ego" in the Vietnam War, and he chose Hubert Humphrey to continue it. At the Democratic convention, antiwar liberals predictably—and with ample cause—sought to disrupt the Johnson-Humphrey juggernaut by challenging several of the southern delegations, particularly the one from Maddox's Georgia, for being undemocratic and white supremacist. The prowar forces, which a member of Americans for Democratic Action described as an "alliance of northern bosses, labor, and southern reactionaries," preserved control of the convention, rejected the challenges, and nominated Humphrey. Southern delegates generally supported Humphrey as the least objectionable of a bad lot.[28]

The Humphrey campaign made little headway in the South. Through much of the region, as a journalist wrote in regard to Georgia, "no active Democratic politician of statewide stature would touch the campaign." Only in Texas did state Democrats make a serious effort in behalf of Humphrey. There Johnson and Governor John B. Connally, a Johnson protégé, lined up county support for the ticket, and Texas was the only southern state Humphrey carried. Black southerners voted virtually unanimously for Humphrey, and he won most of the Mexican-American, Jewish, and other minority ballots.[29]

Only in the South was the 1968 election a sharply contested tri-party race, and southern voters flocked to the polls. For the only time in the twentieth century, a majority of voting-age southern citizens cast ballots in a presidential election. Although only slightly more than 50 percent of the potential electorate participated, the turnout of approximately 16.8 million voters was by southern standards massive. African Americans, many newly enfranchised by the 1965 Voting Rights Act, and women, evidencing

---

[28] Chester, Hodgson, and Page, *An American Melodrama*, 524, 558. The member of Americans for Democratic Action was Joseph L. Rauh.

[29] Margaret Shannon in *Atlanta Journal and Constitution Magazine*, November 3, 1968; Bartley and Graham, *Southern Politics and the Second Reconstruction*, 126–35.

increased political awareness and involvement, as well as lower-status whites presumably reacting to increased partisan competition, less restrictive voter registration procedures, and the social upheavals in the region, made up the larger portion of the new participants.[30]

Nixon finished first in the region, winning 36 percent of the vote. He carried pluralities and the electoral votes of seven states: Florida, Kentucky, North Carolina, Oklahoma, South Carolina, Tennessee, and Virginia. Receiving 33 percent of the vote, Wallace ran second; he commanded majorities in Alabama and Mississippi and pluralities in Arkansas, Georgia, and Louisiana. Humphrey won a plurality only in Texas, where he finished narrowly ahead of Nixon. He received 31 percent of the southern vote.[31]

For a time, Wallace had appeared to be a formidable national candidate. In late September, 1968, opinion polls reported Wallace to be the choice of 21 percent of the potential electorate, placing him only 7 percentage points behind Humphrey. Thereafter the AFL-CIO waged an all-out attack on the former governor of a low-wage, right-to-work state. Wallace's choice of an air force general, Curtis E. LeMay, also turned out badly, with LeMay professing a partiality toward atomic weapons and a concern that the American public was too irresolute about their use in warfare. Wallace received 13.5 percent of the national vote, and the South provided well over half the ten million ballots cast for him.[32]

Wallace's candidacy failed to deny Nixon a majority in the electoral college, but it did have an enormous impact on electoral politics. The Wallace campaign exposed a broad and unanticipated undercurrent of discontent among ordinary white working people. As a result, journalists discovered Middle America and wrote of a new populism. In a special report on "The Troubled American," *Newsweek* explained, "The yawning gap between the intellectual and the common man, between the governors and the governed, lies at the heart of the New Populism." Middle

[30] Carol A. Cassel, "Change in Electoral Participation in the South," *Journal of Politics*, XLI (1979), 907–17; Harold W. Stanley, *Voter Mobilization and the Politics of Race: The South and Universal Suffrage, 1952–1984* (New York, 1987).

[31] Republican National Committee, *The 1968 Elections*.

[32] Chester, Hodgson, and Page, *An American Melodrama*, 609–710.

Americans, so polling data suggested, were fed up with black rioting, militant student antiwar protest, school busing programs,
rising crime rates, promiscuous sexual activity, relativist values, social engineering, and the prosperity gap that separated the rich
and the affluent upper-middle class from themselves.[33]

Richard M. Scammon and Ben J. Wattenberg, two Democratic
party operatives who evaluated the 1968 presidential campaign,
decided that the results hinged on what they called the Social
Issue. Most voters, Scammon and Wattenberg pointed out, were
"unyoung, unpoor, unblack." The absolute-typical "Middle
Voter," according to them, was a "forty-seven-year-old housewife
... whose husband is a machinist." Whistling past the Democratic
southern graveyard, they perceived Humphrey's disaster in the
region as having to do with the Democrats' reputation for being
"soft on crime" and with the way the party was positioned relative
to " 'kidlash,' morals, and disruption." Race was a factor, but since
opinion polls disclosed that the number of "strict segregationists"
in the region had dropped 20 percentage points between 1964
and 1968, they argued that the influence of racism per se could
easily be exaggerated. The Democratic strategy should be, Scammon and Wattenberg concluded, to emphasize economic issues
and to "split off the Race Issue from the Social Issue." Instead of
viewing "law and order" as code words for bigotry and suppression, Democrats should stand for law and order and racial
progress.[34]

In the South, a wave of moderate candidates arrived at similar
conclusions. Eschewing racial demagoguery, New South candidates sought to appeal to ordinary white and black voters by combining a common-folk campaign style with the advocacy of moderately progressive policies. Despite differences among them, the
victorious gubernatorial candidates that emerged from the disruptive politics of the 1960s were in the main young, political
outsiders, religious, and—at least in their political imagery—sincere. Their basic strategy was to combine the Wallace voters with

[33] "The Troubled American," *Newsweek*, October 6, 1969, pp. 28–73, p. 67 quoted; Christopher Lasch, *The True and Only Heaven: Progress and Its Critics* (New York, 1991), 476–532.

[34] Richard M. Scammon and Ben J. Wattenberg, *The Real Majority: An Extraordinary Examination of the American Electorate* (New York, 1970), 45, 70, 180, 285.

the Humphrey voters and thereby to overwhelm the Nixon partisans. A number of them were so successful in identifying culturally with a wide range of southern voters that they appealed to most segments of society and abated the sharp class and racial conflicts of the previous decade.

The southwide success of the "populist" moderates was so general as to be remarkable. James Clotfelter and William R. Hamilton explained, "New men—a self-styled 'country lawyer' named Dale Bumpers in Arkansas, a peanut farmer named Carter in Georgia, a no-liquor-no-tobacco Panhandle Presbyterian elder named Reubin Askew in Florida—defeated better-known Democrats to win nomination and then defeated Republican gubernatorial candidates by margins ranging from 4-to-3 to 2-to-1. . . . They were neither racists nor limousine liberals." Clotfelter and Hamilton might also have mentioned Mississippi's William L. Waller, a former district attorney from Jackson who had twice unsuccessfully attempted to convict Byron de la Beckwith of the murder of NAACP field secretary Medgar Evers; Congressman Edwin W. Edwards, who credited his gubernatorial victory in Louisiana to a "coalition of blacks, farmers, people from South Louisiana of French Cajun descent;" Lieutenant Governor John C. West of South Carolina, the victor over Albert Watson, a Goldwater Republican whose campaign was so blatantly racist to embarrass not only black citizens but a considerable number of newly sensitive whites; Robert W. Scott, who had won the North Carolina statehouse in 1968; and Wendell Ford, an outsider who disrupted Kentucky's debilitating Democratic factionalism by defeating former Governor Bert T. Combs. Not all of the "new men" were Democrats. Winfield Dunn, an amiable dentist from Memphis who remarked that if elected governor of Tennessee he would have to learn how to operate from behind a desk, and A. Linwood Holton, a church elder and Sunday-school teacher in Virginia, were successful New South candidates for the Republicans.[35]

---

[35] James Clotfelter and William R. Hamilton, "But Which Southern Strategy?" *South Today*, April, 1971, p. 6; Edwards quoted in *The Two-Party South*, by Lamis, 111; Larry Sabato, "New South Governors and the Governorship," in *Contemporary Southern Politics*, ed. James F. Lea (Baton Rouge, 1988), 194–213; Larry Sabato, *Goodbye to Good-Time Charlie: The American Governor Transformed, 1950–1975* (Lexington, Mass., 1978); Bartley and Graham, *Southern Politics and the Second Reconstruction*, 136–63.

The region's new breed of governors often used their inaugural addresses to announce a new era in race relations. "I say to you quite frankly that the time for racial discrimination is over," Jimmy Carter declared. "Our people have already made this major and difficult decision. . . . No poor, rural, weak, or black person should ever have to bear the additional burden of being deprived of the opportunity of an education, a job, or simple justice." In South Carolina, Governor West promised to "eliminate from our government every vestige of discrimination because of race, creed, sex, religion, or any other barrier to fairness for all citizens." In Virginia, Governor Holton vowed to "see that no citizen of the commonwealth is excluded from full participation in both the blessings and responsibility of our society because of his race." And so it went across the region. During the early 1970s, for the first time in the twentieth century, southern chief executives endorsed equality before the law.[36]

The blossoming of an attractive and articulate southern leadership that accepted national ideals had a striking impact on the American media. Long debased as a region afflicted by racism, ignorance, poverty, and violence, the South quickly became a land of swiftly arriving prosperity and expanding racial cooperation. In a special issue of *Ebony* on the "South today," Lerone Bennett, the editor, wrote, "Wherever one turned, in *Harper's*, in the New York *Times*, in the *Atlantic Monthly*, there were rhapsodic litanies on the New South—a South that had turned its back on the horrors of the past; a South that was too busy to hate, a South that was hard at work out-doing the Yankees, a South of hustle and bustle, of new buildings, new roads, and new factories." Bennett permitted himself an element of hyperbole, but certainly the popular image of the South had improved considerably. Television networks aired special reports on the "new voices in the South," and *Time* magazine placed Governor Carter on its cover. By the midseventies, the South had become a part of the flourishing Sunbelt and

[36] Carter Inaugural Address, Atlanta *Constitution,* January 13, 1971; West Inaugural Address, *The State,* January 20, 1971; Holton Inaugural Address, Richmond *News-Leader,* January 18, 1970. See also Askew Inaugural Address, Miami *Herald,* January 6, 1971; and Bumpers Inaugural Address, *Arkansas Gazette* (Little Rock), January 13, 1971.

the "southern way of life" had become the "southern style of life."[37]

Journalists often referred to the new southern governors as populists. That label may have described their election campaigns, but their executive policies were anything but Populist, in the historical sense of the term. They stressed centralized government, businesslike management, state planning, and the delegation of decision making to experts. Virtually all the southern chief executives undertook government reorganization. Usually they followed the procedures adopted in Tennessee, where, as Governor Dunn explained, "We had a businessman's study of state government." When implemented, the reorganization "revolutionized the way state government is run based on the unique insights we got from the businessmen." During the late 1960s and early 1970s, five states—Florida, Georgia, Louisiana, North Carolina, and Virginia—adopted new constitutions, and Arkansas, Kentucky, and Texas wrote new constitutions that the voters rejected. By the midseventies, all the southern states except Kentucky and Virginia had strengthened their executive branches by permitting governors to succeed themselves.[38]

The renewed drive for efficient and centralized government complemented the continuing commitment to economic growth. Far from being Populists, the "new voices in the South" were business-oriented promoters "of new buildings, new roads, and new factories." As Larry Sabato has pointed out, they were "far less progressive on economic policy than many of the populist, segregationist governors of earlier times." The majority of the southern states opened offices in Washington to lobby for federal dollars for development, and state industrial promotion agencies pursued new industry in the North and abroad. During the 1970s Georgia opened foreign offices in Brussels, São Paulo, Tokyo, and

---

[37] Lerone Bennett, Jr., "Old Illusions and New Souths," *Ebony,* August, 1971, p. 35; *Time,* May 31, 1971; Steve Oney, "How Others See the South," *Atlanta Journal and Constitution Magazine,* January 7, 1979.

[38] Winfield Dunn Interview, in Southern Oral History Program, Bass-DeVries Southern Politics Series, 1947–1974, Southern Historical Collection; Sabato, "New South Governors and the Governorship"; James Clotfelter, "Populism in Office; or, Whatever Happened to Huey Long?" *New South,* Spring, 1973, pp. 56–61.

Toronto, and George Busbee, Carter's successor as governor, was a "frequent international traveler in quest of new industry." Britain's premier newspaper informed its readers that the new southern governors were "traveling widely, at home and abroad, informing people about the modernization of their states and striving to win new respect and new investment." [39]

As a result of these policies, the trends in southern taxing and spending continued unabated. The region further solidified its reputation for low and regressive taxation. At the end of the 1970s all the southern states ranked well below the national average in per capita state and local collections. Arkansas, Alabama, Mississippi, Tennessee, South Carolina, and North Carolina collected the least taxes per capita in the nation.[40]

More so than elsewhere, the southern states relied heavily on sales taxes. Income, death (estate, inheritance, and gift), property, and business taxes were relatively low. Louisiana, Oklahoma, and Texas, however, collected business taxes well above the national average as a result of the severance taxes they imposed on mineral extraction. During the early 1970s Alabama, Kentucky, and Tennessee placed severance taxes on coal, and Governor Askew pushed through Florida's legislature a corporate income tax. With that, only Texas assessed no income taxes at all. The region's propensity for general and selective sales taxes placed the relatively greatest tax burdens on less affluent residents.[41]

Although prosperity permitted the southern states to improve public services, expenditures continued to lag behind national norms in most categories. At the end of the 1970s all the southern states still trailed the national average in educational funding per pupil. Alabama, Mississippi, Arkansas, Tennessee, South Carolina, and North Carolina spent the least per public-school pupil in av-

[39] Sabato, "New South Governors and the Governorship," 200; Dick Petty in Savannah News-Press, October 10, 1982; Numan V. Bartley, The Creation of Modern Georgia (2nd ed.; Athens, Ga., 1990), 208–37; James C. Cobb, The Selling of the South: The Southern Crusade for Industrial Development, 1936–1980 (Baton Rouge, 1982); James C. Cobb, Industrialization and Southern Society, 1877–1984 (Lexington, Ky., 1984), 99–164; Frank Vogl in Times (London), September 29, 1977.

[40] Bureau of the Census, Government Finances in 1978–1979 (1980).

[41] Eva Galambos, State and Local Taxes in the South, 1973 (Southern Regional Council, 1973); Bureau of the Census, State Government Finances in 1979 (1980).

erage daily attendance of all the states in the nation, and Georgia and Kentucky placed among the bottom ten states. The southern states fared better in rankings of public-school expenditures as a percentage of personal income. On that scale, the southern states were only slightly behind the national average. Federal aid to southern education kept conditions from being worse than they were. At the end of the 1970s one-quarter of Mississippi's public-school budget came from the federal government.[42]

Most southern states spent significantly more on roads and highways than states elsewhere did, and southern spending for health and hospitals exceeded the national average. Southern states provided fewer services, though, and expenditures for such welfare programs as aid to families with dependent children was substantially below national averages. In 1975 the Louisiana legislature adopted a right-to-work provision, thereby solidifying the former Confederate states behind open-shop policies regarding labor unions. In 1975 a study of the "business climate" of American states that equated "excellence" with "low taxes, low levels of public assistance, restrictive labor legislation, and a low level of government spending and debt" found the states ranking "highest" to be Texas, Alabama, Virginia, South Dakota, South Carolina, North Carolina, Florida, and Arkansas. As an economist matter-of-factly stated, "One of the classical public policies recommendations for a state is to induce the in-migration of profitable businesses by tax breaks and to encourage the out-migration of unemployables by low levels of public assistance to the least fortunate."[43]

To be sure, the new southern chief executives in the main demonstrated a higher level of social responsibility than their predecessors had shown. They promoted fair employment practices

[42] National Education Association, *Rankings of the States* (Washington, D.C., 1981).

[43] Bernard L. Weinstein and Robert E. Firestine, *Regional Growth and Decline in the United States: The Rise of the Sunbelt and the Decline of the Northeast* (New York, 1978), 135; Mancur Olson, "The Causes and Quality of Southern Growth," in *The Economics of Southern Growth*, ed. E. Blaine Liner and Lawrence K. Lynch (Durham, N.C., 1977), 129; Peter A. Lupsha and William J. Siembieda, "The Poverty of Public Services in the Land of Plenty: An Analysis and Interpretation," in *The Rise of the Sunbelt Cities*, ed. David C. Perry and Alfred J. Watkins (Beverly Hills, Calif., 1977), 169–90; Bureau of the Census, *Government Finances in 1978–1979*.

and, increasingly, affirmative action in public institutions. They were for the most part environmentally conscious and favored as much ecological reform as rapid economic and metropolitan growth would permit. They were usually selective about the types of new industries they attempted to lure to their states, although the economic plight of much of the rural South and the general lust for economic development produced many compromises. They supported modest tax reforms and improvements in transportation, health services, and education to the extent that fiscal conservatism and a good business atmosphere would allow.

The policies of the new governors confirmed the triumph of the moderates and completed the transfer of power from county courthouses to metropolitan boardrooms. After an era of disruptive conflict, a new leadership restored social stability and ratified the ideological dominance of an ethos of economic growth. During the 1970s and later, southern political and business leaders accepted the civil rights legislation of the mid-1960s, relied on an "expanding economy" to elevate the living standards "for all our citizens—both Negro and white"—and looked to an "ever increasing level of education" to ensure employment opportunities. Senator Ralph W. Yarborough of Texas explained that regional businessmen and politicians no longer fought blacks and labor but cooperated with them. No longer was an appointed state committee complete without black representation, and a legislator from South Carolina found it "surprising" how closely the chamber of commerce and labor leaders worked together. "I think that is significant," he mused.[44]

The increase in the number of black voters and public officials buttressed the forces of moderation. By the end of the 1960s about six in ten black citizens were registered to vote, compared with approximately two-thirds of white citizens. With increased black voting came an expanding number of black public officials,

[44] "What We Believe" (Statement by Alabama Chamber of Commerce and other business groups), April, 1965, in White House Central Files (Human Rights), Papers of Lyndon B. Johnson, Lyndon Baines Johnson Library, Austin, Tex.; Senator Ralph Yarborough Interview, Rex Carter Interview, both in Southern Oral History Program, Bass-DeVries Southern Politics Series, 1947–1974, Southern Historical Collection. Carter was speaker of the South Carolina house of representatives.

some seventeen hundred of them by the midseventies. Given the total number of offices available in the South, the proportion of black incumbents was far smaller than the relative size of the black population, but the impact of African-American political participation was considerable, both in moderating southern politics and in encouraging black support for moderate policies.[45]

Particularly significant was the increase in the number of black city officials. Most African-American mayors in the South resided in towns. After Maynard Jackson became mayor of Atlanta in 1973, however, black power in the city halls of the metropolitan South became relatively common. Because black city officials faced the same policy choices as their white predecessors, policy changed relatively little. "Black politicians were recruited, generally, from the black middle class," David R. Goldfield has written, "and held the same political objectives as their white colleagues." As Julian Bond observed in the mid-1970s, "many of the region's black elected officials have turned out to be only slightly better than the white officials whose places they took." Clarence N. Stone has concluded from his study of Atlanta that Maynard Jackson's regime "produced significant gains for the black middle class, but little for the black poor and working class." Black leadership did permit African Americans to be a part of the system and to receive whatever patronage merit systems, centralized purchasing, and the like permitted.[46]

In the moderate New South, voices of discord received a limited hearing. In the elections of 1970 and 1971, former governors Orval E. Faubus and Jimmie H. Davis attempted comebacks, and the voters of Arkansas and Louisiana decisively rejected them. Similarly, the voters retired those incumbents identified with eco-

[45] United States Commission on Civil Rights, *Political Participation* (1968); David Campbell and Joe R. Feagin, "Black Politics in the South: A Descriptive Analysis," *Journal of Politics*, XXXVII (1975), 129–62; Bass and DeVries, *The Transformation of Southern Politics*, 41–56; Mildred Elizabeth Sanders, "Electorate Expansion and Public Policy: A Decade of Political Change in the South" (Ph.D. dissertation, Cornell University, 1978).

[46] David R. Goldfield, *Black, White, and Southern: Race Relations and Southern Culture, 1940 to the Present* (Baton Rouge, 1990), 191, p. 199 Bond quoted; Clarence N. Stone, *Regime Politics: Governing Atlanta, 1946–1988* (Lawrence, Kans., 1989), 177; James W. Button, *Blacks and Social Change: Impact of the Civil Rights Movement in Southern Communities* (Princeton, 1989).

nomic liberalism. In the 1970 Democratic primary in Texas, Senator Ralph Yarborough, who really did demonstrate Populist inclinations, lost to Lloyd M. Bentsen, a member of the conservative wing of the state Democratic party. In the 1970 general election, Senator Albert Gore, who after the death of Estes Kefauver in 1963 was perhaps the most prominent progressive member of the southern Senate delegation, fell victim to the Social Issue—and a conservative Republican. A. S. "Mike" Monroney of Oklahoma, who had begun his national legislative career during the New Deal and had remained aligned with its ideals, lost his seat in 1968, and Fred R. Harris, another Democrat from Oklahoma who was elected senator in 1964 and who became increasingly liberal while in office, heeded the opinion polls and did not seek reelection in 1972. Republicans replaced both Monroney and Harris in the Senate.

Displaying a stubborn resilience, liberal insurgents challenged the political establishments in Virginia and Texas. Henry E. Howell, a charismatic proponent of popular reform, led a largely personal following that sought to gain control of Virginia's Democratic party. Although elected lieutenant governor in 1971, Howell twice failed to win the statehouse. Subsequent to Yarborough's defeat, Frances T. "Sissy" Farenthold, whom a journalist described as "a crusading liberal, a woman, a Roman Catholic," led a resurgence of the game but outgunned liberal faction of the Democratic party in Texas. That effort also failed.[47]

The influence of the old-guard southern Democrats declined significantly in Congress. Richard B. Russell, the longtime head of the southern congressional caucus and the heart of the Bourbon position in Congress, died in 1971. The loss of Senator Russell and Senator Byrd from the Senate floor would by itself have seriously weakened southern influence. The death, retirement, or defeat during the late 1960s and early 1970s of a dozen other veteran senators, along with numerous members of the House, represented a considerable upheaval. In 1974 national Democrats in the House actually challenged southern leadership by restricting the authority of committee and subcommittee chairs. They

[47] Lamis, *The Two-Party South,* 199.

even stripped three southern Democrats of their committee chairmanships. By that time, a host of Republicans and two black Democrats—Barbara Jordan of Houston and Andrew Young of Atlanta—had undermined the unity of the southern congressional delegation.[48]

Even in an age of moderation, there was no shortage of southern conservatives. A study published in 1975 reported that the South was still "decidedly the most conservative regional bloc in Congress." Within the Republican party, Senator Thurmond of South Carolina and Senator Jesse Helms of North Carolina—the latter elected in 1972—anchored the far right side of the political spectrum, while legatee Democratic senators such as James Eastland and John H. Stennis of Mississippi, John McClellan of Arkansas, and Herman Talmadge of Georgia ensured a conservative presence in Democratic councils. Yet even the most dedicated conservatives adapted to the new political currents. Thurmond employed a black aide and adjusted his stance on racial matters, not in the expectation of earning black votes but simply to remain politically respectable. McClellan and Talmadge failed to meet the challenge and suffered defeat in 1978 and 1980 respectively.[49]

George Wallace neither bent nor suffered political rejection for his rigidity. Lurleen Wallace died of cancer in 1968, and Albert Brewer, the lieutenant governor and a former Wallace protégé, inherited the Alabama statehouse. Wallace needed Alabama as a base for a renewed presidential effort in 1972, and consequently he opposed Brewer in the 1970 gubernatorial primary. Brewer was a conservative who enjoyed the advantages of incumbency, who appealed to affluent metropolitan voters, and who struck black citizens as an improvement over Wallace. The national Republican party, hoping to thwart Wallace's presidential ambitions, poured money and support into Brewer's campaign. Brewer ran ahead of Wallace in the first primary, but in the runoff, Wallace

---

[48] The departing Democrats included—besides Gore, Monroney, and Yarborough—Hill of Alabama, Fulbright of Arkansas, Smathers and Holland of Florida, Ellender of Louisiana, Ervin and Jordan of North Carolina, Johnston of South Carolina, and Robinson of Virginia. See Charles S. Bullock III, "The South in Congress: Power and Policy," in *Contemporary Southern Politics*, ed. Lea, 177–93; and Leroy Rieselbach, *Congressional Reform in the Seventies* (Morristown, N.J., 1977).

[49] Ladd and Hadley, *Transformations of the American Party System*, 174.

returned to tried and tested techniques. He denounced Brewer as the "bloc vote" candidate, and his radio advertisements stirred the apprehensions of whites: "How would you like for your wife to get stopped on a dark night on a lonely road by a black state trooper?" The tactics worked, and Wallace won the election.[50]

Clearly, race was by no means defunct as a political concern. In 1969 Kevin P. Phillips, a Republican party operative, analyzed the 1968 presidential election and concluded that it was the prelude to an "emerging Republican majority." Phillips wrote that "the election statistics of 1968 signaled the end of an era." They marked the repudiation of the "Democratic Party for its ambitious social programming and inability to handle the urban and Negro revolutions." According to Phillips, the Democrats lost the upland South when they replaced their "economic populist stance" with a "credo of social engineering," and they lost the lower South because of racial issues. "Inescapably, the Democratic Party in the Deep South was on its way to becoming the Negro party," he judged. Therefore, it was "essential to the GOP" that the Nixon administration accelerate the transformation by vigorously enforcing the 1965 Voting Rights Act. To be successful, he argued, the Republican party needed only to follow a southern strategy, take advantage of racial animosities, and capture most of the votes cast by whites. Phillips concluded that the South was "shaping up as the pillar of a national conservative party."[51]

Racial issues became more complex when the United States Supreme Court extended "affirmative action" to encompass school districts in large southern cities. Prior to the early 1970s positive efforts to achieve racial integration had largely been confined to rural areas, towns, and small cities in the South. *Green v. New Kent County* had in 1968 conferred on school boards the "affirmative duty" to eliminate segregated school systems. In that case the issue was relatively simple. New Kent County, Virginia, had only two schools, one white and one "colored." With the

---

[50] Albert Brewer Interview, in Southern Oral History Program, Bass-DeVries Southern Politics Series, 1947–1974, Southern Historical Collection; Lottman, *The GOP and the South*, 17–22; Greenhaw, *Watch Out for George Wallace*, 213–17.

[51] Kevin P. Phillips, *The Emerging Republican Majority* (New Rochelle, N.Y., 1969), 207, 27, 206, 231, 287, 187.

coming of "freedom of choice" following the 1964 Civil Rights Act, county officials admitted some black students to the "white" school, and otherwise things continued as usual. Busing meant transporting most black students to one school and all whites and 115 blacks to the other. Integration, the justices suggested, could be accomplished "simply by assigning students living in the eastern half of the county to the New Kent School and those living in the western half of the county to the Watkins School." The rural–town–small city South was the only significant part of the nation lacking extensive residential segregation, and school integration, however it might disrupt the social lives of students and however it might antagonize white segregationists, presented no great legal or administrative difficulties. Consequently, Office of Education guidelines and federal court decisions largely accomplished the integration of southern counties.[52]

During this period southern cities generally continued to practice "freedom of choice," which was essentially the same as the "open enrollment" policy employed by most nonsouthern cities. The result was what the United States Commission on Civil Rights termed "racial isolation in the public schools." In the great cities with their massive black ghettos, sprawling housing projects, and expanding suburbs, school segregation was "severe" and "growing." Indeed, because of increased segregation in northern cities, public-school students were more segregated in 1971 than they had been at the time of the *Brown* decision in 1954. Far more so than the relatively stable and residentially diverse southern countryside, the cities presented enormously complicated problems. Not only would the busing of huge numbers of students within urban areas raise practical difficulties, such a policy directly conflicted with the terminology contained in the 1964 Civil Rights Act and the 1966 amendments to the Elementary and Secondary Education Act.[53]

Storming into a thicket where angels might have treaded fearfully, the Court in 1971 opened an assault on school segregation

[52] *Green* v. *County School Board of New Kent County*, 391 U.S. 437, 442 (1968).

[53] *Racial Isolation in the Public Schools: A Report of the U.S. Commission on Civil Rights* (1967), 3; Hugh D. Graham, *The Civil Rights Era: Origins and Development of National Policy, 1960–1972* (New York, 1990), 125–52; Nicolaus Mills, ed., *The Great School Bus Controversy* (New York, 1973).

in southern cities in *Swann* v. *Charlotte-Mecklenburg Board of Education*. "Some justices," J. Harvie Wilkinson III has stated, "saw in Charlotte an extension of Little Rock or Birmingham, the sort of southern resistance they had been dealing with for years." Consequently, the Court accepted the busing plan that an "expert in education administration" appointed by the federal district court devised to transport inner-city black students to outlying white schools and suburban white children in the Charlotte-Mecklenburg school district to inner-city schools. The justices reproved the deliberate thwarting of Supreme Court mandates and decided that, although city integration plans might "be administratively awkward, inconvenient, and even bizarre," they were necessary for eliminating dual school systems. Beginning in the fall of 1971, school busing programs became increasingly common in southern cities.[54]

The Charlotte-Mecklenburg decision applied only to the South, but by the fall of 1971 programs for integrating urban schools were looming in the North as well. A number of factors contributed to the nationalization of the imperative to integrate the public schools. Black protests demanded integration, and the intellectual climate encouraged voluntary efforts. Federal district judges and bureaucrats in the Office of Education began to question northern de facto segregation, while state courts and agencies began to require enforcement of state constitutions. Busing plans remained more common in the South than elsewhere, but their extension northward contributed to making the attack on "racial isolation in the public schools" a national concern.[55]

The "great school bus controversy" was a major issue in the 1972 presidential election. President Nixon maneuvered to avoid being identified with either the civil rights reform of the Great Society or the civil rights negativism of Barry Goldwater. Interested above all in foreign affairs, Nixon was free on domestic issues

[54] J. Harvie Wilkinson III, *From Brown to Bakke: The Supreme Court and School Integration, 1954–1978* (New York, 1979), 39; *Swann* v. *Charlotte-Mecklenburg Board of Education*, 402 U.S. 8, 28 (1971); George R. Metcalf, *From Little Rock to Boston: The History of School Desegregation* (Westport, Conn., 1983), 130–36.

[55] See Mills, ed., *The Great School Bus Controversy*, esp. Christopher Jencks, "Busing: The Supreme Court Goes North," 14–26.

"to pursue contradictory policies for short-term gains," as Hugh
D. Graham has observed. His administration initiated a modest
program to encourage black capitalism and promoted the Philadelphia Plan to open employment to blacks in the construction
trades but otherwise was content with an attitude of "benign neglect" toward civil rights. Nixon reiterated his agreement with the
principle of the *Brown* decision, promised to uphold the decisions
of the Supreme Court, and expressed his "opposition to any compulsory busing of pupils beyond normal geographic school zones
for the purpose of achieving racial balance." The administration's
policies proved to be politically adept. As Republican strategist
Harry S. Dent has written, "Nixon seemed to win the acclaim of
the opponents—much in the majority—while the courts received
the blame." George Wallace insisted that Nixon stood "forth-
rightly on both sides of most questions."[56]

Wallace described busing as "social scheming." Invented by
"anthropologists, zoologists, and sociologists," it threatened the
"health and safety of your child, regardless of color." Wallace entered Florida's Democratic presidential primary in March, 1972,
apparently as a ploy to gain publicity preparatory to setting out
on a third-party campaign. Facing a field of ten Democratic presidential aspirants, he won 42 percent of the vote and finished far
ahead of Hubert Humphrey, Edmund S. Muskie, and the others.
Wallace went on to vanquish the opposition in Tennessee and
North Carolina, and he finished an impressive second in Wisconsin, Pennsylvania, and Indiana. On May 15 at a rally in Maryland,
a would-be assassin grievously wounded Wallace, paralyzing him
from the waist down. On the following day the Alabama governor
finished first in the Maryland and Michigan primaries. At that
point, Wallace had won almost three and a half million votes in
the primaries and was well ahead of Humphrey and Senator
George McGovern, his two nearest rivals. Because his staff had
made little effort to qualify Wallace delegates, his popular vote did
not translate into support at the Democratic convention. It would

[56] Graham, *The Civil Rights Era,* 301–65, p. 302 quoted; Richard M. Nixon, "Statement
About Desegregation of Elementary and Secondary Schools," March 24, 1970, in *Public
Papers of the Presidents of the United States, 1970* (Washington, D.C., 1971), 91–92; Dent, *The
Prodigal South Returns to Power,* 197; Wallace quoted in New York *Times,* August 6, 1971.

have served as a formidable base for a third-party campaign had his injuries not forced him to the sidelines.[57]

George McGovern emerged from the primaries to become the Democratic presidential nominee. Two years after its disastrous 1968 convention, the party had adopted convention rules requiring "affirmative steps" to ensure greater representation for women, minorities, and young people. As a result, women were 36 percent of the delegates in 1972, as compared with 13 percent in 1968, and the proportion of African Americans in the delegations from the former Confederate states grew from one in ten to one in four. The party also became more elitist. The changes in the process for selecting delegates, in Thomas B. Edsall's words, "tilted the balance of party power toward an activist upper-middle class whose interests [were] often in direct opposition to the interests of less active, but larger, blocs of [blue-collar and lower-status] Democratic voters." The convention adopted a notably reformist platform that promised basic changes in welfare, defense, and taxation. The platform also declared, "Transportation of students is another tool to accomplish desegregation." The white southern delegates, many of them horrified at the new Democratic party, cast a plurality of their convention ballots for Wallace.[58]

The 1972 election was anticlimactic. Nixon won an overwhelming national victory, and the Solid South gave all its electoral votes to the president. Nixon won the bulk of the votes cast by those groups which had supported Wallace, and thereby unified the white voters of the region. He commanded 86 percent of the ballots southern white Protestants cast. McGovern fared even more poorly than Humphrey had done four years previously, and like Humphrey, McGovern did well only among minorities. The inability of Wallace to mount a third-party campaign that could have divided white voters doomed whatever chance McGoven may have had in the South.[59]

[57] Wallace quoted in *Watch Out for George Wallace*, by Greenhaw, 40; Carlson, *George C. Wallace and the Politics of Powerlessness*, 133–79.

[58] Thomas Byrne Edsall, *The New Politics of Inequality* (New York, 1984); Black and Black, *The Vital South*, 241–48; Nelson W. Polsby, *Consequences of Party Reform* (New York, 1983).

[59] Bartley and Graham, *Southern Politics and the Second Reconstruction*, 164–83; Ladd and Hadley, *Transformations of the American Party System*, 157–58.

More so than candidates of either major party, Wallace articulated the grievances of huge numbers of Middle Americans and most especially of ordinary southern whites. Journalists observed that "Wallace dealt in nothing so prosaic as literal truth," but in his exaggerations he capitalized on the Social Issue before Scammon and Wattenberg named it. Wallace forced other candidates, a journalist wrote, to acknowledge, at least in their rhetoric, such issues as the "remoteness of government, urban disorder and decay, and an overwhelming sense of frustration." The Alabamian pointed out that the Democratic party no longer served the interests of working people, and he drove home the abashing realization that the most ardent white proponents of busing—and increasingly the black proponents as well—lived in largely white suburbs or sent their own children to private schools.[60]

Wallace's failing lay in his inability to propose solutions for the problems he dramatized. The programs he occasionally did advance were often tinctured with racism and frequently came across as bizarre. As Maddox had learned in Georgia, the American governmental system offered few opportunities for ordinary people to protect their economic and cultural interests. The movement Wallace headed was a highly personalized crusade fueled by the charisma of one individual. Lacking organization and structure, it did not long survive the incapacitation of its leader. When Wallace attempted to revive his campaign for the Democratic nomination in 1976, the effort failed.

Instead, Jimmy Carter swept from the South to become the Democratic presidential candidate. Four years in advance of the 1976 election, Carter and aide Hamilton Jordan formulated a remarkably astute campaign strategy. During the early stages of the Watergate affair, they recognized that in 1976 the character of the candidates would be of more interest than party platforms, that honesty, sincerity, and trust would be of greater concern than specific issues, and that the growing mistrust of politicians and government would benefit an attractive newcomer. They anticipated that the Wallace following would respond to a nonracist alterna-

[60] Chester, Hodgson, and Page, *An American Melodrama*, 280; R. W. Apple, Jr., in New York *Times,* April 23, 1972.

tive that expressed their feelings of alienation, powerlessness, and frustration.[61]

Events validated the Carter campaign scenario. The investigation of the Watergate scandal by a Senate select committee headed by Senator Sam J. Ervin of North Carolina exposed criminal action by the Nixon administration and its Committee to Reelect the President. In the fall of 1973 Vice-President Spiro T. Agnew resigned rather than face federal prosecution, and in August, 1974, President Nixon resigned to avoid impeachment. With the United States government seemingly in collapse, the Organization of Petroleum Exporting Countries quadrupled the price of crude oil, thereby touching off an energy crisis, inflation, and recession. President Gerald R. Ford inherited a disgraced administration and a failing economy.

Little known nationally, Carter consolidated his southern base during the presidential primaries by defeating Wallace in Florida, North Carolina, Georgia, and Tennessee. Outside the South he did well enough in the primaries to ensure his nomination. At the Democratic convention, all sections of the nation supported Carter, but the southern delegates were the most enthusiastic, casting almost nine out of ten of their ballots for the former Georgia governor. Even Wallace endorsed his candidacy.

Carter's nomination, as Alexander P. Lamis has noted, "was a godsend to Southern Democratic leaders." Most of the region's Democrats supported the national ticket. In the campaign, Carter took full advantage of his position as a native son. One Carter commercial that aired in the South began with an announcer saying, "On November 2 the South is being readmitted to the Union. If that sounds strange, maybe a southerner can understand. Only a southerner can understand years of coarse, antisouthern jokes and unfair comparisons." Carter talked of being a "born-again Christian," of heading a government "as filled with love as are the American people," and of cleaning up the "mess in Washington."

[61] Jules Witcover, *Marathon: The Pursuit of the Presidency, 1972–1976* (New York, 1977), 105–18. On Carter and the 1976 campaign, other helpful works include James T. Wooten's *Dasher: The Roots and Rising of Jimmy Carter* (New York, 1978); Martin Schram's *Running for President, 1976: The Carter Campaign* (New York, 1977); and Kandy Stroud's *How Jimmy Won: The Victory Campaign from Plains to the White House* (New York, 1977).

He also promised, "I'll never lie to you." He spoke of tax reform and an energy policy, but his campaign's emphasis was less on specific issues than on trust, honesty, and traditional virtues.[62]

The national contest between Carter and Ford was extremely close, but in the South, Carter won eleven of thirteen states, losing only Oklahoma and Virginia. Wallace sympathizers by and large supported him, and he collected almost half the ballots whites cast in the region at the same time that he was the unequivocal choice of minority voters. In the South and in the nation, Carter won majorities among blue-collar workers, and Ford won the white-collar precincts. By appealing to the alienated and the dispossessed, Carter sealed the expiration of the Wallace movement.[63]

The collapse of the black civil rights movement, the softening of the attitudes of common white folk, and the success of moderate leadership contributed to the stabilization of southern politics during the 1970s and afterward. From the perspective of the new middle class, the New South governors brought to the region enlightened statesmanship. State government became more rational, institutional, and respectable. Gubernatorial administrations dealt far more fairly with black people than had previous regimes, and they encouraged at least in their rhetoric the women's movement. They addressed without notable improbity the rampant metropolitan and economic growth of the 1970s. By most journalistic and academic standards, they compared favorably with their nonsouthern counterparts.

The new political order did not foster democratic participation. In presidential elections, voter participation reached its zenith in the 1968 election. In state politics, the high point came between 1968 and 1971, when more than four in ten potential voters cast ballots in gubernatorial general elections. Black turnout peaked at the same time as white. Thereafter electoral participation declined. The presidential election of 1980 attracted about 45 percent of adult citizens, and gubernatorial elections after 1972 drew hardly more than one-third of the possible electorate. Southern

---

[62] Lamis, *The Two-Party South*, 37; Schram, *Running for President*, 332; Witcover, *Marathon*, 198; Wooten, *Dasher*, 347.

[63] Lamis, *The Two-Party South*, 37–39; Black and Black, *The Vital South*, 329–37.

political participation came closer to approximating the national average, but not as a result of greater southern involvement after the late 1960s but because of the even more rapid decline in nonsouthern turnout.[64]

Turnout was lowest among white and black men with no more than a high-school diploma, and it was highest among the college-educated, particularly women and blacks. In keeping with the politics of New South moderation, the new middle class, along with upward-striving members of the working class and minorities "who believe[d] in and aspire[d] to the culturally dominant standards of reasonableness and legitimacy," dominated the electorate. Even as de jure disfranchisement disappeared, the disorganized and politically atomized lower half to two-thirds of the southern white and black population remained largely outside the political process. Earl Black and Merle Black have concluded that, as a predictable result, "southern governments g[a]ve scant attention and few tangible benefits to those in the bottom half of the social structure."[65]

Despite the coming of two-party political competition, the partisan South of the 1970s had what two political scientists termed a "one-and-a-half" party system. The Democratic party, dominated on the state level by New South moderates, retained most of the local offices in the region, while an increasingly conservative Republican party vied for the more conspicuous positions. Many years before, V. O. Key had argued that enfranchisement and a two-party system would permit southerners to divide over legitimate economic issues and would foster a more liberal southern politics. Even a scholar so perceptive as Key could not have foreseen the changed conditions that would invalidate his optimistic prediction.[66]

[64] Black and Black, *Politics and Society in the South*, 175–94; Stanley, *Voter Mobilization and the Politics of Race*, 4–17.

[65] Black and Black, *Politics and Society in the South*, 193.

[66] John Van Wingen and David Valentine, "Partisan Politics: A One-and-a-Half, No-Party System," in *Contemporary Southern Politics*, ed. Lea, 124–47; Bradley Canon, "Factionalism in the South: A Test of Theory and Revisitation of V. O. Key, Jr.," *American Journal of Political Science*, XXII (1978), 33–57.

CHAPTER XII

THE SUNBELT SOUTH

T HE moderate consensus in the South proved to be remarkably resilient. The civil rights movement had overturned the region's social system, and a growing women's
rights movement further challenged time-honored ways. The disruption of the laws and customs that governed race and gender
encouraged blacks and women to pursue their own ambitions.
The consequence was greater individualism and a far more dynamic and diverse labor market. Metropolitan areas experienced
explosive growth, and migrants from the nation's economically
troubled Snowbelt poured into the region's Sunbelt cities in
search of economic opportunity. Regional folk culture, with its
concern for roots, place, and community, reeled in the wake of
modernist values, consumer affluence, and a labor market no
longer anchored to mill villages and plantations nor defined by
race and gender. Moderate southern state governments promoted
urban and economic growth, offered token opposition to public-
school busing programs, and accepted changes in gender relations while demonstrating little support for an Equal Rights
Amendment to the Constitution. The southern congressional delegation tilted with the remaining northern liberals over the meaning of civil rights reform. Through it all, southern affairs of state
proceeded with delusive placidity.

The storm over busing public-school children prompted several southern states to enact antibusing legislation. North Carolina and Tennessee prohibited the use of state vehicles to transport students for the purpose of achieving racially balanced
enrollments. More attuned to the spirit of the times, however,
were statutes approved in Alabama, Georgia, Louisiana, and South
Carolina that copied virtually verbatim a New York law: "No stu-

dent shall be assigned or compelled to attend any school on account of race, creed, color or national origin, or for the purpose of achieving equality of attendance or increased attendance or reduced attendance at any school." Governor John J. McKeithen of Louisiana could orate, "That is the law in New York; it is now also the law of Louisiana. We ask no special treatment; we demand no concessions. But we do seek and expect to be treated as any other state in the nation." [1]

Because Great Society civil rights legislation and Supreme Court decisions alike treated the South as a special province, southern politicians counterattacked by insisting on equality before the law. During the congressional debates of 1970, Senator John H. Stennis of Mississippi introduced an amendment requiring that the guidelines and other racial policies "be applied uniformly in all regions of the United States." Stennis intoned, "If segregation is wrong in the South, it is wrong in the North." Northern racial liberals replied that the "moral" imperatives of racial justice could be achieved only by exempting the North and enforcing integration in the South "with the utmost diligence." Senator Jacob K. Javits of New York maintained that the debate needed "to be placed on the level it deserves—the moral level"— and therefore that it should focus on the South. Senator Abraham A. Ribicoff of Connecticut deplored the "monumental hypocrisy" of his northern liberal colleagues and argued, "As long as the North hides in lily-white suburbs and as long as they say this is a southern problem, we are not going to attack the basic problem." Congress engaged in a similar debate later in the same year when considering the extension of the 1965 Voting Rights Act. Southern segregationists called for the nationwide protection of voting rights, while northern liberals defended the "moral" position that enforcement of voting rights should be confined to the South. Such inanity confirmed the end of the civil rights era and drained the "moral issue" of whatever validity it might have originally possessed.[2]

[1] Hayes Mizell, "School Desegregation and the Southern Strategy," *New South*, Spring, 1970, p. 41.

[2] "Congress and Federal School Racial Policy," *Congressional Digest*, IL (1970), 106, 116, 115, 122; Judith F. Buncher, ed., *The School Busing Controversy, 1970–1975* (New York,

Southern congressmen and their largely Republican allies held the initiative as the fracas continued. By the fall of 1972, northern senators were conducting a filibuster against civil rights legislation that the southern segregationists were sponsoring. Both President Nixon and President Ford supported the national application of desegregation measures, as well as antibusing legislation. In 1975 and again in 1977, Congress passed and President Ford signed amendments limiting busing and defending "neighborhood schools." The swelling congressional opposition to civil rights experiments and the reluctance of nonsouthern legislators to accord integration the same urgency in the North as in the South testified to the abiding unpopularity of busing. The political climate had changed to where protests and demonstrations were more likely to be in opposition to than in support of integration.[3]

The brabble in Congress had little direct result. The federal courts steered racial policy during the 1970s, and to all appearances they paid scant attention to Congress. Of all the nation's political institutions, the Supreme Court had the deepest investment in school integration. The National Association for the Advancement of Colored People, as well as other establishment civil rights groups and a considerable number of upper-middle-class racial liberals, agreed that school desegregation was the "only solution available if there is to be substantial integration in this generation." The United States Civil Rights Commission had earlier criticized the trend toward "racial isolation in the public schools," and the National Advisory Commission on Civil Disorders—the Riot Commission—had warned, "Our nation is moving toward two societies, one black, one white—separate and unequal." With the federal executive, Congress, and most state governments ever firmer in their antagonism toward busing—in the South, only Reubin Askew of Florida accepted it as a necessary imposition— the Supreme Court persevered.[4]

1975), 99–117; Richard L. Engstrom, "Black Politics and the Voting Rights Act, 1965–1982," in *Contemporary Southern Politics,* ed. James F. Lea (Baton Rouge, 1988), 83–106; Stephen F. Lawson, *In Pursuit of Power: Southern Blacks and Electoral Politics* (New York, 1985), 121–90.

[3] Buncher, ed., *The School Busing Controversy,* 185–200; George R. Metcalf, *From Little Rock to Boston: The History of School Desegregation* (Westport, Conn., 1983), 229–41.

[4] Gary Orfield, *Must We Bus? Segregated Schools and National Policy* (Washington, D.C.,

The Court extended busing outside the South in *Keyes* v. *Denver,* decided in 1973. The justices found complicity on the part of the public officials of Denver in perpetuating racial segregation, and their order imposed what was in effect citywide busing. In *Keyes,* the Court did not enunciate a universal set of conditions sufficient for triggering judicial remedies. Rather, discrimination could be assumed in the South, the Court decided, but had to be proved in the North. Nevertheless, even given the difficulty of proving wrongful intent in the creation of de facto segregation, federal courts ordered busing in a sizable number of nonsouthern cities.[5]

Keyes applied only to the city of Denver. Coloradans made the point explicit the following year when they approved a constitutional amendment barring Denver from annexing neighboring suburban areas, thereby ensuring that the city's problems remained within the city. Busing plans for entire metropolitan areas took effect only in consolidated school districts like Charlotte-Mecklenburg and Louisville–Jefferson County. In large metropolitan areas, there could be no more than a gesture at integration without including the suburbs in busing plans.

In cases involving Richmond and Detroit, the Supreme Court shrank from requiring the outlying districts to help in reducing the racial imbalances in the cities. In the Virginia case, a federal district court, taking into account that Richmond's public-school enrollment was already almost two-thirds black, had ordered a busing plan incorporating suburban Henrico and Chesterfield counties. The United States Court of Appeals for the Fourth Circuit had then overruled the district court on the grounds that the judiciary had no authority to alter a state's internal political boundaries. The Supreme Court, with Justice Lewis Powell of Richmond disqualifying himself, upheld the circuit court by a vote of four to four. Because of the tie, the Detroit case became crucial. In Detroit the situation was like that in Richmond, except that the circuit court had upheld the district court's devising of a busing

---

1978), 7; *Racial Isolation in the Public Schools: A Report of the U.S. Commission on Civil Rights* (1967); *Report of the National Advisory Commission on Civil Disorders* (New York, 1968), 1.

[5] *Keyes* v. *School District Number One, Denver, Colorado,* 413 U.S. 189 (1973); J. Harvie Wilkinson III, *From Brown to Bakke: The Supreme Court and School Integration, 1954–1978* (New York, 1979), 193–203.

plan that required participation by Detroit's suburbs. In a five-to-four decision, the Supreme Court in 1974 rejected the district court's contention that "school district lines are simply matters of political convenience and may not be used to deny constitutional rights." Busing, the Court ruled in *Milliken* v. *Bradley*, does not take precedence over jurisdictional autonomy.[6]

Milliken v. *Bradley* was akin in tenor to *San Antonio* v. *Rodriguez*, decided the year before. In that case, plaintiffs challenged school financing practices in Texas. Like other southern states, the state of Texas aided local school districts through arrangements such as its minimum foundation program, and as elsewhere, the districts augmented the state's allocations with local school taxes. Although poor districts commonly taxed their residents at a higher rate than rich districts, the rich districts could afford substantially higher expenditures per pupil. The Supreme Court agreed that "the Texas system discriminates on the basis of wealth in the manner in which education is provided for its people," but it could discover no constitutional basis for overturning the system. The Court reversed district and circuit court rulings and upheld the procedures employed in Texas.[7]

The Court's approach was in harmony with the upper-middle-class bias of civil rights reform. The *San Antonio* decision assured that the schools most likely to be integrated—those in the southern countryside and those within the cities—would be the most inadequately financed, while the schools least likely to experience anything beyond token desegregation would also be the most generously supported. The Court also upheld a California provision that had the effect of keeping low-rent housing projects out of suburban areas. The *Swann* decision of 1971, which ordered integration in southern cities, and the *Keyes* decision of 1973, which extended court-ordered integration northward, moved the focus of the civil rights debate from the rural and small-town South to the cities, but through it all the more affluent suburbs remained largely outside the fray.[8]

[6] *School Board of City of Richmond, Virginia* v. *State Board of Education of Virginia*, 412 U.S. 92 (1973); *Milliken* v. *Bradley*, 418 U.S. 717 (1974).
[7] *San Antonio Independent School District* v. *Rodriguez*, 411 U.S. 16 (1973).
[8] *James* v. *Valtierra*, 402 U.S. 137 (1971).

Southern critics ranging from Stokely Carmichael to George C. Wallace had long been contemptuous of northern liberals who promoted social experiments for the less privileged while residing in the insulated suburbs of Connecticut, Maryland, and northern Virginia. The Supreme Court's acquiescence in confining integration to working-class and poor whites and blacks in the declining cities and the declining southern outland merely confirmed their analysis. Under such conditions, elaborate busing programs largely betrayed the fond liberal dream that integration would by itself suffice for increasing toleration and accomplishment among students. After reviewing the literature on the subject, one scholar determined, "The main conclusion we can draw from these . . . studies is that busing per se has almost no effect." Some evidence suggested that pupils from educationally deprived backgrounds benefited from attending schools with affluent, educationally advantaged classmates, but that pedagogic arrangement was rarely an option. As Christopher Jencks has concluded, "School desegregation can have a profound effect if it is part of a larger effort to transform relations between blacks and whites, but . . . it has very little effect in and of itself." [9]

The Court's reliance on intracity busing hastened the already brisk exodus of whites to the suburbs. Southern cities, and especially their public schools, were on their way to becoming black enclaves. In an effort to stabilize public-school enrollment, the leadership of the Atlanta NAACP in 1973 joined with other blacks and whites who wielded power in the city to negotiate an end to extensive busing in exchange for the appointment of a black city superintendent and black administrative control of the school system. By then, fewer than a quarter of Atlanta's public-school students were white. In 1970 segregationists created the Southern Independent School Association to assist in the development of private schools, but financial realities limited them to the well-off.

[9] Jennifer L. Hochschild, *The New American Dilemma: Liberal Democracy and School Desegregation* (New Haven, 1984), 59; James S. Coleman *et al.*, *Equality of Educational Opportunity* (Washington, D.C., 1966), esp. 3–24; Christopher Jencks, "Busing: The Supreme Court Goes North," in *The Great School Bus Controversy*, ed. Nicolaus Mills (New York, 1973), 22; Christopher Jencks *et al.*, *Inequality: A Reassessment of the Effect of Family and Schooling in America* (New York, 1972); David L. Horowitz, *The Courts and Social Policy* (Washington, D.C., 1977), 22–67.

The modest growth in the number of private schools—about 6 percent of southern students attended private academies in the early 1970s—provided one more escape for the prosperous who wished to leave integration to the hoi polloi.[10]

The great crusade to integrate the schools that began with the *Brown* decision of 1954 never met the expectations of its sponsors. The schools were the central focus of racial reform through much of the period after World War II, but they proved incapable of accomplishing a social transformation. Desegregation became the norm in educational—indeed in most public—facilities, particularly in the South, but busing programs were so massively unpopular that they tended to discredit civil rights reform generally. In the fall of 1971, nine out of ten southern whites opposed the mandatory transportation of students, as did about half the blacks. "Busing as a means of achieving racial balance in the schools," *Time* magazine ventured, "may well be the most unpopular institution imposed on Americans since Prohibition."[11]

The decline of black civil rights reform coincided with the ascent of the women's rights movement. The black struggle in the South clearly helped shape the women's campaign. Women who participated in the civil rights movement—most obviously those who took part in the Mississippi Freedom Summer of 1964—could hardly avoid drawing parallels between the "treatment of Negroes and treatment of women in our society as a whole." More fundamentally, by rejecting the southern caste system and insisting on individual opportunity, black people repudiated social restrictions based on immutable racial distinctions. In that, they contributed to a redefinition of individual rights. By the late 1960s, as Cynthia Harrison has stated, a growing number of women were also rejecting the validity of social policies determined by immutable characteristics and arguing "that differences between men's and women's roles were culturally based rather than biologically determined."[12]

[10] Clarence N. Stone, *Regime Politics: Governing Atlanta, 1946–1988* (Lawrence, Kans., 1989), 103–107; Margaret Rose Gladney, "I'll Take My Stand: The Southern Segregation Academy Movement" (Ph.D. dissertation, University of New Mexico, 1974).

[11] George H. Gallup in Nashville *Tennessean*, September 13, 1971; "Busing and Strikes: Schools in Turmoil," *Time*, September 15, 1975, p. 35.

[12] Casey Hayden and Mary King, "Sex and Caste," in *Personal Politics: The Roots of Women's*

Still, the differences between the two movements were substantial. Whereas black protest sprang from largely southern roots, the impetus for female rights came from outside the region. Whereas the federal government was excruciatingly reluctant to support black rights until forced to do so by massive protest, it sponsored the women's rights campaign. Whereas southern states massively resisted black gains, the spread of women's issues into the region caused few political ripples.

The decisive boost to an inchoate women's movement came from Congressman Howard W. Smith's insertion of the word *sex* in the 1964 Civil Rights Act. The Virginia congressman shared with the Republican-oriented National Woman's Party a concern that the Civil Rights Act without an amendment of the sort he offered "would not even give protection against discrimination because of 'race, color, religion, or national origin,' to a White Woman, a Woman of the Christian Religion, or a Woman of United States Origin." With his amendment, the Civil Rights Act placed the burgeoning federal civil rights bureaucracy in the service of gender equality. By the end of the 1960s federal agencies had begun, Hugh D. Graham has noted, "to rule almost as aggressively on gender as it had from the beginning on race." As Paul Burstein has pointed out, white women proved to be the "main beneficiaries" of legislation that had originally been designed to aid black men.[13]

Smith's amendment appeared unexpectedly without being preceded by congressional hearings or popular debate. Even within the federal government, women reformers were divided. The strongest faction, the labor-oriented "women's bureau coalition," opposed the amendment, preferring instead a program that upheld the New Deal legacy of family-oriented social reform and special protection for women workers. As the national Democratic party sloughed off its traditional blue-collar and pink-blouse work-

---

Liberation in the Civil Rights Movement and the New Left, by Sara Evans (New York, 1979), 235; Cynthia Harrison, *On Account of Sex: The Politics of Women's Issues, 1945–1968* (Berkeley and Los Angeles, 1988), 220.

[13] Harrison, *On Account of Sex,* 176; Hugh D. Graham, *The Civil Rights Era: Origins and Development of National Policy, 1960–1972* (New York, 1990), 231; Paul Burstein, *Discrimination, Jobs, and Politics* (Chicago, 1985), 192.

ing-class voter base, upper-middle-class Democrats became more influential. They joined their Republican colleagues in support of equal rights for women. The Democrats drawn to that cause were, however, as Hugh Graham has written, a "thin, elite network of top-down reformers, not representatives empowered by a grass-roots social movement." [14]

The task of enlisting recruits fell largely to the President's Commission on the Status of Women, the Citizens' Advisory Council on the Status of Women, and the Interdepartmental Committee on the Status of Women, all created by President Kennedy in the early 1960s and originally dominated by the women's bureau coalition. Much as the United States Civil Rights Commission served as a tax-supported lobbying agency for black civil rights, the presidential agencies, most particularly the Citizens' Advisory Council, promoted gender equality and proved to be what Janet K. Boles has termed a "forerunner in the women's rights movement." By early 1967, when Texas created a state advisory agency, the Citizens' Advisory Council had commissions in all fifty states. By that time the council and its state affiliates had sponsored the formation of the National Organization of Women, which in 1967 endorsed passage of an equal rights amendment that read, "Equality of rights under the law shall not be denied or abridged by the United States or by any State on account of sex." [15]

In 1972 Congress passed the Equal Rights Amendment by lopsided majorities and sent it to the states for ratification. The amendment received vigorous support from the Citizens' Advisory Committee and its state commissions and from virtually all upper-middle-class women's groups, led by the National Federation of Business and Professional Women's Clubs and the National Organization of Women. Most metropolitan newspapers, the National Association of Manufacturers, and other representatives of middle-class respectability endorsed the amendment. Twenty-two states quickly ratified it, and eight more did so in 1973, leaving the amendment eight states short of approval.[16]

[14] Graham, *The Civil Rights Era*, 225.

[15] Janet K. Boles, *The Politics of the Equal Rights Amendment: Conflict and the Decision Process* (New York, 1979), 44; Mary Frances Berry, *Why ERA Failed: Politics, Women's Rights, and the Amending Process of the Constitution* (Bloomington, Ind., 1986), 121.

[16] The campaign for the Equal Rights Amendment is examined by Boles in *The Politics of*

For a time it seemed that even the southern states would support the amendment. In 1971 Virginia's voters approved an equal rights amendment to the state constitution, and in 1972 the voters of Texas endorsed a state amendment assuring equal legal rights by a four-to-one majority. The legislatures in Texas and Tennessee ratified the Equal Rights Amendment by large majorities in the spring of 1972, and soon afterward the Kentucky legislature approved it by a close vote in both houses. Thereafter, the amendment's success in the South ended. In 1974 Tennessee rescinded its ratification, and in 1978 the Kentucky legislature voted to rescind ratification and Governor Julian Carroll vetoed the rescinder. Texas turned out to be the only southern state to endorse the amendment unequivocally. In the end, the states rejected the Equal Rights Amendment, and ten of the fifteen states that never ratified it were southern.[17]

Because of the top-down structure of the women's rights campaign, the forces behind the amendment lacked organized grassroots support, most particularly in the South. When Phyllis Schlafly of Illinois established Stop ERA in late 1972, she quickly won broad southern backing. Many metropolitan business and professional women, along with well-educated suburban homemakers, favored the amendment, but elsewhere in southern society the commitment to it was often less than enthusiastic. Working-class women tended to be suspicious of "county-club feminism." Kathy Kahn, a labor activist, boasted that "most working-class women . . . will never fall prey to the media-created fads which advertise themselves as 'women's liberation.' " A receptionist in Atlanta remarked, "Middle-class women's lib is a trend; working women's liberation is a necessity." Black women, who for generations had been minding the kitchens and nurseries of white women, often held similar views. The women's movement, a black woman observed, "is just a bunch of bored white women with

the Equal Rights Amendment; by Berry in Why ERA Failed; by Jane J. Mansbridge in Why We Lost the ERA (Chicago, 1986); and by Gilbert Y. Steiner in Constitutional Inequality: The Political Fortunes of the Equal Rights Amendment (Washington, D.C., 1983).

[17] Berry, Why ERA Failed, 86–100; Boles, The Politics of the Equal Rights Amendment, 1–8.

nothing to do—they're just trying to attract attention away from the black liberation movement."[18]

The southern cultural mystique tempered the immediate effect of a campaign for women's rights. "The past—not the one validated in schoolbooks but another kind, unanalyzed and undefined—hangs upon Southern women as if they were dispossessed royalty," Shirley Abbott has reminisced. "I never learned," she added, "to construe the female sex as downtrodden or disadvantaged." Academic studies supported Abbott's observations. When Caroline M. Dillman looked for "continuity or change" among southern women, she discovered continuity. "It is going to take time," she wrote, "for them to catch up to women in other parts of the country." Even southern professional women, limited evidence suggests, were less feminist and less committed to individual and career goals.[19]

In a study of the defeat of the Equal Rights Amendment in North Carolina, Donald G. Mathews and Jane S. De Hart found that they "were dealing with two different ways of understanding the universe. One was comfortable with modern social analysis and challenges to tradition; the other believed such critiques eroded the foundation of self and community." The National Organization of Women declared, "We reject the current assumptions . . . that marriage, home and family are primarily women's world. . . . We believe that a true partnership between the sexes demands a different concept of marriage, an equitable sharing of the responsibilities of home and children and of the economic

[18] Donald G. Mathews and Jane Sherron De Hart, *Sex, Gender, and the Politics of ERA: A State and the Nation* (New York, 1990), 145; Kathy Kahn, ed., *Hillbilly Women* (New York, 1973), 19, 183; Helen H. King, "Black Women and Women's Lib," *Ebony*, March, 1971, p. 70; Dolores E. Janiewski, *Sisterhood Denied: Race, Gender, and Class in a New South Community* (Philadelphia, 1985), 152–78; James H. Cone, *For My People: Black Theology and the Black Church* (Maryknoll, N.Y., 1984), 122–39; Irene L. Murphy, *Public Policy on the Status of Women: Agenda and Strategy for the 1970s* (Lexington, Mass., 1973).

[19] Shirley Abbott, *Womenfolks: Growing Up down South* (New Haven, 1983), 31; Rosemary Daniel, *Fatal Flowers: On Sin, Sex, and Suicide in the Deep South* (New York, 1980); Maxine Alexander, ed., *Speaking for Ourselves: Women of the South* (New York, 1984); Caroline Matheny Dillman, "Southern Women: In Continuity or Change?" in *Women in the South: An Anthropological Perspective*, ed. Holly F. Mathews (Athens, Ga., 1989), 8–17; Susan Middleton-Deirn and Jackie Howsden-Eller, "Reconstructing Femininity: The Woman Professional in the South," in *Women in the South*, 57–70.

burdens of their support." Stop ERA campaigned under the slogan You Can't Fool Mother Nature. The difference between those
who supported and those who opposed the constitutional amendment divided the more "advanced" elements of the South's new
middle class from much of the rest of southern society.[20]

The abortion issue complicated and before long overshadowed
the debate concerning the amendment. In 1973 the Supreme
Court, in a case stemming from a challenge to an antiabortion
law in Texas and in a companion case relating to a Georgia law,
declared state legislation that prohibited abortion unconstitutional. Such legislation, the Court declared, violated an individual's right to privacy. Roe v. Wade, the Texas case, touched off an
escalating controversy, with the "moral issue" this time claimed by
the right-to-life defenders of traditional twentieth-century restrictions. Those who opposed abortions—often Catholics and fundamentalist Protestants—tended to hold extremely strong feelings about it. Their passion fascinated journalists and assured
widespread media coverage. At the same time, the religiously
based defense of lower-middle-class morality strengthened the influence of southern television evangelists and helped direct political disaffection into religious channels, which doubtless contributed to the southern moderate political consensus and to the
declining turnout among lower-income voters.[21]

The South proved to be infertile ground for an equal rights
amendment but gender practices changed anyway. More women
entered the work force: in 1970 women made up 39 percent of
it, and in 1980 they amounted to 43 percent. Affirmative-action
measures broadened opportunities, at least for more highly educated women. Julia K. Blackwelder has written, "The work and
family patterns of southern women [underwent a] revolution
wrought by Sunbelt development and the civil rights movement."
Iris, a character in one of Bobbie Ann Mason's short stories, ex-
postulated, "Times are different now, Pappy. We're just as good

[20] Mathews and De Hart, *Sex, Gender, and the Politics of ERA*, x; National Organization of
Women, Statement of Purpose, in *Up from the Pedestal: Selected Writings in the History of American Feminism*, ed. Aileen S. Kraditor (Chicago, 1968), 368; Berry, *Why ERA Failed*, 66.

[21] *Roe* v. *Wade*, 410 U.S. 113 (1973); *Doe* v. *Bolton*, 410 U.S. 179 (1973); Eva R. Rubin,
Abortion, Politics, and the Courts: Roe v. Wade and Its Aftermath (Rev. ed., New York, 1987).

as the men." The incomplete autonomy of southern women showed in the response by Iris' husband: "She gets that from television." Yet, as Blackwelder pointed out, "The economic, demographic, and social changes that have occurred since World War II have diminished the differences between women in the urban South and women in other American cities." [22]

Even while rejecting the Equal Rights Amendment, southern state governments acknowledged changing social practices. Georgia, Kentucky, and Oklahoma enacted relatively comprehensive laws requiring fair employment practices and equal pay in the workplace. Other states passed more limited legislation. North Carolina's provisions for fair practices in employment by the state exempted the highway department, where a majority of the skilled jobholders worked. Enforcement procedures varied from state to state. Still, the requirement of equal pay and fairness in the labor market and the prohibition of discrimination in the financing of housing and in other areas became relatively common in the region. Southern state governments were hardly pioneers in the drive for racial and gender equality, but by accommodating change rather than practicing massive resistance to it, they demonstrated the new directions in southern politics.[23]

Amid the debates over busing, equal rights, and abortion, the southern population and economy expanded rapidly. In the 1960s the southern states reversed a long-standing historical trend when more people moved into the region than moved out of it. The immigrants of the 1960s were overwhelmingly white and often well educated, and they moved mainly to Florida, Texas, and Virginia. The rest of the South continued to lose people to other parts of the country. In the 1970s states throughout the region

[22] Julia Kirk Blackwelder, "Race, Ethnicity, and Women's Lives in the Urban South," in *Shades of the Sunbelt: Essays on Ethnicity, Race, and the Urban South*, ed. Randall M. Miller and George E. Pozetta (Westport, Conn., 1988), 78, 88; Bobbie Ann Mason, *Shiloh and Other Stories* (New York, 1982), 104.

[23] Susan Deller Ross, *The Rights of Women* (New York, 1973), 291–347; *Shana Alexander's State-by-State Guide to Women's Legal Rights* (Los Angeles, 1975), 166–75; Susan Deller Ross and Ann Barcher, *The Rights of Women* (Rev. ed.; New York, 1983); David F. Ross, "State and Local Governments," in *Employment of Blacks in the South: A Perspective on the 1960s*, ed. Ray Marshall and Virgil L. Christian, Jr. (Austin, Tex., 1978), 70–106; Franklin J. James *et al., Minorities in the Sunbelt* (New Brunswick, N.J., 1984).

reported a net inflow, and the newcomers included both whites and blacks. A black electrician in Chicago whose father had moved north acknowledged, "I'm moving south for the same reasons my father came here from Mississippi. He was looking for a better way of life." [24]

By 1980 approximately two in ten southern residents had been born outside the region. Florida was in a category by itself, with the southern-born constituting less than half its population, and it skewed the proportion of outsiders for the South as a whole. Even so, the presence of people from other places was conspicuous not only in Florida. During the 1970s the southern population increased from fifty-six million to sixty-eight million and the southern work force from twenty-one million to twenty-nine million. By 1980 per capita personal income in Florida, Texas, and Virginia approximated the national average, and taking cost-of-living differences into account, the income gap between southern and national norms was no longer a chasm.

The demographic and economic expansion in the South and West contrasted with the hard times the North was experiencing. National corporations had long pursued a "southern strategy" of escaping labor unions and high wages by moving production facilities south. With the success of American Cold War policies making much of the world safe for multinational corporations, the southern strategy became a Third World strategy that pursued an even cheaper and more docile labor force. When Arab nations in 1973 declared an oil embargo and the Organization of Petroleum Exporting Countries escalated the price of petroleum, the resulting energy crisis exacerbated the manufacturing problems of the midwestern and northeastern industrial belt. The resulting recession of the mid-1970s was the most severe since World War II, and for a decade thereafter periodic recessions and bouts of "stagfla-

[24] David R. Goldfield, *Promised Land: The South Since 1945* (Arlington Heights, Tex., 1987), 216; Timothy G. O'Rourke, "The Demographic and Economic Setting of Southern Politics," in *Contemporary Southern Politics*, ed. Lea, 9–33; Randall M. Miller, "The Development of the Modern Urban South: An Historical Overview," in *Shades of the Sunbelt*, ed. Miller and Pozetta, 1–20; Earl Black and Merle Black, *Politics and Society in the South* (Cambridge, Mass., 1987), 3–49.

tion" racked the nation and most particularly the northern Rust Belt.[25]

The southern states weathered the storm relatively well. The regional economy gained from federal military outlays during the late sixties and early seventies. At the height of military expansion in 1968, war spending provided jobs for an estimated 8 percent of the nonagricultural work force in the South. The energy crisis created a demand for domestically produced fuels that meant an economic boom for Kentucky and the rest of the Appalachian coal region and for the states that supplied oil and natural gas, especially Texas, Louisiana, and Oklahoma. The price of coal reached unheard-of levels, and only federal price controls prevented an even greater economic bonanza in the Southwest.[26]

The eversion of the customary images of North and South received its most influential expression in Kirkpatrick Sale's *Power Shift,* which appeared in 1975. Sale described an area stretching from North Carolina to southern California that had gained "enormous economic importance . . . , an importance all the more remarkable in that it has come about only in the last thirty years, changing the pleasant little backwaters and half-grown cities into an industrial and financial colossus." The new colossus, Sale suggested, had an "economy built upon money from Washington and a culture devoted unreservedly to growth." Its "six basic pillars" were agribusiness, defense, advanced technology, oil and natural-gas production, real estate and construction, and tourism and leisure. A Manhattan journalist, Sale was by no means gratified by what he perceived to be a "cowboy culture" delinquent in morality but rich in right-wing politics, racist excesses, and repressive impulses. Yet, in his view, national developments had "quite simply shifted the balance of power in America away from the Northeast and toward the Southern Rim."[27]

[25] E. Blaine Liner and Lawrence K. Lynch, eds., *The Economics of Southern Growth* (Durham, N.C., 1977); Bernard L. Weinstein and Robert E. Firestine, *Regional Growth and Decline in the United States: The Rise of the Sunbelt and the Decline of the Northeast* (New York, 1978).

[26] C. S. Pyun, *Impacts of Defense Procurement on the Mid-South Economy* (Memphis, 1973), 32; Bruce J. Schulman, *From Cotton Belt to Sun Belt: Federal Policy, Economic Development, and the Transformation of the South, 1938–1980.*

[27] Kirkpatrick Sale, *Power Shift: The Rise of the Southern Rim and Its Challenge to the Eastern Establishment* (New York, 1975), 18–20, 55, 6.

Whatever Sale's misgivings, his depiction of a vibrant and burgeoning region quickly became standard fare in the national media. The nation's image of the South, as well as southern people's image of themselves, had been improving since the coming of the New South governors in the early 1970s. In February, 1976, the New York *Times* ran a series of front-page articles in which it gave currency to the name Sunbelt. Thereafter, virtually every national magazine carried articles, usually flattering, about the newly discovered Sunbelt South, and even the *Times* of London published a special supplement devoted to the "New South." As Carl Abbott has observed, the name Sunbelt "passed from coinage to cliché in 1976 and 1977."[28]

The South's new-won respectability extended well beyond the printed page. The family television series *The Waltons,* Senator Sam J. Ervin as chair of the Senate Watergate hearings, and "Country" Charlie Pride, the first successful black country-music artist, typified the new, improved Sunbelt South. "Good ole boys" rather than grotesque racists now drove the pickup trucks, and they, according to *Time* magazine, possessed a well-intentioned "devil-may-care lightheartedness" rather than a propensity for racial violence. Lillian Carter, the president's mother, and Miss Jane Pittman, the black protagonist in an acclaimed television drama, personified the strength and wisdom of southern women. The once benighted region had become, Fred Hobson has written, "what one might call a superior South—a region cleaner, less crowded, more open and honest, more genuinely religious and friendly, and suddenly more racially tolerant than any other American region." Hobson added: "The role of moral superiority appears a strange one for Dixie."[29]

Southern music, particularly country music, spread nationwide and won a new respectability. In the early 1960s there were ap-

---

[28] New York *Times,* February 8, 1976–February 13, 1976; *Times* (London), September 29, 1977; Carl Abbott, "New West, New South, New Region," in *Searching for the Sunbelt: Historical Perspectives on a Region,* ed. Raymond A. Mohl (Knoxville, Tenn., 1990), 9; Gene Burd, "The Selling of the Sunbelt: Civic Boosterism in the Media," in *The Rise of the Sunbelt Cities,* ed. David C. Perry and Alfred J. Watkins (Beverly Hills, Calif., 1977), 129–50.

[29] "Those Good Ole Boys," *Time,* September 27, 1976, p. 47; Fred Hobson, *Tell About the South: The Southern Rage to Explain* (Baton Rouge, 1983), 14, 354; Jack Temple Kirby, *Media-Made Dixie: The South in the American Imagination* (Rev. ed., Athens, Ga., 1986).

proximately eighty country-music radio stations in the nation; by the mid-1970s all-country stations numbered more than a thousand. Country music of the 1970s was more commercial and more sexually explicit than it had been, but it continued to portray sinful people attempting to cope with infidelity, heartbreak, and suffering. Considerably more often than not, country music was politically conservative. Merle Haggard's "Okie from Muskogee" and "Fightin' Side of Me" were, as James C. Cobb has noted, musical versions of America—Love It or Leave It bumper stickers. Tammy Wynette expressed traditional gender views when she sang "Don't Liberate Me, Love Me." Even the more representative releases, such as Tanya Tucker's "Would You Lay with Me in a Field of Stone?" and Loretta Lynn's "Your Squaw's on the Warpath," gave voice to the wider sexual freedom and the enhanced status of women without endorsing the implications of women's liberation.[30]

Southern rock music also earned a national following during the 1970s. In the late 1950s and early 1960s such rock 'n' roll recording artists as Elvis Presley of Mississippi, Jerry Lee Lewis of Louisiana, and Buddy Holly of Texas dominated the music charts, but southern-inspired rock 'n' roll succumbed in the midsixties to the British Invasion, led by the Beatles and the Rolling Stones. The British Invasion muted regional distinctions in music and circumscribed the appeal of rock 'n' roll. The Allman Brothers Band of Macon, Georgia, popularized southern rock during the 1970s. "Much southern rock," Stephen R. Tucker has commented, "evoked explicit images of southern culture and aggression, the superiority of rural life, and unbridled individualism." Both country and southern rock came with hefty doses of nostalgia, and both depicted a commercial, individualized, and newly self-confident region.[31]

[30] James C. Cobb, "From Muskogee to Luckenbach: Country Music and the 'Southernization' of America," *Journal of Popular Culture*, XVI (1982), 84, 88; Paul DiMaggio *et al.*, "Country Music: Ballad of the Silent Majority," in *The Sounds of Social Change*, ed. R. Serge Denisoff and Richard A. Peterson (Chicago, 1972), 38–55; Bill C. Malone, *Southern Music, American Music* (Lexington, Ky., 1979).

[31] Stephen R. Tucker, "Rock, Southern," in *Encyclopedia of Southern Culture*, ed. Charles Reagan Wilson and William Ferris (Chapel Hill, N.C., 1989), 1027; Frye Gaillard, *Race, Rock, and Religion: Profiles from a Southern Journalist* (Charlotte, N.C., 1982).

The new "southern chic" was partly the result of ballyhoo by the region's boosters. "Regional progress," Carl Abbott has written, "could suddenly be defined in terms of convergence or kinship with the dynamic West, as part of a new leading sector marked by fast growth and fast living." Rather than having to defend a backward part of the country, southern promoters were in the unaccustomed position of advertising their region as trend-setting. *Sunbelt* became a popular name for new business firms, and the southern-based press, most notably the magazine *Southern Living*, celebrated the southern way of life with its year-round golf games and barbecue cookouts.[32]

Yet the South's place in the national economy had changed rather less than Kirkpatrick Sale led readers to believe. In important ways the region remained a dependency of economic power headquartered elsewhere. Thierry J. Noyelle and Thomas M. Stanback have pointed out in their study of American cities that the southern pattern of growth "has differed markedly from that in the snowbelt." The decimation of manufacturing in the Snowbelt not only cost the nation many of its higher-wage, unionized industrial jobs but also was an aspect of the structural shift from production to service, most crucially to services connected with the "complex of corporate activities" supporting the great multinational corporations. While manufacturing jobs moved to the Third World, the corporations' main offices, along with the commercial-banking, advertising, and other ancillary business and financial services they required, remained in the United States— by and large in the Snowbelt and in California. The transition from producing things in the Snowbelt to overseeing the production of things in Mexico, Indonesia, and the South lay behind much of the economic crisis in the North during the 1970s.[33]

Southern metropolitan areas became larger, more complex, and more sophisticated, but to a striking degree they remained what Arthur F. Raper and Ira De A. Reed three and a half decades earlier had called "branch-house" cities. Economic and popula-

---

[32] Abbott, "New West, New South, New Region," 16; Bradley R. Rice, "Searching for the Sunbelt," in *Searching for the Sunbelt*, ed. Mohl, 212–23; Burd, "The Selling of the Sunbelt."

[33] Thierry J. Noyelle and Thomas M. Stanback, Jr., *The Economic Transformation of American Cities* (New York, 1984), 18.

tion growth made the South a far more profitable consumer market than it had been, and national firms managed from New York and Chicago opened or increased the size of regional offices in favored southern cities. The well-developed airports and shipping and warehousing infrastructure in southern metropolises were the hardware of regional distribution hubs. Southern metropolitan areas retained closer ties with their hinterlands and with agriculture than did the larger Snowbelt cities, and the national firms headquartered in the South were apt to produce foods and beverages or provide retail and distribution services. Unlike the Snowbelt, the South continued to gain manufacturing jobs in the 1970s, and employment in the public sector and in health services expanded throughout the nation. But for the more substantial southern cities, distribution, consumer, and retail services were the chief engine of population growth.

Houston, Miami, and New Orleans joined Atlanta and Dallas as regional metropolises. Houston and Miami were the South's most important international centers. Houston specialized in petroleum and energy-related equipment, trade, and services. Miami was the gateway for commerce with Latin America. New Orleans, at the core of the mammoth complex of chemical plants, grain elevators, and port facilities stretching along the Mississippi River to Baton Rouge, regained some of the economic significance it had lost earlier in the century. Dallas remained the South's preeminent financial center. The Dallas–Fort Worth metropolitan area, with its balance between high-wage manufacturing and diversified services, was the region's largest metropolitan area. Its population of almost three million in 1980 placed it just ahead of Houston in size.

Regional capitals increased in number during the postwar years. By the 1970s, they included Charlotte, North Carolina; Jackson, Mississippi; Shreveport, Louisiana; and Little Rock. In booming south Florida were three of the eight southern metropolitan areas that had more than one million people in 1980: Miami, Tampa–St. Petersburg, and Fort Lauderdale–Hollywood. The economy of the area owed not only to the international trade of Miami but to tourism and retirement living, diversified manufacturing, real estate and construction, and drug smuggling, as well.

San Antonio, Norfolk-Portsmouth, and several smaller regional capitals remained closely tied to the military-industrial complex.[34]

Throughout the region, much of the economic and population growth was in the suburbs. Corporate and government offices and the operations of banking and insurance firms and other companies providing services to businesses and individuals often located in suburban areas, as did much of the region's manufacturing and warehousing. As Carl Abbott has remarked, "Suburbs are increasingly self-sustaining as economic entities that are able to generate their own jobs." Atlanta, so often hailed as the premier city of the New South, exhibited in slightly exaggerated form the main trends of metropolitan development. By the mid-1970s only 12 percent of the metropolitan work force held jobs within the city itself, and a host of businesses had followed their customers to where they lived and worked. Between 1963 and 1972 retail sales inside the city limits increased by 78 percent; in the metropolitan area around the city they grew by 286 percent. In 1963 the city of Atlanta had 4,276 retail firms, and there were 3,870 in the rest of the metropolitan area. In 1972 the city of Atlanta had 4,605 retail firms, and there were 7,948 in the suburbs. "Of all the major sunbelt cities," Abbott pointed out in 1981, "Atlanta stands at the greatest social and economic disadvantage in relation to its suburban ring." Other southern cities were not much better off. Christopher Silver commented that Richmond "had become a city polarized between its core and its periphery, between poor and affluent, between black and white."[35]

Central business districts remained important. The building booms of the 1950s and especially the 1960s had multiplied the high-rise office buildings that often contained the executive suites of banks, law firms, government agencies, and corporations. The complementary hotels, restaurants, entertainment providers, trade and convention centers, and athletic stadiums frequently

[34] *Ibid.;* Perry and Watkins, eds., *The Rise of the Sunbelt Cities.*

[35] Carl Abbott, *The New Urban America: Growth and Politics in Sunbelt Cities* (Chapel Hill, N.C., 1981), 185, 229; Numan V. Bartley, "1940 to the Present," in *A History of Georgia,* ed. Kenneth Coleman (2nd ed.; Athens, Ga., 1991), 339–60; Christopher Silver, *Twentieth-Century Richmond: Planning, Politics, and Race* (Knoxville, Tenn., 1984), 175; Gurney Breckenfeld, "Refilling the Metropolitan Doughnut," in *The Rise of the Sunbelt Cities,* ed. Perry and Watkins, 231–58.

occupied land on which lower-income black housing had once stood. Service employees—janitors, maids, waitresses, and such—were essential, and their pay became the economic base for many inner-city minority neighborhoods. One study concluded, "Low wages in service industries are as important to a city's export industries as are low taxes."[36]

The orgy of urban renewal ended during the 1970s. The election of Richard M. Nixon as president and the passage of the Housing and Community Development Act shifted federal priorities away from large construction. At the same time, the expanding number of blacks in city halls made bulldozing black neighborhoods a more debatable proposition. By the late seventies Atlanta, Birmingham, New Orleans, and Richmond were among the southern cities that had black mayors, and in many places neighborhood political associations had gained influence. Such developments broadened the narrow base of leadership that had previously determined policy in most southern cities. Black mayors, besides being constrained by the same realities that had limited the policy options of white mayors, faced deteriorating city economies. Unsurprisingly, they followed their predecessors in promoting economic growth. Mayor Andrew Young of Atlanta was particularly known for his efforts to entice foreign investments to the city.[37]

The change in the objectives of federal programs led some southern cities to restore districts of historical distinction. In Charleston, New Orleans, Richmond, and Savannah, downtown areas received rehabilitation, and some cities rebuilt smaller neighborhoods, such as Beale Street in Memphis. Monuments to the civil rights movement were relatively numerous, and the reenactments of events in the struggle for civil rights such as the march from Selma to Montgomery and the demonstrations in Birmingham became the "Confederate veterans' parades of the

[36] Daniel R. Fusfeld and Timothy Bates, *The Political Economy of the Urban Ghetto* (Carbondale, Ill., 1984), 162.

[37] Miller, "The Development of the Modern Urban South," 1–20; Christopher Silver, "The Changing Face of Neighborhoods in Memphis and Richmond, 1940–1985," in *Shades of the Sunbelt,* ed. Miller and Pozetta, 93–126; David R. Goldfield, *Black, White, and Southern: Race Relations and Southern Culture, 1940 to the Present* (Baton Rouge, 1990), 181–95.

late twentieth century," in David R. Goldfield's phrase. But although the new style of southern historicism improved the appearance of some inner-city districts and brought in visitors at tourist prices, it also made the housing too expensive for its former residents, and in that regard differed little from clear-and-build urban renewal.[38]

The South continued to attract investments from both national and foreign sources in an increasingly international world economy. In 1981 an Atlanta journalist observed with pride rather than consternation that "most of the prime properties in town are controlled by interests head-quartered elsewhere: New York, Dallas, Boston, Toronto, Hamburg, Amsterdam, Al Kuwait." South Carolinians sometimes referred to portions of the I-85 as the autobahn, because of the large number of German firms along the highway. Foreign firms located in the South, according to a report the Federal Reserve Bank in Atlanta released in 1982, because it offered "abundant, low-cost, hard-working, non-union labor; cheap and abundant land and utilities; low work-stoppage rates; low taxes; good climate; conservative, pro-business state government; and a nice place to raise a family." The international economy also presented a problem. A development official in Alabama complained that "industrial jobs are going out the back door [to the Third World] faster than we can get them in the front door." [39]

To critics, the "almost touching lust of . . . chambers of commerce for new chemical plants, glassy-mazed office parks, and instant subdivisions" appeared to be constructing a Sunbelt South that was less than lustrous. A Washington journalist speculated that a northern Virginia interstate highway was designed by Dante: "No mortal highway engineer, no mere planner of urban sprawl, could have possibly concocted such a heinous scheme." John

[38] David R. Goldfield, "The City as Southern History: The Past and the Promise of Tomorrow," in *The Future South: A Historical Perspective for the Twenty-First Century*, ed. Joe P. Dunn and Howard L. Preston (Urbana, Ill., 1991), 33; David R. Goldfield, *Cotton Fields and Skyscrapers: Southern City and Region, 1607–1980* (Baton Rouge, 1982), 151–58.

[39] Neil Shister, "Who Owns Atlanta?" *Atlanta Magazine*, January, 1981, p. 51; Goldfield, "The City as Southern History," 37; Bank report quoted in Atlanta *Journal and Constitution*, February 14, 1982; Alabama official quoted in "The Sunbelt South: Industrialization in Regional, National, and International Perspective," by James C. Cobb, in *Searching for the Sunbelt*, ed. Mohl, 36.

Egerton meditated, "We had built glittering cities of steel and glass, but they looked for all the world like the cities of the North, and they emptied out at night as our commuters retreated to the suburban Grosse Pointes we had built beyond the moated loops of our freeways." The most telling commentary concerned southern values. Marshall Frady lamented that "the South has been mightily laboring to re-create itself into a tinfoil-twinkling simulation of Southern California, and in the process has unwittingly worked on itself a species of spiritual impoverishment." Tobacco Road had been paved, and purebred cattle grazed on Jeeter Lester's defunct cotton patch, but the evidence suggested that more than a few southerners were ambivalent about what they saw.[40]

Thoughtful observers speculated about the nature of regional cultural distinctiveness and the future of an identifiable southern culture. "If pondering and examining the mind and the soul of Dixie had seemed a Southern affliction before 1945," Fred Hobson has observed, "it assumed epidemic proportions in the three decades thereafter." George B. Tindall japed that during the sixties and early seventies academic symposia on the "changing South" became "one of the flourishing minor industries of the region." Clearly, the South was changing, but as Tindall also pointed out, the Vanishing South was staging "one of the most prolonged disappearing acts since the decline and fall of Rome."[41]

In the late 1950s Harry S. Ashmore, the progressive editor of the *Arkansas Gazette,* and Henry Savage, a conservative advocate of state rights from South Carolina, wrote thoughtfully about their native region. The two men approached their subject from widely different perspectives, but on one issue they were in agreement. Ashmore entitled his work *An Epitaph for Dixie,* and Savage concluded that it was "irretrievably foreordained that, year by year, the South will be more American and less Southern." Writing at approximately the same time as Ashmore and Savage, two econ-

---

[40] Marshall Frady, *Southerners: A Journalist's Odyssey* (New York, 1980), 281–82; Neal R. Peirce, *The Great Plains States of America: People, Politics, and Power in the Nine Great Plains States* (New York, 1973), 102; John Egerton, *Shades of Gray: Dispatches from the Modern South* (Baton Rouge, 1991), 254; Atlanta *Journal and Constitution,* February 1, 1982.

[41] Hobson, *Tell About the South,* 297; George Brown Tindall, *The Ethnic Southerners* (Baton Rouge, 1976), 224, ix.

omists documented in their book *This Changing South* the economic, demographic, and cultural upheavals that "might well hasten the day when the South, once perhaps the most distinctively 'different' American region, will have become in most such matters virtually indistinguishable from the other urban-industrial areas of the nation." Later studies by social scientists and economists usually arrived at a similar conclusion. Like Frank E. Smith in *Look Away from Dixie,* some wondered if the "very concept" of the South had "any future value for the nation, or even for those who live in the South." [42]

Some scholars and journalists vigorously defended southern exceptionalism. Historian Francis Butler Simkins held that the South might be changing but that it remained—in the phrase that he used as the title of a book—the everlasting South. In an earlier volume, Simkins had written, "The South is an attitude of mind and a way of behavior just as much as a territory." The essays in *The Everlasting South* developed that thesis, and he introduced them with the reflection that "it can be argued that the region, despite many changes, is as much different from the rest of the United States today as it was in 1860." Similarly, the contributors to a collection entitled *The Lasting South* generally defended the proposition that "the South has gone on being the South, both despite controversy and because of it, and it will continue to go on being the South." Simkins and most of the contributors to *The Lasting South* expressed an affinity with southern traditions and a skepticism toward the changes taking place in the region. As one of the editors of the collection observed of the South, "Modernity is its most deadly enemy." [43]

Most academic historians were reluctant to pen an "epitaph for Dixie" even though they welcomed the expansion of national values in the region. As a participant in a symposium phrased it,

[42] Harry S. Ashmore, *An Epitaph for Dixie* (New York, 1957); Henry Savage, Jr., *Seeds of Time: The Background of Southern Thinking* (New York, 1959), 274; John H. Maclachlan and Joe S. Floyd, Jr., *This Changing South* (Gainesville, Fla., 1956), 151; Frank E. Smith, *Look Away from Dixie* (Baton Rouge, 1965), 3.

[43] Francis Butler Simkins, *A History of the South* (New York, 1953), ix; Francis Butler Simkins, *The Everlasting South* (Baton Rouge, 1963), xii; Louis D. Rubin, Jr., and James J. Kilpatrick, eds., *The Lasting South: Fourteen Southerners Look at Their Home* (Chicago, 1957), x, 2.

"Unusual courage will be required to paddle out of brackish intellectual waters into the mainstream of history." Particularly during the 1960s, when urbanization and industrialization made the South ever more like the rest of the nation, the region behaved as bizarrely as ever. To explain the paradox, historians searched for a central theme of southern history that would capture the essence of regional culture. They usually turned to psychological interpretations. Among the more provocative efforts to define a central theme were accounts that stressed the region's historical uniqueness, romanticism, extremism, mythology, and most of all white psychological racism. They did not, however, succeed in explaining the core of southern culture or the truculence of white southern resistance to desegregation.[44]

The popular equivalent of the search for a central theme was the literature of "guilt and shame." Usually written by white journalists and often in autobiographical form, it was intense and personalized. Writers like Lillian E. Smith, Pat Watters, and James McBride Dabbs were driven less by a sense of personal guilt than by a feeling of shame for the behavior of their homeland. Such an author, in Fred Hobson's words, "agonized and brooded over the South . . . and felt compelled to pour out his feelings about the South and about himself as a Southerner." The literature of guilt and shame normally focused on race relations and on the failure of the region's white people to recognize the humanity of black people. The spate of works put into words the anguish felt by some white southerners over the region's harsh resistance to the civil rights movement. By the 1970s the increasingly stylized genre was losing much of its appeal. In the Sunbelt "even books of that sort were written from a new spirit of Southern confidence, and authorship no longer appeared a life and death matter."[45]

Black power spurred the national ethnic revival and heralded

[44] Rembert W. Patrick, "The Deep South, Past and Present," in *The Deep South in Transformation: A Symposium,* ed. Robert B. Highsaw (University, Ala., 1964), 129; C. Vann Woodward, *The Burden of Southern History* (New York, 1960); Frank E. Vandiver, ed., *The Idea of the South: Pursuit of a Central Theme* (Chicago, 1964); Patrick Gerster and Nicholas Cords, eds., *Myth and Southern History* (Chicago, 1974); Numan V. Bartley, "Writing About the Post–World War II South," *Georgia Historical Quarterly,* LXVIII (1984), 1–18.

[45] Fred Hobson, "A South Too Busy to Hate," in *Why the South Will Survive,* by Fifteen Southerners (Athens, Ga., 1981), 47; Hobson, *Tell About the South,* 353.

the coming of a multiculturalism that fit nicely with the developing multinational economy. Hispanic Americans, Native Americans, homosexuals, and other population groups sought to promote their own identities and interests in an increasingly fragmented nation. In the clamor of ethnicity, some scholars began to see white southerners as an ethnic group. Despite the statistical confluence of South and North, survey research demonstrated measurable differences in attitude between white southerners and northerners. The data John Shelton Reed analyzed led him to conclude that the differences between the values of white southerners and those of Americans generally were "similar in kind, if not degree, to those of the immigrant ethnic groups." Religion and family shaped the white southern mentality in much the same way they did the outlooks of Jewish Americans and the several ethnic constituencies of American Catholicism. Such a view largely conceded the decline of a distinctive regional culture and left the South just another piece in the national mosaic.[46]

The concept of the Sunbelt rested on the assumption that booming metropolitan and economic growth transcended other considerations and made South Carolina much like southern California. The future of southern distinctiveness continued to command ink and paper, but the weight of Sunbelt logic suggested that the "lasting South" might not last very long. When in 1981 "fifteen southerners" collaborated on the volume *Why the South Will Survive,* the effort was less than convincing. In the introduction to the collection of essays, Clyde N. Wilson affirmed that the South "may prove in the long run more able to survive change without losing its identity than can America at large," but the essays offered limited support to the proposition. The spirit of the book was closer to the caution of Cleanth Brooks, who concluded, "The best one can say is that a venerable tradition has not been wholly lost—that there remains at least a foundation upon which to rebuild."[47]

[46] John Shelton Reed, *The Enduring South: Subcultural Persistence in Mass Society* (Lexington, Mass., 1972), 11; Lewis M. Killian, *White Southerners* (New York, 1970); George Brown Tindall, *The Ethnic Southerners.*

[47] Clyde N. Wilson, "Introduction: Should the South Survive?" in *Why the South Will Survive,* by Fifteen Southerners, 8; Cleanth Brooks, "The Enduring Faith," *ibid.,* 211; Louis D. Rubin, Jr., ed., *The American South: Portrait of a Culture* (Baton Rouge, 1980).

In *Why the South Will Survive,* William C. Havard speculated about the possibility of preserving the "best of the [southern] tradition" in a newly modernized region. That notion was during the 1970s a popular one. A growing number of commentators, rather than anxiously awaiting southern absorption into the national mainstream, expressed second thoughts. John Egerton in *The Americanization of Dixie: The Southernization of America* captured much of the new outlook. The South, rather than eliminating its more objectionable features and becoming an integral part of a successful and meritorious society, seemed instead to be abandoning the best features of southern culture and adopting the least admirable traits of the North. "The South and the nation," Egerton wrote, "are not exchanging strengths as much as they are exchanging sins." In any event, the disruption of the Cold War consensus and the economic travails of the North left the South bereft of a mainstream to join.[48]

In 1969 political leaders, professional people, businessmen, and educators from twelve southern states created the L. Q. C. Lamar Society to encourage a more cautious and better-planned approach to economic growth and regional change. A participant explained that the South yet had time to control "urbanization and shape it into more graceful, more human, and more livable cities than those in other regions." The Lamar Society inspired the formation of the Southern Growth Policies Board, which adopted the slogan Southern Growth Without Northern Mistakes. Terry Sanford, a former governor of North Carolina and a founder of the Growth Policies Board, argued that the South should give up trying to reconstitute itself into the "familiar wastelands" of New Jersey. Organized in 1971 and headquartered at the Research Triangle in North Carolina, the board addressed ecological issues and attempted to frame an "overall design plan" for metropolitan and economic growth.[49]

[48] William C. Havard, "The Distinctive South: Fading or Reviving?" in *Why the South Will Survive,* by Fifteen Southerners, 44; John Egerton, *The Americanization of Dixie: The Southernization of America* (New York, 1974), xx.

[49] Joel L. Fleishman, "The Southern City: Northern Mistakes in Southern Settings," in *You Can't Eat Magnolias,* ed. H. Brandt Ayers and Thomas H. Naylor (New York, 1972), 170; Terry Sanford, "The End of Myths: The South Can Lead the Nation," *ibid.,* 322; H.

The Lamar Society and the Growth Policies Board represented a significant if inchoate undertaking. During the years after World War II, the southern leadership had attempted to guide the region's economic development to suit the needs of northern investors. During the 1970s the Growth Policies Board and the southern governors who were members of it talked of preserving a "southern style of life" more compatible with the image promoted by Sunbelt boosters. Reubin Askew, a board member who described the South as an "unfinished frontier," declaimed, "We have an opportunity in the South to fashion our frontier into whatever we want to make it." The chairman of the board, David L. Boren of Oklahoma, asked, "How do we retain the community spirit that is so strong? How do we keep alive the values that make our . . . section so vital?"[50]

The neo-Confederate effort to bend southern growth to southern values proved short-lived. The Southern Growth Policies Board soon abandoned its slogan of Southern Growth Without Northern Mistakes to become a regional propaganda agency for economic development, a function that it had at least in spirit originally been designed to combat. The board's role in planning continued, but its basic purpose came to be what Joel Garreau has described as "easily the most sophisticated regional economic pressure group in North America." When in 1976 northeastern and midwestern political leaders organized to protect Snowbelt interests, the Growth Policies Board took the lead in defending the Sunbelt from Yankee politicians who objected to the southward flow of federal funds and corporate investment.[51]

The Lamar Society and the Growth Policies Board bespoke a growing self-confidence in regional accomplishments but could not transmute that into a successful revolt against the South's de-

Brandt Ayers, "The L. Q. C. Lamar Society," *ibid.*, 368–71; *The Future of the South* (Southern Growth Policies Board, 1974).

[50] Askew and Boren quoted in *Myth, Media, and the Southern Mind*, by Stephen A. Smith (Fayetteville, Ark., 1985), 120, 121; Robert H. McKenzie, "Of New Souths Rising," in *The Rising South: Southern Universities and the South*, ed. Robert H. McKenzie (University, Ala., 1976), 1–10.

[51] Joel Garreau, *The Nine Nations of North America* (Boston, 1981), 130; Jay Dilger, *The Sunbelt-Snowbelt Controversy: The War over Federal Funds* (New York, 1982).

pendent status in the national economy. The South gained greater influence and respect in national affairs, as Kirpatrick Sale had suggested, but rhetoric about the South shaping its own destiny had by the late 1970s become increasingly hollow. The Sunbelt imagery, Carl Abbott has noted, "allowed the newest New South to deny its dependence on and subordination to the North," but the denial proved to be unconvincing.[52]

The combination of pride and resentment that contributed to the southern quasi revolt against northern economic domination also influenced the drive toward excellence in higher education. When in 1965 Allan M. Cartter published a study of "southern university education," he concluded "that the region cannot as yet boast of a single outstanding institution on the national scene. It has a fair share of good universities, but perhaps more than its share of poor ones." He correctly predicted, however, a brighter future.[53]

"By 1970," Clarence L. Mohr has stated, "Southern universities were fully engaged in a serious effort to equal or surpass their peer institutions in other areas." Southern universities in 1968 granted just under two in every ten of the nation's doctorates and received just over two in every ten federal research and development dollars. The civil rights movement freed higher education of the burden of segregation. Not only had desegregation become a requirement for successfully competing for federal and foundation grants but the abandonment of racial restrictions enhanced the prestige of southern universities whose faculties had long been denigrated as curators of backwoods "seg" schools. "We've tried to escape our provincialism by becoming more regional and national and even international in scope," a faculty member explained. "We have become more selective in the students we accept, more cosmopolitan in our hiring of faculty, more sophisticated in the nature and level of our graduate programs

[52] Abbott, "New West, New South, New Region," 16.

[53] Allan M. Cartter, "Qualitative Aspects of Southern University Education," *Southern Economic Journal*, XXXII (1965), 39–69, p. 63 quoted; Cartter, "The Role of Higher Education in the Changing South," in *The South in Continuity and Change*, ed. John C. McKinney and Edgar T. Thompson (Durham, N.C., 1965), 277–97.

and our research activities." As John Egerton reported in 1967, "The big state universities of the South are on the make."[54]

Affluence and the baby boom had the same effect on higher education in the South as they did elsewhere in the nation. During the 1960s southern college enrollment doubled; by 1970 more than two million students attended institutions within the region. Two-year junior and community colleges proliferated. State officials and university administrators mounted vigorous programs of academic development in the colleges as well as the universities. A majority of southern states embraced a relatively clearly conceived educational hierarchy extending from "flagship" state universities, through technological institutes, universities with local missions, and four-year colleges, to two-year institutions. Some states like Texas and Alabama adopted a more haphazard approach.[55]

During the 1970s a number of southern universities joined the upper echelon of higher education in the nation. The rating of universities is an inexact enterprise, but a study Paul K. Conkin undertook in the 1980s separately rated the nation's large public universities and its elite private institutions on the basis of their financial support, library holdings, faculty reputations, student abilities, and scholastic traditions. Conkin placed the University of North Carolina and the University of Texas among the nation's ten best public universities, and the University of Virginia and the University of Georgia among the second ten. No universities in the South made it onto Conkin's list of the top ten private universities in the nation, but Duke, Emory, Rice, and Vanderbilt were in the second ten. Conkin did not rate technological schools, but clearly the Georgia Institute of Technology, Texas A and M, and possibly one or two others would have qualified for high rankings.[56]

[54] Clarence L. Mohr, "Postwar Visions and Cold War Realities: The Metamorphosis of Southern Higher Education, 1945–1965" (Paper presented at Porter L. Fortune, Jr., History Symposium, University of Mississippi, October 7, 1992), 16; Egerton, *Shades of Gray,* 15, 6.

[55] Mohr, "Postwar Visions and Cold War Realities"; *Fact Book on Higher Education in the South* (Southern Regional Education Board, 1962–).

[56] Paul K. Conkin, "The Rating Game," *Vanderbilt Magazine,* Spring, 1988, pp. 25–38.

Such accomplishments were impressive, but southern universities failed to develop their own niche in the educational world
as northeastern private universities and midwestern state universities had done. They simply became better at doing what other
schools did. The increased financial resources and prestige of
southern schools permitted them to load their faculties, particularly in the liberal arts, with Ivy League graduates, who looked to
their alma maters for intellectual guidance and ratification. The
craving for government funds turned faculty and administrators
toward a focus on federally defined objectives. Too, what might
be termed the Triangle Park syndrome enmeshed some universities and influenced others, primarily in scientific and engineering fields. Land-grant universities had long been committed to
public service as well as to research and instruction, and on the
model of North Carolina's Triangle Park, many seized the opportunity to assist in the economic growth of the region. "University-
industry collaboration, university-based 'incubator' facilities for
high-tech start-up firms, and state-aided technology parks," Robert C. McMath has commented, "sprang up all over the South."[57]

The enlistment of universities in the campaign for economic
growth was eminently practical. The pursuit of technological sophistication was itself a part of the anticolonial upsurge that
sought to escape the traditional practice of importing technology
from the North. Nevertheless, harnessing the universities to the
needs of corporate enterprise constricted academic inquiry.
Surely the most innovative academic program in the twentieth-
century South was the Institute for Research in Social Science at
the University of North Carolina. During the 1920s, 1930s, and
1940s, the institute sponsored pathbreaking studies in southern
regionalism. Thereafter, in the words of two historians, it "entered
into contracts with the Air Force for a series of studies of Soviet
industrial capacities and a study of day-and-night populations of
Soviet and American 'target cities,' and with the Public Health
services for studies of urbanization in connection with the build-

[57] Robert C. McMath, Jr., "Variations on a Theme by Henry Grady: Technology, Modernization, and Social Change," in *The Future South*, ed. Dunn and Preston, 92.

ing of the Savannah River atomic energy plant." The University of North Carolina became one of the pillars of the Research Triangle.[58]

As southern institutions of higher learning looked to the new middle class for undergraduate students and recruited graduate students nationally and internationally, they became more removed from the southern people. Most predominantly white institutions did recruit black students—even students who did not play football or basketball—and thereby placed pressure on the predominantly black colleges. Affirmative action assured blacks, women, and other protected groups favored access to professional and graduate schools. The South still had probably more than its share of mediocre institutions, but by the end of the 1970s it also was the home of some of the best. The region failed to sever its intellectual dependence on the North, and as Robert McMath has suggested, the enlistment of higher education in the service of corporate technology held "little promise for region specific improvements."[59]

The neo-Confederate campaign for autonomy largely failed, but between massive resistance and the Sunbelt South, the nature of southern identity underwent a crucial change. By the 1970s the new white suburban middle class had replaced the county-seat elite as the leading conveyers of southern consciousness. John Shelton Reed found that members of the suburban upper-middle class—"educated, urban, white-collar, well-informed respondents"—were the people most apt to identify with the new "self-congratulatory" southernism. The southern consciousness they bore correlated negatively with traditional values. The same upper-middle-class people who were "intensely conscious of the place and role of their society, its economy and its culture," were also the people most likely to "have lost—often they've consciously rejected—many elements of their traditional, 'folk' culture." They were the population group least committed to com-

---

[58] Guy Benton Johnson and Guion Griffis Johnson, *Research in Service to Society: The First Fifty Years of the Institute for Research in Social Science at the University of North Carolina* (Chapel Hill, N.C., 1980), 121; Allen Tullos, *Habits of Industry: White Culture and the Transformation of the Carolina Piedmont* (Chapel Hill, N.C., 1989), 294–302.

[59] McMath, "Variations on a Theme by Henry Grady," 92.

munalism, familism, racism, fatalism, and the like. The same forces that heightened regional consciousness—education, urbanization, demographic mobility—also undermined traditional values. The most self-consciously southern of southerners had come to be not defenders of the old regime but promoters of the new order.[60]

By 1980 approximately one-quarter of the southern work force held professional, proprietary, or managerial positions, which was probably a relatively accurate indicator of the size of the southern middle—or statistically speaking, upper-middle—class. The suburbs became more self-contained, and the costlier suburbs became more insulated. People more often moved from one metropolitan suburb to another, while fewer migrated from the city to the more prestigious portions of the city's periphery. Many of the new arrivals came from outside the region. In such ways, affluent southern suburbanites lived little differently from those elsewhere in the nation.

They did have their own style, which was often exaggerated by a press fascinated with the Sunbelt. The articles in *Southern Living* could easily lead readers to think that white men spent an inordinate part of their time on their backyard patios wearing "blazers, eating hors d'oeuvres, and looking as if they would rather be inside watching the Redskins-Cowboys game" as Reed has put it. The women of the magazine's features strove to be graceful hostesses and to be genteel and ladylike. Aside from nuances of style and manners, however, southern suburbanites were consumers scarcely different from the suburbanites elsewhere in the country. They shopped at the same chain stores and watched the same programs on television. They even voted for politicians who were as bland as those elsewhere.[61]

Compared with the national upper-middle class, the white southern segment was more provincial, more religious, and more conservative. In the South, however, its members were in the van-

[60]John Shelton Reed, *Southerners: The Social Psychology of Sectionalism* (Chapel Hill, N.C., 1983), 31; John Shelton Reed, *One South: An Ethnic Approach to Regional Culture* (Baton Rouge, 1982), 125.

[61]John Shelton Reed, *Southern Folk, Plain and Fancy: Native White Social Types* (Athens, Ga., 1986), 63.

guard of social and ideological change. As the prime beneficiaries of the postwar suburban boom, they were the most attuned to rapid economic development and entrepreneurial individualism. They were best situated to replace dependence on kin and personal relationships with impersonal market forces and contractual relationships. Though they often lagged in their willingness to accept the further liberation of blacks and women, they did accept the need to subordinate social relations to the requirements of the market and the bottom line.

The logic of their position—at least in its ideal form—supported the coming of a market society that further commodified both environment and people and subjected them more directly to the demands of the marketplace. The effect of modernist culture was to liberate individuals from restrictive cultural conventions and to sustain a commitment to self-fulfillment, self-achievement, and self-advancement. Autonomous individualism increasingly replaced the folk-culture, predominantly masculine, hell-of-a-fellow individualism of the past. The creation of a social system that upheld autonomous individualism and formal legal equality expanded the social and economic roles of women and African Americans and other minorities. It also required the southern people to cope with perplexing social disruptions.

Southern suburbanites, like those elsewhere, were likely to be busy. Work—not family—defined identity. Educated women pursued careers as an avenue to self-fulfillment in a society that no longer accorded much deference to mothers and homemakers. The residents of the affluent but disaggregated reaches of the metropolitan South led the trend toward individualistic forms of improvement. Jogging, health foods, and the noisy rebuff of tobacco took on the guise of moral commitments. The works of novelists like Barry Hannah and Richard Ford suggested the social and cultural nihilism and rootlessness of the southern upper-middle class.[62]

Divorce became more common, smaller families the norm, and a declining proportion of households sheltered traditional nuclear families. Divorce and even desertion lost much of their

[62] Richard Ford, *The Sportswriter* (New York, 1986); Barry Hannah, *Ray* (New York, 1981).

stigma as marriage forfeited its moral and religious sanctity. In the pursuit of secular salvation through material enrichment, men and women changed marital partners far more frequently than ever before. The decimation of family was a phenomenon common to all levels of southern metropolitan society, but in the more prestigious neighborhoods it marked the erosion of elite support for the institution. As Christopher Jencks has commented, affluent couples could "afford the luxury of supporting two households." At the same time, the rates of divorce and illegitimacy among southern whites lagged behind those in the more advanced portions of the nation.[63]

In 1980 blue-collar workers made up 46 percent of the region's labor force. Some 14 percent of employed southerners held craft or skilled positions, and almost one-third were operatives, laborers, and blue-collar service employees. Another one-quarter of the region's workers were in predominantly pink-blouse clerical and sales occupations. Blue-collar and pink-blouse employees made up three-quarters of the southern work force and included most blacks and those whites who during the 1950s and 1960s had often been stereotyped as rednecks and who in the Sunbelt seventies became good ole boys and good ole girls.

A considerable number of working-class families parlayed two incomes into middle-class life-styles in the less prestigious suburbs. Others, unable to afford the available suburban dwellings, escaped the public-school busing, taxes, and crime of the cities by moving into mobile homes. Joel Garreau exaggerated when he wrote, "Trailers are becoming the most typical southern architectural form," but he was correct in noting that "Dixie has embraced the mobile home." Female-headed households were abundant among those working families that lived in or on the margin of poverty.[64]

Working-class families accepted much of modern consumer culture at the same time that they resisted the attendant changes in values. Many whites opposed the Supreme Court's rulings in

---

[63] Christopher Jencks, "Deadly Neighborhoods," *New Republic*, June 13, 1988, p. 30; Andrew Hacker, *Two Nations: Black and White, Separate, Hostile, and Unequal* (New York, 1992), 67–92; Andrew Hacker, *The End of the American Era* (New York, 1977).

[64] Garreau, *The Nine Nations of North America*, 142–43.

favor of affirmative action and criminal rights, and many blacks and whites disapproved of its toleration of pornography and abortion and its banning of prayer from the schools. By all indications, they were uneasy with modernist values and the replacement of moral strictures with legal prerogatives. They provided much of the audience for television evangelists and much of the social base for the New Religious Right, which by 1980 had become a potent political movement. In the main, however, working-class southerners accommodated in practice the cultural changes they opposed intellectually.[65]

Family life was no more stable in working-class neighborhoods than in the upscale suburbs. Social disintegration reached its apex in the metropolitan ghettos. The more highly paid working-class blacks joined the black middle class in abandoning the inner city, leaving behind them economic stagnation, unemployment, and social isolation. As William Julius Wilson has documented, "rates of inner-city joblessness, teenage pregnancies, out-of-wedlock births, female-headed families, welfare dependency, and serious crime . . . did not reach catastrophic proportions until the mid-1970s."[66]

More typical working-class families fared better in degree if not in kind. In the fictional working-class households created by Bobbie Ann Mason, virtually all women worked at menial jobs while they wondered about their former husbands or watched their marriages disintegrate or questioned why they had not disintegrated or why they ever happened in the first place. Mason's working-class people were immersed in popular culture, especially television. Whereas Faulkner had insisted that the past was not dead or even past, a Mason character explained, "The main thing you learn from history is that you can't learn from history. That's what history is."[67]

[65] Samuel S. Hill, Jr., and Dennis E. Owen, *The New Religious Right in America* (Nashville, 1982), 15–66; Christopher Lasch, *The True and Only Heaven: Progress and Its Critics* (New York, 1991), 407–532.

[66] William Julius Wilson, *The Truly Disadvantaged: The Inner City, the Underclass, and Public Policy* (Chicago, 1987), 3.

[67] Mason, *Shiloh and Other Stories;* Bobbie Ann Mason, *In Country* (New York, 1985), 226.

The writers of the Southern Renaissance, who dominated southern literature until the midfifties and continued to influence it thereafter, had grown up before World War II. They were the products of communities in which, Louis D. Rubin has written, "all was fixed and ordered, and everyone knew everyone else, and who he was, and how and what his family was, and in which life seemed to hold few surprises." No matter how complex their narratives, William Faulkner and his generation had depicted a community-based society in which the past sat in judgment on the present. When Faulkner christened characters Montgomery Ward Snopes or Watkins Products Snopes, he did so not in tribute to consumerism but in derogation of their family lineage.[68]

By the 1970s a new generation of writers dealt with a different region. The assumptions and perceptions upon which their works rested differed radically from those of their predecessors. Most significant was the almost complete absence of southern consciousness, historical awareness, and community and family verities. Fred Hobson, who analyzed the works of southern writers born during and after World War II, was struck by the "absence of nurturing family, community, and religion, those staples of traditional southern life and literature." The result was "characters who inhabit shopping malls and drive-ins with no idea of and no concern for what was there fifty years before, no idea of how they fit into the whole picture, temporally or spatially." Insofar as communities entered the narrative at all, they were the female and black communities of Jill McCorkle, Alice Walker, and Ernest Gaines.[69]

In the 1970s the moderate consensus was triumphant. The South had accepted desegregation, at least to a greater extent than other regions, and it had for the most part accepted the new woman of postindustrial America. "Ohio baiting" to some degree superseded "Mississippi bashing" as a national pastime. Even the

[68] Louis D. Rubin, Jr., *Writers of the Modern South: The Faraway Country* (Seattle, 1963), 5; Louis D. Rubin, Jr., "Is the Southern Literary Renascence Over? A Sort of Cautionary Epistle," in *The Rising South*, ed. Noble and Thomas, 72–91; Richard H. King, *A Southern Renaissance: The Cultural Awakening of the American South, 1930–1955* (New York, 1980).

[69] Fred Hobson, *The Southern Writer in the Postmodern World* (Athens, Ga., 1991), 13, 18.

sterner critics of the region's progress could hardly deny a Florida editor's assertion that "it beats the hell out of pellagra." The new southern world was prosperous, progressive, and individualized. As in Lee Smith's fictional *Oral History*, the old family homeplace still stood, but it had become an appropriately decaying part of a successful theme park called Ghostland.[70]

[70] Gene Patterson quoted in *The Nine Nations of North America*, by Garreau, 148; Lee Smith, *Oral History* (New York, 1983), 292.

THE SOUTH SINCE
1945

S AVE for Georgia, the Solid South firmly repudiated its native son in the presidential election of 1980. Republican Ronald Reagan won almost 60 percent of the votes cast by white southerners. Jimmy Carter carried most of the ballots marked in black precincts, and he did well among other minorities, but he was the choice of only 36 percent of southern whites. He did best among older and lower-income whites, but relatively few lower-status citizens voted. Reagan carried the South and won overwhelmingly in the West to coast to a national victory.[1]

Carter's campaign faced severe handicaps. A recession, double-digit inflation and interest rates, and high unemployment, along with the Democratic party's usual morass of foreign policy problems, largely doomed Carter's effort. So too did the Social Issue. The Democratic party platform favored affirmative action, federally funded abortions, and busing, and it endorsed the Equal Rights Amendment to the point of denying party support to candidates who opposed the amendment and encouraging boycotts of states that refused to ratify it. Reagan's Republican platform disavowed busing and abortion, ignored the Equal Rights Amendment, demanded prayer be allowed in the schools, and advocated family values. Both the Republican candidate and his party's platform called for a return to state and local rights and to free-enterprise economics. "In this present crisis, government is not

---

[1] Alexander P. Lamis, *The Two-Party South* (New York, 1984), 21–26; Earl Black and Merle Black, *The Vital South: How Presidents Are Elected* (Cambridge, Mass., 1992), 307–12. An independent candidate, John B. Anderson, won most of the votes that did not go to Reagan or Carter.

the solution to our problem," Reagan asserted in his inaugural address; "government is the problem."[2]

Reagan promised to achieve a free-market society by deregulating the economy, trimming the federal bureaucracy, limiting government, privatizing as many public services as possible, and increasing defense spending. At the same time he pledged to protect family values by halting the government's social engineering and its intrusion into the private lives of citizens. The two propositions—a free-market society and family values—were of course broadly incompatible. A free-market ideology stressed individual self-interest, material acquisitiveness, and the commodification of people as paid labor. Family values, at least in any traditional sense, required people—in the past particularly women—to sublimate self-interest for the achievement of family and community goals, to sacrifice material gain to personal relationships, and to place children and family above vocation. "In the name of traditional virtue," Alan Wolfe has observed, Reagan's conservative program gave a "free hand to business practices that destroy neighborhoods, separate families, promote hedonism, encourage mobility, and plan obsolescence."[3]

Reagan's victory and his overwhelming reelection in 1984 were a repudiation of Democratic social engineering and a setback for domestic reform by judicial fiat. The Reagan administration largely wrote off blacks and other minorities, the poor, and the working class in favor of business, professional, and corporate progress. Clearly, the election of 1980 was an event of some consequence. At the same time, the extent of the "Reagan Revolution" could be exaggerated. In many ways the Reagan program was a relatively natural outcome of national priorities and policies of the postwar era.

Soon after the end of World War II, national Democrats adopted a program of Cold War liberalism composed of an Amer-

[2] Gerald M. Pomper, "The Nominating Contests," in *The Election of 1980: Reports and Interpretations,* by Gerald M. Pomper *et al.* (Chatham, N.J., 1981), 1–37; Henry A. Plotkin, "Issues in the Presidential Campaign," *ibid.,* 38–64; "Inaugural Address of President Ronald Reagan," *ibid.,* 190.

[3] Alan Wolfe, *America's Impasse: The Rise and Fall of the Politics of Growth* (New York, 1981), 232.

ican Century foreign policy, corporate prosperity, economic expansion, defense spending, domestic anticommunism, and civil rights for black people. The popular-front liberals, who were the heirs to the New Deal and the proponents of detente with the Soviet Union abroad and social reform at home, were the chief ideological opponents of the Cold War liberals within the Democratic party. In the ensuing intraparty civil war, President Harry S. Truman and the Americans for Democratic Action relied primarily on discrediting popular-front liberals by associating them with Communist subversion. In the process of destroying the grass-roots-oriented popular front, Cold War liberals moved away from the mass coalition that sustained the New Deal. For two decades after World War II, the New Deal coalition continued to elect Democrats to office, but in policy matters Cold War liberals looked to corporations and the upper-middle class and to labor leaders rather than workers and civil rights organizations rather than blacks.[4]

Popular-front liberalism offered the most obvious hope for a progressive politics in the South. Most southerners identified with the Democratic party, the New Deal, and domestic reform. The South remained a conservative enclave not because of its people but because of its political institutions, most particularly disfranchisement. The Great Depression and World War II had exposed the bankruptcy of the old order in the region and had moved a disparate company of change-oriented southerners into opposition to the old regime. The popular front, centered in the Southern Conference for Human Welfare, led the effort to organize ordinary southerners behind a program of social reform. Arguing that the need of the hour was "political and industrial democracy" rather than desegregation, popular-front liberals endeavored to create a bond of mutual interest between white and black workers, especially through support for labor-union orga-

[4] Bruce J. Schulman, *From Cotton Belt to Sunbelt: Federal Policy, Economic Development, and the Transformation of the South, 1938–1980* (New York, 1991); Allen J. Matusow, *The Unraveling of America: A History of Liberalism in the 1960s* (New York, 1984); Godfrey Hodgson, *America in Our Time* (New York, 1976); Christopher Lasch, *The True and Only Heaven: Progress and Its Critics* (New York, 1991); Richard Klimmer, "Liberal Attitudes Toward the South, 1930–1965" (Ph.D. dissertation, Northwestern University, 1976).

nization and enfranchisement. The basic problem was the fact that the forces of Bourbon Democracy controlled the levers of power in a stunted political domain of disfranchisement, malapportionment, one-party rule, and deeply institutionalized practices of white supremacy.

The Southern Conference and its allies looked to national liberals for help in broadening the southern electorate and enrolling southerners in unions. The crucial test was Operation Dixie, the southern organizing drive of the Congress of Industrial Organizations. Operation Dixie failed, in large part of course because of the truculent opposition from the ruling elite in the region, but also because it fell victim to the internal war for control of Democratic party politics. Cold War liberals demonstrated greater interest in purging popular-front liberals than in organizing workers. The federal government branded the Southern Conference a Communist front, and the Truman administration and its allies identified Henry A. Wallace and his supporters with treason. The emergence of a Republican version of anticommunism in the form of McCarthyism further discredited mass-based social reform.

The elimination of the popular-front liberals in the South was a victory for the county-seat governing class that directed the public affairs of the region. During 1948 the Truman administration and the Democratic party diverted the thrust of party reform away from class issues to the promotion of civil rights for blacks in the South. To the most disgruntled elements among the southern governing elite, Truman's modest civil rights program posed as much of a long-term threat as did popular-front policies, and unlike the New Deal, the Truman program had little support within the southern electorate. The extreme Bourbons reacted by organizing the States' Rights Democratic party to punish the national Democrats. The failure of the Dixiecrats demonstrated the extent to which the New Deal and World War II had bound the South to the rest of the nation. Much of the regional Democratic establishment, no matter how much it may have sympathized with the Dixiecrats, was unwilling to abandon the national party and to jeopardize congressional seniority and federal patronage and spending in the region.

The revolts of both the liberals and the Dixiecrats ended in defeat. County-seat conservatives continued to dominate southern politics, and indeed after 1948 both national Democrats and Republicans courted regional congressional conservatives, whose power and prestige rose steadily in Washington. As it turned out, the sweeping upheavals of World War II had little effect on southern politics, except in the short term to strengthen the position of the Bourbon conservatives. The Truman administration continued to pay lip service to civil rights and to lay the foundation for a policy of symbolic equality that would gradually reform the Jim Crow system in the South, reinforce the moral superiority of white Americans, and improve the nation's image in world affairs. The federal judiciary moved ever closer to restoring the Fourteenth Amendment to the Constitution, and northern liberals became ever more enamored of civil rights reform in the wicked South.

The national approach to civil rights conformed closely to the propositions propounded by Gunnar Myrdal in his epic *An American Dilemma,* which structured informed discussions of racial issues for two decades after its publication in 1944. Myrdal defined the race problem not in terms of social, economic, or class relationships but as a moral and psychological problem for individual white Americans. The solution was education and responsible leadership, whereby the masses of whites and most especially southern whites could be taught tolerance. Because social deprivation, economic competition, and ignorance exacerbated prejudice, economic growth, education, and desegregation in the South would undermine racial bias and permit the flowering of the American Creed "of liberty, equality, justice, and fair opportunity for everybody." [5]

In 1954 the Supreme Court overturned the separate-but-equal doctrine in *Brown* v. *Board of Education,* and in 1955 it enunciated

[5] Gunnar Myrdal, *An American Dilemma: The Negro Problem and Modern Democracy* (New York, 1944), lxx; Walter A. Jackson, *Gunnar Myrdal and America's Conscience: Social Engineering and Racial Liberalism, 1938–1987* (Chapel Hill, N.C., 1990), 272–371; David W. Southern, *Gunnar Myrdal and Black-White Relations: The Use and Abuse of "An American Dilemma," 1944–1969* (Baton Rouge, 1987). For a vigorous and influential reaffirmation of Myrdal's argument a decade after the publication of *An American Dilemma,* see Gordon Allport, *The Nature of Prejudice* (Reading, Mass., 1954).

its gradualist with-all-deliberate-speed compliance doctrine. Southern political elites responded with a program of massive resistance to desegregation. The fury of the massive-resistance counterattack gave pause to federal judges and encouraged the Eisenhower and Kennedy administrations to do even less than they might have been inclined to do. The champions of massive resistance had no program beyond purblind defense of the old order, but they did successfully prevent anyone else from taking constructive action. By promoting a politics of race, they impaired the position of progressive politicians in the region and helped make the once honorable sobriquet of *liberal* a term of derision. By sharply drawing the line on desegregation, county governing elites contributed to the national tendency to make black civil rights a surrogate for all other social and class issues. In the end their intransigence helped convince federal bureaucrats and judges that elected state and local officials were too irresponsible to determine policy and thereby contributed to the coming of a national program of social engineering.

Ultimately, the scorched-earth inflexibility of massive resistance endangered the economic progress of the region and provoked a moderate countermobilization. When segregationist leaders closed public schools in Arkansas and Virginia, metropolitan business leaders and suburbanites came to the defense of public education and continued economic expansion. To growth-oriented moderates, desegregation with economic growth was preferable to segregation without it. White moderates allied with middle-class blacks and gradually shifted the direction of southern policy. By the time the South did accept token desegregation, the region had in the main achieved "modernization," a transformation accomplished under a regimen of white-male supremacy.

Despite the limited goals of the open-schools movement, the victory of the metropolitan moderates over the county-seat establishment was a historic and lasting triumph that was ratified by the Supreme Court's legislative reapportionment decisions of the early 1960s. Prior to the ascension of the moderates, the South was distinctively different from the rest of the nation in significant part because of two factors. The southern social system rested on de jure white supremacy in the form of enforced segregation along with disfranchisement and other related practices while that of the rest of the nation did not. The southern governing class was a rural-oriented colonial ruling elite that differed fundamentally from the corporate business and financial establishment and allied upper-middle-class suburbanites who ruled much of the rest of the nation. The moderate victory brought to power in the South metropolitan corporate leaders who had much in common with their northern peers and who accepted the demise of strict Jim Crow segregation. Thereafter, the South became considerably more like the non-South.

The southern moderates bulldozed urban black neighborhoods and accepted federal funds for urban renewal projects and expressways. They eagerly pursued northern investments and offered low taxes, minimal public services, and a good business atmosphere in exchange. They constructed vocational schools but allowed the public schools to remain relatively underfunded. They accepted token desegregation and cooperated with black middle-class leaders.

In early 1960 black college students launched the sit-in movement. Although the bus boycotts elevated Martin Luther King, Jr., to leadership and expressed the growing discontent of black southerners, the sit-ins directly challenged the Jim Crow edifice. Young, upwardly mobile blacks demanded entry into the white marketplace. The initial phase of the movement was local and spontaneous, but the direction of events soon passed to civil rights organizations. The Student Nonviolent Coordinating Committee and the southern wing of the Congress of Racial Equality shifted the thrust of movement toward the southern countryside with voter registration and community-organizing projects. The Southern Christian Leadership Conference endeavored to force federal intervention with its campaigns in Albany, Birmingham, St. Augustine, Selma, and elsewhere.

During the first half of the 1960s the black revolt dominated southern affairs, but civil rights activists remained largely within the Cold War consensus. That gradually changed. Of particular significance in radicalizing SNCC and CORE field workers was the refusal of the federal government to protect voter registrants and organizers. Although the power of the county-seat conservatives

461

had been broken on the state level through most of the region, they still commanded affairs in the southern hinterlands, and they used public authority to suppress civil rights activities.

The field workers found themselves beset by paradoxes. They became ever more hostile toward a federal government and its department named Justice that had promised to protect voter registrants and then refused to do so, while at the same time they remained dependent on federal power. Outside the metropolitan areas—indeed inside many of them—white southern law-enforcement officials and vigilantes would surely have crushed the movement had it not been for the passive presence of FBI agents and other federal officials. SNCC and CORE activists began as committed integrationists, but not only did they become enamored of the virtues of rural and small-town black culture but they became increasingly annoyed with the tendency of the national news media to ignore death and brutality when the victims were black while sensationalizing the murder of white workers, especially during the Mississippi Freedom Summer of 1964 and the Selma campaign of 1965.

SNCC and CORE sought white support, but the enlistment of northern volunteers during the Freedom Summer bred conflict between those attuned to black southern rural culture and those from upper-middle-class northern suburbs. Even as SNCC and CORE staff members moved toward black consciousness, they became more hostile toward economically successful African Americans who preferred to cooperate with rather than confront local white power. As field workers became immersed in the pre–market society of the rural black South, they promoted reforms that would hasten its entry into the expanding market society. Such experiences contributed to divisions within SNCC and CORE and to the emergence of a black-power strategy and a rejection of nonviolence.

Martin Luther King, Jr., and the Southern Christian Leadership Conference occupied the center of the civil rights movement. King's teachings, especially his emphasis on nonviolence, established the tone of the movement. In the beginning King talked of nonviolent "creative tension" wherein blacks, by challenging segregation, would force southern whites to confront the moral dilemma structured by the regional caste system. That failing, King turned to mass demonstrations to focus national attention on southern segregation and to force federal intervention in the region. By the time King's staff opted for confrontation in Birmingham, creative tension was aimed at the living rooms and dens of a national television audience.

The great demonstrations in Birmingham and Selma succeeded in discrediting de jure segregation, and the resulting national demand for reform in the South forced a reluctant federal government to respond. King came to understand, more clearly than activists in SNCC and CORE, that concentrated mass violence, even when directed against blacks, would bring media attention and "creative tension." The Civil Rights Acts of 1964 and 1965 accomplished the original aims of the movement. De jure segregation collapsed. At least in a legal sense, black southerners enjoyed the same civil rights as white southerners.

The civil rights legislation also created a "crisis of victory." As King pointed out, the civil rights movement had dealt largely with surface issues—the right to drink a cup of coffee, to vote, to compete with whites for jobs. As important as such civil rights were, they did not address basic questions of poverty and power, and they did not question national practices or institutions. They remained within the parameters established by Gunnar Myrdal. Yet huge numbers of black people were poor and unskilled, and the South had made the transition from rural to urban within a social order based on white supremacy. During 1965 the American invasion of the southern half of Vietnam and the massive riot in the Watts section of Los Angeles vastly complicated the search for solutions.

The civil rights movement broke asunder. The National Association for the Advancement of Colored People became more conservative in its approach to civil rights issues. SNCC and CORE adopted a black-power strategy aimed toward the organization of the black masses in the inner-city ghettos. King called for a Marshall Plan for the cities and soon launched a poor people's campaign to achieve it. Remaining true to nonviolence and assimilation, King endeavored to rally the dispossessed of all creeds and colors behind a program of social reform. The failure of the black-power strategy and the death of King brought to an end the most promising efforts to achieve national social justice.

The "crisis of victory" sundered the national liberal consensus on civil rights. Black power gave rise to a general ethnic revival that during the 1970s took the form of multiculturalism, a movement Gunnar Myrdal three decades after *An American Dilemma* dismissed as "intellectual romanticism" on the part of upper- and upper-middle-class liberals. Thoughtful white southerners grappled with new realities. Leslie W. Dunbar asked in 1966, "Does the Negro community need another white social worker as much as it needs . . . a small business loan, the money his or her education cost? Should we ever again build a large public-housing project within or close to an all Negro community, knowing in advance that it would add to already weak community cohesiveness? Should we bus children in large numbers away from Negro neighborhoods, thus weakening the influence of the school as a community center? Should there be any white policemen in Negro neighborhoods?"[6]

The Johnson administration responded with its Great Society. Although flawed in its premises, the Johnson program never received a fair test. In Washington the internal affairs of Vietnam were more important than social reform in the United States, and war expenditures dwarfed those allocated to the antipoverty program. The high point of the Johnson administration's commitment to reform may have been the president's June, 1965, speech at Howard University, when he called for "not just equality as a right and a theory but equality as a fact and as a result." The Moynihan Report, which starkly exposed the extent of social disorganization and family disintegration in the black ghettos, provided the inspiration for Johnson's address. As one of the president's aides explained, civil rights reform had reached the point where "you can go to school with us, we'll educate you, train you, we'll get better housing. . . . But we haven't really fixed it at the base, which is money, security, family holding together, and some power that is given to them by their money." Johnson entitled his

---

[6] Gunnar Myrdal, "The Case Against Romantic Ethnicity," *Center Magazine,* July–August, 1974, pp. 26–30; Leslie W. Dunbar, *A Republic of Equals* (Ann Arbor, Mich., 1966), 123–24.

speech "To Fulfill These Rights." President Truman's Committee on Civil Rights had labeled its report *To Secure These Rights.* They had been secured, and Johnson promised fulfillment.[7]

Rather than being received as a somewhat paternal but nevertheless well meaning reform effort, "To Fulfill These Rights" and the Moynihan Report touched off a storm of controversy. Black critics interpreted the Johnson administration as blaming the victims of discrimination for their plight. SNCC refused to attend the White House conference "To Fulfill These Rights," as did some individual black activists. By the time the conference convened in 1966, the antiwar movement, black power, urban rioting, a white backlash, and other disruptions made the conference academic, and the Johnson administration devoted its efforts to preventing passage of antiadministration resolutions rather than seeking reform solutions.[8]

The breakup of the civil rights consensus accelerated the trend toward "managerial liberalism." The federal bureaucracy had achieved considerable success in managing the economy and promoting military Keynesianism. As David A. Horowitz has noted, the Kennedy and Johnson administrations "placed great faith in bureaucratic structures and managerial methods of conflict resolution." The Civil Rights Act of 1964 gave the federal bureaucracy the authority to impose an administrative structure on civil rights reform, and federal judges, having long ago lost confidence in the ability of ordinary citizens and the democratic process to accomplish court objectives, allied with the bureaucrats to chart new directions in civil rights matters. Affirmative action, desegregation guidelines, public-school student busing, and minority preference contracts poured forth. The social engineering approach to civil rights was elitist, both in the sense that it most effectively served the interests of educated and successful blacks and in the sense that it paid little attention to the democratic

[7] Lyndon B. Johnson, "To Fulfill These Rights: Remarks of the President at Howard University," June 4, 1965 (Copy), in White House Central Files, Name File (Lee White), Lyndon Baines Johnson Library, Austin, Tex.; Harry McPherson Oral History Interview, March 24, 1969, p. 19, in Johnson Library.

[8] Daniel Patrick Moynihan, *The Negro Family: The Case for National Action* (Washington, D.C., 1965); Lee Rainwater and William L. Yancey, *The Moynihan Report and the Politics of Controversy* (Cambridge, Mass., 1967).

process and the interests of ordinary whites. It was, in the words of one study, a "revolution whose manifesto is a court decision and whose heroes are bureaucrats, judges, and civil rights lawyers." It was also utterly unpopular.[9]

For two decades after World War II, northern liberals and southern moderates, in spite of the overwhelming evidence to the contrary, insisted that the font of southern racism was poor and working-class whites. During the 1960s that tenet came closer to being true. The failure of the Bourbons to deliver on massive-resistance promises, and the inability of the moderates during the 1960s to restore social stability stirred the restiveness of lower-middle-class and working-class whites. Suburban middle-class whites gained greater economic prosperity in the advancing South and, as federal court interpretations unfolded, exemption from busing and other civil rights problems; blacks—especially middle-class blacks—benefited from Great Society programs and affirmative action. Rural and working-class southern whites gained little while losing control of their lives and being expected to pay the costs of desegregation.

George C. Wallace of Alabama emerged to express the alienation and discontent of ordinary white southerners. Wallace was accurate in pointing out that bureaucrats, judges, intellectuals, and upper-middle-class liberals "looked down their noses" at southern white common folk. He was largely correct in insisting that elitist liberals were "pluperfect hypocrites" who themselves avoided anything beyond token desegregation in their suburbs and private schools. The hypocrisy of white northern liberals was probably the only thing that patrician James J. Kilpatrick, radical Stokely Carmichael, and rabble-rouser George Wallace agreed on. Wallace's 1968 presidential campaign clearly structured the basic political divisions in the South, and it called national attention to the growing disaffection not only of ordinary white southerners but of white common folk throughout the nation.[10]

[9] David Alan Horowitz, "White Southerners' Alienation and Civil Rights: The Response to Corporate Liberalism," *Journal of Southern History*, LIV (1988), 199, 173; Gary Orfield, *The Reconstruction of Southern Education: The Schools and the 1964 Civil Rights Act* (New York, 1969), 1.

[10] Wallace quoted in *George C. Wallace and the Politics of Powerlessness: The Wallace Campaigns*

"The South provided a frontier for the country's strong sense of idealism and adventure," John Herbers has observed. During the late 1960s the civil rights struggle moved north, and the moral commitment of white liberals declined precipitously. Journalists discovered the "forgotten American" and heralded the advent of a new populism. Senator Edward Kennedy of Massachusetts observed that most Wallace supporters were "not motivated by racial hostility or prejudice. They are decent, respectable citizens who feel that their needs and their problems have been passed over by the tide of recent events. . . . They feel that the established system has not been sympathetic to them and their problems of everyday life—and in large measure they are right." Racism was an integral part of the reaction of both white southerners and white northerners, but as David Horowitz has pointed out, a "leading issue for those outside this world [of liberal elitism] was a sense of lost control over lives and communities."[11]

During the second half of the 1960s, federal bureaucrats and judges achieved the desegregation of the rural, small-town, and small-city South. The common-white-folk protest led by Wallace failed to win visible gains. Black voters became more influential. An increasing number of whites, particularly those resident in the more prosperous suburbs, came to accept desegregation. These and other factors contributed to the consolidation of the rule of the moderates. The 1970 elections ushered into office a wave of attractive New South moderates who accepted equal rights and relied on economic growth to solve social problems. Southern state politics settled into a moderate consensus that continued through the 1970s and beyond.

Most of the southern states refused to ratify the Equal Rights Amendment, but they adapted to the changing status of both

---

for the Presidency, 1964–1976, by Jody Carlson (New Brunswick, N.J., 1981), 144; Kilpatrick quoted in The Crisis of Conservative Virginia: The Byrd Organization and the Politics of Massive Resistance, by James W. Ely, Jr. (Knoxville, Tenn., 1976), 98; Carmichael quoted in A Prophetic Minority, by Jack Newfield (New York, 1966), 111.

[11] John Herbers, The Lost Priority: What Happened to the Civil Rights Movement? (New York, 1970), 107; Kennedy quoted in Catch the Falling Flag: A Republican's Challenge to His Party, by Richard J. Whalen (Boston, 1972), 269; Horowitz, "White Southerners' Alienation and Civil Rights," 200.

blacks and women by enacting state laws supporting equal rights. The expansion of legal equality corresponded to the central intellectual trends of the era. Modernist thought, with its relativist morality, secular bias, and existential focus, encouraged individualism. The spreading market society fostered individual self-interest and the pursuit of self-fulfillment and individual achievement. Southern economic prosperity offered opportunities for individuals who possessed the requisite ambition, education, social background, and single-mindedness, and the consumer society encouraged two-income families.

Such social developments wreaked havoc on traditional southern folk culture. Women's liberation was perhaps a more profound break with the past than the civil rights movement had been. Traditional women's behavior, as Maxine Alexander has observed, was the "very heart of the experience of community." More than men, women devoted themselves "to family, to the land, and to survival itself," as well as to religion and community. As growing numbers of women abandoned their wonted roles to seek identity and self-fulfillment in the marketplace, the folk cultures that were another part of southern distinctiveness went into decline. The new metropolitan South was not only "too busy to hate" but also, cynics added, "too self-interested to care." When Carter won the presidency in 1976, his evocation of roots, place, faith, and moral verities appealed in the urban South more to nostalgia than to reality.

By 1980 the southern work force was just under one-half white male, just over one-third white female, just under 10 percent black male, and just under 10 percent black female. The breakdown of plantations, mill villages, and similar places of settled employment freed white males to respond to the demands of the market. The civil rights movement and federal legislation permitted blacks to become a more dynamic part of the labor force. Women's liberation and the loosening of traditional restraints opened female access to market demands. Together, they completed the commodification of much of the southern adult population. A dynamic, free-flowing work force unburdened by labor union membership, unity, or much in the way of state protection or social legislation complemented the drive for economic growth while it undermined family, community, and the spiritual aspects of religion. It was, in James C. Cobb's words, a "conservative capitalist's dream come true." At the same time, Shirley Abbott has pointed out, "The disintegration of a culture is a melancholy event." [12]

The coming of the Sunbelt South was just reward for southern sacrifices and accomplishments. The national image of the long-scorned region improved steadily through the first half of the 1970s. By the second half of the decade, it had become a "superior South" filled with promise and progress. The economic hardships of the Snowbelt accentuated the success story in the South. The situation gave rise to a neo-Confederate campaign to cast off northern economic and intellectual domination, but that inchoate campaign failed. In terms of material reward and instant gratification, the South offered far more to its citizens than it had done in the past. There was also truth in the observation by Lester Maddox that "in our zeal to fulfill our material needs we have neglected to put proper emphasis on human and spiritual needs." [13]

The cultural changes sweeping over the region found a more ready acceptance in the prospering suburbs than in the lower-income districts. Many ordinary southerners—especially the whites among them—viewed with bewilderment the decline of previously honored customs. The managerial and judicial liberalism of the 1960s and 1970s aided individuals in a position to take advantage of opportunities, but it offered little in the way of social reform. In 1980 the white upper-middle class was conservative, particularly on economic matters. The white lower-middle class and working class were conservative, primarily on cultural issues.

The situation was ripe for the culmination of the Republican southern strategy. Ronald Reagan promised the business and professional middle class a free-market economy, and he appealed to

---

[12] Maxine Alexander, ed., *Speaking for Ourselves: Women of the South* (New York, 1977), 3; James C. Cobb, "The Sunbelt South: Industrialization in Regional, National, and International Perspective" in *Searching for the Sunbelt: Historical Perspectives on a Region,* ed. Raymond A. Mohl (Knoxville, Tenn., 1990), 39; Shirley Abbott, *Womenfolks: Growing Up down South* (New Haven, 1983), 44.

[13] *Speaking Out: The Autobiography of Lester Garfield Maddox* (Garden City, N.Y., 1975), 170.

the New Religious Right by pledging a return to family values. National liberals had difficulty countering the Republican appeal. They too lauded individual rights, economic growth, defense spending, and a belligerently anticommunist foreign policy. The liberals wanted to expand individual rights into areas once deemed to be in the private sphere while maintaining regulatory authority over the economy. The Reagan conservatives wanted to expand individual rights in the economic sphere while avoiding interference in local and family matters. Neither offered social solutions to social problems. Neither afforded much of measurable value to the lower half to two-thirds of the population. It was hardly surprising that most black southerners remained loyal to the party of civil rights, and the large majority of whites supported the Reagan candidacy.

The glory days of the Sunbelt South were brief. Declining energy prices after 1980 eroded one of the pillars of the southern economy, and with the economic recovery of the Snowbelt, Sunbelt prosperity no longer seemed unique. Some southern states did considerably better than others, but all flourished, at least in comparison with the past. The region was no longer the nation's number-one economic problem nor the nation's number-one moral problem, but economic and racial problems persisted. The South was no longer a land of depleted and gullied farms, but the exploitation of the environment continued and probably became more severe. The expanding service economy produced low-pay and dead-end jobs, while corporate and professional people prospered, thereby widening the gap between the working class and the affluent. A black bourgeoisie fared well, while ordinary blacks struggled to make ends meet, and violence and social disorganization among the black poor increased. The expanding market society absorbed the labor of blacks and women, though imperfectly, especially in the case of poor and inner-city blacks. The South was prosperous and progressive, and southerners were free to pursue personal self-fulfillment through career and achievement.

CRITICAL ESSAY ON AUTHORITIES

The New South came of age during the same period that the publishing industry underwent an epochal expansion. Because events in the region attracted national and international attention, the literature on the South after World War II is enormous. In addition, a huge amount of archival material has become available. A central problem facing students in most areas of New South history is not a shortage of research sources but a surfeit. In this study, I have most often consulted manuscript collections in areas where the published literature was not entirely adequate (as for the early postwar period) or where the subject was of such importance that I deemed the research necessary despite the existence of an excellent secondary literature (as for the civil rights movement).

GENERAL STUDIES

The best study of the South for the period before 1945 is George Brown Tindall's *The Emergence of the New South, 1913–1945* (Baton Rouge, 1967), which is Vol. X of *A History of the South*, ed. Wendell Holmes Stephenson and E. Merton Coulter. Gunnar Myrdal's *An American Dilemma: The Negro Problem and Modern Democracy* (New York, 1944) is an epic work that set the tone for the civil rights debate during the postwar era. V. O. Key, Jr.'s *Southern Politics in State and Nation* (New York, 1949), another classic work, dominated the study of southern politics for decades. Rupert B. Vance's *All These People: The Nation's Human Resources in the South* (Chapel Hill, N.C., 1945), one of the regional studies sponsored by the Institute for Research in Social Science at the University of North Carolina, is a compendium of information about the South in the early 1940s.

471

Some of the most perceptive studies of the postwar South are collections of essays. Assessments of the nature and extent of southern development include *The South in Continuity and Change,* ed. John C. McKinney and Edgar T. Thompson (Durham, N.C., 1965); *Change in the Contemporary South,* ed. Allan P. Sindler (Durham, N.C., 1963); *The Deep South in Transformation: A Symposium,* ed. Robert B. Highsaw (University, Ala., 1964); *Perspectives on the South: Agenda for Research,* ed. Edgar T. Thompson (Durham, N.C., 1967); *Perspectives on the American South: An Annual Review of Society, Politics, and Culture,* Vols. I and II, ed. Merle Black and John Shelton Reed (New York, 1981–84), Vols. III and IV, ed. James C. Cobb and Charles R. Wilson (New York, 1985–87); *From the Old South to the New: Essays on the Transitional South,* ed. Walter J. Fraser, Jr., and Winfred B. Moore, Jr. (Westport, Conn., 1981); *Contemporary Southern Political Attitudes and Behavior: Studies and Essays,* ed. Lawrence W. Moreland *et al.* (New York, 1982); *Developing Dixie: Modernization in a Traditional Society,* ed. Winfred B. Moore, Jr., *et al.* (Westport, Conn., 1988); and *The Future South: A Historical Perspective for the Twenty-First Century,* ed. Joe P. Dunn and Howard L. Preston (Urbana, Ill., 1991).

The South and the Sectional Image: The Sectional Theme Since Reconstruction, ed. Dewey W. Grantham, Jr. (New York, 1967); *The Southerner as American,* ed. Charles Grier Sellers, Jr. (Chapel Hill, N.C., 1960); *The Idea of the South: Pursuit of a Central Theme,* ed. Frank E. Vandiver (Chicago, 1964); and *The South Today: One Hundred Years After Appomattox,* ed. Willie Morris (New York, 1965), focus on the question of southern distinctiveness during a period of sectional strife and generally cheer for the full incorporation of the region into the national mainstream. Welcoming change while expressing caution about the consequences of southern industrialization and urbanization are *You Can't Eat Magnolias,* ed. H. Brandt Ayers and Thomas H. Naylor (New York, 1972); *Two Decades of Change: The South Since the Supreme Court Desegregation Decision,* ed. Ernest M. Lander and Richard J. Calhoun (Columbia, S.C., 1975); *The Rising South: Changes and Issues,* ed. Donald R. Noble and Joab L. Thomas (University, Ala., 1976); and *The Rising South: Southern Universities and the South,* ed. Robert H. McKenzie (University, Ala., 1976).

Among numerous journalistic accounts, the works of Neal R. Peirce are particularly valuable. *The Great Plains States of America: People, Politics, and Power in the Nine Great Plains States* (New York, 1973); *The Deep South States of America: People, Politics, and Power in the Seven Deep South States* (New York, 1974); and *The Border South States: People, Politics, and Power in the Five Border South States* (New York, 1975) together cover the thirteen southern states, often with great insight. Joel Garreau's *The Nine Nations of North America* (Boston, 1981) devotes attention to the southern region from an interesting perspective, and Pat Watters' *The South and the Nation* (New York, 1969) is an analysis by a veteran southern journalist. Fred Powledge's *Journey Through the South: A Rediscovery* (New York, 1979); Chet Fuller's *I Hear Them Calling My Name: A Journey Through the South* (Boston, 1981); and William Least Heat Moon's *Blue Highways: A Journey Through America* (Boston, 1982) differ quite fundamentally from such earlier travel accounts as Ray Sprigle's *In the Land of Jim Crow* (New York, 1949) and Carl T. Rowan's *Go South to Sorrow* (New York, 1957). Among collections of essays by leading southern journalists are Marshall Frady's *Southerners: A Journalist's Odyssey* (New York, 1980); John Egerton's *Shades of Gray: Scenes from the Modern South* (Baton Rouge, 1991); and *Dixie Dateline: A Journalistic Portrait of the Contemporary South*, ed. John B. Boles (Houston, 1983).

ECONOMIC AND DEMOGRAPHIC DEVELOPMENT

Gavin Wright's *Old South, New South: Revolutions in the Southern Economy Since the Civil War* (New York, 1986), the best general survey of regional economic development, stresses the profound changes that occurred during and after World War II. The underdeveloped state of the southern economy at the time of World War II is examined in Douglas F. Dowd's "A Comparative Analysis of Economic Development in the American South and West," *Journal of Economic History*, XVI (1956), 558–74; William H. Nicholls' "The South as a Developing Area," *Journal of Politics*, XXVI (1964), 22–40; and Arthur Goldschmidt's "The Development of the U.S. South," *Scientific American*, CCIX (1963), 225–32. Perceptive discussions of the South's place in the nation include Joseph Persky's "Regional Colonialism and the Southern Economy," *Review of Radical Political Economics*, IV (1972), 73–86, and "The South: A Colony at Home," *Southern Exposure*, I (1973), 15–22; and Immanuel Wallerstein's "What Can One Mean by Southern Culture?" in *The Evolution of Southern Culture*, ed. Numan V. Bartley (Athens, Ga., 1988).

Three excellent studies examine the decimation of southern agriculture: Gilbert C. Fite, *Cotton Fields No More: Southern Agriculture, 1865–1980* (Lexington, Ky., 1984); Pete Daniel, *Breaking the Land: The Transformation of Cotton, Tobacco, and Rice Cultures Since 1880* (Urbana, Ill., 1985); and Jack Temple Kirby, *Rural Worlds Lost: The American South, 1920–1960* (Baton Rouge, 1987). Other useful accounts include James H. Street's *The New Revolution in the Cotton Economy: Mechanization and Its*

Consequences (Chapel Hill, N.C., 1957); Anthony M. Tang's *Economic Development in the Southern Piedmont, 1860–1950: Its Impact on Agriculture* (Chapel Hill, N.C., 1958); Arthur M. Ford, Ray Marshall, and Allen Thompson's *Status and Prospects of Small Farmers in the South* (Atlanta, 1976); and *Holding On to the Land and the Lord: Kinship, Ritual, Land Tenure, and Social Policy in the Rural South,* ed. Robert L. Hall and Carol B. Stack (Athens, Ga., 1982).

The poverty of southern agriculture was a continuing problem during the postwar years. Its extent and causes are probed in Arthur M. Ford's *Political Economics of Rural Poverty in the South* (Cambridge, Mass., 1973); George Thomas' *Poverty in the Nonmetropolitan South: A Causal Analysis* (Lexington, Ky., 1972); and Brian Rungeling *et al.*'s *Employment, Income, and Welfare in the Rural South* (New York, 1977). Ralph A. Felton's *These My Brethren: A Study of 570 Negro Churches and 1542 Negro Homes in the Rural South* (Madison, N.J., 1950) is a depiction of the living conditions of the black poor. Morton Rubin, *Plantation County* (Chapel Hill, N.C., 1951) and the National Education Association, *Wilcox County, Alabama: A Study of Social, Economic, and Educational Bankruptcy* (Washington, D.C., 1967), two studies of the same county, suggest the persistence of rural poverty.

The mechanization and depopulation of southern agriculture sparked a massive migration from farm to city and from South to North and West. Jack Temple Kirby's "The Southern Exodus, 1910–1960: A Primer for Historians," *Journal of Southern History,* XLIV (1983), 585–600, is a good introduction to the subject. Examining the exodus from the region are Neil Fligstein's *Going North: Migration of Blacks and Whites from the South, 1900–1950* (New York, 1981); Nicholas Lemann's *The Promised Land: The Great Migration and How It Changed America* (New York, 1991); Flora Gill's *Economics and the Black Exodus: An Analysis of Negro Emigration from the Southern United States, 1910–1970* (New York, 1979); and Daniel M. Johnson and Rex R. Campbell's *Black Migration in America: A Social and Demographic History* (Durham, N.C., 1981).

Studies of southern industrial growth abound, and many of them are quite good. *Essays in Southern Economic Development,* ed. Melvin L. Greenhut and W. Tate Whitman (Chapel Hill, N.C., 1964), is a well-conceived collection, and one of the essays—Clarence H. Danhof's "Four Decades of Thought on the South's Economic Problems"—is effective in placing postwar development in its historical context. Three works sponsored by the Committee of the South of the National Planning Association are impressive examinations of regional development during the period just after World War II: Glenn E. McLaughlin and Stefan Robock, *Why In-*

dustry Moves South: A Study of Factors Influencing the Recent Location of Manufacturing Plants in the South (1949); Frederick L. Deming and Weldon A. Stein, *Disposal of Southern War Plants* (1949); and Calvin B. Hoover and B. U. Ratchford, *Economic Resources and Policies of the South* (1951). Providing extremely useful data on the decade after World War II are Hammer and Company's *Post-War Industrial Development in the South* (Atlanta, 1956), and *Senate Documents*, 84th Cong., 2nd Sess., "Selected Materials on the Economy of the South: Report of the Committee on Banking and Currency." Harvey S. Perloff *et al.*'s *Regions, Resources, and Economic Growth* (Baltimore, 1960) is helpful in placing southern development within a national context.

The changing southern economy made the South—at least statistically—more like the rest of the nation, a point documented in such works as John M. Maclachlan and Joe S. Floyd, Jr.'s *This Changing South* (Gainesville, Fla., 1956) and John C. McKinney and Linda Brookover Bourque's "The Changing South: National Incorporation of a Region," *American Sociological Review*, XXXVI (1971), 399–412. Studies of southern economic progress and problems include Albert W. Niemi, Jr.'s *Gross State Product and Productivity in the Southeast* (Chapel Hill, N.C., 1975); Thomas H. Naylor and James Clotfelter's *Strategies for Change in the South* (Chapel Hill, N.C., 1975); *The Economics of Southern Growth*, ed. E. Blaine Linder and Lawrence K. Lynch (Durham, N.C., 1977); and Bernard L. Weinstein and Robert E. Firestine's *Regional Growth and Decline in the United States: The Rise of the Sunbelt and the Decline of the Northeast* (New York, 1978).

James C. Cobb's *The Selling of the South: The Southern Crusade for Industrial Development, 1936–1980* (Baton Rouge, 1982) and *Industrialization and Southern Society, 1877–1984* (Lexington, Ky., 1984) are superior accounts of the extent to which southern state governments sponsored industrial development. The federal government also promoted southern economic growth, a subject skillfully addressed in Bruce J. Schulman's *From Cotton Belt to Sunbelt: Federal Policy, Economic Development, and the Transformation of the South, 1938–1980* (New York, 1991). Examining the warfare state in the South are Roger E. Bolton's *Defense Purchases and Regional Growth* (Washington, D.C., 1966); C. S. Pyun's *Impacts of Defense Procurement on the Mid-South Economy* (Memphis, 1973); and the special spring issue of *Southern Exposure* in 1973 concerning "the military and the South."

As studies of agriculture suggest, southern economic development was uneven. J. Wayne Flynt's *Dixie's Forgotten People: The South's Poor Whites* (Bloomington, Ind., 1979) is a good survey of the general subject of southern poverty, and Jacqueline Jones's *The Dispossessed: America's Underclasses from the Civil War to the Present* (New York, 1992) is an inclusive study that places the issue within a national context. Excellent on the causes and consequences of the continuing economic problems in Appalachia are Harry M. Caudill's *Night Comes to the Cumberlands: A Biography of a Depressed Area* (Boston, 1963) and *Theirs Be the Power: The Moguls of Eastern Kentucky* (Urbana, Ill., 1983); and John Gaventa's *Power and Powerlessness: Quiescence and Rebellion in an Appalachian Valley* (Urbana, Ill., 1980). D. W. Meinig's *Imperial Texas: An Interpretive Essay in Cultural Geography* (Austin, Tex., 1969) is a suggestive study with implications that extend beyond a single state, and Francis B. Burdine's "Regional Economic Effects of Petroleum Industry Development in Texas, 1900–1970" (Ph.D. dissertation, University of Texas, 1976) demonstrates that the pumping of oil, like the mining of coal, did not necessarily contribute to local economic development. The persistence of wage differentials between the South and the rest of the nation is discussed in Victor R. Fuchs and Richard Perlman's "Recent Trends in Southern Wage Differentials," *Review of Economics and Statistics,* XLII (1960), 292–300; H. M. Douty's "Wage Differentials: Forces and Counterforces," *Monthly Labor Review,* XCI (1968), 74–81; and Robert J. Newman's *Growth in the American South: Changing Regional Employment and Wage Patterns in the 1960s and 1970s* (New York, 1984).

That black southerners benefited relatively little from the early years of postwar economic development is documented by James D. Cowhig and Calvin L. Beale in "Relative Socioeconomic Status of Southern Whites and Nonwhites, 1950–1960," *Southwestern Social Science Quarterly,* XLIV (1964), 113–24; and by Vivian W. Henderson in *The Economic Status of Negroes: In the Nation and in the South* (Southern Regional Council, [1961]). The 1964 Civil Rights Act did materially benefit black workers, a point developed in John J. Donohue and James Heckman's "Continuous Versus Episodic Change: The Impact of Civil Rights Policy on the Economic Status of Blacks," *Journal of Economic Literature,* XXIX (1991), 1603–43. The results were uneven, however, as is demonstrated in Herbert R. Northup and Richard L. Rowan's *Negro Employment in Southern Industry* (Philadelphia, 1970); James Louis Walker's "Economic Development, Black Employment, and Black Migration in the Nonmetropolitan Deep South" (Ph.D. dissertation, University of Texas, 1974); and *Employment of Blacks in the South: A Perspective on the 1960s,* ed. Ray Marshall and Virgil L. Christian, Jr. (Austin, Tex., 1978).

THE CITIES AND THE SUNBELT

The literature on southern urban and metropolitan expansion is extensive and often extremely good. *The Urban South,* ed. Rupert B. Vance and Nicholas J. Demerath (Chapel Hill, N.C., 1954), is an indispensable study of early postwar urban development. The best overview of southern urbanization is David R. Goldfield's "The Urban South: A Regional Framework," *American Historical Review,* LXXXVI (1981), 1009–34, and see also his *Cotton Fields and Skyscrapers: Southern City and Region, 1607–1980* (Baton Rouge, 1982). Otis Dudley Duncan *et al.*'s *Metropolis and Region* (Baltimore, 1960) and Thierry J. Noyelle and Thomas M. Stanback, Jr.'s *The Economic Transformation of American Cities* (New York, 1984) are invaluable in relating southern metropolises to those elsewhere in the nation.

A number of generally excellent works examine southern cities from a Sunbelt perspective. They include *The Rise of the Sunbelt Cities,* ed. David C. Perry and Alfred J. Watkins (Beverly Hills, Calif., 1977); Carl Abbott's *The New Urban America: Growth and Politics in Sunbelt Cities* (Rev. ed.; Chapel Hill, N.C., 1987); *Sunbelt Cities: Politics and Growth Since World War II,* ed. Richard M. Bernard and Bradley R. Rice (Austin, Tex., 1983); *Searching for the Sunbelt: Historical Perspectives on a Region,* ed. Raymond A. Mohl (Knoxville, Tenn., 1990); and Raymond A. Mohl *et al.*'s *Essays on Sunbelt Cities and Recent Urban America* (College Station, Tex., 1990). The diversity of southern cities is explored in Franklin J. James *et al.*'s *Minorities in the Sunbelt* (New Brunswick, N.J., 1984) and *Shades of the Sunbelt: Essays on Ethnicity, Race, and the Urban South,* ed. Randall M. Miller and George E. Pozetta (Westport, Conn., 1988). Kirkpatrick Sale's *Power Shift: The Rise of the Southern Rim and Its Challenge to the Eastern Establishment* (New York, 1976) is important for its role in defining the Sunbelt phenomenon and in directing attention to southern metropolitan areas.

Floyd Hunter's *Community Power Structure: A Study of Decision Makers* (Chapel Hill, N.C., 1953) is an extremely influential examination of the leadership of Atlanta, an analysis confirmed by Ivan Allen, Jr.'s *Mayor: Notes on the Sixties* (New York, 1971). Carol Estes Thometz' *The Decision-Makers: The Power Structure of Dallas* (Dallas, 1963) arrives at conclusions similar to those reached by Hunter's study. Of all southern cities, Atlanta has been the most thoroughly researched. Other significant studies include Lorraine Nelson Spritzer's *The Belle of Ashby Street: A Political Biography of Helen Douglas Mankin* (Athens, Ga., 1982); Harold H. Martin's *William Berry Hartsfield: Mayor of Atlanta* (Athens, Ga., 1978); Floyd Hunter's *Community Power Succession: Atlanta's Policy-Makers Revisited* (Chapel

Hill, N.C., 1980); Truman A. Hartshorn's *Metropolis in Georgia: Atlanta's Rise as a Major Transaction Center* (Cambridge, Mass., 1976); and Clarence N. Stone's *Regime Politics: Governing Atlanta, 1946–1988* (Lawrence, Kans., 1989).

Robert L. Crain's *The Politics of School Desegregation: Comparative Case Studies of Community Structure and Policy-Making* (Chicago, 1968) is a valuable study of southern urban leadership. Edward F. Haas's *DeLesseps S. Morrison and the Image of Reform: New Orleans Politics, 1946–1961* (Baton Rouge, 1974) is an extremely good biography. Charles H. Levine's *Racial Conflict and the American Mayor: Power, Polarization, and Performance* (Lexington, Mass., 1974) and Jimmie Lewis Franklin's *Back to Birmingham: Richard Arrington, Jr., and His Times* (Tuscaloosa, Ala., 1989) explain developments in Birmingham after the civil rights demonstrations of 1963.

Among the better studies of other southern cities are Christopher Silver's *Twentieth-Century Richmond: Planning, Politics, and Race* (Knoxville, Tenn., 1984); Don H. Doyle's *Nashville Since the 1920s* (Knoxville, Tenn., 1985); David M. Tucker's *Memphis Since Crump: Bossism, Blacks, and Civic Reformers, 1948–1968* (Knoxville, Tenn., 1980); and Charles W. Johnson and Charles O. Jackson's *City Behind a Fence: Oak Ridge, Tennessee, 1942–1946* (Knoxville, Tenn., 1981). Karl E. Taeuber and Alma F. Taeuber's *Negroes in Cities: Residential Segregation and Neighborhood Change* (Chicago, 1965) documents the growth of racial segregation along with the expansion of cities. William H. Barnwell's *In Richard's World: The Battle of Charleston, 1966* (Boston, 1968) captures the social distance that separated the white middle class from the black inner-city poor.

SOUTHERN POLITICS

The best study of southern politics during the post–World War II era is Earl Black and Merle Black's *Politics and Society in the South* (Cambridge, Mass., 1987). Dewey W. Grantham's *The Life and Death of the Solid South: A Political History* (Lexington, Ky., 1988) is the best general treatment of twentieth-century politics. *The Southern Political Scene, 1938–1948,* ed. Taylor Cole and John H. Hallowell (Gainesville, Fla., 1948), and *The American South in the 1960s,* ed. Avery Leiserson (New York, 1964), both book versions of special issues of the *Journal of Politics,* are well-conceived essay collections. *The Changing Politics of the South,* ed. William C. Havard (Baton Rouge, 1972); Numan V. Bartley and Hugh D. Graham's *Southern Politics and the Second Reconstruction* (Baltimore, 1975); and Jack Bass and Walter DeVries' *The Transformation of Southern Politics: Social Change and*

Political Consequences Since 1945 (New York, 1976) are important studies. *Southern Elections: County and Precinct Data, 1950–1972,* comp. Numan V. Bartley and Hugh D. Graham (Baton Rouge, 1978), is a useful compilation. Robert Sherrill's *Gothic Politics in the Deep South: Stars of the New Confederacy* (New York, 1968) is a readable work emphasizing the outrageous side of southern politics.

Frederic D. Ogden's *The Poll Tax in the South* (University, Ala., 1958) and Cortez A. M. Ewing's *Primary Elections in the South: A Study in Uniparty Politics* (Norman, Okla., 1953) are good introductions to southern disfranchisement. Examining the breakdown of disfranchisement and the short-term growth in voter participation are Carol A. Cassel's "Change in Electoral Participation in the South," *Journal of Politics,* XLI (1979), 907–17; and Harold W. Stanley's *Voter Mobilization and the Politics of Race: The South and Universal Suffrage, 1952–1984* (New York, 1987). William C. Havard and Loren P. Beth's *The Politics of Mis-Representation: Rural-Urban Conflict in the Florida Legislature* (Baton Rouge, 1962) is the best study of a southern state legislature; W. D. Workman, Jr.'s *The Bishop from Barnwell: The Political Life and Times of Senator Edgar A. Brown* (Columbia, S.C., 1963) is the best biography of a southern state legislator; Malcolm E. Jewell's *Legislative Representation in the Contemporary South* (Durham, N.C., 1967) is the best general study of southern legislatures; and Paul T. David and Ralph Eisenberg's *Devaluation of the Urban and Suburban Vote: A Statistical Investigation of Long-Term Trends in State Legislative Representation* (Charlottesville, Va., 1961) is a competent examination of malapportionment. Gubernatorial administrations are evaluated in several state studies, the best of which are David R. Colburn and Richard K. Scher's *Florida's Gubernatorial Politics in the Twentieth Century* (Tallahassee, Fla., 1980) and Harold P. Henderson and Gary L. Roberts' *Georgia Governors in an Age of Change: From Ellis Arnall to George Busbee* (Athens, Ga., 1988). James R. Scales and Danney Goble's *Oklahoma Politics: A History* (Norman, Okla., 1982) and Paul Luebke's *Tar Heel Politics: Myths and Realities* (Chapel Hill, N.C., 1990) are among the better state studies that have regional implications.

SOUTHERN LIBERALS

The aborted revival of southern liberalism after World War II is competently analyzed in two Ph.D. dissertations: Patricia Ann Sullivan, "Gideon's Southern Soldiers: New Deal Politics and Civil Rights Reform, 1933–1948" (Emory University, 1983), and Randall Lee Patton,

"Southern Liberals and the Emergence of a 'New South,' 1938–1950" (University of Georgia, 1990). Thomas A. Krueger's *And Promises to Keep: The Southern Conference for Human Welfare* (Nashville, 1967) and Linda Reed's *Simple Decency and Common Sense: The Southern Conference Movement, 1938–1963* (Bloomington, Ind., 1991) cover the Southern Conference, although the conference's objectives are best stated in Stetson Kennedy's *Southern Exposure* (Garden City, N.Y., 1946) and *Outside the Magic Circle: The Autobiography of Virginia Foster Durr*, ed. Hollinger F. Barnard (University, Ala., 1985). The decimation of southern radicalism and the transformation of liberalism into moderation is traced in Anthony P. Dunbar's *Against the Grain: Southern Radicals and Prophets, 1929–1959* (Charlottesville, Va., 1981) and Morton Sosna's *In Search of the Silent South: Southern Liberals and the Race Issue* (New York, 1977).

Biographies of prominent southern liberals include Anne C. Loveland's *Lillian Smith, A Southerner Confronting the South* (Baton Rouge, 1986); Warren Ashby's *Frank Porter Graham, A Southern Liberal* (Winston-Salem, N.C., 1980); Charles W. Eagles' *Jonathan Daniels and Race Relations: The Evolution of a Southern Liberal* (Knoxville, Tenn., 1982); John A. Salmond's *A Southern Rebel: The Life and Times of Aubrey Willis Williams, 1890–1965* (Chapel Hill, N.C., 1983) and *Miss Lucy of the CIO: The Life and Times of Lucy Randolph Mason, 1882–1959* (Athens, Ga., 1988); Virginia Van der Veer Hamilton's *Lister Hill, Statesman from the South* (Chapel Hill, N.C., 1987); and Charles L. Fontenay's *Estes Kefauver: A Biography* (Knoxville, Tenn., 1980). Ellis Gibbs Arnall's *The Shore Dimly Seen* (New York, 1946) and *What the People Want* (New York, 1948) are important statements about one wing of progressive thought, and Arnall's career is treated in Harold Paulk Henderson's *The Politics of Change in Georgia* (Athens, Ga., 1991).

Earl K. Long and James E. Folsom were the most prominent heirs to the South's rural populist tradition. Among the more helpful of numerous works on Long and Louisiana politics are Michael L. Kurtz and Morgan D. Peoples' *Earl K. Long: The Saga of Uncle Earl and Louisiana Politics* (Baton Rouge, 1990); A. J. Liebling's *The Earl of Louisiana* (New York, 1961); Stan Opotowsky's *The Longs of Louisiana* (New York, 1960); Allan P. Sindler's *Huey Long's Louisiana: State Politics, 1920–1952* (Baltimore, 1956); and Perry H. Howard's *Political Tendencies in Louisiana* (Rev. ed.; Baton Rouge, 1971). Carl Grafton and Anne Permaloff's *Big Mules and Branchheads: James E. Folsom and Political Power in Alabama* (Athens, Ga., 1985) and George E. Sims's *The Little Man's Big Friend: James E. Folsom in Alabama Politics, 1946–1958* (University, Ala., 1985) deal perceptively with Folsom.

SOUTHERN CONSERVATIVES

The classic work on the old-guard Bourbon Democrats is Jasper Berry Shannon's *Toward a New Politics in the South* (Knoxville, Tenn., 1949), which coined the term *county seat governing class*. Charles Wallace Collins' *Whither Solid South? A Study in Politics and Race Relations* (New Orleans, 1947) is the most influential statement of Bourbon views. The best general study of the Dixiecrat movement is Robert A. Garson's *The Democratic Party and the Politics of Sectionalism, 1941–1948* (Baton Rouge, 1974), and the most thorough examination of the Dixiecrat campaign is Ann Mathison McLaurin's "The Role of the Dixiecrats in the 1948 Election" (Ph.D. dissertation, University of Oklahoma, 1972). Other significant studies include Sarah McCulloh Lemmon's "The Ideology of the 'Dixiecrat' Movement," *Social Forces*, XXX (1951), 162–71; Emile B. Ader's *The Dixiecrat Movement: Its Role in Third Party Politics* (Washington, D.C., 1955); William D. Barnard's *Dixiecrats and Democrats: Alabama, 1942–1950* (University, Ala., 1974); Richard C. Ethridge's "Mississippi's Role in the Dixiecrat Movement" (Ph.D. dissertation, Mississippi State University, 1971); Glen Jeansonne's *Leander Perez, Boss of the Delta* (Baton Rouge, 1977); and Nadine Cohodas' *Strom Thurmond and the Politics of Southern Change* (New York, 1993).

The most comprehensive examination of the massive resistance to desegregation is Numan V. Bartley's *The Rise of Massive Resistance: Race and Politics in the South During the 1950s* (Baton Rouge, 1969). The best study of the Citizens' Council movement is Neil R. McMillen's *The Citizens' Council: Organized Resistance to the Second Reconstruction, 1954–1964* (Urbana, Ill., 1971). Also helpful on the Citizens' Councils are several journalistic studies, including John Bartlow Martin's *The Deep South Says, Never* (New York, 1957); James Graham Cook's *The Segregationists* (New York, 1962); and Hodding Carter III's *The South Strikes Back* (Garden City, N.Y., 1959). Other good studies relating to massive resistance include Benjamin Muse's *Ten Years of Prelude: The Story of Integration Since the Supreme Court's 1954 Decision* (New York, 1964); Reed Sarratt's *The Ordeal of Desegregation: The First Decade* (New York, 1966); and Earl Black's *Southern Governors and Civil Rights: Racial Segregation as a Campaign Issue in the Second Reconstruction* (Cambridge, Mass., 1976).

The important role played by the Byrd organization in the coming of massive resistance is investigated in Benjamin Muse's *Virginia's Massive Resistance* (Bloomington, Ind., 1961); Robbins L. Gates's *The Making of Massive Resistance: Virginia's Politics of Public School Desegregation, 1954–1956* (Chapel Hill, N.C., 1964); J. Harvie Wilkinson III's *Harry Byrd and the Changing Face of Virginia Politics, 1945–1956* (Charlottesville, Va., 1968); and James W. Ely, Jr.'s *The Crisis of Conservative Virginia: The Byrd Organization and the Politics of Massive Resistance* (Knoxville, Tenn., 1976). The Richmond *News Leader* published its editorials promoting resistance in pamphlet form as *Interposition: Editorials and Editorial Page Presentations* (Richmond, 1956).

Among numerous state studies helpful on the activities of old-guard southern Democrats, James Silver's *Mississippi: The Closed Society* (Rev. ed.; New York, 1966) is particularly revealing. Gilbert C. Fite's *Richard B. Russell, Senator from Georgia* (Chapel Hill, N.C., 1991) is an outstanding biography of the leader of the anti–civil rights forces in Congress, and David Daniel Potenziani's "Look to the Past: Richard B. Russell and the Defense of Southern White Supremacy" (Ph.D. dissertation, University of Georgia, 1981) is also helpful and is more critical of Russell. M. Carl Andrews' *No Higher Honor: The Story of Mills E. Godwin, Jr.* (Richmond, 1970) is a biography of a leading member of the Byrd organization who made the transition from massive resistance to conservative moderation to Republicanism. William Bryan Crawley, Jr.'s *Bill Tuck: A Political Life in Harry Byrd's Virginia* (Charlottesville, Va., 1987) and Bruce J. Dierenfield's *Keeper of the Rules: Congressman Howard W. Smith of Virginia* (Charlottesville, Va., 1986) deal with two other top ranking members of the Byrd organization. Herman E. Talmadge's *Talmadge: A Political Legacy, A Politician's Life* (Atlanta, 1987) is one of the few memoirs written by massive resistance leaders. *Speaking Out: The Autobiography of Lester Garfield Maddox* (Garden City, N.Y., 1975) is more revealing, however.

SOUTHERN MODERATES

Two excellent works crucial to an understanding of the southern moderates are *Southern Businessmen and Desegregation*, ed. Elizabeth Jacoway and David R. Colburn (Baton Rouge, 1982), and *Contemporary Southern Politics*, ed. James F. Lea (Baton Rouge, 1988). M. Richard Cramer's "School Desegregation and New Industry: The Southern Community Leaders' Viewpoint," *Social Forces*, XLI (1963), 384–89, is a particularly important article. Alfred O. Hero, Jr.'s *The Southerner and World Affairs* (Baton Rouge, 1965) is a far more comprehensive study than its title implies. The works of Samuel Lubell, especially *The Future of American Politics* (2nd ed.; Garden City, N.Y., 1956) and *Revolt of the Moderates* (New York, 1956), contain perceptive sections on the influence of moderates in politics. William Peters' *The Southern Temper* (Garden City, N.Y.,

1959) surveys the state of southern moderation in the late 1950s. David R. Colburn's "Florida's Governors Confront the *Brown* Decision: A Case Study of the Constitutional Politics of School Desegregation, 1954–1970," in *An Uncertain Tradition: Constitutionalism and the History of the South*, ed. Kermit L. Hall and James W. Ely, Jr. (Athens, Ga., 1989), and William H. Chafe, *Civilities and Civil Rights: Greensboro, North Carolina, and the Black Struggle for Freedom* (New York, 1981) contain critiques of moderation's limitations.

A number of southern moderates recorded their observations and experiences in book form. Luther H. Hodges' *Businessman in the Statehouse: Six Years as Governor of North Carolina* (Chapel Hill, N.C., 1962) is particularly revealing. Among other important such works are Hodding Carter's *Southern Legacy* (Baton Rouge, 1950); Harry S. Ashmore's *An Epitaph for Dixie* (New York, 1958); Brooks Hays's *A Southern Moderate Speaks* (Chapel Hill, N.C., 1959); Ralph W. McGill's *The South and the Southerner* (Boston, 1963); Frank E. Smith's *Congressman from Mississippi* (New York, 1964); and Francis Pickens Miller, *Man from the Valley: Memoirs of a Twentieth-Century Virginian* (Chapel Hill, N.C., 1971). Orval Eugene Faubus describes his peculiar career in two volumes of *Down from the Hills* (Little Rock, Ark., 1980–86). Tom R. Wagy's *Governor LeRoy Collins of Florida, Spokesman for the New South* (University, Ala., 1985) is among the best of a number of biographies of moderates that include Jim Lester's *A Man from Arkansas: Sid McMath and the Southern Reform Tradition* (Little Rock, Ark., 1976); Ann Hodges Morgan's *Robert S. Kerr: The Senate Years* (Norman, Okla., 1977); and Lee Seifert Green's *Lead Me On: Frank Goad Clement and Tennessee Politics* (Knoxville, Tenn., 1982).

BLACK SOUTHERNERS

The best study of the reentry of black people into southern politics is Donald R. Matthews and James W. Prothro's *Negroes and the New Southern Politics* (New York, 1966). Other extremely helpful studies include Daniel C. Thompson's *The Negro Leadership Class* (Englewood Cliffs, N.J., 1963); Everett Carll Ladd, Jr.'s *Negro Political Leadership in the South* (Ithaca, N.Y., 1966); William R. Keech's *The Impact of Negro Voting: The Role of the Vote in the Quest for Equality* (Chicago, 1968); Harry Holloway's *The Politics of the Southern Negro: From Exclusion to Big City Organization* (New York, 1969); M. Elaine Burgess' *Negro Leadership in a Southern City* (Chapel Hill, N.C., 1962); Steven F. Lawson's *Voting Rights in the South, 1944–1969* (New York, 1976) and *In Pursuit of Power: Southern*

Blacks and Electoral Politics, 1965–1982 (New York, 1985); and James W. Button's *Blacks and Social Change: Impact of the Civil Rights Movement in Southern Communities* (Princeton, 1989).

Useful accounts relating to particular states include Hugh D. Price's *The Negro and Southern Politics: A Chapter in Florida History* (New York, 1957); Andrew Buni's *The Negro in Virginia Politics, 1902–1965* (Charlottesville, Va., 1967); Idus A. Newby's *Black Carolinians: A History of Blacks in South Carolina from 1895 to 1968* (Columbia, S.C., 1973); Darlene Clark Hine's *Black Victory: The Rise and Fall of the White Primary in Texas* (Millwood, N.Y., 1979); and Jason Berry's *Amazing Grace: With Charles Evers in Mississippi* (New York, 1973). Good examinations of black political participation on the local level are Hanes Walton, Jr.'s *Black Politics: A Theoretical and Structural Analysis* (New York, 1972); John Rozier's *Black Boss: Political Revolution in a Georgia County* (Athens, Ga., 1982); Robert J. Norrell's *Reaping the Whirlwind: The Civil Rights Movement in Tuskegee* (New York, 1985); and Lawrence J. Hanks's *The Struggle for Black Political Empowerment in Three Georgia Counties* (Knoxville, Tenn., 1987).

TWO-PARTY POLITICS AND NATIONAL POLICIES

The emergence of two-party politics in the South is most perceptively examined in Alexander Heard's *A Two-Party South?* (Chapel Hill, N.C., 1952) and Alexander P. Lamis' *The Two-Party South* (New York, 1984). Other important works include Bernard Cosman's *The Case of the Goldwater Delegates: Deep South Republican Leadership* (University, Ala., 1966) and *Five States for Goldwater: Continuity and Change in Southern Presidential Voting Patterns* (University, Ala., 1966); *Election '64: A Ripon Society Report* (Cambridge, Mass., 1965); John C. Topping, Jr., *et al.*'s *Southern Republicanism and the New South* (Cambridge, Mass., 1966); Michael S. Lottman's *The GOP and the South* (Cambridge, Mass., 1970); and Wayne Greenhaw's *Elephants in the Cottonfields: Ronald Reagan and the New Republican South* (New York, 1982).

State studies of Republicanism include Walter Dean Burnham's "The Alabama Senatorial Election of 1962: Return of Inter-Party Competition," *Journal of Politics*, XXVI (1964), 798–829; Paul Casdorph's *A History of the Republican Party in Texas, 1865–1965* (Austin, Tex., 1965); and Peter D. Klingman's *Neither Dies Nor Surrenders: A History of the Republican Party in Florida, 1867–1970* (Gainesville, Fla., 1984). The first postwar Republican governor of a former Confederate state is favorably evaluated in John L. Ward's *The Arkansas Rockefeller* (Baton Rouge, 1978) and Cathy Kunzinger Urwin's *Agenda for Reform: Winthrop Rockefeller as Governor of Arkansas, 1967–1971* (Fayetteville, Ark., 1991). Tracing the growth of Republican strength in presidential politics are Donald S. Strong's *The 1952 Presidential Election in the South* (University, Ala., 1956), *Urban Republicanism in the South* (University, Ala., 1960), "Further Reflections on Southern Politics," *Journal of Politics,* XXX (1971), 239–56, and *Issue Voting and Party Realignment* (University, Ala., 1977); and O. Douglas Weeks's "The South in National Politics," *Journal of Politics,* XXVI (1964), 221–40.

The best study of the South in national politics is Earl Black and Merle Black's *The Vital South: How Presidents Are Elected* (Cambridge, Mass., 1992). Everett Carll Ladd, Jr.'s *Transformations of the American Party System: Political Coalitions from the New Deal to the 1970s* (New York, 1975) includes a good examination of the South's changing place in the national party system. Other useful studies are Paul T. David *et al.*'s *The South* (Baltimore, 1954), which is Vol. III of *Presidential Nominating Politics in 1952,* and Allan P. Sindler's "The Unsolid South: A Challenge to the Democratic National Party," in *The Uses of Power: Seven Cases in American Politics,* ed. Alan F. Westin (New York, 1962). Robert F. Burk's *Symbolic Equality: The Eisenhower Administration and Black Civil Rights* (Knoxville, Tenn., 1984) is particularly valuable, but also helpful are James C. Duram's *A Moderate Among Extremists: Dwight D. Eisenhower and the School Desegregation Crisis* (Chicago, 1981); J. W. Anderson's *Eisenhower, Brownell, and the Congress: The Tangled Origins of the Civil Rights Bill of 1956–1957* (University, Ala., 1964); and Charles Whalen and Barbara Whalen's *The Longest Debate: A Legislative History of the 1964 Civil Rights Act* (Washington, D.C., 1985).

Especially helpful on national policies as they related to the South are Michal R. Belknap's *Federal Law and Southern Order: Racial Violence and Constitutional Conflict in the Post-Brown South* (Athens, Ga., 1987); Kenneth O'Reilly's *Racial Matters: The FBI's Secret File on Black America, 1960–1972* (New York, 1989); Allen J. Matusow's *The Unraveling of America: A History of Liberalism in the 1960s* (New York, 1984); and Hugh Davis Graham's *The Civil Rights Era: Origins and Development of National Policy, 1960–1972* (New York, 1990). Carl M. Brauer's *John F. Kennedy and the Second Reconstruction* (New York, 1977) is the most useful work on its subject, although Burke Marshall's *Federalism and Civil Rights* (New York, 1964) is the best statement of Kennedy administration policy toward the southern civil rights movement. Studies evaluating Lyndon B. Johnson from various perspectives include Robert Dallek's *Lone Star Rising: Lyn-*

don Johnson and His Times, 1908–1960 (New York, 1991); Robert A. Caro's *The Years of Lyndon Johnson: The Path to Power* (New York, 1982) and *The Years of Lyndon Johnson: Means of Ascent* (New York, 1992); Paul K. Conkin's *Big Daddy from the Pedernales: Lyndon B. Johnson* (Boston, 1986); and Eric F. Goldman's *The Tragedy of Lyndon Johnson* (New York, 1969).

The crucial election of 1968 is examined in Lewis Chester *et al.*'s *An American Melodrama: The Presidential Campaign of 1968* (New York, 1969); Richard M. Scammon and Ben J. Wattenberg's *The Real Majority: An Extraordinary Examination of the American Electorate* (New York, 1971); and Kevin P. Phillips' *The Emerging Republican Majority* (New Rochelle, N.Y., 1969). Harry S. Dent, an aide to Senator J. Strom Thurmond of South Carolina, examines the evolution of the Republican southern strategy in *The Prodigal South Returns to Power* (New York, 1978). The most helpful available works on George C. Wallace are Jody Carlson's *George C. Wallace and the Politics of Powerlessness: The Wallace Campaigns for the Presidency, 1964–1976* (New Brunswick, N.J., 1981); Harold G. Grasmick's "Social Change and the Wallace Movement in the South" (Ph.D. dissertation, University of North Carolina, 1973); Marshall Frady's *Wallace* (New York, 1968); and Bill Jones's *The Wallace Story* (Northport, Ala., 1966).

Journalistic accounts that focus on Jimmy Carter's 1976 presidential campaign include Jules Witcover's *Marathon: The Pursuit of the Presidency* (New York, 1977); Martin Schram's *Running for President, 1976: The Carter Campaign* (New York, 1977); and James T. Wooten's *Dasher: The Roots and Rising of Jimmy Carter* (New York, 1978). Jimmy Carter's *Why Not the Best?* (New York, 1975) is the former president's most interesting statement. Gary M. Fink's *Prelude to the Presidency: The Political Character and Legislative Leadership Style of Governor Jimmy Carter* (Westport, Conn., 1980) is a good study of Carter's governorship, and Charles O. Jones's *The Trusteeship Presidency: Jimmy Carter and the United States Congress* (Baton Rouge, 1988) is the best available study of the Carter presidency. Works that focus on the 1980 election include Gerald Pomper *et al.*'s *The Election of 1980: Reports and Interpretations* (Chatham, N.J., 1981) and *The Hidden Election: Politics and Economics in the 1980 Presidential Campaign,* ed. Thomas Ferguson and Joel Rogers (New York, 1981), which includes a particularly helpful historical assessment of the election by Walter Dean Burnham.

THE CIVIL RIGHTS MOVEMENT

The literature on the southern civil rights movement is vast, and much of it is extremely good. David J. Garrow's massive editorial project *Martin Luther King, Jr., and the Civil Rights Movement* (18 vols.; Brooklyn, 1989) is invaluable. It brings together important previously unpublished material and significant previously published articles into a single collection. *Martin Luther King, Jr., and the Civil Rights Movement* is the essential beginning point for the study of the movement. A number of individual volumes are cited below.

Helping to explain the movement's origins are Doug McAdam's *Political Process and the Development of Black Insurgency, 1930–1970* (Chicago, 1982); August Meier and Elliott Rudwick's *Along the Color Line: Explorations in the Black Experience* (Urbana, Ill., 1976); and Jack M. Bloom's *Class, Race, and the Civil Rights Movement* (Bloomington, Ind., 1987). Among a number of good oral histories are *My Soul Is Rested: Movement Days in the Deep South Remembered*, ed. Howell Raines (New York, 1977); *The Voices of Negro Protest in America*, ed. H. Haywood Burns (New York, 1963); and *Voices of Freedom: An Oral History of the Civil Rights Movement from the 1950s Through the 1980s*, ed. Henry Hampton and Steve Fayer (New York, 1990). Also useful is *The Eyes on the Prize Civil Rights Reader: Documents, Speeches, and Firsthand Accounts from the Black Freedom Struggle, 1954–1990*, ed. Clayborne Carson *et al.* (New York, 1991).

The Civil Rights Movement in America, ed. Charles W. Eagles (Jackson, Miss., 1986), is an unusually good collection of essays, and *Women in the Civil Rights Movement: Trailblazers and Torchbearers, 1941–1965*, ed. Vicki L. Crawford *et al.* (Brooklyn, 1990), is a helpful work on a generally neglected subject. Among surveys of the civil rights movement, Manning Marable's *Race, Reform, and Rebellion: The Second Reconstruction in Black America, 1945–1982* (Jackson, Miss., 1984) is the most interpretative and the most interesting, Robert Weisbrot's *Freedom Bound: A History of America's Civil Rights Movement* (New York, 1990) places the southern movement within a national context, and David Goldfield's *Black, White, and Southern: Race Relations and Southern Culture, 1940 to the Present* (Baton Rouge, 1990) provides the fullest coverage of the southern movement.

THE *BROWN* DECISION AND DESEGREGATION

Helpful on the National Association for the Advancement of Colored People are Robert L. Zangrando's *The NAACP Crusade Against Lynching,*

1909–1950 (Philadelphia, 1980); Mark V. Tushnet's *The NAACP's Legal Strategy Against Segregated Education, 1925–1950* (Chapel Hill, N.C., 1987); Langston Hughes's *Fight for Freedom: The Story of the NAACP* (New York, 1962); and *Standing Fast: The Autobiography of Roy Wilkins* (New York, 1982). Also helpful is Louis E. Lomax' *The Negro Revolt* (New York, 1963), which criticizes NAACP strategy.

The NAACP focused its legal attack on the schools, the early phase of which is covered in the United States Commission on Civil Rights' report *Equal Protection of the Laws in Public Higher Education* (1960). The most comprehensive study of the Supreme Court's school desegregation decision is Richard Kluger's *Simple Justice: The History of Brown v. Board of Education and Black America's Struggle for Equality* (New York, 1975). Good studies of the federal judiciary and the problem of enforcement include J. W. Peltason's *Fifty-Eight Lonely Men* (2nd ed.; Urbana, Ill., 1971); Frank T. Read and Lucy S. McGough's *Let Them Be Judged: The Judicial Integration of the Deep South* (Metuchen, N.J., 1978); and Jack Bass's *Unlikely Heroes* (New York, 1981). *With All Deliberate Speed: Segregation-Desegregation in Southern Schools*, ed. Don Shoemaker (New York, 1957) reports on the progress of desegregation following the *Brown* decision.

Aldon D. Morris' *The Origins of the Civil Rights Movement: Black Communities Organizing for Change* (New York, 1984) is the best study of black activism during the 1950s. Works on the Montgomery bus boycott include *The Walking City: The Montgomery Bus Boycott, 1955–1956*, ed. David J. Garrow (Brooklyn, 1989), which is Vol. VII of *Martin Luther King, Jr., and the Civil Rights Movement*, ed. Garrow; *The Montgomery Bus Boycott and the Women Who Started It: The Memoir of Jo Ann Gibson Robinson*, ed. David J. Garrow (Knoxville, Tenn., 1987); Martin Luther King, Jr.'s *Stride Toward Freedom: The Montgomery Story* (New York, 1958); Norman W. Walton's "The Walking City: A History of the Montgomery Bus Boycott," *Negro History Bulletin*, XX (1956), 17ff., 27ff., 102ff., 147ff.; L. D. Reddick's "The Bus Boycott in Montgomery," *Dissent*, III (1956), 107–17; and J. Mills Thornton's "Challenge and Response in the Montgomery Bus Boycott of 1955–1956," *Alabama Review*, XXXIII (1980), 163–235. The Tallahassee boycott is covered in Charles U. Smith and Lewis M. Killian's *The Tallahassee Bus Boycott* (New York, 1958) and Lewis M. Killian and Charles U. Smith's "Negro Protest Leaders in a Southern Community," *Social Forces*, XXXVIII (1960), 253–62. Adam Fairclough's "The Preachers and the People: The Origins and Early Years of the Southern Christian Leadership Conference, 1955–1959," *Journal of Southern History*, LII (1956), 401–40, is an important article that suggests the limitations of black protest during the 1950s.

Massive resistance dominated the late 1950s, and the crucial test for it was Little Rock. Helpful studies include Irving J. Spitzberg, Jr.'s *Racial Politics in Little Rock, 1954–1964* (New York, 1987); David E. Wallace's "The Little Rock Central Desegregation Crisis of 1957" (Ph.D. dissertation, University of Missouri, 1977); Corinne Silverman's *The Little Rock Story* (Rev. ed.; University, Ala., 1959); *Little Rock, U.S.A.: Materials for Analysis,* ed. Wilson Record and Jane Cassels Record (San Francisco, 1960); and Henry M. Alexander's *The Little Rock Recall Election* (Eagleton Institute, 1960). Significant memoirs include Robert R. Brown's *Bigger Than Little Rock* (Greenwich, Conn., 1958); Virgil T. Blossom's *It Has Happened Here* (New York, 1959); Daisy Bates's *The Long Shadow of Little Rock: A Memoir* (New York, 1962); and "The Story of Little Rock—As Governor Faubus Tells It," *U.S. News and World Report,* June 20, 1958, pp. 101–106. Colbert S. Cartwright, a Little Rock resident, offers a particularly persuasive analysis in "Lesson from Little Rock," *Christian Century,* LXXIV (1957), 1193–94; and in "The Improbable Demagogue of Little Rock, Ark.," *Reporter,* October 17, 1957, pp. 23–25.

Ernest Q. Campbell's *When a City Closes Its Schools* (Chapel Hill, N.C., 1960) and Bob Smith's *They Closed Their Schools: Prince Edward County, Virginia, 1951–1964* (Chapel Hill, N.C., 1965) are good studies of two Virginia communities where schools were closed to avoid desegregation. The New Orleans school desegregation crisis is examined in the Louisiana State Advisory Committee's *The New Orleans School Crisis: Report to the United States Commission on Civil Rights* (New Orleans, 1961); Earlean Mary McCarrick's "Louisiana's Official Resistance to Desegregation" (Ph.D. dissertation, Vanderbilt University, 1964); Morton Inger's *Politics and Reality in an American City: The New Orleans School Crisis of 1960* (New York, 1969); and Edward L. Pinney and Robert S. Friedman's *Political Leadership and the School Desegregation Crisis in New Orleans* (New York, 1963). Other noteworthy studies of desegregation crises include Walter Lord's *The Past That Would Not Die* (London, 1966), on the desegregation of the University of Mississippi, and Calvin Trillin's *An Education in Georgia: Charlayne Hunter, Hamilton Holmes, and the Integration of the University of Georgia* (1964; rpr. Athens, Ga., 1991).

THE STUDENT NONVIOLENT COORDINATING COMMITTEE,
THE CONGRESS OF RACIAL EQUALITY, AND DIRECT ACTION

By the time of the New Orleans school crisis, black students had launched the sit-in movement. Among the best of numerous accounts of the movement are *We Shall Overcome: The Civil Rights Movement in the United States*, ed. David J. Garrow (3 vols.; Brooklyn, 1989), that is, Vols. IV–VI of *Martin Luther King, Jr., and the Civil Rights Movement*, ed. Garrow; James H. Laue's *Direct Action and Desegregation, 1960–1962: Toward a Theory of the Rationalization of Protest* (Brooklyn, 1989), which is Vol. XV of the same set; and Martin Oppenheimer's *The Sit-In Movement of 1960* (Brooklyn, 1989), which is Vol. XVI of the set. Miles Wolff's *Lunch at the Five and Ten: The Greensboro Sit-Ins* (New York, 1970) details the beginning of the sit-in campaign. Important articles on the changing nature of the movement are John M. Orbell's "Protest Participation Among Southern Negro College Students," *American Political Science Review*, LXI (1967), 446–56; and Anthony M. Orum and Amy W. Orum's "The Class and Status Bases of Negro Student Protest," *Social Science Quarterly*, IL (1968), 521–33.

Pat Watters and Reese Cleghorn's *Climbing Jacob's Ladder: The Arrival of Negroes in Southern Politics* (New York, 1967), written by two veteran southern journalists and based largely on Voter Education Project records, remains the best general study of the civil rights movement. Jack Newfield's *A Prophetic Minority* (New York, 1966) is also a useful work. Several reports by the Southern Regional Council, including *The Student Protest Movement: Winter, 1960* (Atlanta, 1960) and *The Student Protest Movement: A Recapitulation* (Atlanta, 1961), are helpful, as are two comparative studies: Emilie Schmeidler, "Shaping Ideas and Action: CORE, SCLC, and SNCC in the Struggle for Equality, 1960–1966" (Ph.D. dissertation, University of Michigan, 1980), and Jacquelyne Johnson Clarke, *These Rights They Seek: A Comparison of the Goals and Techniques of Local Civil Rights Organizations* (Washington, D.C., 1962).

Clayborne Carson's *In Struggle: SNCC and the Black Awakening of the 1960s* (Cambridge, Mass., 1981) is the best study of the Student Nonviolent Coordinating Committee. Also valuable are Howard Zinn's *SNCC: The New Abolitionists* (Boston, 1964) and Emily Stoper's *The Student Nonviolent Coordinating Committee: The Growth of Radicalism in a Civil Rights Organization* (Brooklyn, 1989), which is Vol. XVII of *Martin Luther King, Jr., and the Civil Rights Movement*, ed. Garrow. The most useful of several memoirs written by SNCC activists are James Forman's *The Making of Black Revolutionaries: A Personal Account* (New York, 1972) and Cleveland Sellers' *The River of No Return: The Autobiography of a Black Militant and the Life and Death of SNCC* (New York, 1973).

August Meier and Elliott Rudwick's *CORE: A Study in the Civil Rights Movement, 1942–1968* (New York, 1973) is an excellent account of the Congress of Racial Equality, as well as a significant commentary on the civil rights movement generally. James Farmer's *Lay Bare the Heart: An Autobiography of the Civil Rights Movement* (New York, 1985) is an important memoir. CORE achieved a southern presence by sponsoring the freedom rides, which are ably examined in Catherine A. Barnes's *Journey from Jim Crow: The Desegregation of Southern Transit* (New York, 1983) and in a perceptive memoir, James Peck's *Freedom Ride* (New York, 1962).

Good studies of the Mississippi Freedom Summer include Len Holt's *The Summer That Didn't End* (London, 1966); William McCord's *Mississippi: The Long, Hot Summer* (New York, 1965); Sally Belfrage's *Freedom Summer* (New York, 1965); *Letters from Mississippi*, ed. Elizabeth Sutherland (New York, 1965); Tracy Sugarman's *Stranger at the Gates: A Summer in Mississippi* (New York, 1966); Nicholas Von Hoffman's *Mississippi Notebook* (New York, 1964); Doug McAdam's *Freedom Summer* (New York, 1988); and Nicolaus Mills's *Like a Holy Crusade: Mississippi 1964—The Turning of the Civil Rights Movement in America* (Chicago, 1992). The role of the Delta Ministry is examined in Bruce Hilton's *The Delta Ministry* (Toronto, 1969). Mary Aickin Rothschild's *A Case of Black and White: Northern Volunteers and the Southern Freedom Summers, 1964–1965* (Westport, Conn., 1982) and Nicholas J. Demerath *et al.*'s *Dynamics of Idealism: White Activists in a Black Movement* (San Francisco, 1971) are good on northern volunteers in southern summer campaigns. The difficulties encountered in voter registration projects are covered in Frederick M. Wirt's *Politics of Southern Equality: Law and Social Change in a Mississippi County* (Chicago, 1970) and Neil R. McMillen's "Black Enfranchisement in Mississippi: Federal Enforcement and Black Protest in the 1960s," *Journal of Southern History*, XLIII (1977), 351–72.

KING AND THE SOUTHERN CHRISTIAN LEADERSHIP CONFERENCE

The Montgomery bus boycott elevated Martin Luther King, Jr., to prominence. The best biography of King is David J. Garrow's *Bearing the Cross: Martin Luther King, Jr., and the Southern Christian Leadership Conference* (New York, 1986). *Martin Luther King, Jr.: Civil Rights Leader, Theologian, Orator*, ed. David J. Garrow (3 vols.; Brooklyn, 1989), that is, Vols. I–III of *Martin Luther King, Jr., and the Civil Rights Movement*, ed. Garrow, is an excellent collection of essays. Garrow's *The FBI and Martin Luther King, Jr.* (New York, 1981) is also helpful. Among numerous other biographies of King, David L. Lewis' *King: A Critical Biography* (New York, 1970) is particularly good, and Stephen B. Oates's *Let the Trumpet Sound:*

The Life of Martin Luther King, Jr. (New York, 1982) catches the mood of the movement. Adam Fairclough's *To Redeem the Soul of America: The Southern Christian Leadership Conference and Martin Luther King, Jr.* (Athens, Ga., 1987) is the best study of King's organization, and Eugene Pierce Walker's "A History of the Southern Christian Leadership Conference, 1955–1965: The Evolution of a Southern Strategy for Social Change" (Ph.D. dissertation, Duke University, 1978) is also extremely good. *Testament of Hope: The Essential Writings of Martin Luther King, Jr.,* ed. James Melvin Washington (San Francisco, 1986), is a valuable collection. King's *Strength to Love* (Philadelphia, 1963) is one of the most revealing of the books by King, and Coretta Scott King's *My Life with Martin Luther King, Jr.* (New York, 1969) and Ralph David Abernathy's *And the Walls Came Tumbling Down* (New York, 1989) are useful memoirs. Richard Lentz's *Symbols, the News Magazines, and Martin Luther King* (Baton Rouge, 1990) is a provocative work that helps explain King's national popularity.

Glenn T. Eskew's "But for Birmingham: The Local and National Movements in the Civil Rights Struggle" (Ph.D. dissertation, University of Georgia, 1993) is an outstanding study of the crucial Birmingham campaign. Other important works on Birmingham include *Birmingham, Alabama, 1956–1963: The Black Struggle for Civil Rights,* ed. David J. Garrow (Brooklyn, 1989), which is Vol. VIII of *Martin Luther King, Jr., and the Civil Rights Movement,* ed. Garrow; and Robert Gaines Corley's "The Quest for Racial Harmony: Race Relations in Birmingham, Alabama, 1947–1963" (Ph.D. dissertation, University of Virginia, 1979). William Dorman's *We Shall Overcome* (New York, 1964) devotes a lengthy section of his journalistic report to the Birmingham demonstrations, and Charles Morgan, Jr.'s *A Time to Speak* (New York, 1964) and Martin Luther King, Jr.'s *Why We Can't Wait* (New York, 1964) record the observations of participants in the Birmingham crisis. The role of police commissioner Eugene Connor is included in William A. Nunnelley's *Bull Connor* (Tuscaloosa, Ala., 1991).

The Albany Movement is examined by Howard Zinn in *Albany: A Study in National Responsibility* (Atlanta, 1962) and *The Southern Mystique* (New York, 1964), and by John A. Ricks III in " 'De Lawd' Descends and Is Crucified: Martin Luther King, Jr., in Albany, Georgia," *Journal of Southwest Georgia History,* II (1984), 3–14. David R. Colburn's *Racial Change and Community Crisis: St. Augustine, Florida, 1977–1980* (New York, 1985), and *St. Augustine, Florida, 1963–1964: Mass Protest and Racial Violence,* ed. David J. Garrow (Brooklyn, 1989), which is Vol. X of *Martin Luther King, Jr., and the Civil Rights Movement,* ed. Garrow, are good on the Southern Christian Leadership Conference's campaign in that city. Detailing the demonstrations in Selma are David J. Garrow's *Protest at Selma: Martin Luther King, Jr., and the Voting Rights Act of 1965* (New Haven, 1978); Charles E. Fager's *Selma, 1965* (New York, 1974); C. L. Chestnut, Jr., and Julia Cass's *Black in Selma: The Uncommon Life of J. L. Chestnut, Jr.* (New York, 1990); and Stephen L. Longenecker's *Selma's Peacemaker: Ralph Smeltzer and Civil Rights Mediation* (Philadelphia, 1987). Charles Fager's *Uncertain Resurrection: The Poor People's Washington Campaign* (Grand Rapids, 1969) is the most complete work on its subject.

BLACK POWER AND THE DECLINE OF THE MOVEMENT

Stokely Carmichael and Charles V. Hamilton's *Black Power: The Politics of Liberation in America* (New York, 1967) and Stokely Carmichael's *Stokely Speaks: Black Power Back to Pan-Africanism* (New York, 1971) are the most noteworthy efforts to explain black power as it emerged in the Student Nonviolent Coordinating Committee. Robert L. Allen's *Black Awakening in Capitalist America: An Analytic History* (Garden City, N.Y., 1969) and Julius Lester's *Look Out Whitey: Black Power's Gon' Get Your Mama* (New York, 1968) are among numerous works on black power, and Harold Cruse's *Rebellion or Revolution* (New York, 1968) and Earl Ofari's *The Myth of Black Capitalism* (New York, 1970) are good critiques.

John Herbers' *The Lost Priority: What Happened to the Civil Rights Movement?* (New York, 1970) helps explain the decline of black protest. Charles E. Silberman's "Beware the Day They Change Their Minds," *Fortune*, November, 1965, pp. 150ff., describes the response of civil rights groups to the enactment of federal civil rights legislation, and Silberman's *Crisis in Black and White* (New York, 1964) and Leslie W. Dunbar's *A Republic of Equals* (Ann Arbor, Mich., 1966) perceptively assess the state of the movement. The busing debate is discussed in George R. Metcalf's *From Little Rock to Boston: The History of School Desegregation* (Westport, Conn., 1983); *The Great School Bus Controversy*, ed. Nicolaus Mills (New York, 1973); *The School Busing Controversy, 1970–1975*, ed. Judith F. Buncher (New York, 1975) and Gary Orfield's *The Reconstruction of Southern Education: The Schools and the 1964 Civil Rights Act* (New York, 1969) and *Must We Bus? Segregated Schools and National Policy* (Washington, D.C., 1978). Richard A. Pride and J. Davis Woodward's *The Burden of Busing: The Politics of Desegregation in Nashville, Tennessee* (Knoxville, Tenn., 1985) and Robert A. Pratt's *The Color of Their Skin: Education and*

Race in Richmond, Virginia, 1954–1989 (Charlottesville, Va., 1992) are good studies of two southern cities.

Major studies that draw different conclusions about the educational effects of segregation and integration in the schools are *Racial Isolation in the Public Schools: A Report of the U.S. Commission on Civil Rights* (1967); James S. Coleman *et al.*'s *Equality of Educational Opportunities* (Washington, D.C., 1966); and Christopher Jencks *et al.*'s *Inequality: A Reassessment of the Effect of Family and Schools in America* (New York, 1972). J. Harvie Wilkinson III's *From Brown to Bakke: The Supreme Court and School Integration, 1954–1978* (New York, 1979) is an important study that stresses the elitism of social reform by judicial decree, and David Alan Horowitz' "White Southerners' Alienation and Civil Rights: The Response to Corporate Liberalism, 1956–1965," *Journal of Southern History*, LIV (1988), 173–200, is a good study of "managerial liberalism" and the popular reaction to it.

WOMEN'S RIGHTS

The drive for black rights sparked demands for individual rights for other groups. Cynthia Harrison's *On Account of Sex: The Politics of Women's Issues, 1945–1968* (Berkeley and Los Angeles, 1988) is good on the emergence of the women's rights movement. Sara Evans' *Personal Politics: The Roots of Women's Liberation in the Civil Rights Movement and the New Left* (New York, 1979) and Carl M. Brauer's "Women Activists, Southern Conservatives, and the Prohibition of Sex Discrimination in Title VII of the 1964 Civil Rights Act," *Journal of Southern History*, IL (1983), 37–56, link the women's rights movement with black civil rights protest in the South. Good studies of the defeat of the Equal Rights Amendment include Janet K. Boles's *The Politics of the Equal Rights Amendment: Conflict and the Decision Process* (New York, 1979); Gilbert Y. Steiner's *Constitutional Inequality: The Political Fortunes of the Equal Rights Amendment* (Washington, D.C., 1985); Mary Frances Berry's *Why ERA Failed: Politics, Women's Rights, and the Amending Process of the Constitution* (Bloomington, Ind., 1986); and Jane J. Mansbridge's *Why We Lost the ERA* (Chicago, 1986). The only significant work to study the amendment's defeat in the South is Donald G. Mathews and Jane Sherron DeHart's *Sex, Gender, and the Politics of ERA: A State and the Nation* (New York, 1990).

Susan Deller Ross's *The Rights of Women* (New York, 1973) and Ross Barcher and Ann Barcher's *The Rights of Women* (Rev. ed.; New York, 1983) summarize state laws relating to equal rights. Eva R. Rubin's *Abor-*

tion, Politics, and the Courts: Roe v. Wade and Its Aftermath (Rev. ed.; New York, 1987) is a solid study of its subject, and Christopher Lasch's *The True and Only Heaven: Progress and Its Critics* (New York, 1991) is an important national study that helps explain cultural conservatism in the South.

SOUTHERN SOCIETY

Pete Daniel's *Standing at the Crossroads: Southern Life Since 1900* (New York, 1986) is the only general social history of the recent South. William T. Polk's *Southern Accent: From Uncle Remus to Oak Ridge* (New York, 1953) emphasizes the distinction between the "traditional" rural and small-town South and the "modern" urban South. Various works by Robert Coles, most particularly *Farewell to the South* (Boston, 1963), contain fascinating interviews. Floyd C. Watkins and Charles Hubert Watkins' *Yesterday in the Hills* (Athens, Ga., 1963) is a revealing commentary on the nature of southern change. A special issue of *Ebony* in August, 1971, on the "South today," is an extremely good evaluation of the changes wrought by desegregation. John Shelton Reed's *Southerners: The Social Psychology of Sectionalism* (Chapel Hill, N.C., 1983) and *Southern Folk, Plain and Fancy: Native White Social Types* (Athens, Ga., 1986) are good on the life-styles of white southern social groups.

The best study of a southern subregion is James C. Cobb's *The Most Southern Place on Earth: The Mississippi Delta and the Roots of Regional Identity* (New York, 1992). David L. Cohn's *Where I Was Born and Raised* (Boston, 1948) is a firsthand account of the same region. A comparison of the two books suggests a great deal about the changes that have taken place in the South. Helpful among numerous community studies are H. C. Nixon's *Lower Piedmont Country: The Uplands of the Deep South* (University, Ala., 1946); Solon T. Kimball and Marion Pearsall's *The Talladega Story: A Study in Community Process* (University, Ala., 1954); Elizabeth Rauh Bethel's *Promiseland: A Century of Life in a Negro Community* (Philadelphia, 1981); Hylan Lewis' *Blackways of Kent* (Chapel Hill, N.C., 1955); Marion Pearsall's *Little Smoky Ridge: The Natural History of a Southern Appalachian Neighborhood* (University, Ala., 1959); Catherine H. C. Seaman's "Kinship and Land Tenure in a Piedmont County: A Diachronic Study of a Heterogeneous Community in the South" (Ph.D. dissertation, University of Virginia, 1969); and William Hildra Baker's "The Economics of a Small Southern Town" (Ph.D. dissertation, University of Alabama, 1963).

The expansion of the metropolitan white southern middle class is welcomed in William H. Nicholls' *Southern Tradition and Regional Progress* (Chapel Hill, N.C., 1960) and Leonard Reissman's "Social Development and the American South," *Journal of Social Issues,* XXII (1966), 101–16. White middle-class values are criticized in such works as Wilma Dykeman's "The Man in the Gray Flannel Sheet," *Progressive,* February, 1959, pp. 8ff. E. Franklin Frazier's *Black Bourgeoisie* (Glencoe, Ill., 1957) and Lois Benjamin's *The Black Elite: Facing the Color Line in the Twilight of the Twentieth Century* (Chicago, 1991) are excellent national studies, as is Bart Landry's *The New Black Middle Class* (Berkeley and Los Angeles, 1987), which exaggerates the size of its subject by an overly generous definition of *middle class.* John R. Salter, Jr.'s *Jackson, Mississippi: An American Chronicle of Struggle and Schism* (Malabar, Fla., 1987) examines one of numerous examples of class conflict within the black community.

Two excellent studies of white working-class attitudes are Robert Emil Botsch's *We Shall Not Overcome: Populism and Southern Blue-Collar Workers* (Chapel Hill, N.C., 1980) and David Hirsh Tabb's "Attitudes Toward Economic Equality in the South: A Study of the Political Ideology of the Poor" (Ph.D. dissertation, University of North Carolina, 1969). White textile workers are examined in John Kenneth Moreland's *Millways of Kent* (Chapel Hill, N.C., 1958); Herbert Lahne's *The Cotton Mill Worker* (New York, 1944); Harriet L. Herring's *Passing of the Mill Village: Revolution in a Southern Institution* (Chapel Hill, N.C., 1949); Jacquelyn Dowd Hall *et al.'s Like a Family: The Making of a Southern Cotton Mill World* (Chapel Hill, N.C., 1987); Jacquelyn Dowd Hall *et al.'s* "Cotton Mill People: Work, Community, and Protest in the Textile South, 1880–1940," *American Historical Review,* XCI (1986), 245–86; and Douglas Flamming's *Creating the Modern South: Millhands and Managers in Dalton, Georgia, 1884–1984* (Chapel Hill, N.C., 1992).

Other helpful studies include B. M. Wofford and T. A. Kelly's *Mississippi Workers: Where They Come from and How They Perform* (University, Ala., 1955); J. Kenneth Moreland's "Kent Revisited: Blue-Collar Aspirations and Achievements," in *Blue Collar World: Studies of the American Worker,* ed. Arthur B. Shostak and William Gomberg (Englewood Cliffs, N.J., 1964); Ethelyn Davis' "Careers as Concerns of Blue-Collar Girls," in *Blue Collar World,* ed. Shostak and Gomberg; *Working Lives: The "Southern Exposure" History of Labor in the South,* ed. Marc S. Miller (New York, 1980); Ronald L. Lewis' *Coal Miners in America: Race, Class, and Community Conflict, 1780–1980* (Lexington, Ky., 1988); and Crandall A. Shifflett's *Coal Towns: Life, Work, and Culture in Community Towns of Southern Appalachia, 1880–1960* (Knoxville, Tenn., 1991).

Jacqueline Jones's *Labor of Love, Labor of Sorrow: Black Women, Work, and the Family from Slavery to the Present* (New York, 1985) is an excellent overview of its subject. Molly Crocker Dougherty's *Becoming a Woman in Rural Black Culture* (New York, 1978) and Theodore R. Kennedy's *You Gotta Deal with It: Black Family Relations in a Southern Community* (New York, 1980) are helpful works. Other useful studies of southern women include Mary Martha Thomas' *Riveting and Rationing in Dixie: Alabama Women and the Second World War* (Tuscaloosa, Ala., 1987); Dolores E. Janiewski's *Sisterhood Denied: Race, Gender, and Class in a New South Community* (Philadelphia, 1985); *Southern Women*, ed. Caroline Matheny Dillman (New York, 1988); *Women in the South: An Anthropological Perspective*, ed. Holly F. Mathews (Athens, Ga., 1989); Southeast Women's Employment Coalition's *Women of the South: Economic Status and Prospects* (Lexington, Ky., 1986); and Priscilla C. Little and Robert C. Vaughan's *A New Perspective: Southern Women's Cultural History from the Civil War to Civil Rights* (Charlottesville, Va., 1989). *Hillbilly Women*, ed. Kathy Kahn (Garden City, N.Y., 1973), is an extremely good oral history of working white women, and *Speaking for Ourselves: Women of the South*, ed. Maxine Alexander (New York, 1977), is a helpful oral history, as well.

Memoirs that contribute to an understanding of southern social developments include Anne Moody's *Coming of Age in Mississippi* (New York, 1968); Ben Robertson's *Red Hills and Cotton: An Upcountry Memoir* (Columbia, S.C., 1942); Maya Angelou's *I Know Why the Caged Bird Sings* (New York, 1969); Shirley Abbott's *Womenfolks: Growing Up down South* (New Haven, 1983); Rosemary Daniell's *Fatal Flowers: On Sin, Sex, and Suicide in the Deep South* (New York, 1980); and Melton A. McLaurin's *Separate Pasts: Growing Up White in the Segregated South* (Athens, Ga., 1987). Geraldine Moore's *Behind the Ebony Mask* (Birmingham, Ala., 1961) and A. G. Gaston's *Green Power: The Successful Way of A. G. Gaston* (Birmingham, Ala., 1968) are interesting observations by two members of Birmingham's black bourgeoisie. *On Shares: Ed Brown's Story*, ed. Jane Maguire (New York, 1975), is a remembrance by a black tenant farmer. Roy G. Taylor's *Sharecroppers: The Way We Really Were* (Winston, N.C., 1984) tells a white tenant farmer's story.

ORGANIZED LABOR

F. Ray Marshall's *Labor in the South* (Cambridge, Mass., 1967) is the best general history of organized labor in the region, and his *The Negro and Organized Labor* (New York, 1965) is also helpful. Philip S. Foner's

Women and the American Labor Movement: From World War I to the Present (New York, 1980) and *Organized Labor and the Black Worker, 1619–1981* (New York, 1982) are useful surveys. Barbara Sue Griffith's *The Crisis of American Labor: Operation Dixie and the Defeat of the CIO* (Philadelphia, 1988) is a valuable if somewhat narrowly focused study of the crucial organizing effort in the South, and Lucy Randolph Mason's *To Win These Rights: A Personal Story of the CIO in the South* (New York, 1952) is a good firsthand account. Among the more useful studies of union labor in the South are Paul David Richards' "The History of the Textile Workers Union of America, CIO, in the South, 1937 to 1945" (Ph.D. dissertation, University of Wisconsin, 1978); Joseph Y. Garrison's "Paul Revere Christopher, Southern Labor Leader, 1910–1974" (Ph.D. dissertation, Georgia State University, 1977); Charles R. Perry's *Collective Bargaining and the Decline of the United Mine Workers* (Philadelphia, 1984); Horace Huntley's "Iron Ore Miners and Mine Mill in Alabama, 1933–1952" (Ph.D. dissertation, University of Pittsburgh, 1977); Robert J. Norrell's "Caste in Steel: Jim Crow Careers in Birmingham, Alabama," *Journal of American History*, LXXIII (1986): 669–94; Robert Korstad and Nelson Lichtenstein's "Opportunities Found and Lost: Labor, Radicals, and the Early Civil Rights Movement," *Journal of American History*, LXXV (1988), 786–811; and *Organized Labor in the Twentieth-Century South*, ed. Robert H. Zieger (Knoxville, Tenn., 1991). J. R. Dempsey's *The Operation of the Right-to-Work Laws* (Milwaukee, 1961) is good on its subject.

PUBLIC SERVICES

The absence of a history of public education in the modern South is a serious void. The Fund for the Advancement of Education sponsored a comprehensive investigation of southern public schools in the early 1950s that resulted in publication of Harry S. Ashmore's *The Negro and the Schools* (Chapel Hill, N.C., 1954); Ernst W. Swanson and John A. Griffin's *Public Education in the South: Today and Tomorrow* (Westport, Conn., 1955); and Truman M. Pierce *et al.*'s *White and Negro Schools in the South: An Analysis of Biracial Education* (Englewood Cliffs, N.J., 1955). Southern educational developments during the 1950s are surveyed in the essays prepared by the staff of the Southern Education Reporting Service, in *Southern Schools: Progress and Problems,* ed. Patrick McCauley and Edward D. Ball (Nashville, 1959). Beyond that, researchers must rely on state studies and official statistics.

James W. Martin and Glenn D. Morrow's *Taxation of Manufacturing in the South* (University, Ala., 1948) and Eva Galambos' *State and Local Taxes in the South, 1973* (Southern Regional Council, 1973) are helpful works. The Southern Regional Council issued periodic reports, such as *Public Assistance in the South* (Southern Regional Council, 1966), calling attention to the poverty of public services in the region. Edward H. Beardsley's *A History of Neglect: Health Care for Blacks and Mill Workers in the Twentieth-Century South* (Knoxville, Tenn., 1987) is the most penetrating study of health care in the region, and Thomas R. Ford's *Health and Demography in Kentucky* (Lexington, Ky., 1964) is a particularly helpful state study.

LITERATURE, THOUGHT, AND HIGHER EDUCATION

Excellent studies of the changing intellectual climate in the region include Fred Hobson's *Tell About the South: The Southern Rage to Explain* (Baton Rouge, 1983); Daniel Joseph Singal's *The War Within: From Victorian to Modernist Thought in the South, 1919–1945* (Chapel Hill, N.C., 1982); and Richard H. King's *A Southern Renaissance: The Cultural Awakening of the American South, 1930–1955* (New York, 1980). Other works that help to illuminate themes in southern literature and thought include F. Garvin Davenport, Jr.'s *The Myth of Southern History: Historical Consciousness in Twentieth-Century Southern Literature* (Nashville, 1967); Keith F. McKean's *Cross Currents in the South* (Denver, 1960); Samuel Chase Coale's "The Role of the South in the Fiction of William Faulkner, Carson McCullers, Flannery O'Connor, and William Styron" (Ph.D. dissertation, Brown University, 1970); Australia T. Henderson's "In Loathing and Love: Black Southern Novelists' Views of the South, 1954–1964" (Ph.D. dissertation, University of Iowa, 1978); Alice Walker's "The Black Writer and the Southern Experience," *New South,* Fall, 1970, pp. 23–26; and Sylvia Jenkins Cook, *From Tobacco Road to Route 66: The Southern Poor White in Fiction* (Chapel Hill, N.C., 1976).

Important studies of southern literature include Louis D. Rubin, Jr.'s *Writers of the Modern South: The Faraway Country* (Seattle, 1963); Walter Sullivan's *Death by Melancholy: Essays on Modern Southern Fiction* (Baton Rouge, 1972) and *A Requiem for the Renascence: The State of Fiction in the Modern South* (Athens, Ga., 1972); Floyd C. Watkins' *The Death of Art: Black and White in the Recent Southern Novel* (Athens, Ga., 1970) and *In Time and Place: Some Origins of American Fiction* (Athens, Ga., 1977); John M. Bradbury's *Renaissance in the South: A Critical History of the Literature, 1920–1960* (Chapel Hill, N.C., 1963); C. Hugh Holman's *The Roots of*

Southern Writing: Essays on the Literature of the American South (Athens, Ga., 1972) and *The Immoderate Past: The Southern Writer and History* (Athens, Ga., 1977). *Flannery O'Connor: Mystery and Manners,* ed. Sally Fitzgerald and Robert Fitzgerald (New York, 1969), and *The Living Novel: A Symposium,* ed. Granville Hicks (New York, 1957), are solid essay collections. Cleanth Brooks's *William Faulkner: First Encounters* (New Haven, 1983) and Lawrence H. Schwartz's *Creating Faulkner's Reputation: The Politics of Modern Literary Criticism* (Knoxville, Tenn., 1988) are good studies of the most important writer of the southern renaissance. Fred Hobson's *The Southern Writer in the Postmodern World* (Athens, Ga., 1991) is a particularly fine study of the works of younger southern writers who grew up in the postwar South.

There is no history of higher education in the recent South, although Clarence L. Mohr's "Postwar Visions and Cold War Realities: The Metamorphosis of Southern Education, 1945–1965" (Paper presented at Porter L. Fortune, Jr., History Symposium, University of Mississippi, October 7, 1992), is extremely suggestive, as is Allan M. Cartter's "Qualitative Aspects of Southern University Education," *Southern Economic Journal,* XXXII (1965), 36–69. The annual *Fact Book on Higher Education in the South* (Southern Regional Education Board, 1962–) provides ample statistics. Paul K. Conkin, one of America's leading intellectual historians, offers a knowledgeable appraisal of southern universities in "The Rating Game," *Vanderbilt Magazine,* Spring, 1988, pp. 25–38. Histories of individual universities abound, but three excellent studies are broadly representative. Paul K. Conkin's *Gone with the Ivy: A Biography of Vanderbilt University* (Knoxville, Tenn., 1985) is a study of an elite private university, Thomas G. Dyer's *The University of Georgia: A Bicentennial History, 1785–1985* (Athens, Ga., 1985) is an examination of a major state university, and Robert C. McMath, Jr., *et al.*'s *Engineering the New South: Georgia Tech, 1885–1985* (Athens, Ga., 1985) is a history of a leading technical university.

IMAGES AND DILEMMAS

Jack Temple Kirby's *Media-Made Dixie: The South in the American Imagination* (Rev. ed.; Athens, Ga., 1986) is good on the changing national image of the South. Also helpful are Edward D. C. Campbell, Jr.'s *The Celluloid South: Hollywood and the Southern Myth* (Knoxville, Tenn., 1981) and *The South and Film,* ed. Warren French (Jackson, Miss., 1981). Richard Klimmer's "Liberal Attitudes Toward the South, 1930–1965" (Ph.D.

dissertation, Northwestern University, 1976) is a significant study based on an analysis of northern liberal publications. C. Vann Woodward's *American Counterpoint: Slavery and Racism in the North-South Dialogue* (Boston, 1964), *The Burden of Southern History* (Rev. ed.; Baton Rouge, 1968), and *Thinking Back: The Perils of Writing History* (Baton Rouge, 1986) are important studies that examine the South's place within the Union and the influence of history on southern thought.

Arguing with varying degrees of intensity that the South will continue as a distinctive region are *The Lasting South: Fourteen Southerners Look at Their Home,* ed. Louis D. Rubin, Jr., and James J. Kilpatrick (Chicago, 1957); Francis Butler Simkins' *The Everlasting South* (Baton Rouge, 1963); *The American South: Portrait of a Culture,* ed. Louis D. Rubin, Jr. (Baton Rouge, 1980); and *Why the South Will Survive,* by Fifteen Southerners (Athens, Ga., 1981). John Shelton Reed's *The Enduring South: Subcultural Persistence in Mass Society* (Lexington, Mass., 1972) makes clear that white southerners did hold opinions that differed from those of white Americans generally. As George Brown Tindall suggests in *The Ethnic Southerners* (Baton Rouge, 1976), some studies have treated white southerners as an ethnic group. Among the most significant of such works are Lewis M. Killian's *White Southerners* (New York, 1970) and John Shelton Reed's *One South: An Ethnic Approach to Regional Culture* (Baton Rouge, 1982). At the same time, the South became more closely integrated into national culture, a point rather ruefully made in John Egerton's *The Americanization of Dixie: The Southernization of America* (New York, 1974).

Racial issues dominated much of the debate in the postwar South, and Gunnar Myrdal's *An American Dilemma: The Negro Problem and Modern Democracy* (New York, 1944) established the framework for thinking about race. Two extremely good studies examine the making of *An American Dilemma* and assess its influence: David W. Southern, *Gunnar Myrdal and Black-White Relations: The Use and Abuse of "An American Dilemma," 1944–1969* (Baton Rouge, 1987), and Walter A. Jackson, *Gunnar Myrdal and America's Conscience: Social Engineering and Racial Liberalism, 1938–1987* (Chapel Hill, N.C., 1990). One of several articles that attempt and generally fail to locate a moral conflict is Ernest Q. Campbell's "Moral Discomfort and Racial Segregation: An Examination of the Myrdal Hypothesis," *Social Forces,* XXXIX (1961), 228–34. Charles H. Stember's *Education and Attitude Change: The Effect of Schooling on Prejudice Against Minority Groups* (New York, 1961) and Judith Caditz' *White Liberals in Transition: Current Dilemmas of Ethnic Integration* (New York, 1976) convincingly question the proposition that racial toleration was indigenous to the educated and comfortable.

RELIGION

E. Franklin Frazier's *The Negro Church in America* (New York, 1963) is the classic study of its subject. Also important is Joseph R. Washington, Jr.'s *Black Religion: The Negro and Christianity in the United States* (Boston, 1964). See also, by the same author, *The Politics of God* (Boston, 1967). Ruby Funchess Johnson's *The Religion of Negro Protestants: Changing Religious Attitudes and Practices* (New York, 1956) and Charles V. Hamilton's *The Black Preacher in America* (New York, 1972) are helpful works. Lower-class black religion is examined in Joseph R. Washington, Jr.'s *Black Sects and Cults* (Garden City, N.Y., 1972) and Hans A. Baer's *The Black Spiritual Movement: A Religious Response to Racism* (Knoxville, Tenn., 1984).

The black-theology movement generated a substantial literature. Perhaps the best examination and critique is James H. Cone's *For My People: Black Theology and the Black Church* (Maryknoll, N.Y., 1984). See also Cone, *Black Theology and Black Power* (New York, 1969). Other helpful works include Gayraud S. Wilmore's *Black Religion and Black Radicalism: An Interpretation of the Religious History of the Afro-American People* (2nd ed.; Maryknoll, N.Y., 1983); *The Black Church in America*, ed. Hart M. Nelsen et al. (New York, 1971); and Hart M. Nelsen and Anne K. Nelsen's *Black Church in the Sixties* (Lexington, Ky., 1975). *Black Theology: A Documentary History*, ed. Gayraud S. Wilmore and James H. Cone (Maryknoll, N.Y., 1979), is a good collection.

Samuel S. Hill, Jr., is the premier student of white southern religion. His works include his and Robert G. Torbet's *Baptists North and South* (Valley Forge, Pa., 1964); his *Southern Churches in Crisis* (New York, 1967); Hill et al.'s *Religion and the Solid South* (Nashville, 1972); his *The South and the North in American Religion* (Athens, Ga., 1980); his and Dennis E. Owen's *The New Religious Political Right in America* (Nashville, 1982); and *Religion in the Southern States: A Historical Study*, ed. Hill (Macon, Ga., 1983). Gene McLean Adams' "An Analytical Study of Southern Religion of the 1970s as Based on Samuel S. Hill, Jr.'s Southern Culture-Religion Thesis" (Ph.D. dissertation, Florida State University, 1980) is also helpful. Other useful studies include Kenneth K. Bailey's *Southern White Protestantism in the Twentieth Century* (New York, 1964); David M. Reimers' *White Protestantism and the Negro* (New York, 1965); Andrew Michael Manis' *Southern Civil Religions in Conflict: Black and White Baptists and Civil Rights, 1947–1957* (Athens, Ga., 1987); John Lee Eighmy's *Churches in Cultural Captivity: A History of the Social Attitudes of Southern Baptists* (Rev. ed.; Knoxville, Tenn., 1987); Gibson Winter's *The Suburban Captivity of the Churches* (New York, 1962); and Donald W. Dayton and

Robert K. Johnson's *The Variety of American Evangelicalism* (Knoxville, Tenn., 1991).

William G. McLoughlin, Jr.'s *Billy Graham: Revivalist in a Secular Age* (New York, 1960) is the best biography of Graham. Also helpful are the same author's *Modern Revivalism: Charles Grandison Finnery to Billy Graham* (Rev. ed.; New York, 1959); Lowell D. Streiker and Gerald S. Stober's *Religion and the New Majority: Billy Graham, Middle America, and the Politics of the Seventies* (New York, 1972); and Marshall Frady's *Billy Graham: A Parable of American Righteousness* (Boston, 1979). David Edwin Harrell, Jr.'s *Oral Roberts: An American Life* (Bloomington, Ind., 1985) is a superior biography, and his *White Sects and Black Men in the Recent South* (Nashville, Tenn., 1971) and *All Things Are Possible: The Healing and Charismatic Revivals in Modern America* (Bloomington, Ind., 1975) are good on their subjects.

Erskine Caldwell's *Deep South: Memory and Observation* (New York, 1969) is a perceptive commentary. Other helpful works on white Protestantism include Ernest Q. Campbell and Thomas F. Pettigrew's *Christians in Racial Crisis: A Study of Little Rock's Ministry* (Washington, D.C., 1959); Will D. Campbell's *Race and the Renewal of the Church* (Philadelphia, 1962); C. Dwight Dorough's *The Bible Belt Mystique* (Philadelphia, 1974); Harry Groff Lefever's "Ghetto Religion: A Study of the Religious Structures and Styles of a Poor White Community in Atlanta, Georgia" (Ph.D. dissertation, Emory University, 1971); and Howard Dorgan's *Giving Glory to God in Appalachia: Worship Practices of Six Baptist Subdenominations* (Knoxville, Tenn., 1987). Examining television ministries are Jeffrey K. Hadden and Charles E. Swann's *Prime Time Preachers: The Rising Power of Televangelism* (Reading, Mass., 1981); *New Christian Politics*, ed. David G. Bromley and Anson Sharpe (Macon, Ga., 1984); Peter G. Horsfield's *Religious Television: The American Experience* (New York, 1984); Peter G. Horsfield *et al.*'s "The Mediated Ministry," *Journal of Communication*, XXXV (1985), 89–156; and Steve Bruce's *The Rise and Fall of the New Christian Right: Conservative Protestant Politics in America, 1978–1988* (New York, 1988) and *Pray TV: Televangelism in America* (New York, 1990).

INDEX

Carlton, Doyle, Jr., 259
Carmichael, Stokely, 342, 343, 352–
53, 355, 362, 375, 422, 466, 493
Caro, Robert A., 486
Carroll, Julian, 426
Carson, Clayborne, 300, 312, 487,
490
Carter, Asa, 203, 204
Carter, Hodding, III, 33, 353, 354,
481, 483
Carter, Jimmy, 391, 399–402, 413–
15, 455, 468, 486
Carter, Lillian, 432
Cartter, Allan M., 445, 500
Cartwright, Colbert S., 489
Casdorph, Paul, 484
Cash, Wilbur J., 128; *The Mind of the
South,* 5–6, 74
Cass, Julia, 493
Cassel, Carol A., 479
Catholic church, 44, 272, 284, 376,
428, 442
Caudill, Harry M., 120, 476
Census Bureau, 128
Chafe, William H., 168, 367, 483
Channing, Steven A., 163
Chapel Hill, N.C., 215
Charleston, S.C., 141–42, 253, 437
Charleston *News and Courier,* 142
Charlotte, N.C., 140, 220, 410, 435
Charlotte *Post,* 304
Charlottesville, Va., 242, 245
Chattanooga, Tenn., 303, 386
Chattanooga *Times,* 303
Cherry, Francis, 215
Cherry, R. Gregg, 85
Chester, Lewis, 486
Chestnut, C. L., Jr., 493
Child Development Group of Missis-
sippi, 368–69
Christian, Virgil L., Jr., 476
Christian-American Association, 41
Churches. *See* Black churches; Reli-
gion

Cigarette industry. *See* Tobacco indus-
try
CIO. *See* AFL-CIO; Congress of Indus-
trial Organizations (CIO)
CIO-PAC, 38–39
Cities. *See* Urban areas
Citizens' Advisory Council on the
Status of Women, 425
Citizens' Board of Inquiry into Hunger and Malnutrition, 289
Citizens' Council, 200, 202, 205
Citizens' Councils, 199–207, 218,
226, 242, 244, 245, 248, 252, 253,
255, 388, 481
Citizens' Councils of America, 200
Citizens for Eisenhower, 102
Civil rights: and Truman administration, 57, 74–75, 77–78, 82–83, 85,
95–97, 321, 458, 459, 464–65; in
1940s, 68–69, 74–78, 81; and
"symbolic equality," 69–70; whites'
defensive attitudes toward, 74; Dixiecrat opposition to, 82–83, 85, 86,
87, 95; and Eisenhower administration, 232–33, 235, 311; and Johnson administration, 235, 321, 339–
40, 341, 347, 365–66, 370–75,
378; and Nixon administration,
411, 419; and Ford administration,
419; social engineering approach
to, 465–66
Civil Rights Act of 1964, pp. 339,
365, 370–75, 383, 409, 424, 463,
465
Civil Rights Act of 1965, p. 463
Civil Rights Act of 1968, pp. 361–62,
378
Civil Rights Commission, 171, 409,
419, 425, 488, 494
Civil rights movement: student involvement in, 153, 298–301, 303–
305, 345–46, 461; and bus boycotts, 176–82, 461; and black
churches, 178, 292, 308–309; non-

Public welfare, 157, 210, 211, 217, 403, 498
Pyun, C. S., 475

Quint, Howard H., 162

Race relations: Lillian E. Smith on, 4–5, 64–65; in Faulkner, 5, 35–36; violence against African Americans, 6, 76–77; in Wright, 6–7, 35; during World War II, 12–15; Myrdal on, 13, 35, 65–67, 184, 200, 297, 343, 344, 459, 463; "separate but equal" doctrine of, 15, 147, 154–55, 160, 167, 341–42; Supreme Court cases on, 15; and business-oriented political moderates, 23; Southern Conference on Human Welfare on, 28; and worker solidarity, 28–29, 60–61; and Southern Regional Council, 29–30; conservatives on, 37; in CIO, 60–62; in labor unions, 60–62, 72–73; "symbolic equality" in, 69–70; in southern towns of 1940s–1950s, 108, 109, 117–18; and desegregation of education, 158–71; Martin Luther King, Jr., on, 184; Folsom on, 206–208; Earl Long on, 206–208; and prejudice of working class against African Americans, 278–80; and multiculturalism, 379–80, 441–42, 464; and moderate governors in 1960s, 400; bibliography on, 501–502. See also African Americans; Civil rights movement; Integration; Racism; Segregation; White supremacy; Whites
Racial diplomats, 174–76, 185, 186, 303
Racism: Lillian E. Smith on, 4–5, 64–65; Double V campaign against, 7; against northern black solders in South during World War II, 8; and business-oriented political moder-

ates, 23; conservatives on, 37; Myrdal on, 66–67, 343; and Citizens' Councils, 199–207; of Wallace, 211, 395; of white working class, 278–80, 466; institutional, 343; of Maddox, 391–93; in southern culture, 441; motivations for, 467. See also Segregation; White supremacy
Radio, 17
Railroad Brotherhoods, 39
Railroads, 17–18, 148
Rainach, William M., 207, 212
Raines, Howell, 487
Raleigh, N.C., 57, 215, 299
Raleigh News and Observer, 25, 57
Randolph, A. Philip, 232
Raper, Arthur F., 3, 7–8, 144–45, 264, 434
Ratchford, B. U., 475
Rauh, Joseph, 348, 349
Rayburn, Sam, 198, 237–38
Read, Frank T., 488
Reagan, Ronald, 455–56, 469–70
Reconstruction Finance Corporation, 20
Record, Jane Cassels, 489
Record, Wilson, 489
Reddick, L. D., 488
Redstone Arsenal, 119
Reed, John Shelton, 442, 448, 449, 472, 495, 501
Reed, Linda, 480
Regional Council of Negro Leadership, 169
Reid, Ira De A., 3, 7–8, 144–45, 264, 434
Reimers, David M., 502
Reissman, Leonard, 2, 262, 496
Religion: Catholic church, 44, 272, 284, 376, 428, 442; black churches, 178, 183, 290, 291–94, 308–309, 376–77; metropolitan churches, 270–71; of middle class, 270–77; in O'Connor's fiction,

189, 191–94, 213, 247; county elites in, 190; Southern Manifesto supported by, 198; Citizens' Councils in, 199, 206; Nixon ticket in, 239, 397; school closings in, 241, 243–44, 460; save-the-schools campaign in, 244, 245–46; integration of education in, 246–47, 256–57, 408–409, 420–21; Perrow Commission, 247; economic development in, 265; integration of public facilities in, 265; religion in, 285; sit-ins in, 299; freedom rides in, 306; SNCC's projects in, 316; moderates in, 399; race relations in 1960s in, 400; new constitution of, 401; business climate of, 403; equal rights amendment approved in, 426; migration to, in 1960s, 429; income in, 430

Virginia Committee for Public Schools, 244

Virginia Resolution, 188

Virginia State College, 154

Virginia Union University, 313

VISTA, 367

Vocational and technical schools, 158

Volstead Act, 189

Von Hoffman, Nicholas, 491

Voter Education Project (VEP), 313

Voter registration: by NAACP and local black political associations, 26; NAACP's involvement in, 26, 318; by Southern Conference, 50; statistics on, 171–72, 404; literacy tests for, 172; obstacles to African-American, 172, 173–74; SCLC's involvement in, 185, 312, 318, 328; Long's protection of, in Louisiana, 212; CORE's involvement in, 312, 317, 319, 461; and Kennedy administration, 312–13; SNCC's role in, 312–14, 461; Voter Education Project for, 313; bibliography on, 491

Voting behavior: of African Americans, 171–76, 396, 397, 415–16; in 1960s–1980s, 415–16

Voting rights: and disfranchisement of African Americans, 15, 24, 26, 31–34, 36, 159, 172–73; and white primary elections, 15, 26; and poll tax, 24, 26, 50, 75, 80, 83, 172, 310; and voter registration, 26; for African Americans, 171–76; Eisenhower administration legislation on, 232–33, 235; and Kennedy administration, 309–10, 312–13

Voting Rights Act of 1965, pp. 339–40, 341, 375, 408, 418

Wagy, Tom R., 483

Walker, Alice, 129, 453, 499

Walker, Eugene Pierce, 492

Walker, Jack L., 303

Walker, James Louis, 476

Walker, Wyatt T., 292, 325, 328, 334

Wallace, David E., 489

Wallace, George C.: 1958 gubernatorial campaign of, 211; opposition of, to school desegregation, 254, 373, 382–83, 422, 467; on political parties, 381, 413; 1962 gubernatorial campaign of, 382; 1964 presidential campaign of, 383; 1966 gubernatorial campaign of wife of, 390–91; 1968 presidential campaign of, 393–95, 397; 1970 gubernatorial campaign of, 407–408; assassination attempt on, 411; on busing, 411, 413; 1972 presidential campaign of, 411–12; failings of, 413; Carter endorsed by, 414; on hypocrisy of white northern liberals, 466; bibliography on, 486

Wallace, Henry A.: and Southern Conference for Human Welfare, 39, 53–54; charges of Communism against, 51–52, 63, 364, 458; dis-